T0385553

The Cybersecurity Guide to Governance, Risk, and Compliance

The Cybersecurity Guide to Governance, Risk, and Compliance

Dr. Jason Edwards

New Braunfels
TX, USA

Griffin Weaver

San Antonio
TX, USA

WILEY

Library of Congress Cataloging-in-Publication Data applied for

Hardback ISBN: 9781394250196

Cover Design: Wiley
Cover Image: © Andriy Onufriyenko/Getty Images

Set in 10.5/13pt Muli by Straive, Chennai, India
Printed and bound by CPI Group (UK) Ltd, Croydon, CR0 4YY

C9781394250196_240424

Dedication by Griffin Weaver

As I present this book on cybersecurity and governance, coauthored with immense dedication and passion, my thoughts turn not only to the profound complexities of our digital world but also to the incredible journey that has led me here. As a legal expert deeply entrenched in the nuances of cybersecurity, I've embarked on this endeavor with a singular purpose: to bridge the gap between theoretical knowledge and practical application in a field that is as challenging as it is essential.

To my wife, Whitney, and our three children, Harper, Gideon, and Flynn, my journey in this field is a testament to the balance between pursuing professional passions and cherishing the invaluable support of family. It is with this balanced perspective that I've approached the writing of this book, aiming to infuse it not just with legal and technical insights but also with the underlying values of dedication, curiosity, and perseverance.

Cybersecurity and the law are not just areas of professional interest to me; they are vital pillars upon which our digital society rests. In writing this book, my hope is to illuminate these complex subjects for a diverse audience, from students who are just beginning their academic pursuits to seasoned practitioners looking to deepen their understanding and enhance their skills.

The landscape of cybersecurity is ever-evolving, and with it, the legal frameworks that govern our digital interactions. It is my earnest desire that this book serves as a beacon, guiding readers through the intricacies of cybersecurity and governance with clarity, depth, and relevance. May it inspire you to explore further, question deeper, and contribute to the shaping of a secure, ethical digital future.

Dedication by Jason Edwards

This book is dedicated to my family, whose unwavering support and love have been the cornerstone of my endeavors; to my wife, Selda, whose wisdom and strength have been my guiding light; and to my children, Michelle, Chris, Ceylin, and Mayra, who inspire me daily to be the best version of myself. The book is a testament to my professional journey and a reflection of the values and resilience you have instilled in me.

I acknowledge my fellow veterans and colleagues in the cybersecurity community, who have been comrades and mentors on this challenging yet rewarding path. Your camaraderie and insights have been invaluable in shaping the perspectives shared on these pages. A special acknowledgment goes out to those who serve in silence, dedicating their lives to the safety and security of our digital world.

This book is also dedicated to educators, students, and professionals in cybersecurity and related fields. May this work serve as a beacon, guiding you through the complexities of governance, risk, and compliance in our ever-evolving digital landscape. Your commitment to learning and adapting will drive us forward in these unprecedented times.

And, with a wry smile, I dedicate this book to the indomitable spirits of the "A7" project team. For two years, we waded through a quagmire of confusion and challenges that often teetered on the edge of chaos. Yet, against all odds, we emerged victorious. This dedication is a salute to our collective perseverance, ingenuity, and slightly warped sense of humor that saw us through the hellish yet unforgettable adventure of "A7."

Contents

Purpose of the Book

The first step in any journey of understanding is to clarify the why. This book was born out of a need for comprehensive yet practical insights into cybersecurity governance, risk management, and compliance. Navigating these complex domains can be a daunting task without a reliable roadmap. This book aims to guide, elucidating the pathways through the labyrinth of cyber threats and security measures, organizational policies, and regulatory requirements.

This book aims to bridge the knowledge gaps in the dynamic cybersecurity field. While many resources tackle the subject, they often focus on a narrow aspect, leaving you to stitch together various pieces of information. This guide takes a different approach to provide a holistic understanding of cybersecurity from a governance, risk, and compliance perspective.

A critical aspect of cybersecurity is compliance. Compliance is not just about checking off boxes on a list. Instead, it is about integrating practices safeguarding an organization's data and digital assets. This book strives to provide insights that can elevate an organization's compliance activities from mere tasks to strategic initiatives, thus enhancing the resilience of the enterprise against cyber threats.

Professional development is a continual process. The pace of technological change necessitates that professionals in the field of cybersecurity continually upgrade their skills and understanding. This book is designed to be a valuable tool in that process, providing in-depth insights and practical approaches that can be applied in various professional settings.

The regulatory landscape related to cybersecurity is multifaceted and ever-evolving. Without a clear understanding of these complexities, an organization can easily find itself noncompliant and vulnerable. This book aims to aid you in navigating this challenging environment, providing you with the knowledge needed to build a cybersecurity program that aligns with regulatory requirements.

While this book strongly focuses on financial compliance, the insights and guidance can be applied to all industries. Cyber threats and the need for effective cybersecurity measures are universal issues impacting businesses of all sizes and sectors. Therefore, this guide can be beneficial for a diverse range of professionals.

Finally, this book is not just about learning but also about sharing experiences. You contribute to the book's purpose by exploring the content and applying the insights in your professional environment. By adding your expertise to the collective wisdom, you can help others navigate their cybersecurity journey.

Target Audience

The subject of cybersecurity touches a wide range of professionals. One of the key strengths of this book is its cross-industry applicability, which means it can benefit a diverse audience. This guide targets cybersecurity professionals, from those beginning their careers to seasoned experts. It provides foundational knowledge and in-depth insights into cybersecurity governance, risk, and compliance.

Compliance officers are another primary audience for this book. These professionals ensure that their organizations adhere to the necessary regulations and standards. Compliance officers can more effectively align their practices with the organization's cyber risk management efforts with a clear understanding of cybersecurity principles.

IT professionals can gain substantial value from this guide, whether directly involved in cybersecurity or not. Cybersecurity is not a stand-alone function; it is deeply interwoven with other IT practices. Therefore, understanding cybersecurity principles can aid IT professionals in designing, implementing, and maintaining systems and networks that are resilient against cyber threats.

For business executives, understanding cybersecurity is about much more than technology; it is about ensuring business continuity and preserving stakeholder trust. This book aims to give executives the knowledge they need to make informed decisions related to cybersecurity and drive cyber risk governance in their organizations.

The book is equally valuable for boards of directors. Boards are responsible for overseeing risk, including cyber risk. With the knowledge in this guide, board members can play a more active role in directing their organization's cybersecurity strategy and ensuring compliance with relevant regulations.

Legal professionals can also find value in this book. As laws and regulations related to cybersecurity continue to evolve, legal professionals must stay informed. This guide can help them understand cybersecurity's technological and compliance aspects, enabling them to provide more practical advice and support to their clients or organizations.

Regulators are the final primary audience for this book. Effective regulation requires a deep understanding of the subject being regulated. This guide can support regulators in developing and implementing effective cybersecurity regulations by providing comprehensive insights into cybersecurity from a governance, risk, and compliance perspective.

Structure of the Book

As authors, we have crafted this book to offer a well-rounded and engaging journey through cybersecurity governance, risk, and compliance. The book is thoughtfully divided into specific sections, each concentrating on a unique aspect of the subject. These sections are filled with in-depth discussions, practical tips, and real-world examples that help bring the subject to life.

Our book is not just for sequential reading from cover to cover. We have designed it so you can read specific sections depending on your immediate needs or interests. Each chapter is independent, providing a focused exploration of a distinct cybersecurity dimension. This means you can always revisit or explore new sections at your own pace and according to your requirements.

Throughout the book, we have highlighted key themes such as the crucial role of cybersecurity in an organization's strategy, the use of risk management in cyber defense, and the importance of compliance in safeguarding against cyber threats. We believe that understanding these themes is fundamental to grasping the complex world of modern cybersecurity.

We've also included over 70 Key Risk Indicators (KRIs) and Key Performance Indicators (KPIs) and references to relevant regulations, standards, and online resources. These additions are intended to aid you in measuring your cybersecurity efforts and to provide extra material for your learning.

We want you to understand and act on what you learn. So, after each section, we offer a few actionable recommendations. With over 1300 suggestions in the book, we are equipping you with the tools to translate the knowledge into practical steps.

One of our favorite features of the book is the real-life case studies and examples. They illustrate the concepts we are discussing and help you envision how they can be applied in real-world situations.

Finally, we have mapped the Federal Financial Institutions Examination Council (FFIEC) Information Security Handbook to the National Institute of Standards and Technology Cybersecurity Framework (NIST CSF). This will serve as a guide, helping you navigate these critical regulatory and guidance documents. It will enable you to understand their connections and overlaps for an efficient approach to compliance, thus bolstering your cybersecurity stance.

Foreword by Wil Bennett

Over the past 30 years in cybersecurity, I've witnessed its transformation from a simple defense mechanism to an intricate architecture interwoven with governance, risk, compliance, leadership, technology, and business strategies. This evolution was unimaginable three decades ago.

Having worked extensively in crafting and steering cybersecurity strategies, I've been fortunate to observe the expertise and dedication of Jason and Griffin closely. Their combined strengths in cybersecurity strategy, regulatory remediation, and legal aspects have proved crucial in meeting contemporary cybersecurity challenges.

The Cybersecurity Guide to Governance, Risk, and Compliance represents the wealth of knowledge and practical insights that Jason and Griffin possess. Having collaborated with Jason at USAA, I can attest to his unwavering commitment and strategic expertise in cybersecurity, especially in regulatory remediation. Similarly, Griffin's expertise in legal aspects has significantly shaped our understanding of cybersecurity laws and regulations.

This book delves deeply into the multifaceted realm of cybersecurity in today's age. Designed for professionals across the board, from seasoned cybersecurity veterans to business leaders, auditors, and regulators, this guide integrates the latest technological insights with governance, risk, and compliance (GRC). Every chapter brims with actionable recommendations from the authors' vast experience and forward-thinking vision.

Readers will find a comprehensive range of topics, from key performance indicators and cutting-edge technological advancements to risk management strategies and regulatory insights. This book stands not just as a testament to the knowledge of Dr. Jason Edwards and Griffin Weaver but also as a beacon guiding those eager to navigate current and future cybersecurity challenges.

In sum, this book is more than a text – it's an enlightening compass for traversing the dynamic terrain of cybersecurity governance, risk management, and compliance. I wholeheartedly endorse this guide as a pivotal resource for anyone striving for cybersecurity excellence and resilience.

—Wil Bennett
Vice President,
Chief Information Security Officer
CISSP

Foreword by Gary McAlum

In an era of constant digital evolution and deepening ties between governance, risk, compliance, and cybersecurity, *The Cybersecurity Guide to Governance, Risk, and Compliance* emerges as a pivotal resource. This guide combines practical insights with actionable strategies, providing a detailed road map through the complexities of modern cybersecurity.

During my tenure as Chief Security Officer at USAA, I had the privilege of working with Griffin Weaver and Dr. Jason Edwards. Griffin's expertise as a cyber attorney enhanced our cybersecurity strategies, ensuring their robustness and alignment with regulatory requirements. Dr. Jason Edwards' strategic approach and practical experiences significantly contributed to our efforts, and their insights are evident in this book.

Jason and Griffin have crafted a versatile guide suitable for beginners, educators, cybersecurity professionals, and executive leaders. With over 1300 actionable recommendations, KPIs, and KRIs, it offers a comprehensive route to a more secure cyber environment. From my role as Chief Information Security Officer, I appreciate the guide's exploration of cutting-edge topics like AI, cloud, and quantum computing, providing insights into their potential impacts on security and compliance.

This guide's coverage of governance, leadership, legal frameworks, and regulatory nuances ensures organizations can establish resilient cybersecurity postures. Each chapter delivers actionable knowledge, making the guide thorough and practical.

In summary, this book is a testament to the authors' expertise and commitment to advancing cybersecurity knowledge. It's a valuable resource for anyone in the field of cybersecurity, governance, risk, and compliance.

—Gary McAlum
Senior Vice President,
Chief Information Security Officer
CISSP

CHAPTER 1

Governance, Risk Management, and Compliance

"Cybersecurity governance empowers us with wisdom, risk management equips us with foresight, and compliance holds us accountable to our commitment to protecting our digital assets. Together, they form an unbreakable shield against cyber adversaries."

Integrating governance, risk, and compliance (GRC) into an organization's operations offers considerable advantages, including improved decision-making, increased operational efficiency, strengthened reputation, and cost reductions. It is essential to align GRC with business goals to leverage its potential and ensure optimal efficiency. Both theoretical principles and practical insights show the inherent business value and distinctive benefits offered by GRC when it is smoothly embedded within an organization's strategic framework.

UNDERSTANDING GRC

GRC is a crucial concept that guides organizations toward efficient operation. It offers an integrated, holistic approach to corporate governance, risk management, and regulatory compliance. Understanding the concept of GRC and its components, their interrelations, and their importance across industries forms the basis of this section.

Governance is managing a company to ensure it meets its statutory and legal obligations, while risk management involves identifying, assessing, and controlling threats to an organization's capital and earnings. Compliance refers to an organization's conformance with regulatory requirements and industry standards.

It is crucial to comprehend the significance of GRC across industries. Whether healthcare, finance, or information technology (*IT*), every industry faces unique risks, governance issues, and regulatory requirements. Understanding GRC allows organizations in these diverse sectors to address these issues effectively.

Emphasizing security, the banking industry is compelled to confront a diverse range of threats. The Graham–Leach–Bliley Act (*GLBA*) and the Dodd–Frank Act in the United States require the implementation of robust compliance mechanisms to strengthen institutional security against regulatory violations. Concurrently, banks need to handle risks tied to lending and market volatility, necessitating a reliable risk management system designed to enhance financial security. Furthermore, the industry must have strong cybersecurity measures to face the ever-present danger of cyber threats.

On the other hand, the healthcare sector faces strict patient data protection regulations like the Health Insurance Portability and Accountability Act (*HIPAA*) in the United States, requiring compliance systems. They also face risks related to patient safety and cybersecurity, calling for risk management, and require good governance to ensure quality healthcare delivery.

In the digital age, where cyber threats are rising, the IT industry faces unique GRC challenges. For instance, they must comply with data protection regulations like the General Data Protection Regulation (*GDPR*) in the EU, manage risks related to cybersecurity, and maintain good governance for efficient and ethical operation.

Understanding GRC and its components provides a road map to navigate industries' complex operational landscape. It offers a framework to efficiently address the challenges related to GRC, allowing organizations to maintain their competitive edge.

Recommendations:

- **Get Acquainted with GRC**: Start by individually understanding GRC definitions and concepts. Then, explore how these components interrelate and support each other in a business context.
- **Understand the GRC Context**: Comprehend how GRC applies to your specific industry. Research your industry's regulatory requirements, risk landscape, and governance challenges.
- **Learn GRC from Others**: Look into how organizations in your industry and other sectors have implemented GRC. There may be successful case studies that can offer insights and guidance.
- **Broaden Your View on GRC**: While focusing on your industry is crucial, keep an open mind about GRC practices in other sectors. There may be innovative solutions that can be applied to your context.
- **Stay Updated on GRC**: The world of GRC is dynamic, with regulations, risks, and governance structures evolving. Keep yourself updated about these changes to maintain your organization's GRC readiness.

THE BUSINESS CASE FOR GRC

The business case for GRC extends beyond simply meeting regulatory requirements. Implementing GRC in a business context can offer many benefits, promote alignment with business objectives, and significantly enhance operational efficiency. The case for GRC becomes compelling when considering these aspects.

At the heart of GRC lies the integration of GRC activities traditionally managed in isolation. This integration offers numerous benefits. It allows for more informed decision-making, efficient resource use, and improved organizational performance. When a business has a holistic view of its risks, it is better equipped to identify and mitigate potential threats before they become costly. Through a GRC approach, the organization's leadership gains visibility into the possible areas of noncompliance, thereby allowing for proactive remediation and the opportunity to avoid regulatory penalties.

The alignment of GRC activities with business objectives is a strategic imperative that fosters business growth and resilience. By embedding GRC into strategic planning, an organization can ensure its initiatives align with its risk appetite and adhere to relevant regulations. This alignment leads to achieving objectives and enhances shareholder confidence in the organization.

Operational efficiency is another critical benefit derived from GRC implementation. Organizations can achieve significant cost savings by eliminating the overlap of activities and streamlining processes across GRC. Furthermore, GRC promotes a culture of transparency and accountability, which leads to better governance and operational excellence.

Despite the myriad benefits of GRC, implementing it is not without its challenges. Organizations often struggle with defining roles and responsibilities, managing change, and sustaining commitment toward GRC. The following sections will delve into these aspects further, offering practical insights into how to overcome these challenges.

Recommendations:

- **Establish a Unified GRC Approach**: Integrate your GRC activities. This integrated approach will not only lead to cost savings but will also ensure that the organization has a comprehensive view of its risks and compliance status.
- **Align GRC with Business Objectives**: Incorporate GRC strategies as a central component of your organization's strategic planning process. This not only ensures your GRC practices are tightly aligned with your business goals, but it also provides a roadmap for balancing your business ambitions with your tolerance for risk and compliance requirements.
- **Promote Operational Efficiency**: Utilize GRC as a powerful instrument to boost operational efficiency in your organization. By refining your processes and eliminating redundancies across the GRC domains, you can

facilitate smoother operations and a more cost-effective approach to managing the business.

- **Embrace Transparency**: Cultivate a culture of transparency within your organization. This proactive approach promotes improved accountability among all stakeholders and bolsters governance practices, leading to better decision-making and overall trust within the organization.
- **Prepare for Challenges**: Expect and plan for hurdles you may encounter during the implementation of your GRC program. Preparing for these challenges in advance by establishing a strong change management strategy can lead to more successful outcomes and help ensure the organization is ready to adapt to the required changes.

GOVERNANCE: LAYING THE FOUNDATION

Regarding the interlinked concepts of GRC, governance encompasses the structured set of practices and protocols by which an organization is directed, managed, and controlled. It sets the fundamental tone for the entire organization, establishing clear roles, defining responsibilities, and setting the course for accountability. An organization rooted in strong governance principles lays a solid, unshakeable foundation for GRC. This is because it outlines the strategic direction of the business and forms the mechanisms for reaching these goals, all while meeting the required ethical standards and legal prerequisites.

Good governance, a nonnegotiable part of any successful organization, is constructed from several vital elements. These include a comprehensible and well-defined organizational structure, decision-making processes that are effective and well established, transparent leadership that is accountable to stakeholders, strong and clear communication mechanisms, and routine performance evaluations to keep track of progress and areas of improvement. When these elements are put into place with careful consideration and are allowed to function efficiently, governance becomes the driving force that propels an organization toward achieving its strategic goals. Concurrently, it ensures that all conduct within the organization is ethical and that all activities comply with relevant laws and regulations.

However, it is critical to note that the concept of governance is not a standardized, universally applicable entity. The requirements and practices that govern an organization can vastly differ across industries, as varying regulatory requirements dictate them, the nature of different business models, and diverse risk profiles. Discerning these differences is integral to successfully implementing governance practices tailored to meet your organization's needs. Despite the broad variance across sectors, a common thread binds successful governance practices across industries – the delicate balance between meeting legal and ethical obligations while simultaneously achieving business objectives.

Understanding the intricacies of governance, its core elements, and how its implementation may vary across industries forms the primary step toward crafting a comprehensive GRC strategy. It prepares the groundwork for managing risk effectively and ensuring unwavering compliance. As we delve deeper into the subsequent chapters, we will unpack how governance intertwines with risk management and compliance to give rise to a holistic GRC approach.

Recommendations:

- **Grasp the Role of Governance**: It is crucial to thoroughly comprehend governance's importance and function in the GRC framework. It should be noted that governance sets the tone for an organization's operations and management style, providing a structured and systematic approach to decision-making.
- **Familiarize with Key Elements**: Delving into the intricacies of good governance requires a solid understanding of its essential components. These include a transparent organizational structure, robust decision-making processes that encourage involvement and accountability, and leadership that stands accountable for their actions and decisions.
- **Appreciate Industry Variations**: Acknowledging that governance practices differ significantly depending on the industry is key. Each industry has unique characteristics and demands, requiring a bespoke approach to governance. Therefore, adjusting your governance strategies to suit your organization's industry's specific needs and regulatory requirements is essential.
- **Strike a balance**: It is crucial to strike a delicate balance in governance practices, ensuring business objectives are met while adhering to legal and ethical obligations. This means crafting strategies that drive growth and profitability and uphold a strong commitment to ethical standards and legal compliance.
- **Lay the Foundation**: Strong governance is a fundamental basis for a robust GRC strategy within an organization. It underpins managing risk, ensuring compliance, and driving organizational growth. Hence, establishing strong governance can lay a firm foundation for a successful GRC strategy.

RISK MANAGEMENT: MANAGING UNCERTAINTIES

Risk management is a cornerstone of GRC. It instills a systematic methodology for identifying, assessing, and addressing an organization's uncertainties. Acting as a guardrail, risk management steers organizations safely amidst uncertain tides, keeping them on track toward their strategic goals. Understanding risk management – its definition, significance, the part it plays within GRC, and the variations in its approach across different industries – is paramount to a robust and wide-ranging GRC strategy.

At its core, risk management encapsulates pinpointing, evaluating, reducing, and consistently monitoring risks. It demands an in-depth comprehension of prospective threats, the likelihood of their manifestation, and the potential repercussions they can bring. By illuminating these aspects, risk management equips organizations with the necessary knowledge to make informed decisions regarding the strategies and mechanisms they should adopt to alleviate these risks.

Risk management's role within the broader GRC framework is pivotal and cannot be downplayed. When left unattended or poorly managed, risks can unleash repercussions, from severe financial losses to irreversible damage to the organization's reputation. By folding risk management into the GRC strategy, organizations are better primed to handle uncertainties, reduce potential harm, and increase their resilience.

However, akin to governance, approaches to risk management are not universal and must be tailored to fit the distinct needs of different industries. For example, the nature, scale, and implications of risks within the banking sector can drastically differ from those within the healthcare or technology sectors. Consequently, each industry necessitates a bespoke risk management strategy that accurately captures and addresses its unique risk profile.

Understanding risk management and its integral role within the GRC framework enables organizations to navigate uncertainty effectively. This knowledge equips them with the tools to anticipate, mitigate, and adapt to potential threats and risks, thereby maintaining resilience in the face of adversity. As the business environment continues evolving and presents new challenges, this grasp of risk management within the broader GRC context becomes an essential asset for sustainable and successful business operations.

Recommendations:

- **Comprehend Risk Management**: An essential first step in any GRC strategy is developing a clear and in-depth understanding of risk management, its importance, and its position within the broader GRC landscape. Grasping the concept of risk management allows you to perceive the possible obstacles your organization might face and to establish effective strategies to mitigate them.

- **Implement Systematic Processes**: To effectively manage risk, it is essential to implement methodical procedures for identifying, assessing, mitigating, and continually monitoring risks. This structured approach allows for the early detection and appropriate management of potential risks, ultimately safeguarding your organization's strategic objectives.

- **Customize Your Approach**: Recognize that the approach to risk management is not one-size-fits-all. Each industry has a distinct risk profile, so your risk management strategies must be adapted to fit these unique requirements and vulnerabilities, ensuring a robust and effective risk management framework.

- **Incorporate into GRC**: Risk management is not an isolated function; it must be seamlessly integrated into your organization's broader GRC framework. This integration ensures a cohesive strategy, promoting effective governance and compliance while actively managing risk.

- **Stay Resilient**: Leveraging risk management enhances your organization's resilience, enabling it to respond to uncertainties and adapt to change effectively. You can ensure your organization remains robust and flexible, even in unexpected challenges, by continuously monitoring and managing risks.

COMPLIANCE: ADHERING TO REGULATIONS AND STANDARDS

Compliance is the third pillar of GRC, emphasizing adherence to external regulatory requirements and internal policies. It involves keeping up with ever-changing laws and regulations and ensuring that business operations, processes, and practices align with these rules. In the broader context of GRC, compliance aids in mitigating risk and fortifying governance.

The importance of compliance in any organization cannot be understated. Noncompliance can result in legal penalties, financial losses, and reputational damage, even threatening the organization's survival. Moreover, maintaining compliance can be challenging in a complex and interconnected business environment, where rules and regulations are constantly evolving. Yet, it is an endeavor that organizations must undertake to protect themselves and their stakeholders.

Compliance challenges and requirements can vary across industries like governance and risk management. For example, financial institutions must comply with strict banking regulations, healthcare organizations must adhere to patient privacy laws, and tech companies face data security and privacy rules. Understanding these variations is crucial for establishing effective compliance procedures and controls.

In a rapidly changing regulatory environment, compliance must be dynamic and adaptive. Keeping abreast of regulatory changes, interpreting their implications, and implementing necessary changes securely are essential. This requires a well-coordinated effort involving various organizational functions, including legal, human resources, finance, operations, and IT.

Compliance is not just about rule-following; it is about building trust. A compliant organization earns the trust of its stakeholders, including customers, employees, investors, and regulators. This trust translates into business reputability, customer loyalty, and long-term success.

Recommendations:

- **Understand Compliance**: Grasp the importance of compliance and its role within GRC. Understand that compliance is not just about adhering to laws but also about earning stakeholder trust.
- **Keep Abreast of Changes**: Stay informed about new laws and regulations in a rapidly changing regulatory environment. Regularly assess their impact on your business and make necessary adjustments.
- **Acknowledge Industry Variations**: Recognize that compliance requirements can vary significantly across industries. Develop a compliance strategy that aligns with your specific industry regulations.

- **Invest in Compliance Training**: Dedicate resources to compliance training to ensure all employees thoroughly understand its importance. Familiarity with relevant regulations and internal policies is crucial, as it equips employees with the knowledge necessary to make informed decisions and behave ethically within the scope of their roles.
- **Establish a Strong Compliance Culture**: Cultivating a robust culture of compliance within your organization should be a top priority. This involves instilling the values of integrity and accountability and making adherence to rules, regulations, and ethical standards a fundamental part of your organization's identity. A strong compliance culture can help prevent violations, promote ethical behavior, and enhance your organization's reputation.

THE INTERSECTION OF GOVERNANCE, RISK, AND COMPLIANCE

In the broader tapestry of the GRC framework, GRC are not isolated threads. They intertwine, interact, and affect one another. The subtle art of balancing these components and the critical role of leadership in accomplishing this form the bedrock of an effective GRC strategy.

GRC work together to form a harmonious trifecta, each contributing unique aspects to the GRC framework. Governance lays the foundational structure for the organization, setting the tone for decision-making, accountability, and performance assessment. It provides the necessary leadership and strategic vision, aligning the organization's actions with its business objectives while ensuring ethical conduct and regulatory compliance.

Risk management, the second component of this triad, adds a layer of protection to this foundation. It provides the mechanisms for identifying, evaluating, and mitigating risks that might derail an organization from achieving its objectives. The risk management function works in close conjunction with governance. While governance sets the strategic direction, risk management ensures that potential roadblocks are identified and managed, allowing the organization to navigate uncertainties and remain on course.

Compliance forms the third and equally critical component of the GRC framework. It ensures that the organization's activities and processes align with external regulatory requirements and internal policies. Compliance works closely with both governance and risk management. It ensures that governance structures and procedures align with regulatory requirements and adds another layer of scrutiny to the risk management process by identifying and managing compliance risks.

Despite each component's distinct role, maintaining a balance between GRC is crucial. Overemphasis on any one part can lead to an imbalance, disrupting the efficacy of the GRC framework. For example, overly rigid compliance procedures may stifle innovation, while an overzealous approach to risk management may impede strategic growth. Conversely, a lack of governance could lead to a chaotic and inefficient organizational environment. Therefore, it is crucial to strike the right balance, understand these components' interplay, and integrate them effectively.

Leadership plays a decisive role in this integration process. Leaders set the tone for GRC within an organization. They are responsible for fostering a culture that values and practices robust governance, risk-aware decision-making, and stringent compliance. Leaders are the stewards of the organization's strategic vision, driving the execution of the GRC framework in alignment with this vision. They are instrumental in implementing governance structures, endorsing risk management practices, and promoting a culture of compliance.

Moreover, leaders must be active champions of GRC, demonstrating the importance of GRC through their actions. This involves setting clear expectations, providing the necessary resources and support for GRC initiatives, and ensuring that the performance evaluation systems align with the organization's GRC objectives. In this way, they can drive the successful integration of GRC, enabling the organization to achieve its objectives while managing uncertainties and adhering to regulatory requirements.

Understanding how GRC work together and striking the right balance among these components is critical. Equally essential is the role of leadership in driving this integration and fostering a culture that values GRC. With a sound understanding of these elements, organizations can leverage their GRC framework effectively to drive strategic success, manage risks, and ensure regulatory compliance.

Recommendations:

- **Understand the Intersection**: Grasp how GRC work together in a GRC framework. Understand how these elements interrelate and support each other.
- **Maintain Balance**: Balance GRC. While each component is essential, none should overshadow the others.
- **Recognize Leadership's Role**: Acknowledge leadership's pivotal role in GRC integration. Leaders should champion GRC initiatives and promote a culture of good governance, effective risk management, and strict compliance.
- **Incorporate GRC into Strategy**: Make GRC an integral part of your organization's strategy. This integration will help align GRC activities with your business goals and objectives.
- **Measure GRC Performance**: Establish metrics to measure the effectiveness of your GRC activities. Regularly evaluate your GRC performance and make necessary adjustments.

GRC FRAMEWORKS AND STANDARDS

GRC is integral to any organization's structure, ensuring business sustainability and resilience. To streamline and structure these elements, GRC frameworks and standards are utilized. They provide structured guidance as blueprints to help organizations design, implement, and maintain their GRC programs effectively.

The primary role of GRC frameworks is to simplify complexity. They organize myriad regulations, standards, and best practices into comprehensible models. These models, or frameworks, then serve as a roadmap, guiding organizations on how to align their business operations with governance, manage risks systematically, and comply with relevant regulations and standards.

GRC frameworks are diverse and multifaceted, each offering unique perspectives and strategies. Among these, some of the most recognized frameworks include the National Institute of Standards and Technology Cybersecurity Framework (NIST CSF), the Committee of Sponsoring Organizations of the Treadway Commission (COSO) Framework, ISO 31000, and Control Objectives for Information and Related Technologies (COBIT), each designed to address specific aspects of GRC in unique ways.

The NIST CSF addresses risk management. The framework provides standards, guidelines, and best practices for managing cybersecurity-related risk. NIST CSF's core comprises five functions – Identify, Protect, Detect, Respond, and Recover – offering a high-level, strategic view of an organization's cybersecurity risk management. With the increasing prevalence of cyber threats in today's digital landscape, NIST CSF has become vital to many organizations' overall GRC strategies. Its focus on continuous improvement and adaptation to the changing cyber risk landscape makes it an effective tool for managing and mitigating cybersecurity risk.

The COSO Framework is a globally recognized standard. Developed in the United States, the COSO Framework is a resource for enterprise risk management, internal control, and fraud deterrence. The beauty of the COSO Framework lies in its comprehensive model, which includes five internal control components – control environment, risk assessment, control activities, information and communication, and monitoring activities. These components are applied to manage fraud and enhance organizational performance across three broad categories: operations, reporting, and compliance. With its holistic approach, the COSO Framework provides a structured basis for organizations to establish a robust GRC strategy.

ISO 31000, on the other hand, takes a focused approach to risk management. Developed by the International Organization for Standardization, ISO 31000 outlines a systematic approach to risk management that can be applied across all sectors. It provides guidelines and principles for designing, implementing, and maintaining risk management processes within an organization. The strength of ISO 31000 lies in its universality, meaning it can be used by any organization, regardless of its size, nature, or complexity. The framework emphasizes integrating risk management into all organizational processes, creating a risk-aware culture, and enhancing strategic decision-making.

Meanwhile, COBIT provides a unique lens for GRC through its focus on IT governance. Developed by ISACA, COBIT provides a comprehensive framework designed explicitly for IT governance. It outlines a set of generic processes for the management of IT, with each method defined together with process inputs and outputs, key process activities, process objectives, performance measures, and an elementary maturity model. COBIT's primary strength is its focus on aligning IT processes with business objectives, ensuring that organizations can leverage IT as a strategic enabler while managing associated risks and meeting compliance requirements.

It is crucial to note that choosing a GRC framework depends on the organization's specific needs, size, and context. Therefore, it is vital to understand each framework, its components, and how it aligns with the organization's business operations and strategy. Choosing the wrong framework could lead to ineffective GRC implementation and might fail to address specific organizational risks and challenges.

Implementing a GRC framework involves a series of steps, from understanding the chosen framework to mapping it to the organization's processes and finally to the continuous monitoring and refinement of the system. It is not a one-size-fits-all approach; instead, it should be customized to fit the unique needs and context of the organization.

GRC frameworks are not static; they must adapt to the dynamic business environment. As new risks emerge and regulations change, organizations must revisit their GRC framework to ensure it remains effective and relevant. Regular audits, reviews, and updates should be part of the GRC program to keep pace with this dynamism.

Lastly, effective GRC implementation is not solely about choosing and applying the proper framework. It requires buy-in from all levels of the organization, from top leadership to frontline employees. This collective commitment fosters a culture of good governance, risk awareness, and compliance adherence, driving the organization toward its strategic goals and sustainable success.

Recommendations:

- **Familiarize with Frameworks**: Start with a comprehensive understanding of GRC frameworks and standards. Consider the unique aspects, benefits, and limitations of each to provide a foundation for informed decision-making.
- **Match Framework to Needs**: Match the chosen framework with your organization's specific needs, size, and context. An alignment with your business strategy, operations, and risk landscape is essential for effective GRC implementation.
- **Customize and Adapt**: GRC frameworks should be customized and adapted to your organization's unique context. Regular reviews and updates are necessary to maintain their relevance and effectiveness.
- **Ensure Organizational Buy-in**: Seek buy-in from all levels of the organization, from leadership to frontline employees. This will foster a culture of good governance, risk awareness, and compliance adherence.

GRC TOOLS AND TECHNOLOGIES

The inherent complexity of managing GRC necessitates using specialized tools and technologies. Beginning with the discussion on the importance of these tools, it is evident they significantly help organizations automate and streamline their GRC activities. These solutions pave the way for efficient risk identification, assessment, and mitigation. Furthermore, they enhance compliance monitoring and reporting while offering an integrated perspective on the organization's overall GRC status.

Numerous GRC tools are available in the market, each boasting different features and capabilities. This section outlines the typical characteristics of GRC tools, such as risk assessment capabilities, compliance tracking, incident management, policy management, and reporting features. Understanding these features can guide organizations in choosing a tool that best meets their GRC needs.

In the realm of GRC, RSA Archer stands at the forefront, making a name for itself as one of the leading solutions in the industry. RSA Archer provides an array of modules spanning areas such as risk management, compliance management, and policy management. A standout feature of this tool is its ability to offer a holistic view of risks at every level of an organization. RSA Archer truly shines regarding scalability, making it an excellent fit for large organizations that grapple with intricate risk and compliance requirements across various domains. Furthermore, it facilitates collaboration across business units and promotes a uniform understanding and approach toward managing risk and compliance.

IBM OpenPages, another prominent player in the field, delivers a flexible, modular solution to GRC. Designed to provide a comprehensive view of risk and compliance, OpenPages successfully integrates disparate risk management activities across organizations. One of its distinguishing features is its cognitive capabilities, leveraging AI to offer advanced analytics and automation. The tool is highly adaptable and boasts seamless integration capabilities with other systems. For organizations aiming to tailor their GRC solutions to their specific needs, IBM OpenPages provides a flexible and robust platform.

MetricStream, a robust GRC platform, offers a broad spectrum of solutions, including risk management, compliance management, policy management, and audit management. MetricStream excels with its user-friendly interface, robust functionality, and the capacity to support many GRC initiatives on a single platform. Adding to its appeal, MetricStream's mobile capabilities ensure on-the-go access to GRC data, making it a versatile and convenient tool for modern, dynamic businesses.

ServiceNow GRC takes a distinctive approach by amalgamating GRC with IT service management. This seamless integration is beneficial for organizations aligning IT functions with GRC initiatives. By fusing business context with risk data across IT processes, ServiceNow GRC aids organizations in managing and mitigating IT risks. This results in consistent compliance and reduced audit costs, delivering value across the organization's operational landscape.

NAVEX Global offers a GRC platform primarily focusing on ethics and compliance management. This platform provides various services, including risk management, policy management, and a whistleblower hotline, all aimed at fostering an ethical, compliant corporate culture. NAVEX Global is renowned for its strong compliance training and case management capabilities. This tool provides an end-to-end solution for ethics and compliance programs, ensuring organizations maintain the highest standards of conduct.

SAP GRC is a robust enterprise solution covering various aspects such as risk management, compliance management, and policy management. Given its seamless integration with other SAP modules and its potent analytics capabilities, SAP GRC is preferred for organizations that are deeply invested in SAP infrastructure and require a tightly integrated GRC solution. From a risk management perspective, SAP GRC offers predictive analytics that enables companies to forecast risks and take preventive measures, reinforcing its standing as a top-tier GRC tool.

LogicGate offers an accessible GRC platform distinguished by its highly configurable nature. LogicGate empowers organizations to create customized GRC applications tailored to their specific needs, which can be accomplished without coding knowledge. The platform's visual approach aids in understanding complex GRC processes and workflows, making it a particularly appealing choice for organizations seeking a visually driven, adaptable GRC solution. Whether for risk identification, assessment, or mitigation, LogicGate allows businesses to create their unique path in their GRC journey.

Evaluating and selecting GRC tools requires a systematic approach. It involves understanding the organization's GRC needs, defining the tool requirements, reviewing different tools, and selecting a tool that best meets them. This section offers a guide to this evaluation and selection process.

Implementing a GRC tool is not a one-off task; it is an ongoing process. Post-implementation, the tool's performance should be monitored, and updates or modifications should be made as necessary. This ensures that the tool continues to provide value and support the organization's evolving GRC needs.

Lastly, while GRC tools are valuable, they are not a magic solution. They should complement, not replace, the organization's GRC processes. The human element – involving decision-making, judgment, and ethical considerations – still plays a crucial role in GRC.

Recommendations:

- **Understand Tool Functions**: Begin by understanding the various functions and benefits of GRC tools. This understanding can inform the criteria for tool selection and ensure that the chosen tool meets the organization's GRC needs.

- **Define Requirements**: Clearly define your tool requirements. Consider factors like functionality, ease of use, scalability, integration capabilities, vendor support, and cost.
- **Review Options**: Review the various GRC tools in the market. Understand their features, strengths, and weaknesses and how they align with your tool requirements.
- **Monitor and Update**: Post-implementation, regularly monitor the tool's performance and make necessary updates or modifications. This ensures that the tool continues to meet your evolving GRC needs.
- **Maintain Human Element**: GRC tools are valuable but cannot replace the human element. Involving decision-making, judgment, and ethical considerations remain crucial in GRC.

BUILDING A GRC CULTURE

GRC extends beyond processes, frameworks, and tools, intimately involving people and culture. The emphasis is on cultivating a GRC culture wherein each individual within the organization comprehends and embodies GRC principles. This perspective introduces the concept of a GRC culture and explicates its significance. A robust GRC culture nurtures a proactive approach toward GRC and encourages every organization member to take ownership of these elements.

Fostering a GRC culture requires a systematic and methodical approach. Initially, this process necessitates gaining leadership buy-in. The critical role of leaders cannot be overstated, as they set the tone, model GRC behaviors, and prioritize GRC at a strategic level. They are the primary drivers of cultural change, and their actions and attitudes significantly shape employee behaviors.

Subsequently, the importance of training and communication in establishing a GRC culture comes to the forefront. For effective GRC, employees need a comprehensive understanding of what GRC implies, its relevance, and their specific roles. Regular training programs, interactive sessions, and consistent communication instill GRC principles in employees.

The journey then progresses toward the implementation of an ethical framework. This framework outlines the expected behaviors and principles that steer decision-making within the organization. It forms a critical aspect of GRC culture, ensuring that GRC are carried out with integrity and transparency.

Furthermore, there is a necessity to incorporate GRC into everyday operations. GRC should not be perceived as a separate or isolated function but should be integrated into all business activities. Such integration lets employees understand how their daily tasks impact the organization's GRC objectives.

Lastly, using incentives and rewards plays a significant role in cultivating a GRC culture. Acknowledging and rewarding behaviors compliant with GRC can motivate employees to adhere to GRC principles consistently. However, the reward system must be meticulously designed to prevent unintended consequences.

Recommendations:

- **Leadership Buy-in**: Secure leadership buy-in for building a GRC culture. Leaders play a critical role in setting the tone and modeling GRC behaviors.
- **Training and Communication**: Invest in regular exercise and clear communication to help employees understand GRC principles and their roles in implementing them.
- **Establish Ethical Framework**: Develop an ethical framework to guide decision-making. This ensures that GRC are conducted with integrity.
- **Integrate GRC**: Weave GRC into daily business activities. This enables employees to see the relevance of GRC in their day-to-day tasks.
- **Incentivize GRC Behaviors**: Recognize and reward GRC-compliant behaviors. However, ensure that the reward system is carefully designed to avoid unintended consequences.

THE ROLE OF GRC IN STRATEGIC PLANNING

Strategic planning is a vital activity that shapes the direction and future of an organization. It requires a clear understanding of the organization's vision, mission, and potential challenges and opportunities that may influence achieving its strategic objectives. Herein lies the significant role of GRC in strategic planning.

GRC provides a comprehensive framework that supports strategic planning by helping organizations understand and manage potential risks and compliance obligations. It guides how organizations set strategic objectives and make decisions that align with their governance structures, risk appetite, and regulatory requirements.

Incorporating GRC in strategic planning begins with understanding the organization's governance structure. It helps set the strategic direction by defining roles, responsibilities, and accountabilities. It provides the basis for decision-making, ensuring that strategic decisions align with the organization's vision, mission, and ethical standards. Governance helps maintain strategic focus, facilitating effective coordination of activities and maximizing the use of resources to achieve strategic objectives.

Risk management, a significant component of GRC, plays an instrumental role in strategic planning. It helps organizations identify potential threats and opportunities that may impact their strategic objectives. Through risk management, organizations can develop strategies that are resilient and adaptable to uncertainties. It gives them the foresight to anticipate risks and establish effective mitigating mechanisms. As such, risk management transforms strategic planning from a static process to a dynamic one capable of navigating the complex and uncertain business landscape.

Compliance, the third pillar of GRC, ensures that strategic planning aligns with the legal and regulatory obligations of the organization. Compliance helps organizations understand the regulatory environment in which they operate, informing them about the laws, regulations, and standards they must comply with while pursuing their strategic objectives. By integrating compliance into strategic planning, organizations can avoid legal pitfalls, protect their reputation, and foster trust with stakeholders.

Balancing the components of GRC in strategic planning is a critical task. Too much emphasis on one element may undermine the others, leading to a skewed strategic approach. This balance requires leadership to understand the interconnectedness of GRC and how they collectively contribute to strategic success.

Leadership plays an essential role in integrating GRC into strategic planning. Leaders create a GRC-oriented culture, demonstrating a commitment to good governance, effective risk management, and regulatory compliance. They ensure that GRC principles are ingrained in the organization's strategic planning process, guiding it toward its strategic goals while operating within acceptable risk and regulatory compliance.

In essence, GRC plays a fundamental role in strategic planning. It provides a structured approach to setting strategic objectives, making informed decisions, managing potential risks, and ensuring regulatory compliance. By integrating GRC into strategic planning, organizations can create resilient strategies capable of withstanding uncertainties and delivering sustainable success.

Recommendations:

- **Integrate GRC in Strategy**: Recognize GRC as a strategic imperative and integrate it into your strategic planning process. This ensures that strategies are resilient and adaptable to potential risks.
- **Guide Ethical Conduct**: Use GRC to guide ethical conduct in strategic planning. Align strategic goals with your organization's values and ethical standards.
- **Manage Change**: Leverage GRC to manage changes effectively. Ensure that strategic modifications do not compromise governance standards or compliance obligations.
- **Drive Continuous Improvement**: Utilize GRC for continuous improvement. Use GRC tools and methodologies to assess the effectiveness of strategic plans and identify areas for improvement.

Chapter Conclusion

Understanding the significant role of GRC in businesses provides a rich insight into their crucial functions in shaping the strategic direction of organizations. These aspects are deeply interwoven, creating a sturdy yet adaptable foundation that guides the operation and direction of businesses.

Governance forms the structural backbone of an organization, guiding and controlling its operations and decision-making processes. However, it is important to note that governance is not merely about having an established organizational structure and running day-to-day processes efficiently. It further emphasizes transparency in operations and decision-making, accountability for actions and outcomes, and effective leadership that motivates and directs the workforce toward achieving organizational goals. By establishing and ensuring strong governance, businesses set a solid platform that guides them on a clear path toward their strategic objectives while consistently maintaining high ethical integrity.

Risk management forms another critical, dynamic component within businesses. It represents an ongoing process that requires systematic and logical methods for identifying, assessing, and addressing potential risks. If not properly managed, these potential risks could cause businesses to deviate significantly from their strategic path, causing financial, reputational, or operational damage. Therefore, risk management is not a static function that can be established once and left to run its course. It is an ever-evolving process that must be continually reviewed and adjusted to align with the changing business landscape and risk profiles.

On the other hand, compliance is not to be overlooked as a significant part of achieving business objectives. It ensures that a business aligns its operations, strategies, and goals with the relevant laws, regulations, and ethical standards applicable to its industry and operational context. Beyond merely being a legal obligation, compliance is a strategic necessity that builds trust among stakeholders, promotes accountability throughout the organization, and contributes significantly to sustained success.

When these critical elements of GRC are harmoniously blended, they form a resilient and adaptable structure that allows businesses to navigate the complexities of the modern commercial world effectively. This is not about treating GRC as an added layer or an afterthought, but viewing it as an integrated, indispensable framework that guides the organization's strategic planning and operations. Businesses that can effectively comprehend, incorporate, and implement these GRC principles position themselves for long-lasting success in a rapidly evolving and increasingly regulated business environment. They enable themselves to anticipate and react effectively to changes, maintain ethical and regulatory compliance, and pursue their strategic objectives confidently and efficiently.

Case Study: GRC Implementation at SpectraCorp

Harper, the newly appointed CEO of SpectraCorp, a tech-based multinational firm, quickly identified a significant issue in her new role. There was no defined GRC structure. The lack of an integrated GRC system has caused disjointed decision-making, risk exposures, and recurring noncompliance issues. Realizing the criticality of GRC for operational efficiency and resilience, Harper set out to initiate comprehensive GRC implementation.

First, Harper laid the foundation by establishing a governance structure. She implemented board committees to supervise strategic decisions and insisted on creating a transparent reporting structure to enhance accountability. Harper also initiated regular audits and controls, ensuring SpectraCorp's governance aligned with industry best practices.

Next, she turned her attention to risk management. By leveraging her background in data analytics, she introduced advanced risk assessment tools that provided in-depth insights into potential risks. This shift allowed SpectraCorp to anticipate and mitigate potential threats before they become full-blown, improving its operational efficiency and financial resilience.

The third pillar of Harper's GRC strategy was compliance. She built a team to ensure the company adhered to regulatory requirements in all jurisdictions where SpectraCorp operated. Recognizing the dynamic nature of regulatory environments, she adopted a proactive approach, leveraging technology to track and adapt to changes in real time.

Harper understood the need for GRC integration to ensure that all three components – GRC – worked harmoniously. She championed the implementation of an enterprise-wide GRC framework that considered SpectraCorp's specific needs and challenges. This structure was further complemented by a GRC tool that enhanced efficiency and provided necessary oversight.

Recognizing the importance of a GRC-oriented culture, Harper initiated extensive employee training programs and made GRC a part of the organizational DNA. She faced challenges, including resistance to change and a lack of understanding about GRC. However, her steadfast commitment and the deployment of best practices ensured a successful GRC implementation.

CHAPTER 2

The Landscape of Cybersecurity

"In cybersecurity, the destination is not a point but a direction.
The goal is not to achieve perfection, but relentless improvement."

Cybersecurity is a critical concern across all sectors in our increasingly digital world. A comprehensive understanding is necessary, from identifying underlying principles and trends to understanding the technological challenges and opportunities. Regulatory influences and skill gaps further complicate the scenario. The discussion becomes even more nuanced as we consider sector-specific contexts such as the financial industry, healthcare, government, and general businesses. Each sector faces unique cyber threats, data protection issues, technology dependencies, staffing concerns, and compliance impacts. The path to robust cybersecurity lies in recognizing and addressing these factors effectively.

COMPREHENSIVE OVERVIEW OF CYBERSECURITY MATURITY

The progression of the digital era has deeply interwoven the realms of technology, business, and everyday life, thus compelling us to reassess the measures we adopt to protect and secure our information landscape. As the possibilities enabled by technology expand, so do the risks and threats in cyberspace. This amplified cybersecurity landscape defines new paradigms in our professional and personal lives.

The shift toward digitization, which the global pandemic has further accelerated, has essentially turned cybersecurity into a universal concern. Where once the onus of cyber protection might have been seen as resting with IT departments, today, the responsibility extends to everyone, from executives at the helm to individuals using digital services in their homes. The democratization of technology has paralleled the democratization of digital risks.

In business, this has had profound implications. Organizations are no longer merely physical entities but digital structures, their boundaries extended and often blurred by the internet. As a result, cybersecurity threats are driving significant changes in business operations and strategy. Information security is about safeguarding data and ensuring operational continuity, maintaining customer trust, protecting brand reputation, and meeting regulatory requirements.

Moreover, organizations today are critically dependent on many technologies, from cloud services and big data platforms to mobile applications and IoT devices. These technologies have created unprecedented efficiencies and opportunities but have also made new vulnerabilities and entry points for cyber attackers. The threat landscape has expanded and diversified, with cybercriminals continually evolving their strategies and tools in response to cybersecurity advancements.

On the other hand, the same transformative technologies are also enabling more robust defenses. For instance, artificial intelligence (AI) and machine learning are increasingly employed in cybersecurity solutions, allowing for real-time threat detection and rapid response. These systems can analyze vast amounts of data to identify patterns and anomalies that may indicate a cyber threat, significantly outpacing traditional, manual approaches to cybersecurity. The cybersecurity landscape, therefore, is one of perpetual cat-and-mouse, a constant race between those aiming to exploit the digital world and those working to protect it.

Regulation, too, is playing a crucial role in this landscape. As the impacts of data breaches and cyberattacks become increasingly tangible, governments worldwide are responding with stricter data protection laws and cybersecurity regulations. These regulations obligate businesses to prioritize cybersecurity, often requiring them to reshape their processes, systems, and culture. Meanwhile, these regulations also drive demand for cybersecurity skills, which is currently outstripping supply.

The world is undergoing a digital revolution, and the maturation of cybersecurity is a fundamental part of this journey. It defines the way we do business, the way we govern, and even the way we live as individuals.

Recommendations:

- **Emphasize Shared Responsibility**: With digitization becoming ubiquitous, cybersecurity is no longer the sole responsibility of IT departments; it now extends to everyone. Creating a security-conscious culture where every employee understands their cybersecurity role is essential. This approach includes regular training and awareness sessions for staff at all levels.

- **Integrate Cybersecurity into Business Strategy**: In the digital age, organizations are not merely physical entities but are extended and often blurred by the internet. Therefore, cybersecurity should be integral to business operations and strategies. This approach means considering cybersecurity during business decision-making, including new initiatives, partnerships, and investments.

- **Address Emerging Technology Risks**: The growing reliance on various technologies, from cloud services and big data platforms to mobile applications and IoT devices, brings new vulnerabilities and entry points for cyber attackers. Adopting robust security measures, regular risk assessments, and constant vigilance for these technologies can help manage these risks.
- **Leverage AI and ML for Cybersecurity**: AI and machine learning advancements offer opportunities for more robust cybersecurity defenses. These technologies enable real-time threat detection and rapid response, significantly outpacing traditional, manual approaches. Incorporating these tools into the cybersecurity strategy can help stay ahead of emerging threats.
- **Align with Regulatory Requirements**: Complying with relevant laws and regulations is vital with an increasing global focus on data protection and cybersecurity. This process includes keeping abreast of regulation changes, implementing required safeguards, and shaping business processes, systems, and culture to ensure ongoing compliance.

CYBERSECURITY IN THE FINANCIAL INDUSTRY

The financial industry sits in the crosshairs of global cybercrime due to its significant economic and data-rich environment. This sector is frequently targeted for a good reason: it provides lucrative opportunities for cybercriminals eager to exploit weaknesses for financial gain. The methods used by these digital adversaries are evolving and growing in sophistication, encompassing a wide array of strategies from advanced persistent threats (APTs), often state-sponsored, to ransomware attacks that lock institutions out of their critical systems until a ransom is paid.

Furthermore, the financial industry is equally susceptible to insider threats where rogue employees or individuals with inside access can cause substantial damage. This is coupled with a rising trend in socially engineered attacks, in which cybercriminals craft deceptive schemes to trick employees into unwittingly granting them access to the organization's sensitive information or systems. This human element of cybersecurity poses a unique challenge, as it requires technical defenses and continuous education and awareness among staff members.

In addition to the direct threats from cybercriminals, the financial industry contends with complex data protection and privacy laws. International standards such as the Payment Card Industry Data Security Standard (PCI-DSS) necessitate stringent protective measures around payment information. Simultaneously, the US Gramm–Leach–Bliley Act (GLBA) expands these requirements to all personally identifiable information. These laws enforce strict rules for data handling, consent, and breach notification, thus increasing the cyber-security responsibilities of financial institutions.

Yet, the financial industry's challenges do not stop with direct attacks and regulatory compliance. The sector is transforming digitally, increasing its vulnerability to cyber threats. Financial services are increasingly offered through digital platforms – from mobile banking applications and digital wallets to advanced algorithmic trading systems. Each touchpoint expands the attack surface, providing potential entry points for cybercriminals to exploit. This rapid digitization is reshaping the sector and escalating its cybersecurity needs' urgency and complexity.

However, addressing these challenges is hindered by a considerable skills gap. Cybersecurity in the financial sector is a field of unique specificity and complexity. It requires experts who understand the technical aspects of cyber-security and the business processes, regulatory requirements, and the particular technologies used in finance. This level of expertise is in short supply, leading to a talent gap that many financial institutions struggle to bridge. This staffing issue can often result in inadequate defenses, slow incident response times, and a lack of foresight in strategic cybersecurity planning.

Finally, the financial sector's regulatory and compliance landscape presents its challenges. While these frameworks are integral to protecting consumers and preserving the integrity of the global financial system, they can be both a boon and a bane. They act as drivers, compelling financial institutions to maintain high cybersecurity standards and accountability. However, they can also be a burden as they often involve complex, rapidly evolving requirements that demand significant resources to understand, implement, and maintain. The struggle to ensure compliance while enabling efficient and innovative financial services is a delicate balance, further emphasizing the intricacies of cybersecurity in the financial industry.

Recommendations:

- **Strengthen Cyber Defenses**: Recognize the financial industry's significant cyber threats, from state-sponsored APTs to ransomware attacks. Regularly update and bolster your organization's cybersecurity defenses to detect, prevent, and respond to these evolving threats. This involves deploying advanced security technologies, monitoring systems for unusual activity, and implementing effective incident response plans.
- **Prioritize Insider Threat Management**: Be aware of the risks posed by insider threats. Implement stringent access controls, user behavior analytics, and regular audits to identify and mitigate potential threats within your organization. Also, consider implementing a policy of least privilege, where employees only have access to the information they need to perform their duties.
- **Promote Cybersecurity Awareness**: Tackle socially engineered attacks by prioritizing employee education and awareness. Regular training

sessions, simulated phishing exercises, and updates on the latest scam techniques can empower your staff to recognize and avoid falling prey to these schemes. The human element in cybersecurity should not be underestimated, as every staff member can serve as a potential line of defense against cyberattacks.

- **Comply with Data Protection Standards**: Keep up with complex data protection and privacy regulations like PCI-DSS and GDPR. Ensure your organization has stringent data handling, consent, and breach notification procedures. Regular audits and compliance checks should be carried out to ensure ongoing adherence to these regulations and mitigate the risk of noncompliance penalties.
- **Manage Digital Transformation Risks**: As the financial industry increasingly digitizes, managing the associated cyber risks effectively is essential. Regularly assess the security of digital platforms such as mobile banking applications and algorithmic trading systems. Each new touchpoint should be scrutinized for potential vulnerabilities and secured accordingly.
- **Bridge the Skills Gap**: Acknowledge the significant skills gap in cybersecurity in the financial sector. Invest in training and development for your current staff and consider partnering with educational institutions or cybersecurity organizations to attract and cultivate the talent you need. Furthermore, outsourcing certain cybersecurity functions to reputable third-party providers can be a viable option to supplement internal expertise.
- **Balance Compliance and Innovation**: Lastly, acknowledge the challenges of managing regulatory compliance while fostering innovation. Develop strategies to maintain high cybersecurity standards and accountability without stifling the ability to deliver efficient and innovative financial services. It is a delicate balance but achievable with the right approach and consistent effort.

CYBERSECURITY IN THE HEALTHCARE INDUSTRY

The healthcare sector is uniquely vulnerable in the cybersecurity landscape due to several factors: the sensitive nature of the data involved, the critical importance of its services, and its growing dependence on complex, interconnected technologies. Unlike other industries, a cybersecurity incident in healthcare can directly impact human lives, making the stakes exceedingly high.

Patient data, encompassing everything from medical histories to genetic profiles, is among the most sensitive and valuable types of personal information. This data breach can have severe consequences, from identity theft and fraud to potential impacts on insurability and employment. Moreover, the very nature of medical information means it cannot be changed or replaced in the same way as, for example, a compromised credit card number – a medical history compromised once, it remains compromised.

At the same time, healthcare providers are increasingly leveraging digital technologies to improve patient care. Electronic Health Records (EHRs), telemedicine platforms, wearable health monitors, and network-connected medical devices are commonplace. While these technologies offer immense benefits, they also vastly expand the potential attack surface for cybercriminals, creating new vulnerabilities and complexities.

Regulations such as the Health Insurance Portability and Accountability Act (HIPAA) in the United States set stringent standards for the protection and privacy of patient data. These regulations ensure that healthcare providers take appropriate measures to safeguard patient information, whether stored in a physical filing cabinet or a cloud-based EHR system. However, the sheer volume and diversity of healthcare data and the need for rapid, often real-time access to this information make achieving compliance a significant challenge.

The evolution of medical technology presents another set of challenges. Network-connected medical devices, from infusion pumps to MRI machines, are now essential tools in healthcare. However, these devices often run on outdated software, have limited built-in security features, and require continuous availability, making them attractive targets for cybercriminals. Similarly, the advent of telemedicine and remote patient monitoring, accelerated by the COVID-19 pandemic, has introduced additional cybersecurity risks that the healthcare sector is still learning to manage effectively.

Complicating matters further, the healthcare sector faces a significant cybersecurity skills gap. Many healthcare organizations lack the necessary expertise to secure their complex IT environments. This field demands technical cybersecurity skills and an understanding of clinical workflows, patient care processes, and the particular regulatory requirements of healthcare. Filling this skills gap is a pressing issue, as the shortage of cybersecurity expertise can result in unsecured systems, delayed detection of breaches, and ineffective incident response.

Lastly, the regulatory frameworks governing healthcare add another layer of complexity. While these frameworks are crucial for patient safety and data protection, their stringent and often dynamic requirements can be challenging to navigate. Compliance efforts can consume substantial resources and attention, potentially diverting them from other essential tasks. Moreover, the consequences of noncompliance, ranging from hefty fines to reputational damage, further emphasize the critical role of cybersecurity in healthcare.

Recommendations:

- **Establish Strong Data Protection Measures**: Patient data, including medical histories and genetic profiles, is highly sensitive and valuable. Its breach can have severe consequences, from identity theft to insurability and employment. Hence, implementing stringent data protection measures, including encryption, secure data handling procedures, and robust access controls, is vital.

- **Manage Technology-Related Risks**: As healthcare providers increasingly leverage digital technologies like EHRs, telemedicine platforms, wearable health monitors, and network-connected medical devices, the potential cyberattack surface expands. Regular cybersecurity audits, vulnerability assessments, and up-to-date security tools can help manage these new risks.

- **Ensure HIPAA Compliance**: Compliance with regulations like the Health Insurance Portability and Accountability Act (HIPAA) is a significant challenge due to the volume and diversity of healthcare data and the need for rapid access to this information. However, achieving this compliance is crucial to safeguarding patient information and avoiding penalties. Consider regular third-party audits to ensure all cybersecurity practices adhere to these standards.

- **Secure Medical Devices**: Network-connected medical devices, which often run on outdated software and have limited built-in security features, are attractive targets for cybercriminals. Specialized cybersecurity measures should be taken to secure these devices, including secure device configurations, ongoing device monitoring, and timely software updates.

- **Address the Cybersecurity Skills Gap**: The healthcare sector faces a significant cybersecurity skills gap, demanding technical skills and an understanding of clinical workflows, patient care processes, and regulatory requirements. Investing in the recruitment, retention, and upskilling of cybersecurity professionals in this field is vital. Partnerships with academic institutions or online learning platforms can help keep the workforce updated with the latest cybersecurity.

- **Navigate Regulatory Frameworks**: While regulatory frameworks are crucial for patient safety and data protection, their stringent and often dynamic requirements can be challenging. Allocate resources for continuous monitoring of regulatory changes and maintaining compliance. Consider outsourcing or automating compliance tasks to free up resources for other critical tasks.

- **Create a Cybersecurity Culture**: Cultivating a cybersecurity culture is crucial to addressing healthcare's complex cybersecurity issues. This includes regular cybersecurity training for all staff and fostering an environment where cybersecurity is everyone's responsibility.

CYBERSECURITY IN THE GOVERNMENT SECTOR

Governments manage a uniquely broad and sensitive range of data, encompassing everything from citizens' personal information to classified national security details. This wealth of high-value information makes the government sector a prime target for cyber threats of various kinds – state-sponsored attacks, cyber espionage, politically motivated hacktivism, and more. The potential ramifications of a successful attack are vast, extending beyond financial or reputational damage to potentially impacting national security or public safety. This immense responsibility creates a pressing need for governments to maintain rigorous cybersecurity defenses.

Protecting public and classified data is a fundamental obligation in the government sector. Ensuring this data's confidentiality, integrity, and availability is complex. It requires a comprehensive, multilayered defense strategy, encompassing everything from robust encryption techniques to secure data storage practices, stringent access controls, and rigorous audit trails. Governments must ensure various information types, from individual tax records and health data to classified national defense or diplomatic communications documents.

Like many other sectors, governments increasingly rely on technology, introducing cybersecurity challenges. The breadth of government technologies is vast, from public service portals for tasks like license renewals or tax payments to sophisticated military communication systems and national infrastructure control systems. Each of these technologies must be securely managed to prevent unauthorized access and service disruption; a task made all the more challenging by their often highly interconnected nature.

The growing complexity and sophistication of cyber threats have amplified the need for skilled cybersecurity professionals in the government sector. However, attracting and retaining this talent can be a significant challenge. The public sector often faces stiff competition from private industry, which can typically offer more competitive salaries and career growth opportunities. Furthermore, government cybersecurity work's high-stress, high-stakes nature can make these roles challenging to fill and retain.

Government agencies also have to navigate an often complex and demanding landscape of regulatory requirements. These regulations are frequently more stringent than those in the private sector, reflecting government entities' higher stakes and unique obligations. Compliance with these regulations is mandatory and can drive the adoption of robust cybersecurity practices. However, the complexity and evolving nature of these requirements can also consume significant resources and potentially divert attention away from other essential cybersecurity tasks. These regulations also require ongoing investment in compliance expertise, systems, and processes.

The military represents a unique government facet with distinctive cybersecurity challenges and responsibilities. To safeguard a nation's security, the military is often at the forefront of cyber warfare, dealing with sophisticated and persistent cyber threats. These range from state-sponsored attacks designed to breach defense systems and gain strategic advantages to the potential disruption of critical military infrastructure.

One of the fundamental challenges for the military is protecting highly sensitive data and mission-critical systems. This includes everything from classified operational plans to weapons systems data, personnel records, and communication systems. A breach in these areas could compromise national security and potentially endanger lives. Furthermore, the modern battlefield is becoming increasingly digital, with technologies like drones, AI, and satellite communication playing key roles. These digital technologies create additional attack vectors that could be exploited if not adequately secured.

The military is also at the forefront of offensive cybersecurity, defending against cyber threats and actively engaging in cyber operations where necessary. These threats could include disrupting enemy communication systems, infiltrating foreign networks to gather intelligence, or launching pre-emptive strikes against perceived threats. Such activities require an elevated level of cyber proficiency, requiring an expert workforce capable of defending our networks and systems and carrying out sophisticated offensive operations.

In addition, the military faces similar challenges as the broader government sector regarding regulatory compliance and talent acquisition. Military-specific regulations often add additional layers of complexity, and attracting the necessary cybersecurity talent can be challenging given the high-stress, high-stakes nature of military work. Nonetheless, the critical importance of the military's mission and the potential consequences of breaches make cybersecurity an essential priority in this sector. With a constant and vigilant eye on the evolving cyber landscape, the military continues to adapt and strengthen its defenses against the ever-present and evolving cyber threats.

Overall, the government sector's cybersecurity challenges are vast and complex. They encompass the technical aspects of securing a wide array of sensitive data and technologies and the organizational and policy factors, including talent management, regulatory compliance, and allocating limited resources. Despite these challenges, the critical importance of government services and the potential consequences of breaches make cybersecurity an essential priority.

Recommendations:

- **Establish Multilayered Defense Strategies**: Recognizing the vast range of sensitive data managed by governments, from citizens' personal information to classified national security details, it is imperative to implement a comprehensive, multilayered cybersecurity defense strategy. This strategy includes using robust encryption techniques, secure data storage practices, stringent access controls, and rigorous audit trails to ensure data confidentiality, integrity, and availability.

- **Ensure Secure Technology Management**: Given the breadth of technologies governments use, from public service portals to military communication systems and national infrastructure control systems, secure management of these technologies is crucial. Regular security audits, penetration testing, and vulnerability assessments should be conducted to identify and fix potential security flaws. The interconnected nature of these systems demands thorough risk assessments to understand the potential cascading impacts of a security breach.

- **Invest in Cybersecurity Talent**: Address the significant need for skilled cybersecurity professionals in the public sector. This may involve creating attractive career paths within government cybersecurity, offering competitive compensation, and exploring partnerships with academic institutions for a steady influx of talent. Ongoing staff training can also aid in retention and ensure your workforce is equipped with the latest cybersecurity knowledge.

- **Manage Regulatory Compliance**: Given the stringent regulatory landscape that government entities must navigate, significant investment in compliance expertise, systems, and processes is required. Make compliance integral to your cybersecurity strategy and stay updated with evolving regulations. Regular reviews should be carried out to ensure continued compliance, thus minimizing potential penalties and protecting your organization's reputation.

- **Secure Military Cyber Infrastructure**: In the military sector, where cyber warfare poses constant threats, securing highly sensitive data and mission-critical systems should be a priority. This includes protecting classified operational plans, weapons systems data, personnel records, and communication systems. As the modern battlefield becomes increasingly digitized, additional measures must be taken to secure new technologies such as drones, AI, and satellite communication systems.

- **Develop Offensive Cybersecurity Capabilities**: Recognize that the military is not only a defender but also an active player in cyber operations. Develop teams and capabilities to carry out sophisticated offensive operations when necessary, such as disrupting enemy communication systems or infiltrating foreign networks for intelligence. These efforts require a highly skilled and specialized workforce, emphasizing the need for a comprehensive talent strategy.

- **Allocate Resources Wisely**: Lastly, understand the organizational and policy aspects of cybersecurity, including talent management, regulatory compliance, and resource allocation. Given the government sector's vast and complex challenges, cybersecurity should be a top budget priority. Constant monitoring, review, and adjustment of cybersecurity strategies should be carried out to ensure their continued effectiveness in an evolving threat landscape.

CYBERSECURITY IN SMALL TO LARGE ENTERPRISES

Businesses of all sizes and sectors must grapple with cybersecurity threats, from small startups to multinational corporations. Each faces unique cyber risks, whether an emerging fintech innovator, a growing e-commerce platform, or a vast supply chain network. These threats are broad and multifaceted, from sophisticated phishing schemes, supply chain attacks, and malicious insider activities to APTs, Distributed Denial of Service (DDoS) attacks, and ransomware campaigns.

As digitization continues to permeate every aspect of business, the risks associated with cyber threats are more substantial than ever. The internet's global reach, the ubiquity of mobile devices, and the growing reliance on cloud-based services have all contributed to an expanded cyberattack surface. Consequently, businesses must be particularly mindful of securing digital assets, protecting network infrastructures, and building resilience against potential cyber incidents.

Data protection is pivotal for businesses of all kinds. This involves safeguarding sensitive corporate data and protecting customer information, trade secrets, intellectual property, and financial data. Achieving this is vital for regulatory compliance, maintaining customer trust, preserving brand reputation, and ensuring operational continuity.

Moreover, various business-specific technologies necessitate robust cybersecurity measures. These include Customer Relationship Management (CRM) systems, Enterprise Resource Planning (ERP) systems, proprietary software, e-commerce platforms, and various third-party applications. Each system presents unique vulnerabilities, which could serve as potential entry points for cybercriminals. Therefore, businesses must implement multifaceted defense mechanisms, such as robust access controls, continuous monitoring, regular vulnerability assessments, and incident response plans, to protect these critical technologies.

The issue of talent shortage in the cybersecurity field is a significant hurdle for businesses. The demand for cybersecurity expertise vastly outstrips supply, leading to a critical talent gap. Companies often struggle to recruit, retain, and upskill professionals with cybersecurity skills and competencies. This problem is particularly acute for small and medium-sized enterprises (SMEs), which may lack the resources to compete with larger organizations for top talent.

Finally, the role of compliance and regulatory frameworks in shaping businesses' cybersecurity approaches cannot be overstated. Compliance with regulations, such as GDPR, CCPA, and NYDFS, and sector-specific laws like HIPAA or PCI-DSS is an absolute necessity for many businesses. These requirements dictate the minimum data protection and cybersecurity standards and assure stakeholders, customers, and partners that a company takes its cybersecurity responsibilities seriously. However, the ever-evolving regulatory landscape poses another layer of complexity to the cybersecurity challenge, requiring businesses to stay abreast of changes and ensure ongoing compliance.

Recommendations:

- **Implement a Holistic Cybersecurity Strategy**: Considering the multifaceted cyber threats businesses face today, from phishing schemes to DDoS attacks and ransomware campaigns, it is essential to develop a comprehensive cybersecurity strategy. This includes using up-to-date security tools, implementing secure network configurations, establishing incident response and recovery procedures, and providing regular cybersecurity training for all employees.
- **Secure Digital Assets and Network Infrastructures**: With the continuous permeation of digitization in businesses, securing digital assets and

network infrastructures is a critical priority. Regular cybersecurity audits and vulnerability assessments should be conducted to detect potential weaknesses. A secure backup strategy should also be implemented to ensure business continuity during a cyber incident.

- **Prioritize Data Protection**: Protecting corporate and customer data, trade secrets, intellectual property, and financial information should be a core aspect of your cybersecurity strategy. This involves implementing robust encryption, data handling procedures, stringent access controls, and rigorous auditing systems. Data protection standards are essential for regulatory compliance, customer trust, and brand reputation.

- **Safeguard Business-Specific Technologies**: Given the range of business-specific technologies, such as CRM and ERP systems, proprietary software, and e-commerce platforms, businesses should protect these technologies from cyber threats. This includes continuously monitoring these systems, implementing strong access controls, conducting regular vulnerability assessments, and having incident response plans in place.

- **Address the Talent Gap in Cybersecurity**: With the significant shortage of cybersecurity talent, businesses must invest in the recruitment, retention, and upskilling of professionals in this field. Consider partnerships with academic institutions or online learning platforms to keep your team updated with the latest cybersecurity. Outsourcing cybersecurity to a trusted partner can be a viable option for smaller organizations.

- **Maintain Regulatory Compliance**: Given the crucial role of compliance and regulatory frameworks, businesses should stay updated on regulation changes such as GDPR, CCPA, NYDFS, HIPAA, or PCI-DSS. Allocate resources to maintain compliance and consider regular third-party audits to ensure all cybersecurity practices adhere to these standards. Understanding and complying with these requirements mitigates potential penalties and signals stakeholders that your business is committed to cybersecurity.

Chapter Conclusion

The intricate world of cybersecurity in today's era is a complex domain filled with varied challenges and opportunities, requiring ongoing vigilance and adaptation. This is evident across different fields, including the financial and healthcare industries, government institutions, and a broad spectrum of businesses, each facing unique cybersecurity aspects.

In the financial realm, continuous threats from cybercriminals owing to the potential benefits of breaking its defenses are a significant concern. The sector encounters APTs, ransomware, insider threats, and socially engineered attacks. This industry's multifaceted nature, data protection needs, rapid technological evolution, and lack of skilled personnel present unique obstacles. However, the challenges also pave the way for using sophisticated technologies, including AI and machine learning, to enhance the security infrastructure.

The healthcare field, entrusted with extremely sensitive patient data, confronts its unique cybersecurity issues. The consequences of data breaches can be devastating, and the historical delay in executing cybersecurity measures amplifies these issues. The exponential growth of medical technology and devices has drastically expanded the potential attack areas for cybercriminals. Issues with regulatory compliance and scarcity of cybersecurity skills further complicate the situation. Nevertheless, the need to safeguard patient safety and data catalyzes the development of innovative cybersecurity solutions.

The government, responsible for protecting sensitive and often classified information, remains a prime target for cyber threats. Threats include state-sponsored attacks, cyber espionage, and politically driven hacktivism. Security breaches in this sector can have extensive repercussions domestically and internationally, making cybersecurity a high-stakes pursuit. Despite challenges in talent acquisition and stringent regulation compliance, there lies the potential for the government sector to spearhead cybersecurity innovation and exhibit leadership in cyber defense.

Regardless of size or industry, general businesses face various cyber threats as digital technology becomes increasingly integrated into their operations. The expanding attack surface for cybercriminals, the necessity for data protection, the integration of diverse business-specific technologies, and staffing gaps in cybersecurity all pose substantial challenges. However, these hurdles spur businesses to remain agile, promoting a culture that encourages innovation and proactive security measures.

Common threads run through the cybersecurity narrative across all sectors, including the universal need for data protection, reliance on technology, prevalent skills gaps in cybersecurity, and regulatory requirement impacts. Cybersecurity, therefore, is a dynamic and evolving field filled with intricacies and complexities. To understand it fully, one must engage in a journey of ongoing learning and adaptation, continuously reassessing strategies, defenses, and readiness.

Case Study: TechGiant Inc.'s Holistic Approach to Information Security

Meet "TechGiant Inc.," an influential multinational technology company recognized for pushing the boundaries of innovation and maintaining a significant market presence. At TechGiant, Rob, the company's Chief Information Security Officer (CISO), is responsible for developing and implementing the organization's cybersecurity strategy.

Given its industry stature and the vast wealth of proprietary and customer data it holds, TechGiant represents a prime target for cybercriminals. Rob faced the same array of threats familiar to the financial sector, such as APTs, ransomware attacks, and socially engineered attacks. Understanding the high stakes involved, Rob knew he needed to develop and execute a comprehensive, resilient cybersecurity strategy to safeguard the company's sensitive data, uphold its industry reputation, and maintain customer trust.

One critical aspect Rob had to factor into his strategy was TechGiant's ongoing digital transformation. As with many leading-edge companies, TechGiant's push toward digitalization was a double-edged sword. On the one hand, digital transformation opened doors for increased efficiency, innovation, and market competitiveness. On the other hand, it vastly expanded the potential attack surface for cybercriminals, introducing many new access points that could be exploited if not adequately secured.

Rob observed that TechGiant's dependence on various technology platforms and systems – from CRM and ERP systems to e-commerce platforms and cloud-based data storage solutions – represented both a strength and a vulnerability. To address this, he emphasized implementing stringent access controls, establishing continuous security monitoring mechanisms, and conducting regular vulnerability assessments to identify and address potential security weaknesses promptly.

Another significant challenge Rob faced in his role was the notable skills gap in cybersecurity. Despite TechGiant's stature and appeal as a top-tier employer, attracting and retaining professionals with specialized cybersecurity skills was no easy task. The shortage of such talent is an issue shared across sectors. To address this, Rob spearheaded the creation of a two-pronged approach. First, he championed ongoing training programs for existing staff to bolster their cybersecurity skills. Second, he forged partnerships with reputable cybersecurity recruitment firms to attract top talents for specialized roles.

Additionally, Rob had to navigate the complexity of regulatory frameworks and their impact on TechGiant's cybersecurity approach. He knew that adhering to regulations like GDPR, CCPA, and sector-specific regulations was not just an option but a necessity. However, Rob also understood that the dynamic nature of these regulatory requirements and the resources needed to ensure compliance could quickly become overwhelming. To address this, he spearheaded the creation of a dedicated compliance team within his department. This team was tasked with staying abreast of changing regulatory requirements, ensuring the company's ongoing compliance, and allowing the rest of the cybersecurity team to focus on protecting the company from cyber threats.

By taking the time to thoroughly understand the unique threats faced by TechGiant and the shared challenges experienced across sectors, Rob developed a more effective and mature cybersecurity strategy tailored to the organization's specific needs. The journey was filled with complexities and challenges. Still, through careful planning, strategic decision-making, and continual adaptation, Rob has illustrated how businesses can navigate the intricate cybersecurity landscape.

CHAPTER 3

Cybersecurity Leadership: Insights and Best Practices

"As leaders, our task isn't just to manage the present and prepare for the ever-changing future. Cybersecurity isn't static; it's an ongoing challenge that demands continuous learning and adaptation."

Effective leadership in cybersecurity requires a unique set of traits, robust team-building strategies, personal development, and the ability to foresee and prepare for future trends. Ethical decision-making, proficient incident management, and the capacity to balance business objectives with cybersecurity requirements form the core principles. The future of cybersecurity leadership hinges on sound mentoring practices and well-thought-out succession planning. For personal development, achieving a healthy work–life balance is paramount.

THE ESSENTIAL TRAITS OF A CYBERSECURITY LEADER

Steering a successful cybersecurity program requires a clear and comprehensive strategic vision. This vision, once formulated, provides the blueprint for all future activities and goals. Embodying a sense of absolute certainty, even in the face of adversity, is crucial for a leader. It is not enough to have an idea; one must act upon it decisively. Any hesitance or equivocation could compromise the initiative, leading to failure. Being a visionary leader in cybersecurity involves creating a well-defined strategic vision and articulating this vision effectively enough to inspire and guide the team.

The second crucial trait for a cybersecurity leader is exemplary communication skills. A leader should be able to demystify complex security concepts, translating them into a language easily understood by everyone involved. This communication prowess is vital for explaining the nuances of intricate technological ideas to a wide array of audiences, including technical teams, nontechnical stakeholders, and high-level executives.

Deep technological understanding is the third pillar of effective cybersecurity leadership. It is incumbent upon a cybersecurity leader to stay at the forefront of emerging trends and technologies. The world of cybersecurity evolves at an astonishing pace, and leaders must immerse themselves in continuous learning to maintain an understanding of the latest tools, techniques, and threats.

Ethical decision-making forms the fourth crucial trait. A successful cybersecurity leader must display an unwavering commitment to high standards of integrity, regardless of the complexity or contentiousness of a situation. This entails prioritizing privacy and trust, making these values fundamental in their decision-making process. Leading by example helps set a precedent for ethical conduct throughout the cybersecurity industry.

Finally, resilience is essential in the rapidly changing, high-stakes world of cybersecurity. Overcoming obstacles and adversities is part and parcel of the job, and leaders must cultivate the ability to rebound and persevere. Fostering a culture of tenacity and adaptability is critical for teams to respond effectively to the continually evolving landscape of cyber threats. Just as resilience can be built over time in individuals, a resilient culture can be nurtured within an organization, providing a robust foundation for responding to challenges.

Recommendations:

- **Visionary Leadership:** In cybersecurity, having a clear strategic vision and effectively communicating it is key. This vision will guide the cybersecurity team's activities and goals. A visionary leader can confidently make decisions and take action without hesitating or hedging their bets.
- **Effective Communication:** Cybersecurity leaders must translate complex security concepts into language all stakeholders can understand. They must be skilled at explaining complex topics to diverse audiences, including technical teams and nontechnical stakeholders.
- **Technological Acumen:** A cybersecurity leader must keep up-to-date with the latest cybersecurity technologies and trends. They must maintain a strong understanding of the technical aspects of their field to lead their teams effectively.
- **Ethical Decision-Making:** Upholding high standards of integrity is crucial, even in complex or challenging situations. In cybersecurity, leaders must ensure that ethical considerations are central to their decision-making processes.
- **Resilience:** Cybersecurity is a fast-paced, constantly changing field. Leaders in this area must foster a culture of perseverance and adaptability to respond to evolving cyber threats effectively. Resilience is key to overcoming challenges and adversities in this field.

BUILDING AND LEADING EFFECTIVE CYBERSECURITY TEAMS

Effective team construction is a foundational aspect of any high-performing organization. Spotting the right talents and skills is central to this process. It is increasingly recognized that the competition for top talents will be even more intense. Companies that provide their employees additional flexibility may find themselves at an advantage. Within cybersecurity, the challenge lies in identifying the unique mix of competencies necessary for various roles. This task requires a deep understanding of essential technical skills and an appreciation for the softer skills that enable teamwork and fuel innovation.

The role of trust and positive team culture cannot be overstated in fostering collaboration and enhancing the success of a team as a whole. Leaders within the cybersecurity realm must nurture an atmosphere that champions transparency, respect, and open dialogue. They must adopt a growth mindset, promoting learning and innovation as key driving factors for individual and collective success. Creating such an environment reframes mistakes as opportunities for learning, cultivating a culture centered on growth and development.

Innovation is the engine that drives the technology industry, and cybersecurity is no exception to this rule. Given the rapidly changing landscape of cyber threats, fostering continuous innovation and creativity in developing response strategies is crucial. Leaders must encourage their teams to think creatively, challenge existing norms, and innovate problem-solving approaches.

Conflict resolution forms a vital element of team leadership. The high-stakes, fast-paced nature of cybersecurity can often lead to conflicts and disagreements. Leaders must emphasize open dialogue, empathy, and fair treatment when dealing with such situations. Developing quick and practical strategies to identify and handle conflicts is crucial to maintaining a productive and harmonious team.

Lastly, maintaining team efficiency and productivity requires effective performance management. Implementing clear performance metrics, offering constructive feedback, and acknowledging accomplishments enable employees to comprehend their roles and responsibilities better and inspire them to excel. Setting clear expectations and recognizing achievements are key to fostering a motivated and engaged workforce.

Recommendations:

- **Prioritize Skill Identification:** Make a conscious effort to learn about the essential technical and soft skills required in your cybersecurity team. This awareness will help you identify the right talent, ensuring your team has a balanced skill set necessary for success.
- **Cultivate a Growth Mindset:** Actively encourage a culture of transparency, respect, and open dialogue. Embrace a growth mindset that views mistakes as opportunities for learning, fostering a supportive and developmental environment.

- **Encourage Innovation:** Challenge your team to think creatively and avoid questioning the status quo. Promoting a culture of innovation can lead to more effective problem-solving strategies in the dynamic field of cybersecurity.
- **Develop Conflict Resolution Strategies:** Be proactive in handling potential conflicts within the team. Open Communication, empathy, and fairness should be the pillars of your conflict resolution strategy, ensuring a harmonious and productive work environment.
- **Implement Performance Management:** Regularly review performance metrics, provide constructive feedback, and celebrate achievements. Clear expectations and recognition will boost your team's motivation and engagement, increasing productivity and efficiency.

ADAPTING TO EMERGING TRENDS IN CYBERSECURITY LEADERSHIP

Innovation and adaptability are paramount in the realm of cybersecurity leadership. Cybersecurity is characterized by a rapidly changing landscape and swift progress, underscoring the necessity to stay up-to-date with emerging technologies. Equally important is understanding how to integrate these technological advancements into cybersecurity measures and protocols. Such an undertaking calls for an unwavering dedication to continuous learning and the ability to swiftly adapt to novel technological trends, thus emphasizing the need for perpetual evolution in cybersecurity practices.

Furthermore, the role of proactiveness cannot be overstated in cybersecurity. Given the increasingly complex interplay between Technology and business, it is almost inevitable that a discourse on one will invariably include the other. Therefore, predicting potential threats has become an essential aspect of cybersecurity leadership. Harnessing the power of data and analytics can allow for the accurate forecasting of potential cyber threats. This, in turn, empowers organizations to develop and implement robust defensive strategies designed to protect their digital infrastructure.

Recent developments across the globe have highlighted the significance of effective leadership in remote work environments. The transition to remote working practices necessitates the creation of a conducive environment that encourages collaboration, creativity, and innovation, irrespective of the geographical location of team members. Therefore, refining and developing skills for leading remote teams effectively have emerged as a pressing requirement in the modern digital workspace.

Cybersecurity leaders should also emphasize active engagement with the global cybersecurity community. This kind of involvement can facilitate a fruitful exchange of knowledge, keeping abreast with the latest threats and creating opportunities for collaboration and mutual assistance. Participation in this global community can assist organizations in maintaining a vanguard approach to their cybersecurity strategies, thus enabling them to navigate the continuously shifting cybersecurity landscape effectively.

Finally, future-proofing leadership skills are a critical component of cybersecurity leadership. The incessant speed of change that characterizes cybersecurity requires leaders to commit to continuous learning and skill enhancement. This commitment is not just a mere aspiration but a vital necessity for cybersecurity leadership, just as it is for any other field of endeavor. Leaders in the field of cybersecurity should perceive their skills not as fixed assets but as dynamic resources that need constant nurturing and upgrading, ready to meet the challenges of the future.

Recommendations:

- **Embrace Technological Adaptability:** Actively follow emerging technologies and understand how to incorporate them into cybersecurity practices. This will require a commitment to lifelong learning and rapid adaptation to technological changes.
- **Anticipate Threats:** Use data and analytics to predict potential cyber threats. The insights obtained can help in developing robust defensive strategies for your organization.
- **Master Remote Work Leadership:** With the global shift toward remote working, it is vital to master the skills to lead remote teams effectively. Foster an environment that promotes collaboration, creativity, and innovation, irrespective of physical location.
- **Engage with Global Cybersecurity Community:** Regular interaction with international peers in the cybersecurity field can provide valuable insights, keep you updated on the latest threats, and reveal opportunities for collaboration.
- **Future-proof Leadership Skills:** Continuous learning and skill enhancement are vital in the rapidly evolving cybersecurity landscape. Embrace a mindset of ongoing education to stay effective as a leader in this dynamic field.

STRATEGIC DECISION-MAKING IN CYBERSECURITY LEADERSHIP

The role of data-driven decision-making has undeniably grown to become an integral part of strategic leadership within cybersecurity. In cutting-edge organizations where new ideas and products frequently challenge the confines of existing Technology, striking the right balance between fostering a spirit of innovation and ensuring appropriate levels of user privacy and security is imperative. By effectively leveraging data, analytics, and intelligence, leaders in the field of cybersecurity can make informed decisions that strike this delicate balance, giving due consideration to innovation and user privacy and security.

Furthermore, incorporating risk management strategies forms another indispensable facet of strategic decision-making in cybersecurity. The notion of absolute privacy, especially within the technological and cybersecurity context, is more a mirage than a reality. Hence, cybersecurity leaders should be deliberate about incorporating risk assessments into their decision-making frameworks. This proactive approach to identifying and addressing potential vulnerabilities aids in ensuring the maximum possible level of security for the users and the organization.

Financial acumen is significant in any leadership role, and cybersecurity is no different. The tech industry is characterized by a dynamic where traditional approaches often yield innovation. To effectively manage cybersecurity initiatives, leaders should understand and be able to manage their role's financial dimensions. Without robust financial acumen, allocating resources optimally and justifying the costs associated with innovative security measures could pose considerable challenges.

Securing stakeholder alignment is another critical aspect of cybersecurity leadership. In successful business models, the customer is often metaphorically placed at the epicenter of all activities, akin to a valued guest at a party where the company plays the host. Cybersecurity leaders must strive to align their objectives with the overall organizational goals, consistently placing the customer at the heart of their decision-making process.

Lastly, compliance with legal and regulatory stipulations should be woven into the very fabric of all cybersecurity strategies. In a world where data has assumed a role as valuable as precious commodities like oil, the diligent protection of this resource is of utmost importance. By factoring in legal and regulatory requirements as integral components of their cybersecurity strategy, leaders can safeguard their organizations from potential legal complications while maintaining the trust and confidence of their stakeholders.

Recommendations:

- **Prioritize Data-Driven Decisions:** Leverage analytics and intelligence to make informed decisions prioritizing user privacy and security. Embrace a data-driven approach to balance innovation with user safety.
- **Incorporate Risk Management:** Regularly conduct risk assessments to proactively identify and address potential vulnerabilities. Strive to integrate risk management into all aspects of your decision-making process.
- **Develop Financial Acumen:** Understand and manage the financial aspects of your cybersecurity programs. This understanding is critical to effectively allocating resources and justifying innovative security measures' costs.
- **Ensure Stakeholder Alignment:** Align your objectives with the overall organizational goals, keeping the customer at the center of your decision-making process. Strive for constant alignment to maintain stakeholder trust.

- **Uphold Legal and Regulatory Compliance:** Protect your organization by incorporating legal and regulatory requirements into your cybersecurity strategy. This adherence helps mitigate legal complications and maintain stakeholder trust.

DEVELOPING THE NEXT GENERATION OF CYBERSECURITY LEADERS

Mentorship programs play a crucial role in nurturing future leaders in cybersecurity. The philosophy behind effective mentorship involves pushing people to their limits to refine their skills and abilities, molding them into better versions of themselves. Establishing robust mentorship programs within an organization can significantly help groom potential cybersecurity leaders. These programs can give mentees the necessary knowledge, guidance, and experience to thrive in leadership roles. The essence of mentorship also lies in sharing invaluable lessons learned, passing on practical wisdom, and guiding the mentees toward making informed decisions that would benefit the organization.

Another crucial element in grooming future cybersecurity leaders is succession planning. Good companies do not just let leadership roles fall to whoever seems available now; they plan for it. Succession planning involves identifying and preparing potential leaders long before a transition is needed. This early identification and preparation ensure continuity of leadership, minimize disruptions in the organization's cybersecurity posture, and instill confidence in the organization's stakeholders. A structured approach to succession planning can help pinpoint the right talent, hone their skills, and ensure they are ready to take on leadership roles when the time comes.

Promoting diversity and inclusion within an organization is ethically correct and can yield significant benefits. Diverse teams bring different perspectives, experiences, and ideas to the table, leading to better decision-making and representation of all stakeholders. Fostering a diverse and inclusive cybersecurity workforce and leadership can bring innovative solutions to complex problems. By embracing diversity, organizations can tap into a wider pool of talent, leading to enhanced problem-solving and decision-making capabilities, thereby strengthening the organization's cybersecurity defenses.

Continuous learning and development through training and educational initiatives are other essential aspects for aspiring cybersecurity leaders. Cybersecurity is fast-evolving and dynamic, requiring leaders to be constant learners. Growth and comfort rarely coexist, and to excel in a challenging field like cybersecurity, potential leaders must step out of their comfort zones. Regular training sessions, workshops, conferences, and educational programs can provide potential leaders with up-to-date knowledge and skills needed for their roles. These initiatives can prepare them for the challenges they may face and equip them with the tools to navigate the rapidly evolving cybersecurity landscape.

Lastly, effective leadership transition strategies are paramount to maintaining a solid security posture during changes in leadership roles. A significant change, like a leadership transition, carries a certain level of responsibility within a technology-focused organization. Current cybersecurity leaders must ensure smooth transitions that uphold the integrity and security of the organization. Carefully planned leadership transition strategies can mitigate risks, maintain stability, and ensure the continuity of the organization's cybersecurity initiatives.

Recommendations:

- **Strengthen Mentorship Programs:** Invest in robust mentorship programs to nurture potential cybersecurity leaders. Emphasize practical guidance and experience sharing, pushing individuals to refine their skills and excel in leadership roles.
- **Prioritize Succession Planning:** Initiate a structured approach to succession planning, identifying and preparing potential leaders for their future roles early. This early preparation can ensure continuity and minimize disruptions in your cybersecurity posture.
- **Promote Diversity and Inclusion:** Foster a diverse and inclusive workforce. The varied perspectives this brings can enhance your problem-solving and decision-making capabilities, strengthening your cybersecurity defenses.
- **Invest in Training and Educational Initiatives:** Implement regular training sessions, workshops, and educational programs to keep your cybersecurity team up-to-date with the fast-evolving cybersecurity landscape. Constant learning prepares potential leaders for their challenging roles.
- **Implement Leadership Transition Strategies:** Develop effective strategies for leadership transitions to maintain a strong security posture during such changes. Smooth transitions uphold the integrity and security of the organization, mitigating risks and ensuring continuity.

PERSONAL DEVELOPMENT FOR CYBERSECURITY LEADERS

Maintaining a healthy work–life balance cannot be overstated, especially in a demanding field like cybersecurity. While challenging, achieving this equilibrium is vital as it contributes significantly to productivity, stress reduction, and creativity fostering. A balanced life allows cybersecurity professionals to recharge, refresh their perspectives, and develop novel approaches to managing cyber threats. Moreover, organizations that promote a good work–life balance can attract and retain top talents in the field, given that an equilibrium between professional and personal life is an increasingly sought-after factor in job selection.

Emotional intelligence is another vital component of effective leadership in cybersecurity. Developing emotional intelligence can lead to a better understanding of team dynamics and individual motivations, contributing to a compelling and harmonious work environment. Emotional intelligence goes beyond the technical skills required in cybersecurity; it involves positively understanding, using, and managing one's emotions to relieve stress, communicate effectively, empathize with others, and overcome challenges. Leaders with high emotional intelligence can foster better interpersonal relationships, which are fundamental in a team-based environment like cybersecurity.

Time management skills are imperative for cybersecurity leaders due to the job's dynamic and often critical nature. Cybersecurity leaders must make timely decisions and take immediate action, particularly during a potential or ongoing cyberattack. Effective time management includes prioritizing tasks, working efficiently, and delegating when necessary in a role where every second counts. Excellent time management skills can decide between successfully mitigating a threat or suffering a security breach.

Professional networking and community engagement and involvement are crucial for continuous personal development and staying ahead in cybersecurity. By building a robust professional network and engaging actively in the cybersecurity community, leaders can share knowledge, gain insights into emerging threats, and foster collaborative problem-solving approaches. Participation in community initiatives can also present opportunities for thought leadership and influence in the field.

Lastly, crafting and maintaining a personal brand is strategic for cybersecurity leaders. Developing a personal brand involves establishing oneself as a reliable and credible figure in the field, which can lead to increased influence and reach. It is about demonstrating through actions and contributions to the field rather than merely making claims. A solid personal brand can also drive meaningful change in the industry by influencing trends and shaping conversations around cybersecurity issues.

Recommendations:

- **Prioritize Work–Life Balance:** Establish protocols that ensure a healthy work–life balance. Encourage staff to take time off for rejuvenation, enhancing their productivity and creativity in managing cyber threats.

- **Cultivate Emotional Intelligence:** Promote initiatives that foster emotional intelligence among your team. Understanding and managing emotions can enhance interpersonal relationships, leading to a more effective and harmonious work environment.

- **Improve Time Management Skills:** Invest in training that develops time management skills. In the dynamic field of cybersecurity, time is always at a premium.

- **Enhance Networking and Community Involvement:** Encourage your team to participate actively in the cybersecurity community. Sharing knowledge and insights with peers can help you stay ahead of emerging threats and foster collaborative problem-solving approaches.

- **Build a Personal Brand:** Demonstrate thought leadership, significantly influence trends, and shape conversations around cybersecurity issues. A solid personal brand can boost credibility and reach in the industry.

INCIDENT MANAGEMENT AND CRISIS LEADERSHIP

Recognizing that security incidents are inevitable for organizations in the digital age forms a foundational premise in cybersecurity leadership. This awareness of an impending "when" rather than an "if" drives the development of comprehensive preparation and mitigation strategies. Acknowledging this creates an ever-prepared environment to address and manage incidents effectively, mitigating potential impacts and ensuring swift recovery.

Crisis communication holds paramount importance when dealing with security incidents. During crises, transparent, clear, and timely Communication is crucial in maintaining control, minimizing panic, and ensuring efficient and effective incident response. Cybersecurity leaders must communicate effectively with stakeholders, including their teams, other organizational departments, and potentially affected clients or users.

Leadership in the incident response team is critical to directing coordinated action during a security incident. This role involves understanding the dynamics of the incident, making data-driven decisions, and ensuring a streamlined and efficient response. Guiding the incident response team effectively is a significant aspect of cybersecurity leadership, as it can significantly influence the incident's eventual impact and the organization's recovery time.

The importance of post-incident analysis and learning cannot be overstated. Evaluating incidents after they have been effectively contained and managed provides a valuable learning opportunity. A thorough examination can reveal vulnerabilities, ineffective response strategies, or areas requiring further training or education. Cybersecurity leaders must conduct these analyses meticulously to derive actionable insights to enhance future defenses and responses.

Finally, a comprehensive understanding of incident response's legal and regulatory aspects is essential. Cybersecurity leaders must navigate a complex landscape of laws, regulations, and compliance requirements during and after a security incident. This understanding is vital for protecting the organization's data, reputation, and legality, and it helps to prevent potential legal complications or penalties associated with noncompliance or mishandling of data.

Recommendations:

- **Be Prepared for Incidents:** Cultivate a mindset that anticipates potential security incidents. This involves developing comprehensive preparation and mitigation strategies to manage incidents effectively when they occur.

- **Communicate Effectively:** During a security incident, prioritize clear, transparent, and timely Communication to maintain control and minimize panic. Ensure that all stakeholders are informed and that any misinformation is quickly corrected.

- **Lead the Incident Response Team:** Guide your incident response team effectively. Make data-driven decisions and ensure a streamlined and coordinated response to mitigate the impacts of the security incident.
- **Learn from Incidents:** After managing a security incident, conduct a thorough post-incident analysis. Use this analysis to identify improvement areas and strengthen your organization's defenses and response strategies.
- **Understand Legal and Regulatory Aspects:** Stay updated on the latest laws, regulations, and compliance requirements related to cybersecurity. This will help you navigate the legal landscape during and after a security incident and protect your organization from potential legal complications.

LEADING CYBERSECURITY CULTURE AND AWARENESS

Emphasizing a Security-First Culture is a strategic priority that underscores the role of any cybersecurity leader. This necessitates a cultural shift toward proactive, innovative security practices that pervade all aspects of the organization. Embracing this transformative approach marks the cornerstone of effective cybersecurity leadership, as it fosters a climate where security is prioritized and valued by all organization members rather than being seen as just the responsibility of a specific team. This cultural transition is not just a reaction to the latest trends, but is a proactive stance in anticipating and mitigating potential security risks.

Creating effective Training Programs and Initiatives is pivotal to improving the organization's cybersecurity posture. By developing and implementing innovative training programs, cybersecurity leaders can foster an environment where all stakeholders participate actively in maintaining cybersecurity. These programs, tailored to different roles and levels within the organization, educate employees about their role in safeguarding the organization's digital assets and the potential risks of noncompliance. Beyond the traditional confines of classroom training, these initiatives can include hands-on exercises, cyber drills, simulations, and gamified experiences to foster engagement and better retention.

Engagement and Communication form a fundamental pillar in shaping a cybersecurity culture. Recognizing cybersecurity as an ongoing process rather than a static product is essential. This notion urges cybersecurity leaders to transform cybersecurity into a continuous organizational conversation. Establishing open channels for Communication, encouraging feedback, and promoting transparent discussions about security issues can strengthen this process. Engaged employees who understand their roles in the security ecosystem can serve as an organization's first defense against cyber threats.

Reward and Recognition Programs can effectively drive positive cybersecurity behaviors. These initiatives can instill a proactive, security-first culture by rewarding and recognizing individuals or teams for contributing to cybersecurity through innovative ideas, diligent security practices, or outstanding incident response. These programs can also encourage employees to stand up for cybersecurity, promoting ownership and responsibility for the organization's security posture.

Regular Assessments and Improvements are integral to maintaining and enhancing the effectiveness of cybersecurity culture and awareness programs. This ongoing evaluation cycle seeks to identify areas of improvement, inefficiencies, and potential blind spots in the organization's cybersecurity culture. Leaders can gain valuable insights into cybersecurity awareness and organizational behaviors using various assessment tools and methodologies. Continuous improvement, driven by these insights, ensures that cybersecurity programs evolve alongside the rapidly changing cyber threat landscape and the organization's specific needs.

Recommendations:

- **Security-First Culture:** Instill a security-first mindset across the organization. This involves fostering a climate where all employees prioritize and value security.
- **Training Programs and Initiatives:** Develop and implement innovative training programs that encourage active participation in maintaining cybersecurity.
- **Engagement and Communication:** Make cybersecurity an ongoing conversation within the organization. Establish open channels for Communication and feedback to promote engagement and understanding.
- **Reward and Recognition Programs:** Recognize and reward positive cybersecurity behaviors and initiatives. This will help foster a sense of ownership and responsibility among employees.
- **Regular Assessments and Improvements:** Continuously evaluate and improve the organization's cybersecurity culture and awareness programs. This will ensure they remain practical and relevant in the face of evolving cyber threats.

THE ETHICAL DIMENSION OF CYBERSECURITY LEADERSHIP

The crucial role of the ethical dimension in cybersecurity leadership is undeniably immense, with its influence being indispensable in guiding the actions and decisions of those at the helm. Ethical Decision-Making's intricate art and invaluable skills are key to effective leadership within this expansive field. Leaders' essential role shapes an organization's ethical framework, particularly within cybersecurity's broad-reaching and sensitive domain. These leaders essentially become the moral compass for their teams, guiding their actions, directing their efforts, and ensuring that decisions mirror the highest possible standards of integrity and responsibility. They are the torchbearers of ethical values, setting benchmarks for behavior and maintaining a vigilant eye on adherence to ethical standards.

The two interconnected and fundamental principles of Privacy and Data Protection are central to these ethical practices. These are pivotal elements that form the cornerstone of any ethical cybersecurity practice. Upholding individuals' rights to privacy, protecting sensitive data, and maintaining a secure digital environment are foundational to a successful and credible cybersecurity strategy. The significance of these facets becomes magnified when one considers the potential damage and repercussions that can arise from a breach of trust, both on an individual and organizational level. As a cybersecurity leader, prioritizing user and data privacy helps foster an environment of trust, assurance, and confidence that benefits the users and all stakeholders involved. This approach further cements the organization's commitment to ethical conduct, reinforcing its reputation as a trusted entity.

Another significant aspect of ethical leadership in cybersecurity is the creation of safe, secure, and anonymous mechanisms for Whistleblowing and Reporting. It is not uncommon for breaches, flaws, or unethical practices to remain unnoticed or unreported, especially in large organizations where the scale of operations can make such oversights more likely. Therefore, establishing secure and anonymous avenues for staff, stakeholders, and users to raise these issues is critically important. Doing so helps preserve the integrity of security practices and fosters a culture of trust, transparency, and shared responsibility within the organization. It encourages everyone within the organization to uphold ethical standards and creates an environment where potential threats can be mitigated proactively.

Maintaining Compliance with Ethical Standards is another critical responsibility of cybersecurity leaders. The digital technology world is evolving rapidly, and with it comes the ever-increasing volume of data, leading to an intricate and challenging ethical minefield. Ensuring that every operation, piece of data, and action taken strictly adhere to established ethical standards and guidelines becomes a paramount concern. This ongoing task involves handling vast swathes of data, often sensitively, with utmost care and converting them into valuable insights while strictly adhering to ethical norms. It is about navigating the complexities of the digital landscape while ensuring that ethical standards are not compromised.

The critical task of Educating and Encouraging Ethical Behavior forms a significant part of the cybersecurity leader's role. Embedding ethical conduct within an organization's culture necessitates more than a series of rules, regulations, or policies. It requires an active and visible commitment from the leadership to promote and uphold ethical behavior at all levels of the organization. This includes providing necessary and regular training, maintaining open and transparent channels of Communication, and leading by example. The consistent and unwavering promotion of ethical behavior builds a robust and ethical cybersecurity culture that extends beyond the IT department to permeate the entire organization. This comprehensive approach ensures that ethical behavior becomes an intrinsic part of the organizational fabric, guiding actions, decisions, and interactions at all levels.

Recommendations:

- **Embrace Ethical Leadership:** Commit yourself to lead by example in all cybersecurity matters. This commitment extends beyond compliance with laws to incorporate your organization's and society's values and norms. Understand the ethical implications of your decisions and strive to make choices that uphold the highest standards of integrity.
- **Prioritize Privacy and Data Protection:** Make protecting user data and privacy a central component of your cybersecurity strategy. Develop and implement policies prioritizing data protection, ensuring data collection and usage transparency. Regularly review these policies to ensure they continue to meet the evolving challenges in data protection and privacy.
- **Foster a Whistleblowing Culture:** Develop and promote safe and anonymous avenues for whistleblowing and reporting within your organization. Reinforce the importance of these channels to your team and encourage their use. Make sure to act on reports received to demonstrate their value and impact.
- **Promote Ethical Compliance:** Ensure your organization's cybersecurity practices comply with established ethical standards and guidelines. Regularly review these practices to ensure they uphold the highest ethical standards. Use the vast amounts of data your organization handles responsibly, ensuring it is turned into ethically obtained insights.
- **Encourage Ethical Behavior:** Actively promote ethical behavior within your organization. Provide regular training and Communication about ethical standards and practices in cybersecurity. Demonstrate these practices in your leadership and reward ethical behavior in your team to foster a culture of integrity and responsibility.

BALANCING BUSINESS OBJECTIVES AND CYBERSECURITY

In our world, where digital interconnectivity has become the norm rather than the exception, organizations face the demanding challenge of protecting their digital assets. Equally important is the need for organizations to ensure that Cybersecurity Measures seamlessly integrate with and support their Business Goals. This is a tightrope walk that demands an immense degree of creativity and innovation from cybersecurity leaders. Their ultimate aim is to ensure that the organization's security initiatives not only shield it from threats but also boost its strategic objectives and steer it toward its desired direction.

Adding complexity to this delicate balancing act is the practice of Risk-Based Decision-Making. This process entails making well-informed, calculated decisions considering the security needs and the organization's business requirements. The goal is to preserve customer trust, which is invaluable in today's digital marketplace, and mitigate potential financial implications arising from a data breach or other cybersecurity incidents. This dual-focus strategy helps organizations balance maintaining their security infrastructure and achieving their business goals.

Another essential facet of the cybersecurity leadership role is careful Financial Planning for Cybersecurity. In a world where the threat of cybercrime looms large and is ever-present, budgeting and resource allocation for cybersecurity initiatives take on heightened importance. This planning is crucial as every dollar invested in cybersecurity can save many more by protecting the organization from the financial and reputational damage a cybersecurity breach can inflict. Therefore, cybersecurity leaders must have a solid financial management understanding to allocate resources effectively.

In this digital era marked by rapid technological advances, Technology is critical to supporting business objectives while bolstering cybersecurity measures. As digital Technology evolves exponentially, cybersecurity leaders face the challenge of harnessing cybersecurity technologies that protect the organization and enhance and support its business operations. This task requires navigating through potential difficulties and challenges but is crucial for maintaining a robust cybersecurity framework that complements business growth.

Lastly, but equally importantly, is communicating the value of Cybersecurity. Cybersecurity leaders are charged with the crucial task of articulating the business benefits of robust cybersecurity practices. This communication should help stakeholders and decision-makers understand that cybersecurity is not a one-off task but a continuous process integral to the organization's success. By effectively communicating the importance and value of cybersecurity, leaders can ensure the proper prioritization of cybersecurity measures and foster a culture of security awareness across the organization. This communication strengthens the organization's security posture and reinforces its commitment to safeguarding its digital assets.

Recommendations:

- **Foster Innovation:** Commit to fostering innovation within your cybersecurity practices. Doing so can ensure that your security measures align with and enhance your organization's business objectives.
- **Embrace Risk-Based Decision-Making:** Implement risk-based decision-making processes in your cybersecurity strategies. Consider both the security needs and the business requirements when making decisions to maintain customer trust and minimize financial implications.
- **Prioritize Financial Planning:** Take the time to budget and allocate resources for cybersecurity initiatives carefully. Recognize the importance of these investments in protecting every aspect of your business and mitigating potential financial and reputational damages.
- **Leverage Technology:** Utilize the most effective and relevant cybersecurity technologies to protect and enhance your business operations.

Stay updated with the latest advancements in cybersecurity technology and leverage them to your advantage.

- **Communicate Value:** Continually articulate the business benefits of robust cybersecurity measures to all stakeholders and decision-makers in your organization. Help them understand that cybersecurity is an ongoing process integral to the organization's success.

LEARNING FROM MILITARY LEADERSHIP

The realm of cybersecurity leadership can draw a wealth of meaningful insights from the field of military leadership. One of the core principles of military leadership that can significantly enhance the cybersecurity decision-making process is Disciplined Decision-Making. This principle suggests that the freedom to navigate the challenging terrain of cybersecurity can be achieved by applying disciplined, structured thinking. It underscores that clear, deliberate decisions made under high-pressure situations are pivotal in maintaining a robust cybersecurity environment.

Moreover, the concept of a transparent Chain of Command and Communication, a key element in military operations, is equally crucial in cybersecurity. Ensuring that there is a well-defined hierarchy and that effective communication channels exist between different tiers of the organization can streamline processes, promote efficiency, and foster a sense of unity among team members. It enables swift responses to incidents and ensures that every team member understands their responsibilities, which is critical in a field as rapidly evolving and as crucial as cybersecurity.

Another noteworthy lesson cybersecurity can take from military leadership is the emphasis on Training and Preparedness. Just as military forces train tirelessly to be prepared for various potential scenarios, cybersecurity teams must also be well prepared to anticipate and respond to multiple threats and incidents. By incorporating military-style training methodologies, cybersecurity leaders can foster an environment that allows for continuous learning, growth, and resilience, even in the face of setbacks and failures. This approach instills a mindset that views setbacks not as final but as stepping stones toward improvement and ultimate success.

Risk Management and Situation Analysis, another critical component of military leadership, is equally vital to strengthening cybersecurity defenses. Cybersecurity leaders can significantly enhance their ability to anticipate potential threats by adopting military-style strategies for risk assessment and situational analyses. Moreover, they can design more effective approaches to mitigate these threats, leading to a more secure and resilient cyber environment.

Finally, military leadership's emphasis on Team Cohesion and Morale can also be adopted fruitfully in cybersecurity. The essence of this concept lies in the understanding that a united team is much more potent than the sum of its members. By fostering a culture of unity, mutual respect, and shared purpose among their groups, cybersecurity leaders can motivate their teams to work together more effectively. This team unity can drive them to overcome even the most daunting cybersecurity challenges.

Recommendations:

- **Embrace Disciplined Decision-Making:** Implement disciplined, structured thinking in your decision-making processes. This approach can help you navigate complex, high-pressure decisions in cybersecurity more effectively.
- **Establish Clear Chains of Command and Communication:** Create clear hierarchical structures and effective communication channels in your organization. This can enable swift incident response and ensure everyone is on the same page.
- **Prioritize Training and Preparedness:** Adopt military-style training methodologies to prepare your teams for various threats and incidents. Cultivate an environment that promotes learning and growth, even in the face of setbacks.
- **Leverage Risk Management and Situation Analysis:** Utilize military strategies for risk assessments and situational analyses to better anticipate and mitigate potential threats. This can lead to a more secure and resilient cybersecurity environment.
- **Foster Team Cohesion and Morale:** Cultivate a sense of unity, mutual respect, and shared purpose among your team members. This can significantly enhance teamwork and drive your team to overcome even the most challenging cybersecurity objectives.

FUTURE TRENDS AND PREPARING FOR WHAT'S NEXT

The twin pillars of adaptation and innovation are critical for survival in cybersecurity. The cybersecurity landscape is dynamic and constantly evolving, mandating a similar continuous evolution in strategies, systems, and leadership. As such, cybersecurity leaders must be fully immersed in the ever-changing cybersecurity trends, proactively engaging with information that can shape the future of their organization's security posture. This proactive approach, combined with an engaged understanding of the field, can equip leaders with the necessary insight to predict how these trends could potentially impact their organization's security landscape and thereby guide them in formulating efficient countermeasures.

The Cyber Threat Landscape is a prime area of continuous change in cybersecurity. With threats evolving in sophistication and potential destructiveness at an alarming pace, leaders need to adopt a mindset that fosters innovation and resiliency. Rather than being restrained by obstacles, leaders should focus on overcoming hurdles and continuously seeking new ways to redefine problems and solutions. The emphasis here should lie in transforming challenges into opportunities, facilitating improvement and growth within the cybersecurity environment.

Another key player in the cybersecurity world is the advent and adoption of Emerging Technologies. As technological advancements continue to permeate all aspects of our lives, it is incumbent upon leaders to comprehend not only the potential benefits of these technologies but also the potential security implications they may harbor. This calls for constant vigilance, an unending learning cycle, and the ability to adapt swiftly to ensure that security measures evolve in parallel with technological progress.

Also crucial in the ever-evolving cybersecurity world is the need for a Scalable Cybersecurity Program. As threats and technologies continue to morph and expand, so must the cybersecurity programs designed to combat them. These programs should be designed with scalability and flexibility at their core, allowing for a change in direction as required. This inherent flexibility will enable organizations to confront new challenges head-on, maintaining an effective security posture even amidst the rapidly changing cybersecurity landscape.

Further, the practice of Succession Planning and Developing Future Leaders is of paramount importance. As the cybersecurity field morphs and evolves, it will necessitate a generation of leaders capable of navigating this unpredictable terrain. Placing trust in and investing resources in the next generation of cybersecurity leaders will play a pivotal role in cybersecurity programs' ongoing success and resilience. This involves recruiting and training the right talent to be agile, innovative, and well-informed leaders capable of steering the cybersecurity ship through choppy waters.

Recommendations:

- **Stay Informed on Cybersecurity Trends:** Cybersecurity leaders should make a conscious effort to remain updated about the latest trends in the field. This can involve attending relevant webinars, reading industry reports, and networking with other professionals.

- **Understand the Evolving Cyber Threat Landscape:** Regularly conduct threat assessments to understand the emerging threats and their potential impact on your organization. Use these insights to devise effective countermeasures.

- **Embrace Emerging Technologies:** Stay abreast of emerging technologies and understand their potential security implications. Implement security measures that are capable of adapting to rapid technological changes.

- **Develop a Scalable Cybersecurity Program:** Design your cybersecurity program with scalability and flexibility. This will allow it to adapt and evolve alongside the changing threats and technologies.

- **Invest in Succession Planning and Developing Future Leaders:** Invest time and resources in identifying and training future leaders. Foster an environment that encourages learning and adaptation, preparing them to lead in the dynamic field of cybersecurity.

Chapter Conclusion

Navigating the dynamic terrain of cybersecurity, leadership is perceived less as a fixed achievement and more as an enduring expedition. This journey calls for a profound understanding of the process as a continuous one, demanding resilience, versatility, and an unwavering commitment to lifelong learning. Such a mindset forms the bedrock for successfully steering through the intricate waters of cybersecurity.

Reflection and continual self-enhancement form an integral part of this leadership journey. It involves reaching milestones and gleaning lessons from each encounter, irrespective of whether it was a triumph or a setback. Surrounding oneself with a network of seasoned professionals and mentors can deliver invaluable insights, perspectives, and feedback, all contributing to an ongoing cycle of personal and professional evolution.

Staying motivated and inspired during challenging times is another pivotal element of this journey. Although the cybersecurity landscape is laden with potential threats and challenges, it offers numerous opportunities for innovation and progression. The ability to remain inspired, sustain a creative mindset, and consistently innovate, even in the face of adversity, distinguishes a true cybersecurity leader.

The leadership journey also significantly emphasizes the leader's legacy and contributions. A leader's influence reverberates beyond their tenure, reflecting in the legacy they leave behind and the positive transformations they initiate. The goal of a genuinely efficacious cybersecurity leader should be to forge a lasting impact on their organization and its people, thereby enriching the landscape of cybersecurity.

Irrespective of the challenges faced or victories savored, each leadership journey leaves behind a unique footprint. The hope is that the insights provided throughout this guide will illuminate and enhance your pathway in cybersecurity leadership's complex yet rewarding domain.

Case Study: The Transformation of Cybersecurity Leadership at CyberFusion Inc.

In the bustling city of Techville, nestled among innovative tech startups and well-established tech giants, stood CyberFusion Inc., a promising company specializing in network security solutions. The company was recognized for its cutting-edge technologies but struggled with a significant challenge: ineffective cybersecurity leadership. This was until Kurt, a seasoned IT professional, became the Chief Information Security Officer (CISO).

Kurt joined CyberFusion Inc. with a wealth of knowledge and a clear, strategic vision for the company's cybersecurity program. He knew that having a comprehensive cybersecurity program was more than just about being technologically adept; it was about being resilient, ethical, and communicative with stakeholders across the organization. Kurt believed that "leadership is about making others better as a result of your presence and making sure that impact lasts in your absence," a sentiment expressed by Sheryl Sandberg.

As a result of this belief, Kurt undertook a company-wide assessment to understand the current cybersecurity landscape and identify areas for improvement. This process involved technical reviews and considered team morale, communication channels, and existing training programs. Kurt also made it a point to communicate his findings and recommendations transparently to all stakeholders.

Kurt adopted a culture of trust and respect in leading the cybersecurity team. He focused on talent identification, selecting the right blend of skills and competencies for diverse cybersecurity roles. He fostered an environment that encouraged creative problem-solving and innovative approaches to cybersecurity, addressing conflicts promptly and fairly. As Bill Gates said, "We always overestimate the change that will occur in the next two years and underestimate the change that will occur in the next ten," he aimed to prepare his team for the long-term challenges of cybersecurity.

Under Kurt's leadership, CyberFusion Inc. began to see a transformation. The cybersecurity team was more efficient and motivated, and the organization became more aware and respectful of cybersecurity policies and procedures. Kurt also ensured that he stayed abreast of emerging technologies and anticipated threats by leveraging data analytics, thus preparing for potential cyber threats effectively.

Kurt's approach to leadership at CyberFusion Inc. truly embodied the insights and recommendations provided in this guide. His continuous journey of learning, reflection, motivation, innovation, and leaving a positive legacy has made a significant difference in the company's cybersecurity posture. His story serves as a reminder that effective leadership, coupled with an understanding of cybersecurity, can make a substantial difference in a company's journey.

CHAPTER 4

Cybersecurity Program and Project Management

"In the complex world of cybersecurity, remember that simplicity can be the highest form of sophistication. To create robust and efficient systems, sometimes less is indeed more."

Program and project management play pivotal roles in cybersecurity, dictating how security efforts are structured and implemented. Understanding these concepts, their relevance to cybersecurity, and their unique nuances within this context is crucial. Various cybersecurity projects can be categorized and managed using fundamental project management techniques, spanning the life cycle to budgeting. Agile project management, a modern, flexible approach, is highly applicable to cybersecurity. Beyond this, the management of overarching cybersecurity programs requires significant attention. Central to these efforts are communication and collaboration within cybersecurity projects. The importance of effective program and project management is ever-present, and in this rapidly changing field, the need for continual learning and adaptation is paramount.

PROGRAM AND PROJECT MANAGEMENT IN CYBERSECURITY

Change is a fundamental component of our world and its functioning, which applies significantly to project and program management. Businesses implement strategic methodologies to navigate challenges, capitalize on newfound opportunities, and institute crucial enhancements. Project and program management form the structured spine of an organization's growth trajectory.

In essence, projects are temporal initiatives with defined starting and ending points instituted to deliver a distinct outcome, service, or product. Each project is like a solo journey with a clear objective and termination. Conversely, programs encompass interconnected projects managed collectively to achieve benefits and efficiencies that would otherwise be elusive if these initiatives were managed separately.

When these principles are applied to cybersecurity, they produce a complex and multifaceted environment. This sphere incorporates diverse stakeholders, variable risks, and numerous strategic objectives. It becomes clear that directing these cybersecurity projects or programs is not a trivial task. Instead, it demands an in-depth understanding of cybersecurity and project and program management tenets.

Every organization presents a distinct array of cybersecurity challenges, which can originate from several fronts. Some may arise from the particular technology deployed by the firm, while others might be driven by the organization's operational nature or regulatory stipulations. Organizations frequently launch a set of projects to address these issues. Each project is a unique endeavor with a clear target – resolving a specific problem or enhancing a particular component of the organization's cybersecurity posture.

In conjunction, the concept of programs adopts a broader view. In the context of cybersecurity, a program is a strategic undertaking that consolidates multiple projects. This initiative aims to provide overarching direction and coordination, assuring that the results of individual projects dovetail with the organization's broader cybersecurity goals and strategies.

Thus, a structured approach to problem-solving and continual improvement is indispensable in the convoluted world of cybersecurity. This is precisely where project and program management principles become an invaluable asset.

Recommendations:

- **Understand the Landscape:** Gain a comprehensive understanding of your organization's unique cybersecurity landscape. This includes recognizing the risks associated with the technology you have deployed and understanding how the nature of your business and regulatory requirements impact your cybersecurity needs.

- **Implement Project Management Principles:** Apply project management principles to tackle your cybersecurity challenges. Each project should be designed to solve a specific problem or enhance a particular aspect of your cybersecurity posture.

- **Adopt a Program Mindset:** Do not view your cybersecurity initiatives as standalone projects. Instead, adopt a program mindset, considering how each project aligns with your cybersecurity goals and strategies. This will help ensure that all your initiatives work together to improve your cybersecurity posture.

- **Use a Structured Approach:** In the complex world of cybersecurity, a structured approach is crucial. Use project and program management principles to guide your initiatives and ensure that you are continuously improving your cybersecurity posture.

- **Continual Improvement:** Embrace the idea of continuous improvement. Just as project and program management involves iterative processes, your approach to cybersecurity should also involve continual adjustments and enhancements based on learning from past projects and current threats.

TYPES OF CYBERSECURITY PROJECTS

The domain of cybersecurity primarily focuses on the implementation and maintenance of robust protective measures designed to safeguard both physical and digital assets. This involves many activities, some of which revolve around introducing and upgrading security software. This software usually includes, but is not limited to, antivirus programs, systems designed to detect and prevent unauthorized access or intrusion, as well as firewalls intended to monitor and control incoming and outgoing network traffic based on predetermined security rules. Each deployment of this nature effectively aims to strengthen and enhance an organization's digital defenses against the numerous and ever-evolving cyber threats in today's interconnected world.

In addition to digital security, the integrity of physical security systems is equally important in a comprehensive security strategy. Projects in this category frequently involve the installation of physical security apparatus. One example is biometric scanners, which provide sophisticated access control by authenticating individuals based on their unique physical characteristics. Other examples include closed-circuit television (CCTV) systems for surveillance and deterrence, network routers to handle and direct data traffic, and physical firewalls to further safeguard the network from potential cyber threats. The effectiveness of an organization's cybersecurity strategy is often reliant on the strength of these physical security measures and should, therefore, not be overlooked.

Another crucial component of a comprehensive security strategy is compliance. This involves ensuring that the organization's security measures and protocols align with regulatory requirements and industry-specific security standards. Projects under this category often include conducting internal audits to assess the current state of compliance, carrying out gap analyses to identify areas that need improvement, and implementing corrective actions to address the identified vulnerabilities. The primary goal of these activities is to maintain compliance with the law. However, they also play a critical role in establishing and maintaining trust with the organization's customers and stakeholders by demonstrating that their data is handled securely and their privacy is respected.

Lastly, network security enhancements are critical to improving an organization's resilience against cyber threats. Projects in this category might involve measures to strengthen encryption standards, thereby making data harder for unauthorized individuals to read. Others might focus on establishing protocols for secure remote access, critical to the current climate of increased remote work. Additional efforts might involve hardening network devices against potential attacks. The inherent vulnerabilities in interconnected digital systems mean that any cybersecurity strategy should prioritize network security.

Recommendations:

- **Embrace Software Upgrades:** Regularly review and update your security software, including antivirus programs and intrusion detection systems. By keeping your software current, you enhance the ability of your plans to detect and counter new threats.
- **Strengthen Physical Security:** Do not underestimate the importance of physical security measures. Invest in advanced devices like biometric scanners and CCTV systems. Regularly review and update these systems to ensure they meet the evolving security needs of your organization.
- **Prioritize Compliance:** Familiarize yourself with the regulatory and industry-specific security standards your organization needs to meet. Conduct regular internal audits and gap analyses, and be proactive in implementing corrective actions to ensure full compliance.
- **Enhance Network Security:** Regularly review your network security measures. This could involve upgrading encryption standards, establishing secure remote access protocols, or hardening network devices against potential attacks. Keeping your network secure is an ongoing process that requires constant attention.
- **Continual Education:** Stay updated on the latest trends and developments in the cybersecurity domain. This knowledge will allow you to anticipate potential threats and adapt your organization's security strategy accordingly. This could involve attending webinars, subscribing to industry publications, or participating in relevant training programs.

PROJECT MANAGEMENT FUNDAMENTALS APPLIED TO CYBERSECURITY

The broad and encompassing realm of project management includes numerous indispensable concepts that directly apply to cybersecurity. A more profound comprehension of these principles allows for more effective and efficient execution of cybersecurity projects. Such principles cover areas including, but not limited to, understanding the life cycle of a project, defining its scope, creating and maintaining a schedule, effectively allocating resources, handling the budget, and managing associated risks. Delving into these principles aims to build a robust foundation that can effectively guide the management of cybersecurity projects.

The life cycle of a project refers to the sequence of stages it undergoes, beginning with the initial spark of conception and concluding with the ultimate wrap-up and review of the completed project. In the context of cybersecurity, these stages could involve the initial identification of a particular security need or vulnerability, followed by the creation of a comprehensive response plan. This leads to the execution of predetermined security measures before culminating in a final review to assess the project's effectiveness and gather learnings for future initiatives. The ability to effectively manage each stage of this life cycle is vital, as it can significantly influence the ultimate success of a cybersecurity project.

Defining the scope of a project involves detailing the specific goals, deliverables, features, and tasks that will collectively constitute the project. When dealing with cybersecurity, the scope might include identifying the exact systems that need protection, outlining the potential threats against which safeguards need to be erected, and pinpointing the appropriate protective measures to be deployed. Defining the scope with clarity and precision helps manage expectations, ensuring that all team members are aligned and that their collective efforts are coordinated and focused.

The creation of a project schedule is another fundamental aspect of project management. This involves laying out the timeline for the project, including establishing deadlines for each task. Within cybersecurity, the speed of the response can often be the determining factor in minimizing the potential damage that can arise from a cyber incident. As such, scheduling in cybersecurity projects must balance the need for meeting deadlines with the necessity for rapid execution to manage potential threats effectively.

Resource allocation is yet another pivotal component of project management, which involves designating the necessary personnel, equipment, and funds for each task involved in the project. In cybersecurity, this might involve deciding which team members are best suited to work on specific tasks, determining the required tools and resources, and designating a portion of the project's budget for each task. Effectively allocating resources is vital to avoid overstretching, ensuring that each task is executed to the best possible standard.

The creation and management of a budget within project management involves estimating the costs associated with the project and ensuring these align with the resources that have been allocated. This might include calculating the costs of new software, hardware, personnel training, and other factors regarding cybersecurity. Budget management is crucial to avoid cost overruns and ensure the project delivers maximum value for the resources invested.

Finally, risk management is a vital component of project management, and perhaps nowhere is this more true than cybersecurity. This involves identifying, assessing, prioritizing potential risks, and implementing strategies to minimize their impact. Given the unpredictability and potential severity of cyber threats, effective risk management can be a deciding factor in the prevention of breaches and in reducing the impact when breaches occur.

Recommendations:

- **Understand the Life cycle:** Commit to a thorough understanding of the project life cycle in the context of cybersecurity. This involves identifying security needs, creating response plans, executing security measures, and reviewing the project's outcomes. Recognizing the importance of each stage will lead to more successful project execution.

- **Define the Scope:** Be clear and comprehensive when defining the scope of your cybersecurity projects. This includes identifying the systems to be protected, the threats to counter, and the protective measures to implement. A well-defined scope can greatly enhance project efficiency and effectiveness.

- **Prioritize Scheduling:** Ensure the creation of a well-considered schedule that balances the need for rapid response with meeting set deadlines. The ability to act swiftly can often be a deciding factor in minimizing the potential damage from cyber threats.

- **Master Resource Allocation:** Develop a deep understanding of effectively allocating resources, including personnel, tools, and budget. Ensuring that each task has the necessary resources can significantly enhance the overall success of your cybersecurity projects.

- **Emphasize Risk Management:** Continually improve your risk management skills. Being able to identify, assess, prioritize, and mitigate risks is an essential skill in the cybersecurity field. Effective risk management can significantly decrease security breaches' chances and potential impact.

AGILE PROJECT MANAGEMENT FOR CYBERSECURITY

The following discussion delves into the principles and methodologies of Agile Project Management and their practical application within cybersecurity projects. The methodologies of Agile, including popular systems like Scrum and Kanban, have their roots in the software development industry. Still, they present significant advantages when applied in the field of cybersecurity.

The philosophy of Agile Project Management places a high premium on concepts such as iterative progress, flexibility, and the active involvement of stakeholders. These principles can be of significant value in dealing with the dynamic nature of cyber threats and the consequent need for rapidly evolving security responses. Agile's emphasis on iterative progress lends itself to the continuous improvement and refinement of security measures. Meanwhile, its inherent flexibility allows for efficient adaptation to evolving threat scenarios. Furthermore, active stakeholder involvement helps ensure that devised security solutions align with the broader business needs and objectives, resulting in more effective and appropriate security implementations.

Within the Agile methodology, various sub-methodologies can be effectively employed in managing cybersecurity projects. These include Scrum and Kanban, which offer unique advantages in this context. Scrum is particularly effective for projects with defined objectives but without a delineated solution. The iterative nature of Scrum lends itself to the progressive discovery and implementation of solutions, as it allows for constant refinement and improvement. On the other hand, Kanban is well suited for ongoing cybersecurity tasks, including threat monitoring and incident response. The visual nature of Kanban boards provides a straightforward way for teams to track, manage, and prioritize tasks effectively, making it an invaluable tool in cybersecurity.

Incorporating Agile principles in the management of cybersecurity projects brings several substantial benefits. It allows for faster response times in the face of security threats, enhancing an organization's ability to prevent or mitigate potential damages. The flexibility inherent in Agile methodologies enables cybersecurity teams to adapt more quickly and effectively to evolving threat landscapes. Furthermore, Agile promotes improved collaboration among team members, facilitating the sharing of expertise and knowledge. Regular feedback loops, a core component of Agile methodologies, ensure that corrective measures can be identified and implemented swiftly. This ability to respond rapidly can be pivotal to reducing potential damage from cyber threats. Finally, Agile approaches promote transparency in project progress and risk management, enabling more informed and effective decision-making processes.

Recommendations:

- **Embrace Iterative Progress:** Understand and value the principle of iterative progress inherent in Agile methodologies. This approach allows for continuously improving your security measures and can lead to more effective strategies to counter cyber threats.
- **Leverage Flexibility:** Use the flexibility built into Agile project management to adapt to evolving threat scenarios swiftly. This adaptability is particularly beneficial in the dynamic field of cybersecurity, where threats constantly change and evolve.
- **Foster Stakeholder Involvement:** Ensure the active involvement of stakeholders in your cybersecurity projects. This involvement can help align security solutions with business needs and objectives, enhancing your cybersecurity strategy's effectiveness.
- **Utilize Suitable Methodologies:** Choose an appropriate Agile methodology depending on your project requirements. Scrum can benefit projects with defined objectives but unknown solutions, while Kanban can be advantageous for ongoing tasks such as threat monitoring and incident response.
- **Prioritize Feedback Loops:** Regularly use feedback loops to ensure swift identification and implementation of corrective measures. This can significantly reduce potential damage from cyber threats and enhance the overall security of your systems.

MANAGING CYBERSECURITY PROGRAMS

Multiple projects with unique objectives and challenges are at the heart of a cybersecurity program. Managing a program of this nature is a complex task that necessitates aligning these disparate projects toward a unified goal: enhancing the organization's cybersecurity posture. This task is not straight-forward and calls for the precise orchestration of resources, time, and efforts across different projects harmoniously and coherently. It is akin to conducting a symphony where every musician, or in this case, every project, contributes to a united, harmonious whole.

Governance is the framework and processes through which the cyberse-curity program is overseen and controlled. The importance of effective gov-ernance in such programs cannot be overstated. It ensures that the program aligns with the organization's strategic objectives, adheres to the best prac-tices in the industry, and complies with the necessary regulatory requirements. Governance does not simply exist for oversight; it plays a significant role in decision-making related to the direction of the program, allocation of resources, management of risk, and engagement of stakeholders.

Another pivotal aspect of managing cybersecurity programs is the set-ting of strategic objectives. These objectives elucidate what the cybersecurity program intends to achieve in the long run. The objectives could be manifold, ranging from enhancing system resilience, reducing system vulnerabilities, and achieving regulatory compliance to improving threat detection capabilities. These strategic objectives serve as guiding stars, directing the entire cyberse-curity program.

Alongside strategic objectives, Key Performance Indicators (KPIs) are measurable milestones that track progress toward these objectives. In a cybersecurity program, KPIs could encompass metrics such as the num-ber of vulnerabilities identified and rectified, the time to respond to secu-rity incidents, or even the level of employee awareness about cybersecurity protocols. These KPIs help assess the program's effectiveness and identify improvement areas.

Stakeholder management is another crucial element in a cybersecurity pro-gram. Stakeholders in such a program could include a wide range of individuals and groups, from senior management and employees to customers, regula-tory bodies, and even the general public. Managing these stakeholders involves informing them about the program's progress, actively addressing their concerns, and incorporating feedback.

Effective stakeholder management can significantly enhance the buy-in for the cybersecurity program and improve its overall success. It bridges the gap between the program and the people it affects, promoting transparency, com-munication, and trust. By keeping stakeholders informed, addressing their con-cerns, and integrating their feedback, an organization can foster a supportive environment for its cybersecurity program.

To sum up, managing a cybersecurity program is a complex and multifac-eted process, encompassing the alignment of multiple projects, program gov-ernance, setting strategic objectives and KPIs, and stakeholder management. Each of these elements, while individually significant, must work in harmony to establish an effective cybersecurity program that aligns with an organization's goals, meets compliance requirements, and is capable of responding to the ever-evolving landscape of cyber threats.

By comprehensively understanding these facets, organizations can better navigate the complex task of managing cybersecurity programs, leading to more robust cyber defenses, better compliance with regulations, and a more secure operational environment.

Recommendations:

- **Unify Your Projects:** Consider all your cybersecurity initiatives as parts of a larger whole. Ensure each project contributes to the overarching objective of strengthening your organization's cybersecurity posture. This could involve regular alignment meetings or integrated project management tools.
- **Establish Strong Governance:** Develop a robust governance framework for your cybersecurity program. This should involve clear processes for decision-making, resource allocation, risk management, and stakeholder engagement. Regularly review and update this framework to ensure it remains relevant and practical.
- **Set Clear Strategic Objectives:** Define what your cybersecurity program aims to achieve long term. These goals could be related to system resilience, vulnerability reduction, regulatory compliance, or threat detection. Ensure these objectives are clear, measurable, and aligned with your organization's strategy.
- **Use Key Performance Indicators:** Develop and track KPIs to measure progress toward your strategic objectives. These could include metrics like the number of vulnerabilities addressed, incident response times, or levels of employee cybersecurity awareness. Regularly review these KPIs to assess your program's effectiveness and identify areas for improvement.
- **Manage Your Stakeholders:** Engage actively with all stakeholders, from senior management and employees to customers and regulators. Keep them informed about the program's progress, address their concerns, and incorporate feedback where possible. Effective stakeholder management can enhance buy-in for your program and contribute to its overall success.

COMMUNICATION AND COLLABORATION IN CYBERSECURITY PROJECTS

A communication plan is a blueprint that details key aspects of project information dissemination: identifying who should be kept in the loop, defining the information they require, scheduling when they should receive this information, and strategizing how this information will be delivered. Within cybersecurity, a communication plan is pivotal to ensure all stakeholders, including team members, senior management, customers, and more, are duly informed about the project's progress, imminent risks, and other pertinent details. This tool is indispensable for managing expectations, streamlining decision-making processes, and cultivating trust within the project environment.

Deeply rooted in the essence of a communication plan is stakeholder analysis. This process involves identifying and understanding the stakeholders involved in a project. It necessitates considering their interests, gauging their influence, and comprehending their expectations. The insights gleaned from a thorough stakeholder analysis are critical for managing their involvement effectively and appropriately. In a cybersecurity project, stakeholders could be varied, ranging from IT staff, senior management, and external regulators to clients. An understanding of the needs, concerns, and expectations of each stakeholder group is a powerful guide to inform communication strategies, decision-making approaches, and risk management tactics.

Beyond the communication plan and stakeholder analysis, the role of collaboration tools in facilitating efficient teamwork in cybersecurity projects is noteworthy. Such tools may include project management software, communication platforms, shared databases, and other technologies that synergize team efforts toward effective project execution. The field of cybersecurity is marked by rapid evolution, and as such, leveraging advanced collaboration tools can significantly enhance the speed and quality of project execution.

Expanding further on the communication plan, it is worth noting that its importance extends beyond just keeping stakeholders informed. It also contributes to transparency, allowing everyone involved in the project to understand current affairs. This level of transparency can increase trust among team members, foster a stronger team culture, and improve overall project performance. Additionally, a well-structured communication plan can serve as a reference document, helping to keep the project on track and reducing misunderstandings.

Drilling down into the stakeholder analysis, it is also crucial to remember that understanding the power dynamics between different stakeholders can be just as important as understanding their individual needs and expectations. This can inform how to approach and communicate with each stakeholder, helping to avoid conflicts and build stronger relationships. Also, understanding what each stakeholder values most makes it possible to align the project's objectives more closely with their interests, leading to greater overall satisfaction and project success.

Finally, the power of collaboration tools extends beyond just facilitating communication and coordination. These tools can also provide a centralized platform for storing and accessing all project-related information, helping to ensure everyone is working with the latest and most accurate data. In addition, many of these tools come with features like task tracking, document sharing, and real-time updates, which can further enhance productivity and collaboration. These technologies are increasingly crucial in today's interconnected world, where teams often must collaborate across different time zones and locations.

Recommendations:

- **Prioritize Communication:** Develop a comprehensive communication plan at the outset of your cybersecurity project. This plan should outline who needs to be informed, what information they need when needed, and how it will be conveyed. Regularly review and update this plan to keep it relevant throughout the project.
- **Conduct a Thorough Stakeholder Analysis:** Spend time identifying and understanding the stakeholders in your project. Analyze their interests, influence, and expectations. This understanding will inform your communication strategies, decision-making processes, and risk management tactics.
- **Leverage Collaboration Tools:** Use advanced collaboration tools to facilitate efficient teamwork. This could include project management software, communication platforms, and shared databases. Choosing tools that best fit your team's needs can significantly improve the speed and quality of project execution.
- **Foster Transparency:** Use your communication plan to foster transparency in your project. Share regular updates with all stakeholders, and make sure everyone has access to the same information. This can build trust, strengthen team culture, and improve project performance.
- **Understand Power Dynamics:** As part of your stakeholder analysis, understand the power dynamics between stakeholders. This can inform how you approach and communicate with each stakeholder, helping to avoid conflicts and build stronger relationships.

A GUIDE FOR PROJECT MANAGERS IN CYBERSECURITY

If you are a project manager specializing in cybersecurity, your role is comprehensive, encompassing the project's leadership from initiation to completion. Your primary responsibilities include crafting a clear project scope, developing a robust project plan, coordinating team members and resources, managing associated risks, and offering timely reports on the project's progress. Your role entails managing stakeholders, ensuring accurate and prompt communication, and facilitating informed decision-making processes.

A project manager in the cybersecurity domain requires an amalgamation of technical prowess and managerial expertise. The technical acumen should encapsulate a solid knowledge base of cybersecurity concepts, an understanding of the involved systems, and proficiency in using the tools pertinent to this field. On the managerial front, essential skills include project planning, resource management, risk management, and effective communication. In a rapidly evolving cybersecurity field, the ability to learn swiftly, adapt to changes seamlessly, and operate under pressure are invaluable assets.

The journey to becoming an effective project manager in cybersecurity does not stop with acquiring the necessary skills. Continued professional development and acquiring industry-recognized certifications are paramount. Numerous certification programs are available that can augment your knowledge and boost your credibility in the field. Some of the renowned certifications include Project Management Professional (PMP), Certified Information Systems Security Professional (CISSP), and Certified in Risk and Information Systems Control (CRISC).

Successful execution of cybersecurity projects is not a product of chance but a result of strategic thinking, proactive planning, and effective execution. Adherence to best practices is essential for achieving project objectives. These practices include defining project objectives and scope with utmost clarity, crafting detailed project plans, prioritizing effective communication, proactively managing risks, and continuously learning and adapting to the evolving cybersecurity landscape.

Digging deeper into the role of a cybersecurity project manager, one may also have to deal with budgeting and financial aspects. This could include estimating project costs, managing the project's budget, and ensuring that financial resources are utilized efficiently. Your role may also involve identifying potential cost savings or efficiencies that could improve the project's economic performance.

Moreover, a project manager in cybersecurity often acts as the liaison between the technical team and nontechnical stakeholders. This involves translating technical jargon into layperson's terms for stakeholders to understand, and vice versa, interpreting the stakeholders' needs and expectations into technical requirements for the team. This role requires excellent communication and interpersonal skills and the ability to navigate between different languages and cultures within the organization.

Furthermore, project managers in cybersecurity must also keep abreast with the latest trends and developments in the field. Cyber threats continually evolve, and staying updated with the latest threat landscape is crucial for effective risk management. This might involve participating in relevant forums and communities, attending seminars and webinars, or subscribing to industry reports and newsletters.

Lastly, apart from just managing the project, a project manager in cybersecurity also plays a critical role in promoting a culture of cybersecurity within the organization. This could involve organizing awareness programs, training employees, and advocating for the adoption of secure practices. This strengthens the organization's overall security posture and improves the success rate of cybersecurity projects.

Recommendations:

- **Enhance Your Skillset:** Develop a strong foundation in cybersecurity's technical and managerial aspects. Keep yourself updated with the latest trends and developments in the field. Acquire the necessary certifications to boost your credibility and enhance your knowledge.

- **Emphasize Communication:** Prioritize effective and timely communication with all stakeholders. Strive to translate complex technical jargon into simpler terms for nontechnical stakeholders. Foster a culture of openness and transparency in your team.
- **Be Proactive:** Adopt a proactive approach toward planning and risk management. Anticipate potential challenges and prepare contingency plans in advance. Continuously monitor the project's progress and make necessary adjustments.
- **Foster a Culture of Cybersecurity:** Promote a culture of cybersecurity within your organization. Organize awareness programs, train employees, and advocate for secure practices. This will not only strengthen the organization's security posture but also improve the success rate of your projects.
- **Prioritize Continuous Learning:** Embrace the rapidly evolving nature of the cybersecurity field. Engage in continuous learning and professional development. Utilize relevant forums, seminars, and industry reports to update yourself with the latest threat landscape.

Chapter Conclusion

As cyber threats grow more complex and pervasive, organizations across the globe find themselves needing to step up their defensive strategies. The role of effective program and project management in cybersecurity initiatives cannot be understated. Integral to these strategies is the understanding and applying comprehensive program and project management principles, helping to align multiple projects, manage resources efficiently, ensure regular and effective communication, and pave the way for achieving strategic cybersecurity objectives.

Organizations must adapt and continually improve their cybersecurity strategies in an era of rapid technological advances and increasing digital interconnectivity. Cybersecurity initiatives, therefore, need to be fluid ready to shift in response to new threats or emerging technologies. This adaptability is made possible through effective program and project management, which establishes the mechanisms and processes that allow for proactive adjustments and continuous improvement.

Program and project management is the backbone that provides structure to cybersecurity initiatives. It ensures that all actions are purposeful, align with the organization's broader security objectives, and contribute to systematically and proactively tackling cybersecurity threats.

In the realm of cybersecurity, each action can have far-reaching implications. A well-planned project can shore up defenses, close loopholes, and protect valuable data, while a poorly managed one can leave gaps that cybercriminals can exploit. Hence, a project manager's ability to define project scopes clearly, allocate resources wisely, and manage timeframes effectively are all critical skills that can directly influence an organization's security posture.

The cybersecurity landscape is constantly in flux, shaped by new technologies, emerging threats, and evolving regulations. Cybersecurity project managers must be agile and ready to adapt their strategies to these changes. This calls for a continuous learning and improvement culture, where new knowledge is regularly integrated into existing practices.

This continual improvement is not restricted to technical know-how alone. It extends to project management methodologies, team collaboration strategies, and stakeholder communication. Whether adopting a new agile management methodology, introducing a new collaboration tool, or improving the clarity of project reports, every improvement contributes to the overall effectiveness of cybersecurity initiatives.

Cybersecurity is comprehensive and varied, and staying abreast of current trends, best practices, and advancements is an ongoing task. Fortunately, numerous resources are available for further learning and professional development. Professional certifications such as PMP, CISSP, and CRISC offer structured learning opportunities and globally recognized qualifications.

Besides certifications, industry forums and conferences provide platforms to interact with peers, learn from industry leaders, and stay updated on the latest in the field. Furthermore, a wealth of knowledge can be found in cybersecurity and project management publications. These resources provide invaluable insights, case studies, and guidance, helping professionals navigate cybersecurity project management's complex and often challenging world.

Case Study: Proactive Program Management at Acme Tech

Acme Tech, a leading technology solutions provider, had a reputation for its innovative products, but struggled with cybersecurity incidents. Recognizing the importance of strengthening its security posture, the company initiated a comprehensive cybersecurity program to overhaul its existing infrastructure and processes. The charge was led by Kim, an experienced project manager, newly certified in cybersecurity management.

Kim started by understanding the importance of differentiating between programs and projects in the cybersecurity context. She identified the larger strategic objectives – improving the security posture, meeting compliance requirements, and implementing robust incident response mechanisms – and categorized them into distinct projects under the overarching cybersecurity program. This clear differentiation helped align multiple projects, each with specific deliverables and timelines.

Focusing on project management fundamentals, Kim outlined the scope, scheduling timelines, allocated resources, and budget for each project within the program. For instance, she led a software deployment project for an updated intrusion detection system, considering the hardware requirements, compatibility with existing systems, and the need for personnel training. She prioritized risk management in every project, identifying potential vulnerabilities and working out contingency plans.

When Kim's team was tasked with a significant network security enhancement project, they employed Agile project management methodologies. The project was divided into smaller, manageable iterations, allowing quicker feedback and more efficient troubleshooting. By applying principles of Scrum and Kanban, the team maintained flexibility, adapting their strategies in real time and ensuring their efforts were closely aligned with the changing threat landscape.

Communication was vital to Kim's management approach. She designed detailed communication plans and conducted stakeholder analyses, ensuring everyone, from the IT staff to senior management, was informed and engaged throughout the program's execution. She leveraged various collaboration tools, enabling efficient teamwork and promoting unity within her team.

As a cybersecurity project manager, Kim was aware of her roles and responsibilities, and she continually updated her skills and competencies to match the evolving demands of the job. She leveraged her professional development certifications to enhance her credibility and effectiveness. Her commitment to continuous learning and adaptation was reflected in her leadership style, fostering a culture of improvement within her team.

The result was a well-executed cybersecurity program that significantly enhanced Acme Tech's security posture, decreased the frequency of cybersecurity incidents, and improved the overall confidence of its clients. The experience underscored the importance of effective program and project management in cybersecurity, emphasizing communication, strategic alignment, risk management, continuous improvement, and the value of professional development.

CHAPTER 5

Cybersecurity for Business Executives

"Success in cybersecurity doesn't just mean protection today; it means anticipation, innovation, and the audacity to face tomorrow's threats head-on."

The intricate and demanding nature of the cybersecurity landscape calls for the deep involvement of business leaders to ensure robust protection. Business leaders play a central role in cybersecurity, tasked with numerous duties and responsibilities. Understanding the business implications of cyber threats is crucial, as is recognizing the role of cybersecurity as a driving force for business growth and its interplay with business strategies. It is also necessary to appreciate executives' perspectives on cybersecurity, their challenges, and their key roles in this field. Close collaboration between business leaders and cybersecurity teams is critical. Leaders need to understand essential cybersecurity concepts, which can aid in making informed business decisions, setting a cybersecurity risk tolerance, staying updated through training and awareness, comprehending legal and regulatory aspects, and adapting to future cybersecurity trends.

WHY BUSINESS EXECUTIVES NEED TO BE INVOLVED IN CYBERSECURITY

Security, per the renowned cybersecurity expert Bruce Schneier, is not simply a product but an ongoing process. In the modern era, where digital systems are extensively interconnected, finding a business that remains untouched by the risk of cyber threats is nearly impossible. A single breach can lead to grave financial losses, considerably erode customer trust, and damage a company's reputation. This makes Cybersecurity not just a concern limited to the IT department but an enterprise-wide risk that can critically affect the functioning of business operations. Given this high-stakes scenario, it becomes imperative for business executives to have a thorough understanding and active management role in Cybersecurity.

Cybersecurity extends beyond mere prevention of threats; it plays a critical role as a business enabler. A robust cybersecurity framework safeguards its valuable information assets, ensuring the uninterrupted operation of business processes while protecting the company's reputation. Providing a secure environment where customers can conduct business with peace of mind significantly contributes to customer retention and attraction, acting as a growth catalyst.

As the business landscape becomes increasingly complex, the once clear line separating business strategy from Cybersecurity has begun to blur. Data has become a critical business asset in the digital age, primarily due to the growing reliance on digital platforms. Protecting this asset is now a strategic concern that directly influences crucial business decisions. This necessitates business executives to thoroughly understand the implications of Cybersecurity on business strategy and ensure that they are effectively aligned.

Moreover, Cybersecurity is now integral to maintaining and enhancing a company's competitive advantage. A robust cybersecurity framework can protect the company's proprietary information, critical infrastructure, and digital assets from potential competitors and threats. It can also enable businesses to provide better customer service by ensuring data privacy and system availability, making the company more attractive to prospective clients and partners.

Additionally, Cybersecurity also plays a pivotal role in regulatory compliance. Many industries have strict data protection and privacy regulations, and failure to comply can result in heavy penalties. Therefore, a strong understanding of Cybersecurity can help business executives navigate these regulatory landscapes, reduce compliance risk, and maintain the organization's credibility in the eyes of regulators, customers, and partners.

Finally, understanding Cybersecurity is also essential for business continuity and disaster recovery planning. In a cyber incident, having a well-crafted recovery plan can minimize downtime, data loss, and financial damage. It can also ensure the quick restoration of normal business operations, helping maintain customer trust and reputation. Thus, the role of Cybersecurity extends far beyond just protection – it is a cornerstone of a resilient and thriving business in today's digital age.

Recommendations:

- **Prioritize Cybersecurity:** Begin by acknowledging Cybersecurity's significant role in your business. Understand that it is not just a support function but an enabler of your operations, customer trust, and overall growth.
- **Integrate Cybersecurity into Strategy:** Ensure that Cybersecurity becomes a fundamental part of your business strategy. This means incorporating

cybersecurity considerations into decision-making, long-term planning, and risk assessments.

- **Stay Informed:** Commit to regularly learning about the evolving landscape of cyber threats and protections. Familiarize yourself with crucial cybersecurity principles, emerging trends, and best practices in the industry.
- **Embrace Compliance:** Make a concerted effort to understand your industry's regulatory environment around data protection. Use this understanding to ensure your organization meets or exceeds all necessary compliance requirements, thus avoiding potential penalties and damage to your reputation.
- **Invest in Disaster Recovery:** Develop a robust disaster recovery and business continuity plan that considers potential cyber incidents. This includes having clear procedures for responding to breaches, backup strategies for critical data, and plans for communicating with customers and other stakeholders during an incident.

ROLES AND RESPONSIBILITIES OF BUSINESS EXECUTIVES IN CYBERSECURITY

In our increasingly connected digital world, the role of business executives in overseeing and driving cybersecurity efforts is not just crucial but inevitable. The landscape of cyber threats is ever-evolving and affects every facet of an organization. Therefore, it has become an executive responsibility to ensure the company's cybersecurity initiatives are proactive, comprehensive, and adequately resourced.

Steering and strategically aligning cybersecurity efforts has become a central obligation for business leaders. This responsibility encompasses defining a clear and well-articulated vision and strategy for Cybersecurity. It necessitates a comprehensive understanding of the organization's mission and goals, as this vision must echo the larger business objectives. The alignment of Cybersecurity and business strategy effectively weaves Cybersecurity into the fabric of all business operations, helping to create a secure infrastructure that facilitates rather than hinders the accomplishment of the organization's mission.

The decision-making role of executives extends significantly into cybersecurity investments. Resource allocation in Cybersecurity – financial, technological, or human – requires careful thought and strategic planning. Understanding the organization's risk profile is crucial for making informed decisions about the appropriate investments in technology, personnel, and training. Assessing the current cybersecurity infrastructure, understanding the cyber risks associated with the business sector, and analyzing the potential impact of a breach on the business are all critical components of this understanding.

Beyond strategic planning and resource allocation, executives play an indispensable role in cultivating a cybersecurity-conscious culture within the organization. This role involves promoting awareness of cybersecurity threats and safeguards among all employees, fostering a sense of responsibility for protecting the organization's digital assets. Ensuring adherence to the company's cybersecurity policies is equally important, as even the best policy is ineffective if not properly enforced. Organizational culture plays a significant role in how effectively cybersecurity policies are adopted and adhered to, and this culture is substantially influenced by executive leadership.

In addition to internal responsibilities, executives must also navigate the complex terrain of legal and regulatory requirements related to Cybersecurity. Executives must have a solid understanding of the legal landscape in which their business operates, including relevant data protection laws, industry regulations, and contractual obligations. Regularly reviewing and updating practices are essential to stay compliant as regulations evolve.

Lastly, the role of a business executive also extends to the arena of external engagement. Communication and cooperation with external stakeholders and partners, including suppliers, customers, and regulatory bodies, are integral to a comprehensive cybersecurity strategy. Whether it is information sharing, joint initiatives, or contract negotiations, executives play a pivotal role in ensuring that cybersecurity considerations are adequately addressed and that partnerships do not expose the organization to unnecessary cyber risks.

Recommendations:

- **Immerse in Strategy:** Make a deliberate effort to understand your organization's mission and objectives and align them with your cybersecurity strategy. This alignment will help to ensure that cybersecurity efforts support and enable the broader business goals.
- **Invest Wisely:** Allocate resources to Cybersecurity based on a comprehensive understanding of your organization's risk profile. Consider potential threats, business sector-specific risks, and the potential impact of a breach when deciding on investments in technology, personnel, and training.
- **Foster a Cybersecurity Culture:** Encourage cybersecurity awareness among all employees and foster a culture that values Cybersecurity. Use your influence as a leader to promote responsible behavior and adherence to your organization's cybersecurity policies.
- **Stay Compliant:** Familiarize yourself with the legal and regulatory landscape related to Cybersecurity in your industry. Ensure your organization's practices align with these requirements and regularly review and update them as regulations evolve.
- **Engage Externally:** Take an active role in engaging with external stakeholders on cybersecurity matters. Whether it is information sharing, joint initiatives, or contract negotiations, ensure that cybersecurity considerations are appropriately addressed in your interactions with external parties.

EFFECTIVE COLLABORATION BETWEEN BUSINESS EXECUTIVES AND CYBERSECURITY TEAMS

The journey toward achieving cyber resilience is not a solitary one but a collective effort that requires engagement from every stratum of an organization. Central to this endeavor are top-level executives. Their understanding and active participation are pivotal to guiding the organization's strategic trajectory, particularly in response to the ever-evolving landscape of cyber threats. Their influence permeates various aspects of the organization, driving the broader business strategy and ensuring the company's resilience in the face of cyber threats.

A key element fostering the synergy between executive leadership and the cybersecurity team is robust, transparent, and frequent communication. Communication channels must be kept open and active, ensuring a constant flow of information. This interchange enables executives to maintain an up-to-date understanding of the organization's cybersecurity posture while guaranteeing that the cybersecurity team aligns its efforts with the business's strategic direction and broader objectives. Regular briefings, updates, and strategic discussions facilitate mutual understanding, helping to align priorities and ensuring that decisions are informed and holistic.

Beyond clear communication, shared objectives and goals must mark the relationship between executive leadership and the cybersecurity team. These common aims should be centered around the effective management of cyber risks and should seamlessly align with the broader business strategy. This shared vision echoes the organization's strategic objectives and ensures that cybersecurity efforts are laser-focused on protecting the most vital business assets and processes. This intricate alignment of Cybersecurity and business strategies underscores the critical role of Cybersecurity in ensuring the smooth and successful functioning of the organization.

Leadership support is another aspect that profoundly impacts the effectiveness of the cybersecurity team. Creating a supportive and understanding environment around the cybersecurity program can boost morale and drive effectiveness. When executives show that they appreciate the efforts of the cybersecurity team and are willing to invest resources into their work, it emboldens the team to take necessary and decisive actions. This supportive environment emphasizes that Cybersecurity is a vital function of the organization and not just an ancillary requirement or a nod to compliance.

The role of executives extends far beyond strategy formulation and planning. Their active involvement is crucial during incident response and crisis management. This involvement is not limited to awareness of the response plans but should extend to their development. By participating in the design and execution of these plans, executives can ensure they are comprehensive, considering all aspects of the business that could be impacted. This hands-on approach illustrates that Cybersecurity is a top priority for the organization, providing direction and strategic insight.

In the event of a cyber incident, the leadership and decision-making abilities of executives can significantly impact the management of the crisis and the extent of its consequences. With a broad perspective, executives are well positioned to make decisions that balance business continuity, stakeholder communication, regulatory obligations, and other crucial aspects. Their steady presence can reassure the rest of the organization and external stakeholders during unsettling times. Effectively navigating a crisis significantly contributes to an organization's cyber resilience, underscoring executives' crucial role in a comprehensive cybersecurity strategy.

Recommendations:

- **Facilitate Communication:** Maintain open and regular communication channels with your cybersecurity team. Regular updates and discussions will help both sides understand each other's goals and concerns, leading to more effective decision-making.
- **Align Goals:** Ensure that the objectives and goals of your cybersecurity team align with the broader business strategy. This alignment will ensure that cybersecurity efforts are directed toward safeguarding your organization's most critical assets and processes.
- **Foster Support:** Create a supportive environment for your cybersecurity program. Show appreciation for your cybersecurity team's work and invest in their efforts. This will empower your team and highlight the importance of Cybersecurity within your organization.
- **Engage in Planning:** Be actively involved in incident response and crisis management planning. Your involvement will ensure that plans are comprehensive and consider the potential impacts on all aspects of your business.
- **Lead Through Crises:** Show strong leadership during cyber incidents. Your leadership and decision-making abilities will be crucial in managing the crisis and minimizing its impact. Your presence can provide reassurance to your organization and stakeholders during challenging times.

KEY CYBERSECURITY CONCEPTS FOR BUSINESS EXECUTIVES

The rapidly shifting landscape of Cybersecurity requires business executives to possess a robust understanding of several fundamental concepts. Cybersecurity is not a static field. Instead, it is an arena of constant change, where new threats emerge and technology advances at breakneck speed. As a result, it is incumbent on executives to ensure they are well-versed in key topics within this domain, which are integral for the protection and prosperity of their organizations.

Understanding cyber risks and threats is the heart of these fundamentals. It is pivotal to recognize that cyber risks are not abstract concepts but potential sources of significant harm related to the technical infrastructure, the utilization of technology, or even the company's reputation. Risks emerge from the likelihood of a cybersecurity incident and the subsequent impact on the organization. On the other hand, threats are potential causes of these unwanted incidents, be they malicious actors, malware, or system vulnerabilities, leading to system disruptions or data breaches. A solid grasp of the different types of risks and threats can aid executives in identifying areas of vulnerability within their organization and ensuring necessary safeguards are in place.

Simultaneously, a basic familiarity with cybersecurity technologies and controls is indispensable for executives. While they do not need to delve into the minutiae of these technologies, a foundational understanding of their purpose, effectiveness, and potential limitations is essential. This knowledge spans various tools and procedures like firewalls acting as a first-line defense, intrusion detection systems identifying malicious activity, and encryption technologies safeguarding sensitive information. By appreciating how these elements work in concert to shield the organization's information assets, executives can make more informed decisions about technology investments and strategic priorities.

In the age of digitalization, data protection and privacy have emerged as critical aspects of Cybersecurity. The increasing regulatory focus on data privacy means executives must understand the imperative of protecting personal and sensitive data from an ethical and legal perspective. This goes beyond just preventing data breaches. It includes ensuring appropriate data handling practices, respecting customer privacy, and maintaining compliance with domestic and international regulations. Understanding the potential ramifications of data breaches, ranging from regulatory penalties to reputational damage, is crucial to this awareness.

Understanding security metrics and reporting is critical to an executive's cybersecurity knowledge toolkit. Often presented as dashboards or reports, these metrics provide valuable insights into the organization's cybersecurity performance. They might include data on incident response times, patch management, or the number of detected threats. This data-driven approach allows executives to assess the effectiveness of the organization's cybersecurity strategy, enabling them to make informed decisions about resource allocation, risk management, and strategic planning. Moreover, they can be useful for communicating with other stakeholders, such as board members or regulators, about the organization's cybersecurity posture. By fully comprehending these metrics, executives can become more proactive and data-driven in their cybersecurity leadership, fostering a more secure and resilient organization.

Recommendations:

- **Expand Cyber Threat Awareness:** Increase your understanding of cyber risks and threats. Learn about the different types of risks, their sources, and how they could potentially impact your organization. Your enhanced knowledge will allow you to identify vulnerabilities within your organization and ensure necessary safeguards are in place.

- **Familiarize with Cybersecurity Technologies:** Develop a basic familiarity with cybersecurity technologies and controls. While you do not need to delve deep into the technicalities, understanding their purpose, effectiveness, and potential limitations can significantly enhance decision-making regarding technology investments and strategic priorities.
- **Emphasize Data Protection and Privacy:** Take steps to understand better the importance of data protection and privacy in the age of digitalization. Learn about the legal and ethical implications of data breaches and work to improve data handling practices and compliance with domestic and international regulations.
- **Utilize Security Metrics and Reporting:** Learn how to interpret security metrics and reporting. Understanding these will provide insights into your organization's cybersecurity performance and help you make informed decisions about resource allocation, risk management, and strategic planning.
- **Promote Data-Driven Leadership:** Use your understanding of security metrics and reporting to become more proactive and data-driven in your cybersecurity leadership. This approach will foster a more secure and resilient organization. Regularly engage with these metrics to keep your strategies and decisions grounded in concrete data.

INCORPORATING CYBERSECURITY INTO BUSINESS DECISION-MAKING

Cyber risk assessment is a vital precursor to any decision-making process in our highly interconnected world, where new business ventures frequently hinge on digital capabilities. Whether an organization is contemplating launching an innovative digital service, forging strategic partnerships, or exploring untapped market segments, each prospective endeavor carries inherent cyber risks. Such risks, however, should not be seen merely as potential threats but also as opportunities for growth, given the proper management and control strategies. The assessment process goes beyond the primary identification of risks. It delves deeper into understanding the broader implications of the organization's cybersecurity posture.

Assessing cyber risk is dissecting an organization's cybersecurity infrastructure's overall health and resilience. The process should evaluate how existing measures can hold up against the potential impacts of a breach and how they can be fortified further. These assessments provide invaluable insights, enabling executives to balance potential benefits and associated risks, culminating in balanced, strategic decision-making that protects and propels the organization.

The digitization of businesses has heightened the relevance of Cybersecurity in business continuity planning. Today's organizations are heavily reliant on digital technologies for their operations. While enabling efficient and advanced operations, this dependency also means businesses are more vulnerable to disruptions resulting from cyber incidents. A single, well-orchestrated cyberattack can paralyze business operations, cause significant reputation damage, and result in substantial financial losses. Therefore, integrating cybersecurity considerations into business continuity and disaster recovery plans is necessary.

Business executives should champion the integration of Cybersecurity within these plans. Doing so ensures the organization is well prepared to confront potential cyber threats and can swiftly return to normal operations following an incident. This approach should focus on reinforcing the resilience of essential business processes and functions, minimizing downtime, and guaranteeing quick recovery during a cyberattack. Emphasizing Cybersecurity in business continuity planning is vital to ensure the organization's survival and sustained prosperity amidst an ever-evolving threat landscape.

The intricate interplay between Cybersecurity and vendor and supply chain management is another critical area of focus. Numerous vendors and supply chain partners can access a company's systems and sensitive data, so these connections often represent potential cyberattack entry points. This inherent vulnerability underscores the need to integrate cybersecurity considerations into vendor selection and relationship management processes. Implementing stringent cybersecurity standards, regular audits, and robust incident response plans with all partners are necessary to strengthen these potentially vulnerable links in the chain.

Moreover, Cybersecurity plays a pivotal role in fostering and maintaining strong customer relationships. In our data-centric world, where data breaches have unfortunately become commonplace, customers are increasingly mindful of the safety and security of their personal information. Organizations that make a demonstrable commitment to Cybersecurity not only protect their customers' data but also enhance their reputation, trustworthiness, and customer loyalty. Executives, therefore, should ensure that their cybersecurity measures are clearly articulated in all customer communications and deeply ingrained across all customer touchpoints, from product design to after-sales service.

Making Cybersecurity a priority can significantly differentiate an organization in a fiercely competitive business landscape. When businesses put Cybersecurity at the forefront, they can drive customer trust and loyalty, leading to enduring relationships and increased customer lifetime value. The potential reputational and financial dividends of a robust and visible cybersecurity posture are substantial, making it an integral aspect of an organization's strategic vision.

Recommendations:

- **Understand the Cyber Risk Landscape:** Take the initiative to deepen your understanding of cyber risk. Learn about its potential impact on new ventures, strategic partnerships, and entry into new markets. With this knowledge, you can evaluate risks and devise effective mitigation strategies.

- **Integrate Cybersecurity into Business Continuity Plans:** Advocate for integrating cybersecurity considerations into business continuity and disaster recovery plans. This approach ensures your organization is resilient and prepared for potential cyber threats, minimizing downtime, and facilitating quick recovery.
- **Strengthen Vendor and Supply Chain Management:** Consider Cybersecurity a vital factor in vendor selection and relationship management. Implement rigorous cybersecurity standards and conduct regular audits to ensure your vendors and partners adhere to them, thus reducing the risk of breaches.
- **Prioritize Cybersecurity in Customer Relations:** Ensure cybersecurity measures are evident and communicated to your customers across all touchpoints. Doing so can build trust and loyalty and differentiate your organization in the marketplace.
- **Commit to Learning:** Familiarize yourself with established cybersecurity frameworks and best practices. This foundational understanding will enable you to implement robust cybersecurity measures effectively and develop a culture of cyber resilience within your organization.

DEVELOPING A CYBERSECURITY RISK APPETITE

Establishing a cybersecurity risk appetite necessitates an in-depth understanding of two foundational terms: "risk appetite" and "risk tolerance." Risk appetite embodies the risk an organization is prepared to accept to pursue its objectives. It is a strategic component that shapes the course of decision-making processes, defining the contours of an acceptable risk landscape. When considered through the lens of Cybersecurity, risk appetite becomes a measure of acceptable risk levels tied to various categories of data or systems. It furnishes a benchmark for determining the extent and depth of the cybersecurity measures that need to be implemented, helping organizations find a balanced approach between being overly protective, which can limit innovation, and being too lenient, which can lead to vulnerabilities.

Conversely, risk tolerance concerns the level of variance from this established risk appetite that an organization is willing to withstand. It is an operational aspect that addresses the real-world complications and nuances of implementing a risk strategy. Understanding the interplay between risk appetite and risk tolerance is vital, as it aids in tailoring a cybersecurity strategy in harmony with the organization's risk threshold.

The next crucial phase in this journey involves harmonizing the cybersecurity risk appetite with overarching business objectives. This step goes beyond merely aligning the two; it is about integrating cybersecurity considerations into the very essence of business strategy. This integration ensures that risk management initiatives are not disjointed or peripheral efforts. Instead, they are focused on protecting those assets and processes that drive the organization's mission and strategic goals.

Such congruence nurtures an organizational culture that perceives Cybersecurity not as a secondary, supportive function but as a core business component. This perspective prompts a proactive approach to Cybersecurity, where all stakeholders recognize its significance and actively participate in maintaining the organization's cybersecurity posture. In this culture, Cybersecurity is not an afterthought but a foundational aspect of every initiative, decision, and operation in the organization.

The cybersecurity landscape is in perpetual flux, characterized by emerging threats, evolving vulnerabilities, and advancing defensive measures. This dynamic nature necessitates an organization's cybersecurity risk appetite to be equally agile and adaptable. It requires an openness to routine reviews, updates, and necessary adjustments in response to the shifting threat landscape, changing business goals, or evolving regulatory environments.

Risk appetite is not a static statement set in stone but an evolving guideline that adapts in tandem with these changes. This fluidity ensures that the organization's risk management approach remains relevant, effective, and aligned with its changing environment and strategic objectives. Regularly revisiting and refining risk appetite ensures an organization stays resilient in the face of emerging challenges and is adept at identifying, managing, and mitigating cyber risks in real time.

Recommendations:

- **Master the Fundamentals:** Make an effort to thoroughly understand the concepts of "risk appetite" and "risk tolerance." By appreciating the nuances and interplay between these terms, you can effectively shape your organization's cybersecurity strategy and risk management approach.

- **Integrate Cybersecurity with Business Strategy:** Prioritize the integration of your cybersecurity risk appetite with your overarching business goals. Ensure risk management initiatives center around protecting assets and processes crucial to your organization's mission and strategic objectives.

- **Create a Proactive Cybersecurity Culture:** Foster a culture where Cybersecurity is seen as an essential business function rather than an auxiliary support role. This shift will prompt a proactive approach to Cybersecurity among all stakeholders within the organization.

- **Stay Agile and Adaptable:** Remember that your organization's cybersecurity risk appetite should be fluid and adaptable. It should be open to regular reviews and adjustments in response to changes in the threat landscape, organizational objectives, and regulatory environments.

- **Commit to Learning:** Familiarize yourself with leading cybersecurity risk management frameworks and guidelines. This foundational understanding will aid in successfully implementing and managing your organization's cybersecurity measures, ultimately bolstering its resilience against cyber threats.

TRAINING AND AWARENESS FOR BUSINESS EXECUTIVES

Tailored cybersecurity training programs are a powerful tool in an executive's cyber resilience arsenal. These are not generic one-size-fits-all solutions but bespoke educational experiences tailored to executives' unique roles, responsibilities, and decision-making scenarios. By distilling complex cybersecurity concepts into actionable insights, these programs equip executives with an in-depth understanding of their organization's cyber risks. Moreover, they illuminate the myriad cybersecurity controls that executives can deploy to safeguard their digital assets, thus arming them with the knowledge to develop and implement effective cybersecurity strategies.

In addition to specific training programs, maintaining a consistent awareness of rapidly evolving cyber threats and trends is vital to executive education. Cybersecurity is a dynamic battlefield where threats mutate and vulnerabilities shift rapidly. This continuous evolution necessitates regular briefings and updates for executives, ensuring they remain abreast of the latest cyber threats, novel attack methodologies, and preventive measures. This vigilant awareness empowers them to anticipate risks, respond effectively to incidents, and make informed decisions that bolster the organization's cyber defenses.

Engagement in broader industry forums, associations, and roundtables can further supplement executive training and awareness. These platforms provide a valuable opportunity to exchange insights with peers, learn from others' experiences, and assimilate industry best practices. They offer a panoramic view of the cybersecurity environment beyond the confines of one's organization, fostering a richer understanding of the broader cyber ecosystem. Additionally, active participation in these forums underscores a commitment to collective cyber resilience, contributing to the industry-wide advancement of cybersecurity norms and practices.

The culmination of these elements – tailored training, vigilance of emerging trends, and active industry participation – creates a well-rounded and effective cybersecurity awareness framework for business executives. This robust framework facilitates navigation of the tumultuous cyber-threat landscape and lays the groundwork for a proactive and resilient organizational cybersecurity posture.

Recommendations:

- **Implement Tailored Training Programs:** Recognize the importance of bespoke cybersecurity training programs that cater to executives' unique roles, responsibilities, and decision-making scenarios. Develop and participate in such programs to ensure a deep understanding of your organization's specific cyber risks and appropriate control measures.
- **Stay Vigilant of Emerging Trends:** Cybersecurity is an ever-evolving field. Regularly update your knowledge base through briefings and updates to keep abreast of the latest cyber threats, novel attack methodologies, and

preventive measures. This vigilance will empower you to anticipate risks, respond effectively to incidents, and make informed decisions, reinforcing your organization's cyber defenses.

- **Engage in Industry Forums:** Participation in broader industry forums, associations, and roundtables can provide valuable insights from your peers and the opportunity to assimilate industry best practices. These platforms offer a broader perspective of the cybersecurity environment, enhancing your understanding of the broader cyber ecosystem.
- **Contribute to Collective Resilience:** Active involvement in industry forums not only equips you with more knowledge but also allows you to contribute to the collective resilience of the cyber ecosystem. By sharing your experiences and insights, you can aid in advancing cybersecurity norms and practices across your industry.
- **Foster a Well-rounded Awareness Framework:** Embrace the combination of tailored training, awareness of emerging trends, and active industry participation to develop a comprehensive cybersecurity awareness framework. Such a robust framework will assist in navigating the complex cyber-threat landscape and lay the groundwork for a proactive and resilient organizational cybersecurity posture.

LEGAL AND REGULATORY CONSIDERATIONS FOR BUSINESS EXECUTIVES

Cybersecurity, once seen purely as a domain of technical expertise, has undergone a dramatic transformation. Today, it is universally recognized as a broad-based enterprise-wide risk that permeates every aspect of an organization. The expansive nature of Cybersecurity means it now intersects with several areas, including those that carry considerable legal and regulatory significance. In our modern, heavily regulated business environment, the legal and compliance aspects of Cybersecurity are becoming increasingly prominent and demand serious attention.

A deep and detailed understanding of legal obligations related to Cybersecurity is now a fundamental requirement for executives in all types of organizations, irrespective of size or sector. These obligations can arise from many sources, including various data protection laws that governments have implemented around the globe, sector-specific cybersecurity regulations that may apply, and legal mandates for disclosing cyber incidents. There are also internationally recognized standards, such as the General Data Protection Regulation (GDPR) in the European Union and the California Consumer Privacy Act (CCPA) in the United States.

Grasping the intricacies of these diverse legal and regulatory mandates is vital for executives as they navigate the intricate maze of legal compliance in Cybersecurity. A deep and nuanced understanding of these obligations allows executives to guide their organizations adeptly, minimizing the likelihood of encountering potential legal pitfalls and mitigating the risk of penalties and legal actions.

However, the responsibility of executives in this context goes beyond merely understanding the legal landscape. They also play a pivotal role in fostering a strong culture of regulatory compliance within their organizations. This critical task starts with setting the tone at the top. In other words, executives must demonstrate their unwavering commitment to Cybersecurity through their decisions, actions, and communications.

This process's vital element involves strategically allocating resources to enhance compliance efforts. This might include investing in state-of-the-art technology solutions that can provide robust cybersecurity protection, hiring personnel with specialist skills and qualifications, and ensuring employees receive ongoing training in cybersecurity awareness and best practices. Executives also play a central role in endorsing the creation and stringent application of robust policies and procedures designed to fulfill regulatory requirements.

Additionally, the fallout from cybersecurity failures extends well into the legal realm, with potentially severe consequences for executives. The repercussions are no longer limited to organizational penalties such as regulatory fines and reputational damage; executives themselves can face serious legal consequences. There may be a barrage of lawsuits from a wide range of stakeholders – customers, shareholders, and employees – who could have been negatively affected by a cyber incident.

Some jurisdictions have laws that hold executives personally accountable for significant cybersecurity failures. This means executives could face personal legal consequences, including hefty fines and, in some cases, imprisonment. This important development further underscores executives' crucial role in managing cybersecurity risk within their organizations.

In this context, Cybersecurity is about more than simply safeguarding IT infrastructure. It protects the organization from potential risks, including operational disruption, financial loss, legal repercussions, and reputational damage. Consequently, executives must view Cybersecurity not just as a technical challenge but as a key component of their broader enterprise risk management strategy, deeply integrated into every aspect of their organizational operations.

Recommendations:

- **Commit to Learning:** Make a conscious effort to understand the diverse legal obligations related to Cybersecurity that affect your organization. This will require understanding various data protection laws, sector-specific regulations, and international standards such as GDPR and CCPA.
- **Cultivate a Culture of Compliance:** As an executive, you must foster a strong culture of regulatory compliance within your organization. This involves setting an example through your actions and decisions, investing in resources to enhance compliance efforts, and endorsing the development and implementation of robust policies and procedures.

- **Prepare for Legal Consequences:** Understand that the fallout from cybersecurity failures can extend to personal legal consequences. Familiarize yourself with the laws in your jurisdiction that might hold executives personally accountable for significant cybersecurity failures.
- **Integrate Cybersecurity into Enterprise Risk Management:** Recognize that Cybersecurity is an integral component of your broader enterprise risk management strategy. Approach it not merely as a technical challenge but as an enterprise-wide risk that affects every aspect of your organization.
- **Invest in Training:** Allocate resources for ongoing cybersecurity training for yourself and your employees. A well-informed workforce is your best defense against cyber threats, and continuous learning is crucial, given the dynamic nature of the cybersecurity landscape.

THE FUTURE OF BUSINESS EXECUTIVE ENGAGEMENT IN CYBERSECURITY

As technological landscapes become and metamorphose, the risks associated with these advancements also transfigure, bringing about an ensuing shift in executive responsibilities toward managing these new-age risks.

The cyber threat landscape is substantially overhauling with emerging trends and challenges like artificial intelligence, machine learning, the Internet of Things (IoT), quantum computing, and blockchain technology. These technological advancements are dissolving the boundaries between physical and virtual security, compelling executives to reevaluate, revamp, and refine their approach to Cybersecurity, aiming for an integrated and holistic view of risk that encompasses both realms.

Consequently, the role of executives in Cybersecurity is transitioning from a reactive posture to a more proactive and anticipatory stance. Executives are now not merely required to manage and mitigate cyber risks reactively; they are increasingly expected to comprehend the intricate interplay between technological innovation and security. They are called to envision and navigate the labyrinth of evolving threats, technological innovations, and business impacts. In this new paradigm, security is not just a protective measure but a competitive differentiator and a catalyst for business transformation, which can drive trust and customer loyalty when appropriately leveraged.

Simultaneously, secure adaptation to new business models and technologies necessitates an intricate understanding of the complex interdependencies that bind business processes, technologies, and cyber risks. It is about understanding the potential ripple effects a single vulnerability can have across an interconnected digital ecosystem and the cascading impacts of a cyber incident on business continuity, brand reputation, regulatory compliance, and customer trust. When blended with strategic foresight, this nuanced understanding will enable executives to craft a comprehensive and resilient security strategy that enables and actively fuels digital transformation while effectively managing and mitigating cyber risks.

In essence, as Cybersecurity becomes a marathon rather than a sprint, it demands long-term strategic planning, consistent investment, and relentless executive vigilance. As stewards of their organization's digital destiny, executives must stay at the forefront of technological advances, emerging cyber threats, and evolving regulatory landscapes. This is a marathon that every executive needs to run, in pace with the changing cyber threat landscape, to ensure the continued resilience and growth of their organizations in a digitally interconnected world.

Recommendations:

- **Adopt a Proactive Stance:** With the rapidly evolving technological landscape, executives must transition from a reactive to a proactive cybersecurity posture. Anticipate potential threats associated with new trends such as artificial intelligence, IoT, and blockchain, and develop preemptive strategies to manage these risks.
- **Seek Holistic Understanding:** Aim to understand the intricate interplay between technological innovations and security. This understanding will allow you to effectively manage risks and leverage security as a competitive differentiator, driving trust and customer loyalty.
- **Comprehend Complex Interdependencies:** Develop a deep understanding of the interdependencies among business processes, technologies, and cyber risks. Recognize the potential ripple effects of a single vulnerability across an interconnected digital ecosystem, including impacts on business continuity, brand reputation, and customer trust.
- **Strategize for Long-term Security:** Cybersecurity is a marathon, not a sprint. This demands long-term strategic planning and consistent investment. Leverage your understanding of the interplay between technology and security to craft a comprehensive and resilient security strategy that manages risks and fuels digital transformation.
- **Maintain Relentless Vigilance:** Stay abreast of the latest technological advances, emerging cyber threats, and evolving regulatory landscapes. Constant vigilance is crucial to managing cybersecurity risks and ensuring your organization's continued resilience and growth in the digital era.

Chapter Conclusion

The critical importance of executive involvement in cybersecurity has been persistently emphasized, highlighting the various roles, responsibilities, and expectations placed on executive leaders. With ever-changing technological environments, the landscape of cyber threats continues to evolve, necessitating an unwavering, firm commitment to cybersecurity, which must be ingrained in every level of the organization, from top leadership to the most junior employee.

A commitment to improving cybersecurity is necessary today, teeming with cyber threats. The domain of cyber threats is in constant flux, perpetually unveiling new threats and vulnerabilities. Adapting swiftly to these emerging threats and vulnerabilities is vital for organizations, requiring operational dedication and significant executive commitment. This devotion from the top echelons of an organization ensures continuous support, investment, and enhancement of the organization's cybersecurity standing. It is about fostering a culture of cybersecurity that infiltrates every aspect of the organization, from strategic planning to daily operations.

The future role of business executives in cybersecurity calls for a dramatic shift in perspective. Cybersecurity has transformed from an IT issue to a strategic business concern directly impacting an organization's bottom line. The fallout from a cyber incident can reverberate throughout an organization, impacting not just technical systems but also customer trust, brand reputation, regulatory compliance, and financial performance.

As such, executive involvement in cybersecurity needs to venture beyond the conventional scopes of risk management. It should no longer be perceived merely as a cost center or a necessary evil but as a strategic facilitator that can enhance business value. Executives ought to consider how they can utilize cybersecurity as a tool for business enablement, fostering customer trust, gaining a competitive advantage, and acting as a catalyst for innovation and digital transformation. Adopting this comprehensive and futuristic approach to cybersecurity will distinguish successful businesses in the digital age.

Case Study: Engaging Cybersecurity at Spectrum Enterprises

Spectrum Enterprises, a multinational technology company specializing in AI and machine learning solutions, grappled with the rapidly evolving world of Cybersecurity. Recent waves of sophisticated cyberattacks in their industry segment raised alarms within the organization and the broader business community. Spectrum's CEO, Wil, even though he had no formal background in technology or Cybersecurity, quickly acknowledged the gravity of the situation. He resolved to engage proactively and personally in addressing the pressing cybersecurity needs of the company.

Wil's journey started with education. Recognizing the vital role knowledge plays in Cybersecurity; he established a tailored training program to gain a deep understanding of cyber risks and threats. But he did not stop at his personal development. Wil expanded this training program to include all top-level executives, transforming Cybersecurity from a niche concern into a company-wide dialogue. This initiative demystified Cybersecurity and its specific risks related to their sector, cultivating a more aware and appreciative company culture of Cybersecurity's importance.

With this newfound knowledge, Wil began integrating Cybersecurity into business strategy and operations. He led a strategic revision of business plans to incorporate comprehensive cyber risk assessments for new business opportunities. He championed Cybersecurity in business continuity planning, ensuring Spectrum could maintain operations despite cyber disruptions. He prioritized Cybersecurity in vendor and supply chain management, fortifying Spectrum's entire operational chain against potential breaches. This holistic approach ensured that Cybersecurity became integral to every business decision at Spectrum Enterprises, strengthening the company's defense against cyber threats.

Wil worked closely with the legal and Cybersecurity teams to ensure regulatory compliance. Understanding the legal obligations related to Cybersecurity became a priority for him. He allocated resources and workforce to streamline compliance activities, setting the tone for a culture of proactive and meticulous cybersecurity compliance across the organization.

Inevitably, despite all precautions, Spectrum Enterprises faced a cyber incident. A group of criminals breached their system, exploiting a zero-day vulnerability. However, thanks to the robust communication channels between the executives and the cybersecurity team and the incident response strategy they had developed together, Spectrum was able to contain the threat swiftly. The incident's impact was minimized, and the company could quickly return to normal operations.

The cyber incident was a wake-up call, driving Wil to reassess the company's cybersecurity posture. He led an effort to improve cybersecurity engagement at the executive level continuously. They reviewed their incident response strategy, identified areas for improvement, and initiated changes. This commitment to learning from challenges and enhancing its cybersecurity stance made Spectrum more resilient against future threats.

The Spectrum Enterprises case is a tangible illustration of how executive engagement in Cybersecurity can shape a company's resilience against cyber threats. It underscores how such engagement drives business success in the increasingly digital world.

CHAPTER 6

Cybersecurity and the Board of Directors

"Embracing Cybersecurity is not a burden; it's a strategic advantage. By investing in our digital defenses, the board enhances our competitive edge and paves the way for innovation and growth."

The corporate board of directors has a pivotal role in managing cybersecurity within an organization. Their responsibilities encompass understanding the perspectives of the board and cybersecurity executives and addressing their expectations, challenges, and strategies for managing cyber risks. Effective communication strategies and recommendations for reporting to the board are also crucial aspects of their role. Standards such as those from the FFIEC shed light on the extent of board involvement required in cybersecurity. Integrating cybersecurity deeply into the corporate culture is essential to ensure a security-focused mindset across all levels. Legal and regulatory considerations also need to be acknowledged. The board's involvement in cybersecurity will become even more significant as the digital landscape continues to evolve.

THE CRITICAL ROLE OF THE BOARD IN CYBERSECURITY

The rapidly evolving cyber landscape has transformed cybersecurity from a technical issue to a critical board-level concern. The potential consequences of cyber risks on corporate governance are far-reaching and can severely impact a company's reputation, operational efficiency, and financial health. In this context, the role of the board of directors in overseeing cyber risk management becomes paramount. This involves ensuring adequate resources for robust cybersecurity programs, establishing a well-defined cyber risk appetite, ensuring strict compliance with legal and regulatory requirements, and overseeing effective crisis management and incident response mechanisms.

The board's role in cybersecurity extends beyond mere risk management. It encompasses strategic planning, policy setting, and ensuring that the organization's cybersecurity efforts perfectly align with its business objectives. This necessitates a deep understanding of the cyber threats the organization faces, the potential impact of these threats on various aspects of the business, and the measures in place to mitigate them. It is about having a holistic view of the organization's cyber risk landscape and ensuring that all aspects of cybersecurity are integrated into the broader business strategy.

Ensuring that the organization has the necessary resources to manage cyber risks effectively is another critical aspect of the board's role in cybersecurity. This includes not only financial resources but also human resources equipped with the right skills and expertise. The board may need to approve significant investments in advanced cybersecurity technologies, comprehensive staff training programs, and external consultants or services. It is about ensuring that the organization has the capacity and capabilities to anticipate, prevent, detect, and respond to cyber threats.

Establishing a cyber risk appetite is another important responsibility of the board. This involves determining the level of cyber risk the organization is willing to accept to pursue its business objectives. The board must strike a delicate balance between the need for innovation and digital transformation, which often involves taking calculated risks, and the need to protect the organization's valuable assets and sensitive information. It is about making informed decisions considering digital initiatives' potential rewards and risks.

The board also has a crucial role in ensuring compliance with legal and regulatory requirements related to cybersecurity. This includes thoroughly understanding the relevant laws and regulations, ensuring that the organization's cybersecurity policies and practices fully comply with these requirements, and overseeing the organization's response to any regulatory inquiries or investigations. It is about fostering a culture of compliance and ensuring that the organization meets and exceeds regulatory expectations.

Finally, the board must oversee the organization's crisis management and incident response plans. This involves ensuring the organization is well prepared to respond effectively to a cyber incident, minimize the damage, and recover as quickly and smoothly as possible. It is about resilience and the ability to bounce back from cyber incidents with minimal disruption to the business. The board must ensure that the organization has a well-tested and regularly updated crisis management plan, a clear incident response process, and a communication strategy to manage the fallout from a cyber incident.

Recommendations:

- **Understand the Cyber Landscape:** Board members should educate themselves about the evolving cyber landscape and the threats their organization faces. This can be achieved through regular briefings from the organization's cybersecurity team, external consultants, or industry experts.

- **Integrate Cybersecurity into Strategic Planning:** The board should ensure that cybersecurity is integrated into the organization's strategic planning process. This involves considering cyber risks when making strategic decisions and ensuring that the organization's cybersecurity efforts align with its business objectives.

- **Invest in Cybersecurity Resources:** The board should ensure the organization has the resources to manage cyber risks effectively. This may involve approving investments in cybersecurity technologies, staff training, or external consultants.

- **Establish a Cyber Risk Appetite:** The board should work with management to establish a cyber risk appetite. This involves determining the level of cyber risk the organization is willing to accept to pursue its business objectives.

- **Oversee Compliance and Incident Response:** The board should oversee the organization's compliance with legal and regulatory requirements related to cybersecurity and its response to cyber incidents. This involves understanding the relevant laws and regulations, ensuring that the organization's cybersecurity policies and practices comply with these requirements, and overseeing the organization's response to any regulatory inquiries or investigations.

PERSPECTIVES FROM THE BOARD OF DIRECTORS

This section delves deeper into the board's perspective on cybersecurity, their expectations regarding cyber risk management, and the challenges they face in addressing cybersecurity. The board's viewpoint is instrumental in shaping the organization's cybersecurity strategy and ensuring it aligns with the overall business objectives. However, board members often face challenges in understanding the technical aspects of cybersecurity and translating them into business terms.

The board's expectations regarding cyber risk management are high. They expect the organization to have a robust cybersecurity program that includes risk identification and assessment, risk mitigation strategies, incident response plans, and ongoing monitoring and reporting. For example, they would expect the organization to have a system in place to identify potential cyber threats, assess their potential impact, develop strategies to mitigate these risks, plan to respond to cyber incidents, and monitor and report on the effectiveness of these measures. They also expect the organization to comply with all relevant legal and regulatory requirements, such as the General Data Protection Regulation (GDPR) in the European Union or the California Consumer Privacy Act (CCPA) in the United States.

However, board members often face challenges in addressing cybersecurity. These challenges include a lack of technical expertise, difficulty understanding the rapidly evolving cyber threat landscape, and the need to balance cybersecurity with other business priorities. For instance, a board member with a background in finance might struggle to understand the technical aspects of a cyber threat or the specifics of a cybersecurity solution. They may also find it challenging to keep up with the rapidly evolving cyber threat landscape, with new threats emerging and existing threats becoming more sophisticated. Balancing cybersecurity with other business priorities, such as growth, innovation, and customer satisfaction, can be challenging. They may also struggle to communicate effectively with cybersecurity executives and to understand the technical jargon often used in cybersecurity reports and briefings. For example, terms like "zero-day vulnerability," "phishing," or "DDoS attack" might be unfamiliar to board members without a technical background.

In addition to these challenges, board members may face difficulties integrating cybersecurity considerations into strategic decision-making processes. They may struggle to understand how cybersecurity risks can impact strategic objectives and how to incorporate these risks into strategic planning. For example, they may find it challenging to understand how a cyberattack could disrupt supply chains, impact customer relationships, or affect the launch of a new product or service.

Furthermore, board members may face challenges in understanding cybersecurity initiatives' return on investment (ROI). They may struggle to quantify cybersecurity investments' benefits and understand how these investments contribute to the organization's overall performance and value. For example, they may find it challenging to know how investing in a new cybersecurity technology can reduce the risk of a data breach, improve customer trust, or enhance operational efficiency.

Finally, board members may face challenges overseeing the organization's cybersecurity strategy implementation. They may struggle to understand the progress, the effectiveness of the measures implemented, and the gaps that must be addressed. For example, they may find it challenging to understand the findings of cybersecurity audits, the implications of security incidents, or the effectiveness of incident response plans.

Despite these challenges, the board's role in cybersecurity is crucial. By understanding the risks, setting high expectations for cyber risk management, and overcoming the challenges, board members can play a pivotal role in enhancing the organization's cybersecurity posture and resilience.

Recommendations:

- **Develop Cybersecurity Knowledge:** Board members should take steps to develop their knowledge of cybersecurity. This could include attending training sessions, reading industry reports, or consulting with external experts.
- **Set Clear Expectations:** The board should set clear expectations for the organization's cyber risk management. This includes risk identification and assessment expectations, risk mitigation, incident response, and compliance with legal and regulatory requirements.

- **Address Challenges Proactively:** The board should proactively address the challenges they face in addressing cybersecurity. This could include seeking technical advice, staying updated on the latest cyber threats, and balancing cybersecurity with other business priorities.
- **Improve Communication:** The board should work to improve communication with cybersecurity executives. This could involve developing a common language, asking for reports to be presented in business terms, and using visual aids to help understand complex issues.
- **Stay Involved:** The board should stay involved in the organization's cybersecurity efforts. This includes regular updates on the organization's cyber risk profile, progress in implementing the cybersecurity program, and any significant cyber incidents.

PERSPECTIVES FROM CYBERSECURITY EXECUTIVES

This section delves into the perspective of cybersecurity executives, focusing on their views on board engagement, the communication of cyber risks to the board, and the alignment of cybersecurity strategy with business objectives. As key players in managing the organization's cyber risks, cybersecurity executives often face the challenge of translating technical issues into business terms and aligning the cybersecurity strategy with the organization's business objectives.

Communicating cyber risks to the board is a key responsibility of cybersecurity executives. They must translate technical issues into business terms that the council can understand. For example, they might need to explain the potential impact of a cyber threat on the organization's operations, reputation, or financial performance. They must also present the risks in the context of the organization's risk appetite and business objectives. This requires a deep understanding of both cybersecurity and business strategy. For instance, they might need to explain how a proposed cybersecurity measure can help mitigate a specific cyber risk while supporting a strategic business objective.

Aligning the cybersecurity strategy with business objectives is another important task for cybersecurity executives. They must ensure that the cybersecurity program supports the organization's strategic goals and does not hinder innovation or business growth. This requires balancing security and usability and risk mitigation and cost. For example, they might need to ensure that cybersecurity measures do not unnecessarily restrict the use of digital technologies crucial for business innovation and growth.

However, cybersecurity executives often face challenges in fulfilling these responsibilities. They may struggle to communicate effectively with board members who lack a technical background. They may find it difficult to translate complex cybersecurity issues into business terms that the board can understand. They may also struggle to align the cybersecurity strategy with business objectives, particularly when conflicting priorities or constraints exist. For instance, they might work to balance the need for strong cybersecurity controls with business agility and speed.

Despite these challenges, cybersecurity executives are crucial in enhancing the organization's cybersecurity posture. By effectively engaging with the board, communicating cyber risks in business terms, and aligning the cybersecurity strategy with business objectives, they can help the organization navigate the complex cyber threat landscape and build solid cyber resilience. Their role is not just about managing cyber risks; it is also about enabling the organization to leverage digital technologies safely and effectively to achieve its business objectives.

Recommendations:

- **Engage the Board:** Cybersecurity executives should actively engage the board in cyber risk management. This includes regular updates on the organization's cyber risk profile, progress in implementing the cybersecurity program, and any significant cyber incidents.
- **Communicate Effectively:** Cybersecurity executives should communicate cyber risks to the board in business terms. This includes translating technical issues into business risks, presenting the risks in the context of the organization's risk appetite and business objectives, and using visual aids to help the board understand complex issues.
- **Align with Business Objectives:** Cybersecurity executives should align the cybersecurity strategy with the organization's objectives. This requires balancing security and usability and risk mitigation and cost.
- **Seek Board Support:** Cybersecurity executives should seek the board's support for cybersecurity initiatives. This includes support for resource allocation, policy approval, and culture change initiatives.
- **Promote a Cybersecurity Culture:** Cybersecurity executives should promote a cybersecurity culture within the organization. This includes awareness and training programs, clear and enforceable policies, and a positive security climate.

THE BOARD'S RESPONSIBILITIES IN CYBERSECURITY

The board of directors plays a pivotal role in overseeing cyber risk management. Their responsibilities extend beyond the traditional governance roles and into the realm of cybersecurity, where they are expected to ensure that the organization has adequate resources for cybersecurity programs, establish a cyber risk appetite, ensure compliance with legal and regulatory requirements, and oversee crisis management and incident response.

The board's role in overseeing cyber risk management is a critical one. They are tasked with ensuring that the organization has a comprehensive understanding of the cyber threats it faces and the potential impact of these threats on the organization's operations, reputation, and bottom line. They must ensure the organization has a robust cybersecurity program, including risk identification and assessment, risk mitigation strategies, incident response plans, and ongoing monitoring and reporting. The board must also ensure that the organization's cybersecurity efforts align with its overall business objectives and risk appetite.

Another key board responsibility is ensuring the organization has adequate resources for its cybersecurity programs. This includes not only financial resources but also human resources with the right skills and expertise. The board may need to approve investments in cybersecurity technologies, staff training, and external consultants or services. They must also ensure that the organization has the processes and procedures to manage cyber risks effectively.

Establishing a cyber risk appetite is another important responsibility of the board. This involves determining the level of cyber risk the organization is willing to accept to pursue its business objectives. The board must balance the need for innovation and digital transformation with protecting the organization's assets and information. They need to work with management to define the organization's cyber risk appetite and to ensure that it is communicated clearly throughout the organization.

The board also has a role in ensuring compliance with legal and regulatory requirements related to cybersecurity. This includes understanding the relevant laws and regulations, ensuring that the organization's cybersecurity policies and practices comply with these requirements, and overseeing the organization's response to any regulatory inquiries or investigations. The board must ensure that the organization has a compliance program that includes regular audits and reviews of the organization's cybersecurity practices.

Finally, the board must oversee the organization's crisis management and incident response plans. This involves ensuring the organization is prepared to respond effectively to a cyber incident, minimize the damage, and recover as quickly as possible. The board must ensure that the organization's incident response plan is tested regularly and updated to reflect changes in the cyber threat landscape.

Recommendations:

- **Understand the Cyber Landscape:** Board members should educate themselves about the evolving cyber landscape and the threats their organization faces. This can be achieved through regular briefings from the organization's cybersecurity team, external consultants, or industry experts.
- **Set Clear Expectations:** The board should set clear expectations for the organization's cyber risk management. This includes risk identification and assessment expectations, risk mitigation, incident response, and compliance with legal and regulatory requirements.
- **Allocate Adequate Resources:** The board should ensure the organization has the resources to manage cyber risks effectively. This may involve approving investments in cybersecurity technologies, staff training, or external consultants.

- **Establish a Cyber Risk Appetite:** The board should work with management to establish a cyber risk appetite. This involves determining the level of cyber risk the organization is willing to accept to pursue its business objectives.
- **Oversee Compliance and Incident Response:** The board should oversee the organization's compliance with legal and regulatory requirements related to cybersecurity and its response to cyber incidents. This involves understanding the relevant laws and regulations, ensuring that the organization's cybersecurity policies and practices comply with these requirements, and overseeing the organization's response to any regulatory inquiries or investigations.

EFFECTIVE COMMUNICATION BETWEEN THE BOARD AND CYBERSECURITY EXECUTIVES

Effective communication between the board and cybersecurity executives is not just important but crucial for managing cyber risks effectively. This involves several key steps, including developing a common language, presenting cyber risks in business terms, determining the frequency and format of cybersecurity reporting to the board, and utilizing external experts to facilitate communication.

Developing a common language improves communication between the board and cybersecurity executives. This involves translating technical jargon into business terms that the board can understand. It is about simplifying complex technical terms and ensuring they are relevant and meaningful in business. It also involves defining key terms and concepts so everyone understands their meaning. This shared language can help to bridge the gap between the technical and business perspectives and facilitate more effective discussions about cyber risks and strategies.

Presenting cyber risks in business terms is another important aspect of effective communication. Cybersecurity executives must explain the potential impact of cyber threats on the organization's operations, reputation, and bottom line. They must present the risks in the context of the organization's risk appetite and business objectives. They also need to explain the measures in place to mitigate these risks and the effectiveness of these measures. This involves describing these measures' technical aspects, strategic implications, and benefits. For example, they might need to explain how a particular cybersecurity measure can help to protect the organization's brand reputation, enhance customer trust, or support compliance with regulatory requirements.

Determining the frequency and format of cybersecurity reporting to the board is also essential. The board needs regular updates on the organization's cyber risk profile, progress in implementing the cybersecurity program, and any significant cyber incidents. The format of these reports should be clear and concise, with visual aids to help the board understand complex issues. This might involve using dashboards, charts, or other visual tools to present data in a way that is easy to understand and digest. The frequency of these reports should be sufficient to keep the board informed but not so frequent as to overwhelm them with information.

Finally, utilizing external experts can be a useful strategy for facilitating communication between the board and cybersecurity executives. External experts can provide an independent perspective on the organization's cyber risks and the effectiveness of its cybersecurity program. They can also help to translate technical issues into business terms and to facilitate discussions on complex topics. This can be particularly useful when dealing with difficult or contentious issues, where an independent perspective can help to clarify the issues and facilitate a more productive discussion.

In addition to these strategies, it is also important for both the board and cybersecurity executives to be open to feedback and willing to learn from each other. This involves sharing information, listening, and seeking to understand each other's perspectives. Doing so can build a stronger partnership and work together more effectively to manage the organization's cyber risks.

Recommendations:

- **Develop a Common Language:** The board and cybersecurity executives should work together to develop a common language for discussing cyber risks. This involves translating technical jargon into business terms and defining key terms and concepts.
- **Present Risks in Business Terms:** Cybersecurity executives should present cyber risks in business terms. This involves explaining the potential impact of cyber threats on the organization's operations, reputation, and bottom line and presenting the risks in the context of the organization's risk appetite and business objectives.
- **Determine Reporting Frequency and Format:** The board and cybersecurity executives should agree on the frequency and format of cybersecurity reporting to the board. The reports should be clear and concise, with visual aids to help the board understand complex issues.
- **Utilize External Experts:** The board and cybersecurity executives should consider utilizing external experts to facilitate communication. External experts can provide an independent perspective on the organization's cyber risks and the effectiveness of its cybersecurity program, and they can help to translate technical issues into business terms.
- **Promote Open and Honest Communication:** The board and cybersecurity executives should promote an open and honest communication culture. This involves creating a safe environment where people can raise concerns, ask questions, and share ideas without fear of criticism or punishment.

SPECIFIC RECOMMENDATIONS FOR REPORTING TO THE BOARD

This section provides specific recommendations for reporting to the board. It covers defining metrics and KPIs for board reporting, developing dashboards and visual aids, highlighting progress and achievements, providing context for security incidents and breaches, and suggesting proactive steps and strategic initiatives.

Defining metrics and KPIs for board reporting is a crucial first step. These metrics and KPIs should be aligned with the organization's business objectives and risk appetite. They should provide a clear and concise view of the organization's cyber risk profile, the effectiveness of its cybersecurity program, and the progress in implementing the cybersecurity strategy. The metrics and KPIs should be understandable, relevant, and actionable.

Developing dashboards and visual aids can significantly enhance the effectiveness of board reporting. Dashboards provide a visual representation of the organization's cyber risk profile and the status of its cybersecurity program. They can highlight key metrics and KPIs, show trends over time, and provide a quick overview of the organization's cyber risk posture. Visual aids, such as graphs and charts, can help to explain complex issues and to present data in a more digestible format.

Highlighting progress and achievements is another essential aspect of board reporting. This involves showcasing the organization's successes in managing cyber risks, implementing the cybersecurity strategy, and achieving its cybersecurity objectives. It also recognizes the efforts of the cybersecurity team and other stakeholders in the organization.

Providing context for security incidents and breaches is also crucial. The board needs to understand the nature of the incident, the impact on the organization, the response actions taken, and the lessons learned. The reporting should also include an incident assessment regarding the organization's risk appetite and business objectives.

Finally, suggesting proactive steps and strategic initiatives can help to engage the board in the organization's cybersecurity efforts. This involves proposing actions that the board can take to support the cybersecurity program, such as approving investments, endorsing policies, or advocating for a strong cybersecurity culture. It also suggests strategic initiatives to enhance the organization's cyber resilience, such as adopting new technologies, partnering with external organizations, or participating in industry forums.

Recommendations:

- **Define Metrics and KPIs:** The organization should define metrics and KPIs for board reporting. These should be aligned with the organization's business objectives and risk appetite, and they should provide a clear and concise view of the organization's cyber risk profile and the effectiveness of its cybersecurity program.

- **Develop Dashboards and Visual Aids:** The organization should develop dashboards and visual aids for board reporting. These should visually represent the organization's cyber risk profile and the status of its cybersecurity program and highlight key metrics and KPIs.
- **Highlight Progress and Achievements:** The organization should highlight its progress in managing cyber risks, implementing the cybersecurity strategy, and achieving its cybersecurity objectives. This should include recognizing the efforts of the cybersecurity team and other stakeholders in the organization.
- **Provide Context for Incidents:** The organization should provide context for security incidents and breaches in its board reporting. This should include an explanation of the nature of the incident, the impact on the organization, the response actions taken, and the lessons learned.
- **Suggest Proactive Steps:** The organization should suggest proactive steps and strategic initiatives that the board can take to support the cybersecurity program. This could include approving investments, endorsing policies, or advocating for a strong cybersecurity culture.

INSIGHTS FROM THE FFIEC AND OTHER STANDARDS ON BOARD INVOLVEMENT

This section provides an overview of relevant guidelines and standards, applies FFIEC insights to broader industries, and compares FFIEC with other standards on board involvement. The FFIEC and different standards provide valuable guidance on the board's role in cybersecurity, and their insights can be applied to organizations in all industries.

The FFIEC, or the Federal Financial Institutions Examination Council, is a US government interagency body that provides uniform principles, standards, and report forms for examining financial institutions. The FFIEC has issued several guidelines and handbooks on cybersecurity, which provide detailed guidance on the board's role in overseeing cyber risk management.

The FFIEC's guidelines emphasize the importance of board involvement in cybersecurity. They state that the board should approve the organization's cybersecurity program, oversee its implementation, and hold management accountable for its effectiveness. They also note that the board should ensure the organization has adequate resources for its cybersecurity program and complies with all relevant legal and regulatory requirements.

The FFIEC's insights can be applied to organizations in all industries, not just financial institutions. Good governance, risk management, and compliance principles are universal, and the specific guidance on board involvement in cybersecurity is highly relevant in today's cyber threat landscape.

Some other standards and frameworks guide board involvement in cybersecurity. These include the NIST cybersecurity Framework, the ISO 27001 standard, and the COSO Enterprise Risk Management Framework. These standards and frameworks provide similar guidance on the role of the board in cybersecurity, although there are some differences in emphasis and detail.

Recommendations:

- **Understand the FFIEC Guidelines:** The board should familiarize themselves with the FFIEC guidelines and other relevant standards on board involvement in cybersecurity. This can provide valuable guidance on their role and responsibilities in overseeing cyber risk management.
- **Apply the FFIEC Insights:** The board should apply the FFIEC's insights to their organization, regardless of the industry. Good governance, risk management, and compliance principles are universal, and the specific guidance on board involvement in cybersecurity is highly relevant in today's cyber threat landscape.
- **Compare Different Standards:** The board should compare the FFIEC guidelines with other standards and frameworks, such as the NIST cybersecurity Framework, the ISO 27001 standard, and the COSO Enterprise Risk Management Framework. This can provide a broader perspective on their role in cybersecurity and help to identify best practices.
- **Stay Updated:** The board should stay updated on the latest cybersecurity standards and guidelines developments. This can help them to keep their knowledge current and to adapt their approach as the cyber threat landscape evolves.
- **Seek Expert Advice:** The board should seek advice from experts in cybersecurity and governance. This can help them to understand the implications of the standards and guidelines and to apply them effectively in their organization.

CYBERSECURITY GOVERNANCE: EMBEDDING CYBERSECURITY IN CORPORATE CULTURE

Cybersecurity governance is not a standalone concept but is deeply intertwined with corporate culture. The board plays a significant role in shaping this culture, promoting awareness and training across the organization, and integrating cybersecurity into the corporate strategy. This role is not just about setting policies or overseeing compliance; it is about influencing attitudes, behaviors, and decisions throughout the organization.

The board's role in shaping the cybersecurity culture is pivotal. A robust cybersecurity culture is one where every employee, from the top executives to the frontline staff, understands the importance of cybersecurity and their role in protecting the organization's assets and information. The board can influence this culture by setting the tone at the top, demonstrating a commitment to cybersecurity, and holding management accountable for fostering a cybersecurity-conscious environment. This might involve endorsing a cybersecurity policy, supporting cybersecurity initiatives, or recognizing employees demonstrating good cybersecurity practices.

Promoting awareness and training across the organization is another key board responsibility. Cybersecurity is not just the responsibility of the IT department; it is everyone's responsibility. The board should ensure that the organization has a comprehensive cybersecurity awareness and training program that educates all employees about the cyber threats they face and the actions they can take to mitigate them. This might involve approving resources for training programs, promoting participation in these programs, or monitoring the effectiveness of these programs.

Integrating cybersecurity into the corporate strategy is also crucial. Cybersecurity should not be seen as a cost or a compliance requirement but as a strategic enabler. The board should ensure that cybersecurity considerations are integrated into the organization's strategic planning, investment decisions, and risk management practices. This might involve asking strategic questions about cybersecurity in board meetings, considering cybersecurity risks in investment decisions, or incorporating cybersecurity metrics into the organization's risk management framework.

In addition to these responsibilities, the board must also lead by example. This involves not just talking about cybersecurity but also demonstrating a commitment to cybersecurity in their behaviors and decisions. For instance, they might need to use secure communication channels, follow good password practices, or participate in cybersecurity training. By doing so, they can send a strong message to the rest of the organization about the importance of cybersecurity.

Finally, the board needs to maintain a forward-looking perspective on cybersecurity. The cyber threat landscape constantly evolves, and the organization's cybersecurity governance needs to evolve. This involves staying informed about emerging cyber threats, technological developments, and best practices in cybersecurity governance. It also involves being open to change and adapting the organization's cybersecurity governance. By doing so, the board can help the organization stay ahead of the curve and build strong cyber resilience.

Recommendations:

- **Shape the Cybersecurity Culture:** The board should actively shape the organization's cybersecurity culture. This involves setting the tone at the top, demonstrating a commitment to cybersecurity, and holding management accountable for fostering a cybersecurity-conscious environment.
- **Promote Awareness and Training:** The board should ensure the organization has a comprehensive cybersecurity awareness and training program. This program should educate all employees about the cyber threats they face and the actions they can take to mitigate them.
- **Integrate Cybersecurity into Strategy:** The board should ensure that cybersecurity considerations are integrated into the organization's

strategic planning process, investment decisions, and risk management practices.

- **Lead by Example:** The board should lead by example in demonstrating a commitment to cybersecurity. This can involve participating in cybersecurity training, staying informed about cyber threats, and advocating for strong cybersecurity practices.
- **Monitor the Cybersecurity Culture:** The board should monitor the organization's cybersecurity culture. This can involve regular surveys or assessments to gauge employees' awareness and attitudes toward cybersecurity and identify improvement areas.

LEGAL AND REGULATORY CONSIDERATIONS FOR THE BOARD

The board's responsibilities include understanding legal obligations related to cybersecurity, ensuring regulatory compliance, and managing the legal consequences of cybersecurity failures. The board must clearly understand the legal obligations related to cybersecurity. This includes laws and regulations at the local, national, and international levels and industry-specific regulations. These legal obligations relate to data protection, privacy, breach notification, and more. The board should be informed of legal landscape changes that could impact the organization's cybersecurity posture.

In addition to understanding the legal landscape, the board should be aware of various guidance and standards that can help shape the organization's cybersecurity strategy. For instance, the FFIEC IT Examination Handbook provides a wealth of information on managing cybersecurity risks, including developing and implementing a comprehensive information security program, formal project management processes, and business continuity planning. The board should ensure that such guidance is considered when formulating the organization's cybersecurity policies and procedures.

Ensuring regulatory compliance is another key responsibility of the board. Compliance with cybersecurity regulations is not just about avoiding penalties; it is also about demonstrating to stakeholders that the organization takes cybersecurity seriously. The board should ensure that the organization has a robust compliance program, which includes regular audits and reviews of the organization's cybersecurity practices. This includes adhering to regulations such as the Gramm–Leach–Bliley Act, which requires financial institutions to explain their information-sharing practices to their customers and to safeguard sensitive data.

The board should also know the various tools and resources available to help manage cybersecurity risks. For example, the FFIEC cybersecurity Assessment Tool can help institutions identify risks and determine cybersecurity preparedness. The board should use such tools to enhance the organization's cybersecurity posture.

Finally, the board must be prepared to manage the legal consequences of cybersecurity failures. This could include regulatory penalties, lawsuits, and reputational damage. The board should ensure that the organization has a crisis management plan providing a legal response strategy and that this plan is tested and updated regularly. This includes having a comprehensive business continuity program to mitigate the consequences of system interruptions, natural disasters, and unauthorized intrusions.

In conclusion, the board is crucial in managing the organization's cybersecurity risks. This involves understanding the legal and regulatory landscape, ensuring regulatory compliance, leveraging available tools and resources, and preparing for potential cybersecurity incidents. By fulfilling these responsibilities, the board can help ensure the organization is well positioned to manage its cybersecurity risks effectively.

Section Recommendations:

- **Stay Informed:** The board should stay informed about the legal obligations related to cybersecurity. This can be achieved through regular briefings from the organization's legal team or external legal consultants.
- **Ensure Compliance:** The board should ensure that the organization has a robust compliance program. This should include regular audits and reviews of the organization's cybersecurity practices.
- **Prepare for Legal Consequences:** The board should be prepared to manage the legal consequences of cybersecurity failures. This involves a crisis management plan that includes a legal response strategy.
- **Engage Legal Experts:** The board should engage legal experts to advise on cybersecurity matters. These experts can provide valuable insights into the legal implications of cyber risks and the organization's legal obligations.
- **Promote a Culture of Compliance:** The board should promote a culture of compliance within the organization. This involves setting the tone at the top and demonstrating a commitment to legal and regulatory compliance.

THE FUTURE OF BOARD INVOLVEMENT IN CYBERSECURITY

The future of cybersecurity is marked by several emerging trends and challenges that will shape the board's role in managing cyber risks. These trends include the increasing sophistication of cyber threats, the growing reliance on digital technologies, the evolving regulatory landscape, and the rise of new technologies such as artificial intelligence and the Internet of Things.

Cyber threats are becoming more sophisticated and harder to detect. Attackers use advanced techniques and tools, including artificial intelligence and machine learning, to bypass security measures and launch targeted attacks. This trend is expected to continue, with attackers becoming more innovative and persistent in their efforts to compromise systems and steal data.

The growing reliance on digital technologies is another trend that will impact the board's role in cybersecurity. Digital transformation is no longer a choice but a necessity for businesses to stay competitive. However, this digital shift is expanding the attack surface and creating new vulnerabilities that must be managed. The board must ensure that the organization's digital transformation efforts are accompanied by robust cybersecurity measures to protect against potential cyber threats.

The regulatory landscape for cybersecurity is also evolving. Governments and regulatory bodies worldwide are introducing new laws and regulations to protect data and privacy and ensure that organizations take adequate measures to protect against cyber threats. The board must stay informed about these regulatory changes and ensure the organization complies with all relevant laws and regulations.

The rise of new technologies, such as artificial intelligence and the Internet of Things, is another trend that will shape the board's role in cybersecurity. These technologies offer numerous benefits but also introduce new risks and challenges. The board must understand these risks and ensure the organization takes appropriate management measures.

In response to these trends and challenges, the board's role in cybersecurity is expected to become more strategic and proactive. The board will need to engage more deeply with cybersecurity issues, and their role will likely extend beyond oversight and into areas such as strategy formulation, risk management, and crisis response. The board must ensure the organization's cybersecurity strategy is forward-looking, adaptable, and regularly reviewed and updated to reflect changes in the cyber threat landscape.

Finally, the board will need to prepare for future cyber threats. This involves staying informed about emerging threats, understanding their potential impact on the organization, and ensuring it is ready to respond effectively. The board must ensure the organization's cybersecurity strategy is forward-looking, adaptable, and regularly reviewed and updated to reflect changes in the cyber threat landscape. The board must also foster a continuous learning and improvement culture to ensure the organization is always ready to face the next cyber threat.

Recommendations:

- **Stay Informed:** The board should stay informed about emerging trends in the cyber landscape and their implications for the organization's cyber risk profile and cybersecurity strategy.
- **Adapt to Evolving Role:** The board should be prepared to adapt its role in cybersecurity as it evolves. This could involve engaging more deeply with cybersecurity issues and extending their role into strategy formulation, risk management, and crisis response.
- **Prepare for Future Threats:** The board should ensure the organization is prepared for future cyber threats. This involves staying informed about

emerging threats, understanding their potential impact on the organization, and providing its forward-looking and adaptable cybersecurity strategy.

- **Promote a Proactive Approach:** The board should promote a proactive approach to cybersecurity. This involves anticipating and preparing for cyber threats rather than reacting to them.
- **Review and Update Strategy:** The board should ensure the organization's cybersecurity strategy is regularly reviewed and updated to reflect changes in the cyber threat landscape.

Chapter Conclusion

The significance of board involvement in cybersecurity is paramount. Through their oversight of cyber risk management, dedication to allocating sufficient resources, and role in molding the organization's cybersecurity culture, the board plays a crucial role in building a cyber-resilient organization. The path forward for boards and cybersecurity executives involves a commitment to continuous improvement in cyber governance. This encompasses staying informed about emerging trends and threats, continuously reviewing and updating the organization's cybersecurity strategy, and fostering a cybersecurity awareness and responsibility culture.

The board's engagement in cybersecurity is about safeguarding the organization from cyber threats and empowering the organization to leverage digital technologies and innovate confidently. By adopting a proactive and strategic approach to cybersecurity, the board can contribute to building a cyber-resilient organization that is prepared to face the future.

Furthermore, the board's involvement in cybersecurity is a testament to their commitment to the organization's safety and success. By overseeing cyber risk management, they ensure the organization is protected from threats and prepared to respond and recover should a breach occur. Their commitment to providing adequate resources is a testament to their understanding that cybersecurity is not a one-time effort but a continuous process that requires investment in technology, people, and training.

The board's role in shaping the organization's cybersecurity culture is also significant. They set the tone at the top, signaling to all employees that cybersecurity is not just the IT department's responsibility but everyone in the organization. This culture of shared responsibility is crucial in ensuring that all employees are vigilant and proactive in protecting the organization from cyber threats.

Looking ahead, the board and cybersecurity executives must commit to continuous improvement in cyber governance. This means staying abreast of the ever-evolving cyber threat landscape, regularly reviewing and updating the organization's cybersecurity strategy to ensure it remains effective and relevant, and fostering a cybersecurity awareness and responsibility culture.

The board's engagement in cybersecurity is also about enabling the organization to harness the power of digital technologies and innovate securely. By understanding the risks associated with these technologies and ensuring that appropriate safeguards are in place, the board can help the organization leverage these technologies to drive growth and innovation.

In essence, by taking a proactive and strategic approach to cybersecurity, the board plays a pivotal role in building a cyber-resilient organization. An organization that is not just equipped to defend against cyber threats but also prepared to confidently and securely leverage the opportunities presented by the digital age.

Case Study: Cybersecurity Board Governance at TechPioneer Inc.

TechPioneer Inc., a leading technology company, was amid rapid growth and expansion. However, increased cyber threats and vulnerabilities accompanied this exciting development phase. The board of directors, under the leadership of Chairperson Nilosh, recognized the urgent need for a robust cybersecurity governance framework to protect the company's valuable assets and hard-earned reputation.

Nilosh, with her deep and nuanced understanding of the evolving cyber landscape, was acutely aware that the board's involvement in cybersecurity was not just important but crucial. She took the initiative to conduct a comprehensive review of the company's existing cybersecurity strategy. She aimed to ensure it was robust, comprehensive, and aligned with the company's business objectives and risk appetite. She also emphasized defining clear metrics and KPIs for board reporting. She understood the need for developing dashboards and visual aids to enhance the effectiveness of board reporting, making complex cybersecurity issues more understandable for all board members.

Under Nilosh's dynamic leadership, the board of TechPioneer Inc. took a proactive role in shaping the company's cybersecurity culture. They went beyond their supervisory role and actively promoted awareness and training. They were instrumental in integrating cybersecurity into the corporate strategy. Nilosh understood that a strong cybersecurity culture was one where every employee, regardless of their role or position in the company, understood the importance of cybersecurity. She believed everyone had a role in protecting the organization's assets and information.

Legal and regulatory considerations were also a key focus for Nilosh. She ensured that the board clearly understood the legal obligations related to cybersecurity. She confirmed that the company complied with all relevant laws and regulations, whether local, national, or international. She also prepared the board to manage the legal consequences of potential cybersecurity failures. She ensured that a crisis management plan was in place, which included a legal response strategy, and that this plan was tested and updated regularly.

Looking ahead, Nilosh recognized the need for the board to stay informed about emerging trends and adapt their approach accordingly. She was committed to continuous improvement in cyber governance. She made it a priority to remain knowledgeable about emerging threats, and she ensured that the organization's cybersecurity strategy was forward-looking and adaptable. She understood that the cyber threat landscape was constantly evolving and that the company's cybersecurity strategy needed to evolve.

In conclusion, Nilosh's leadership in cybersecurity governance at TechPioneer Inc. serves as a model for other companies. Her proactive approach, commitment to continuous improvement, and focus on integrating cybersecurity into the corporate culture and strategy have helped to build a cyber-resilient organization. Her story underscores the pivotal role the board of directors can play in managing cyber risks and protecting the company's assets and reputation.

Thirty Example Questions for Board Members to Ask About Cybersecurity
Navigating the complex landscape of cybersecurity requires board members to ask insightful questions that can help them understand the organization's cybersecurity posture, identify potential vulnerabilities, and guide the development of robust cybersecurity policies and procedures. Here are 30 questions that board members can ask about cybersecurity, each accompanied by a brief explanation:

1. **What is our current cybersecurity strategy, and how does it align with our business objectives?** This question helps the board understand the organization's approach to managing cyber risks and how it supports achieving business goals.
2. **What are the top cyber risks that our organization faces?** Understanding the most significant cyber threats allows the board to assess whether the organization's cybersecurity measures are appropriately focused.
3. **How are we assessing and managing these risks?** This question delves into the organization's risk management processes, providing insight into how cyber risks are identified, evaluated, and mitigated.
4. **What cybersecurity frameworks or standards are we following?** Knowing which frameworks or standards guide the organization's cybersecurity practices can help the board evaluate their comprehensiveness and effectiveness.

5. **How are we ensuring compliance with relevant laws and regulations related to cybersecurity?** Compliance with cybersecurity laws and regulations is crucial to avoid legal penalties and reputational damage.

6. **What resources (financial, human, technological) are we dedicating to cybersecurity?** This question helps the board assess whether the organization has the resources to manage cyber risks effectively.

7. **Do we have a dedicated cybersecurity team, and who leads it?** Understanding the structure and leadership of the cybersecurity function can provide insights into its effectiveness.

8. **How are we promoting cybersecurity awareness and training across the organization?** A strong cybersecurity culture, underpinned by understanding and training, is key to reducing human-related cyber risks.

9. **What measures do we have in place to protect sensitive data?** Given the potential consequences of data breaches, the board should understand how the organization protects its sensitive data.

10. **How do we respond to a cyber incident, and how often do we test our incident response plan?** Effective incident response is crucial to minimize the impact of a cyber incident.

11. **What is our process for staying informed about the latest cyber threats and trends?** Staying up-to-date with the evolving cyber threat landscape is key to maintaining a robust cybersecurity posture.

12. **How do we measure the effectiveness of our cybersecurity program?** Understanding the metrics used to evaluate the cybersecurity program can help the board assess its success.

13. **What is our cyber risk appetite, and how was it determined?** The board should understand the level of cyber risk the organization is willing to accept in pursuit of its business objectives.

14. **How do we incorporate cybersecurity considerations into our strategic planning and** investment decisions? This question can help the board assess whether cybersecurity is being integrated into business strategy and operations.

15. **How do we communicate about cyber risks and incidents internally and externally?** Effective communication about cyber risks and incidents is crucial for managing stakeholder expectations and maintaining trust.

16. **How do we protect our network and systems from unauthorized access?** Understanding the organization's access control measures can provide insights into its defenses against cyberattacks.

17. **What is our approach to managing third-party cyber risks?** Given the potential cyber risks associated with third-party relationships, the board should understand how these are managed.

18. **What cybersecurity insurance do we have, and what does it cover?** Cybersecurity insurance can provide financial protection against the costs of a cyber incident, but it is essential to understand its scope and limitations.

19. **How do we ensure our software and systems' secure development and maintenance?** Secure development and maintenance practices can help prevent software and system vulnerabilities that cyberattackers could exploit.

20. **How do we protect our remote workers and manage the associated cyber risks?** The increased remote working is crucial to understanding the associated cyber risks and protective measures.

21. **What is our approach to data backup and recovery?** Effective data backup and recovery measures are key to ensuring business continuity during a cyber incident.

22. **How do we manage the cybersecurity risks associated with emerging technologies (e.g., AI, IoT) that we use?** As the organization adopts emerging technologies, it is essential to understand and manage the associated cyber risks.

23. **How do we handle the encryption of sensitive data?** Encryption is key to protecting sensitive data, particularly when transmitted or stored.

24. **What is our policy on software updates and patch management?** Regular software updates and effective patch management are crucial for protecting against known vulnerabilities.

25. **How do we monitor our systems and networks for potential cyber threats?** Continuous monitoring can help detect potential cyber threats early, allowing for a quicker response.

26. **What is our approach to user identity and access management?** Effective identity and access management ensures that only authorized individuals can access the organization's systems and data.

27. **How do we handle the physical security of our IT infrastructure?** Physical security is an often overlooked aspect of cybersecurity, but it is crucial for protecting the organization's IT infrastructure.

28. **What is our policy on mobile device security?** With the widespread use of mobile devices for work purposes, understanding the organization's approach to mobile device security is important.

29. **How do we ensure the security of our cloud services?** Understanding the associated security measures is crucial as more organizations move to the cloud.

30. **What plans do we have for improving our cybersecurity posture in the future?** This forward-looking question can help the board understand the organization's strategies for enhancing its cybersecurity measures.

CHAPTER 7

Risk Management

"Effective risk management in the digital realm is not about building impenetrable fortresses, but rather about forging resilient organizations capable of adapting and evolving in the face of ever-changing cyber threats."

Risk management, a critical component of cybersecurity governance, entails various elements. Starting from a basic understanding of risk management and its importance, one must also navigate the complexities of the risk management life cycle, FFIEC handbooks, governance frameworks, and risk assessment techniques. The field encompasses diverse risk types, including third-party, technology, cybersecurity, compliance, and legal risks. Insights into effective monitoring and reporting mechanisms are equally important. Overall, a deep understanding of risk management from a business perspective is crucial, coupled with practical guidance on adhering to compliance requirements and implementing best practices.

RISK MANAGEMENT IN THE BUSINESS

Risk management is a concept intrinsic to the fabric of any successful business. It refers to identifying, assessing, and controlling threats that an organization might face. These threats or risks could stem from various sources, including financial uncertainties, strategic management errors, legal liabilities, accidents, and natural disasters.

Understanding the importance of risk management is vital for an organization's resilience and longevity. It equips a business with the tools to preemptively recognize potential risks, prepare for them, and develop mitigation strategies.

This, in turn, can enhance operational efficiency, ensure regulatory compliance, and foster stakeholder confidence.

A successful risk management practice is woven into the everyday fabric of the organization. It should not be an afterthought but a fundamental business strategy building block. This requires understanding the organization's business model, objectives, and the industry within which it operates. Risk management is not just about risk avoidance; it is about making informed decisions that balance potential risks against benefits.

The role of laws, regulations, and rules in guiding risk management practices cannot be overstated. These frameworks provide a structure for risk management, establishing clear standards and guidelines that organizations must follow. Regulations can emanate from various governmental or nongovernmental bodies, giving guidance on acceptable levels of risk and mandated protective measures.

Laws and regulations about risk management may differ across countries and industries. Therefore, organizations must stay abreast of these laws and implement necessary measures to remain compliant. Noncompliance could lead to penalties, reputational damage, and loss of customer trust.

While regulations establish minimally acceptable standards, they should not be the end goal of an organization's risk management efforts. Instead, they should be a foundation for more robust and comprehensive risk management strategies. Risk management should, therefore, be a forward-looking exercise, going beyond compliance and focusing on the organization's long-term sustainability and success.

Finally, the successful integration of risk management into business operations relies on the organization's culture. When risk awareness is ingrained into the corporate culture, it encourages employees at all levels to consider risks in their decision-making processes, fostering a more resilient and adaptable organization.

Recommendations:

- **Understand Risk Management Fundamentals:** Embrace risk management as a core business strategy rather than a separate entity. Recognize its role in enhancing operational efficiency, ensuring regulatory compliance, and fostering stakeholder confidence. To identify and assess potential threats effectively, spend time understanding your business model, objectives, and industry.

- **Incorporate Regulatory Frameworks:** Familiarize yourself with the laws, regulations, and rules that guide risk management practices in your industry and jurisdiction. Use them as a foundation to establish clear standards and guidelines within your organization, ensuring compliance to avoid penalties, reputational damage, and loss of customer trust.

- **Stay Updated with Regulatory Changes:** Actively monitor changes to laws and regulations about risk management within your industry and jurisdiction. Implement the necessary measures to remain compliant, as noncompliance could harm your organization.

- **Go Beyond Compliance:** Treat regulatory standards as the bare minimum and aim to build upon them. Develop robust risk management strategies for compliance and the organization's long-term sustainability and success. Make risk management a forward-looking exercise.
- **Build a Risk-Aware Culture:** Integrate risk awareness into your corporate culture. Encourage employees at all levels to consider potential risks in their decision-making processes. This will foster a more resilient and adaptable organization. Conduct regular training and workshops to keep your team informed and prepared.

UNDERSTANDING THE RISK MANAGEMENT LIFE CYCLE

The risk management life cycle is an iterative process designed to provide a systematic approach to identifying, assessing, responding to, and monitoring risks. It begins with identifying risks and recognizing potential threats that could adversely affect the organization's objectives. This stage involves not just identifying risks but also their documentation. Several methods can facilitate risk identification, including brainstorming sessions, historical data analysis, risk checklists, and scenario analysis.

Upon identifying potential risks, the next step in the risk management life cycle is to assess and analyze these risks. This involves determining the likelihood of each risk occurring and its impact on the organization if it did happen. Risk assessment provides a way to prioritize risks based on their potential effect on the business. Tools such as risk matrices and heat maps can help visualize and classify risks, aiding in this process.

The third phase involves developing strategies to mitigate and control identified risks. Risk mitigation involves implementing measures to reduce the likelihood of risks occurring or reducing their potential impact. These measures can take various forms, from implementing robust security protocols to mitigate cybersecurity risks to diversifying suppliers to reduce supply chain risks. The chosen risk mitigation strategies should align with the organization's risk appetite and strategic objectives.

Monitoring and reporting form the fourth stage of the risk management life cycle. This involves monitoring identified risks and the effectiveness of the implemented control measures. Regular monitoring ensures that the organization remains aware of its risk landscape and can respond to changes promptly. Conversely, reporting involves communicating risk information to relevant stakeholders, including the management team, the board of directors, and regulators. Reporting should be clear and concise and provide all the necessary information for decision-making.

The final stage of the risk management life cycle is continuous improvement. No risk management process is perfect; there will always be areas that can be improved. This phase involves reviewing the risk management process, identifying areas of weakness, and implementing changes to enhance its effectiveness. Continuous improvement ensures the risk management process remains practical and relevant despite the ever-changing risk landscape.

Recommendations:

- **Recognize and Document Risks:** Initiate the risk management life cycle by identifying potential threats affecting the organization's objectives. Use various methods to facilitate this, including brainstorming sessions, historical data analysis, risk checklists, and scenario analysis. Document all identified risks systematically.
- **Assess and Prioritize Risks:** Analyze each risk by determining its likelihood and the impact it could have on the organization. Leverage tools such as risk matrices and risk heat maps to visualize and classify risks. Prioritize them based on their potential effect on the business.
- **Develop Risk Mitigation Strategies:** Once risks have been prioritized, design and implement strategies to mitigate and control these risks. Measures could range from implementing robust security protocols for cybersecurity risks to diversifying suppliers for supply chain risks. Align these strategies with the organization's risk appetite and strategic objectives.
- **Establish Routine Monitoring and Reporting:** Continuously monitor the identified risks and the effectiveness of control measures implemented. Regular updates will ensure that the organization can respond promptly to changes in the risk landscape. Develop clear, concise, comprehensive reports for relevant stakeholders, facilitating informed decision-making.
- **Pursue Continuous Improvement:** Review the risk management process regularly, identifying weak spots and areas for improvement. Adapt your approach to keep it effective and relevant in the face of changing risks. Remember that no risk management process is perfect, and continuous enhancement is critical to successful risk management.

FFIEC HANDBOOKS AND RISK MANAGEMENT GUIDANCE

The Federal Financial Institutions Examination Council (*FFIEC*) is an interagency body of the US government that sets standards for examining financial institutions. It publishes handbooks that provide comprehensive guidance on various aspects of risk management, particularly for financial institutions. These handbooks are invaluable for understanding and implementing effective risk management practices.

One such resource is the FFIEC Information Security Handbook, which provides detailed guidance on risk management requirements for financial institutions. The handbook outlines key processes such as risk identification, risk measurement, risk mitigation, risk monitoring, reporting, and metrics for program improvement.

Risk Identification (Page 9 of the handbook): An effective information security program should have documented processes to identify threats and vulnerabilities continuously. Risk identification should produce groupings of threats, including significant cybersecurity threats. A taxonomy for categorizing threats, sources, and vulnerabilities can help identify risk.

Risk Measurement (Page 12 of the handbook): Management should develop risk measurement processes that evaluate the inherent risk to the institution. The risk measurement process should be used to understand the institution's inherent risk and determine the risk associated with different threats. Management should use its measurement of the risks to guide its recommendations for and use of mitigating controls.

Risk Mitigation (Page 13 of the handbook): Once management has identified and measured the risks, it should develop and implement an appropriate plan to mitigate those risks. This plan should include understanding the extent and quality of the current control environment. When evaluating the strength of controls or the ability to mitigate risk, the institution should consider the system of controls rather than any discrete control.

Risk Monitoring and Reporting (Page 47 of the handbook): Risk monitoring is a process by which the institution tracks information about its inherent risk profile and identifies gaps in the effectiveness of risk mitigation activities. Risk reporting is a process that produces information systems reports that address threats, capabilities, vulnerabilities, and inherent risk changes. The reporting process should provide a method of disseminating those reports to appropriate members of management.

Metrics (Page 47 of the handbook): A mature and effective information security program uses metrics to improve the program's effectiveness and efficiency. Management should develop metrics demonstrating the extent to which the security program is implemented and whether the program is effective. Metrics are used to measure security policy implementation, conformance with the information security program, the adequacy of security services delivery, and the impact of security events on business processes.

The FFIEC handbooks cover various topics, including IT Examination, Outsourcing Technology Services, and Business Continuity Management. Each handbook explores specific risk areas and guides the management of these risks. The handbooks aim to ensure that financial institutions have robust risk management systems to safeguard their operations and customers from various risks.

Key principles and objectives underpin the FFIEC's guidance. One of the primary objectives is to ensure that financial institutions maintain sound risk management practices consistent with the size and complexity of their operations. Other objectives include fostering transparency in risk management processes, promoting accountability for managing risks, and ensuring institutions have adequate resources to manage risks effectively.

Compliance with FFIEC handbooks is expected for financial institutions operating in the United States. Compliance entails more than merely ticking off a checklist; it requires a deep understanding of the handbooks' principles and guidelines. The FFIEC encourages institutions to integrate guidance into risk management strategies and processes.

Noncompliance with FFIEC guidance can have severe implications for financial institutions, including potential enforcement actions by regulators. Therefore, understanding and implementing FFIEC handbooks is not optional; it is a necessary part of sound risk management for any financial institution.

Recommendations:

- **Leverage FFIEC Handbooks:** Use the FFIEC handbooks, such as the Information Security Handbook, as your primary resource to understand and implement effective risk management practices. These provide detailed guidance on key processes like risk identification, measurement, mitigation, monitoring, and metrics for program improvement.

- **Implement Risk Identification:** Develop documented processes to continuously identify threats and vulnerabilities, as Page 9 of the Information Security Handbook suggests. Use a taxonomy for categorizing threats, sources, and vulnerabilities to support the risk identification process.

- **Develop Risk Measurement Processes:** Follow the guidance on Page 12 of the handbook to evaluate the inherent risk to your institution. Use the risk measurement process to understand and determine risks associated with different threats. Utilize these measurements to guide recommendations for and use of mitigating controls.

- **Plan and Implement Risk Mitigation:** After identifying and measuring risks, design and implement an appropriate plan to mitigate these risks, as advised on Page 13 of the handbook. Evaluate the strength of controls considering the overall system rather than any individual control.

- **Regularly Monitor and Report Risk:** Monitor your institution's inherent risk profile and identify gaps in the effectiveness of risk mitigation activities, as recommended on Page 47 of the handbook. Develop reports addressing threats, capabilities, vulnerabilities, and inherent risk changes, disseminating them to relevant management team members.

- **Utilize Metrics for Improvement:** Adopt metrics to enhance the effectiveness and efficiency of your security program, as outlined on Page 47 of the handbook. These metrics should demonstrate the extent of security program implementation and its effectiveness, including measuring security policy implementation, conformance with the security program, adequacy of security services delivery, and the impact of security events on business processes.

- **Comply with FFIEC Guidelines:** Compliance with FFIEC guidance is crucial for financial institutions operating in the United States. It requires a thorough understanding of the principles and guidelines in the handbooks. Integrate this guidance into your risk management strategies and processes.

- **Be Mindful of Noncompliance Implications:** Noncompliance with FFIEC guidance can lead to serious repercussions, including potential enforcement actions by regulators. Therefore, understanding and implementing the FFIEC handbook is not just optional but a necessary part of sound risk management for any financial institution.

GOVERNANCE AND RISK MANAGEMENT FRAMEWORK

An integral part of an effective risk management strategy lies in having a firm governance structure in place. The Board of Directors and Senior Management perform key roles within this structure, shaping the organization's strategic direction and defining the risk appetite. They guide the organization through its strategic objectives while ensuring that the risk management processes align seamlessly with these broader strategic goals. The tone set at the top by these influential figures can permeate all levels of the organization, fostering a healthy and responsive risk culture.

A step-by-step, structured approach proves beneficial to develop a robust risk management framework. It begins with identifying and systematically categorizing the risks an organization may face. Once these risks are laid bare, the next step involves defining the roles and responsibilities concerning risk management. Clear delineation of duties prevents overlap or gaps, enabling efficient handling of potential risks. Following this, developing risk management policies and procedures tailored to the organization's specific needs and context forms the backbone of this framework. Implementing risk monitoring and reporting mechanisms completes this framework, providing a means for continual assessment and course correction.

Understanding and defining the organization's risk appetite and tolerance is crucial. Risk appetite is the quantum of risk an organization is willing to accept in pursuing strategic objectives. It serves as a guiding principle for what kind of risks the organization is ready to take to achieve its goals. On the other hand, risk tolerance measures the variability in outcomes an organization can comfortably withstand without jeopardizing its operations or goals. These two elements should serve as guiding parameters for risk management decisions. It's not enough to define these; it is equally essential to ensure that this understanding is communicated and understood throughout the organization, influencing actions and decision-making at all levels.

Strategic planning is not complete without the incorporation of risk management. This integration ensures that potential risks are carefully considered when setting strategic objectives. The process includes identifying and assessing the risks linked to strategic options, embedding risk management into the strategic decision-making process, and ensuring the strategic plans are resilient and adaptive to changes in the risk landscape.

Lastly, the dual aspects of reporting and accountability play a critical role in effective risk management. Reporting ensures the communication of relevant risk information to all stakeholders, allowing for informed decision-making based on understanding the current risk landscape. Meanwhile, accountability ensures that all employees know their specific roles in managing risks and know they will be held responsible for their performance. This level of ownership can foster a strong risk culture, encouraging proactive risk management. It promotes an environment where risks are actively identified and mitigated, and new strategic opportunities are recognized and capitalized.

Recommendations:

- **Establish a Strong Governance Structure:** Ensure the Board of Directors and Senior Management actively shape the organization's strategic direction and define the risk appetite. They should ensure that risk management processes align with broader strategic goals and foster a healthy risk culture.

- **Develop a Structured Risk Management Framework:** Adopt a step-by-step approach to develop a robust risk management framework. This includes identifying and categorizing risks, defining roles and responsibilities in risk management, developing policies and procedures tailored to your organization's specific needs, and implementing risk monitoring and reporting mechanisms.

- **Define Risk Appetite and Tolerance:** Clearly understand and define the organization's risk appetite (the amount of risk the organization is willing to accept in pursuit of its goals) and risk tolerance (the variability in outcomes an organization can withstand without jeopardizing its operations or goals). These should serve as guiding principles for risk management decisions and should be effectively communicated and understood throughout the organization.

- **Integrate Risk Management into Strategic Planning:** Ensure that risk management is integral to strategic planning. This includes identifying and assessing risks associated with strategic options, embedding risk management into the strategic decision-making process, and ensuring that strategic plans are resilient and adaptive to changes in the risk landscape.

- **Prioritize Reporting and Accountability:** Establish clear reporting mechanisms to communicate relevant risk information to all stakeholders for informed decision-making. Simultaneously, instill a sense of accountability among employees about managing risks and hold them responsible for their performance. This promotes a strong risk culture and encourages proactive risk management.

- **Encourage a Culture of Opportunity Recognition:** Foster an environment where risks are actively identified and mitigated and new strategic opportunities are recognized and capitalized on. This approach allows the organization to transform potential risks into business opportunities.

RISK APPROVALS AND THE ROLE OF COMMITTEES

In most organizations, risk management is a multifaceted and comprehensive process that requires various stakeholders' concerted efforts to ensure its efficacy. A key player in the realm of risk management is the Risk Council. This governing body, composed of senior executives drawn from diverse departments within the organization, is entrusted with overseeing and guiding the risk management processes, setting the direction for strategic risk decisions, and endorsing the organization's risk appetite. This council typically deliberates on high-risk choices, such as those involving new market entries or product launches.

While the Risk Council is the central body, other committees, like the Audit Committee, Compliance Committee, or Information Security Committee, often support the risk governance framework. These committees focus on specific risk areas, providing expertise and insight contributing to comprehensive risk management. For instance, the Audit Committee ensures proper financial controls, while the Compliance Committee ensures adherence to regulatory requirements.

At a granular level, departmental or functional teams manage specific risks within their purview. Each risk level is carefully defined, ensuring that risks are managed effectively and efficiently, with more significant risks escalated for higher-level decision-making.

The Chief Information Security Officer (CISO) plays a pivotal role in risk approvals, particularly cybersecurity-related ones. The CISO, by their specialized knowledge and expertise, leads the organization's efforts in identifying potential threats, formulating security protocols, and supervising their implementation. In the context of risk approval, the CISO's insights guide the organization in making informed decisions about cybersecurity risks. They may recommend adopting novel security technologies or strategizing the response to an emerging security threat. Sometimes, if the cost or feasibility of mitigating a risk is prohibitive, the CISO may suggest accepting the risk. In all these cases, the CISO's insights are invaluable for decision-making.

Risk reporting is another crucial element in the risk governance structure. The regular circulation of detailed risk reports helps inform all stakeholders about the organization's risk landscape, facilitating informed decision-making. These reports may include Key Risk Indicators (KRIs) and Key Performance Indicators (KPIs), metrics that quantitatively measure risk exposure and the effectiveness of risk management efforts, respectively. KRIs might include indicators like the number of security incidents, while KPIs might measure the time taken to detect a security breach. To assist in developing relevant and meaningful KRIs and KPIs, this book includes a ready-to-use list.

Recommendations:

- **Establish a Risk Council:** A central governing body comprising senior executives from various departments. This council oversees and guides risk management processes, sets the strategic direction for risk decisions, and endorses the organization's risk appetite. The council also makes high-risk decisions, such as those related to new market entries or product launches.

- **Form Specific Risk Committees:** Specific committees like the Audit, Compliance, and Information Security Committees support the risk governance framework. These committees focus on particular risk areas and provide expertise and insight contributing to comprehensive risk management. For example, the Audit Committee ensures proper financial controls, while the Compliance Committee ensures adherence to regulatory requirements.

- **Assign Risk Management Roles to Departmental Teams:** Departmental or functional teams manage specific risks within their scope. Each risk level is carefully defined to ensure risks are managed effectively and efficiently, with significant risks escalated for higher-level decision-making.

- **Appoint a Chief Information Security Officer (CISO):** The CISO plays a crucial role in risk approvals, especially cybersecurity-related. The CISO leads efforts to identify potential threats, formulate security protocols, and supervise their implementation. The CISO's expertise guides the organization in making informed decisions about cybersecurity risks and strategies.

- **Implement Regular Risk Reporting:** Regular circulation of detailed risk reports keeps all stakeholders informed about the organization's risk landscape, facilitating informed decision-making. These reports may include KRIs and KPIs, which offer a quantitative measure of risk exposure and the effectiveness of risk management efforts, respectively.

- **Develop Relevant KRIs and KPIs:** KRIs might include indicators like the number of security incidents, while KPIs might measure the time to detect a security breach. Developing relevant and meaningful KRIs and KPIs is crucial for understanding and managing risk effectively. Some ready-to-use lists of KRIs and KPIs can be found in supplementary materials like the appendix of this book.

RISK IDENTIFICATION AND ANALYSIS

Risk identification forms the initial step in the comprehensive process of risk management. Particularly within the cybersecurity domain, risk identification requires the meticulous detection and documentation of potential threats, vulnerabilities, and impacts that could compromise an organization's information systems. As the digital landscape continually evolves, techniques to facilitate risk identification have expanded. These methods span from interviews and surveys to brainstorming sessions, *SWOT* analysis (Strengths, Weaknesses, Opportunities, Threats), and *PESTEL* analysis (Political, Economic, Social, Technological, Environmental, Legal).

Interviews and surveys, for instance, involve engaging with individuals within the organization who possess pertinent knowledge or experience that may aid in risk identification. Brainstorming sessions provide a more collaborative approach, pooling various perspectives and experiences to identify potential risks. SWOT and PESTEL analyses facilitate a broader understanding of the context in which cybersecurity risks can emerge, such as technological trends or legal requirements.

Integrating scenario analysis into risk identification can significantly improve its efficacy in uncovering cybersecurity risks. Scenario analysis involves constructing hypothetical situations representing potential, realistic cybersecurity threats or issues. These scenarios can vary widely, from a potential data breach due to an unpatched software vulnerability to a ransomware attack that could disrupt the entire operation. By outlining these scenarios, the organization can identify potential vulnerabilities, pathways an attacker might exploit, and the potential impact of such incidents on the organization.

After identifying potential risks, risk rating and assessment form the next pivotal steps. These methodologies offer an organized way to prioritize the discovered risks based on the probability of their occurrence and their potential impact. Methods for performing these assessments vary widely, from qualitative techniques like expert judgment and risk matrices to quantitative methods such as probabilistic risk assessment and statistical analysis.

Risk analysis tools and models further refine our understanding of these risks by quantifying their potential impacts on the organization. These tools include risk simulation models, sensitivity analysis, and decision trees, all of which help assess the magnitude of risks and provide insights into how risks could evolve under different circumstances.

Two key concepts in risk assessment are inherent and residual risk. Inherent risk refers to the level of risk present in a process or activity without considering any controls or mitigation measures. In contrast, residual risk is the risk that remains after implementing risk mitigation measures. Understanding these two types of risks and their relation to controls and mitigation strategies is vital for effective cybersecurity risk management.

As another layer to the risk management process, stress testing plays a significant role. It involves assessing the organization's systems and processes under extreme but plausible events. For instance, stress testing in cybersecurity might involve simulating a severe cyberattack on the organization's systems to see how well the organization could withstand the attack and recover. This allows the organization to assess its resilience and identify potential areas for improvement.

An organization can significantly enhance its ability to understand and manage cybersecurity risks through risk scenario creation, identification, assessment, and stress testing. When used effectively, these practices can help the organization develop robust risk mitigation strategies, ensuring high resilience in the face of cybersecurity risks.

Recommendations:

- **Review the entire chapter on Risk Assessments.**
- **Identify Risks:** The first step in risk management involves identifying potential risks. Techniques used for risk identification can include interviews and surveys, brainstorming sessions, SWOT analysis (Strengths, Weaknesses, Opportunities, Threats), and PESTEL analysis (Political, Economic, Social, Technological, Environmental, Legal).
- **Rate and Assess Risks:** Once identified, risks must be prioritized based on their likelihood and impact. Assessment methodologies can vary from qualitative techniques like expert judgment and risk matrices to quantitative methods like probabilistic risk assessment and statistical analysis.
- **Use Risk Analysis Tools:** Risk simulation models, sensitivity analysis, and decision trees are used to quantify the potential impact of risks on an organization. These tools help us understand the magnitude of risks and how they could evolve under different circumstances.
- **Understand Inherent and Residual Risks:** Inherent risk refers to the risk level of a process or activity without any controls or mitigation measures in place. In contrast, residual risk refers to the remaining risk after implementing risk mitigation measures. Understanding these two types of risks is crucial for effective risk management.
- **Conduct Risk Scenarios and Stress Testing:** These techniques involve analyzing the potential impact of extreme events or changes in various risk factors on an organization. This provides insight into the organization's vulnerability to severe but plausible events, assisting in developing robust risk mitigation strategies.

THIRD-PARTY RISK MANAGEMENT

In today's intricately interconnected business landscape, third-party risks have emerged as a significant challenge that can substantially threaten an organization's operations and reputation. These risks emanate from the organization's relationships with third-party entities such as suppliers, contractors, and service providers. A data breach at a vendor's end or a sudden disruption in the supply chain can wreak havoc, leading to operational issues, financial losses, and potentially irreparable damage to the organization's reputation.

Conducting a diligent vendor risk assessment is pivotal to effectively managing third-party risks. This process requires a comprehensive evaluation of prospective vendors on multiple fronts. Factors such as financial stability, operational capabilities, adherence to laws and regulations, and robustness of security measures are thoroughly assessed. These elements help determine whether a vendor can fulfill the organization's requirements and manage risks effectively.

Services like BitSight and other vendor risk assessment providers are indispensable in this evaluation process. They furnish ratings and comprehensive reports that measure a vendor's cybersecurity performance, thereby assisting organizations in assessing and keeping a constant vigil on their third-party risk. These insights provide a granular understanding of a vendor's security posture and enable more informed decision-making regarding vendor selection and ongoing management.

Contract management forms another essential pillar of third-party risk management. It encompasses establishing unambiguous contractual terms and conditions, outlining roles and responsibilities, setting performance benchmarks, and ensuring suitable risk transfer provisions. Contracts should be precise and transparent to prevent misunderstandings that could jeopardize the relationship or expose the organization to unnecessary risks.

Active and continuous monitoring of third-party relationships ensures vendors adhere to their contractual obligations and manage risks effectively. Such tracking can involve regular performance reviews to verify that vendors meet service level agreements, audits to confirm regulatory compliance, and recurrent risk assessments to identify and address emerging threats.

In addition to preventive measures, having an incident response plan for third-party risks is paramount. This plan outlines steps to manage incidents involving third parties, such as data breaches or service disruptions. It includes procedures to identify the incident swiftly, contains it, mitigate its impact, and restore normal operations. Effective communication is also critical to such scenarios, with processes for notifying all relevant stakeholders about the incident. Finally, the organization must also extract learnings from the incident, implementing changes to prevent recurrence and strengthen their third-party risk management.

In summary, third-party risk management is a complex but essential aspect of today's business landscape. With the right approaches and tools, organizations can protect themselves and ensure their third-party relationships are robust, secure, and value-adding.

Recommendations:

- **Recognize Third-Party Risks:** In an interconnected business world, relationships with third parties like suppliers, contractors, and service providers can bring considerable risks. These can range from data breaches to supply chain disruptions, potentially significantly affecting an organization's operations and reputation.

- **Conduct Vendor Due Diligence:** To manage third-party risks effectively, performing due diligence and risk assessment on potential vendors is essential. This includes evaluating their financial stability, operational capabilities, compliance with laws and regulations, and security measures, thus ensuring they can meet your organization's needs and handle risks proficiently.

- **Leverage Vendor Risk Assessment Providers:** Companies like BitSight are pivotal to managing third-party risks. They provide ratings and reports on a vendor's cybersecurity performance, which can help your organization assess and monitor the risk associated with each third party.

- **Manage Contracts Effectively:** Contract management is critical to third-party risk management. It is about setting clear contractual terms and conditions, defining responsibilities and expectations, setting performance metrics, and ensuring risk transfer provisions are in place.
- **Monitor Third Parties Continuously:** Ongoing oversight of third-party relationships is vital. Regular performance reviews, audits, and risk assessments can help ensure that vendors continue to fulfill their obligations and manage risks effectively.
- **Have a Third-Party Incident Response Plan:** Be prepared for incidents involving third parties. A response plan for data breaches or service disruptions can help mitigate their impact. This plan should include steps to identify and contain the incident, recover operations, notify relevant stakeholders, and learn from the event to prevent future occurrences.

REGULATORY EXPECTATIONS FOR THIRD-PARTY RISK MANAGEMENT

Over recent years, regulators have steadily increased their focus on managing risks associated with third-party involvement, particularly in technology and cybersecurity. These aspects have gained increasing attention due to the high potential risk they pose to organizations and the immense importance of understanding these risks. In addition, it has become crucial for organizations to be aware of the expectations and stipulations set by regulatory bodies to mitigate these potential threats and vulnerabilities.

In the broad spectrum of risks, those related to technology and cybersecurity stand out. These encapsulate many threats and potential weak points tied to the usage of modern technology and the digital landscape of the internet. These include, but are not limited to, situations like data breaches, the failure of crucial systems, and various cyberattacks. The risks associated with these scenarios are not to be underestimated, as they can cause substantial operational disruptions, lead to significant financial losses, and irreparably damage an organization's standing and reputation in the market.

To manage and mitigate these technology and cybersecurity risks, organizations can utilize a range of diverse techniques. These techniques range from proactive measures such as vulnerability scanning and penetration testing, which aim to identify weaknesses before they can be exploited, to more evaluative procedures like security risk assessments and comprehensive IT audits. These methodologies all serve the same purpose: to help pinpoint potential weak points in an organization's IT infrastructure and processes and assess the potential ramifications if these weak points were exploited.

There is a multitude of cybersecurity frameworks and controls that have been established to assist organizations in managing these technology and cybersecurity risks. For instance, the National Institute of Standards and Technology

(NIST) has developed a Cybersecurity Framework. This framework provides extensive standards, guidelines, and best practices to aid organizations in effectively managing cybersecurity-related risks. Another relevant example is ISO 27001, a comprehensive standard that outlines best practices for establishing, implementing, maintaining, and continually improving an information security management system (ISMS).

In addition to all the measures to prevent and mitigate risks, it is equally critical to have contingency plans for incident response and recovery. This involves having a plan to manage and recover from any technology or cybersecurity incidents effectively. Such a plan typically includes identifying and containing the incident, completely eradicating the threat, recovering systems and data, and conducting a post-incident review. The latter aims to glean valuable lessons from the incident that can be used further to improve the organization's resilience and response capabilities.

Furthermore, regulatory bodies expect organizations to have robust and comprehensive third-party risk management programs. These programs should include the organization's technology and cybersecurity risks and the risks associated with their third parties. This involves conducting a meticulous due diligence process on the technology and cybersecurity practices of third parties, continuously monitoring these risks to ensure they remain in control, and having a well-prepared response plan for any incidents that may involve third parties.

Given the high stakes and potential repercussions, organizations must invest time, resources, and effort into understanding, managing, and mitigating technology and cybersecurity risks. They must meet and, if possible, exceed the expectations set forth by regulatory bodies to ensure they can continue to operate effectively in an increasingly digital and interconnected world.

Recommendations:

- **Review OCC Bulletin 2023–2122:** The guidance is worth reading even for nonfinancial Institutions. https://www.occ.gov/news-issuances/bulletins/2023/bulletin-2023-22a.pdf.
- **Regulatory Focus on Third-Party Risks:** In today's technology-centric business environment, regulators increasingly emphasize managing third-party risks, particularly those related to technology and cybersecurity. These risks, encompassing data breaches, system failures, and cyberattacks, can lead to operational disruptions, financial losses, and reputational damage.
- **Techniques for Technology Risk Assessment:** Various methodologies can help assess technology risks. These include vulnerability scanning, penetration testing, security risk assessments, and IT audits. Identifying potential weak spots in an organization's IT systems and processes, these techniques help evaluate their potential impacts.
- **Cybersecurity Frameworks and Controls:** Many frameworks and controls exist to help manage technology and cybersecurity risks. For instance,

the NIST Cybersecurity Framework provides guidelines and practices for managing these risks. Similarly, ISO 27001 presents best practices for an ISMS.

- **Incident Response and Recovery:** Have a plan for managing and recovering from technology and cybersecurity incidents. This plan should include steps to identify and contain the incident, eradicate the threat, recover systems and data, and conduct a post-incident review to determine lessons learned.
- **Regulatory Expectations for Third-Party Risk Management:** Regulators expect organizations to have vital third-party risk management programs encompassing technology and cybersecurity risks. This implies conducting due diligence on third parties' technology and cybersecurity practices, continually monitoring these risks, and having an incident response plan for third-party-related incidents.

COMPLIANCE AND LEGAL RISK MANAGEMENT

Compliance and legal risks refer to the array of potential perils such as lawsuits, hefty fines, crippling sanctions, or considerable reputational damage that a company may have to grapple with if it fails to strictly comply with all the existing laws, established regulations, prescribed industry standards, or the obligations stipulated in contracts. These risks are a universal concern, cutting across every sector of business, thereby making the effective management of these risks a paramount concern and a top-tier priority for any business, irrespective of its scale or industry.

Many diverse factors contribute to the complex landscape of compliance and legal risks. They can arise due to sudden or unexpected changes in the regulatory environment, a lack of a deep understanding or awareness of the prevailing laws, discrepancies or variations in the interpretation of these laws, and instances of noncompliant behavior exhibited by employees, among other reasons. Therefore, businesses must commit resources and invest heavily in comprehensive compliance programs and robust legal risk management strategies to mitigate these omnipresent risks, safeguard their operations, and ensure their continued viability.

Effective compliance programs are not just about superficial adherence to rules and regulations. Instead, they have a much broader and more profound objective. They are instrumental in fostering a culture of integrity, promoting ethical behavior, and instilling a sense of responsibility among all employees regarding their obligations toward compliance. These compliance programs are typically multifaceted, consisting of multiple components such as thorough compliance training programs, a well-defined code of conduct, regular audits to ensure compliance, and whistle-blower policies that encourage employees to report infractions without fearing repercussions. These components work together to form a comprehensive and robust compliance program.

Legal risk management, another crucial aspect, involves proactively iden-tifying potential legal risks and formulating effective strategies to minimize their impact on the business. This risk mitigation process can involve meticu-lous contract management, where every clause of the terms and conditions is carefully reviewed to mitigate potential disputes and misunderstandings. It also includes having contingency plans for adeptly handling litigation, protect-ing the company's intellectual property, and managing other legal matters that may arise in the business.

Engaging competent legal counsel for advice on complex legal issues and keeping up with regulation changes is highly advisable. Legal professionals can provide invaluable guidance in interpreting the myriad laws and regula-tions a business must comply with and ensure the company is on the right path toward achieving and maintaining compliance. By obtaining timely and expert legal advice, a company can avoid compliance pitfalls and legal risks, thus securing its reputation and operations in an increasingly complex regula-tory environment.

Recommendations:

- **Review the more detailed chapters on compliance within this book.**
- **Definition of Compliance and Legal Risks:** Compliance and legal risks refer to potential dangers like lawsuits, substantial fines, harsh sanc-tions, or significant reputational damage a company might face due to noncompliance with existing laws, regulations, industry standards, or contractual obligations. These risks are universally relevant across all business sectors, making their effective management critical to all busi-nesses, regardless of size or industry.
- **Factors Contributing to Compliance and Legal Risks:** These risks can originate from various sources, including sudden regulatory changes, lack of understanding or awareness of current laws, discrepancies in law inter-pretation, or noncompliant behavior by employees. As a result, businesses must invest in comprehensive compliance programs and robust legal risk management strategies to mitigate these risks and protect their operations.
- **Role of Compliance Programs:** Effective compliance programs are not merely about rule adherence; they aim to cultivate a culture of integrity, encourage ethical behavior, and instill a sense of compliance respon-sibility among employees. These programs are typically multifaceted, encompassing components like comprehensive compliance training, a well-defined code of conduct, regular audits to ensure compliance, and whistle-blower policies that encourage reporting infractions without fear of retaliation.
- **Legal Risk Management:** This involves proactively identifying poten-tial legal risks and developing strategies to minimize their impact on the business. This risk mitigation process can include careful contract man-agement, contingency plans for adeptly handling litigation, protecting

the company's intellectual property, and managing other legal matters that may arise during business operations.

- **Engaging Legal Counsel:** It is advisable to seek competent legal counsel for advice on complex legal issues and to stay abreast of regulatory changes. Legal professionals can provide invaluable guidance in interpreting various laws and regulations a business must comply with, ensuring the company maintains compliance. By securing timely and expert legal advice, a company can avoid compliance and legal risks, thus protecting its reputation and operations in a complex regulatory landscape.

MONITORING AND REPORTING

Continuous monitoring and reporting play pivotal roles in risk management. This section will examine monitoring risk management activities, understanding key indicators (KRIs), and reporting to governance and the board. We will also explore the nuances of regulatory reporting requirements and the periodic review and update of the risk management program.

The process of risk management is dynamic and ongoing. Monitoring risk management activities regularly allows organizations to detect changes in risk profiles and make timely adjustments. This includes reviewing and reassessing risks, analyzing risk treatment effectiveness, and ensuring that risk management plans are up-to-date and relevant.

KRIs are vital tools used in risk monitoring. KRIs are measurable factors that indicate the level of risk exposure in various areas of an organization. They act as an early warning system, allowing management to understand the current risk state and anticipate future changes.

Risk reporting is another crucial part of risk management. Effective communication about risks to the management and the board enables informed decision-making and ensures that risk management aligns with the organization's objectives and risk appetite. Risk reports should be clear, concise, and actionable, providing a snapshot of the current risk landscape and potential future risks.

Regulatory reporting requirements are crucial for organizations, particularly in regulated industries like finance and healthcare. They dictate what risk-related information must be reported to regulators, how often, and in what format. Failing to meet these requirements can result in penalties and reputational damage.

Finally, the risk management program must undergo periodic review and updating. The dynamic nature of the business and risk environment necessitates this. An outdated risk management program may not adequately address new or emerging risks, exposing the organization.

Recommendations:

- **Review the appendix with ready-to-use KRI and KPI examples.**
- **Implement Continuous Monitoring and Reporting:** Monitoring and reporting are critical components of risk management. They involve

observing risk management activities, understanding KRIs, and appreciating the value of reporting to governance and the board. This section also discusses regulatory reporting requirements and the need for periodic review and update of the risk management program.

- **Recommend Dynamic Risk Management Practices:** Risk management is ongoing. Regular monitoring of risk management activities enables organizations to detect shifts in risk profiles and make timely modifications. It encompasses reviewing and reassessing risks, analyzing the efficacy of risk treatment, and ensuring risk management plans remain current and pertinent.

- **Utilize Key Risk Indicators (KRIs):** KRIs are essential tools used in risk monitoring. They are quantifiable factors indicating the level of risk exposure in various organization areas. KRIs function as an early warning system, enabling management to comprehend the current risk state and anticipate future alterations.

- **Promote Regular Risk Reporting:** Risk reporting is another integral aspect of risk management. Effective communication about risks to management and the board facilitates informed decision-making and ensures alignment between risk management, the organization's objectives, and risk appetite. Risk reports should be clear, concise, and actionable, offering an overview of the current risk landscape and potential future risks.

- **Adhere to Regulatory Reporting Requirements:** Regulatory reporting requirements are crucial, especially in regulated industries such as finance and healthcare. These requirements specify what risk-related information must be reported to regulators, the frequency, and the format. Noncompliance can lead to penalties and reputational damage.

- **Conduct Periodic Reviews of the Risk Management Program:** Given the dynamic nature of business and risk environments, the program needs regular reviews and updates. An outdated risk management program may not effectively address new or emerging risks, leaving the organization vulnerable.

Chapter Conclusion

The pivotal role of risk management in business and cybersecurity encompasses various elements, starting with an understanding of its definition, importance, and implications of related laws and regulations. Delving into the risk management life cycle, each stage, from identification to mitigation, monitoring, and reporting, is critical. Valuable guidance for risk management can be found in resources like the FFIEC Handbooks. The responsibility of a Board of Directors and senior management in establishing a robust risk management framework is also a key consideration.

Identifying and assessing risks involves various techniques, stressing the importance of understanding inherent and residual risks. This includes third-party risk management, an area fraught with vendor management challenges, accompanied by regulatory expectations.

In-depth consideration is given to specific risk areas, including technology and cybersecurity, compliance, and legal risk management. Staying informed with evolving regulations and legal standards is crucial. Equally important is monitoring and reporting, which highlights the need for strong risk management programs that adapt to the ever-changing risk environment.

The significance of a proactive stance toward risk management is profound. Rather than treating it as a separate process, risk management should be embedded within all organizational activities. Organizations can bolster their resilience by incorporating risk considerations into every facet of operations, from strategic planning to daily decision-making.

Risk management is a multifaceted process that involves identifying, assessing, mitigating, and monitoring risks. It also necessitates a continuous improvement cycle, where past experiences serve as lessons to refine future strategies. Understanding and managing risks effectively can help organizations avoid potential losses and pinpoint opportunities for improvement and growth.

The growing reliance on external parties, particularly in technology and cybersecurity, has made third-party risk management a significant concern. Effective management of these risks calls for rigorous due diligence processes, contract management, and continuous monitoring, all guided by regulatory standards.

Compliance and legal risk management are other critical aspects of risk management. Keeping up with the evolving legal and regulatory framework, ensuring compliance with all relevant rules, and nurturing a culture of integrity and ethical conduct are fundamental steps in mitigating these risks.

Lastly, organizations can maintain an up-to-date understanding of risk status through effective monitoring and reporting mechanisms. Regular monitoring and transparent reporting ensure alignment of risk management activities with strategic goals and risk appetite. By continually reviewing and updating the risk management program, it remains responsive to the dynamic risk environment.

Case Study: Navigating Risk Management at Phoenix Innovations

Meet Wendell, a risk manager at the burgeoning tech firm Phoenix Innovations. As Phoenix Innovations sought to build its reputation in the tech market, it navigated a labyrinth of complexities associated with risk management. Wendell's expertise was sought to guide the company through a maze of potential risks. This case study follows Wendell's journey as he grapples with these challenges, applying the principles of risk management we have explored in this chapter.

Phoenix Innovations had a proactive approach to risk management. Wendell knew managing risk was not just a solitary process but something that needed to be integrated into every company's operations. With the support of the company's senior management, he worked tirelessly to ensure that risk considerations were factored into strategic planning, daily decision-making, and every other organizational activity. This approach enhanced Phoenix Innovations' resilience and ability to adapt to unforeseen circumstances.

One of the significant concerns Wendell encountered was third-party risk management. Phoenix Innovations' reliance on multiple vendors and external parties, especially in cybersecurity areas, amplified these risks. To manage them effectively, Wendell instituted a system of robust due diligence processes, careful contract management, and continuous monitoring. Each vendor's risk profile was carefully assessed, and contingency plans were drawn up for potential incidents involving third-party risks.

Wendell put significant effort into compliance and legal risk management to keep Phoenix Innovations abreast with evolving regulations and legal standards. This aspect involved regular training sessions, implementing compliance-focused software, and fostering a culture of integrity and ethical conduct. Wendell ensured adherence to all applicable laws and regulations, aiming to mitigate legal and compliance risks as much as possible.

Monitoring and reporting were integral to Wendell's risk management strategy. He set up a system for regular risk monitoring and transparent reporting to keep the company updated about its risk status. By doing this, Wendell could ensure that risk management activities are aligned with Phoenix Innovations' strategic goals and risk appetite.

Through Wendell's journey at Phoenix Innovations, we see the key lessons from this chapter in action. His proactive approach, continuous improvement cycles, third-party risk management, compliance and legal risk mitigation, and effective monitoring and reporting offer practical insights into real-world risk management. Wendell's constant adaptation to the dynamic nature of the risk environment is a testament to the importance of keeping the risk management program updated and relevant, demonstrating the principles we have discussed throughout this chapter.

CHAPTER 8

The NIST Risk Management Framework

"The NIST RMF (Risk Management Framework) is a pillar of cyber-security effectiveness, providing a structured approach to identify, assess, and mitigate risks. It empowers organizations to confidently navigate the turbulent seas of cyber threats, ensuring the preservation of critical assets and fostering a culture of resilience in the face of ever-evolving challenges."

The National Institute of Standards and Technology's Risk Management Framework (NIST RMF) serves as a defining model for cybersecurity management. Understanding the intricacies of the RMF's authorization process and practical implementation methods is vital. The framework plays a significant role in meeting compliance and regulatory expectations, and when integrated into an organization, it aids in risk assessment and management. Additionally, the RMF can be used in technology implementation and managing third-party risks, with an acknowledgment of the challenges faced during implementation and potential solutions to these problems.

THE NIST RISK MANAGEMENT FRAMEWORK

The National Institute of Standards and Technology (NIST) Risk Management Framework (RMF) is integral to any cybersecurity management program. Originating from NIST Special Publication 800-37, it is designed to aid organizations in understanding, managing, and mitigating the risks associated with their information systems. The framework comprises a series of guidelines and recommendations that provide a structured process for integrating cybersecurity into an organization's operations. It's not just about ensuring the safety and integrity of digital assets; it is about aligning cybersecurity with the overall business objectives and risk strategy.

Understanding the NIST RMF begins with its definition. It is a six-step cycle designed to guide organizations through managing their information system-related security risks. This includes categorizing information systems, selecting appropriate security controls, implementing them, assessing their effectiveness, authorizing the information system, and continuously monitoring its security controls.

The NIST RMF did not materialize overnight. It is the result of years of research, feedback, and improvements. The framework has evolved to cater to the ever-changing cybersecurity landscape, reflecting new threats, technologies, and best practices. For instance, it expanded its focus from being a purely federal initiative to becoming a framework that can be adopted by any organization, regardless of size or sector.

The relevance of the NIST RMF in cybersecurity management cannot be understated. In today's digital era, where data breaches and cyber threats are daily, the RMF provides a structured approach to managing these risks. By integrating cybersecurity into the overall risk management process, organizations can align their cyber defense strategy with their business objectives, effectively protect their critical assets, and ensure continuity of operations.

At the heart of the NIST RMF are its six steps: Categorize, Select, Implement, Assess, Authorize, and Monitor. Each step is integral to the framework and contributes to the ongoing risk management cycle. They form a dynamic, iterative process of managing information system-related security risks, keeping pace with the evolving cybersecurity landscape.

Categorizing the information system involves identifying its function, information types, and potential impact should it be compromised. The Select step involves choosing appropriate security controls based on the system's categorization. The Implementation step involves integrating these controls into the system. The assessment step evaluates the effectiveness of these controls in mitigating risks. The Authorize step consists in deciding whether the system's chances are acceptable. Lastly, the Monitoring step involves monitoring the security controls to ensure they remain effective as time passes and circumstances change.

In the subsequent sections, we will delve deeper into these concepts, exploring the RMF's authorization process, providing a step-by-step analysis of the RMF in practice, discussing its relevance to regulatory expectations, and examining how it can be integrated into an organization. Furthermore, we will discuss its applicability in risk assessment and management, technology implementation, overcoming challenges, and managing third-party risks.

Recommendations:

- **Commit to Learning the RMF:** Make a conscious effort to familiarize yourself with the NIST RMF. Begin by exploring its definitions, evolution, and importance to cybersecurity management. This foundational understanding will serve as a basis for successfully implementing the framework.

- **Recognize the Multifaceted Nature of RMF:** Acknowledge the comprehensive nature of the NIST RMF. It is more than just a set of guidelines – it involves six steps that interrelate and synergize to produce effective cybersecurity management, a recognition that will aid in embracing the framework's intricacies.

- **Acknowledge the RMF Relevance:** Understand that the NIST RMF applies to businesses of all sizes and natures. It ensures everyone can take appropriate steps to safeguard their systems and data regardless of their organization's size.

UNDERSTANDING RMF'S AUTHORIZATION PROCESS

The authorization process is a critical component of the RMF, designed to ensure that all operational risks associated with an information system are identified, assessed, and accepted by a designated authority. This process is not just about gaining approval to operate; it is about demonstrating that the necessary safeguards and countermeasures are in place and functioning as expected. More than a mere rubber-stamp process, authorization involves serious deliberation about the risk profile of the information system and whether it falls within acceptable risk parameters.

Authorization within the RMF is based on a concept known as risk-based decision-making. Under this concept, the decision to authorize an information system is made based on a comprehensive understanding of the system's risk profile. This risk profile is determined by thoroughly evaluating the system's security controls, threat landscape, vulnerability exposure, and the potential impact of a compromise on the organization's operations and objectives.

Key to the authorization process is the Security Authorization Package. This package is a collection of documents that describe the information system, its operational environment, security controls, and risk assessment results. The authorizing official uses this package to make an informed decision about whether to authorize the system.

The authorizing official plays a critical role in the RMF's authorization process. This individual, usually a senior executive or manager, is responsible for deciding whether the information system's risk is acceptable. This decision is made based on the information provided in the Security Authorization Package and the organization's risk tolerance and business objectives. The decision to authorize an information system is not taken lightly; it involves a thorough understanding of its risk profile and a willingness to accept it.

However, the authorization process does not end with the approval to operate. Instead, it extends to continuous monitoring and ongoing authorization. Continuous monitoring involves regular reviews and assessments of the information system's security controls to ensure they function as expected. This includes monitoring system changes or operational environments affecting its risk profile.

Ongoing authorization, on the other hand, is a concept that reflects the dynamic nature of information system-related risks. Under this concept, the authorizing official's decision to authorize the system is regularly reviewed and reassessed. This ensures that the decision remains valid in light of changing circumstances, new vulnerabilities, and emerging threats.

In the next section, we will delve deeper into each of the six steps of the RMF, providing a detailed analysis of how each step is carried out in practice. Each step will be broken down, examined, and discussed in the context of practical applications. We will also look at how each step fits into the broader picture of the RMF, contributing to a comprehensive and ongoing risk management process.

Recommendations:

- **Conceptualize Authorization:** Familiarize yourself with the concept of authorization within the RMF, including its role and the security authorization package. These insights will allow you to appreciate its relevance in protecting your systems and data.
- **Understand the Role of an Authorizing Official:** Recognize the importance of the authorizing official in the RMF's authorization process. Their expertise and authority play a vital role in the execution of security plans and continuous monitoring.
- **Adopt Continuous Monitoring:** Implement continuous monitoring and ongoing authorization in your cybersecurity management practice. This lets you remain updated on your system's security status and modify the security controls when required.

NIST RMF IN PRACTICE: STEP-BY-STEP ANALYSIS

Implementing the NIST RMF involves a meticulous and iterative process. It is not a set-and-forget approach but an ongoing cycle that continually assesses, responds to, and monitors risks. This section looks at the six steps involved in the RMF, providing insights into their practical application and how they contribute to effective risk management.

The first step in the RMF is to Categorize the Information System. This process involves understanding the information system's purpose, the data it handles, and the potential impact if it were compromised. A system's category is determined based on federal guidelines in FIPS 199 and NIST SP 800-60. It is important to note that the categorization step sets the stage for the rest of the RMF process, informing the selection of security controls and the system's overall risk strategy.

Once the system is categorized, the next step is to Select Security Controls. These controls are safeguards or countermeasures designed to protect the system's information. The selection is guided by the system's category, with a higher category necessitating more robust controls. The control selection is based on NIST SP 800-53, which provides a security controls and enhancement catalog. A vital aspect of this step is tailoring the selected controls to the specific needs and circumstances of the organization and its information system.

After the controls have been selected, they need to be Implemented. This step involves integrating the chosen controls into the system's operational environment. Each control's implementation must be documented, describing how it fulfills the system's security requirements. Implementation involves technical measures, management, and operational controls, such as risk assessment processes, personnel security, and incident response procedures.

Following implementation, the next step is to Assess the Security Controls. This involves determining if the controls are implemented correctly, operating as intended, and producing the desired outcome concerning meeting the security requirements. Assessments are conducted based on NIST SP 800-53A, which provides guidelines for assessing the effectiveness of security controls.

Once the assessment is complete, the information system must be Authorized. This is where the authorizing official makes a risk-based decision about whether the system can operate. This decision is based on the Security Authorization Package, which includes the system's security plan, security assessment report, and plan of action and milestones. This authorization decision is not permanent; it is subject to review and reassessment based on ongoing monitoring activities.

Finally, the last step in the RMF process is to Monitor Security Controls. This involves keeping an eye on the security controls to ensure they continue to meet the system's security requirements. Monitoring activities include status reporting, impact analyses of changes to the system, security control assessments, and ongoing risk determination and acceptance.

Organizations can manage their information system risks effectively by following this six-step process. However, it is important to note that the RMF is not a one-size-fits-all solution. It needs to be tailored to the specific needs and circumstances of the organization and its information systems.

Recommendations:

- **Embrace Categorization:** Understand the purpose and data your information system handles, including the potential impact if compromised. Categorize your system based on federal guidelines (Federal Information Processing Standards (FIPS) 199 and NIST Special Publication (SP) 800--60), setting a foundation for your risk strategy.
- **Select Security Controls:** Choose appropriate safeguards or countermeasures to protect your system's information, influenced by your system's category. Use NIST SP 800-53 for guidance, and tailor the controls to your organization's needs.

- **Implement Selected Controls:** Integrate the chosen controls into your system's operational environment, documenting each control's implementation. This step involves technical, management, and operational controls.
- **Assess Your Security:** Determine if your controls are implemented correctly, operating as intended, and meeting the security requirements. Use NIST SP 800-53A as a guide to assess the effectiveness of your security controls.
- **Obtain Authorization:** Have an authorizing official make a risk-based decision on the system's operability. Based on the Security Authorization Package, this decision must be reviewed and reassessed through ongoing monitoring activities.
- **Monitor Security Controls:** Ensure your security controls continue to meet the system's security requirements through continuous monitoring, which includes status reporting, impact analyses, and ongoing risk determination and acceptance. Tailor the six-step RMF process to fit your organization's specific needs.

APPLICABILITY TO REGULATORY EXPECTATIONS

One of the key aspects of the NIST RMF is its ability to support compliance with regulatory requirements. Today's regulatory landscape is complex, with various federal and industry-specific regulations imposing different requirements for cybersecurity. The RMF, with its flexible and comprehensive approach, can assist organizations in meeting these varied requirements.

The role of the RMF in compliance begins with its fundamental goal: managing information system-related risks. Regulations require organizations to protect their information systems and data, and the RMF provides a structured process for achieving this goal. By following the RMF, organizations can demonstrate a systematic approach to identifying, assessing, and responding to risks.

Alignment with federal and industry regulations is another strength of the RMF. Federal regulations, such as the Federal Information Security Management Act (FISMA), explicitly reference the NIST standards that underpin the RMF. Similarly, industry regulations, like the Health Insurance Portability and Accountability Act (HIPAA) and the Payment Card Industry Data Security Standard (PCI DSS), have requirements that align with the RMF's steps and controls. By implementing the RMF, organizations can streamline their compliance efforts, meeting multiple regulatory requirements through a single, unified process.

But the RMF is not just about achieving compliance; it is about maintaining it. Regulatory expectations are not static; they change as new threats emerge and technology evolves. The RMF, with its emphasis on continuous monitoring and ongoing authorization, supports organizations in keeping pace with these changes. By continually reviewing and updating their risk management processes and security controls, organizations can ensure that their compliance efforts remain practical and current.

The RMF's applicability to regulatory expectations is not limited to the United States. Its risk management principles are universally applicable, making it a valuable tool for organizations operating in jurisdictions with cybersecurity regulations. This global applicability adds another layer of value to the RMF, making it a versatile tool for managing cybersecurity risks and regulatory compliance.

Recommendations:

- **Understand the Role of RMF in Regulatory Compliance:** Recognize the vital role the RMF plays in meeting regulatory requirements. Its main objective, managing information system-related risks, aligns directly with most regulations. By employing RMF, organizations can demonstrate a systematic approach to identifying, assessing, and addressing risks, thus fulfilling regulatory expectations.

- **Leverage RMF for Alignment with Regulations:** Take advantage of the alignment between the RMF and various federal and industry regulations. Federal regulations like FISMA directly reference NIST standards, and industry regulations like HIPAA and PCI DSS align with RMF's steps and controls. Implementing the RMF allows organizations to streamline their compliance efforts, meeting multiple regulatory demands through a unified process.

- **Utilize RMF for Ongoing Compliance:** Remember that the RMF is not just about achieving compliance; it is also about maintaining it. Regulatory expectations evolve along with emerging threats and technological advancements. Therefore, use the RMF's emphasis on continuous monitoring and ongoing authorization to keep your organization's risk management processes and security controls updated and practical.

- **Apply RMF for Global Regulatory Compliance:** Realize that the RMF's applicability extends beyond the United States. Its risk management principles apply universally, making it a helpful tool for organizations operating under international jurisdictions with cybersecurity regulations. By leveraging the RMF's global applicability, you can efficiently manage cybersecurity risks and regulatory compliance no matter where your organization operates.

- **Stay Updated with the RMF:** As the RMF is designed to adapt to regulatory expectations changes, stay updated and ensure your organization is continually aligned. Regularly review and update your risk management processes, security controls, and the RMF implementation to ensure your compliance efforts remain current and effective.

INTEGRATING NIST RMF INTO AN ORGANIZATION

Adopting the NIST RMF is merely the first step on a transformation journey. Integrating the RMF into the organization's operations, culture, and day-to-day procedures involves dedicated effort and strategic planning. The RMF is not a static document to be shelved once developed; instead, it is a dynamic system that should be deeply woven into how an organization approaches cybersecurity.

The RMF requires broad organizational buy-in and support to initiate the integration process. This extends beyond the confines of the IT department, reaching out to include executives, managers, and individual employees across the spectrum of the organization. It is crucial that everyone within the organization comprehends the significance of the RMF and understands their unique role in its successful implementation. Achieving this understanding could necessitate various approaches such as dedicated training sessions, regular communications and briefings, and explicit incorporation of RMF-related responsibilities into job descriptions and performance metrics. Establishing a pervasive cybersecurity culture within the organization is a concerted effort.

Subsequently, the RMF must be modified and tailored to align with the organization's distinctive requirements. No two organizations are exactly alike, and a one-size-fits-all approach is unlikely to yield optimal results. The RMF is designed to be a flexible framework that can be adapted based on various parameters, including the organization's size, the nature of its industry, its risk tolerance, and other critical factors. The tailoring process should not be undertaken in isolation but should be a collaborative effort involving stakeholders from across the organization. Through this process, the RMF reflects the organization's unique context, enabling it to manage risks effectively.

Once the customized RMF is in place, the spotlight shifts to training and education. Staff and stakeholders must grasp the "what," the "why," and the "how" of the RMF. They need to comprehend why the RMF is indispensable, how it provides a structured approach to managing cybersecurity risks, and how to execute their RMF-related duties diligently. Training and education should not be viewed as a one-time event but as an ongoing necessity to account for staff turnover, organizational structure or business objectives changes, and RMF updates. This continuous learning approach helps maintain the RMF's relevance and effectiveness in a rapidly changing cyber risk landscape.

In the final integration stage, robust procedures and thorough documentation are paramount to validate the RMF's effective implementation. This entails chronicling the organization's RMF processes, maintaining detailed records of RMF activities, and regularly reviewing and updating these documents. This comprehensive documentation provides tangible evidence of the organization's compliance with the RMF, aids in audits and reviews, and plays a critical role in identifying areas for improvement. Furthermore, it creates a historical record of risk management activities, providing invaluable insights for future strategy and decision-making.

However, integrating the RMF into an organization is not a one-and-done affair – it is an ongoing commitment, a marathon rather than a sprint. The cyber risk landscape and an organization's needs and circumstances are not static. Therefore, regular reviews and updates ensure the RMF remains aligned with the evolving risk environment and the organization's dynamic needs. This commitment to continual improvement underlines the living, breathing nature of the RMF – not a mere document but a foundational pillar of the organization's cybersecurity strategy.

Recommendations:

- **Establishing Organizational Commitment:** Begin by promoting the importance of the RMF within your organization. This should include all staff levels, from executives and managers to individual employees. Arrange informational sessions and regular communications, and reflect RMF responsibilities in job descriptions and performance assessments. This will ensure that everyone understands their role and the significance of the RMF in maintaining cybersecurity.

- **Customize the RMF for Your Organization:** Tailor the RMF to meet your organization's specific requirements. Understand that each organization is unique, and factors such as size, industry, and risk tolerance will affect how you implement the RMF. Engage stakeholders from across the organization in this process to ensure that the customized RMF accurately reflects the organization's needs.

- **Prioritize Training and Education:** Once you have a tailored RMF, educate staff about it. Staff need to understand not only the "what" but also the "why" and "how." Please explain why the RMF is crucial, how it aids the organization, and how to execute its specific RMF-related duties. Ensure that training is an ongoing process to account for changes like staff turnover, organizational modifications, and updates to the RMF itself.

- **Implement Documentation and Procedures:** To monitor the implementation of the RMF, create a comprehensive system of procedures and documentation. This should include documenting your RMF processes, maintaining records of RMF-related activities, and routinely revising these documents. This will provide proof of your organization's RMF compliance and help identify areas that need improvement.

- **Keep the RMF Updated:** Recognize that integrating the RMF into your organization is a continuous commitment. The RMF should be regularly reviewed and updated as your organization evolves to align with your needs and circumstances. Regular check-ins and reassessments can ensure the RMF is living and evolving along with your organization.

USING NIST RMF FOR RISK ASSESSMENT AND MANAGEMENT

The National Institute of Standards and Technology's (NIST) RMF aims to support organizations in pinpointing, scrutinizing, and navigating the convoluted landscape of cybersecurity risks. As an instructive tool, the RMF equips organizations with the knowledge and guidance required to make astute decisions regarding allocating resources and establishing controls, thereby amplifying their cybersecurity robustness. This process of diligent evaluation and action, in turn, bolsters the security infrastructure against potential cyber threats and mitigates vulnerabilities.

One of the integral constituents of the RMF is the risk assessment phase, undertaken at the outset of the system categorization and iterated consistently throughout the RMF process. This significant stage involves the identification of plausible threats to the system, exposure to potential vulnerabilities, and the conceivable repercussions if an adverse event were to transpire. The results derived from this risk assessment act as the catalyst in determining the security controls to be implemented and guide the decision-making procedure throughout the entirety of the RMF process.

Upon completion of the risk assessment, a critical juncture in the RMF process occurs in managing the identified risks. Here, the RMF delineates a comprehensive catalog of security controls based on NIST Special Publication 800-53. These controls are designed to temper the identified risks' potential impacts. The security controls incorporate technical implementations such as installing firewalls and data encryption and management strategies like personnel training and drafting incident response plans. The judicious selection of these controls necessitates striking a delicate equilibrium between effective risk mitigation and the resource allocation needed for their efficacious implementation.

Yet, the RMF's approach to risk management does not cease with the implementation of controls. The framework emphasizes the importance of continuous vigilance in monitoring and responding to potential risks. This fundamental aspect of risk management is tackled in the final phase of the RMF, aptly named "monitoring security controls." Constant surveillance detects any deviations in the system or environment that might alter risk levels. In response to these changes, the RMF advises that the risk assessment be updated accordingly, and modifications to the security controls should be made if warranted.

To cap it all, it is important to underscore that while the RMF offers a holistic and comprehensive risk management process, it is intended to be harmoniously integrated with other risk management practices employed within an organization. For instance, should an organization already use another RMF for broader enterprise risks, it is highly recommended that the RMF be coordinated and aligned with it. This ensures a consistent, unified approach to risk management, fostering an even more fortified and resilient organizational cybersecurity stance.

Recommendations:

- **Understand and Implement NIST RMF:** Familiarize yourself with the NIST RMF, its steps, and its objectives. Recognize its core purpose – to assist organizations in identifying, assessing, and managing cybersecurity risks. This understanding is instrumental in making well-informed resource allocation and control establishment decisions.
- **Incorporate Risk Assessment:** Emphasize the risk assessment process, which is integral to the RMF. This process involves identifying potential

threats, vulnerabilities, and the impacts of adverse events. Be mindful that the outcomes of this process significantly influence the selection of security controls and drive decision-making throughout the RMF process.

- **Leverage Security Control Selection:** Post-risk assessment, focus on managing the identified risks via security control selection. Utilize the comprehensive catalog of security controls provided by RMF. Strike a balance between risk mitigation and the resources required to implement these controls.

- **Commit to Risk Monitoring and Response:** Stress on risk management's monitoring and response aspects within the RMF. Understand that continuous monitoring helps detect system or environment changes that may affect risk levels. In line with this, regularly update your risk assessment and adjust your security controls as necessary.

- **Integrate with Other Risk Management Practices:** Remember that while the RMF provides a comprehensive risk management process, it is meant to work with other risk management practices in your organization. Therefore, ensure the coordination of RMF with any other RMF your organization might use to maintain a consistent approach to risk.

NIST RMF AND TECHNOLOGY IMPLEMENTATION

Technology is a double-edged sword in the context of cybersecurity. On the one hand, it opens up new possibilities for efficiency, innovation, and growth. On the other hand, it introduces new vulnerabilities and complexities, which, if not managed correctly, can lead to significant risks. This is where the NIST RMF comes into play, offering a systematic process to manage risks associated with technology implementation.

Securing technology deployments is a major part of this process. Whether it is new software, a hardware update, or a cloud migration, the RMF provides a structured approach to managing the associated risks. This begins with categorizing the information system and selecting, implementing, and assessing the appropriate security controls. By following the RMF, organizations can ensure that their technology deployments are secure from the start, minimizing the risk of future issues.

Moreover, the RMF applies not only to traditional technologies but is also flexible enough to be used with emerging technologies. Whether artificial intelligence, quantum computing, or Internet of Things devices, the RMF provides a robust, adaptable framework for managing these technologies' unique risks. This is critical to today's fast-paced digital world, where technology constantly evolves and new cybersecurity threats emerge.

Another important aspect of technology implementation is integrating existing security technologies and solutions. An organization might already have a range of security measures, from firewalls and antivirus software to intrusion detection systems and data loss prevention tools. The RMF is designed to work alongside these measures, ensuring they are appropriately integrated and effectively manage risks.

Furthermore, the RMF is essential in the secure system development life cycle. It aids in building security into the system from the beginning and maintaining that security throughout its life cycle. This encompasses everything from the initial design and development of the system through its deployment and operation to its eventual decommissioning.

Recommendations:

- **Recognize Technology's Double-Edged Nature:** Accept and understand that technology introduces new vulnerabilities and complexities while providing opportunities for efficiency and growth. The NIST RMF can help you manage these risks effectively.
- **Secure Technology Deployments:** Use the RMF for securing all technology deployments, be it software updates, hardware upgrades, or cloud migrations. Following the RMF's structured approach – categorizing the information system and selecting, implementing, and assessing appropriate security controls – can help ensure your technology deployments are secure and risk-minimized.
- **Embrace Flexibility for Emerging Technologies:** Use the flexible nature of the RMF to manage risks associated with emerging technologies like artificial intelligence, quantum computing, or Internet of Things devices. Adapting RMF to the unique dangers presented by these technologies is crucial in a rapidly evolving digital landscape.
- **Integrate Existing Security Measures:** Ensure the RMF complements existing security measures, like firewalls, antivirus software, intrusion detection systems, and data loss prevention tools. The RMF should work alongside these measures, facilitating appropriate integration and enhancing their effectiveness in managing risks.
- **Utilize RMF for Secure System Development:** Use the RMF in the secure system development life cycle. It can help build security into the system from the start and maintain it throughout its life cycle, from the initial design and development phase through deployment and operation to eventual decommissioning.

CHALLENGES AND SOLUTIONS IN IMPLEMENTING NIST RMF

As beneficial as the NIST RMF is, its implementation is not without challenges. These challenges can stem from various sources – resource constraints and organizational resistance. It is essential for organizations to be aware of these potential hurdles and to approach them strategically to ensure the successful implementation of the RMF.

Organizations' common challenge is the initial time and resource investment needed to implement the RMF. The comprehensive nature of the RMF requires significant input from various stakeholders across the organization, often leading to resource strain. However, this initial investment pays dividends in the long run by reducing the likelihood of costly cybersecurity incidents and helping organizations navigate regulatory requirements more smoothly.

Another hurdle is often the complexity of the RMF. Understanding and implementing the various steps of the RMF, along with the multitude of potential security controls, can be daunting. This can be addressed by investing in training for staff and stakeholders and seeking external expertise where needed.

Furthermore, organizational resistance can be a significant barrier to RMF implementation. Change can be significantly tricky when it impacts daily operations and workflows. Overcoming this requires strong leadership, clear communication about the benefits of the RMF, and a commitment to supporting employees through the transition.

Lastly, organizations might face difficulties in keeping up with the continuous nature of the RMF. Cybersecurity is not a one-time project but an ongoing risk management process that requires constant vigilance. This can be facilitated by integrating RMF activities into regular operational procedures and using automated tools to support continuous monitoring.

To address these challenges, a continuous improvement mindset is essential. Cybersecurity is a constantly evolving field, and so should the organization's approach to managing its risks. This includes regularly reviewing and updating the RMF processes and staying abreast of developments in the field.

Recommendations:

- **Anticipate Initial Resource Strain:** Be prepared for the significant initial time and resource investment required for RMF implementation. While the process may strain resources at first, remember that this investment can reduce the likelihood of costly cybersecurity incidents and smooth regulatory navigation in the future.

- **Invest in Training and External Expertise:** Counter the complexity of the RMF with a commitment to staff and stakeholder training. If needed, seek external expertise to understand and implement the various steps and many potential security controls involved in the RMF.

- **Exercise Strong Leadership:** Tackle organizational resistance through strong leadership and clear communication about the RMF's benefits. Ensure that your team understands the importance of this framework and offers support through the transition phase.

- **Integrate RMF into Regular Operations:** Keep pace with the RMF's continuous nature by integrating its activities into your regular operational procedures. Employ automated tools for constant monitoring to manage cybersecurity as an ongoing process, not a one-time project.

- **Adopt a Continuous Improvement Mindset:** Understand that cybersecurity is an evolving field. Consistently review and update your RMF processes and stay updated on developments in the area. Maintain a growth mindset to improve and adjust your approach to managing cybersecurity risks.

NIST RMF AND THIRD-PARTY RISK MANAGEMENT

In the contemporary interconnected business sphere, risks associated with third parties have rapidly surfaced as a matter of substantial concern. These third-party entities, suppliers, contractors, service providers, or business partners can inadvertently introduce vulnerabilities into an organization's information system. To efficiently manage these risks, the NISTRMF provides a systematic approach.

The initial stage in this risk management process is comprehending the nature and breadth of potential third-party risks. These risks can encompass a wide range of threats, from data breaches due to deficient security measures adopted by the third party to nonadherence with pertinent regulations. Additional risks can emerge from a lack of visibility and control over the practices of these third parties. Organizations can use the RMF to categorize and prioritize these risks based on their potential impact. This assessment enables organizations to strategize their risk management plans effectively.

The deployment of security controls represents a vital element in mitigating third-party risks. The RMF steers organizations in choosing apt controls for managing their third-party relationships. These controls may necessitate contractual measures, such as embedding security stipulations in contracts, and technical strategies, like ensuring secure data transmission between the organization and the third party.

Yet, the mere execution of controls does not provide a comprehensive solution. Managing third-party relationships is an iterative process that necessitates consistent monitoring and assessment. This is where the RMF's "continuous monitoring" phase comes to the forefront. It advocates for organizations to periodically scrutinize their third-party relationships, evaluate the efficacy of the implemented controls, and make necessary adjustments.

In conclusion, it is essential to note that third-party risk management should not be viewed in isolation. Instead, it should be amalgamated with the organization's broader risk management practices. The RMF facilitates this smooth integration, ensuring a consistent and unified approach to risk management that permeates every facet of the organization. This comprehensive application of risk management strategies enhances an organization's resilience to potential threats, bolstering overall cybersecurity integrity.

Recommendations:

- **Understand the Scope of Third-Party Risks:** Recognize the breadth of risks third parties can introduce, ranging from potential data breaches due to their security lapses to noncompliance with regulations. Utilize the RMF to categorize and prioritize these risks to craft a corresponding risk management strategy.

- **Implement RMF-guided Security Controls:** Apply security controls to manage third-party risks as guided by the RMF. These controls could be contractual, such as including explicit security requirements in contracts, or technical, like ensuring secure data transmission between your organization and the third party.

- **Regularly Monitor and Assess Third-Party Relationships:** Understand that managing third-party relationships is an ongoing process that necessitates continuous monitoring and assessment. The RMF's continuous monitoring step can guide you in regularly reviewing these relationships, implementing controls' effectiveness, and making necessary adjustments.

- **Integrate Third-Party Risk Management with Overall Practices:** Ensure that third-party risk management is not treated as a separate process but is integrated with your organization's overarching risk management practices. The RMF can facilitate this integration, providing a consistent approach to risk management across your organization.

- **Regularly Review Third-Party Risks:** As third-party relationships evolve, so do the associated risks. Periodically review these risks, especially in the face of changing relationships or emerging technologies, and adjust your risk management strategy accordingly. The RMF's focus on continuous monitoring can aid in this regular review process.

Chapter Conclusion

Diving deeper into the NIST RMF, we see that it embodies a highly adaptive and extensive structure for governing risks associated with information systems. Its flexibility and comprehensiveness come from its six-step process encompassing every facet of risk management, from information system categorization to monitoring implemented security controls. Thus, the RMF offers an all-encompassing view of cybersecurity risk management.

The RMF's role in risk management is not static; instead, it is designed to evolve in response to the dynamic nature of cyber threats, technological advancements, and shifting regulatory landscapes. This evolution reflects the framework's inherent flexibility and underscores the importance of constant updates and improvements in the RMF methodology. Hence, staying abreast of developments within the RMF and the broader cybersecurity landscape is imperative for organizations aiming to maintain a robust security posture.

Looking toward the future, the importance of the RMF as a tool for effective cybersecurity risk management cannot be overstated. Its systematic, step-by-step approach provides organizations with a roadmap for identifying, assessing, managing, and monitoring cybersecurity risks. As such, it is expected that the RMF will continue to be a mainstay in organizations' cybersecurity toolkits.

Furthermore, organizations should aspire to harmonize the RMF with their overarching risk management strategy. Integrating the RMF into the broader risk management architecture ensures a holistic and coordinated approach to risk management. This integration can encompass various practices and technologies to enhance the organization's risk resilience.

Effective RMF implementation requires strategic foresight, a commitment to continuous learning, and active engagement from all stakeholders. The success of the RMF lies not only in understanding its mechanics but also in appreciating its strategic relevance and potential impact. Thus, organizations should consider making a substantial investment in resources for comprehending and implementing the RMF, including targeted training and capacity-building initiatives.

To this end, strategic planning should be a priority. It involves identifying the necessary resources, defining roles and responsibilities, and laying a roadmap for RMF implementation. This planning stage is crucial to align the RMF with the organization's goals and to ensure that all stakeholders understand their part in the process. Organizations should also encourage continuous learning and improvement, regularly reviewing and updating their RMF processes based on feedback and changing circumstances.

Finally, the significance of stakeholder engagement in RMF implementation cannot be overstated. Organizations can foster a culture of cybersecurity awareness and responsibility by involving everyone – from top management to frontline employees. After all, cybersecurity is not solely the domain of IT departments; it is a collective responsibility that requires everyone's participation.

Case Study: OmniTech Corporation and NIST RMF Implementation

OmniTech Corporation, a rising player in the technology industry, was committed to fortifying its cybersecurity posture. After suffering a minor breach due to a third-party vendor's negligence, the company acknowledged the urgency to overhaul its approach to risk management. At the center of this mission was Meltem, OmniTech's recently appointed Chief Information Security Officer (CISO), charged with navigating the complex waters of cybersecurity governance.

Meltem decided to utilize the NIST RMF as her guiding compass, recognizing its all-encompassing nature and potential for managing cyber risks more effectively. Given OmniTech's diverse technology portfolio, the flexibility and robustness of the NIST RMF were particularly appealing.

In the first phase, Meltem spearheaded an initiative to categorize the company's information systems, aligning her efforts with the initial steps of the NIST RMF. She also incorporated stakeholders from different departments, fostering a sense of shared responsibility and collective action toward cybersecurity. Meltem was aware that the successful integration of the RMF required organizational buy-in and the support of her colleagues from all levels of the organization.

Meltem then proceeded to select and implement the appropriate security controls, tailoring them to OmniTech's specific needs. She managed to secure the integration of cutting-edge security technologies into the company's systems, aligning them with the RMF's guidelines. During this phase, Meltem encountered resistance and challenges, particularly from the operational departments concerned about the changes impacting their workflows. She addressed these challenges by emphasizing the long-term benefits and ensuring that sufficient training and support were provided to all employees.

As OmniTech ventured into continuous monitoring of its implemented controls, Meltem leveraged automated tools and solutions to maintain efficiency. Simultaneously, she established procedures for regular assessment and ongoing authorization to create a culture of continuous improvement.

In her role, Meltem also dealt with third-party risk management, an area where OmniTech had previously faltered. She ensured appropriate security controls were implemented in all third-party relationships and continuously monitored for effectiveness.

The journey was demanding, but Meltem's strategic and inclusive approach paid off. Through implementing the NIST RMF, OmniTech Corporation significantly improved its risk posture, enhanced its resilience against cybersecurity threats, and fostered a security-aware culture within the organization. Meltem's story emphasizes the importance of strategic planning, stakeholder engagement, continuous improvement, and customization of the RMF to fit the organization's unique needs, underlining the critical lessons learned from OmniTech's NIST RMF journey.

SAMPLE RMF AUTHORIZATION DOCUMENT PACKAGE

An RMF Authorization Package is a collection of documents that comprehensively understand the risk associated with an information system. This package makes risk-based decisions on whether to authorize system operation or take appropriate actions. Below is an example of an RMF Authorization Package for a hypothetical system.

This package, while comprehensive, is hypothetical and may need adjustments based on an organization's specific requirements and the nature of the information system.

RMF Authorization Package for Hypothetical Information System

1. **System Categorization Document**
   - **System Name:** Hypothetical Information System
   - **System Owner:** John Doe

- **Information Types:** Confidential Business Information, User Personal Identifiable Information
- **System Impact Level:** Moderate

2. **Security Plan (SP)**
   - **System Name:** Hypothetical Information System
   - **Responsible Entity:** IT Department, XYZ Corporation
   - **System Operational Status:** Operational
   - **Security Control Selection:** Based on system impact level, organizational risk assessment, legal requirements
   - **System Interconnection/Information Sharing:** Detailed descriptions of system interconnections and the information shared with external systems
   - **List of applied security controls and their implementation details. For instance, AC-1 (Access Control Policy and Procedures):** Access to the Hypothetical Information System is regulated by an extensive policy outlining user roles and privileges

3. **Security Assessment Report (SAR)**
   - **Assessment Team:** Internal Security Assessment Team
   - **Assessment Method:** Combination of automated scanning tools, manual checks, and interviews with system stakeholders
   - **Assessment Results:** Details of the assessment results for each security control. For instance, AC-1 (Access Control Policy and Procedures): The access control policies are well-documented and implemented. All users are given access privileges based on their roles

4. **Plan of Action and Milestones (POA&M)**
   - **Weakness Identified:** Weak encryption techniques used for data storage
   - **Recommended Corrective Action:** Implement advanced encryption techniques
   - **Responsible Personnel:** IT Department
   - **Estimated Completion Date:** MM/DD/YYYY

5. **Risk Assessment Report (RAR)**
   - **Risk Assessment Method:** Followed NIST 800-30 Guide for Conducting Risk Assessments
   - **Identified Risks:** Details of risks identified during the risk assessment. For instance, unauthorized data access due to weak encryption
   - **Risk Level:** Moderate
   - **Recommended Risk Response:** Mitigation by implementing advanced encryption techniques

6. **Security Control Assessment (SCA)**
   - **Assessed Security Controls:** All security controls defined in the Security Plan

- **Assessment Results:** Details of the assessment results for each security control
- Potential vulnerabilities and areas for improvement

7. **Authorization Decision Document**
   - **System Name:** Hypothetical Information System
   - **Decision:** (Authorized, Authorized with conditions, Denied)
   - **Authorizing Official:** Jane Smith, Chief Information Security Officer
   - **Decision Rationale:** Detailed rationale for the decision, considering the security assessment results, risk assessment results, and overall business objectives

CHAPTER 9

Cybersecurity Metrics

"Cybersecurity metrics fuel our journey towards a safer digital world. Let's measure our progress, ignite our potential, and soar above the challenges that come our way."

Cybersecurity metrics are measurable indicators that help organizations assess their cybersecurity standing, risk levels, and the effectiveness of their cybersecurity strategies. The importance of these metrics, the distinction between *Key Performance Indicators* (KPIs) and *Key Risk Indicators* (KRIs), their roles in decision-making and resource allocation, and their role in ensuring compliance are all critical to understanding. Challenges associated with defining, interpreting, and utilizing these metrics are also important to consider. Understanding the core components of KPIs and KRIs and strategies for incorporating them into the cybersecurity framework can significantly enhance an organization's cybersecurity management approach.

UNDERSTANDING CYBERSECURITY METRICS

Embarking on the journey through the convoluted landscape of cybersecurity without appropriate metrics is akin to finding oneself lost in a vast, lightless forest without a single guiding light. This challenge of grappling with the complexities and uncertainties of cybersecurity would be akin to an aimless journey through unchartered territory. An attempt to accurately appraise an organization's existing cybersecurity position, identify potential vulnerabilities or blind spots within its protective structures, or evaluate the real-world impact and effectiveness of its cybersecurity plans and initiatives without these guiding metrics would be an uphill battle but an insurmountable challenge.

A frequent misunderstanding often pervades the discussions on security – it is often assumed that the primary goal of security is to avert risk altogether. However, this perspective only skims the surface of the true purpose of security. The underlying truth is that security is not about wholly eradicating risk. Instead, it involves a more nuanced approach: managing these risks competently and effectively. This philosophy forms the bedrock of cybersecurity metrics. These metrics are not merely instruments or tools designed for avoiding or eliminating threats; they serve a far more strategic purpose. They offer a comprehensive, methodical, and data-centric strategy for comprehending, controlling, and, over time, substantially reducing these risks with high efficacy. In the execution of this critical endeavor, specific key metrics emerge as essential navigational tools. KPIs and KRIs are among these critical tools, serving pivotal roles in guiding organizations toward these all-important objectives.

Cybersecurity metrics are expansive, covering many elements within their broad ambit. They encapsulate technical parameters and process-centric metrics, providing a holistic view of an organization's cybersecurity posture. At one end of the spectrum, we find technical indicators that reveal the readiness and resilience of the system against cyber threats. These include the detection rates of intrusions, the blocking rates of malware, and the closure times of vulnerabilities. These technical indicators offer an immediate, though profoundly insightful, snapshot of the system's defensive prowess against relentless cyber threats.

On the flip side, at the other end of the spectrum, we find process-oriented metrics taking center stage. These metrics, incorporating elements such as the time taken to respond to incidents, the efficiency of patch management processes, and the outcomes of compliance audits, provide an in-depth, penetrative gaze into the operational efficiency of an organization's cybersecurity practices. They shed light on cybersecurity's procedural and administrative aspects, offering insights into how well the organization's processes support its defensive strategies.

The significance of these metrics extends far beyond their immediate utility. They are not merely data sources but generate a veritable treasure trove of data-driven insights invaluable for organizational leadership and those occupying decision-making roles. When these insights are diligently interpreted, correctly understood, and strategically applied, they can inform and empower decision-makers. They can guide leaders in making astute, strategic choices in critical areas such as resource allocation, strategic planning, risk mitigation, and regulatory compliance.

Beyond empowering decision-makers, these metrics provide organizations with a pathway to transition from a reactive posture to a more proactive stance in cybersecurity. They are the keys that can unlock the transformation of cybersecurity from an intimidating challenge into a strategic asset. By harnessing these metrics effectively, organizations can move from merely responding to threats to anticipating and preempting them, thereby turning the tables on the ever-evolving landscape of cybersecurity.

Recommendations:

- **Embrace Metrics:** Dedicate time and resources to understanding the importance of cybersecurity metrics. Familiarize yourself with the technical and process-oriented indicators. Building foundational knowledge about intrusion detection rates, malware blocking rates, vulnerability closure times, incident response times, patch management efficiency, and compliance audit results will help shape your organization's cybersecurity strategy.

- **Understand Risk Management:** Begin viewing security as managing risks rather than avoiding them. Strive to develop a systematic, data-driven approach to comprehend, control, and eventually lessen these risks. This mindset shift will form the basis of a robust and proactive cybersecurity infrastructure.

- **Incorporate KPIs and KRIs:** Incorporate KPIs and KRIs into your cybersecurity strategy. Understand their roles and how they can guide your organization toward managing cybersecurity risks more effectively.

- **Utilize Insights:** Spend time understanding how to interpret and apply the insights derived from your cybersecurity metrics. These can guide strategic decisions in critical areas such as resource allocation, strategic planning, risk mitigation, and regulatory compliance.

- **Foster Proactiveness:** Work toward shifting your organization's stance from reactive to proactive when dealing with cybersecurity. Use the insights from your metrics to anticipate and preempt potential threats, turning cybersecurity from a daunting challenge into a strategic advantage.

- **Regular Review and Updates:** Ensure your cybersecurity strategies and metrics are regularly reviewed and updated to reflect evolving threats and risks. Cybersecurity is dynamic, and staying updated is key to maintaining solid defenses.

- **Strengthen the Human Element:** Train your team to understand and utilize cybersecurity metrics effectively. Empower them to apply these insights to their daily roles, thus strengthening the overall cybersecurity posture of your organization.

- **Encourage Cross-Department Collaboration:** Break down silos between IT, operations, and other departments. Encourage a collaborative approach to cybersecurity, where insights and implications from metrics are understood and acted upon across the organization.

- **Involve Leadership:** Engage organizational leadership in understanding and acting on cybersecurity metrics. Leaders can champion the importance of these metrics and drive strategic decisions based on their insights.

- **Foster a Culture of Security:** Lastly, go beyond processes and metrics to foster a security culture within your organization. A shared understanding and commitment to cybersecurity can significantly enhance your organization's ability to anticipate, detect, and respond to threats.

THE IMPORTANCE OF METRICS IN CYBERSECURITY

Metrics in the realm of cybersecurity occupy a critical position of real significance. Metrics function as the pivotal compass that navigates the organization through its often-complex cybersecurity journey, offering quantifiable and concrete evidence of the effectiveness or ineffectiveness of current cybersecurity strategies. Additionally, they shed light on critical areas that may need reevaluation, improvement, or reinforcement. Metrics form a solid performance baseline that serves as a reference point against which future outcomes can be juxtaposed to evaluate progression, identify emerging trends, and observe shifts in the cybersecurity landscape.

The continuous evaluation and adaptation of cybersecurity metrics are essential to the organization's cybersecurity apparatus. They are indispensable in adjusting cybersecurity controls in response to shifting threat landscapes and evolving business needs. The wisdom encapsulated in Albert Einstein's words, "Not everything that can be counted counts, and not everything that counts can be counted," finds a poignant application in cybersecurity metrics. For instance, simply tallying the number of attempted cyberattacks may not provide an insightful or useful metric if it does not correlate to any meaningful outcome.

On the other hand, certain unquantifiable or qualitative factors, such as the level of employee awareness regarding sophisticated phishing attacks or the general cybersecurity hygiene maintained within the organization, might significantly impact cybersecurity posture but may pose challenges when attempting to measure accurately. Thus, establishing effective cybersecurity metrics involves balancing quantitative and qualitative aspects while remaining focused on the broader cybersecurity objectives.

Effective cybersecurity metrics must be tailored to fit the organization's unique requirements, risks, and objectives. They should not merely serve as measuring instruments but should be able to drive actionable insights that empower the organization to enhance its cybersecurity posture continuously. They should guide the organization toward the right mitigation strategies and countermeasures, offering critical feedback that improves cybersecurity performance. Therefore, the continuous evaluation, fine-tuning, and adaptation of KPIs and KRIs are necessary to maintain relevancy and meaningfulness over time.

The ultimate aim of cybersecurity metrics should steer the organization toward a data-driven cybersecurity posture. In a data-driven approach, decisions are rooted in concrete evidence and sound analysis rather than mere conjecture or intuition. By providing an empirical foundation for decision-making, this approach significantly enhances the effectiveness and accuracy of cybersecurity practices and promotes a culture of transparency and accountability within the organization. It assists stakeholders in understanding the current state of cybersecurity, the logic behind specific cybersecurity decisions, and the reasoning behind allocating resources, thus fostering an environment of trust and confidence.

Recommendations:

- **Understand the Importance of Metrics:** Acknowledge that cybersecurity metrics are pivotal to the organization. They provide concrete evidence of the effectiveness of your current cybersecurity strategies and highlight areas that may need improvement. Recognize that metrics form a baseline for evaluating progression, identifying trends, and observing shifts in the cybersecurity landscape.
- **Continuously Evaluate and Adapt Metrics:** Ensure you evaluate and adapt your cybersecurity metrics. These are key in adjusting cybersecurity controls in response to shifting threat landscapes and evolving business needs. Do not just focus on counting events but on what is significant and contributes to meaningful outcomes.
- **Balance Quantitative and Qualitative Aspects:** Understand that effective cybersecurity metrics require a balance of quantitative and qualitative elements. While some metrics are easy to count, others, such as employee awareness regarding phishing attacks or general cybersecurity hygiene, are more challenging to measure but equally important.
- **Tailor Metrics to Your Organization:** Ensure your cybersecurity metrics are tailored to fit your organization's unique requirements, risks, and objectives. They should serve as measuring instruments and drive actionable insights to enhance your cybersecurity posture continuously.
- **Constantly Fine-tune KPIs and KRIs:** Keep your KPIs and KRIs relevant and meaningful by continuously evaluating, fine-tuning, and adapting them according to your cybersecurity landscape and organizational needs.
- **Strive for a Data-driven Cybersecurity Posture:** Aim to steer your organization toward a data-driven cybersecurity posture. Base decisions on concrete evidence and sound analysis rather than conjecture or intuition. By doing this, you enhance the effectiveness and accuracy of cybersecurity practices, promote transparency and accountability, and foster an environment of trust and confidence.
- **Communicate Clearly with Stakeholders:** Use metrics to assist stakeholders in understanding the current state of cybersecurity, the reasoning behind specific decisions, and the logic behind resource allocation. Clear and effective communication can help build trust and confidence in your cybersecurity initiatives.

THE ROLE OF METRICS IN DECISION-MAKING AND RESOURCE ALLOCATION

Cybersecurity metrics function as critical benchmarks in managing an organization's cybersecurity posture. They represent quantifiable data points that drive informed decision-making processes, directing the allocation of resources within the organization. More specifically, these metrics yield concrete insights into the performance of security controls, expose potential vulnerabilities, and assess risk levels.

These tangible insights serve as a backbone for various decisions, such as budget allocation for cybersecurity initiatives, assignment of personnel to specific roles or tasks, development of internal cybersecurity policies, and strategic planning for broader cybersecurity measures. Each decision relies on the accurate and timely information that cybersecurity metrics provide, facilitating a data-driven approach to managing and enhancing an organization's cybersecurity posture.

In this landscape, risk management emerges as a vital component. KRIs are specialized metrics that assist organizations in identifying, assessing, and prioritizing risks. KRIs offer a measurable and quantifiable view of an organization's risk exposure, yielding a clear understanding of potential losses and the effectiveness of the existing controls to manage and mitigate those risks. This granular insight is fundamental in shaping informed decisions around resource allocation, with a keen focus on risk mitigation strategies.

Despite KPIs and KRIs' value individually, a comprehensive understanding of an organization's cybersecurity health necessitates a balanced approach, incorporating both metrics types. KPIs are essential for evaluating the efficacy and performance of cybersecurity efforts, while KRIs offer a full view of the risk landscape, unearthing potential vulnerabilities and areas of concern.

When KPIs and KRIs are used in tandem, they offer a panoramic, in-depth view of the cybersecurity environment. This combined perspective provides a nuanced and comprehensive understanding of an organization's cybersecurity stance, offering rich, actionable insights. This holistic view, resulting from the balance of performance metrics and risk insights, equips decision-makers with the knowledge to formulate robust strategies, efficiently allocate resources, and fortify the organization's cybersecurity posture.

Measuring both performance and risk is to improve the organization's ability to respond and adapt to the ever-evolving landscape of cyber threats. A combined view of KPIs and KRIs empowers organizations to identify gaps in their current strategies, prioritize areas for improvement, and ensure their actions are grounded in data, leading to a more resilient and robust cybersecurity framework.

Recommendations:

- **Recognize the Role of Metrics:** Understand that cybersecurity metrics are essential for managing your organization's cybersecurity posture. They offer quantifiable data points that drive informed decision-making, helping to guide resource allocation and highlight potential vulnerabilities.

- **Utilize Metrics in Decision-Making:** Use the insights derived from cybersecurity metrics for various decisions such as budget allocation for cybersecurity initiatives, assignment of personnel, development of internal cybersecurity policies, and strategic planning for broader cybersecurity measures.

- **Implement Risk Management:** Implement KRIs as part of your cybersecurity metrics. KRIs help identify, assess, and prioritize risks, offering a measurable view of your organization's risk exposure and the effectiveness of your controls to manage and mitigate risks.
- **Balance KPIs and KRIs:** Ensure you have a balanced approach to evaluating your organization's cybersecurity health. KPIs help assess the efficacy and performance of cybersecurity efforts, while KRIs provide a comprehensive view of the risk landscape.
- **Utilize KPIs and KRIs Together:** Use KPIs and KRIs to understand your cybersecurity environment comprehensively. Together, they offer a nuanced view of your cybersecurity stance, providing actionable insights for enhancing your organization's cybersecurity posture.
- **Formulate Robust Strategies:** Use the combined perspective from KPIs and KRIs to formulate robust strategies for your organization. This understanding equips decision-makers with the knowledge to allocate resources efficiently, fortify the organization's cybersecurity posture, and improve its ability to respond to cyber threats.
- **Prioritize Continuous Improvement:** Use the insights from KPIs and KRIs to identify gaps in your current strategies and prioritize areas for improvement. This practice ensures that your actions are grounded in data, leading to a more resilient and robust cybersecurity framework.
- **Adapt to the Evolving Threat Landscape:** Understand that measuring both performance and risk is crucial in improving your organization's ability to adapt to the evolving landscape of cyber threats. Continuously reassess your KPIs and KRIs to ensure they remain relevant and insightful in the face of new and emerging threats.

DIFFERENTIATING BETWEEN KPIs AND KRIs

KPIs represent metrics designed to gauge the effectiveness of an organization's implemented cybersecurity controls. They measure how successfully the organization's cybersecurity strategies, measures, and initiatives maintain security and mitigate threats. These outcome-based measures are usually quantitative, enabling objective performance assessment against predefined targets.

For instance, a few examples of cybersecurity KPIs might include the percentage of systems patched within a specified time frame, the average time taken to detect and respond to a security incident, or the rate of false positives flagged by the organization's intrusion detection system. Other KPIs could involve the rate of successful system backups, the number of successful recoveries from backups, or the time taken to restore services after a cybersecurity incident. These KPIs directly reflect the effectiveness of the organization's cybersecurity protocols and processes.

KRIs are signposts in the organization's cybersecurity risk landscape. Unlike KPIs that focus on performance, KRIs provide quantifiable, often forward-looking

measurements of potential risks, threats, and vulnerabilities that might negatively impact the organization's cybersecurity posture in the future. KRIs enable
organizations to gauge risk exposure, assisting in risk identification, measurement, and mitigation.

Examples of KRIs might include the number of unpatched or out-of-date
systems, the percentage of employees who fail a phishing awareness test, or
the number of high-risk vulnerabilities identified in a recent penetration test.
Further, KRIs could involve the number of days since the last detected intrusion,
the percentage of systems not updated with the latest security patches, or the
number of security alerts generated over a specific period. These KRIs help
organizations understand their risk exposure and assess the potential impact
on their cybersecurity stance.

While KPIs and KRIs are essential metrics used in cybersecurity governance, their focus areas differ significantly. KPIs primarily evaluate the performance of cybersecurity measures, while KRIs are oriented toward assessing
risk exposure. This distinction between KPIs and KRIs is fundamental to using
these metrics effectively and drawing actionable, meaningful insights from
them. With a precise understanding of these metrics, organizations can leverage them to enhance their cybersecurity posture.

Recommendations:

- **Understand the Role of KPIs:** Recognize that KPIs are metrics designed
  to measure the effectiveness of your organization's cybersecurity controls. KPIs focus on the success of cybersecurity strategies, measures,
  and initiatives in maintaining security and mitigating threats.

- **Incorporate Quantitative Measures in KPIs:** Use quantitative, outcome-
  based measures. This can include aspects such as the percentage of systems patched within a specific time frame, the average time taken to
  detect and respond to a security incident, or the rate of false positives
  flagged by the intrusion detection system.

- **Evaluate Cybersecurity Protocols Using KPIs:** Use KPIs to directly assess
  the effectiveness of your organization's cybersecurity protocols and processes. This could involve measuring the rate of successful system backups, the number of successful recoveries from backups, or the time taken
  to restore services after a cybersecurity incident.

- **Understand the Role of KRIs:** Know that KRIs provide quantifiable
  measurements of potential risks, threats, and vulnerabilities that could
  negatively impact your organization's cybersecurity posture. They help
  gauge risk exposure and assist in risk identification, measurement, and
  mitigation.

- **Incorporate Risk Measures in KRIs:** Use KRIs to assess risk-related
  aspects such as unpatched or out-of-date systems, the percentage of
  employees who fail a phishing awareness test, or the number of high-risk
  vulnerabilities identified in a penetration test.

- **Distinguish Between KPIs and KRIs:** Understand that while KPIs and KRIs are essential metrics in cybersecurity governance, they focus on different areas. KPIs primarily evaluate performance, while KRIs are oriented toward assessing risk exposure. This distinction is vital for using these metrics effectively and drawing actionable, meaningful insights from them.
- **Leverage KPIs and KRIs to Enhance Cybersecurity:** Use your understanding of KPIs and KRIs to leverage them effectively and enhance your organization's cybersecurity posture. This might include reassessing your current KPIs and KRIs, establishing new ones, or adjusting your cybersecurity strategies based on the insights drawn from these metrics.

THE ROLE OF METRICS IN COMPLIANCE

In the contemporary regulatory landscape, where regulations are increasingly stringent and complex, achieving compliance is not merely a legal obligation. Rather, it stands as an integral facet of an effective cybersecurity program. Organizations are subject to various regulations depending on their specific industry, geographical location, and the nature of the data they process or store. Each of these regulations stipulates its unique requirements, and noncompliance can lead to heavy penalties, reputational damage, and even business interruption.

In this context, cybersecurity metrics, specifically KRIs, become invaluable tools in facilitating and maintaining compliance. KRIs provide a quantifiable yardstick of potential risks, empowering organizations to effectively identify, evaluate, and manage compliance-related risks. By illuminating the effectiveness or shortcomings of an organization's compliance efforts, KRIs can identify areas for improvement, thereby guiding the prioritization of remediation efforts and policy amendments.

It is essential to understand that different regulations emphasize distinct areas of concern. For example, the Federal Financial Institutions Examination Council (*FFIEC*) primarily targets financial institutions, outlining the cybersecurity expectations for these entities. The Gramm-Leach-Bliley Act (*GLBA*) aims to protect consumers' private financial information, setting the rules for financial institutions about handling and securing this sensitive information. 12 Code of Federal Regulations (*CFR*) 30 Part B sets national banks' and federal savings associations' operational and managerial standards.

On the other hand, the Payment Card Industry Data Security Standard (*PCI DSS*), a contractual, not regulatory requirement, dictates standards for handling and securing cardholder data for entities that process, store, or transmit credit card information. The Sarbanes-Oxley Act (*SOX*) focuses on improving the accuracy and reliability of corporate disclosures made under securities laws. The Cloud Act deals with the regulation of data stored by US-based companies on servers located abroad, and the General Data Protection Regulation (*GDPR*) concentrates on protecting personal data, setting guidelines for the collection and processing of personal information of individuals within the European Union.

Each obligation necessitates an organization to focus on different aspects of its cybersecurity landscape. Using relevant KRIs, organizations can measure the risks associated with these distinct areas and assess the effectiveness of the controls implemented to manage those risks. In this way, KRIs facilitate an organization's compliance efforts, enabling it to adhere to multiple, sometimes overlapping, regulatory requirements effectively. This approach allows organizations to streamline their compliance management processes and reduce the risk of noncompliance and the associated consequences.

Recommendations:

- **Understand the Importance of Compliance:** Recognize that compliance with regulatory requirements is not just a legal obligation but an integral part of an effective cybersecurity program. Depending on your industry, location, and the nature of the data you process, you will be subject to various regulations, each with unique requirements. Noncompliance can result in severe consequences, including penalties and reputational damage.

- **Utilize Cybersecurity Metrics for Compliance:** Use cybersecurity metrics, specifically KRIs, as tools to facilitate and maintain compliance. KRIs provide a measurable gauge of potential risks, enabling your organization to identify, evaluate, and manage compliance-related risks effectively.

- **Use KRIs for Continuous Improvement:** Leverage KRIs to assess the effectiveness of your organization's compliance efforts and identify areas for improvement. This can guide the prioritization of remediation efforts and necessary amendments to policies.

- **Familiarize with Relevant Requirements:** Familiarize yourself with the various requirements relevant to your organization. This could include the FFIEC, GLBA, 12 CFR 30 Part B, PCI DSS, SOX, the Cloud Act, and GDPR. Each regulation focuses on different areas and has unique requirements for maintaining data security.

- **Use KRIs for Regulation-specific Risks:** Understand that each regulation necessitates your organization to focus on different aspects of its cybersecurity landscape. Use relevant KRIs to measure the risks associated with these areas and assess the effectiveness of the controls implemented to manage those risks.

- **Streamline Compliance Processes with KRIs:** Leverage KRIs to adhere effectively to multiple, sometimes overlapping, regulatory requirements. This can streamline your compliance management processes, reducing the risk of noncompliance and its associated consequences.

- **Regularly Update Compliance Strategies:** Keeping your compliance strategies up-to-date is crucial with the regulatory landscape becoming more stringent and complex. Periodically reassess your KRIs and compliance policies and adjust them as needed to align with changes in regulations.

CHALLENGES AND CONSIDERATIONS

Implementing cybersecurity metrics within an organization is not a straightforward task. There are various challenges that organizations may encounter, the first of which is metric overload. Metric overload transpires when an organization attempts to track and analyze an overwhelming number of metrics. This excess can lead to confusion, a lack of focus, and a dilution of the significance of each metric. In such a scenario, critical metrics may be overlooked, or their essential insights could be lost amidst a vast sea of numbers. This is why it is imperative to establish clear priorities and identify key metrics that align with the organization's strategic objectives, risks, and needs. The metrics chosen should be focused and specific, meaningfully understanding the organization's cybersecurity posture.

The second challenge is the risk of reliance on inaccurate or unreliable data. The validity and reliability of cybersecurity metrics hinge upon the quality of the underlying data. If the data is incorrect, incomplete, or outdated, its metrics can be misleading, leading to distorted conclusions and misguided decisions. This emphasizes the need for robust data collection, verification, and management processes. Organizations must ensure that their data sources are reliable, that data collection methodologies are rigorous, and that data is up-to-date and error-free. This also involves regularly reviewing and cleaning the data to maintain its accuracy and reliability.

A third challenge lies in the rapidly evolving landscape of cybersecurity threats and technologies. Cybersecurity is a dynamic field, with new threats emerging and technologies changing rapidly. This dynamic nature of the area requires a continuous evolution and adjustment of the metrics to maintain their relevance, accuracy, and effectiveness. If metrics are not updated regularly to account for these changes, they may become obsolete, irrelevant, or misleading. This necessitates a regular review and adjustment of the metrics, incorporating new data, considering emerging threats, and adapting to technological advancements. Organizations should establish a regular metric review and update process, ensuring their metrics remain relevant, accurate, and reflective of the current cybersecurity landscape.

Another challenge that is often overlooked is the communication and interpretation of metrics. Metrics, by their nature, are technical and numerical, which may make them difficult to understand for nontechnical stakeholders. This calls for clear and effective communication of these metrics, using simple language and visual aids where possible, to ensure that all stakeholders, including those without a technical background, can understand the insights provided by these metrics. This also involves providing context and interpretation for the metrics, explaining what they mean, why they are essential, and their implications for the organization's cybersecurity posture.

Lastly, organizations must know the resource implications of implementing and maintaining cybersecurity metrics. Collecting, analyzing, and reporting on metrics require resources, including time, staffing, and technology. Organizations must be prepared to invest these resources to ensure the successful implementation and effective use of metrics. This involves considering the costs and benefits of different metrics, choosing those that provide valuable insights at a reasonable cost, and allocating adequate resources for their implementation and maintenance.

Recommendations:

- **Avoid Metric Overload:** Be mindful of metric overload when an organization attempts to track and analyze excessive metrics. This can lead to confusion, a lack of focus, and potentially overlooking critical metrics. Establish clear priorities by identifying key metrics that align with your organization's strategic objectives, risks, and needs. The chosen metrics should be focused and specific to provide a meaningful understanding of the organization's cybersecurity posture.

- **Ensure Data Quality:** Recognize the risk of relying on inaccurate or unreliable data. The effectiveness of cybersecurity metrics hinges on the quality of the underlying data. If the data is incorrect, incomplete, or outdated, it could lead to misleading conclusions and misguided decisions. Establish robust data collection, verification, and management processes to ensure your data sources are reliable, rigorous, and up-to-date.

- **Adapt to the Evolving Cybersecurity Landscape:** Understand that the dynamic nature of cybersecurity necessitates continuous evolution and adjustment of metrics. If metrics are not regularly updated to reflect new threats and technological changes, they may become obsolete, irrelevant, or misleading. Periodically review and adjust your metrics, incorporating new data, considering emerging threats, and adapting to technological advancements.

- **Improve Communication and Interpretation of Metrics:** Note that metrics' technical and numerical nature can make them difficult to comprehend, especially for nontechnical stakeholders. Enhance your communication efforts by using simple language and visual aids, and provide context and interpretation for the metrics to help all stakeholders understand their significance and implications.

- **Account for Resource Implications:** Recognize the resource implications of implementing and maintaining cybersecurity metrics. This process requires resources like time, workforce, and technology. Be prepared to invest these resources to ensure the successful implementation and effective use of metrics. Weigh the costs and benefits of different metrics and choose those that provide valuable insights at a reasonable cost. Allocate adequate resources for their implementation and maintenance.

KEY PERFORMANCE INDICATORS (KPIs)

Key Performance Indicators, or KPIs, serve as essential measurement tools for gauging the effectiveness of an organization's cybersecurity controls and initiatives. These metrics provide empirical evidence of the efficiency and effectiveness of the cybersecurity strategies deployed, enabling the organization to quantify the impact of these strategies on its cybersecurity posture. They can cover many aspects, ranging from the time to detect and respond to an incident to the percentage of systems patched within a specified time frame.

Developing effective KPIs is a process that involves several key steps. The first step is to align the KPIs with the organization's broader business objectives. This alignment ensures that the cybersecurity initiatives and the KPIs that measure them directly contribute to the organization's strategic goals. This process may involve discussions with various stakeholders, including business leaders and cybersecurity professionals, to ensure that the KPIs align with business needs and cybersecurity realities.

Once this alignment is achieved, the next step is to define the KPIs clearly and ensure they are measurable. Each KPI should be associated with specific, quantifiable criteria that can be tracked and analyzed over time. It is important to make the definition of the KPIs as precise as possible to avoid ambiguity and ensure consistent interpretation and measurement. Furthermore, the targets set for these KPIs should be realistic and achievable rather than aspirational goals that could lead to disappointment and demotivation. This might involve benchmarking against industry standards or historical performance data to set realistic targets.

Once the KPIs are developed, their effective monitoring and reporting is the next challenge. Regular monitoring of KPIs is essential to track their performance over time and identify any trends, changes, or anomalies. This might involve establishing a routine for traditional data collection and analysis, using automated tools to streamline the process and ensure accuracy.

It's important to establish regular reporting frequencies and formats to ensure timely updates and effective communication of the KPIs. This could be in the form of weekly or monthly reports, depending on the nature of the KPIs and the organization's needs. These reports should present the KPI data in a clear, concise, and understandable manner, using visual aids such as graphs and charts where appropriate to illustrate trends and patterns.

Additionally, integrating KPIs into dashboards can provide a visually appealing and easy-to-understand view of performance trends. Dashboards can be an effective tool for real-time monitoring and reporting KPIs, providing a snapshot of the organization's cybersecurity performance at a glance. They allow for quick identification of areas of concern, enabling swift action to address any issues.

Recommendations:

- **Align with Business Objectives:** Initiate the development of effective KPIs by aligning them with your organization's broader business objectives. Ensure your cybersecurity initiatives and their corresponding KPIs directly contribute to your strategic goals. This process may involve discussions with stakeholders, including business leaders and cybersecurity professionals, to ensure alignment with business needs and cybersecurity realities.

- **Clearly Define and Measure KPIs:** Once alignment is achieved, clearly define your KPIs and ensure they are measurable. Attach specific, quantifiable criteria to each KPI that can be tracked and analyzed over time. Aim for precision in your KPI definitions to avoid ambiguity and ensure consistent interpretation and measurement. Set targets for these KPIs that are realistic and achievable, possibly benchmarking against industry standards or historical performance data.
- **Monitor KPIs Effectively:** Once your KPIs are developed, monitor them regularly to track performance over time and identify trends, changes, or anomalies. This might involve establishing a routine for regular data collection and analysis, potentially using automated tools to streamline the process and ensure accuracy.
- **Establish Reporting Frequencies and Formats:** Set regular reporting frequencies and formats for your KPIs to ensure timely updates and effective communication. This could involve weekly or monthly reports tailored to your organization's needs. Present the KPI data clearly and concisely, using visual aids such as graphs and charts to illustrate trends and patterns.
- **Integrate KPIs into Dashboards:** Integrate your KPIs into dashboards for an easy-to-understand view of performance trends. Dashboards offer a visually appealing real-time monitoring and reporting tool, providing a snapshot of your organization's cybersecurity performance. They allow for the quick identification of areas of concern, enabling swift action to address any issues.

KEY RISK INDICATORS (KRIs)

KRIs play a crucial role in an organization's risk management strategy. They function as a key tool for mapping the organization's risk landscape, providing a quantifiable measure of potential risks and vulnerabilities that could compromise its cybersecurity posture. They can offer insights into various risk factors, ranging from the number of unpatched systems and the percentage of employees who fail a phishing test to the number of high-risk vulnerabilities identified in a penetration test.

The first step in developing effective KRIs involves a comprehensive understanding of the organization's risk tolerance and appetite. Risk tolerance refers to the level of risk the organization is willing to accept before action is required. In contrast, risk appetite is the total amount of risk the organization is willing to accept to pursue its business objectives. Understanding these parameters is essential to ensure the KRIs align with the organization's risk strategy and capabilities.

The next step in this process involves the identification of the organization's critical assets and the associated risks. This could include conducting a thorough risk assessment to identify potential threats, vulnerabilities, and their impact on these assets. The identified risks then form the basis for the KRIs.

Once the KRIs are defined, setting thresholds and triggers for each KRI is essential. These are the values at which a risk becomes unacceptable (entry) and the point at which action must be taken (trigger). Establishing these limits allows for early warning of emerging risks and proactive risk management.

The final aspect of working with KRIs involves their ongoing monitoring and reporting. KRIs should be monitored regularly to track changes and identify emerging trends or threats like KPIs. This could include establishing a routine for regular data collection and analysis and using automated tools to ensure accuracy and timeliness.

Reporting of KRIs should be integrated into the organization's risk management process. This includes presenting the KRI data in a clear, understandable format, highlighting any trends or changes, and explaining their implications for the organization's risk profile. Visual aids such as graphs and charts can be useful for illustrating these trends and making the data more accessible.

KRIs should be reviewed and updated regularly to ensure their continued relevance. The rapidly changing nature of the cybersecurity landscape means that an organization's risks can change rapidly, and the KRIs need to reflect this. Regular reviews also allow adjusting the thresholds and triggers to ensure they remain appropriate in light of changing risks and risk tolerance.

Analysis of KRIs should feed directly into the organization's risk mitigation planning process. By providing a clear, quantifiable picture of the organization's risk profile, KRIs offer actionable insights that can inform decisions about where to focus risk mitigation efforts, which controls to implement, and how to allocate resources effectively. This can significantly enhance the organization's ability to manage and reduce cybersecurity risks.

Recommendations:

- **Understand Risk Tolerance and Appetite:** Understand your organization's risk tolerance (the level of risk you are willing to accept before action is required) and risk appetite (the total amount of risk you are ready to accept to achieve your business objectives). These parameters are essential to align your KRIs with your organization's risk strategy and capabilities.

- **Identify Critical Assets and Associated Risks**: Conduct a thorough risk assessment to identify your organization's critical assets and potential associated threats and vulnerabilities. The risks you identify will form the basis for your KRIs.

- **Set Thresholds and Triggers:** Once your KRIs are defined, set thresholds (the values at which a risk becomes unacceptable) and triggers (the point at which action must be taken). Establishing these limits enables early warning of emerging risks and promotes proactive risk management.

- **Monitor and Report KRIs:** Regularly monitor your KRIs to track changes and identify emerging trends or threats. This could involve establishing a routine for regular data collection and analysis, potentially using automated tools to ensure accuracy and timeliness. Integrate the reporting of KRIs into your risk management process, presenting KRI data in a clear, understandable format, highlighting trends or changes, and explaining their implications for your risk profile.

- **Please review and Update KRIs:** Given the rapidly changing nature of the cybersecurity landscape, review and update your KRIs regularly to ensure they remain relevant and reflect current risks. Also, adjust the thresholds and triggers to remain appropriate in light of changing risks and risk tolerance.

- **Analyze KRIs for Risk Mitigation Planning:** Use your KRIs to inform your risk mitigation planning process. By offering a clear, quantifiable picture of your risk profile, KRIs provide actionable insights that can guide decisions about where to focus risk mitigation efforts, which controls to implement, and how to allocate resources effectively. This approach can significantly enhance your organization's ability to manage and reduce cybersecurity risks.

INTEGRATING KPIs AND KRIs INTO CYBERSECURITY STRATEGY

Incorporating KPIs and KRIs into the cybersecurity strategies of an organization is of paramount importance to establish a stance that is both proactive and reliant on empirical data regarding cybersecurity. This essential integration is not merely about infusing these important metrics into the daily operational activities of the organization. It is also about aligning these metrics with existing, trusted cybersecurity frameworks, such as ISO 27001, the NIST Cybersecurity Framework, or the CIS Critical Security Controls. Such frameworks present a standardized set of guidelines that can aid in defining and setting the metrics, thereby ensuring an invaluable level of consistency and comparability across varying timeframes and different sections within the organization. This harmonious alignment of metrics and frameworks is also beneficial regarding regulatory compliance. Numerous regulations refer to these standard frameworks in their stated requirements.

Crafting effective cybersecurity metrics is far from a responsibility that should fall solely on the IT department. On the contrary, it demands the concerted efforts and collaboration of various organizational functions. For instance, the finance department can make significant contributions by providing insights on the financial repercussions of potential cybersecurity risks, thereby aiding in quantifying potential losses in terms of KRIs. The human resources department, on the other hand, can offer valuable insights into the behavior of employees and training needs. This input can inform the KPIs related to user awareness and training. Operational functions can provide practical insights into the execution and efficiency of controls. By nurturing and encouraging such cross-functional collaboration, organizations can ensure that their cybersecurity metrics are thorough and accurately represent both their risk and performance.

Once cybersecurity metrics have been created, they should not simply be left as is. Instead, they should be leveraged for continuous improvement. They should be evaluated and updated regularly to reflect the ever-changing landscape of cybersecurity, the introduction of new business objectives, and lessons learned from past performance. For example, if a KPI reveals that a certain control is not performing as effectively as initially expected, the organization should investigate why and make the necessary improvements. Similarly, if a KRI indicates a growing risk trend, the organization should delve into the cause of this trend and implement appropriate measures to manage the risk.

Lastly, but certainly not least, is the importance of communicating KPIs and KRIs to all relevant stakeholders in an effective manner. This entails presenting the data in a way that is both clear and understandable, drawing attention to key findings, and explicating what these findings mean for the organization's cybersecurity posture. Depending on the specific audience, this could involve the preparation of in-depth technical reports for IT personnel, summary dashboards for management, or high-level briefings for board members. It is crucial to tailor the communication to suit the intended audience's needs and level of understanding so they can use the information presented to them to make well-informed decisions. Furthermore, communication should not be a singular event but a consistent part of the organization's reporting cycle. This keeps all stakeholders informed of any progress and emerging issues that must be addressed.

Recommendations:

- **Align Metrics with Frameworks:** KPIs and KRIs must be integrated into your cybersecurity strategy to align with trusted cybersecurity frameworks like ISO 27001, the NIST Cybersecurity Framework, or the CIS Critical Security Controls. These frameworks provide standardized guidelines for defining and setting metrics, promoting consistency, comparability, and regulatory compliance.

- **Foster Cross-Functional Collaboration:** Creating effective cybersecurity metrics is a collective effort involving various functions within your organization. For example, your finance department can offer insights into the financial implications of potential cybersecurity risks, your human resources department can contribute information about employee behavior and training needs, and operational functions can provide practical insights into the execution and efficiency of controls.

- **Regularly Evaluate and Update Metrics:** KPIs and KRIs should be periodically assessed and updated to reflect changes in the cybersecurity landscape, new business objectives, and lessons learned from past performance. If a KPI reveals a control's subpar performance, investigate why and make necessary improvements. Similarly, if a KRI indicates a growing risk trend, delve into its cause and implement appropriate risk management measures.

- **Effectively Communicate Metrics:** Present your KPIs and KRIs clearly and understandably, highlighting key findings and explaining their implications for your cybersecurity posture. Depending on your audience, you might prepare technical reports, summary dashboards, or high-level briefings. Tailor your communication to meet your audience's needs and understanding to facilitate well-informed decisions. Consistent reporting keeps all stakeholders updated on progress and emerging issues.

Chapter Conclusion

As we conclude this chapter, it is clear that cybersecurity metrics, including KPIs and KRIs, are integral components of cybersecurity governance, risk management, and compliance. They serve as fundamental tools for measuring and evaluating the efficacy of an organization's cybersecurity controls, providing a detailed view of the risk landscape, and informing decision-making processes at all levels of the organization.

KPIs are quantifiable measurements of the efficiency and effectiveness of an organization's cybersecurity initiatives and controls. They offer a clear perspective on how well various security strategies perform, providing a platform for accountability and driving performance improvements. Developing these metrics involves aligning them with business objectives, ensuring they are realistic, specific, and measurable, and then systematically tracking and reviewing their progress over time.

In contrast, KRIs shed light on the organization's risk environment. They quantify potential risks and vulnerabilities impacting the organization's cybersecurity posture, informing risk assessment and mitigation efforts. To develop valuable KRIs, it is crucial to understand the organization's risk tolerance and appetite, identify the critical assets and associated risks, and establish relevant thresholds and triggers.

Both KPIs and KRIs require systematic monitoring and reporting mechanisms. Regular reviews, updates, and data-driven adjustments are essential to maintain the relevance and effectiveness of these metrics. Precise, targeted communication of these indicators to stakeholders further enhances their utility, ensuring that decision-makers at all levels are equipped with actionable insights.

Cybersecurity metrics also play a critical role in maintaining compliance with various regulations, industry standards, and best practices. By providing a quantifiable measure of compliance-related risks, they aid organizations in identifying areas needing improvement, prioritizing remediation activities, and demonstrating compliance to auditors and other stakeholders.

However, implementing these metrics is not without its challenges. Organizations often grapple with issues such as metric overload, unreliable data, and the need for continuous adjustments to keep pace with the rapidly evolving cybersecurity landscape. Therefore, effective use of cybersecurity metrics involves choosing the right metrics and managing them effectively.

The application of cybersecurity metrics extends beyond IT and security teams. To gain the most value from these metrics, it is vital to foster cross-functional collaboration, align the metrics with established cybersecurity frameworks, use them as tools for continuous improvement, and commu-nicate them effectively to stakeholders. Cybersecurity metrics are essential navigational tools in this context, guiding the organization toward improved security, risk management, and compliance. By understanding and effec-tively using these tools, organizations can enhance their cybersecurity pos-ture, manage risks more effectively, and demonstrate their commitment to cybersecurity to stakeholders.

Case Study: Transforming TechNova's Defense Landscape

At the advent of a significant data breach that shook TechNova, a promis-ing tech startup, to its core, CEO Robin was utterly disinterested. Despite a sizeable investment in advanced cybersecurity tools and skilled resources, the incident exposed severe vulnerabilities in the company's defensive land-scape. The breach directly hit their data reserves and impacted the com-pany's reputation, potentially jeopardizing its future growth trajectory. Robin was perplexed, as TechNova had implemented several cutting-edge cyber-security measures, anticipating a robust and secure defense system.

Upon an in-depth analysis of the incident, a glaring gap was unveiled. TechNova had invested in high-quality cybersecurity measures, but the organization lacked a comprehensive and objective understanding of its performance. Additionally, the company had not fully considered the risks lurking in the complex digital landscape. While their defenses were robust, the lack of insight into their effectiveness and blind spots rendered them incomplete.

To address this issue, Robin turned to the guiding principles outlined in this book and was introduced to the indispensable value of cybersecurity metrics. She quickly grasped how these metrics could provide a detailed, quantifiable assessment of the organization's cybersecurity health and risk exposure. Inspired and determined, she spearheaded identifying and imple-menting relevant KPIs and KRIs within TechNova's cybersecurity strategy.

For KPIs, Robin emphasized metrics that would give insight into the effectiveness and efficiency of their cybersecurity controls. These included the percentage of systems patched within a designated timeframe, the average time to detect and respond to a security incident, and the rate of successful versus false positive detections in their intrusion detection system. These KPIs were designed to offer a clear performance snapshot of the security measures in place.

In parallel, Robin ensured the establishment of KRIs, which would shed light on potential risks and vulnerabilities within the organization. These included the number of systems still pending security patches, the proportion of employees susceptible to phishing scams, and the count of high-risk vulnerabilities identified during their regular penetration testing. KRIs provided a valuable tool to quantify the risks faced by TechNova objectively, guiding their risk management strategy.

However, Robin did not stop at simply defining these metrics. She went further, ensuring the identified KPIs and KRIs were intrinsically linked with TechNova's business objectives and aligned with the organization's risk appetite and tolerance. This approach ensured that the cybersecurity strategy was not a standalone effort but a crucial component of the company's overall business direction.

In addition to establishing these metrics, Robin set up a rigorous monitoring and reporting regime. She mandated regular tracking of the KPIs and KRIs, ensuring that the reports were shared widely across the organization and fostering a culture of transparency, accountability, and cross-functional collaboration.

As the weeks turned into months, Robin witnessed a notable improvement in TechNova's cybersecurity posture. The implementation of KPIs and KRIs not only helped the organization ward off potential breaches but also offered actionable insights to optimize their cybersecurity investments and manage risks more effectively.

The most vital lesson that Robin and her team gleaned from this experience was the understanding that cybersecurity is a continuous process rather than a definitive goal. They internalized the importance of perpetual learning, adaptation, and improvement in cybersecurity, recognizing that the journey is more valuable than the destination. Armed with this wisdom and the practical application of cybersecurity metrics, TechNova stands today as a testament to the transformative power of effective cybersecurity management.

CHAPTER 10

Risk Assessments

"Cyber risk assessments are the Sherlock Holmes of the digital world, helping us uncover hidden vulnerabilities and thwart cyber villains before they strike."

Risk assessments are a key building block in establishing a strong cybersecurity program. Risk assessments' function, application, and significance in cybersecurity must be understood thoroughly. This involves grasping basic concepts and types of risk assessments and the varied regulatory perspectives on them. Valuable insights can be gleaned from exploring the viewpoints of the *Federal Financial Institutions Examination Council* (FFIEC), the *National Institute of Standards and Technology* (NIST), and third-party frameworks like *Factor Analysis of Information Risk* (FAIR), Risk IT, and *Operationally Critical Threat, Asset, and Vulnerability Evaluation* (OCTAVE). Practical advice on performing a cybersecurity risk assessment, handling risks related to third parties, and tackling common challenges in risk assessments is essential. Given the ever-evolving cybersecurity landscape, risk assessments' critical role and future implications should not be underestimated.

THE IMPORTANCE OF RISK ASSESSMENTS

Risk assessment is a fundamental process that helps organizations identify, analyze, and evaluate risks affecting their critical functions and information. It is a proactive approach that acts as the first line of defense against cyber threats, allowing organizations to anticipate and mitigate risks before they escalate into full-blown incidents.

The importance of risk assessment in cybersecurity cannot be overstated. In today's hyperconnected environment, threats can come from anywhere – internally, externally, and increasingly from sophisticated cyber-criminals. A comprehensive risk assessment helps uncover vulnerabilities and weaknesses in your systems, processes, and human elements, helping you to develop targeted strategies to protect your organization's most valuable digital assets.

A well-executed risk assessment comprises several vital components. It begins with identifying assets and understanding their value to the organization. This is followed by identifying and evaluating threats and vulnerabilities that could compromise these assets. The next step is to analyze the potential impact if these threats were realized and identify appropriate risk treatment options. Lastly, the risk assessment process involves regular monitoring and review to account for organizational or threat landscape changes.

There are several types of risk assessments that organizations can leverage, each with its unique focus and methodology. These include but are not limited to vulnerability, threat, and impact assessments. Vulnerability assessments identify, quantify, and rank vulnerabilities in a system. On the other hand, threat assessments focus on identifying the potential threats that could exploit these vulnerabilities. Impact assessments evaluate the possible consequences of a successful attack. The choice of a risk assessment type depends on the organization's specific needs, the nature of its assets, and its risk tolerance.

Recommendations:

- **Understand the Importance of Risk Assessment:** Recognize that risk assessment is a proactive approach toward cybersecurity. It helps your organization identify, analyze, and evaluate risks before they become significant incidents. By understanding its importance, you will be more inclined to integrate it as a fundamental process in your organization.

- **Identify Your Assets:** Start by identifying the various assets in your organization and understand their value. This might include hardware, software, data, personnel, and more. By doing this, you will be able to prioritize which assets require more immediate or robust protection.

- **Conduct Different Risk Assessments:** Perform various risk assessments depending on your organization's needs and assets. These might include vulnerability assessments, threat assessments, and impact assessments. Each type of assessment will provide a unique focus and understanding of the risks your organization might face.

- **Evaluate Threats and Vulnerabilities:** Once your assets are identified, the next step is to find and evaluate any threats and vulnerabilities that could compromise these assets. This evaluation helps you understand the extent of potential damage and the likelihood of each risk occurring.

- **Analyze Potential Impacts:** Estimate the possible impact or consequences if the identified threats were to be realized. This includes the cost of potential damage, downtime, loss of reputation, and more.

- **Choose Appropriate Risk Treatment Options:** Identify suitable treatment options based on the risk assessment results. This might include avoiding the risk, mitigating the risk, transferring the risk, or accepting the risk. The choice depends on your organization's risk tolerance.
- **Implement Regular Monitoring and Review:** The cyber threat landscape is continually evolving, and so should your risk assessment strategy. Regularly review and update your risk assessments to account for any changes in your organization or the threat landscape.

THE FFIEC's PERSPECTIVE ON RISK ASSESSMENTS

The FFIEC, a reputable interagency body comprised of several US government agencies, is bestowed with the crucial responsibility of establishing standards for risk assessment within the context of financial institutions. This integral role the FFIEC plays involves fostering a culture that encourages financial institutions to see risk assessments as more than a compliance activity. In the FFIEC's view, risk assessments are not isolated, infrequent movements; they are a regular and foundational part of an organization's operations intertwined with the overall risk management process. While it is not required for any business outside of its remit, the FFIEC can provide excellent guidance to any business.

The integration of risk assessments into the overall risk management process is what distinguishes the FFIEC's approach. The organization does not merely encourage financial institutions to conduct risk assessments but mandates these assessments as part of their compliance. The reasoning is straightforward: consistent and well-executed risk assessments enable institutions to identify their unique vulnerabilities and, in doing so, align their cybersecurity practices with their defined risk profiles. Risk profiles are dynamic, fluctuating with changes in the business environment, technological advancements, and evolving threat landscapes. Thus, risk assessments must be ongoing to capture these changes accurately and promptly.

As the FFIEC points out, risk assessments are pivotal to compliance with its guidelines. In effect, compliance is not an end in itself; instead, it is a byproduct of an efficient risk management process where risk assessments play a significant role. The principle is that compliance naturally follows if an organization understands its risk profile and manages those risks effectively. Hence, the FFIEC's emphasis on risk assessments is more about securing financial institutions from cyber threats and less about ticking regulatory checkboxes.

FFIEC extends its role beyond issuing guidelines by providing many tools and resources designed to facilitate the risk assessment process for organizations. The *Cybersecurity Assessment Tool* (CAT), provided by the FFIEC, stands out in its utility. It is a comprehensive resource tailored to aid financial institutions in identifying their risk level and evaluating the maturity of their cybersecurity programs. The tool allows organizations to compare their capabilities against pre-established criteria, effectively providing a benchmark and a roadmap for continuous improvement. It encourages organizations not just to identify and mitigate risks but also to enhance their cybersecurity controls continuously.

The FFIEC's Information Security Handbook also offers valuable insights into risk assessments. This comprehensive guide is a treasure trove of information security best practices for financial institutions. The handbook dedicates significant attention to risk assessments, signifying its importance in maintaining an organization's security posture.

Within this document, the FFIEC highlights that risk assessments are not standalone activities. Instead, they are deeply entwined within the broader information security risk management process. These assessments form the basis for understanding the potential threats, vulnerabilities, and impacts that an institution may face, which then informs the development and implementation of effective risk mitigation strategies.

The handbook provides detailed guidance on conducting risk assessments, from identifying and assessing potential threats and vulnerabilities to evaluating the effectiveness of existing controls. It emphasizes considering risk from internal and external perspectives, incorporating technological advancements, evolving threat landscapes, and business operations or objectives changes.

The effectiveness of the FFIEC's guidance on risk assessment can be seen in the numerous success stories of financial institutions. Many organizations have strategically implemented the FFIEC's methodologies to identify their most prominent risks. In addition to risk identification, these methodologies have been used to devise robust strategies to mitigate these risks. The result is a marked enhancement of their overall security posture and assured compliance with regulatory requirements. These success stories testify to the efficacy of the FFIEC's approach to risk assessment, underlining the importance of regular risk assessments as a cornerstone of sound cybersecurity practice.

Recommendations:

- **Recognize the Role of the FFIEC:** The FFIEC plays an integral role in establishing standards for risk assessment in financial institutions. Understand its importance in fostering a culture that encourages regular and thorough risk assessments as a key part of an organization's operations.

- **Adopt the FFIEC's Approach to Risk Assessments:** Integrate risk assessments into your overall risk management process. The FFIEC's approach mandates consistent and well-executed risk assessments to identify unique vulnerabilities, align cybersecurity practices, and keep up with changing business environments and threat landscapes.

- **Understand the Role of Compliance:** The FFIEC emphasizes that compliance should not be the end goal but a byproduct of effective risk management. Compliance will naturally follow if your organization understands its risk profile and manages those risks effectively.

- **Utilize the FFIEC's Resources:** The FFIEC provides many tools and resources designed to facilitate the risk assessment process. Consider using the CAT to identify your organization's risk level and evaluate the maturity of its cybersecurity program.

- **Consult the FFIEC's Information Security Handbook:** The handbook provides detailed guidance on conducting risk assessments and maintaining an organization's security posture. It is a comprehensive guide to information security best practices for financial institutions, focusing significantly on risk assessments.

- **Incorporate Regular Risk Assessments:** Risk assessments should be ongoing to capture changes in the business environment, technology, and threat landscape accurately and promptly. They should form the basis for understanding potential threats, vulnerabilities, and impacts.

- **Learn from Success Stories:** Many financial institutions have successfully implemented the FFIEC's methodologies for risk assessments, which have resulted in enhanced security postures and assured compliance with regulatory requirements. Learn from these success stories and apply these methodologies in your organization.

NIST's APPROACH TO RISK ASSESSMENTS

The NIST, an agency under the U.S. Department of Commerce, is known for its holistic and detailed approach to risk assessments. This approach, designed to provide an encompassing view of an organization's risk landscape, ensures that all areas of potential threats are examined, addressed, and accounted for. An all-encompassing approach such as this not only highlights the risk potential but also provides a structured methodology for understanding the overall cybersecurity posture of an organization.

One of NIST's most notable contributions is the *Risk Management Framework (RMF)*, as detailed in NIST Special Publication (SP) 800-37. This comprehensive framework offers a step-by-step guide for integrating risk management into an organization's procedures. It traverses the entire risk management spectrum, from the initial step of categorizing information systems based on the data they handle and their operational nature to the final stage of continuous monitoring and improvement. The RMF's structured and strategic approach to risk management emphasizes the importance of incorporating risk management into an organization's operations.

Within this overarching framework, NIST SP 800-30 plays a critical role by focusing specifically on the nuances of risk assessments. SP 800-30 establishes comprehensive guidelines for executing risk assessments as a critical component of the more extensive risk management process. It underscores the need to identify and assess risk to various elements, including organizational operations, assets, individuals, other organizations, and even the nation. This wide-angle view of potential risk areas demonstrates NIST's commitment to comprehensive risk understanding and management.

NIST's risk assessment approach promotes an iterative and dynamic process. The process begins with identifying threats and vulnerabilities that could impact an organization's information systems. Subsequently, risk is determined by analyzing the potential impact of these threats and vulnerabilities. Based on this risk determination, appropriate controls are chosen and implemented to manage these risks. This structured process ensures that risks are identified and adequately addressed.

Beyond identifying and managing risks, NIST SP 800-30 underscores the importance of continuous feedback and learning. This iterative approach ensures that risk assessments are not static but evolve with the changing threat landscape. By promoting constant feedback, NIST encourages organizations to learn from their previous experiences, adapt their strategies as needed, and improve their risk assessments continually. This forward-thinking stance indicates a comprehensive life-cycle approach where every aspect of the risk management process is constantly refined for effectiveness.

Using NIST's frameworks and guidelines can significantly enhance an organization's risk assessments. The frameworks, including RMF and NIST SP 800-30 guidelines, provide a clear roadmap for conducting practical risk assessments. These guidelines align with industry standards and provide consistency and comprehensiveness, often missing in less structured approaches. By adopting NIST's methodologies, organizations can ensure that their risk assessments are all-inclusive, aligned with prevailing industry standards, and tailored to their unique risk profile. Thus, NIST's approach to risk assessments provides a blueprint for proactive and efficient risk management.

Recommendations:

- **Acknowledge NIST's Approach:** NIST's holistic and detailed risk assessment approach allows organizations to examine, address, and account for all areas of potential threats. It helps to understand the overall cybersecurity posture of an organization.
- **Implement NIST's RMF:** The RMF, as detailed in NIST Special Publication (SP) 800-37, provides a comprehensive guide for integrating risk management into an organization's procedures. Its strategic approach emphasizes the importance of incorporating risk management into operations.
- **Refer to NIST SP 800-30 for Risk Assessment Guidelines:** This document focuses on the nuances of risk assessments, establishing comprehensive guidelines for executing risk assessments as a part of the broader risk management process. It underscores the need to identify and assess risk across various organizational aspects.
- **Follow NIST's Iterative and Dynamic Process:** Identify threats and vulnerabilities, analyze the potential impact, and then choose and implement appropriate controls to manage these risks. This structured process ensures that risks are identified and adequately addressed.
- **Emphasize Continuous Feedback and Learning:** NIST encourages an iterative approach where risk assessments evolve with the changing

threat landscape. The institution encourages organizations to learn from previous experiences and improve risk assessments.

- **Utilize NIST's Frameworks and Guidelines:** NIST's frameworks, including RMF and SP 800-30, provide a roadmap for conducting practical risk assessments. Adopting these methodologies ensures that your risk assessments are all-inclusive, aligned with industry standards, and tailored to your unique risk profile. This adoption leads to proactive and efficient risk management.

- **Recognize the Value of NIST's Life-Cycle Approach:** The organization promotes a comprehensive life-cycle approach where every aspect of the risk management process is continually refined for effectiveness. This forward-thinking stance ensures that organizations stay ahead of evolving cyber threats.

RISK ASSESSMENT FRAMEWORKS

The FAIR presents a quantitative methodology emphasizing a detailed and systematic approach to risk assessments. FAIR revolves around the comprehensive examination and definition of various risk components, their relationships, and how they collectively shape an organization's information and operational risk landscape. This methodology allows for a more granular, mathematical comprehension of risks, turning abstract concepts into quantifiable entities. This transformation is crucial for precision and targeted risk management.

In practice, the FAIR methodology's ability to provide detailed insights into potential risks enables organizations to concentrate on significant risks. This focus facilitates the creation of targeted and precise strategies for risk mitigation. FAIR, therefore, provides a risk management solution that is both precise and applicable, making it an ideal tool for organizations seeking to streamline their risk management processes.

Of particular note is FAIR's reception in the financial sector, where the ability to convert cyber risk into financial terms is of significant value. This unique feature allows for an intuitive understanding of cyber risks and makes it easier for nontechnical stakeholders to grasp the implications of these risks. By translating cyber risk into financial terms, FAIR simplifies the experience and allows for a more targeted and cost-effective approach to risk management.

The Risk IT Framework, pioneered by ISACA, takes a holistic and integrated approach to risk management. The framework's design seamlessly aligns with other globally recognized ISACA frameworks, such as COBIT, facilitating a comprehensive and uniform view of IT risk management. The Risk IT Framework pivots on harmonizing IT risk with business risk, recognizing that they are not separate entities but interlinked components that jointly shape an organization's risk profile.

This holistic view extends to the very fabric of the organization. The Risk IT Framework emphasizes the need for risk management to be a collective responsibility, extending beyond just the IT department to involve the entire organization. This comprehensive involvement fosters a more inclusive and holistic risk management strategy, where diverse perspectives contribute to a more effective risk management approach.

Another noteworthy framework is OCTAVE, developed by the Software Engineering Institute (SEI) of Carnegie Mellon University. OCTAVE presents a flexible framework that promotes an organization-specific approach to identifying and managing security risks. Recognizing that every organization is unique, OCTAVE tailors its risk management approach to align with an organization's specific needs and operational practices.

What sets OCTAVE apart is its focus on organizational risk rather than purely on IT risk. This broader perspective on risk management recognizes that risks are not confined to the IT department but permeate the entire organization. By broadening the scope of risk management, OCTAVE promotes a more comprehensive understanding and management of risks, thereby providing a practical and relevant solution in today's complex and interconnected business environment.

Recommendations:

- **Understand and Apply FAIR Methodology:** The FAIR presents a quantitative approach to risk assessments that allows for a more granular, mathematical comprehension of risks. This methodology transforms abstract risk concepts into quantifiable entities, leading to precise and targeted risk management.

- **Leverage FAIR in Financial Contexts:** FAIR is particularly valuable in the financial sector due to its ability to convert cyber risk into financial terms. Use it to foster an intuitive understanding of cyber risks and make risk management implications more accessible to nontechnical stakeholders.

- **Use the Risk IT Framework by ISACA:** This framework emphasizes the alignment of IT risk with business risk and promotes the collective responsibility for risk management across the entire organization. Use it to cultivate a more inclusive and holistic risk management strategy.

- **Integrate Other ISACA Frameworks:** The Risk IT Framework seamlessly aligns with other globally recognized ISACA frameworks, like COBIT. Take advantage of this integration to facilitate a comprehensive and uniform view of IT risk management.

- **Implement the OCTAVE Framework:** The Operationally Critical Threat, Asset, and Vulnerability Evaluation (OCTAVE) framework promotes an organization-specific approach to identifying and managing security risks. As it focuses on organizational risk rather than just IT risk, it offers a broader perspective on risk management.

- **Adapt the OCTAVE Approach to Your Organization:** Recognizing that every organization is unique, OCTAVE tailors its risk management approach to align with specific operational practices. Use this flexibility to adapt the framework to your organization's needs and circumstances.

- **Encourage Broad Participation in Risk Management:** Risk IT and OCTAVE frameworks emphasize that risk management is not confined to the IT department but is a responsibility that permeates the entire organization. Promote this approach within your organization to enhance the effectiveness of your risk management strategies.

CONDUCTING A CYBERSECURITY RISK ASSESSMENT

A solid cybersecurity risk assessment begins with meticulously defining its scope and objectives. Being lucid about what the evaluation aims to achieve is the linchpin that holds the entire operation together. The goals will answer the critical question of "why" the assessment is being conducted, whether for compliance purposes, to identify vulnerabilities, or to implement new cybersecurity measures. Understanding the objectives will help strategize the risk assessment effectively, ensuring all efforts are aligned with the organization's broader goals.

Meanwhile, the scope demarcates the boundaries of the assessment, setting limits on what will be examined. It could include specific IT systems, data centers, databases, or business processes. The scope could also define the kind of threats to consider, including internal threats, external threats, or both. Being precise about the scope prevents unnecessary broadening of the process, focusing energy and resources only on areas that matter most to the organization.

Once the scope and objectives are set, the next crucial step involves identifying and categorizing your assets. This process, often referred to as an asset inventory, entails logging every resource, be it tangible or intangible, that contributes to the organization's operation and carries value. This includes hardware like servers and workstations, software applications, critical data, intellectual property, and human resources. Each asset should then be classified based on its significance to the organization's functionality, its value, and its role in achieving the company's objectives. This process helps understand the possible impact if any asset is compromised, thereby assisting in prioritizing security measures.

Upon understanding the organization's assets, the next phase includes threat and vulnerability analysis. Threats refer to any event, actor, or action that could exploit a vulnerability to damage your assets. These could range from natural disasters to human errors and malicious cyberattacks. On the other hand, vulnerabilities refer to weaknesses or gaps in the security defenses that make your assets susceptible to threats. A comprehensive understanding of your threat landscape and vulnerabilities lays the groundwork for accurately evaluating your risks.

The ensuing step is risk analysis and evaluation, a process that blends the threat and vulnerability analysis results with the value of the affected assets. It assesses the likelihood of a threat exploiting a vulnerability and its impact on the organization. This evaluation allows you to rank risks based on their potential impact on your organization, providing critical input for your risk treatment strategy.

Finally, perhaps one of the most significant steps of a risk assessment is the comprehensive documentation and reporting of all the information accrued throughout the process. This documentation serves several vital functions; it depicts the organization's current risk posture, provides substantial evidence for compliance audits, provides invaluable input for management decision-making, and creates a benchmark for future risk assessments. It also aids communication across the organization, promoting a shared understanding of risks, their implications, and the chosen mitigation strategies.

Recommendations:

- **Define the Scope and Objectives:** Start your cybersecurity risk assessment by clearly defining its scope and objectives. The objectives will determine "why" the assessment is being conducted, while the scope will demarcate the boundaries of what will be examined.
- **Conduct an Asset Inventory:** Identify and categorize your assets, including tangible and intangible resources contributing to your organization's operation. Classify each asset based on its importance to your organization's functionality, value, and role in achieving your objectives.
- **Conduct Threat and Vulnerability Analysis:** Identify potential threats that could exploit vulnerabilities in your assets and understand the weaknesses or gaps in your security defenses. This understanding lays the groundwork for accurately evaluating your risks.
- **Undertake Risk Analysis and Evaluation:** Evaluate the likelihood of threats exploiting vulnerabilities and their potential impact on your organization. This evaluation will help you rank the risks and form the basis for your risk treatment strategy.
- **Document and Report Findings:** Document all the information accrued throughout the process. This documentation serves multiple functions – it depicts your organization's current risk posture, provides substantial evidence for compliance audits, supports management decision-making, and creates a benchmark for future risk assessments.
- **Communicate the Findings:** Use the documentation to communicate across the organization, promoting a shared understanding of risks, their implications, and the chosen mitigation strategies. This can foster collective responsibility and engagement in managing cybersecurity risks.

MANAGING THIRD-PARTY RISKS

Third-party risks are inherent in relationships your organization maintains with external entities, suppliers, service providers, business partners, or customers. While beneficial for business operations, these relationships extend your cyber risk landscape to include systems and practices beyond your direct control.

Factors such as these entities' cybersecurity posture, regulatory compliance, and internal policies play a significant role in the risk they pose. Acknowledging these potential threats and their implications is the foundational step toward effective third-party risk management.

To accurately evaluate the risks presented by third parties, a thorough investigation and review of their cybersecurity hygiene are required. This investigative process comprises a multifaceted review of their security policies, protocols, procedures, and controls. For instance, examining their policies on password management, access controls, data encryption, and security awareness training could provide insights into their cybersecurity maturity level. Furthermore, their procedures related to software updates, patch management, and threat intelligence could indicate their preparedness to respond to emerging cybersecurity threats.

Auditing third-party systems and processes also forms an integral part of the assessment. Such audits might include vulnerability assessments and penetration tests to discover potential weaknesses malicious actors could exploit. Ideally performed by independent, certified professionals, these tests can provide a reliable evaluation of the third party's security measures.

Evaluating the third party's incident response capabilities is also crucial. Understanding how they detect, respond to, and recover from security incidents can provide valuable insights into their ability to manage potential crises. For instance, you would want to know if they have a dedicated security team, how they handle data breaches, how quickly they can restore operations, and how they learn from security incidents to prevent future occurrences.

Once third-party risks have been identified, the following step involves developing tailored strategies to mitigate these risks. These strategies might include incorporating strict security stipulations into contracts and *service level agreements* (SLAs), implementing robust data access controls, and mandating regular third-party security reviews. Contractual clauses might include the right to audit, requirements for data protection, and the obligation to report security incidents within a stipulated time.

In addition to these measures, establishing a robust incident response plan that includes third parties is crucial. Such a plan should outline the procedures for notifying each other of incidents, coordinating the response, sharing necessary information, and post-incident review.

Nevertheless, managing third-party risks is not a one-and-done event. Given cybersecurity threats' dynamic and evolving nature, monitoring third-party relationships and risk management is indispensable. Regular audits, performance reviews, SLA adherence, and constant communication are all integral to an ongoing third-party risk management program. It is also crucial to stay informed about any significant changes in the third party's business, such as mergers, acquisitions, or changes in leadership, as these could impact their risk profile.

Finally, remember that your organization's reputation is intertwined with your third parties. If they suffer a data breach or other security incident, your organization could face reputational damage, even if your internal systems and procedures are secure. Therefore, it is best to ensure that your third parties maintain adequate security and are responsive in managing and mitigating risks.

Recommendations:

- **Acknowledge Third-Party Risks:** Understand that third-party relationships extend your cyber risk landscape to systems and practices beyond your direct control. Consider factors like these entities' cybersecurity posture, regulatory compliance, and internal policies.
- **Review Third-Party Cybersecurity Hygiene:** Conduct a multifaceted review of third parties' security policies, protocols, procedures, and controls. Examine their practices related to password management, access controls, data encryption, security awareness training, software updates, patch management, and threat intelligence.
- **Conduct Third-Party System Audits:** Perform vulnerability assessments and penetration tests on third-party systems and processes to discover potential weaknesses. Ideally, these should be performed by independent, certified professionals.
- **Evaluate Incident Response Capabilities:** Understand third parties' abilities to detect, respond to, and recover from security incidents. Gain insights into their security team, data breach management, restoration speed, and lessons learned from previous security incidents.
- **Develop Mitigation Strategies:** After identifying third-party risks, create tailored strategies to mitigate these risks. This could involve incorporating strict security stipulations into contracts and SLAs, implementing robust data access controls, and mandating regular third-party security reviews.
- **Create a Robust Incident Response Plan:** Establish a plan outlining procedures for notifying each other of incidents, coordinating the response, sharing necessary information, and conducting post-incident review.
- **Monitor Third-Party Relationships:** Given the evolving nature of cybersecurity threats, regular audits, performance reviews, SLA adherence, and constant communication are essential for an ongoing third-party risk management program. Stay informed about any significant changes in the third party's business.
- **Protect Your** Reputation: Security incidents involving third parties can impact your organization's reputation. Ensure that your third parties maintain adequate security and proactively manage and mitigate risks.

CHALLENGES AND BEST PRACTICES IN RISK ASSESSMENTS

Risk assessments, an integral part of any robust cybersecurity program, can often be complex due to various complicating factors. These challenges can span from fundamental issues like a lack of understanding about the assets that need to be assessed and their potential vulnerabilities to resource constraints regarding workforce and technological capacity. Understanding the scope and scale of what needs to be included in a risk assessment can be daunting, especially for larger organizations with extensive digital infrastructures.

Another hurdle in the risk assessment process is the constantly evolving landscape of cyber threats. Cyber threats are not static; they change and adapt rapidly, fueled by technological advancements and the increasing sophistication of cybercriminals. New forms of malware, techniques of social engineering, and vulnerabilities in new technology are all evolving in real time. Therefore, risk assessments need to account for this dynamic nature of cybersecurity, which can be pretty challenging.

Subjectivity in assessing risk levels can also pose significant problems. Different stakeholders may have varying perceptions of what constitutes a "high" or "low" risk, leading to inconsistencies in the risk assessment. This is further complicated by variations in risk appetite among stakeholders. Some individuals or departments might be more risk-tolerant than others, influencing their judgment when prioritizing risks.

Quantifying risks is another common challenge. Cyber risks are not always easily measurable, mainly when calculating the potential impact of a data breach or cyberattack in financial terms. Indirect costs, such as reputational damage or loss of customer trust, can be challenging to quantify but could impact the organization's long-term health.

To address these challenges, several best practices have proven effective. First, active involvement from all relevant stakeholders is crucial, including but not limited to the IT team. This engagement should involve members from senior management, legal, human resources, public relations, and other key departments. Their collective expertise can provide a more holistic view of the organization's risks and risk appetite, leading to a more comprehensive risk assessment.

Furthermore, shifting the risk assessment perspective from a one-time event to an ongoing process can significantly enhance its accuracy and relevance. As the cybersecurity landscape is dynamic, a risk assessment must be equally fluid, with regular updates, reviews, and revisions. This approach can ensure that the risk assessment remains pertinent in the face of evolving threats and organizational changes.

Using tools and technology can also significantly enhance the effectiveness of risk assessments. Various risk assessment tools and software are available in the market, providing features like automated data gathering, risk calculation, and reporting capabilities. These tools can simplify the process, increase efficiency, and reduce the chance of human error.

Moreover, *artificial intelligence* (AI) and *machine learning* (ML) can offer advanced analytical capabilities, transforming raw data into actionable insights. They can identify patterns and trends that may be missed by human analysts, thereby improving the accuracy of risk assessments.

Technology can also facilitate communication and collaboration among teams. Collaborative platforms can ensure that all relevant personnel are informed and updated about the risk assessment's progress and outcomes. Moreover, technology is pivotal to continuously monitoring the risk landscape, providing real-time alerts about new threats and vulnerabilities.

Finally, an external perspective can often provide valuable insights. Engaging third-party cybersecurity experts for audits or risk assessments can bring an unbiased view and potentially highlight risks internal teams may have overlooked. Their specialized knowledge and experience can add significant value to the risk assessment. In summary, while the challenges to conducting risk assessments are substantial, they can be effectively managed with thoughtful planning, stakeholder involvement, and leveraging the right technology and expertise.

Recommendations:

- **Understand Scope and Scale:** Grasp the complexity inherent in risk assessments, which a variety of factors such as the number and type of assets at risk, potential vulnerabilities in systems and processes, and resource constraints may influence. These complexities make comprehensive risk assessments a challenging but essential endeavor.
- **Acknowledge the Evolving Cyber Threat Landscape:** The landscape of cyber threats is dynamic and changes rapidly due to technological advancements and the growing sophistication of cybercriminals. As such, one of the key challenges in risk assessments is keeping pace with these shifts and evolving threats.
- **Address Subjectivity in Risk Levels:** Remember that perceptions of risk levels can differ among stakeholders, leading to potential inconsistencies in risk assessments. Different departments or individuals within the organization may also have varying risk appetites, which should be considered when assessing and managing risk.
- **Quantify Risks:** The task of quantifying cyber risks, particularly indirect costs such as reputational damage or loss of customer trust, poses a significant challenge. Nonetheless, measuring these risks as accurately as possible is crucial to a comprehensive risk assessment.
- **Involve All Relevant Stakeholders:** Ensure stakeholders from different departments actively participate in risk assessments. This involvement can provide a more holistic view of the organization's risk profile and help establish an organization-wide understanding of risk tolerance.
- **View Risk Assessment as an Ongoing Process:** Risk assessment is not a one-time activity but rather an ongoing process that needs regular updates, reviews, and revisions to keep up with the dynamic nature of the cybersecurity landscape.
- **Leverage Tools and Technology:** Harness the power of risk assessment tools, AI, and ML for efficient and accurate data gathering, risk calculation,

reporting, and advanced analysis. These technologies can enhance the efficiency and accuracy of risk assessments.

- **Facilitate Communication and Collaboration:** Use technology to Foster effective team communication and continuous risk landscape monitoring. This approach can improve team collaboration and ensure they remain vigilant and responsive to changes in the risk environment.
- **Seek an External Perspective:** Enlist the help of third-party cybersecurity experts to gain unbiased insights. Their external perspective can highlight potential risks or vulnerabilities that internal teams may overlook.
- **Leverage Planning, Stakeholder Involvement, and Technology:** Address the challenges of risk assessments by integrating careful planning, comprehensive stakeholder involvement, and strategic use of technology and external expertise. Such a comprehensive approach can significantly enhance the effectiveness of your risk management efforts.

Chapter Conclusion

Comprehensive risk assessments are the cornerstone of any cybersecurity strategy, serving as the lighthouse guiding organizations through the stormy seas of potential threats and vulnerabilities. Identifying the most critical vulnerabilities enables organizations to channel their finite resources effectively and efficiently, focusing on significant risk areas. This focus ensures that the highest threats are dealt with first, significantly enhancing the organization's security. Moreover, risk assessments contribute to more than just a strong security posture; they are vital to a comprehensive, holistic security program.

Regulatory compliance is another crucial area where risk assessments play a key role. Many regulations, standards, and guidelines mandate organizations to conduct risk assessments to ensure adequate security measures. Hence, risk assessments help in providing the necessary documentation and evidence to demonstrate compliance during audits. Organizations can avoid penalties, preserve their reputation, and maintain stakeholder trust by mitigating compliance risk.

Given the continuous evolution of the cybersecurity landscape, organizations must stay informed about emerging threats and vulnerabilities. Hackers constantly devise new ways to breach defenses, exploit vulnerabilities, and compromise systems. Hence, organizations must ensure that their risk assessment methodologies are updated regularly, reflecting the current threat landscape. This vigilance is critical to maintaining a proactive stance against cyber threats.

Organizations can leverage the latest tools and technologies to keep abreast of the dynamic cybersecurity landscape. These tools can automate various aspects of the risk assessment process, improve accuracy, and provide real-time threat intelligence. Moreover, participation in cybersecurity forums, threat intelligence sharing platforms, and professional networks can provide invaluable insights about new threats, mitigation techniques, and best practices.

As we look toward the future, it becomes increasingly evident that risk assessments will continue to be vital to cybersecurity. With the advent of emerging technologies such as AI, quantum computing, and the Internet of Things, the nature and scale of cyber risks are set to change dramatically. These technologies introduce new threats and vulnerabilities that traditional risk assessment methodologies may not adequately cover.

For instance, AI could be exploited by hackers to launch sophisticated attacks that are hard to detect and prevent. Quantum computing could threaten cryptographic systems, potentially making current encryption methods obsolete. The exponential increase in connected devices due to the Internet of Things expands the attack surface significantly, introducing numerous new potential entry points for attackers.

Given these emerging risks, organizations must be prepared to adapt and enhance their risk assessment practices continuously. They must incorporate these new types of risks into their assessments, revise their mitigation strategies, and potentially invest in new security technologies. This evolution will require organizations to be flexible, innovative, and committed to continuous learning. In essence, the importance of risk assessments in cybersecurity cannot be overstated – they are, and will continue to be, a critical tool in the fight against cyber threats.

Case Study: Utilizing Risk Assessments in Cybersecurity: The Journey of Innovative Tech Solutions

Innovative Tech Solutions (ITS), a burgeoning tech startup offering cutting-edge, AI-powered solutions to its growing clientele, grappled with various cybersecurity challenges. Despite implementing comprehensive security measures to safeguard its digital assets, the company continued to experience minor yet concerning security incidents. At this critical juncture, Mayra, the company's astute *Chief Information Security Officer* (CISO), recognized the vital need for a comprehensive and systematic risk assessment. She was cognizant that such a process would not only shed light on their cybersecurity framework's hidden vulnerabilities. Still, she would also be the foundation for a robust, proactive strategy to mitigate potential threats.

Acting upon her insight, Mayra commenced the elaborate risk assessment process by clearly defining its scope. She held a series of collaborative discussions with department heads from across the organization, meticulously outlining the vast array of systems, datasets, and operational processes that formed the lifeblood of ITS. She made a concerted effort to ensure that the risk assessment process was holistic and inclusive, involving every stakeholder in the company, from the tech-savvy IT team to the nontechnical personnel. This approach marked the first and essential step toward developing a comprehensive security program that extended beyond the confines of the IT department and encompassed the organization's entire landscape.

With the scope defined, Mayra embarked on the daunting task of identifying and categorizing the organization's myriad assets. She left no stone unturned, from mission-critical software applications and confidential customer data to vital hardware components and the company's talented human resources. Each purchase was meticulously cataloged and assigned a category based on its importance to the organization's operations and overall strategic objectives. This exhaustive categorization formed the backbone of the subsequent threat and vulnerability analysis.

During this phase, Mayra employed an array of sophisticated risk assessment tools. The deployment of these advanced tools proved to be a pivotal move, automating a significant portion of the process, providing invaluable analytics, and facilitating the continuous monitoring of ITS' evolving risk landscape. This technological leverage expedited the assessment process and enhanced its precision and depth, highlighting vulnerabilities that might have otherwise remained hidden.

Mayra did not overlook the company's extensive network of third-party associations during the risk assessment. Like many other tech startups, ITS had established relationships with various external entities, ranging from suppliers and service providers to strategic business partners. While these relationships were instrumental in driving the company's growth, Mayra was aware that they also introduced additional, indirect cybersecurity risks. Hence, she led her dedicated team in a thorough evaluation of the security postures of each third-party entity. They reviewed their partners' security policies, conducted audits, and scrutinized their incident response capabilities, leaving no room for hidden vulnerabilities.

Beyond the initial assessment, Mayra was committed to implementing long-term measures to ensure the company's security. She recognized that managing third-party risks was not a one-time event but a continuous requirement, so she worked with her team to incorporate stringent security requirements into all contracts. They implemented robust data access controls, regularly reviewed third-party practices, and established a comprehensive incident response plan that included all partners.

The lessons gleaned from the process were far from over after completing the comprehensive risk assessment. They marked a new beginning. Mayra understood the inherent dynamism of cybersecurity risks and the need for risk assessments to be ongoing, living processes rather than static, one-time events. As part of their risk management strategy, regular performance reviews, rigorous audits, and constant communication became part and parcel of the company's culture. With her foresight, diligence, and unwavering commitment to cybersecurity, Mayra revolutionized ITS' approach to risk management. Her leadership enabled the company to preemptively identify and manage risks and instilled a culture of cybersecurity consciousness throughout the organization.

RISK ASSESSMENT TEMPLATE EXAMPLE

The following provides a detailed example of a risk assessment conducted by ITS, a dynamic tech startup specializing in AI-powered solutions. Despite establishing robust security measures, ITS faced minor security incidents, which raised significant concerns for the leadership team. Recognizing the need to fortify their cybersecurity framework and tackle potential threats proactively, the CISO, Mayra, undertook a comprehensive risk assessment. The aim was to scrutinize every element of the organization's cybersecurity landscape, from its assets and potential vulnerabilities to the practices of third-party entities, and devise an effective risk management strategy. This illustrative risk assessment outlines the entire process, from defining the scope to the continual risk assessment strategy, setting a benchmark for future cybersecurity endeavors.

1. **Scope Definition:**
   - **Objective:** Strengthen the cybersecurity framework of ITS to identify and mitigate potential threats.
   - **Key Stakeholders:** CISO (Mayra), IT team, HR, Legal, Operations, Sales, Marketing, and any third-party vendors or partners.
   - **Boundaries:** All digital and physical assets and processes across the organization, including third-party vendors and off-site assets.
   - **Time Frame:** Start Date–End Date.
   - **Risk Assessment Team:** Mayra (CISO), IT security specialists, third-party risk manager, etc.
   - **Compliance Requirements:** Specific cybersecurity or industry regulations that it must adhere to.
2. **Asset Identification, Classification, and Valuation:**
   - **Asset 1:** Customer Database
     - **Type:** Data
     - **Classification:** Confidential
     - **Value:** High (a key component of business operations and customer trust)

- **Asset 2:** Proprietary AI Software
  - **Type:** Intellectual Property
  - **Classification:** Confidential
  - **Value:** Very High (primary product offering and competitive advantage)
- **Asset 3:** Employee Laptops
  - **Type:** Hardware
  - **Classification:** Internal Use
  - **Value:** Medium (used for work-related tasks)
- **Asset 4:** Office Network Infrastructure
  - **Type:** Network
  - **Classification:** Internal Use
  - **Value:** High (core to day-to-day operations and overall productivity)

3. **Threat Identification and Vulnerability Analysis:**
   - **Threat 1:** External Cyberattacks
     - **Associated Vulnerabilities:** Outdated Firewall on office network infrastructure, lack of multifactor authentication for access to the customer database
     - **Potential Impacts:** Data breach, service disruption, reputational damage, financial loss
   - **Threat 2:** Data leakage through third-party associations
     - **Associated Vulnerabilities:** Insufficient security measures at third-party entities, lack of stringent data handling protocols
     - **Potential Impacts:** Intellectual property theft, financial loss, legal repercussions, reputational damage

4. **Risk Analysis, Evaluation, and Prioritization:**
   - **Risk 1:** Breach of customer data due to cyberattacks
     - **Impact:** High (financial loss, reputational damage, potential legal liabilities)
     - **Likelihood:** Medium (due to outdated firewall and lack of Multi-Factor Authentication (MFA))
     - **Priority:** High
   - **Risk 2:** Confidential information leak through third-party associations
     - **Impact:** High (loss of proprietary information, potential legal issues)
     - **Likelihood:** Low (third parties have agreed to enhance their security measures)
     - **Priority:** Medium

5. **Risk Treatment Strategy:**
   - **Risk 1 Treatment:** Update the Firewall, Implement multifactor authentication for all databases, and train employees on safe online practices.
   - **Risk 2 Treatment:** Incorporate stringent security requirements into contracts, conduct Regular audits of third-party practices, and educate third parties on ITS's security standards.

6. **Risk Treatment Implementation:**
   - **Action Plan:** Detailed steps to implement the treatment strategy, including assigned tasks, deadlines, and resources required.
   - **Monitoring Process:** Regular checks to ensure that the treatment strategy is implemented as planned and effective.

7. **Documentation, Reporting, and Communication:**
   - **Findings:** Detailed findings from the risk assessment, including identified risks, vulnerabilities, and potential impacts.
   - **Recommended Actions:** Concrete steps are recommended to mitigate identified risks.
   - **Risk Assessment Report:** Comprehensive document summarizing the process, findings, and recommendations.
   - **Communication Plan:** How and when the findings will be communicated to stakeholders.

8. **Continual Risk Assessment Strategy:**
   - **Review and Update Frequency:** The risk assessment should be reviewed and updated every six months or in response to significant changes to the business, technology, or threat landscape.
   - **Ongoing Monitoring:** Implement tools and processes for continuously monitoring identified and new potential risks.
   - **Continuous Improvement:** Regularly update and improve the risk assessment methodology, tools, and skills based on lessons learned and industry best practices.

CHAPTER 11

NIST Cybersecurity Framework

"Cybersecurity is not a game of chance but a strategic battle, and the NIST CSF equips you with the intelligence and resources needed to make informed decisions, enabling you to outmaneuver threats and emerge victorious."

The National Institute of Standards and Technology Cybersecurity Framework (NIST CSF) is a pivotal structure in cybersecurity. A thorough introduction to the NIST CSF includes its development, purpose, use cases, and overall structure. Further understanding of the NIST CSF involves delving into its core functions, categories, and implementation tiers and profiles. Practical implementation of the Framework is an important part of its application. Using real-world case studies can provide tangible illustrations of the NIST CSF's application, aiding in a better understanding of its effectiveness.

BACKGROUND ON THE NIST CSF

Established by the NIST, an agency of the U.S. Department of Commerce, the CSF originated from Executive Order 13636 titled "Improving Critical Infra-structure Cybersecurity." This directive, issued by President Obama in 2013, demanded a uniform security framework that would methodically address and manage cybersecurity risk cost-effectively, aligned with business requirements, and did not impose additional regulatory requirements on organizations. This ambitious project, engaging various stakeholders from industry, academia, and government, culminated in developing the NIST CSF.

The primary objective of the NIST CSF is to furnish a comprehensive set of industry standards and best practices to assist organizations in managing and mitigating their cybersecurity risks. Unlike rigid, one-size-fits-all regulations, the NIST CSF is designed with remarkable flexibility. It is constructed to accommodate the varied requirements of various organizations, regardless of their size, industry, or the nature and extent of their cyber risk. The Framework is fundamentally a risk-based approach to managing cybersecurity risk and comprises three main components: the Core, the Tiers, and the Profile.

Each of these components serves a specific purpose within the Framework. The Core is a compilation of everyday cybersecurity activities, outcomes, and informative references across sectors, providing the mechanisms to manage cybersecurity risks. The Tiers depict the extent to which an organization's cybersecurity risk management practices demonstrate the characteristics defined in the Framework. Conversely, the Profile aligns the Framework Core's standards, guidelines, and practices with the organization's business requirements, risk tolerance, and resources, enabling a tailored implementation.

The adoption of the NIST CSF has been widespread and multifaceted across various sectors, each finding its unique uses for the Framework. Use cases span the spectrum from small businesses to multinational corporations, from academic institutions to government agencies, each harnessing the Framework's flexibility and common language to their advantage. The Framework provides a universally understandable language for understanding, managing, and expressing cybersecurity risk, catering to internal and external communications. This common taxonomy, combined with the Framework's capacity to adapt to different risk tolerances, accommodate varied business needs, and keep pace with a rapidly changing cyber landscape, has led to its widespread acceptance and implementation.

However, while the numerous advantages of the NIST CSF are recognized and appreciated, it is also essential to consider its limitations. The NIST CSF is not a panacea for all cybersecurity ailments. Implementing the Framework demands a significant commitment from organizations regarding resources – financial, human, and technological – and time. The full realization of the potential benefits of the NIST CSF necessitates a deep-rooted commitment to an ongoing, iterative process of assessing and improving an organization's cybersecurity posture.

Furthermore, the Framework assumes organizations fundamentally understand their risk environment. This presumption can pose challenges for smaller entities with limited resources or those lacking the in-house expertise to understand their risk landscape thoroughly. However, these limitations should be viewed in context and do not detract from the overall utility, value, and effectiveness of the NIST CSF. When used correctly, the NIST CSF can significantly enhance an organization's ability to understand, manage, and reduce its cybersecurity risks.

Recommendations:

- **Understand the CSF:** Take the time to research and understand the background and origins of the NIST CSF. This includes familiarizing yourself with Executive Order 13636 and its role in establishing the Framework.

This knowledge will allow you to better appreciate the reasons behind the creation of the CSF and its significance to cybersecurity today.

- **Explore the Components:** Dedicate time to study the three main components of the NIST CSF – the Core, the Tiers, and the Profile. Understand their purposes and how they work together to provide a comprehensive CSF. This will provide insight into how the Framework can be best applied within your organization.

- **Evaluate Organizational Compatibility:** Assess your organization's size, industry, nature, and extent of cyber risk to understand how well the NIST CSF can be tailored to your needs. Given the Framework's flexibility, determine how it can benefit your organization.

- **Learn the CSF from Others:** Look into how other organizations within and outside your sector have implemented the NIST CSF. This will provide practical insight and examples of how the Framework can be adopted and adapted.

- **Consider the Commitment:** Before implementing the NIST CSF, ensure your organization understands the resource commitment – financial, human, and technological – and the time investment this will entail. Proper preparation and allocation of resources will aid in successfully adopting the Framework.

- **Understand Your Risk Environment:** The NIST CSF assumes an understanding of the organization's risk environment. Ensure you have the in-house expertise or external help to accurately understand and analyze your risk landscape. This will provide the foundation for more effective implementation of the Framework.

- **Commit to Improvement:** Adopting the NIST CSF is an iterative process. Commit to regular assessment and improvements in your organization's cybersecurity posture. This continued commitment will allow for maximum benefits from the NIST CSF.

- **Balance Expectations:** While the NIST CSF provides comprehensive guidelines, it is not a panacea for all cybersecurity issues. Set realistic expectations and understand that it is a tool to enhance your cybersecurity posture rather than a comprehensive solution to all cyber threats.

CORE FUNCTIONS AND CATEGORIES

The NIST CSF is built around five core functions that encapsulate the critical pillars of any effective cybersecurity strategy. These core functions, namely Identify, Protect, Detect, Respond, and Recover, represent a holistic, strategic view of an organization's approach to managing cybersecurity risk. Importantly, these functions are not intended to denote a rigid sequence; instead, they are concurrent and interrelated dimensions that should be considered continuously throughout the life cycle of an organization's information systems. These core functions are further divided into specific categories and subcategories, providing a comprehensive, granular roadmap for cybersecurity outcomes.

The first core function, "Identity," is foundational in developing an organizational understanding to manage cybersecurity risks effectively. This function entails recognizing and documenting the organization's digital ecosystem's systems, assets, data, and capabilities. Within this function, it is crucial to understand the organization's business context, related cybersecurity risks, and how those risks could impact its mission, functions, and stakeholders. This function includes Asset Management, Business Environment, Governance, Risk Assessment, and Risk Management Strategy. Each category further branches into subcategories that provide more detailed and practical actions, such as identifying and documenting software platforms and applications within the organization (Asset Management) or developing and implementing a risk management plan (Risk Management Strategy).

The second function, "Protect," outlines the defensive safeguards necessary to limit or contain the impact of potential cybersecurity events. It emphasizes proactive measures to maintain the integrity and availability of the organization's information systems. This function encompasses Access Control, Awareness and Training, Data Security, Information Protection Processes and Procedures, and Protective Technology. For example, under Access Control, organizations may need to define user roles and associated access levels, implement robust identity verification procedures, and manage permissions and credentials. Under Awareness and Training, organizations would ensure regular personnel training, updating them about potential threats and proper cyber hygiene practices.

The third core function, "Detect,"' defines the activities necessary to identify the occurrence of a cybersecurity event promptly. It underscores the importance of establishing effective monitoring systems to detect anomalies and trigger alerts, facilitating timely response. This function covers Anomalies and Events, Security Continuous Monitoring, and Detection Processes. For instance, organizations may need to establish a baseline for network activity (Anomalies and Events), perform regular audits and scans for vulnerabilities (Security Continuous Monitoring), and implement automated warning systems (Detection Processes).

Next, the "Respond" function comprises the necessary activities to initiate action regarding a detected cybersecurity incident. It focuses on the ability of an organization to contain the impact of a security event and coordinate a systematic response. This includes categories such as Response Planning, Communications, Analysis, Mitigation, and Improvements. For example, an organization might need a clear incident response plan (Response Planning), mechanisms to notify internal and external stakeholders (Communications), methods to analyze the incident's impact (Analysis), and plans to mitigate the incident and prevent recurrence (Mitigation and Improvements).

The "Recover" function identifies the activities needed to restore any capabilities or services impaired due to a cybersecurity incident. It focuses on returning to normal operations safely and promptly while learning from the incident to improve future responses. This includes Recovery Planning, Improvements, and Communications. Here, an organization would implement plans to restore systems and data, make necessary improvements to prevent future incidents and communicate with internal and external stakeholders about the status of recovery operations.

Each function offers a distinct perspective, providing a lens through which an organization can assess, enhance, and benchmark its cybersecurity program. Organizations can identify areas of strength and weakness by evaluating their current activities against these functions, categories, and subcategories.

This helps set clear priorities for investment and effort, drive continuous improvement, and promote accountability. Moreover, these functions and their related categories and subcategories provide a universally understandable language for discussing cybersecurity issues, enabling clear communication among all stakeholders, including technical and nontechnical personnel, senior leadership, and external partners.

Recommendations:

- **Understand Core CSF Functions:** Familiarize yourself with the five core functions of the NIST CSF: Identify, Protect, Detect, Respond, and Recover. Each function encapsulates a critical aspect of a comprehensive cybersecurity strategy. It is important to remember that these are not intended to follow a strict sequence but are concurrent and interrelated aspects to be continuously addressed.

- **Explore the 'Identify'CSF Function:** Understand your digital ecosystem, including systems, assets, data, and capabilities. Develop an understanding of your business context, related cybersecurity risks, and potential impact on your mission, functions, and stakeholders. This includes efforts in Asset Management, Business Environment, Governance, Risk Assessment, and Risk Management Strategy.

- **Implement the "Protect" CSF Function:** Protective measures to maintain the integrity and availability of your organization's information systems. This includes focusing on Access Control, Awareness and Training, Data Security, Information Protection Processes and Procedures, and Protective Technology. For instance, define user roles, implement robust identity verification procedures, manage permissions, and ensure regular personnel training on potential threats and cyber hygiene practices.

- **Enhance the "Detect" CSF Function:** Establish effective monitoring systems to identify cybersecurity events promptly. This includes focusing on Anomalies and Events, Security Continuous Monitoring, and Detection Processes. For example, establish a baseline for network activity, perform regular audits and scans for vulnerabilities, and implement automated warning systems.

- **Focus on the "Respond" CSF Function:** Develop an organized action plan for any detected cybersecurity incident. This includes Response Planning, Communications, Analysis, Mitigation, and Improvement efforts. For instance, have a clear incident response plan, mechanisms for notifying stakeholders, methods for analyzing the incident's impact, and plans for mitigation and preventing recurrence.

- **Plan the "Recover" CSF Function:** Develop plans to restore any capabilities or services impaired due to a cybersecurity incident. This includes Recovery Planning, Improvements, and Communications. Implement strategies to restore systems and data, make necessary improvements to prevent future incidents, and communicate with stakeholders about the status of recovery operations.

- **Benchmark Your Cybersecurity Program:** Use each function as a lens to assess, enhance, and benchmark your cybersecurity program. Identify areas of strength and weakness by comparing your current activities with these functions, categories, and subcategories. This will help set clear priorities for investment and effort, drive continuous improvement, and promote accountability.

- **Leverage the Universal Language of the CSF:** Use the functions, categories, and subcategories provided by the NIST CSF as a universally understandable language for discussing cybersecurity issues. This can promote clear communication among all stakeholders, including technical and nontechnical personnel, senior leadership, and external partners.

IMPLEMENTATION TIERS

The NIST CSF outlines four distinct implementation tiers, representing varying degrees of sophistication in cybersecurity risk management and incorporating these practices into the organization's broader risk management strategies. They are Partial (Tier 1), Risk-Informed (Tier 2), Repeatable (Tier 3), and Adaptive (Tier 4).

Tier 1: Partial

The Partial tier is the most basic level of implementation. Organizations at this stage may possess limited awareness of cybersecurity risks and lack formalized risk management practices. Cybersecurity activities may be erratic, uncoordinated, and implemented ad hoc, often in response to specific incidents. In this tier, there is typically an absence of prioritization of cybersecurity actions, leading to potential inconsistencies and gaps in defenses. However, recognizing the need to improve is an essential first step, and even this basic level can serve as a starting point for further enhancement of cybersecurity risk management.

Tier 2: Risk-Informed

Organizations in the Risk-Informed tier exhibit a greater understanding of cybersecurity risk, with management practices now being developed. At this stage, organizations understand the need for risk management but may lack a coherent, organization-wide approach. Cybersecurity risk management might not fully integrate into the organization's overall risk management strategy, and practices may be inconsistent. Communication about cybersecurity risks may be limited and typically occurs within IT departments.

Tier 3: Repeatable

The Repeatable tier represents a significant advancement in cybersecurity risk management practices. Organizations at this level have a formal and well-documented approach, with regular updates to cybersecurity practices based on the organization's changes and evolution. The risk management strategy is consistently implemented across the organization, with clear communication pathways to share information about cybersecurity risks. Risk-informed policies, processes, and procedures are always applied, enabling the organization to respond quickly to changes in threats, technologies, or business processes.

Tier 4: Adaptive

Organizations in the Adaptive tier display the most advanced implementation of the NIST CSF. They have an agile and dynamic cybersecurity risk management approach characterized by continual improvement and adaptability. They can adapt their cybersecurity practices based on lessons learned and predictive indicators derived from current and past cybersecurity activities. In this stage, cybersecurity becomes a fully integrated part of the organization's culture, with clear, organization-wide communication about cybersecurity risks. This tier is characterized by real-time, continuous improvements based on a mature understanding of the organization's risk environment.

Although there are four distinct tiers, it is crucial to understand that these are not designed as maturity models that organizations should necessarily aim to progress through linearly. Instead, they function as benchmarks, providing reference points that organizations can use to assess their current practices against desired outcomes. By comparing their cybersecurity protocols and activities against the characteristics of each tier, organizations can gain valuable insights into their cybersecurity posture. This comparison can illuminate potential gaps or weaknesses in an organization's cybersecurity practices and can be an invaluable tool for prioritizing improvements and changes.

Determining the appropriate tier for an organization should be a conscious decision informed by a comprehensive understanding of the organization's unique risk landscape. This decision should be driven by the organization's risk management processes and a clear assessment of the potential impact of cybersecurity events on the organization's operations and desired outcomes. It is unnecessary or advantageous for all organizations to strive for the highest tier (Adaptive). Instead, the chosen tier should align with the organization's unique requirements, objectives, resources, risk appetite, and the complexity of its digital environment.

Moving from one tier to another should be a well-considered and deliberate process underpinned by a solid understanding of the organization's cybersecurity risk environment and a coherent strategy for managing that risk. A tier transition is not a minor adjustment but a strategic change in how the organization approaches cybersecurity, and it can have broad implications for the organization's risk management, operational procedures, and resource allocation. For instance, transitioning to a higher tier typically necessitates increasing resources – not just financial but also personnel, training, time, and technical infrastructure. This potential increase should be carefully factored into strategic planning and resource allocation decisions.

It is also crucial to note that transitioning to a higher tier should be accompanied by regular reviews and adjustments to ensure that the organization's risk management strategy remains responsive to changes in its business context and the broader cybersecurity landscape. Such transitions should be part of a continuous improvement process, where feedback loops are established to track the effectiveness of the new measures, and adjustments are made as needed.

Ultimately, moving to a higher tier should be based on a clear-eyed assessment of the organization's cybersecurity status, risk tolerance, operational needs, and strategic objectives. The transition process should be driven by a comprehensive plan that includes the necessary changes to processes and procedures and measures to ensure the organization's readiness to sustain the new level of cybersecurity rigor in the long term.

Recommendations:

- **Understand CSF Implementation Tiers:** The NIST CSF defines four distinct implementation tiers, each representing different levels of cybersecurity sophistication: Partial (Tier 1), Risk-Informed (Tier 2), Repeatable (Tier 3), and Adaptive (Tier 4).
- **Evaluate CSF "Partial" Tier (Tier 1):** This is the most basic level where organizations may have limited awareness of cybersecurity risks and lack formalized risk management practices. Cybersecurity activities may be inconsistent and reactive. Recognize this as a crucial first step toward improving cybersecurity risk management.
- **Assess CSF "Risk-Informed" Tier (Tier 2):** In this tier, organizations exhibit a greater understanding of cybersecurity risk but may lack a coherent, organization-wide approach. Cybersecurity risk management might not be fully integrated into the organization's overall risk strategy, and communication about risks might be limited.

- **Achieve CSF "Repeatable" Tier (Tier 3):** This tier signifies significant advancement. Organizations have a formal and well-documented approach to cybersecurity, consistently implementing risk management strategies. Risk-informed policies, processes, and procedures are always applied, enabling rapid response to changes.
- **Reach CSF "Adaptive" Tier (Tier 4):** This is the highest level, where organizations have an agile and dynamic cybersecurity risk management approach. They continuously adapt and improve practices based on lessons learned and predictive indicators, fully integrating cybersecurity into the organization's culture.
- **View CSF Tiers as Benchmarks:** Remember that these tiers are benchmarks and not linear stages. Use them as reference points to assess current practices against desired outcomes. Comparisons can highlight potential gaps and help prioritize improvements.
- **Determine the Appropriate CSF Tier:** The right tier for an organization should be decided based on the unique risk landscape. This should be driven by the organization's risk management processes and a clear assessment of the potential impact of cybersecurity events. Striving for the highest tier is not always necessary or advantageous.
- **Consider Transitioning Between CSF Tiers:** Moving between tiers should be a strategic decision, informed by understanding the organization's cybersecurity risk environment and a coherent risk management strategy. Transitioning involves changes to risk management, operational procedures, and resource allocation.
- **Factor in Resource Allocation:** Transitioning to a higher tier usually requires increasing resources – financial, personnel, training, time, and technical infrastructure. These potential increases should be carefully factored into strategic planning.
- **Regularly Review and Adjust:** After transitioning to a higher tier, review and adjust to ensure the risk management strategy remains responsive to changes in the business context and cybersecurity landscape. Establish feedback loops to track the effectiveness of new measures.
- **Base Transition on Comprehensive Assessment:** The decision to move to a higher tier should be based on assessing the organization's cybersecurity status, risk tolerance, operational needs, and strategic objectives. The transition process should be planned carefully to ensure the organization's readiness to sustain the new level of cybersecurity rigor in the long term.

PROFILES

Purpose and Use of Profiles

Profiles in the NIST CSF provide a roadmap for advancing from an organization's cybersecurity to its desired state. They are unique to each organization and play a significant role in decision-making processes concerning cybersecurity. They facilitate understanding the outcomes based on business needs, risk tolerance, and resources. Organizations can create both "Current" and "Target" Profiles. A "Current" Profile indicates the cybersecurity outcomes that are currently being achieved, while a "Target" Profile represents the organization's desired cybersecurity outcomes. Comparing these two profiles helps organizations identify gaps and craft a prioritized action plan.

Creating a Profile

Creating a Profile involves mapping the organization's cybersecurity activities against the NIST CSF's categories and subcategories. The first step in this process is collating information about the organization's cybersecurity practices. This information can be obtained from various sources, including business unit heads, process owners, risk management teams, and IT staff. The collected data is then mapped to the appropriate categories and subcategories of the CSF.

Creating a "Target" Profile involves determining the desired cybersecurity outcomes. This usually requires a cross-functional discussion involving business leaders, IT leaders, and other relevant stakeholders. The organization's risk tolerance, sector-specific threats, legal and regulatory requirements, and business goals should all influence the composition of the "Target" Profile.

Customizing Profiles

Profiles can and should be customized to the specific needs of each organization. They should consider industry-specific risks, the organization's risk appetite, and the operational environment. For instance, a healthcare organization might prioritize protecting patient data, while a financial institution might focus on maintaining the integrity of financial transactions. The customization process might involve adding, removing, or altering categories and subcategories based on the organization's requirements.

Profile Examples

Consider, for instance, a manufacturing company with an existing Profile that identifies strong controls in asset management but weak controls in response planning and recovery planning. Their Target Profile might place a greater emphasis on developing these areas. Similarly, a university might have a Profile that shows full awareness and training programs but needs more focus on data security measures, reflecting the need to protect research data and personal information.

Profile Maintenance and Updates

Maintaining and updating the Profile is a continuous process. As business needs change, threat landscapes evolve, and new technologies are introduced, the Profile should be reviewed and updated to reflect these changes. This could be an annual process or triggered by significant business or risk environment changes. The revisions should involve the same cross-functional team involved in the original creation of the Profile, ensuring that all perspectives are considered.

By understanding Profiles in the NIST CSF, organizations gain a strategic tool for managing cybersecurity risks and customizing the Framework's components to their needs. They provide a clear roadmap, highlighting the direction an organization needs to follow to meet its cybersecurity objectives.

Recommendations:

- **Understand Profiles' Purpose:** Profiles in the NIST CSF act as a roadmap for improving an organization's cybersecurity. They are unique to each organization and help cybersecurity decision-making, enabling an understanding of outcomes based on business needs, risk tolerance, and resources. "Current" and "Target" Profiles denote the present and desired cybersecurity outcomes, respectively.

- **Create a Profile:** To create a Profile, first gather information about the organization's cybersecurity practices from various sources, such as business unit heads, risk management teams, and IT staff. Map the collected data to the appropriate categories and subcategories of the CSF. Conduct a cross-functional discussion for "Target" Profiles to determine desired cybersecurity outcomes.

- **Customize Profiles:** Adapt Profiles to the specific needs of each organization. They should consider industry-specific risks, the organization's risk appetite, and the operational environment. Customization can involve adding, removing, or altering categories and subcategories based on the organization's requirements.

- **Analyze Profile Examples:** For instance, a manufacturing company might have a Profile highlighting strong asset management controls but weak response and recovery planning. Their Target Profile would emphasize the improvement in these areas. A university might need to shift focus toward data security measures to protect research data and personal information.

- **Maintain and Update Profiles:** Keep Profiles current with evolving business needs, threat landscapes, and technological introductions. Regular reviews and updates, possibly annually or triggered by significant changes, should be undertaken with the cross-functional team involved in the Profile creation, ensuring all perspectives are included.

- **Utilize Profiles Strategically:** Organizations acquire a strategic tool for managing cybersecurity risks by understanding Profiles in the NIST CSF. They allow the customization of the Framework's components to specific needs and provide a clear direction to achieve cybersecurity objectives.

IMPLEMENTATION

Understanding Organizational Requirements

Embarking on the implementation process of the NIST CSF requires an initial deep dive into the organization's unique characteristics. This includes understanding its specific business objectives, risk tolerance, and the regulatory landscape in which it operates. These characteristics influence how cybersecurity is approached, the allocation of resources, and the prioritization of cybersecurity initiatives.

For instance, a financial institution operating under stringent data protection laws would need to consider the implications of these regulatory guidelines when setting up its cybersecurity posture. Such an organization might place a high premium on customer data protection, implying a low-risk tolerance for data breaches and necessitating stringent controls to secure customer data.

Furthermore, understanding the resources at the organization's disposal, including personnel, technical capabilities, financial resources, and time, is crucial. These resources, which can vary greatly among organizations, will directly influence the organization's cybersecurity practices, the sophistication of its controls, and its overall ability to manage cyber risk. Therefore, an accurate assessment of available resources is integral to implementing the NIST CSF effectively.

Assessing the Current State

The following step involves a thorough assessment of the current state of the organization's cybersecurity practices. It begins with an exhaustive inventory of the organization's systems, assets, data, and capabilities, all needing to be safeguarded from potential cyber threats. The process includes identifying and classifying information systems, databases, networks, and applications and determining their associated criticality and sensitivity.

Subsequently, the organization's existing cybersecurity practices are systematically compared with the functions, categories, and subcategories of the NIST CSF. This creates a "Current" Profile, a clear benchmark for the organization's cybersecurity measures. The "Current" Profile highlights existing cybersecurity capabilities and unveils areas where the organization's defenses may be insufficient, pointing out gaps that require attention.

Defining the Desired State

After ascertaining the current state, the organization defines its desired state of cybersecurity, using the deep understanding of its unique requirements garnered in the previous stages. The desired state, defined in terms of specific outcomes the organization seeks to achieve, is encapsulated in a "Target" Profile.

The "Target" Profile should harmonize with the organization's business objectives, risk management strategy, and regulatory requirements. For example, suppose an organization's business objective involves expanding into new markets. In that case, the "Target" Profile should consider the cybersecurity implications of this expansion, such as the need to comply with new regulations or the increased exposure to cyber threats.

Gap Analysis and Prioritization

The ensuing step systematically compares the "Current" and "Target" Profiles, shedding light on the gaps in the organization's cybersecurity practices. These gaps represent areas where cybersecurity falls short of desired and may include many issues, such as insufficient security controls, lack of employee training, or outdated incident response plans.

Each identified gap is then evaluated and ranked based on several factors, including its associated risk level, the potential impact on the organization if the gap is not addressed, and the resources required to mitigate it. This evaluation and ranking process culminates in a prioritized list of gaps, which forms the backbone of the strategic action plan.

Developing and Executing the Action Plan

The action plan is crucial to the implementation process, providing a detailed roadmap to transition from the "Current" Profile to the "Target" Profile. The plan delineates the specific tasks, initiatives, or actions to address the identified gaps, the resources required for each action, and a timeline for completion.

A crucial aspect of the action plan is ensuring accountability by assigning each action to a specific owner or team. These individuals or groups are responsible for overseeing the execution of their assigned activities, monitoring the progress, and addressing any issues that may arise. Regular progress reviews against the plan facilitate timely adjustments, ensuring that the implementation remains aligned with the organization's objectives and adapts to any changes in the cybersecurity landscape.

Continuous Improvement

Finally, the implementation process concludes with a commitment to continuous improvement, recognizing that implementing the NIST CSF is not a one-off project but an ongoing endeavor. The dynamic nature of the cybersecurity landscape, characterized by the regular emergence of new threats and vulnerabilities, necessitates that organizations remain proactive in monitoring these changes and adjusting their cybersecurity practices accordingly.

Regular updates of the "Current" and "Target" Profiles and the action plan, coupled with consistent monitoring of the cybersecurity environment, ensure that the organization remains resilient and agile in the face of evolving cyber threats. This could involve regular cybersecurity audits, periodic employee training, or adopting new security technologies. In essence, continuous improvement should be seen as a cornerstone of an effective cybersecurity program, reflecting the organization's ongoing commitment to maintaining a robust cybersecurity posture.

Recommendations:

- **Understand Organizational Requirements:** Implementing the NIST CSF requires understanding the organization's business objectives, risk tolerance, and regulatory landscape. These factors influence the cybersecurity approach, resource allocation, and priority setting. The resources, including personnel, technical capabilities, financial resources, and time, must also be understood, as these will directly influence the organization's cybersecurity practices.

- **Assess the Current State:** Evaluate cybersecurity practices, starting with a comprehensive inventory of systems, assets, data, and capabilities. Then, compare the existing cybersecurity practices with the NIST CSF to create a "Current" Profile, highlighting existing capabilities and identifying gaps.

- **Define the Desired State:** After determining the current state, define the desired state of cybersecurity, factoring in unique organizational requirements. The desired state, represented by a "Target" Profile, should align with the organization's business objectives, risk management strategy, and regulatory requirements.

- **Conduct Gap Analysis and Prioritization:** Compare the "Current" and "Target" Profiles to identify gaps in cybersecurity practices. Evaluate each gap based on its associated risk level, potential impact, and the resources needed for mitigation. This process leads to a prioritized list of gaps, forming the basis of the strategic action plan.

- **Develop and Execute the Action Plan:** Create an action plan, providing a detailed roadmap to transition from the "Current" Profile to the "Target" Profile. Assign each action to a specific owner or team for accountability, monitor progress, and make timely adjustments to keep implementation aligned with the organization's objectives and changes in the cybersecurity landscape.

- **Commit to Continuous Improvement:** Implementing the NIST CSF is an ongoing effort due to the dynamic nature of the cybersecurity landscape. Regular updates of the "Current" and "Target" Profiles, consistent monitoring of the cybersecurity environment, and actions such as regular cybersecurity audits, periodic employee training, or adopting new security technologies ensure the organization remains resilient against evolving cyber threats.

Chapter Conclusion

In the constantly evolving world of cybersecurity, threats are growing more sophisticated, and the potential impact on businesses and society is more significant. The need for a comprehensive, flexible, standardized framework to manage and mitigate these risks has never been greater. This is where the NIST CSF comes into play. With its foundation rooted in an executive order from President Obama in 2013, the NIST CSF has emerged as an invaluable tool for organizations seeking to bolster their cybersecurity posture.

The NIST CSF is built around a triad of Cores, Tiers, and Profiles, each adding depth and functionality to the Framework. The Core, consisting of the functions Identify, Protect, Detect, Respond, and Recover, provides a broad overview of an organization's cybersecurity objectives. It offers a common language and a shared perspective that transcends the barriers of industries, sectors, and countries. The Tiers allow organizations to assess their cyber-security maturity and readiness, aiding in identifying strengths and areas for improvement. Finally, the Profiles encapsulate an organization's current cybersecurity state and targeted outcomes, allowing for a comprehensive gap analysis and a pathway toward improved cybersecurity measures.

Implementing the NIST CSF requires a keen understanding of an organization's unique requirements, assessing its current cybersecurity posture, defining a desired state, and developing and executing a strategic action plan. This plan helps bridge the gap between the present and targeted conditions, driving the organization toward enhanced cybersecurity readiness. Continuous improvement, the final step in this journey, involves staying abreast of the ever-changing cybersecurity landscape and adapting as necessary.

The practical implications of the NIST CSF are as varied as the organizations that use it. From small businesses to multinational corporations, from academic institutions to government agencies, the flexibility and adaptability of the NIST CSF allow it to be tailored to the specific needs of any entity. Providing a common language for understanding, managing, and expressing cybersecurity risk internally and externally will enable stakeholders to engage in meaningful conversations about cybersecurity, fostering a collaborative and proactive approach to risk management.

While the NIST CSF offers numerous benefits, it is essential to acknowledge its limitations. It is neither a one-size-fits-all solution nor a panacea for all cybersecurity woes. Its successful implementation requires significant commitment, resources, and an understanding of the organization's risk environment. However, the perceived limitations do not detract from the utility of the NIST CSF; instead, they highlight the importance of integrating the Framework within a broader risk management strategy, reinforcing the notion that effective cybersecurity is a shared responsibility.

The adoption and implementation of the NIST CSF are likely to continue gaining traction. As our reliance on digital systems deepens, the imperative to secure these systems strengthens. Cybersecurity is no longer an isolated IT concern but a critical business issue with far-reaching implications. Organizations are coming to this reality, and frameworks like the NIST CSF will be increasingly pivotal in guiding their cybersecurity endeavors.

The NIST CSF is a testament to the strides in standardizing cybersecurity efforts across different sectors. Its thoughtful structure, flexibility, and adaptability make it a powerful tool for organizations to manage their cybersecurity risks effectively. While it comes with its limitations and challenges, its benefits far outweigh them.

Case Study: Cybersecurity Journey of TechPulse Inc.

TechPulse Inc., a fictional emerging tech company specializing in *Artificial Intelligence* (AI) and *Machine Learning* (ML) solutions, faced increased cybersecurity threats as its operations expanded and its digital footprint grew. Michelle, the company's newly appointed *Chief Information Security Officer* (CISO), recognized the need for a standardized, comprehensive CSF to protect the organization's systems, assets, data, and capabilities. She saw the NIST CSF as a potential game-changer to bolster the company's cybersecurity posture.

As the first step, Michelle began understanding TechPulse's unique organizational requirements. This involved recognizing the company's business objectives, risk tolerance, regulatory obligations, and available resources for cybersecurity. Given the data-sensitive nature of their products, she understood the company's role in the tech industry and the growing need for strong cybersecurity measures. Michelle also considered the company's regulatory requirements, especially considering the nature of the AI and ML solutions they provided.

Michelle then assessed the current state of TechPulse's cybersecurity practices. She organized an exhaustive inventory of all the digital assets, systems, and data that needed protection from potential cyber threats. After identifying these elements, she compared the existing cybersecurity practices with the functions, categories, and subcategories of the NIST CSF. The resulting "Current" Profile reflected the company's cybersecurity status and highlighted gaps that needed immediate attention.

With the understanding of TechPulse's unique needs and current cybersecurity measures, Michelle defined the company's desired cybersecurity state, encapsulated in the "Target" Profile. She ensured this Profile aligned with TechPulse's business goals, risk management strategy, and regulatory requirements. This target was not an end state but an ongoing process of improvement and adjustment in response to the dynamic nature of cybersecurity threats.

Once the "Current" and "Target" Profiles were defined, Michelle performed a gap analysis to identify disparities between TechPulse's existing cybersecurity posture and its desired state. She ranked each gap based on the associated risk level, the potential impact on the organization, and the resources required for mitigation. This informed the strategic action plan, which laid out the pathway to transition from the "Current" Profile to the "Target" Profile, focusing on tasks, initiatives, and actions that needed to be undertaken, with clear lines of responsibility and accountability.

Finally, Michelle championed the cause of continuous improvement at TechPulse, emphasizing the dynamic nature of the cybersecurity landscape. She set up processes for regular updates of the Profiles and action plan and consistent monitoring of the cybersecurity environment. This way, TechPulse stayed agile and resilient, ready to respond to evolving cyber threats effectively.

CHAPTER 12

Cybersecurity Frameworks

"Cybersecurity frameworks are the blueprints that fortify our digital defenses, enabling us to stand firm against the relentless onslaught of cyber adversaries. Embrace them, for in their structure lies our strength."

Various cybersecurity frameworks exist, each with specifics, strengths, and drawbacks. A deeper understanding of these frameworks is essential, especially when considering their implementation within an organization. The relevance and applicability of these frameworks across various sectors, with a particular focus on the financial industry, are highlighted. The adoption process, integration of the frameworks into existing systems, and recommendations for effective deployment are also crucial points of discussion. The overarching goal is to aid in making informed decisions and ensure the selected cybersecurity framework is appropriately tailored to meet the organization's unique needs.

ISO/IEC 27001: INFORMATION SECURITY MANAGEMENT

ISO/IEC 27001 is a globally recognized standard for information security management. It provides a systematic approach to managing sensitive company information, ensuring it remains secure. This includes everything from financial data, intellectual property, and employee details to information entrusted by third parties.

ISO/IEC 27001 lays the foundation for an Information Security Management System (ISMS), requiring the organization to design and implement a coherent and comprehensive suite of information security controls. These controls are not prescribed, allowing flexibility based on the organization's unique needs. The standard covers risk assessment, security policy, asset management, access control, and physical and environmental security.

The ISO/IEC 27001 certification process is rigorous, involving an external audit by an accredited certification body. It provides third-party verification that an organization is following best practices in information security management, which can significantly enhance its reputation and trustworthiness.

While ISO/IEC 27001 can be applied to any organization, regardless of size or industry, it has particular relevance for financial institutions due to the sensitive nature of the data they handle. This section concludes by discussing the implementation of ISO/IEC 27001 in financial institutions, providing practical insights into the process and the unique challenges and opportunities it presents.

Recommendations:

- **Understand the ISO/IEC 27001 Framework:** Develop a comprehensive understanding of the ISO/IEC 27001 framework, including its purpose and the key controls it recommends.
- **Tailor the ISO/IEC 27001 Approach:** Remember that the controls are not prescribed and should be tailored to fit the organization's unique needs. It is not about ticking boxes but about effectively managing information security.
- **Prepare for the ISO/IEC 27001 Audit:** Be prepared for the rigor of the certification process. It can be demanding but offers an excellent opportunity to improve your information security management practices.
- **ISO/IEC 27001 Relevance to Financial Institutions:** For financial institutions, consider the relevance and benefits of ISO/IEC 27001. The sensitive nature of the data these institutions handle makes the standard particularly valuable.
- **Continuous ISO/IEC 27001 Improvement:** Remember that certification is not the end goal. ISO/IEC 27001 requires continuous improvement, ensuring your organization stays ahead of the game in information security management.

COBIT (CONTROL OBJECTIVES FOR INFORMATION AND RELATED TECHNOLOGIES)

COBIT, an acronym for Control Objectives for Information and Related Technologies, is an industry-recognized framework meticulously developed by ISACA, an international professional association focused on IT governance. The purpose of COBIT is to guide the effective management and governance of enterprise Information Technology (IT). This framework consolidates information systems and technology principles with globally accepted business practices and ethical norms, mapping these critical processes across a comprehensive capability spectrum.

The structure of COBIT is distinctly characterized by its six performance levels, each encapsulating a different set of processes and management practices. These capability levels advance from Level 0, denoted as "Non-existent," where no standardized IT processes are present, to Level 5, labeled as "Optimized." At this apex level, IT processes are continuously improved through monitoring, fine-tuning, and automation based on good practices and compliance requirements.

Each capability level symbolizes an incremental enhancement in an organization's ability to control, manage, and govern its IT resources, representing a stepwise escalation in IT governance maturity. In this manner, COBIT functions as an effective benchmark for organizations, allowing them to measure and optimize their IT management strategies.

The COBIT assessment process is methodically designed to gauge the maturity level of an organization's IT governance, providing a clear and objective measure of its IT management capabilities. The process involves a comprehensive evaluation performed by a certified assessor with extensive knowledge and expertise in the COBIT framework. Following this assessment, the organization is assigned a maturity level that corresponds directly with its successful implementation and compliance with the required processes and management practices.

In an age where IT forms the backbone of every business operation, the relevance of COBIT spans industries. It ensures the secure and efficient management of IT resources, enabling organizations to protect themselves from potential IT failures and security breaches and leverage their IT infrastructure for growth and innovation. COBIT empowers businesses to align their IT goals with their business goals, promoting effective communication between business and IT teams and ensuring that technology investments deliver optimal value.

Beyond its foundational role in IT governance, COBIT is a navigational guide for organizations seeking to improve their IT management. It details a clear progression from basic process controls to advanced, integrated, and optimized governance measures. This roadmap supports businesses at every stage of their IT maturity journey, making COBIT a powerful tool for IT transformation.

As this comprehensive framework continues to evolve with global IT trends and standards, a diverse range of organizations from multiple sectors are expected to embrace COBIT. Its practical and thorough approach to IT governance makes it an attractive option for businesses keen on maximizing their IT value while ensuring robust controls and transparency. This potential expansion of COBIT's application would symbolize the acceptance of its best practices across industries, thereby raising the overall standard of IT governance and control globally.

Recommendations:

- **Understand COBIT's Essence**: Take time to comprehend the core principles and structure of the COBIT framework. Investigate its processes, capability levels, and significance to IT governance and management.

This foundational knowledge will be crucial for your organization's successful adoption and implementation of the framework.

- **Train Key Personnel**: Ensure that the key personnel in your organization, particularly those involved in IT governance and management, undergo training in the COBIT framework. This will equip them with the necessary knowledge and skills to effectively implement the framework and ensure your IT strategies align with your business goals.

- **Conduct an IT Governance Assessment**: Evaluate your organization's current IT governance status. Utilize the COBIT framework as a benchmark to identify areas of strength and areas needing improvement. This will provide a clear starting point for your journey toward improved IT governance using the COBIT framework.

- **Create an Implementation Plan**: Based on your organization's IT governance assessment, develop a detailed COBIT implementation plan. This plan should outline the implementation processes, targets for each capability level, timelines, and responsible parties. This structured approach will facilitate a smooth and efficient adoption of the framework.

- **Review and Optimize**: Post-implementation, regularly review your organization's IT governance practices in line with the COBIT framework. Use these reviews to identify gaps or challenges and continuously optimize your practices to ensure they deliver value. This will help to ensure your organization remains at the optimal level of IT governance maturity.

CMMC (CYBERSECURITY MATURITY MODEL CERTIFICATION)

The Cybersecurity Maturity Model Certification (CMMC) is a comprehensive, unified standard meticulously designed for implementing cybersecurity across the Defense Industrial Base (DIB) in the United States. It amalgamates various cybersecurity standards and best practices, mapping these critical controls and processes across a spectrum of maturity levels. These levels extend from basic foundational cybersecurity hygiene practices to advanced, progressive cybersecurity procedures and protocols.

The fundamental structure of the CMMC incorporates five distinct maturity levels, each featuring a set of processes and practices. These levels traverse the path from Level 1, which represents Basic Cyber Hygiene, to Level 5, designated Advanced/Progressive. Each group signifies an incremental advancement in an organization's capability to safeguard sensitive data, embodying an escalation in its maturity in cybersecurity.

The CMMC assessment process is designed explicitly to verify the implementation of practices and procedures. This process involves an evaluation conducted by a certified assessor from a C3PAO (CMMC Third Party Assessment Organization). The company or organization is conferred with a certification level after the assessment. This level corresponds directly to their successful implementation and adherence to the requisite controls and practices, thus providing a clear and objective measure of their cybersecurity maturity.

Given the sensitive nature of financial data, the CMMC holds substantial relevance in the financial industry. It ensures the secure handling of sensitive financial information and protects the organization and its clients from potential security breaches. In addition, the CMMC provides a clear roadmap for organizations to enhance their cybersecurity, outlining steps to advance from basic to more complex security measures.

As the standard develops and evolves, it is anticipated that organizations outside the DIB may also pursue CMMC certification. This potential expansion would reflect the recognition of the CMMC's comprehensive and practical approach to cybersecurity. Furthermore, it would mark the adoption of these robust defense industry practices in other sectors, thus raising the overall standard of cybersecurity across industries.

Recommendations:

- **Understand the CMMC Maturity Levels:** Familiarize yourself with the five maturity levels of the CMMC and understand what each group signifies regarding cybersecurity practices and processes.
- **Evaluate Your Organization with CMMC:** Evaluate your organization's current cybersecurity practices against the CMMC standards. Identify areas for improvement and gaps in current practices.
- **Prepare for the CMMC Assessment:** Be aware that the CMMC requires an assessment by a certified assessor. Prepare your organization accordingly to ensure a successful evaluation.
- **Relevance of CMMC to the Financial Industry:** Consider the significance of the CMMC to the financial industry. Although it was initially developed for the DIB, the principles apply to any sector handling sensitive data.

CIS (CENTER FOR INTERNET SECURITY) CONTROLS

The Center for Internet Security (CIS) Controls a methodically prioritized series of actions, which, when combined, form a robust defense-in-depth set of best practices for cybersecurity. These controls serve as a clear roadmap for conducting comprehensive cybersecurity. The journey commences with rudimentary measures, progressing gradually toward advanced defense mechanisms, thus providing a layer-by-layer approach to securing an organization's digital assets.

The architecture of the CIS Controls is divided into three strategic categories: basic, foundational, and organizational. Basic controls comprise the essential actions for cybersecurity, focusing on critical hygiene factors that provide an initial line of defense. Foundational controls introduce technical and management controls to build upon, taking security to the next level. On the other hand, the organizational controls concentrate on governance, aimed at refining and improving an organization's comprehensive approach to cybersecurity, nurturing a culture of security within the organization.

Implementing CIS Controls can bring about a transformative improvement in an organization's cybersecurity posture. It provides a robust, well-structured framework for safeguarding against known attack vectors and mitigating potential cyber threats. Beyond the defense realm, CIS Controls also serve as a potent tool for security benchmarking. This allows organizations to evaluate and measure their security posture against an industry-accepted set of best practices, offering an objective perspective on cyber defense readiness.

Furthermore, when applied to financial institutions, the CIS Controls manifest as a solid base for protecting sensitive financial data and transactions. The CIS Controls help ensure compliance with regulatory requirements and help uphold the stringent standards of the financial industry. Implementing these controls reinforces the trust of customers and stakeholders by demonstrating the institution's commitment to cybersecurity.

Moreover, adopting the CIS Controls also aids in maintaining a proactive approach toward cybersecurity. They serve as a protective measure and help organizations identify potential weaknesses and areas for improvement. Thus, CIS Controls contribute to developing a mature, comprehensive, and resilient cybersecurity program that not only reacts to threats but anticipates them, reinforcing the trust and confidence of all stakeholders involved.

Recommendations:

- **Start with the Basics:** Begin the implementation of CIS Controls with the basic controls and gradually move to foundational and organizational controls.
- **Tailor to Your Organization:** While the CIS Controls are designed to be universally applicable, they should be tailored to your organization's specific needs and risks.
- **Measure Progress:** Use the CIS Controls for implementation and measuring progress and security posture over time.
- **Continuous Improvement:** View the implementation of the CIS Controls as a constant improvement process rather than a one-time project.

PCI DSS (PAYMENT CARD INDUSTRY DATA SECURITY STANDARD)

The Payment Card Industry Data Security Standard (PCI DSS) is an internationally recognized set of security standards meticulously designed to ensure that all organizations that accept, process, store, or transmit credit card information uphold a secure environment. It is introduced to safeguard cardholder data and is integral to the global effort to combat financial fraud.

At its core, the PCI DSS was engineered to bolster controls encircling cardholder data, reducing the potential for credit card fraud. The standard delves into comprehensive security aspects, from security management, policies, and procedures to more technical areas like network architecture and software design. Its prescriptive requirements, encompass protective measures such as encryption, vulnerability management, and access control, are designed to defend cardholder data from compromise.

The influence of PCI DSS extends significantly into the financial industry, particularly among organizations that handle card payments. This standard guarantees secure cardholder information handling at every step, protecting the organization and its customers from looming threats. It is a cornerstone of trust in the card payment ecosystem, boosting confidence among consumers, merchants, and financial institutions.

The journey to implementing PCI DSS requirements may initially appear daunting, owing to the intricate web of processes involved. The degree of complexity is often dictated by the size of the organization and the complexity of its cardholder data environment. However, this should not deter organizations from pursuing compliance. Organizations can successfully traverse this process through a structured, step-by-step approach and a firm commitment.

Nevertheless, achieving PCI DSS compliance is not a one-time project but a continuous process of maintaining a secure environment. It requires regular review and adaptation to evolving threats and changing business circumstances. Furthermore, the benefits of PCI DSS compliance extend beyond meeting the standard's requirements. It encourages organizations to adopt a culture of security where data protection becomes an integral part of their business operations. It helps organizations identify and fix vulnerabilities, reduce the risk of data breaches, and avoid the hefty fines associated with noncompliance, thereby protecting their reputation and the trust of their customers.

Recommendations:

- **Embrace the Significance**: Grasp the importance and intricacies of the PCI DSS. Please familiarize yourself with its security requirements, objectives, and importance in preventing financial fraud. This fundamental understanding will serve as a basis for a successful journey toward PCI DSS compliance.

- **Develop a Skilled Team**: Assemble a team of professionals skilled in IT, security, and payment systems. Provide them with comprehensive training on the PCI DSS to ensure they are well equipped to lead your organization toward PCI DSS compliance and maintain a secure cardholder data environment.

- **Assess Current Security Measures**: Undertake a thorough review of your cardholder data security measures against the PCI DSS requirements. This assessment will help identify security controls and practice gaps and guide your action plan to bolster your defenses and meet the PCI DSS requirements.

- **Implement a Structured Approach**: Based on the assessment, design a structured plan to address the identified gaps and meet the PCI DSS requirements. This plan should cover data encryption, access control, and vulnerability management. Consider seeking assistance from a Qualified Security Assessor (QSA) to ensure your approach is sound and effective.

- **Cultivate Continuous Compliance**: Remember that PCI DSS compliance is not a one-time event but a continuous journey of maintaining a secure cardholder data environment. Implement a schedule for regular reviews and updates to your security controls and practices. Foster a culture of security within your organization where data protection is integral to your operations, helping you to maintain compliance and protect your organization's reputation and customer trust.

ICFR (INTERNAL CONTROL OVER FINANCIAL REPORTING)

Internal Control over Financial Reporting (ICFR) refers to the wide-ranging, well-defined procedures an organization implements to validate the accuracy and reliability of its financial statements. Rather than merely a discrete operations component, ICFR is intricately woven into the core threads of corporate governance and financial management. When correctly applied, ICFR can engender trust among stakeholders, assuring the truthfulness of the organization's disclosed financial data.

At its core, ICFR comprises several crucial elements: a control environment, risk assessment, control activities, information and communication, and monitoring activities. These diverse components interact cohesively, laying the foundation for an elaborately organized approach to managing possible risks associated with financial reporting.

As the initial layer, the control environment sets the organizational ethos, cultivating a climate of accountability and ethical conduct. A robust risk assessment process, the second element, identifies potential zones of inaccuracies or fraudulent activities. Following this, control activities help devise protocols to counter these identified risks. The information and communication facet is a conduit, ensuring that relevant information circulates effectively within the organizational structure. Lastly, monitoring activities offer a mechanism for evaluating and enhancing the overall control system over time, ensuring its effectiveness.

In compliance and risk management, ICFR emerges as a stalwart protector of the integrity of financial reporting. It serves as a crucial apparatus for adhering to regulatory requirements. As business transactions and regulations grow more complex, the imperative for a fortified internal control system is amplified. By boosting the reliability of financial statements, ICFR can assist organizations in sidestepping expensive errors, discovering both unintentional and intentional fraud, and aligning with fiscal regulations.

However, the effective implementation and maintenance of ICFR call for a clear delineation of roles and responsibilities, a systematic risk identification procedure, the formulation of preventive controls, stringent testing of control efficacy, and a quick response to address any identified shortcomings. It is not a static process but rather a dynamic one, necessitating routine reviews and updates in sync with the fluidity of business processes, regulatory changes, and technological advancements.

ICFR's successful realization is not solely an executive obligation but requires dedication from every stratum of an organization. This begins with the top-level management, responsible for setting the tone, and extends down to each employee entrusted with the execution of control activities in their day-to-day operations. This collective obligation fosters a culture that values accountability, transparency, and continual refinement, a critical cornerstone for maintaining an organization's long-term financial well-being and sustainable growth trajectory.

Recommendations:

- **Recognize the Importance**: Understand the significance of ICFR and its role in ensuring the accuracy and reliability of financial reports. Please familiarize yourself with the key elements of ICFR, their interconnectedness, and how they contribute to mitigating risks tied to financial reporting. This fundamental understanding will be a launching pad for implementing and maintaining ICFR in your organization.
- **Create an ICFR Committee**: Assemble a dedicated team or committee responsible for implementing and overseeing ICFR in your organization. This team should be cross-functional, involving members from finance, operations, and IT, among others, and should ideally be led by a member of senior management to demonstrate the organization's commitment to ICFR.
- **Conduct Risk Assessments**: Regularly conduct risk assessments to identify areas where inaccuracies or fraud could occur in your financial reporting process. Use these risk assessments to design and implement control activities to mitigate these risks, thereby enhancing the integrity of your financial reports.
- **Establish Clear Communication Channels**: Ensure effective communication channels are in place to disseminate pertinent information regarding ICFR throughout the organization. This includes ensuring all employees understand their roles and responsibilities in the control process and the importance of their contribution to maintaining the accuracy and dependability of financial reports.
- **Embrace Continuous Improvement**: Treat ICFR as a dynamic process that requires continuous monitoring, review, and improvement. Establish a routine for assessing the efficacy of your control activities and make necessary adjustments in response to changing business processes, regulatory requirements, and technological advancements. This commitment to continuous improvement will help foster a culture of accountability and transparency, enhancing your organization's long-term financial health and sustainability.

CLOUD SECURITY ALLIANCE CONTROLS

The Cloud Security Alliance (CSA) is an esteemed nonprofit organization that has dedicated itself to formulating and propagating best practices to ensure a secure environment for cloud computing. With its worldwide membership base and participation from industry experts, CSA acts as a vanguard for cloud security, providing an invaluable resource to the global community. The alliance's security guidance and the Cloud Controls Matrix (CCM) provide a meticulously detailed set of information security control objectives, further bolstered by specific security controls tailored to the unique challenges of cloud computing.

The CSA Security Guidance constitutes a comprehensive suite of cloud-centric controls and protective measures that organizations are advised to consider when adopting cloud services. This guidance is underpinned by research from various cloud security experts, offering a wealth of knowledge and actionable insights that are instrumental in securing cloud-based assets. The CCM further consolidates these security measures into a single, actionable, and user-friendly framework, thus providing organizations with robust protocols to protect their data and maintain regulatory compliance in the cloud.

The practical implementation of CSA controls typically involves a delicate equilibrium between maintaining stringent security measures and achieving core business objectives. This balance demands a nuanced understanding of all the implications associated with cloud usage – from overarching governance issues and architectural considerations to the nitty-gritty of daily operations.

Furthermore, the implementation process is not a one-off event but an ongoing commitment to maintaining a secure cloud environment. This often involves continually assessing and adjusting controls in response to evolving threats, technology changes, and business needs. Companies must establish clear lines of accountability and communication to ensure consistent application of the controls. They must also continually educate and train staff to ensure everyone understands and can effectively apply the controls. By doing so, organizations can leverage the power and flexibility of the cloud while maintaining a strong security posture that protects their most valuable digital assets.

Recommendations:

- **Acknowledge CSA's Importance**: Familiarize yourself with the CSA and its role in promoting secure cloud computing practices. Grasp the fundamentals of the CSA Security Guidance and the CCM and their significance in establishing robust cloud security controls. This foundational understanding will be a stepping stone to successfully applying CSA guidelines in your cloud practices.
- **Assemble a Cloud Security Team**: Form a dedicated team of IT and cloud security experts in your organization responsible for implementing and maintaining the CSA's cloud security controls. Ensure that this team receives regular training on the latest CSA guidance and controls, enabling them to safeguard your cloud-based assets effectively.

- **Implement CSA Guidelines**: Utilize the CSA Security Guidance and CCM to establish your organization's comprehensive cloud security controls. This should involve thoroughly assessing your cloud practices and implementing CSA-recommended controls tailored to your cloud environment and business needs.

- **Foster Clear Communication**: Develop effective communication channels to ensure that the CSA's guidelines and controls are clearly understood and consistently applied across your organization. This should involve regular training and updates for all employees involved in cloud operations, ensuring they know their roles in maintaining cloud security and the significance of their contributions.

- **Commit to Continuous Improvement**: Treat your organization's cloud security practices as an ongoing commitment, not a one-time event. Regularly assess and adjust your cloud security controls per the CSA's latest guidance, technological changes, evolving threats, and your organization's business needs. This continuous improvement approach will ensure your cloud environment remains secure, flexible, and aligned with your business objectives.

ISO 27017: CODE OF PRACTICE FOR INFORMATION SECURITY CONTROLS

ISO 27017 represents a comprehensive standard delineating guidelines for implementing information security controls, particularly within the scope of providing and leveraging cloud services. The primary objective of this code of practice is to extend the pre-existing control measures highlighted in ISO 27002 by proffering further implementation guidance that is distinctly crafted to cater to the needs of both cloud service providers and their customer base.

The primary objectives and controls set forth by ISO 27017 are centered around the assurance of data protection within the cloud environment. These controls delve into numerous areas, such as clarifying asset ownership, delineating segregation protocols in cloud computing, safeguarding records, incorporating data encryption, and ensuring virtual machines' security, among other key aspects.

The integration of ISO 27017 entails weaving its guidelines into the fabric of an organization's security framework. A crucial step in this implementation process is a thorough gap analysis. This enables organizations to pinpoint areas that may require improvements or upgrades to align with the controls advocated by ISO 27017 fully.

An important aspect is that ISO 27017 does not function in isolation. It complements and operates in harmony with other ISO standards, particularly ISO 27001, which is dedicated to Information Security Management. Together, these standards present a holistic approach to data security, paying special attention to the unique vulnerabilities and potential risks associated with cloud-based operations.

ISO 27017, therefore, contributes to a robust, multifaceted security infrastructure, addressing unique challenges posed by the cloud. It helps organizations build a strong security posture by offering specific guidance for managing and protecting cloud-based assets. By adopting this standard, organizations can demonstrate their commitment to cloud security, boost stakeholder confidence, and better manage risks in a world increasingly reliant on cloud technologies.

Recommendations:

- **Understand ISO 27017:** Familiarize yourself with ISO 27017, its controls, and its objectives to understand its requirements fully.
- **Conduct a Gap Analysis:** Assess your security practices against the ISO 27017 controls to identify improvement areas.
- **Implement Controls:** Apply the ISO 27017 controls within your organization, tailoring them as necessary to align with your unique needs and context.
- **Integrate with Other Standards:** Combine the use of ISO 27017 with other ISO standards like ISO 27001 to maximize your security efforts.
- **Regularly Review and Improve:** Review your ISO 27017 compliance and continuously seek to improve your security measures.

ISO 27701: PRIVACY INFORMATION MANAGEMENT

ISO 27701 is a significant extension of ISO 27001 and ISO 27002, particularly focusing on managing privacy within an organization's operations. Its chief function is to guide the establishment, implementation, consistent upkeep, and continuous improvement of a Privacy Information Management System (PIMS).

The fundamental components and stipulations of ISO 27701 encompass the proficient management of personal information, carrying out privacy risk assessments, and incorporating privacy considerations into the risk management process of an ISMS. Moreover, it outlines explicit requirements and guidance for Personal Identifiable Information (PII) controllers and PII processors responsible for handling personal data.

In integrating ISO 27701 with ISO 27001, an organization must first have an ISMS that complies with ISO 27001. Upon this foundation, ISO 27701 adds a specific focus on privacy to the pre-existing ISMS, extending its scope to include the management of privacy risks.

Managing privacy and achieving compliance with ISO 27701 entails adhering to many privacy laws, regulations, and contractual clauses. Compliance can be challenging because these can often be complex and vary greatly across jurisdictions. However, ISO 27701 is a beneficial tool that assists organizations in navigating these complexities and achieving compliance with these varying requirements.

ISO 27701 provides a comprehensive framework for organizations to effectively manage and protect personal information. By adopting this standard, organizations can demonstrate their commitment to privacy, enhance stakeholder trust, meet regulatory requirements, and better manage privacy risks in today's data-driven world. It acts as a strategic tool enabling organizations to proactively respond to privacy risks, thereby strengthening their privacy posture and contributing to their overall resilience in a landscape marked by evolving regulatory requirements and privacy expectations.

Recommendations:

- **Understand ISO 27701 and Its Importance**: Acquaint yourself with ISO 27701, its objectives, and its relevance in managing privacy within your organization. Understand how it extends ISO 27001 to include privacy management and comprehend the primary components of a PIMS. This foundational understanding will be a stepping stone to successfully applying ISO 27701 within your organization.
- **Ensure ISO 27001 Compliance**: Ensure your organization has an ISMS that complies with ISO 27001. As ISO 27701 is an extension of ISO 27001, having a compliant ISMS is a prerequisite for integrating privacy management into your security framework.
- **Implement ISO 27701**: Leverage ISO 27701 to establish, implement, and maintain a robust PIMS within your organization. This involves managing personal information proficiently, carrying out privacy risk assessments, and incorporating privacy considerations into your existing risk management process.
- **Monitor Regulatory Compliance**: Regularly assess your organization's compliance with relevant privacy laws, regulations, and contractual clauses. Given the complex and varying nature of these requirements across different jurisdictions, leveraging ISO 27701 can help navigate these complexities and ensure your organization's compliance.
- **Foster a Culture of Privacy**: Promote a culture of privacy within your organization, emphasizing its importance to all staff members. Regular training and communication about the requirements and benefits of ISO 27701 can help to ensure its successful implementation and maintenance. This proactive approach can bolster your organization's privacy posture, enhance stakeholder trust, and enable you to better manage privacy risks in today's data-driven world.

COMPARING AND INTEGRATING DIFFERENT CYBERSECURITY FRAMEWORKS

Understanding the myriad cybersecurity frameworks available in the market today can feel overwhelming. Each framework was developed with distinct purposes and focuses, and a clear understanding of these can greatly assist in pinpointing the one that will resonate most profoundly with your organization's unique requirements. Whether it is the degree of control granularity, regulatory focus, industry specificity, or governance emphasis, each framework offers something distinct.

In comparing these frameworks, key considerations should include the ease of integration within your existing systems, the comprehensiveness of the framework in covering all aspects of cybersecurity, its specific relevance to your industry, and alignment with your organization's risk tolerance and strategic business goals. It is about finding a framework or set of frameworks that dovetail with your cybersecurity strategy, providing robust protection while enabling business agility and growth.

An integrated cybersecurity program can derive significant value from leveraging multiple frameworks concurrently. By mapping controls across different frameworks, you are provided with a comprehensive and layered approach to managing cybersecurity risks, ensuring that every potential vulnerability is identified and addressed. This multilayered approach gives you the advantage of perspective, enabling a more in-depth and comprehensive analysis of security issues.

Due to the apparent complexity, achieving compliance with multiple frameworks might initially seem like an uphill task. However, when planned and executed strategically, it becomes manageable and provides a multifaceted view of your organization's security posture. This multilateral insight offers comprehensive protection, ensuring all possible gaps are identified and plugged in. It also demonstrates to stakeholders – from customers to regulatory bodies – that your organization takes cybersecurity seriously and has implemented robust measures to protect against threats, thus enhancing your organization's reputation and trustworthiness in the digital marketplace.

Recommendations:

- **Understand the Different Frameworks**: Begin by educating yourself and your team about the various cybersecurity frameworks available. Each one has its unique strengths, purposes, and focus areas. Understanding these frameworks will help you identify those most suited to your organization's needs and requirements.
- **Assess Your Current System and Requirements**: Before selecting a framework, thoroughly assess your organization's existing systems, risk tolerance, strategic goals, and the cybersecurity challenges inherent to your industry. This will help you identify frameworks that can integrate smoothly into your existing infrastructure and align well with your organizational goals.
- **Consider Multiple Frameworks**: Rather than restricting yourself to one framework, consider integrating multiple cybersecurity frameworks. This multilayered approach provides comprehensive protection and various

perspectives for managing cybersecurity risks, ensuring every potential vulnerability is covered.

- **Plan for Compliance**: Compliance with multiple frameworks may seem daunting due to its complexity, but with careful planning and strategic execution, it is manageable. Develop a detailed plan for integrating and maintaining compliance with the chosen frameworks, considering aspects like staff training, system upgrades, and ongoing monitoring.
- **Regularly Review and Update Your Strategy**: As cybersecurity threats evolve, so should your cybersecurity strategy. Periodically review and adjust your strategy and the frameworks you use to ensure they provide robust protection for your organization. This helps maintain security and demonstrates to stakeholders your ongoing commitment to cybersecurity. Understand Your Needs: Understand your organization's specific needs and objectives.

FUTURE TRENDS IN CYBERSECURITY FRAMEWORKS

Cybersecurity is an ever-evolving field. With each passing day, the cybersecurity landscape morphs in response to the changing nature of threats and the rapid pace of technological advancements. Cybersecurity frameworks, designed to provide structured and methodical approaches to managing cybersecurity risks, must also transform to keep pace. It is important to note that these transformations are not random. They often follow a specific trajectory dictated by cybersecurity's most critical areas of concern. For example, one can observe a growing focus on privacy and cloud security, which mirrors the shift in how data is stored and accessed in the digital age.

Existing frameworks must also adapt and expand their scope to accommodate emerging technology trends. Among these trends, Artificial Intelligence (AI) and machine learning profoundly influence cybersecurity. These technologies offer promising capabilities for automating threat detection, improving incident response, and identifying vulnerabilities. As a result, we can anticipate the emergence of revisions or new frameworks that integrate AI and machine learning as core components.

However, this integration is not without challenges. AI and machine learning models themselves need to be secure. Bad actors can manipulate them to cause harm, known as adversarial attacks. Therefore, future cybersecurity frameworks would need to address how to leverage AI for cybersecurity and how to secure the AI systems themselves.

Besides, AI can personalize and enhance cybersecurity training and awareness programs, which are crucial components of any cybersecurity framework. Future frameworks will likely incorporate guidelines for using AI in this capacity, making cybersecurity education more interactive and engaging.

AI's potential impact on cybersecurity also extends to regulatory compliance. As AI models become more sophisticated and their use more widespread, regulatory bodies worldwide are beginning to scrutinize AI systems for transparency, fairness, and privacy concerns. Future cybersecurity frameworks may need to incorporate elements related to AI governance, addressing how organizations can maintain compliance while using AI in their cybersecurity initiatives.

Given the rapid pace of technological change, the cybersecurity landscape of tomorrow will undoubtedly be vastly different from today's. Cybersecurity frameworks, therefore, must be living documents – flexible, adaptable, and capable of evolving in tandem with technological advancements and changing threat vectors. Adapting to this ever-changing landscape is not merely about adopting new technologies like AI or adhering to emerging regulations. It also involves cultivating a culture of continuous learning and vigilance, where organizations proactively stay ahead of the curve by anticipating changes, adapting strategies, and integrating new developments into their cybersecurity frameworks. By doing so, organizations can safeguard their digital assets and maintain their trust in this digital age.

Recommendations:

- **Keep Pace with Technological Advancements:** Stay up-to-date with emerging trends in technology, such as AI and machine learning. These advancements are shaping the future of cybersecurity, and your organization needs to understand and embrace them to strengthen security measures.

- **Secure Your AI Systems:** As your organization starts leveraging AI for cybersecurity, also focus on ensuring the security of these AI systems themselves. Guard against adversarial attacks and implement measures to prevent bad actors from manipulating your AI models.

- **Enhance Training Programs:** Consider how AI can enhance your organization's cybersecurity training and awareness programs. Future frameworks will likely include guidelines on using AI in training, making it more interactive and engaging for staff. Stay ahead of the curve by starting to incorporate these strategies now.

- **Maintain Compliance While Using AI:** As regulatory bodies start to scrutinize AI systems for transparency, fairness, and privacy concerns, your organization will need to ensure it remains compliant while leveraging AI in its cybersecurity initiatives. Keep abreast of evolving regulations and incorporate them into your cybersecurity frameworks.

- **Cultivate a Culture of Continuous Learning:** Given the rapid pace of change in the cybersecurity landscape, fostering a culture of continuous learning and vigilance within your organization is crucial. Stay proactive in anticipating changes, adapting strategies, and integrating new developments into your cybersecurity framework to safeguard your digital assets and maintain trust in the digital age.

Chapter Conclusion

In today's digital era, where technology is woven deeply into the fabric of business operations, cybersecurity is not a mere luxury but a fundamental necessity for every organization, regardless of its size or industry. The increasing interconnectedness of business systems, driven by the proliferation of internet-based technologies, has created an environment where data breaches and cyber threats are actual, constant, and potentially catastrophic. Thus, the need for robust cybersecurity measures transcends industry boundaries, affecting everyone from the smallest start-ups to the largest multinationals.

The spectrum of cybersecurity threats is broad, encompassing everything from phishing attacks and ransomware to insider threats and supply chain vulnerabilities. Navigating this landscape can be complex and overwhelming. This is where cybersecurity frameworks come into play. They provide a structured, systematic, and comprehensive approach to managing cybersecurity risks, making them an invaluable tool in the fight against cyber threats.

Each framework has unique strengths and characteristics, tailoring its approach to specific situations, industries, or regulatory requirements. For instance, ISO/IEC 27001 is an internationally recognized standard for ISMSs, often favored by organizations with a global footprint. In contrast, the CMMC is designed for Department of Defense contractors, emphasizing a tiered approach to cybersecurity maturity.

Understanding these differences is vital in choosing a framework that aligns best with your organization's needs, risk tolerance, business objectives, and regulatory landscape. A thoughtful selection process, guided by thorough knowledge and understanding, can significantly augment your cybersecurity efforts, enabling you to leverage the framework's strengths to fortify your defenses.

However, implementing a cybersecurity framework is not just about protecting your organization's digital assets – although that is undoubtedly critical. A robust and effective cybersecurity program should also align with and support the organization's strategic objectives. It should facilitate business growth, enable digital transformation, and help build customer trust. It should not be viewed as an isolated or purely technical function but should be integrated into the overall business strategy.

For instance, a robust cybersecurity program can be a strong selling point, helping win over customers who value their data privacy and security. A robust cybersecurity program can ensure regulatory compliance and avoid costly penalties for businesses in highly regulated industries like finance or healthcare. It can also enable the secure adoption of new technologies, facilitating innovation and digital transformation.

As we navigate this digital era, we must remember that cybersecurity is a journey, not a destination. The cyber threat landscape constantly evolves, with new threats emerging and old ones becoming more sophisticated. Thus, our approach to cybersecurity must also be dynamic, flexible, and adaptive. The cybersecurity frameworks are not meant to be static; they should be tailored to the organization's evolving needs and the changing threat landscape.

In conclusion, in a world increasingly driven by digital technologies, the importance of robust cybersecurity cannot be overstated. Choosing and implementing the right cybersecurity frameworks can significantly secure an organization's digital assets, support its strategic objectives, and ensure its long-term success in this digital age. It is not an easy task, but with the proper knowledge, resources, and commitment, it is certainly an achievable one.

Case Study: Securing Globex Corporation

Globex Corporation is an international finance firm dealing with high-stakes trading. The firm holds sensitive information on multinational companies and high-net-worth individuals. Its security infrastructure has been a patchwork of solutions to specific problems with no cohesive plan. As a result, the company suffered a significant data breach that threatened its credibility and the trust of its clients.

Marc, recently appointed as the new CISO of Globex Corporation, had the task of ensuring that such a data breach never occurred again. Armed with various cybersecurity frameworks, he was ready to overhaul the company's cybersecurity infrastructure.

Marc began by understanding the business needs of Globex Corporation and the regulatory environment in which it operated. Based on this understanding, he found ISO/IEC 27001 and COBIT to be the most suitable frameworks, considering the company's global operations and the need for robust IT governance. ISO/IEC 27001, with its comprehensive approach to information security, would provide a solid base. COBIT, on the other hand, would ensure that Globex's IT practices align with its business objectives.

However, considering Globex's specific line of business, Marc also decided to incorporate the PCI DSS framework to secure cardholder data and the ISF's Standard of Good Practice to reinforce best practices across all aspects of information security. Lastly, he knew the value of monitoring third-party risks due to Globex's extensive partner network. Hence, he decided to use CyberGRX for effective third-party risk management.

Marc oversaw the implementation of these frameworks, coordinating with various departments to ensure everyone understood their roles and responsibilities in this new cybersecurity infrastructure. It was a challenging task, but Marc used his knowledge of these frameworks and his commitment to learning to effectively communicate their importance and relevance to the company's operations and objectives.

The implementation process had its hiccups. For example, integrating controls from different frameworks was not always straightforward, and not every employee was comfortable with the new processes. However, Marc persevered, organizing training sessions, providing resources for self-learning, and setting up channels for employees to voice their concerns and ask questions.

In the end, Globex Corporation had a comprehensive, robust cybersecurity infrastructure that addressed their previous security issues and built a strong foundation for handling future cybersecurity challenges. Globex could now reassure its clients that their data was safe and secure, and Marc could look back on the journey as a time of significant professional growth and achievement.

TOP STRENGTHS OF EACH FRAMEWORK

1. **ISO/IEC 27001: Information Security Management**
   - Internationally Recognized: This provides credibility and confidence to customers, clients, and stakeholders.
   - Comprehensive: It covers all areas of information security, from risk assessment to incident response.
   - Integrative: It can easily be integrated with other standards, such as ISO 27701, for privacy management.
2. **COBIT (Control Objectives for Information and Related Technologies)**
   - Holistic: It covers all IT governance and management aspects beyond security.
   - Business-focused: It is designed to support business objectives and value creation.
   - Detailed and Structured: It provides clear guidance and maturity models for each control objective.
3. **CMMC (Cybersecurity Maturity Model Certification)**
   - Defense-focused: It is designed for Department of Defense contractors, ensuring alignment with specific needs.
   - Maturity-oriented: It provides a clear path for continuous improvement in cybersecurity.
   - Comprehensive: It covers 17 different cybersecurity domains, providing a wide range of coverage.
4. **CIS (Center for Internet Security) Controls**
   - Actionable: It provides a set of clear and concise controls for improving cybersecurity.

- Prioritized: The controls are prioritized to help organizations focus on the most effective measures first.
- Community-driven: A community of IT security experts develops and refines the controls.

5. **PCI DSS (Payment Card Industry Data Security Standard)**
   - Specific: It is tailored for businesses that handle cardholder data, making it highly relevant.
   - Detailed: It provides clear and specific requirements for each area of compliance.
   - Widely Accepted: Compliance is mandatory for many businesses, making it a recognized standard.

6. **ISF's Standard of Good Practice for Information Security**
   - Comprehensive: It covers all aspects of information security, including people, processes, and technology.
   - Business-oriented: It focuses on practical actions that support business objectives.
   - Customizable: It allows organizations to tailor the standard to their specific needs.

7. **ICFR (Internal Control over Financial Reporting)**
   - Financial Focus: It is specifically tailored for financial reporting processes, making it highly relevant for finance-related businesses.
   - Compliance-focused: Compliance with ICFR can help businesses avoid regulatory penalties.
   - Structured: It provides a systematic approach to managing the risks associated with financial reporting.

8. **Cloud Security Alliance Controls**
   - Cloud-specific: It focuses on security issues specifically associated with the cloud, making it relevant in the era of cloud computing.
   - Comprehensive: It covers all areas of cloud security, from data security to disaster recovery.
   - Community-driven: The controls are developed and refined by a community of cloud security experts.

9. **CyberGRX**
   - Third-party Focus: It focuses on managing third-party cyber risk, a significant and growing area of concern.
   - Dynamic: It uses a dynamic and up-to-date view of third-party cyber risk.
   - Scalable: It allows organizations to assess many third parties efficiently.

10. **CyberVadis**
    - Scalable: It uses a SaaS platform to enable scalable and efficient cybersecurity assessments.

- Comprehensive: It covers various cybersecurity domains, from IT security to data protection.
- Continuous Monitoring: It offers constant monitoring capabilities to provide up-to-date risk information.

11. **ISO 27017: Code of Practice for Information Security Controls**
    - Cloud-specific: It provides guidelines for cloud service providers and customers.
    - Internationally Recognized: Like ISO 27001, it provides credibility and confidence.
    - Integrative: It is designed to be used with ISO 27001 and other ISO standards.

12. **ISO 27701: Privacy Information Management**
    - Privacy-focused: It is designed explicitly for managing privacy information, making it highly relevant in an era of increasing privacy concerns.
    - Integrative: It is designed to supplement ISO 27001, allowing integration with existing ISMS.
    - Comprehensive: It covers all aspects of privacy information management, from collection to deletion.

CHAPTER 13

NIST SP 800-53: Security and Privacy Controls Framework

"Cybersecurity controls are not mere gatekeepers; they are the unsung heroes who tirelessly patrol the digital frontier, ensuring our safety and peace of mind."

The National Institute of Standards and Technology (NIST) Special Publication (SP) 800-53 offers comprehensive guidelines addressing security and privacy controls for federal information systems and organizations. Understanding the purpose, applicability, structure, and significance of its control families is crucial. The organization and integration of SP 800-53 with other standards are also discussed, providing insights into its various components, such as the control catalog, privacy controls, supplemental guidance, and the available resources for understanding and implementation. The concept of controls and control families is also simplified, with a detailed discussion of their selection, application, and relationship with other frameworks.

OVERVIEW OF NIST SP 800-53

The NIST SP 800-53 is an essential cybersecurity tool. Its primary objective is to provide guidelines for selecting and specifying security controls for systems that process, store, and transmit information. Its background stems from recognizing growing cybersecurity threats, creating the need for robust, flexible, and responsive measures to ensure information systems security.

Applicability of NIST SP 800-53 extends to all federal information systems except those related to national security. Nevertheless, its core principles are valuable for organizations beyond the federal sphere, offering a robust framework for managing cybersecurity risks. Given its comprehensive nature and alignment with globally recognized standards, it finds relevance across various industries and organizations of different sizes.

When discussing control families and their structure, it is essential to understand that these are groups of related controls to mitigate specific types of risks. Each control family corresponds to a particular security function, and their composition reflects a thorough understanding of security requirements.

NIST SP 800-53 does not exist in isolation but integrates seamlessly with other risk management standards. It aligns with the Risk Management Framework (RMF), which emphasizes the importance of continuous monitoring and real-time risk management. This integration enhances the ability of organizations to create a comprehensive and effective cybersecurity posture.

SP 800-53 has evolved significantly since its inception to adapt to the dynamic cybersecurity landscape. Its revisions address emerging threats and reflect the latest research and understanding of risks, threats, vulnerabilities, and security controls.

Recommendations:

- **Dedicate Time for Comprehensive Review:** Invest quality time to understand the guidelines specified in NIST SP 800-53. These guidelines are essential in developing a robust security controls framework that aligns with industry standards and best practices.

- **Ensure Broad Applicability:** Even if your organization is not a federal body, consider leveraging NIST SP 800-53 for its broad applicability and comprehensive nature. Its principles can fortify any organization's cybersecurity infrastructure.

- **Focus on Control Families:** Pay special attention to the control families detailed in NIST SP 800-53. Understanding these controls and their interrelationships is crucial in mitigating specific types of risks.

- **Explore Integration Possibilities:** Look for opportunities to integrate NIST SP 800-53 with other risk management frameworks within your organization. This approach ensures a holistic security posture.

- **Stay Updated:** Keep an eye on revisions and updates to NIST SP 800-53. The evolving landscape of cybersecurity necessitates the continuous adaptation of such guidelines.

STRUCTURE AND ORGANIZATION OF NIST SP 800-53

NIST SP 800-53 is structured around a Control Catalog, which provides an exhaustive list of controls designed to tackle a wide range of cybersecurity risks. These controls span multiple domains, encompassing a variety of preventive and responsive measures. The catalog is periodically updated, with new controls added to reflect the rapidly evolving threat landscape.

This ensures that the catalog maintains its relevance and effectiveness over time.

Within the Control Catalog are Baselines, a subset of the catalog's controls that offer a starting point for developing a security plan. These baselines are tailored to the unique needs and risk profiles of different systems and organizations, providing a comprehensive, adaptable framework for cybersecurity. This tailoring process allows for adding, modifying, or removing controls based on specific risk considerations, industry regulations, and business requirements.

Alongside security controls, NIST SP 800-53 also features Privacy Controls, which address the need to protect individuals' personal information. These controls help organizations comply with privacy regulations and best practices, promoting stakeholder transparency and trust. They reflect the growing importance of privacy in the digital age and its interconnection with cybersecurity.

Providing more context to the controls are the Supplemental Guidance sections. These sections offer additional insights into the controls' intent, implementation, and assessment. They serve to ensure that organizations have a clear understanding of what is expected and how to achieve the desired security outcomes.

The Appendices and Resources are essential to NIST SP 800-53. They provide more detailed information on various topics and offer practical tools to assist in implementing and managing the controls. These resources can benefit cybersecurity professionals seeking to deepen their understanding of the standard and improve their organization's security posture.

Recommendations:

- **Detailed Examination of Control Catalog:** Conduct a thorough examination of the Control Catalog to identify the controls relevant to your organization's cybersecurity needs.
- **Utilize Baselines Effectively:** To develop your organization's security plan, tailoring it to fit your specific requirements and risk profiles.
- **Prioritize Privacy Controls:** In an age where data privacy is crucial, pay close attention to the privacy controls within NIST SP 800-53. These can guide your organization in safeguarding personal information and compliance with privacy regulations.
- **Benefit from Supplemental Guidance:** Take advantage of the supplemental guidance provided for each control. This guidance can help clarify intent and aid in successfully implementing the rules.
- **Leverage Appendices and Resources:** Utilize the detailed information and tools provided in the appendices and resources. These can significantly aid in understanding and effectively applying the standards outlined in NIST SP 800-53.

UNDERSTANDING CONTROLS AND CONTROL FAMILIES

In NIST SP 800-53, controls are the countermeasures or safeguards an organization deploys to protect its information systems and data from cybersecurity threats. These controls can be technical, administrative, or physical. Control Families, meanwhile, are groups of related controls that work together to tackle specific categories of cybersecurity risks.

Control Families form the backbone of NIST SP 800-53, covering various potential security issues. Understanding the Core Control Families is crucial in grasping the comprehensive security strategy outlined in the standard. These families include but are not limited to Access Control (AC), Audit and Accountability (AU), Incident Response (IR), Risk Assessment (RA), and System and Communications Protection (SC).

The process of Selecting and Applying Controls can be complex. It is driven by an organization's risk management strategy, unique risk profile, and the specific requirements of its information systems. It is important to note that the selection and application of controls is not a one-size-fits-all process. Instead, it requires careful thought, planning, and tailoring to the organization's needs.

Control Enhancements are modifications to the base controls that provide a higher level of security. These enhancements can be added to the base controls based on an organization's specific needs, risk tolerance, and the sensitivity of the information it processes, stores, and transmits.

Control Assessments are key to ensuring the selected controls are correctly implemented and effectively mitigating the identified risks. These assessments are carried out regularly as part of the organization's continuous monitoring strategy.

Finally, the controls and control families within NIST SP 800-53 are isolated. They have a solid relationship with Other Frameworks, such as the NIST Cybersecurity Framework and the ISO/IEC 27001 standard. Understanding these relationships can help organizations build a more integrated, holistic cybersecurity program.

Recommendations:

- **Understand Control Families:** Learn the core control families outlined in NIST SP 800-53. Understanding these is essential to build a comprehensive and effective security strategy.
- **Thoughtful Selection of Controls:** Choose controls that align with your organization's risk management strategy, risk profile, and the specific needs of your information systems.
- **Consider Control Enhancements:** Review the potential for control enhancements in the context of your organization's specific needs and risk tolerance. These can provide additional layers of protection.
- **Regular Control Assessments:** Conduct regular control assessments to ensure the selected controls are effectively implemented and successfully mitigate the identified risks.

- **Connect with Other Frameworks:** Understand the relationship of NIST SP 800-53 controls and control families to other risk management frameworks. This can aid in building a more integrated, comprehensive cybersecurity program.

Chapter Conclusion

Navigating the labyrinth of cybersecurity risks can be an overwhelming task in today's technology-dependent era. Threats are ever-present, and the potential consequences of a security breach can be severe. Thankfully, implementing a robust, industry-proven framework can significantly reduce these risks. A leading solution in this field is the NIST SP 800-53 standard, a comprehensive model built to fortify cybersecurity governance.

The effectiveness of NIST SP 800-53 lies in its well-structured and methodical organization. It has been meticulously designed to assist users by classifying controls into discernible families. Focused areas of this standard include a control catalog, baselines and tailoring, privacy controls, supplemental guidance, and supplementary resources. Each component has been diligently evaluated to cover all potential cybersecurity threats broadly.

You find the controls and control families at the heart of NIST SP 800-53. These represent the actionable and practical measures businesses can integrate into their systems and procedures. Deep dives into the core control families, selection and application of controls, control enhancements, control assessments, and their interplay with other frameworks offer a complete overview of the standard's commitment to all-encompassing cybersecurity defenses.

In addition to its theoretical approach, practical and actionable recommendations have been suggested to help businesses implement NIST SP 800-53 more effectively. The provided guidance aids in successfully integrating the standard's advice into any organizational framework, facilitating the journey from learning about the standard to understanding its nuances and applying it in a real-world scenario.

Beyond mere compliance, understanding and implementing NIST SP 800-53 offers organizations a comprehensive toolkit to enhance their security posture significantly. This standard enables efficient and effective management of cybersecurity risks and establishes a robust framework capable of mitigating current threats while evolving to counteract future challenges.

Consequently, embracing NIST SP 800-53 means more than simply learning a new standard – it means understanding its fundamental principles and applying its profound insights. This knowledge could ignite an organization's journey toward a safer, more secure future. While this exploration of NIST SP 800-53 may be over, it is hoped that it will begin a long-term commitment to robust cybersecurity governance, risk management, and compliance.

Case Study: SecureTech Solutions

SecureTech Solutions, a burgeoning tech start-up, had been grappling with the daunting task of developing a comprehensive cybersecurity framework. Their IT Manager, Dan, was tasked with the challenge. He recognized the significance of a robust cybersecurity strategy in today's digital era and was determined to establish a solid foundation for SecureTech's cybersecurity practices. His objective was clear: to ensure SecureTech's systems were secure, its data was protected, and its reputation was safeguarded.

Dan had always been aware of the importance of the NIST SP 800-53 standard but had found it difficult to navigate its complexities and intricacies. The multitude of control families, the extensive control catalog, and the diversity of guidelines often overwhelmed him. However, he understood that mastering NIST SP 800-53 was not an overnight job. Taking the first recommendation to heart, he committed himself to learning, starting with a foundational understanding of the NIST Risk Management Framework, its evolution, and its relevance to cybersecurity management.

Gradually, Dan began to appreciate the structure of the NIST SP 800-53 standard. He understood its modular organization into control families, which helped him break down the standard into manageable portions. He started by integrating controls from critical control families, such as AC and AU, into SecureTech's existing systems. Dan realized that understanding each control family and their relationships was crucial for effective implementation.

As SecureTech's systems evolved and expanded, Dan constantly reassessed and revised the controls. He found the supplemental guidance NIST SP 800-53 particularly useful, as it offered practical advice on adapting controls to suit SecureTech's unique requirements and circumstances. Here, understanding the controls and control enhancements became abundantly clear.

When Dan finally had a comprehensive set of controls, he did not rest on his laurels. He understood that the rapidly changing cybersecurity landscape meant regular control assessments were necessary. Using NIST SP 800-53's guidance, he developed an assessment plan that ensured SecureTech's cybersecurity measures remained robust and relevant.

This case study of SecureTech and Dan's journey is a testament to the benefits and practicality of implementing NIST SP 800-53. It underscores the need for a commitment to learning, understanding the structure and organization of the standard, integrating controls and control families, and regularly assessing and adapting these controls. These are the key lessons every organization seeking to enhance its cybersecurity posture can draw from this chapter. With NIST SP 800-53 knowledge, organizations like SecureTech can protect their digital assets and ensure success in today's interconnected world.

NIST 800-53 CONTROL FAMILIES AND DESCRIPTIONS

AC: Access Control

The AC family of controls is one of the fundamental cornerstones of information security. It focuses on limiting and managing access to an organization's information systems to prevent unauthorized access. Access control covers everything from user registration and de-registration, user access provisioning, and management of privileged access rights to password management and review of user access rights.

With the rise of cyber threats, organizations must emphasize ensuring that their access controls are robust and effective. As such, the AC family also provides guidelines for session management, remote access, and wireless access controls. It ensures that the policies, procedures, and technical controls applied for access management align with the organization's risk strategy.

Moreover, as organizations expand their digital footprint, the AC family plays a crucial role in ensuring that the principle of least privilege is adhered to, ensuring that users only have the necessary rights to perform their functions.

PE: Physical and Environmental Protection

The Physical and Environmental Protection (PE) family of controls deals with the physical security of an organization's information systems and the environment where they are located. It includes controls to ensure physical access to assets is restricted and monitored and that protection is in place against natural and artificial threats. This involves using security guards, CCTV, locks, badges, and other physical security mechanisms.

In environmental protection, the controls aim to safeguard the organization's information systems from environmental hazards such as floods, fire, dust, electricity failures, and other physical risks. Aspects like temperature and humidity control in data centers are also considered within these controls.

These physical and environmental protections are essential in maintaining an organization's information systems' confidentiality, integrity, and availability. In an era where digital threats are prevalent, organizations should not forget the importance of the physical security of their IT infrastructure.

AT: Awareness and Training

The Awareness and Training (AT) family of controls emphasizes the role of people in the cybersecurity landscape. While technical controls are vital, the human element can become the weakest link in an organization's security posture without proper awareness and training. Therefore, this control family deals with implementing a comprehensive security education program for all users of information systems.

The AT family aims to ensure that users understand their responsibilities concerning system security and are equipped with the knowledge to handle system interactions securely. It covers general security awareness training for all users and targeted training for users with significant security responsibilities.

The third aspect of the AT family deals with the concept of continual learning. The rapidly changing landscape of cyber threats means that security awareness and training cannot be a one-time activity. It should be a continuous process, updated regularly to address emerging threats and vulnerabilities.

PL: Planning

The Planning (PL) family of controls focuses on developing and implementing comprehensive security plans for an organization's information systems. These plans outline the system's security requirements, the controls in place to meet these requirements, and the strategies for maintaining system security. The security plan acts as a road map guiding the organization's security efforts.

A vital aspect of the PL control family is incorporating security into the initial design and development of systems. Organizations can proactively address potential vulnerabilities and threats by adopting a security-first approach in system design, making their systems more secure and resilient.

The PL family also regularly updates and reviews the security plan to ensure it remains relevant in the face of evolving risks and business requirements. The life cycle approach ensures the maintenance of an effective and robust security posture throughout the system.

AU: Audit and Accountability

The AU control family is about tracking, logging, and analyzing activities within an organization's information system. Through this, organizations can ensure that actions can be traced back to a responsible entity, promoting individual accountability and allowing for the detection of potential malicious activity.

The controls within the AU family cover areas such as audit event generation, review, analysis, and reporting, as well as audit storage, protection, and reduction. The aim is to create a comprehensive audit trail that records significant events and allows for detecting and investigating security incidents.

The third component of this control family is accountability. By tracing actions back to individuals, organizations can enforce responsibility for actions taken. Accountability is vital in deterring individuals from engaging in malicious activities, knowing their actions can be tracked.

PM: Program Management

The Program Management (PM) control family emphasizes establishing, implementing, and managing the overarching cybersecurity program. It recognizes that effective security requires a strategic, top-down approach that aligns with the organization's risk strategy and business objectives.

This control family addresses risk management strategy, security authorization process, mission/business process definition, enterprise architecture, and establishing a senior information security officer position. The aim is to ensure that security is not just a technical issue but an integral part of the organization's strategy and culture.

Furthermore, this control family recognizes the need for ongoing management and review of the security program. The security landscape is dynamic and ever-changing. As such, organizations must continually review and update their security program to ensure it remains effective in the face of emerging threats and vulnerabilities.

CA: Assessment, Authorization, and Monitoring

The Assessment, Authorization, and Monitoring (CA) control family deals with verifying the security posture of an organization's information system. It involves the regular testing and evaluation of the implemented security controls to ensure they operate effectively and provide the desired level of security.

This control family covers the initial assessment of security controls, the authorization to operate the system, and continuous monitoring. The aim is to provide ongoing assurance that the system's security controls continue to mitigate identified risks effectively.

Moreover, the CA control family recognizes the importance of an organization's risk appetite in deciding the appropriate levels of authorization and monitoring. By balancing business needs and security requirements, organizations can ensure that the controls provide an acceptable level of risk mitigation without hampering business operations.

PS: Personnel Security

The Personnel Security (PS) control family ensures that individuals accessing an organization's information systems are trustworthy and adequately trained to handle sensitive information. This includes personnel screening, employment agreements, and third-party personnel security.

This control family addresses the risk posed by "insiders" who have authorized access to an organization's systems. By ensuring personnel are trustworthy and understand their responsibilities, organizations can reduce the risk of internal security breaches.

The third component of the PS family focuses on maintaining personnel security throughout an individual's period of employment. This includes ongoing assessments of trustworthiness and the effective management of changes in work.

CM: Configuration Management

The Configuration Management (CM) control family focuses on establishing and maintaining consistent operational, functional, and physical attributes for an organization's systems and components. It includes baseline configuration, configuration change control, and security impact analysis.

The purpose of the CM family is to provide a structured and disciplined approach to managing changes in the system and its environment, ensuring that all changes are documented and approved, and any security implications are considered.

The third component of the CM family involves the ongoing monitoring and review of system configurations. By regularly reviewing and updating configurations, organizations can ensure that their systems continue to operate securely and efficiently, even in the face of evolving threats and changing business requirements.

PT: PII Processing and Transparency

The PII Processing and Transparency (PT) family of controls is a response to the increasing importance of personal data in today's digital world. It focuses on the secure and transparent processing of personally identifiable information (PII), ensuring an individual's privacy rights are respected.

This family of controls covers areas such as privacy notice, PII processing purpose, data minimization, use limitation, and data quality and integrity. It aims to provide individuals with information about the processing of their PII and ensure that this processing is carried out securely and legally.

The PT family also addresses the issue of consent. It provides controls for obtaining and managing consent for processing PII, ensuring individuals have control over their data.

CP: Contingency Planning

The Contingency Planning (CP) family of controls covers preparing and responding to events that could disrupt an organization's operations or compromise its information systems. These controls ensure that organizations recover quickly and efficiently from disruptions and continue providing essential services.

This family of controls addresses areas such as contingency planning, contingency plan testing and exercises, and contingency plan updates. The aim is to provide a framework for managing and reducing the impact of unexpected events.

The CP family's third component involves the system's recovery and reconstitution after an event. Organizations can ensure that they can recover their systems to a known, secure state following a disruption by having a detailed and well-tested contingency plan.

RA: Risk Assessment

The RA family of controls emphasizes the importance of understanding and managing the risks to an organization's information systems. Organizations can proactively mitigate these risks by identifying and analyzing potential threats and vulnerabilities.

This control family covers risk assessment, vulnerability scanning, and risk mitigation. The aim is to provide a systematic and repeatable process for assessing and addressing risks.

The third component of the RA family is the continuous monitoring of risks. By regularly reviewing and updating their risk assessments, organizations can ensure that they are aware of emerging threats and vulnerabilities and can take appropriate action to mitigate these risks.

IA: Identification and Authentication

The Identification and Authentication (IA) family of controls ensures that only authorized individuals can access an organization's information systems. It includes user identification and authentication, device identification and authentication, and authenticator management.

The purpose of the IA family is to prevent unauthorized access to systems and data. By verifying the identity of users and devices, organizations can ensure that only authorized entities have access to their systems.

The third component of the IA family involves the management of authentication mechanisms. Organizations can maintain the integrity of their identification and authentication processes by ensuring that authentication mechanisms are secure and effectively managed.

SA: System and Services Acquisition

The System and Services Acquisition (SA) family of controls addresses the procurement and integration of new systems and services. It includes the system development life cycle, acquisition processes, and third-party services.

This family of controls aims to ensure that security is considered throughout the acquisition process, from the initial requirements definition to the integration and acceptance of the new system or service.

The SA family's third component involves managing supply chain risks. By considering security throughout the supply chain, organizations can ensure that the systems and services they acquire do not introduce new vulnerabilities into their environment.

IR: Incident Response

The Incident Response (IR) family of controls focuses on preparing for and handling security incidents. It includes incident response planning, training, testing, handling, monitoring, reporting, and post-incident analysis.

The IR family aims to ensure that organizations are prepared to respond quickly and effectively to security incidents. Organizations can minimize the impact of incidents and recover more rapidly by having a well-planned and practiced incident response process.

The third component of the IR family involves learning from incidents. By analyzing incidents and their handling, organizations can improve their response processes and take steps to prevent similar incidents.

SC: System and Communications Protection

The SC family of controls addresses protecting information at rest and in transit. It includes boundary protection, cryptographic key management, and network integrity.

The purpose of the SC family is to prevent unauthorized access to and disclosure of information. This involves technical controls, such as encryption and firewalls, and procedural controls, such as secure handling procedures and data destruction.

The third component of the SC family involves the ongoing monitoring and protection of systems and communications. Organizations can ensure their information remains secure by regularly monitoring system activity and updating protections.

MA: Maintenance

The Maintenance (MA) control family focuses on the routine and non-routine maintenance of an organization's information systems. It includes maintenance policies and procedures, timely maintenance, and maintenance tools.

The MA family aims to ensure that systems remain secure throughout their life cycle. This includes providing that maintenance activities do not introduce new vulnerabilities and that systems are returned to a secure state following maintenance.

The third component of the MA family involves the monitoring of maintenance activities. By tracking and reviewing these activities, organizations can ensure that maintenance does not reduce system security.

SI: System and Information Integrity

The System and Information Integrity (SI) control family deals with preventing and detecting errors and malicious activity in an organization's information systems. It includes areas like flaw remediation, malicious code protection, and system monitoring.

The purpose of the SI family is to maintain the integrity of systems and information by preventing unauthorized changes and detecting and correcting errors. This involves technical controls, such as antivirus software and intrusion detection systems, and procedural controls, such as incident handling procedures.

The third component of the SI family involves the ongoing monitoring and protection of system integrity. Organizations can ensure their systems and information remain secure by regularly monitoring system activity and updating protections.

MP: Media Protection

The Media Protection (MP) family of controls protects information stored on physical media. It includes media access, storage, transport, and sanitization.

The MP family aims to prevent unauthorized access to and disclosure of information stored on physical media. This involves technical controls, such as encryption, and procedural controls, such as secure handling procedures and media destruction.

The third component of the MP family involves monitoring and controlling media. By tracking the use and movement of physical media, organizations can ensure that information is not lost, stolen, or accessed by unauthorized individuals.

SR: Supply Chain Risk Management

The Supply Chain Risk Management (SR) family of controls focuses on managing the risks associated with an organization's supply chain. It includes supplier risk management, supply chain protection, and supply chain authenticity.

The SR family aims to ensure that the products and services an organization acquires do not introduce new risks into its environment. This involves technical controls, such as security testing, and procedural controls, such as supplier vetting and contractual agreements.

The third component of the SR family involves the ongoing monitoring and management of supply chain risks. By regularly reviewing their supply chain and addressing identified risks, organizations can ensure the security of their products and services.

CHAPTER 14

The FFIEC: An Introduction

"The FFIEC Examination Handbooks serve as invaluable guides, illuminating the path toward effective risk management and comprehensive cybersecurity practices, empowering organizations to navigate the ever-evolving threat landscape."

This chapter explores the Federal Financial Institutions Examination Council (FFIEC), a crucial organization in financial cybersecurity. We delve into its historical background and significance, understand its key roles and responsibilities, and demystify the FFIEC Examination Handbooks. The chapter concludes with an overview of the FFIEC Cybersecurity Assessment Tool (CAT), illustrating its purpose, components, and how it can be effectively integrated into an organization's cybersecurity program.

FFIEC HISTORY AND BACKGROUND

The establishment of the FFIEC in 1979 was a landmark event in the history of financial regulation in the United States. The FFIEC was formed due to the Financial Institutions Regulatory and Interest Rate Control Act of 1978, a federal law enacted to promote consistent and coordinated standards among financial institutions. The creation of the FFIEC signified a significant shift toward a more streamlined and cohesive approach to regulating the financial sector, addressing the need for uniform standards, regulatory practices, and oversight among the diverse entities within the industry.

The primary objectives of the FFIEC were well defined from the onset. Its mandate was clear – to promote uniform principles, standards, and report forms among financial institutions. These principles and standards encompass

245

many areas, including risk management, consumer protection, lending practices, operational efficiency, and now, an increasingly critical area – cybersecurity. The consistent pursuit of these objectives over the years underscores the FFIEC's unwavering commitment to fostering a coherent and balanced regulatory landscape, vital for ensuring stability, integrity, and public confidence in the financial sector.

The financial industry's landscape has drastically changed since the FFIEC was established, mainly due to technological advancements. Recognizing this evolution, the FFIEC has dynamically adapted its focus and approach. The Council has significantly transitioned from overseeing traditional financial operations to addressing a broader set of challenges and risks the digital era poses. The emphasis on information technology (IT), digital banking, and cybersecurity is a testament to the FFIEC's adaptability and foresight in proactively addressing emerging threats and opportunities.

The FFIEC's role in the financial industry is multifaceted and extends beyond setting guidelines and standards. It also serves as a facilitator of dialogue and mutual understanding among different stakeholders within the industry. Through its initiatives, the Council ensures that the concerns and perspectives of financial institutions are heard, considered, and incorporated into its guidelines and principles. By doing so, the FFIEC effectively bridges the gap between regulatory requirements and the practical realities of operating a financial institution. This balanced approach fosters compliance and cooperation while ensuring the guidelines and standards are pragmatic and responsive to the needs of the industry.

The influence of the FFIEC is not confined to the borders of the United States. In the era of globalization, financial markets worldwide are closely interconnected, and cybersecurity threats are universal, often transcending geographical boundaries. Recognizing this, the FFIEC's guidance, standards, and principles often serve as models for regulatory bodies in other countries. Its guidelines have been adopted or used as reference points by financial regulatory authorities across the globe. This global influence further underscores the FFIEC's leadership role in shaping robust and effective regulatory practices for financial institutions.

Furthermore, the Council's global impact is seen in harmonizing international financial regulatory practices. The FFIEC has helped promote a more consistent and coordinated approach to managing financial and cyber risks worldwide by establishing standards and guidelines that are benchmarks of good practice. Its role in facilitating knowledge sharing and cooperation among global financial regulatory authorities has been instrumental in enhancing the collective capability of the global financial industry in managing challenges and threats, particularly in the cybersecurity domain.

Recommendations:

- **Streamline Financial Regulation:** The FFIEC, established in 1979, is a game-changer for financial regulation in the United States. It shifted toward a more coordinated approach to regulating the financial sector, standardizing practices, and ensuring oversight across diverse entities.

- **Foster Regulatory Coherence:** The FFIEC promotes uniform principles, standards, and reporting formats across financial institutions. This consistency is vital for stability, integrity, and public confidence in the financial sector.
- **Adapt to Technological Changes:** The FFIEC has adapted to significant financial industry changes, primarily due to technological advancements. The Council now focuses on the challenges and risks of the digital era, such as IT, digital banking, and cybersecurity.
- **Facilitate Industry Dialogue:** The FFIEC is not just a regulatory body. It also fosters dialogue among stakeholders in the financial industry, ensuring that their concerns and perspectives are considered in developing guidelines and principles.
- **Influence Global Regulatory Practices:** The reach of the FFIEC extends beyond US borders. Its guidelines serve as a reference for regulatory bodies worldwide, harmonizing international practices and promoting a coordinated approach to managing financial and cyber risks.
- **Enhance Global Cybersecurity:** The FFIEC has played a crucial role in enhancing the global financial industry's ability to manage threats, especially in cybersecurity. It promotes knowledge sharing and cooperation among financial regulatory authorities worldwide.

ROLE AND RESPONSIBILITIES

The FFIEC, an interagency body comprised of several US financial regulatory agencies, is responsible for regulatory oversight of various financial institutions. This includes commercial banks, savings associations, credit unions, and other financial bodies in the United States. Its oversight role is not just a routine duty but a critical part of maintaining the nation's financial stability, especially in the digital age. The FFIEC ensures that these institutions adhere to all applicable federal laws and regulations designed to protect consumers, maintain stability, and bolster public confidence in the nation's financial system.

This oversight role is particularly critical to the realm of cybersecurity. As financial institutions increasingly rely on digital technologies, they become more susceptible to digital threats. To safeguard against these evolving threats, the FFIEC's oversight extends to each institution's cybersecurity practices. They scrutinize their security measures, systems resilience, incident response plans, and overall cyber risk management, ensuring that these institutions are well protected against potential cyber threats.

Beyond its oversight role, the FFIEC is responsible for setting appropriate standards, guidelines, and principles for the financial sector. This function is comprehensive, covering many aspects related to the functioning of financial institutions. These aspects include but are not limited to risk management, IT protocols, lending standards, consumer protection, and the hot-button issue of cybersecurity. The Council constantly monitors developments and trends in the financial sector and the broader economic environment. Based on their observations, they periodically review, revise, and strengthen these standards and guidelines to ensure they are up-to-date and robust.

Developing these guidelines and standards is not a theoretical exercise for the FFIEC. Instead, it is an in-depth process that involves drawing from practical experiences, soliciting expert inputs, conducting extensive research, and using lessons learned from past events. These guidelines and standards reflect the FFIEC's commitment to creating a regulatory environment compliant with the law and practical, relevant, and valuable for institutions.

The FFIEC's responsibilities extend beyond setting guidelines; it also ensures their implementation through examination and compliance processes enforced by the members of the FFIEC council. The Council conducts regular examinations of financial institutions to assess their adherence to federal laws, regulations, and the guidelines set by the FFIEC itself. These examinations are crucial for maintaining a healthy financial ecosystem and identifying potential issues before they escalate.

Besides its regulatory and supervisory roles, the FFIEC also undertakes significant educational and communication initiatives. The Council recognizes that knowledge is power and that informed decisions by financial institutions contribute to a more resilient and robust financial system. Thus, the FFIEC undertakes various initiatives to educate and communicate with the financial industry. It conducts regular training programs, seminars, and workshops; publishes informative handbooks and guides; shares best practices; and disseminates useful information on various aspects of financial management, including cybersecurity. The FFIEC's educational initiatives equip financial institutions with the knowledge and tools to manage their operations effectively and responsibly.

Finally, the FFIEC emphasizes the importance of collaboration in fulfilling its mandate. The Council collaborates extensively with other regulatory bodies, industry associations, and financial institutions to foster a culture of mutual understanding, cooperation, and joint action. By working closely with other entities, the FFIEC can get diverse perspectives, leverage shared resources, and coordinate actions more effectively. This collaborative approach is precious in dealing with cybersecurity threats requiring a united, coordinated, and rapid response. Through collaboration, the FFIEC and its partners can address the collective challenge of cybersecurity and protect the integrity of the nation's financial system.

Recommendations:

- **Recognize the Regulatory Role:** Understand the extent and importance of the FFIEC's regulatory oversight, which will help comply with their standards and guidelines.
- **Stay Updated with Standards:** Stay updated with the latest standards and guidelines issued by the FFIEC, as these can significantly influence an institution's cybersecurity policies.

- **Be Prepared for Examinations:** Be aware of the FFIEC's examination process and prepare for it. Regular internal audits and compliance checks can ensure a smooth examination process.
- **Leverage FFIEC's Educational Resources:** Use the FFIEC's educational resources and training programs to enhance your understanding of complex financial and cybersecurity concepts.
- **Engage in Collaboration:** Proactively engage with the FFIEC and other entities. Open communication and cooperation can significantly enhance your institution's ability to manage and respond to cybersecurity threats.

UNDERSTANDING THE FFIEC EXAMINATION HANDBOOKS

The FFIEC Handbook series is an integral resource as a comprehensive financial institution reference. These handbooks guide these institutions in navigating various aspects of their operational management, with cybersecurity being a focal point of their content. Given the complex and evolving nature of the cybersecurity landscape, the insights offered by these handbooks are invaluable. They understand cybersecurity threats and risks and provide comprehensive management procedures and controls.

These handbooks are not optional readings; their understanding is crucial for the successful operation of any financial institution. This is because they contain a wealth of knowledge on various operational aspects, from managing internal processes to dealing with external regulatory compliance. The handbooks act as an authoritative guide, providing clear and actionable directives to comply with federal laws and regulations, thus ensuring that institutions are meeting their legal obligations and employing best practices for optimal operations.

The key objectives of the FFIEC Handbooks are manifold. First, they offer practical guidance to financial institutions on managing and enhancing different aspects of their operations. This guidance is not just about managing current operations but also extends to improving processes and optimizing performances, ensuring that institutions function at their best. Second, the handbooks aim to establish a uniform approach to examinations. They provide a standardized checklist for institutions and examiners, ensuring consistency, fairness, and comprehensiveness in the examination process.

The handbooks cover an extensive range of topics. The cybersecurity guidelines are particularly critical, given the increasing digital threats and the rising costs of data breaches. These guidelines help institutions develop robust and resilient cybersecurity frameworks aligned with regulatory expectations, facilitating regulatory compliance while enhancing cyber resilience.

The applicability and scope of the FFIEC Handbooks are not limited. They cater to the entire spectrum of financial institutions under federal regulation. This includes the big names with complex operations and smaller, more straightforward institutions. The handbooks recognize the diversity of the financial industry and offer specific advice and instructions that are relevant and useful to different types of institutions. They understand various institutions' unique challenges and requirements and tailor their guidance accordingly, ensuring no institution is unsupported.

Using the FFIEC Handbooks to ensure regulatory compliance is a prudent strategy for any financial institution. These handbooks are not abstract, theoretical documents; they offer practical, real-world recommendations that can be effectively implemented. The handbooks also offer an exhaustive guide to the FFIEC examinations, providing clear directives on preparing for and navigating these examinations successfully. Institutions that utilize the handbooks effectively are better prepared for FFIEC examinations and are more likely to meet their regulatory responsibilities, ensuring continued operation and success in the competitive financial industry.

Recommendations:

- **Obtain the Handbooks:** Acquire the latest editions of the FFIEC Handbooks. They are the most comprehensive resource for understanding your institution's regulatory obligations.
- **Understand the Objectives:** Appreciate the objectives of these handbooks. They aim to ensure consistency in operational practices and regulatory examinations across financial institutions.
- **Review Applicability:** Understand the applicability of the handbooks to your institution, recognizing the tailored advice for different types of financial institutions.
- **Use the Handbooks for Compliance:** Use the FFIEC Handbooks to ensure compliance with federal regulations and successfully navigate FFIEC examinations.
- **Seek Expert Guidance:** When necessary, seek expert guidance to understand better and implement the complex aspects of the handbooks, particularly those relating to cybersecurity.

THE FFIEC CYBERSECURITY ASSESSMENT TOOL (CAT)

The FFIEC CAT is an integral part of the Council's cybersecurity guidelines, designed to help institutions identify their risk levels and determine the maturity of their cybersecurity programs. Understanding the purpose and use of this tool can significantly enhance an institution's capacity to manage cybersecurity threats effectively.

The primary purpose of the CAT is to provide a standardized approach for assessing cybersecurity risks and readiness. It enables institutions to evaluate their risk profiles and cybersecurity preparedness accurately. The CAT catalyzes a proactive approach toward cybersecurity, shifting institutions from reactive threat management to a strategic, risk-based cybersecurity stance.

The components of the CAT are designed to cover all essential areas of cybersecurity. It includes an inherent risk profile, which helps institutions identify the type and level of risk they inherently hold, and a cybersecurity maturity assessment, which measures an institution's preparedness and resilience to potential cyber threats. These components ensure a comprehensive evaluation, considering potential threats and an institution's management capability.

Conducting a cybersecurity assessment using the CAT is a structured process. It begins with identifying an institution's inherent risk profile and evaluating its cybersecurity controls' maturity. By comparing the risk profile and maturity levels, institutions can identify gaps in their cybersecurity strategies and prioritize areas for improvement.

The **Inherent Risk Profile** measures the level of risk posed by an institution's activities, services, and products. The risk profile is determined by the type, volume, and complexity of the institution's operations and the threats it faces. The inherent risk profile helps institutions understand how their activities, technologies, and external threats contribute to cybersecurity risk.

Cyber Risk Management and Oversight addresses the board of directors' oversight and management's development and implementation of an effective enterprise-wide cybersecurity program with comprehensive policies and procedures. This includes governance, risk management, resources, and training and culture. It emphasizes the mitigation of cybersecurity threats and the establishment of appropriate accountability and oversight.

Threat Intelligence and Collaboration involve processes to effectively discover, analyze, and understand cyber threats, with the capability to share information internally and with appropriate third parties. This includes threat intelligence, monitoring and analyzing, and information sharing. It emphasizes acquiring and analyzing information to identify, track, and predict cyber capabilities, intentions, and activities.

Cybersecurity Controls are the practices and processes used to protect assets, infrastructure, and information by strengthening the institution's defensive posture through continuous, automated protection and monitoring. This includes preventative controls, detective controls, and corrective controls. It emphasizes using infrastructure management, access management, device and end-point security, and secure coding to deter and prevent cyberattacks.

External Dependency Management involves establishing and maintaining a comprehensive program to oversee and manage external connections and third-party relationships with access to the institution's technology assets and information. This includes connections and relationship management. It emphasizes identifying, monitoring, and managing external connections and data flows to third parties.

Cyber Incident Management and Resilience includes establishing, identifying, and analyzing cyber events; prioritizing the institution's containment or mitigation; and escalating information to appropriate stakeholders. Cyber resilience encompasses planning and testing to maintain and recover ongoing operations during and following a cyber incident. This includes incident resilience planning strategy, detection, response, mitigation, and escalation reporting. It emphasizes the integration of cybersecurity practices and analytics across lines of business and the automation of the majority of risk--management processes.

Analyzing and understanding the results of a CAT assessment is as crucial as conducting the evaluation itself. The results offer invaluable insights into an institution's cybersecurity strengths and vulnerabilities. Institutions can use these insights to make informed decisions, formulate strategic plans, and allocate resources more effectively toward enhancing their cybersecurity posture.

Integrating the results from the CAT into an institution's cybersecurity program is the final, crucial step. It enables institutions to align cybersecurity strategies with risk profiles and readiness levels. By doing so, they can ensure that their cybersecurity measures are robust and tailored to their specific needs and vulnerabilities.

Recommendations:

- **Understand the Tool:** Commit to learning about the FFIEC CAT. Familiarize yourself with its purpose, structure, and components to understand how it can be utilized to identify and manage cybersecurity risks in your organization.
- **Evaluate Inherent Risk:** Use the CAT to assess your organization's inherent risk profile. This evaluation will help identify the types and levels of risks posed by your organization's activities, services, and products, providing a solid basis for tailoring your cybersecurity strategy.
- **Measure Cybersecurity Maturity:** Implement the cybersecurity maturity assessment component of the CAT to gauge your organization's resilience to potential cyber threats. This measured understanding will guide improvements and strengthen your cybersecurity posture.
- **Analyze the Assessment:** Dedicate resources to analyze your CAT assessment results thoroughly. The insights from this analysis will offer a valuable understanding of your organization's cybersecurity strengths and vulnerabilities, helping you make informed strategic decisions.
- **Integrate Results:** Prioritize integrating your CAT assessment results into your organization's cybersecurity program. This will ensure that your cybersecurity strategies align with your risk profile and readiness levels, leading to more effective and specific protective measures.

THE FFIEC AUDIT HANDBOOK

The FFIEC Audit Handbook is a comprehensive guide that offers a wealth of information on the characteristics of an effective IT audit function. The booklet is designed to serve as a roadmap for examiners and financial institutions, providing them with the necessary tools and knowledge to navigate the complex landscape of IT auditing. The booklet underscores the importance of a well-planned and adequately structured audit program, emphasizing that such a program is instrumental in evaluating risk management practices, internal control systems, and compliance with corporate policies concerning IT-related risks.

The booklet outlines the roles and responsibilities of various stakeholders in the IT audit process. This includes the board of directors, management, and internal or external auditors. Each of these entities plays a crucial role in ensuring the effectiveness of the IT audit function. The board of directors, for instance, provides oversight and direction, while management is responsible for the day-to-day operations of the IT audit function. Internal or external auditors, on the other hand, are tasked with conducting the audits and providing objective assessments of the institution's IT controls and procedures.

One of the key themes in the booklet is the need for the IT audit program to address IT risk exposures throughout the institution. This broad mandate covers many areas, including IT management and strategic planning, data center operations, client/server architecture, local and wide-area networks, telecommunications, physical and information security, electronic banking, systems development, and business continuity planning. The audit program can help the institution identify and mitigate potential risks by addressing these areas, enhancing its overall security posture.

The booklet also delves into how to structure and staff the internal IT audit function. It underscores the importance of independence in the audit function, noting that this is key to ensuring objective and unbiased assessments. The booklet also discusses the need for proper staffing, highlighting that the audit function should be staffed by individuals with the necessary skills and expertise to effectively assess the institution's IT controls and procedures.

Risk assessment and risk-based auditing are other vital topics covered in the booklet. These are critical components of the IT audit process, helping to ensure that the audit function is focused on the areas of highest risk. The booklet guides how to conduct risk assessments and how to use the results of these assessments to inform the audit process.

The booklet also discusses the audit function's role in application development, acquisition, conversions, and testing. It notes that auditors should be involved in these processes to ensure IT controls are appropriately designed and implemented. This involvement can help prevent issues from arising down the line and can contribute to the overall effectiveness of the IT audit function.

Finally, the booklet discusses the potential benefits of outsourcing the internal IT audit function and conducting third-party reviews of technology service providers (TSPs). Outsourcing can be a viable option for institutions that lack the resources or expertise to perform IT audits in-house effectively. Meanwhile, third-party reviews can ensure that TSPs adhere to the necessary standards and best practices.

Recommendations:

- **Establish a Comprehensive IT Audit Program:** Ensure your audit program is well-planned and properly structured. It should evaluate risk management practices, internal control systems, and compliance with corporate policies concerning IT-related risks.

- **Cover All IT Risk Exposures:** Your IT audit program should address IT risk exposures throughout the institution. This includes IT management and strategic planning, data center operations, client/server architecture, local and wide-area networks, telecommunications, physical and information security, electronic banking, systems development, and business continuity planning.
- **Ensure Independence and Proper Staffing of IT Audit:** The IT audit function should be independent and adequately staffed. It should also involve risk assessment and risk-based auditing, audit participation in application development, acquisition, conversions, and testing.
- **Consider Outsourcing and Third-Party Reviews:** If necessary, consider outsourcing the internal IT audit function. Also, consider third-party reviews of TSPs to ensure they meet the required standards.

THE FFIEC BUSINESS CONTINUITY HANDBOOK

Business Continuity Management is a comprehensive guide that offers a wealth of information on managing and preparing for disruptions to critical business functions. It serves as a valuable resource for organizations seeking to enhance their resilience and ensure the continuity of their operations in the face of potential disruptions.

The handbook begins by discussing the importance of governance in business continuity management. It underscores the role of leadership in establishing the strategic direction for business continuity management and fostering a culture of resilience within the organization. The handbook emphasizes that effective governance ensures that business continuity management is integrated into the organization's overall risk management framework and aligns with its strategic objectives.

Risk management is another key topic covered in the handbook. The handbook guides identifying, assessing, and managing the various risks that could disrupt the organization's operations. It emphasizes the need for a systematic and structured approach to risk management, noting that this can help the organization prioritize its efforts and allocate its resources more effectively. The handbook also discusses the importance of regular risk assessments to keep abreast of the evolving risk landscape.

The handbook also delves into the specifics of developing business continuity strategies. It guides how to design strategies tailored to the organization's unique needs and circumstances, considering factors such as the organization's risk appetite, operational requirements, and the potential impacts of various disruption scenarios. The handbook emphasizes that effective business continuity strategies should be flexible and adaptable, capable of addressing a wide range of potential disruptions.

The components of a business continuity plan are also discussed in the handbook. It outlines the key elements that should be included in a business continuity plan, such as recovery objectives, recovery strategies, and communication plans. The handbook also guides testing and maintaining the business continuity plan to ensure its effectiveness.

Finally, the handbook underscores the importance of resilience, communication, and event management in ensuring business continuity. It notes that building strength into the organization's operations can help it absorb shocks and recover quickly from disruptions. Meanwhile, effective communication is crucial for coordinating the organization's response to troubles and keeping stakeholders informed. For its part, event management involves managing the organization's response to a disturbance, from the initial detection of the disruption to the recovery of normal operations.

Recommendations:

- **Strengthen Governance:** Leadership should establish the strategic direction for business continuity management and foster a culture of resilience within the organization. Business continuity management should be integrated into the organization's overall risk management framework and align with its strategic objectives.
- **Enhance Risk Management:** Organizations should adopt a systematic and structured approach to risk management. Regular risk assessments should be conducted to identify, assess, and manage potential risks.
- **Develop Tailored Business Continuity Strategies:** Business continuity strategies should be designed to meet the organization's unique needs and circumstances. These strategies should be flexible and adaptable, addressing many potential disruptions.
- **Create a Comprehensive Business Continuity Plan:** The business continuity plan should include key elements such as recovery objectives, strategies, and communication plans. The plan should be regularly tested and maintained to ensure its effectiveness.
- **Focus on Resilience, Communication, and Event Management:** Building resilience into the organization's operations can enhance its ability to recover from disruptions. Effective communication is crucial for coordinating the organization's response to disruptions and keeping stakeholders informed. Event management involves managing the organization's response to a disruption, from the initial detection to the recovery of normal operations.

THE FFIEC DEVELOPMENT AND ACQUISITION HANDBOOK

The Development and Acquisition Handbook provides guidelines and standards for various IT development and acquisition aspects. It is a valuable resource for organizations seeking to enhance their IT development and acquisition processes, ensuring they align with best practices and regulatory requirements.

The handbook begins by discussing the importance of project management in IT development and acquisition. It underscores the role of project management in coordinating the various activities involved in IT development and acquisition, ensuring they are completed on time, within budget, and to the required quality standards. The handbook emphasizes that effective project management is crucial for ensuring the successful delivery of IT projects.

The system development life cycle is another key topic covered in the handbook. The handbook guides the stages of the system development life cycle, from initial requirements gathering to system implementation and maintenance. It emphasizes the need for a systematic and structured approach to system development, noting that this can help the organization manage the complexity of IT projects and ensure the delivery of high-quality systems.

The handbook also delves into the specifics of alternative development methodologies. It guides the selection and implementation of development methodologies best suited to the organization's needs and circumstances. The handbook emphasizes that the choice of development methodology can significantly impact IT projects' success, affecting project timelines, costs, and quality outcomes.

The handbook also discusses the roles and responsibilities of various stakeholders in IT development and acquisition. It outlines the responsibilities of project managers, developers, testers, and other key roles, emphasizing the importance of clear role definitions and effective collaboration in ensuring the successful delivery of IT projects.

Other topics covered in the handbook include project plans, configuration management, quality assurance, risk management, testing, documentation, and acquisition. The handbook provides detailed guidance on these topics, offering practical advice and best practices to help organizations enhance their IT development and acquisition processes.

Finally, the handbook covers software development techniques, databases, acquisition standards, licenses, and regulatory requirements. It guides applying software development techniques effectively, managing databases efficiently, and complying with acquisition standards and software license agreements. The handbook also provides information on the regulatory requirements organizations must comply with in their IT development and acquisition activities.

Recommendations:

- **Strengthen Project Management:** Effective project management is crucial for successfully delivering IT projects. Organizations should ensure that their project management practices are robust and align with best practices.

- **Adopt a Systematic Approach to System Development:** Organizations should adopt a systematic and structured approach to system development.

This can help manage the complexity of IT projects and ensure the delivery of high-quality systems.

- **Select Appropriate Development Methodologies:** The choice of development methodology can significantly impact the success of IT projects. Organizations should carefully select and implement development methodologies best suited to their needs and circumstances.
- **Define Roles and Responsibilities Clearly:** Clear role definitions and effective collaboration are key to successfully delivering IT projects. Organizations should ensure that the roles and responsibilities of various stakeholders in IT development and acquisition are clearly defined.
- **Complying with Acquisition Standards and Regulatory Requirements:** Organizations must comply with acquisition standards and software license agreements in their IT development and acquisition activities. They must also be aware of and comply with the relevant regulatory requirements.

THE FFIEC INFORMATION SECURITY HANDBOOK

The FFIEC Information Security Handbook is a comprehensive guide that provides guidelines and standards for information security within financial institutions. It is a valuable resource for organizations seeking to enhance their information security practices, ensuring they align with best practices and regulatory requirements.

The handbook begins by discussing the importance of governance in the information security program. It underscores the role of leadership in establishing the strategic direction for information security and fostering a culture of security within the organization. The handbook emphasizes that effective governance ensures that information security is integrated into the organization's overall risk management framework and aligns with its strategic objectives.

Risk identification and mitigation is another key topic covered in the handbook. The handbook guides identifying, assessing, and managing the various risks that could compromise the organization's information security. It emphasizes the need for a systematic and structured approach to risk management, noting that this can help the organization prioritize its efforts and allocate its resources more effectively. The handbook also discusses the importance of regular risk assessments to keep abreast of the evolving threat landscape.

The handbook also delves into the specifics of overseeing third-party service providers. It guides managing the risks associated with outsourcing IT services to third parties. The handbook emphasizes that organizations should conduct thorough due diligence before entering into agreements with third-party service providers and maintain ongoing oversight of these providers to ensure they comply with their contractual obligations and meet the organization's security standards.

Other topics covered in the handbook include policies, procedures, and controls related to cybersecurity, physical security, and network controls.

The handbook provides detailed guidance on these topics, offering practical advice and best practices to help organizations enhance their information security practices.

Recommendations:

- **Strengthen Governance:** Leadership should establish the strategic direction for information security and foster a security culture within the organization. Information security should be integrated into the organization's overall risk management framework and align with its strategic objectives.
- **Enhance Risk Identification and Mitigation:** Organizations should adopt a systematic and structured approach to risk management. Regular risk assessments should be conducted to identify, assess, and manage potential risks.
- **Manage Third-Party Service Providers Effectively:** Organizations should conduct thorough due diligence before outsourcing IT services to third parties and maintain ongoing oversight of these providers to ensure they comply with their contractual obligations and meet the organization's security standards.
- **Implement Robust Policies, Procedures, and Controls:** Organizations should implement robust policies, procedures, and controls related to cybersecurity, physical security, and network controls. These should be regularly reviewed and updated to ensure their effectiveness.
- **Stay Up-to-date with Changes in Technology and Emerging Threats:** Organizations should keep abreast of technological changes and emerging threats. This can help them stay ahead of the curve in managing their information security risks.

THE FFIEC MANAGEMENT HANDBOOK

The FFIEC Management Handbook provides guidelines and standards for IT and risk management within financial institutions. It is a valuable resource for organizations seeking to enhance their IT management practices, ensuring they align with best practices and regulatory requirements.

The handbook begins by discussing the importance of IT governance. It underscores the role of leadership in establishing the strategic direction for IT and fostering a culture of effective IT management within the organization. The handbook emphasizes that effective IT governance is crucial for ensuring that IT is aligned with the organization's business strategy and delivers value to the organization.

Risk identification and mitigation is another key topic covered in the handbook. The handbook guides identifying, assessing, and managing the various risks that could compromise the organization's IT operations. It emphasizes the need for a systematic and structured approach to risk management, noting that this can help the organization prioritize its efforts and allocate its resources more effectively. The handbook also discusses the importance of regular risk assessments to keep abreast of the evolving risk landscape.

The handbook also delves into the specifics of monitoring and reporting. It guides how to monitor the performance of IT operations and how to report on this performance to stakeholders. The handbook emphasizes that effective monitoring and reporting are crucial for ensuring that IT delivers value to the organization and that risks are managed effectively.

The handbook provides detailed guidance on examiners' procedures when conducting an IT examination. It also includes a glossary of terms to help readers understand the terminology used in the handbook.

Recommendations:

- **Strengthen IT/Cyber Governance:** Leadership should establish the strategic direction for IT and foster a culture of effective IT management. IT should be aligned with the organization's business strategy and should deliver value to the organization.
- **Enhance Risk Identification and Mitigation:** Organizations should adopt a systematic and structured approach to risk management. Regular risk assessments should be conducted to identify, assess, and manage potential risks.
- **Improve Monitoring and Reporting:** Organizations should monitor the performance of IT operations and report on this performance to stakeholders. Effective monitoring and reporting are crucial for ensuring that IT delivers value to the organization and that risks are managed effectively.
- **Follow Examination Procedures:** Organizations should follow the procedures provided in the handbook when conducting an IT examination. This can help ensure that the examination is conducted effectively and provides a thorough assessment of the organization's IT management practices.
- **Understand the Terminology:** Organizations should familiarize themselves with the terminology used in the handbook. This can help them understand the guidance provided in the handbook and apply it effectively.

THE ARCHITECTURE, INFRASTRUCTURE, AND OPERATIONS HANDBOOK

The Architecture, Infrastructure, and Operations Handbook is a comprehensive guide that provides guidelines and standards for IT operations within financial institutions. It is a valuable resource for organizations seeking to enhance their IT operations, ensuring they align with best practices and regulatory requirements.

The handbook begins by discussing the importance of governance in IT operations. It underscores the role of leadership in establishing the strategic direction for IT operations and fostering a culture of effective IT management within the organization. The handbook emphasizes that effective governance is crucial for ensuring that IT operations align with the organization's business strategy and deliver value to the organization.

The handbook also guides policies and risk management related to IT operations. It emphasizes the need for a systematic and structured approach to risk management, noting that this can help the organization prioritize its efforts and allocate its resources more effectively. The handbook also discusses the importance of robust policies to guide IT operations.

Data governance is another key topic covered in the handbook. The handbook guides managing the organization's data effectively, ensuring it is accurate, consistent, and secure. The handbook emphasizes that effective data governance is crucial for ensuring the integrity and reliability of the organization's data.

The handbook also delves into the specifics of IT asset management. It guides managing the organization's IT assets effectively, ensuring they are used efficiently and deliver value to the organization. The handbook emphasizes that effective IT asset management is crucial for optimizing the organization's IT resources and managing the risks associated with IT assets.

Other topics covered in the handbook include network and data flow diagrams, board and senior management responsibilities, IT management, and operations personnel. The handbook provides detailed guidance on these topics, offering practical advice and best practices to help organizations enhance their IT operations.

Finally, the handbook underscores the importance of communication and reporting in ensuring effective risk management. It notes that effective communication and reporting are crucial for coordinating the organization's risk management efforts and keeping stakeholders informed about its risk profile.

Recommendations:

- **Strengthen Governance:** Leadership should establish the strategic direction for IT operations and foster a culture of effective IT management. IT operations should align with the organization's business strategy and deliver value to the organization.

- **Enhance Policies and Risk Management:** Organizations should adopt a systematic and structured approach to risk management. They should also have robust policies in place to guide their IT operations.

- **Improve Data Governance:** Organizations should manage their data effectively, ensuring it is accurate, consistent, and secure. Effective data governance is crucial for ensuring the integrity and reliability of the organization's data.

- **Optimize IT Asset Management:** Organizations should manage their IT assets effectively, ensuring they are used efficiently and deliver value to the organization. Effective IT asset management is crucial for optimizing the organization's IT resources and managing the risks associated with IT assets.

- **Enhance Communication and Reporting:** Effective communication and reporting are crucial for coordinating the organization's risk management efforts and keeping stakeholders informed about the organization's risk profile.

THE OUTSOURCING TECHNOLOGY SERVICES HANDBOOK

The Outsourcing Technology Services Handbook is a comprehensive guide that provides guidelines and standards for financial institutions on outsourcing technology services to third-party service providers. It is a valuable resource for organizations seeking to enhance their outsourcing practices, ensuring they align with best practices and regulatory requirements.

The booklet begins by discussing the responsibilities of the board and management in outsourcing technology services. It underscores the role of leadership in establishing the strategic direction for outsourcing and fostering a culture of effective risk management within the organization. The booklet emphasizes that the board and management are ultimately responsible for ensuring that outsourcing activities align with the organization's business strategy and deliver value to the organization.

Risk management is another key topic covered in the booklet. The booklet guides on identifying, assessing, and managing the various risks that could arise from outsourcing technology services. It emphasizes the need for a systematic and structured approach to risk management, noting that this can help the organization prioritize its efforts and allocate its resources more effectively.

The booklet also delves into risk assessment, service provider selection, and contract issues. It guides conducting thorough risk assessments before outsourcing technology services, selecting service providers that meet the organization's needs and standards, and managing contract issues effectively.

Other topics covered in the booklet include ongoing monitoring, business continuity planning, information security, and outsourcing to foreign service providers. The booklet provides detailed guidance on these topics, offering practical advice and best practices to help organizations manage their outsourcing activities effectively.

Finally, the booklet includes examination procedures, laws, regulations, guidance, and appendices on foreign-based third-party and managed security service providers. This additional information can help organizations understand the regulatory landscape for outsourcing and provide them with further guidance on managing specific aspects of their outsourcing activities.

Recommendations:

- **Strengthen Board and Management Responsibilities:** Leadership should establish the strategic direction for outsourcing and foster a culture of effective risk management. Outsourcing activities should align with the organization's business strategy and deliver value to the organization.

- **Enhance Risk Management:** Organizations should adopt a systematic and structured approach to risk management. They should conduct thorough risk assessments before outsourcing technology services and effectively manage the risks arising from outsourcing.

- **Improve Service Provider Selection and Contract Management:** Organizations should select service providers that meet their needs and standards. They should also manage contract issues effectively to protect their interests.

- **Implement Ongoing Monitoring and Business Continuity Planning:** Organizations should monitor their outsourcing activities continuously to ensure that service providers meet their contractual obligations. They should also have robust business continuity plans to manage the risks associated with outsourcing.

- **Ensure Information Security and Manage Outsourced Service Providers:** Organizations should ensure that their information security practices align with best practices and regulatory requirements. They should also effectively manage the risks of outsourcing to foreign service providers.

THE RETAIL PAYMENT SYSTEMS HANDBOOK

The Retail Payment Systems Handbook is a comprehensive guide that provides guidelines and standards for retail payment systems within financial institutions. It is a valuable resource for organizations seeking to enhance their retail payment systems, ensuring they align with best practices and regulatory requirements.

The handbook discusses payment instruments, clearing and settlement processes, card-based electronic payments, and emerging retail payment technologies. It underscores the importance of understanding the different types of payment systems and how they operate. The handbook emphasizes that a thorough understanding of these systems is crucial for effectively managing the risks associated with retail payment systems.

Risk management strategies for payment systems is another key topic covered in the handbook. The booklet provides guidance on managing various types of risks, including payment system, strategic, reputation, credit, liquidity, legal (compliance) risk, and operational risk. It emphasizes the need for a systematic and structured approach to risk management, noting that this can help the organization prioritize its efforts and allocate its resources more effectively.

The handbook also delves into audit, information security, business continuity planning, and vendor and third-party management. It guides conducting audits of retail payment systems, ensuring the security of these systems, planning for business continuity, and managing relationships with vendors and third parties.

Other topics covered in the handbook include examination procedures, a glossary, a schematic of retail payment access channels and payment methods, and laws, regulations, and guidance. The handbook provides detailed guidance on these topics, offering practical advice and best practices to help organizations manage their retail payment systems effectively.

Recommendations:

- **Understand Payment Systems:** Organizations should understand the different types of payment systems and how they operate. This understanding is crucial for effectively managing the risks associated with retail payment systems.
- **Enhance Risk Management:** Organizations should adopt a systematic and structured approach to risk management. They should manage various risks, including payment system, strategic, reputation, credit, liquidity, legal (compliance), and operational risks.
- **Improve Audit, Information Security, and Business Continuity Planning:** Organizations should conduct audits of retail payment systems, ensure the security of these systems, and plan for business continuity. These activities are crucial for managing the risks associated with retail payment systems.
- **Manage Vendors and Third Parties Effectively:** Organizations should effectively manage their relationships with vendors and third parties. This can help ensure these parties meet the organization's standards and not pose undue risks to its retail payment systems.
- **Comply with Laws, Regulations, and Guidance:** Organizations should comply with the relevant laws, regulations, and guidance related to retail payment systems. This can help ensure their systems are compliant and not expose the organization to legal or regulatory risks.

THE SUPERVISION OF TECHNOLOGY SERVICE PROVIDERS HANDBOOK

The Supervision of TSPs is a comprehensive guide released by the FFIEC that provides guidelines and standards for supervising TSPs within financial institutions. It is a valuable resource for organizations seeking to enhance their supervision practices, ensuring they align with best practices and regulatory requirements.

The handbook begins by discussing supervisory policy and examination responsibility. It underscores the importance of having a robust supervisory policy and clearly defining the duties of examining TSPs. The handbook emphasizes that effective supervision is crucial for managing the risks associated with TSPs.

Risk-based supervision is another key topic covered in the handbook. The handbook guides how to implement a risk-based approach to supervision, noting that this can help the organization prioritize its efforts and allocate its resources more effectively. The handbook also discusses the risks associated with TSPs, including strategic, reputation, operational, transaction, and compliance risks.

The handbook also delves into risk management, audit, and internal controls. It guides managing the risks associated with TSPs, conducting audits of these providers, and implementing effective internal controls. The handbook emphasizes that these activities are crucial for managing the risks associated with TSPs.

Other topics covered in the handbook include the roles and responsibilities of various stakeholders in the supervision process, the supervisory programs, and the examination report. The handbook provides detailed guidance on these topics, offering practical advice and best practices to help organizations manage their supervision activities effectively.

Finally, the handbook includes an appendix on the Uniform Rating System for Information Technology (URSIT). This system provides a standardized framework for rating the performance of TSPs, helping organizations assess these providers more effectively.

Recommendations:

- **Strengthen Supervisory Policy and Examination Responsibility:** Organizations should have a robust supervisory policy and clearly define the responsibilities of examining TSPs. Effective supervision is crucial for managing the risks associated with TSPs.

- **Implement Risk-Based Supervision:** Organizations should implement a risk-based approach to supervision. This can help them prioritize their efforts and allocate their resources more effectively.

- **Enhance Risk Management, Audit, and Internal Controls:** Organizations should manage the risks associated with TSPs, conduct audits of these providers, and implement effective internal controls. These activities are crucial for managing the risks associated with TSPs.

- **Define Roles and Responsibilities Clearly:** Organizations should clearly define the roles and responsibilities of various stakeholders in the supervision process. This can help ensure that the supervision activities are coordinated effectively.

- **Use the Uniform Rating System for Information Technology (URSIT):** Organizations should use the URSIT to rate the performance of TSPs. This can help them assess these providers more effectively.

THE WHOLESALE PAYMENT SYSTEMS HANDBOOK

The Wholesale Payment Systems Handbook is a comprehensive guide that provides guidelines and standards for wholesale payment systems within financial institutions. It is a valuable resource for organizations seeking to enhance their wholesale payment systems, ensuring they align with best practices and regulatory requirements.

The handbook begins by discussing various interbank payment and messaging systems, securities settlement systems, and intrabank payment and messaging systems. It underscores the importance of understanding the different types of payment systems and how they operate. The handbook emphasizes that a thorough understanding of these systems is crucial for effectively managing the risks associated with wholesale payment systems.

The handbook also provides information on various systems such as Fedwire, CHIPS, NSS, SWIFT, and CLS Bank. It provides detailed descriptions of these systems, explaining how they work and how they are used in the context of wholesale payments.

Risk management for wholesale payment systems is another key topic covered in the handbook. The handbook guides implementing effective wholesale payment system risk management policies and procedures. It emphasizes that these policies and practices are crucial for managing the risks associated with these systems.

Recommendations:

- **Understand Payment Systems:** Organizations should understand the different types of payment systems and how they operate. This understanding is crucial for effectively managing the risks associated with wholesale payment systems.
- **Familiarize with Various Systems:** Organizations should familiarize themselves with Fedwire, CHIPS, NSS, SWIFT, and CLS Bank. Understanding these systems can help organizations manage their wholesale payments more effectively.
- **Implement Effective Risk Management Policies and Procedures:** Organizations should implement effective risk management policies and procedures for wholesale payment systems. These policies and practices are crucial for managing the risks associated with these systems.

Chapter Conclusion

The FFIEC plays a central and influential role in the United States financial industry. Since its establishment in 1979, the FFIEC has fostered uniformity, ensured best practices, and driven consistency in the supervision and regulation of diverse financial entities nationwide. Its objectives, although steadfast, have evolved and expanded over time to accommodate the dynamic and increasingly digital financial landscape.

The FFIEC is not merely a regulatory body dictating guidelines but a dialogue facilitator, fostering mutual understanding between diverse entities within the industry. The Council bridges regulatory expectations and the practical realities of operating financial institutions, striking a balance between maintaining stability, fostering growth, and advancing innovation. Its influence extends beyond US borders, and it serves as a model for regulatory practices on a global scale.

The Council's primary knowledge dissemination and regulation tool is its detailed Handbooks. These Handbooks cover various topics, including IT Management, Operations, Lending, and Cybersecurity. Through these handbooks, the FFIEC disseminates knowledge, facilitates training, and outlines clear guidelines for compliance. Each handbook reflects a comprehensive understanding of its topic and provides practical recommendations that financial institutions can implement.

The role of the FFIEC, its responsibilities, and the knowledge encapsulated within its Handbooks are invaluable for financial institutions. In the face of rapidly evolving cybersecurity threats, the guidance provided by the FFIEC is an essential resource for any entity aiming to ensure the security and reliability of its operations. As financial institutions navigate cybersecurity governance, risk management, and compliance, they can rely on the FFIEC to provide a consistent, comprehensive, and practical roadmap to success.

CHAPTER 15

U.S. Federal Cybersecurity Regulations

"A Cybersecurity Leader must navigate the complex world of U.S. Cybersecurity Regulations and Requirements, unlocking the tools and understanding necessary to ensure compliance and protect sensitive information."

The complexities of U.S. Cybersecurity Regulations and Requirements can be quite intricate. Key pieces of legislation, guidelines, and standards like the Gramm–Leach–Bliley Act (GLBA), Sarbanes–Oxley Act (SOX), and Payment Card Industry Data Security Standard (PCI DSS) play significant roles. It is essential to understand their historical context, crucial provisions, impacts on privacy and data security, compliance measures, enforcement mechanisms, and interactions with other regulations. Through a detailed exploration, individuals can gain the knowledge necessary to understand and navigate the diverse landscape of cybersecurity regulations and requirements in the United States.

GRAMM–LEACH–BLILEY ACT (GLBA)

The Gramm–Leach–Bliley Act, commonly known as GLBA, is a pivotal piece of legislation in the United States that shapes the financial industry's approach to cybersecurity. Historical context is critical to understanding why the GLBA was enacted. Passed by the U.S. Congress in 1999, GLBA repealed part of the Glass–Steagall Act of 1933, enabling commercial banks, investment banks, securities firms, and insurance companies to consolidate. While the primary motive was to allow banking institutions to compete globally with fewer restrictions, there was a need for proper safeguards to ensure customer privacy and data security, thus paving the way for GLBA.

One of the main provisions of GLBA, SEC. 501 is the Protection of Non-public Personal Information. Financial institutions must establish appropriate standards to protect customers' nonpublic personal information. The Act places a duty on financial institutions to keep customer data safe and maintain their privacy.

GLBA has had a significant impact on privacy and data security. It was one of the first legislations that recognized the importance of protecting customer information in the digital age. By necessitating financial institutions to explain their information-sharing practices to their customers and protect sensitive data, the Act set a precedent for privacy and data security in the finance sector.

Compliance and enforcement of GLBA are handled primarily by the Federal Trade Commission (FTC). Financial institutions must provide annual privacy notices to customers, outlining how they share and protect their data. Financial institutions can face severe financial and reputational penalties if noncompliant.

The GLBA does not operate in isolation. It interacts with regulations such as the Fair Credit Reporting Act (FCRA) and the Health Insurance Portability and Accountability Act (HIPAA). For instance, where GLBA protects customer information privacy, HIPAA safeguards patient health information (PHI), establishing a network of interrelated regulations.

Recommendations:

- **Deep Dive into GLBA:** Gain a comprehensive understanding of GLBA, including its historical context, key provisions, impacts on privacy and data security, and how it interacts with other regulations.
- **Understanding SEC. 501:** Focus particularly on understanding SEC. 501 of the GLBA is the cornerstone provision for protecting nonpublic personal information.
- **Privacy Policy Review:** Financial institutions should regularly review their privacy policies and practices to ensure compliance with GLBA requirements.
- **Enhance Data Security:** Prioritize implementing robust data security measures to protect customer information as stipulated by GLBA.
- **Collaborate with Legal Teams:** Given the complexities of GLBA and its interplay with other regulations, financial institutions should work closely with their legal teams to ensure full compliance.

THE HEALTH INSURANCE PORTABILITY AND ACCOUNTABILITY ACT (HIPAA)

HIPAA, or the Health Insurance Portability and Accountability Act, is a cornerstone regulation in the healthcare industry, pivotal for safeguarding sensitive PHI. Its inception aimed at establishing stringent rules to protect the privacy and security of individual health data, setting a standardized practice that health-related organizations must adhere to, and ensuring PHI remains confidential and secure.

Central to HIPAA are its foundational rules: the Privacy Rule, the Security Rule, and the Breach Notification Rule. The Privacy Rule emphasizes the protection of PHI, setting standards on who is allowed access to health information and under what circumstances. The Security Rule focuses primarily on electronic PHI (ePHI), detailing strategies and safeguards to protect ePHI from cyber threats, data breaches, and other potential vulnerabilities. The Breach Notification Rule mandates the steps organizations must take following a breach of unsecured PHI, such as notifying affected individuals and necessary authorities.

Two primary entities manage PHI: covered entities and business associates. Covered entities typically involve healthcare providers, health plans, and healthcare clearinghouses directly involved in the handling and managing of health records. On the other hand, business associates are third-party entities providing services to covered entities coming into contact with PHI.

The management of PHI is key to HIPAA compliance. Organizations must ensure that PHI, which encompasses medical records, treatment histories, payment records, and other sensitive information, is adequately protected. Processes and protocols must be established to ensure this sensitive information's safe handling, transmission, and storage.

HIPAA is not a one-time compliance effort. Organizations must continuously update their practices, procedures, and systems to align with HIPAA's evolving standards. This effort involves regular risk assessments, system upgrades, and employee training to ensure that the entirety of the organization operates in harmony with HIPAA's regulations.

HIPAA's framework is adaptive, changing as technology evolves and introduces new tools, systems, and potential vulnerabilities into the healthcare landscape. Organizations must stay abreast of technological advancements, assessing and implementing new technologies that enhance the security and efficiency of PHI handling while maintaining compliance.

Failure to comply with HIPAA regulations can result in significant consequences. Penalties range from monetary fines to criminal charges, depending on the severity and nature of the violation. Organizations must be thorough in their compliance efforts, ensuring that all aspects of their operations align with HIPAA's requirements.

Continuous learning and adaptation are crucial. HIPAA's regulations are not static; staying updated with their modifications and updates is imperative for ongoing compliance. Regular training and awareness programs should be a part of organizations' strategies to ensure all staff members are current with HIPAA's requirements and best practices.

By grounding operations in the guidelines outlined above, organizations can foster a secure environment, resilient against potential threats and conducive to safeguarding sensitive patient information. This facilitates compliance and fortifies trust with patients and stakeholders, ensuring that the sanctity of health information is upheld.

Recommendations:

- **Adopt a Robust Risk Management Strategy:** Prioritize establishing a comprehensive risk management strategy that meticulously aligns with the HIPAA Security Rule. Regularly conduct thorough risk assessments to identify vulnerabilities and implement necessary safeguards, ensuring the confidentiality, integrity, and availability of Protected Health Information (PHI).

- **Educate and Train Staff Regularly:** Develop continuous education and training programs for all staff members, focusing on HIPAA regulations, potential risks, and best practices. Ensuring every team member is well-versed with HIPAA compliance requirements and updated on recent changes will bolster the organization's defenses against potential violations and breaches.

- **Implement Strong Authentication Processes:** Enhance the security of PHI by implementing robust authentication processes. Ensure that only authorized individuals have access to sensitive information, employing strategies such as multifactor authentication, unique user identifiers, and regular password updates to fortify access control mechanisms by the HIPAA Security Rule.

- **Develop and Maintain Clear Policies and Procedures:** Craft and continuously update well-defined policies and procedures that encapsulate the multifaceted aspects of HIPAA compliance. These should serve as practical guides, detailing the processes and protocols necessary for safeguarding PHI, reporting breaches, and ensuring ongoing compliance with HIPAA standards.

- **Stay Updated on Regulatory Changes and Technological Advancements:** Stay abreast of changes in HIPAA regulations and evolving technological advancements that impact the healthcare industry. Commit to adopting new technologies and practices that enhance the protection of PHI, ensuring that your organization's compliance strategies are always aligned with current laws and best practices.

INTERAGENCY GUIDELINES ESTABLISHING INFORMATION SECURITY STANDARDS (12 CFR 30 PART B)

The Interagency Guidelines Establishing Information Security Standards, also known as 12 CFR 30 Part B, were introduced to protect the security and confidentiality of customer records and information. The guidelines are crucial in defining sound practices concerning the proper disposal and Protection of consumer report information.

These guidelines have a crucial role within financial institutions. They provide a framework for developing and implementing administrative, technical, and physical safeguards to protect customer information. The guidelines help financial institutions in reducing operational risk and enhancing data security.

Over the years, several versions of the Interagency Guidelines have been released to keep pace with the evolving cybersecurity landscape. Each version aims to incorporate the latest best practices and standards to ensure the safety of customer information.

The guidelines lay out specific requirements for a Customer Information Security Program. Each institution must design a comprehensive written program, including administrative, technical, or physical safeguards to protect customers' information. Risk Assessment and Management is a core part of these guidelines. Institutions must identify reasonably foreseeable internal and external threats that could result in unauthorized disclosure, misuse, alteration, or destruction of customer information.

Implementation and Testing of Information Security Programs are mandated under these guidelines. Financial institutions must regularly test the information security program's key controls, systems, and procedures to ensure effectiveness. Oversight of service providers is an essential aspect of the guidelines. Institutions must exercise appropriate due diligence in managing and monitoring their service providers to ensure customer information's safety.

The guidelines also necessitate having response programs for unauthorized access to customer information. Institutions must have an incident response plan detailing how to react during a security breach. Lastly, reporting requirements and compliance play a vital role. Institutions must report any incidents of unauthorized access to customer information that could result in substantial harm or inconvenience to the customer.

Recommendations:

- **Understand the Guidelines:** Familiarize yourself with the Interagency Guidelines, including their purpose, role within financial institutions, and existing versions.
- **Develop a Comprehensive Security Program**: Institutions should develop a comprehensive written security program per the guidelines to protect their customers' information.
- **Emphasize Risk Management:** Regular risk assessments should be conducted to identify potential threats to customer information, and appropriate management strategies should be implemented.
- **Ensure Oversight of Service Providers:** Due diligence in managing and monitoring service providers is crucial to safeguard customer information.
- **Establish a Robust Response Plan:** Institutions should have a robust incident response plan to react effectively to security breaches.

PAYMENT CARD INDUSTRY DATA SECURITY STANDARD (PCI DSS)

The Payment Card Industry Data Security Standard, PCI DSS, is a comprehensive and globally recognized security standard initiated in 2004. This standard was a cooperative measure from leading card brands such as Visa, MasterCard,

American Express, Discover, and JCB. Their collective initiative aimed to address the rapidly growing credit card fraud issues while enhancing cardholder data security internationally.

A rising trend of financial cybercrime and data breaches has created an urgent need for an industry-wide security measure. Hence, these card companies developed a unified set of regulations, later known as the PCI DSS. This was a significant step toward safeguarding the sensitive information processed, stored, or transmitted by organizations dealing with card payments.

The PCI DSS encompasses a set of 12 essential requirements, which are organized around six control objectives. The first objective focuses on building and maintaining a secure network and systems. This involves installing and maintaining a firewall to protect cardholder data and not using vendor-supplied defaults for system passwords and other security parameters.

The second objective underscores the need to protect cardholder data. It mandates the Protection of stored cardholder data and the encryption of the transmission of cardholder data across open, public networks. Following these guidelines ensures that valuable cardholder data is adequately safeguarded.

The third objective pertains to maintaining a Vulnerability Management Program. This includes using antivirus software or programs and developing and maintaining secure systems and applications. This program is instrumental in identifying and mitigating potential security threats.

The fourth objective outlines the need for implementing strong access control measures. This necessitates restricting access to cardholder data by business need-to-know, unique identification of individuals with computer access, and restriction of physical access to cardholder data. These measures aim to limit unauthorized access to sensitive data.

The fifth objective discusses the regular monitoring and testing of networks. It requires tracking and monitoring all access to network resources and cardholder data and periodic testing of security systems and processes. This ongoing scrutiny helps detect any possible breaches or anomalies early.

The sixth and final objective emphasizes maintaining an information security policy. This policy must address information security for all personnel. This encourages a security-conscious work environment and ensures employees understand their role in maintaining data security.

In terms of compliance, an annual assessment of the PCI DSS is mandatory for most businesses that process card payments. This evaluation, carried out either by a Qualified Security Assessor (QSA) for larger businesses or a self-assessment for smaller ones, confirms that all organizations involved in card payment processing meet the stringent security requirements set by the PCI DSS.

In the financial industry, the PCI DSS assumes an instrumental role. Given the highly sensitive nature of cardholder data processed, stored, or transmitted within the sector, strict compliance with the PCI DSS is not merely an option – it is a necessity. This is not just about achieving a compliance certificate; it is about maintaining a continuous state of compliance to ensure the ongoing Protection of cardholder data. Adhering to the PCI DSS is not just a regulatory obligation but also a practice that strengthens customers' trust in the security protocols of the entity handling their data.

Recommendations:

- **Familiarize with the Standard:** It is essential to understand the objectives and requirements of the PCI DSS.
- **Embrace a Security-First Culture:** Compliance should be seen not as a yearly event but as part of an ongoing, dynamic process. Maintaining a state of continuous compliance demands a security-first culture.
- **Regular Compliance Assessment:** Regular audits should be performed to identify any gaps in compliance, and immediate corrective measures should be taken.
- **Training and Awareness:** Regular training sessions should be organized for all employees handling cardholder data to create awareness about PCI DSS and the importance of safeguarding cardholder information.
- **Employ Encryption:** To prevent unauthorized access and data theft, all cardholder data should be encrypted during transmission across open public networks.

SARBANES–OXLEY ACT (SOX)

The Sarbanes–Oxley Act, often called SOX, was enacted in 2002 as a response to large-scale corporate and accounting scandals, including those affecting Enron, Tyco International, and WorldCom. The primary objective of SOX is to protect shareholders and the general public from accounting errors and fraudulent practices in enterprises.

The impact of SOX on information security is profound. Section 404 of the Act, which requires annual evaluation and reporting of internal control over financial reporting, has implications for information security, given that many controls depend on information systems.

Compliance with SOX is mandatory for all publicly traded companies in the United States. However, it also has implications for privately held companies, especially those looking to go public. Compliance involves demonstrating that all business records, including electronic records and electronic messages, are saved for "not less than five years."

Due to the nature of their business, financial institutions are particularly affected by SOX. As institutions that handle significant financial transactions and sensitive customer data, robust controls and transparency are crucial to maintaining public trust and investor confidence.

However, complying with SOX is not without its challenges. It requires significant resources to document and test internal controls. The Act's requirements can be vague, leading to differing interpretations and implementations.

Despite these challenges, effective implementation of SOX can lead to improved internal controls, greater transparency, and increased investor confidence.

Recommendations:

- **Understand SOX:** Ensure you are familiar with the requirements of SOX, particularly as they relate to information security.
- **Invest in Compliance:** Allocate adequate resources to meet SOX compliance requirements. This could include both personnel and technology investments.
- **Document Processes:** Create detailed documentation of all financial controls and processes and ensure they are regularly reviewed and updated.
- **Train Staff:** All relevant staff should be trained in SOX compliance requirements. This training should be refreshed regularly.
- **Seek Expert Advice:** Given the complexity of SOX compliance, seeking advice from legal and financial experts may be beneficial.

THE CLOUD ACT

The Clarifying Lawful Overseas Use of Data Act, better known as The Cloud Act, was signed into law in the United States in March 2018. The legislation was conceived against a backdrop of escalating cross-border data disputes and was intended to modernize data storage and law enforcement access regulations, providing a framework for law enforcement agencies to access data stored in foreign countries.

A crucial provision of The Cloud Act is the establishment of bilateral agreements between the United States and other countries, which govern access to data stored in the respective countries. These agreements, known as executive agreements, enable foreign governments to bypass the Mutual Legal Assistance Treaty (MLAT) process, which can be slow and cumbersome, in favor of a more streamlined process.

The Act also includes the rule of comity assessment, providing a route for service providers to challenge data access orders that might conflict with foreign laws. In addition, it clarifies that the Stored Communications Act (SCA) warrants jurisdiction, confirming that US law enforcement can demand data about any individual (regardless of their citizenship or where the data is stored), provided a company subject to US jurisdiction stores the data.

However, The Cloud Act has not been without controversy, and its impact on data privacy and security is a hotly debated topic. Privacy advocates argue that the Act infringes on user privacy by allowing governments to access personal data stored in the cloud without the legal safeguards that would ordinarily apply in a domestic context.

The Cloud Act presents challenges from a compliance perspective, particularly for cloud service providers. These entities must navigate complex legal landscapes, balancing the need to comply with the Act and other conflicting domestic or foreign laws. It is also important to note that noncompliance with the Act's provisions can result in penalties.

The Cloud Act has undoubtedly reshaped the data privacy landscape in the era of cloud technology and digitalization. The Act will remain essential to the conversation as international data access concerns evolve.

Recommendations:

- **Understand The Cloud Act:** Familiarize yourself with The Cloud Act's provisions, rationale, and impact on data privacy and security.
- **Analyze Data Handling Practices:** Review your data handling and storage practices to ensure compliance with the Act.
- **Develop a Response Plan:** Establish a plan to respond effectively to government data access requests while ensuring compliance with the Act and other relevant laws.
- **Review Service Provider Agreements:** If you use cloud services, review your provider's terms and conditions to understand how they handle legal requests for data.
- **Monitor Developments:** Stay informed about ongoing developments related to the Act and international data privacy laws to ensure continued compliance.

INTERNAL REVENUE SERVICE PUBLICATION 1075

Publication 1075 by the Internal Revenue Service (IRS), commonly called IRS 1075, is a comprehensive set of regulations stipulating the standards for federal, state, and local agencies, including other entities like contractors, that deal with Federal Tax Information (FTI). This regulatory framework is a roadmap for implementing adequate security controls that protect sensitive tax information against threats like unauthorized access, usage, disclosure, disruption, alteration, or destruction.

From a cybersecurity perspective, IRS 1075 is crucial in fortifying the protective barriers around sensitive data. By promoting and enforcing adherence to robust cybersecurity practices, it seeks to mitigate the potential cyber threats targeting the privacy and security of FTI.

The data protection requirements set forth by IRS 1075 are extensive and multifaceted, underlining the importance of maintaining a comprehensive cybersecurity program. These requirements span many areas, forming a holistic and well-rounded cybersecurity strategy.

Access controls are central to data security, ensuring only authorized individuals can access the sensitive FTI. Detailed provisions for audit trails and accountability mechanisms ensure that all data transactions and manipulations are logged, fostering transparency and traceability.

Awareness and training emphasize the critical role of educated and vigilant human assets in maintaining cybersecurity. Configuration management pertains to the secure setup of IT systems to minimize potential vulnerabilities that hackers could exploit. Contingency planning emphasizes the necessity for well-planned response and recovery measures in case of cybersecurity incidents, ensuring business continuity and minimizing damage.

Incident response guidelines ensure the rapid detection, response, and recovery from security incidents to limit the impact and prevent potential recurrences. Maintenance ensures that systems are updated and vulnerabilities patched regularly to minimize risks.

Media protection concerns the safe storage and disposal of physical and digital media containing FTI. The guidelines regarding personnel security underscore the importance of vetting individuals who have access to FTI to prevent insider threats. Physical and environmental protection rules are designed to safeguard the hardware and data centers where FTI is stored from physical threats.

System and information integrity involves measures to protect data from being modified or destroyed without authorization. System and communications protection protects network communications to prevent data breaches or leaks. System and services acquisition underscores the importance of including security considerations when procuring systems or outsourcing services.

Compliance with IRS 1075 is monitored stringently by the IRS Office of Safeguards through self-assessment and on-site reviews. Entities must submit an annual Safeguard Security Report (SSR) to demonstrate their compliance with IRS 1075's data protection requirements.

The IRS Office of Safeguards has the authority to enforce penalties or sanctions for noncompliance, with consequences ranging from fines to loss of access to FTI. This combination of stringent standards and enforcement mechanisms underscores the importance of cybersecurity in protecting sensitive tax information.

Recommendations:

- **Familiarize with IRS 1075:** Understand the scope and requirements of IRS 1075, mainly if your organization handles FTI.
- **Develop a Security Plan:** Establish a comprehensive security plan that meets all requirements outlined in IRS 1075.
- **Regular Compliance Checks:** Conduct audits and reviews to identify potential compliance gaps.
- **Continual Training:** Ensure all personnel handling FTI are provided with regular training on IRS 1075 requirements and the importance of data protection.
- **Maintain a Strong Incident Response Plan:** Be prepared for potential data breaches or incidents with a robust incident response plan aligning with IRS 1075 guidelines.

CRIMINAL JUSTICE INFORMATION SERVICES (CJIS) SECURITY POLICY

The Criminal Justice Information Services (CJIS) Security Policy was developed by the Federal Bureau of Investigation (FBI) to establish appropriate controls to protect the entire lifecycle of Criminal Justice Information (CJI) from creation through dissemination.

The CJIS Security Policy encompasses 13 areas, each focusing on specific security requirements. These policy areas address various aspects of information security within the criminal justice domain.

One policy area is Information Exchange Agreements, which outline the requirements for establishing agreements between agencies to exchange CJI securely. Another area is Security Awareness Training, which emphasizes the need for training programs to educate personnel about security risks, best practices, and the proper handling of CJI.

Incident Response is another important policy area establishing procedures for detecting, reporting, and responding to security incidents involving CJI. Auditing and Accountability is a policy area emphasizing comprehensive auditing mechanisms to ensure Accountability, detect unauthorized activities, and monitor compliance with security policies.

Access Control is a critical policy area that covers measures to control and manage access to CJI systems and data. This includes Authentication, authorization, and access privilege management. Identification and Authentication is another area that focuses specifically on verifying the identity of individuals accessing CJI systems, utilizing methods such as passwords, biometrics, or multifactor Authentication.

Configuration Management is a policy area that addresses the procedures for managing and maintaining the secure configuration of systems and devices that handle CJI. Media Protection is another area that highlights the secure handling, storage, transportation, and disposal of physical media containing CJI.

Physical Protection is an essential policy area that emphasizes the need for physical security measures to safeguard CJI facilities, equipment, and storage areas. Systems and Communications Protection focuses on security requirements for CJI systems, networks, and communication channels, including encryption, intrusion detection systems, and firewalls.

Information Assurance is a policy area that encompasses measures to ensure the integrity, confidentiality, and availability of CJI. This includes data backup, disaster recovery planning, and encryption. Personnel Security addresses the requirements for screening, background checks, and security clearances for personnel with access to CJI.

Lastly, Configuration Management for Remote Access is a policy area explicitly addressing the security measures and controls for managing remote access to CJI systems and data.

Compliance with the CJIS Security Policy is assessed through audits conducted by the CJIS Systems Agency (CSA) or a representative thereof. The CSA determines the frequency and processes of these audits, which examine an agency's adherence to the requirements outlined in the policy areas. The audits ensure the secure handling of CJI at all times and promote a robust security posture within the CJI environment.

Recommendations:

- **Understand the CJIS Security Policy:** Ensure you understand the objectives and requirements of the CJIS Security Policy.
- **Develop a Comprehensive Security Plan:** Establish a thorough security plan that meets all the requirements outlined in the CJIS Security Policy.
- **Regular Audits:** Perform routine audits to identify any compliance gaps and address them promptly.
- **Employee Training:** Offer regular training to employees on the CJIS Security Policy requirements and the importance of protecting CJI.
- **Incident Response Plan:** Have a robust incident response plan to react swiftly to potential data breaches or security incidents.

DEFENSE FEDERAL ACQUISITION REGULATION SUPPLEMENT (DFARS)

The Defense Federal Acquisition Regulation Supplement (DFARS), commonly known as DFARS, is a set of regulations that Department of Defense (DoD) government acquisition officials – and those contractors doing business with DoD – must follow in the procurement process involving defense-related goods and services.

DFARS contains numerous clauses and provisions that impose specific obligations on contractors. DFARS clause 252.204-7012 notably mandates that contractors implement adequate security on all covered contractor information systems that process, store, or transmit protected defense information.

Compliance with DFARS requires a thorough understanding of the cybersecurity requirements and developing and maintaining an adequate security system to protect covered defense information. The DoD can audit contractors for compliance with DFARS.

Navigating DFARS compliance can be challenging, but it is essential for maintaining a business relationship with the DoD. It requires substantial resources and a deep understanding of the regulations. However, achieving DFARS compliance can lead to a significant competitive advantage, improved cybersecurity, and the potential for more government contracts.

Recommendations:

- **Gain DFARS Knowledge:** Familiarize yourself with the DFARS requirements, especially if you are a contractor or plan to do business with the DoD.

- **Commit Resources:** Allocate sufficient resources to ensure DFARS compliance. This may involve both personnel and technology investments.
- **Develop an Adequate Security System:** Establish a security system that meets the DFARS requirements for protecting covered defense information.
- **Continual Training:** Provide regular DFARS training to all relevant staff to ensure understanding and compliance.
- **Please seek Expert Advice:** Given the complexity of DFARS, it may be beneficial to consult with experts in the field.

DEPARTMENT OF DEFENSE CLOUD COMPUTING SECURITY REQUIREMENTS GUIDE

The DoD Cloud Computing Security Requirements Guide (SRG) provides security requirements and guidance for migrating missions to the cloud. The SRG is intended to ensure that all DoD cloud usage is secure and that all associated data is adequately protected while facilitating a consistent risk-based decision-making process for cloud services.

The SRG lays out a range of cloud security requirements across different security levels and categories of data. These requirements are grouped into governance, risk management, compliance, human capital, operations, incident response, contingency planning, network security, systems and services acquisition, and identity and access management.

For compliance with the SRG, cloud service providers are assessed by the Defense Information Systems Agency (DISA) or authorized Third-Party Assessment Organizations (3PAOs). The rigorous compliance process requires cloud service providers to demonstrate robust security measures in line with the SRG's requirements. Reporting is also a key part of the compliance process, ensuring transparency and Accountability.

Recommendations:

- **Study the Guide:** Understand the DoD Cloud Computing SRG's requirements, especially if you are a cloud service provider or a DoD mission planning to use cloud services.
- **Build a Secure System:** Develop a cloud system that aligns with the security requirements stipulated in the SRG.
- **Prepare for Assessments:** Prepare your systems and processes for the rigorous assessment process required for SRG compliance.
- **Implement Robust Reporting:** Ensure robust and transparent reporting mechanisms are in place, in line with the SRG requirements.
- **Stay Updated:** Keep abreast of any updates or changes to the SRG to ensure ongoing compliance.

FAMILY EDUCATIONAL RIGHTS AND PRIVACY ACT (FERPA)

FERPA is a federal law in the United States that allows parents to access their children's education records, seek to have the documents amended, and have some control over disclosing personally identifiable information from the education records. When a student turns 18 or enters a postsecondary institution at any age, the rights under FERPA transfer from the parents to the student.

FERPA's data protection requirements focus on protecting the privacy of student's education records. This includes any information directly related to a student and maintained by an educational agency or institution or a party acting for the agency or institution.

Compliance with FERPA is enforced by the U.S. Department of Education, which can withhold federal funding from institutions that violate FERPA. The Department also handles complaints from parents and students about potential FERPA violations.

Managing FERPA compliance can be challenging, but a robust data governance policy, regular training, and proactive management of education records can help educational institutions comply with the Act's requirements and protect students' privacy rights.

Recommendations:

- **Understand FERPA:** If you are involved in an educational institution, familiarize yourself with the requirements of FERPA.
- **Robust Data Governance:** Implement a robust policy addressing FERPA requirements.
- **Regular Training:** Train staff on FERPA's requirements and the importance of protecting student's education records.
- **Proactive Record Management:** Regularly review and manage education records to ensure FERPA compliance.

SEC RULES 17A-4 AND 18A-6

SEC Rule 17a-4 specifies the types of records that broker-dealers must preserve and the periods for such preservation. It dictates that certain records must be kept for not less than six years. The rule also requires that electronic records be preserved in a non-rewritable, non-erasable format, commonly known as write once, read many (WORM) formats.

SEC Rule 18a-6, on the other hand, pertains to the retention of records by nationally recognized statistical rating organizations. It imposes requirements similar to those in Rule 17a-4, emphasizing the need for the secure preservation of relevant records.

For compliance, broker-dealers and rating organizations must adhere to the rules in their recordkeeping practices. The SEC conducts inspections and examinations to assess compliance with these and other rules.

Given the potential financial and reputational risks associated with non-compliance, it is crucial to develop and implement robust recordkeeping practices that meet the requirements of these rules. Regular training and audits can also help maintain compliance.

Recommendations:

- **Understand the Rules:** If you are a broker-dealer or a nationally recognized statistical rating organization, familiarize yourself with the requirements of Rules 17a-4 and 18a-6.
- **Develop Robust Recordkeeping Practices**: Implement practices that align with the recordkeeping requirements of these rules.
- **Regular Training and Audits:** Conduct regular training and audits to ensure understanding and adherence to the rules.

SECTION 508

Section 508 of the Rehabilitation Act is up next for discussion. It relates to accessibility requirements for federal agencies and assessing their compliance. Section 508 was enacted to eliminate information technology barriers and make new opportunities available for people with disabilities. It seeks to develop technologies that offer more employment opportunities and allow everyone, including people with disabilities, to take full advantage of the internet and intranet.

The accessibility requirements outlined in Section 508 encompass a broad range of areas, including web-based intranet and internet information and applications, software applications and operating systems, video and multimedia products, telecommunications products, desktop and portable computers, and more. The goal is to ensure that all digital technologies are accessible to all users, including those with disabilities.

Compliance with Section 508 is assessed through automated tests and manual checks. The assessment covers different areas such as proper text equivalents for images, easy navigation for keyboards, use of colors, readability of text, and more.

Enforcement of Section 508 compliance happens primarily through a complaint process or a lawsuit filed by a person with a disability. Additionally, non-compliance could also potentially affect federal funding.

Recommendations:

- **Understand the Law:** Familiarize yourself with the requirements of Section 508 and its applicability to your agency or organization.
- **Incorporate Accessibility:** Consider accessibility at the start of a project to avoid more significant challenges later.
- **Conduct Regular Assessments:** Regularly test your digital technologies for accessibility using automated and manual methods.
- **Provide Training:** Regularly train all relevant staff members on accessibility requirements and best practices.

FEDERAL INFORMATION SECURITY MANAGEMENT ACT (FISMA)

FISMA, the Federal Information Security Management Act, was enacted as part of the Electronic Government Act 2002. Its primary objective is protecting government information, operations, and assets from natural and artificial threats. FISMA has played an ever-increasing role in raising awareness about cybersecurity within the federal government and has explicitly emphasized the importance of implementing a "risk-based policy for cost-effective security."

Under FISMA, federal agencies are mandated to develop, document, and implement an agency-wide program that provides comprehensive security for the information systems supporting their operations and assets. This program encompasses a broad range of requirements, including robust training programs aimed at educating personnel about cybersecurity risks, periodic and thorough risk assessments to identify vulnerabilities, the establishment of robust policies and procedures, and the implementation of an effective process to address identified vulnerabilities and potential threats, among others.

To ensure compliance with FISMA, stringent assessments are conducted to evaluate different components of an agency's information security program and its strict adherence to FISMA requirements, Office of Management and Budget (OMB) policy, and relevant guidelines provided by the National Institute of Standards and Technology (NIST). These assessments have become increasingly rigorous and comprehensive, reflecting the evolving nature of cybersecurity threats and the critical need to safeguard government information and assets effectively.

Furthermore, agencies must report the status of their information security programs to OMB annually, providing a comprehensive and in-depth overview of their efforts in safeguarding government information and assets. These reports undergo thorough scrutiny, focusing on demonstrating continuous improvement and proactive measures to mitigate emerging threats and vulnerabilities.

FISMA continues to play a pivotal and exponentially growing role in promoting a proactive, adaptive, and risk-based approach to cybersecurity within the federal government. By mandating robust security programs and conducting rigorous assessments, FISMA aims to enhance the Protection of sensitive government information, strengthen the resilience of critical operations, and improve the overall security posture of federal agencies in the face of increasingly sophisticated and persistent cyber threats.

Recommendations:

- **Understand FISMA:** Familiarize yourself with the requirements of FISMA, especially if you are involved in federal government operations.
- **Develop a Security Program:** Develop an agency-wide program that addresses FISMA's requirements for security.

- **Regular Assessments:** Conduct periodic risk assessments to identify and address vulnerabilities.
- **Compliance Reporting:** Regularly report the status of your information security program, as required by FISMA.
- **Keep Updated:** Stay updated on changes to FISMA, OMB policy, and applicable NIST guidelines.

FEDERAL INFORMATION PROCESSING STANDARD (FIPS) 140-2

The Federal Information Processing Standard (FIPS) 140-2, or FIPS 140-2, is a U.S. government standard that lays out cryptographic module specifications, including hardware and software components. The standard is organized into four levels, each representing a varying degree of security. Level 1 represents the most basic security requirements, while Level 4 embodies the most rigorous security provisions.

This standard extends across multiple areas, encapsulating aspects such as the specification of cryptographic modules, the design of ports and interfaces, the assignment of roles, provisions of services, Authentication protocols, finite state models, physical security measures, and more. Each area of focus contributes to the robust security fabric that FIPS 140-2 seeks to foster within organizations.

Ensuring compliance with FIPS 140-2 is executed via the Cryptographic Module Validation Program (CMVP). The CMVP represents a collaborative initiative between the NIST in the United States and the Communications Security Establishment (CSE) in Canada. Products that successfully undergo and pass the stringent testing process prescribed by the CMVP are then added to an officially validated product list.

By achieving compliance with FIPS 140-2, organizations can demonstrate that their cryptographic modules meet the stringent security requirements laid out by this recognized standard. This not only can enhance the confidence of customers and other stakeholders in the organization's security measures, but it can also be essential for certain organizations that must comply with specific regulations or handle sensitive information. In this way, FIPS 140-2 serves as a critical benchmark for information security and offers a roadmap for organizations seeking to enhance their cryptographic security practices.

Recommendations:

- **Familiarize with FIPS 140-2:** Understand the requirements of FIPS 140-2 if you are involved in developing or using cryptographic modules.
- **Follow the Standard:** Ensure the cryptographic modules meet the requirements of FIPS 140-2.
- **Understand the Levels:** Understand the different FIPS 140-2 levels to choose the appropriate one for your needs.
- **Plan for Validation:** Prepare your cryptographic modules for the CMVP testing process.

Chapter Conclusion

The landscape of U.S. cybersecurity regulations and requirements is expansive, spanning multiple financial, educational, military, and federal sectors. Key legislation and policy directives guide this intricate realm, each carrying unique implications and requirements.

The GLBA is one such piece of legislation, crucially impacting financial institutions and their obligations to protect nonpublic personal information. Delving into its historical context, key provisions, and influence on privacy and data security helps provide a deep understanding of the regulatory expectations within the financial industry.

The Interagency Guidelines Establishing Information Security Standards offer valuable insights into customer information security program expectations, touching on risk assessment, management, implementation, and testing aspects. This set of guidelines illustrates the rigorous standards set for financial institutions.

PCI DSS is another key standard, particularly within the financial sector, underscoring its requirements and the importance of compliance assessment. The considerable influence of PCI DSS on card security and the financial sector's integrity highlights its role within the broader cybersecurity ecosystem.

Legislations such as the SOX and the Cloud Act have significantly transformed how organizations handle information security and data privacy. IRS Publication 1075 imposes stringent data protection requirements and compliance expectations, emphasizing the critical role of cybersecurity within federal tax operations.

The CJIS Security Policy and the DFARS each present unique security requirements and compliance considerations. The Department of Defense Cloud Computing SRG further dictates security expectations within the DoD's cloud environments.

Finally, regulations such as the Family Educational Rights and Privacy Act (FERPA), SEC Rules 17a-4 and 18a-6, and Section 508 carry distinct implications for privacy, record-keeping, and accessibility. The Federal Information Security Management Act and the FIPS 140-2 establish crucial security requirements and cryptographic standards for federal information systems.

These frameworks are accompanied by actionable suggestions that guide organizations through their unique compliance paths. This comprehensive view of cybersecurity regulations empowers individuals and organizations to effectively manage the complexities of cybersecurity governance, risk management, and compliance.

Case Study: CyberSecure's Compliance Journey

Nilsu, the newly appointed Chief Information Security Officer (CISO) of the fictional company CyberSecure Inc., was charged with ensuring the company complied with all relevant cybersecurity regulations. The task was daunting given the company's varied clientele, from financial institutions to educational entities and federal agencies.

The book "The Ultimate Cybersecurity Guide to Governance, Risk, and Compliance" proved an invaluable resource for Nilsu. She took the first recommendation from each regulation section of chapter 13 seriously – to familiarize herself with each regulation. This foundational understanding proved critical to helping her identify which laws were pertinent to CyberSecure Inc. and its clients.

She then began to implement the recommended practices from each section systematically. For example, in ensuring compliance with the GLBA, she implemented a comprehensive security program, periodically reassessing and improving it. Taking a cue from the Interagency Guidelines, she also set up a robust risk assessment and management framework. When tackling SOX compliance, Nilsu took special care to implement effective internal controls for financial reporting.

Recognizing the importance of communication, Nilsu kept her team and the board updated about the company's compliance status and any changes in the regulations that affected them. Inspired by the FISMA section, she also reported regularly to the board about the state of the company's information security program, giving them a clear picture of their risk posture.

By the end of her first year as CISO, Nilsu had significantly improved CyberSecure Inc.'s regulatory compliance posture. She reflected on the critical lessons from the chapter – the importance of understanding each regulation, implementing robust systems and controls, conducting regular reviews, and communicating effectively. Thanks to the recommendations from this guide, Nilsu had a roadmap to navigate the complex waters of cybersecurity governance, risk management, and compliance, positioning CyberSecure Inc. as a trusted partner in their clients' digital journeys.

CHAPTER 16

State-level Cybersecurity Regulations

"Navigate the complexities of state-level regulations, embracing their power to fortify businesses and drive cybersecurity advancements."

The United States is home to a diverse landscape of state-level regulations, each presenting its own set of complexities. State and federal compliance alignment is critical to navigating this intricate system. These regulations are not static; they evolve continuously, influenced by various factors shaping the broader cybersecurity field. States such as California, New York, Massachusetts, Nevada, Texas, Florida, Illinois, Oregon, Colorado, Ohio, Maryland, Virginia, Washington, Maine, and Utah have distinctive regulatory landscapes. These unique characteristics can potentially pose specific business challenges within each jurisdiction. Understanding the nuances of these regulations is key to formulating effective strategies for compliance. In this context, a comprehensive understanding is crucial to remain compliant and anticipate future changes and trends in this dynamic regulatory environment.

STATE-LEVEL CYBERSECURITY REGULATIONS

State-level regulations, in essence, are legal frameworks put into place by individual states to manage and control activities within their jurisdiction. They range across various sectors, and one area that has seen significant state intervention recently is cybersecurity. The growing concerns about data privacy and the increasing rate of cybercrime drive the enactment of state-level cybersecurity regulations. States have begun to prioritize establishing cybersecurity laws as part of their commitment to protect businesses and consumers in their territory.

Understanding these state-level regulations is crucial for businesses operating within the United States, as they often have to comply with many laws depending on the states they operate in or have customers. The onus falls on organizations to ensure they are familiar with the individual laws, their obligations under these laws, and the penalties for noncompliance. While federal regulations may lay the groundwork, state-level regulations can vary significantly, often providing additional protections and obligations.

Despite their importance, state-level regulations present a complex tapestry of rules and requirements. They can be intricate and distinct, reflecting each state's diversity and needs. The disparity across these laws can lead to confusion and pose considerable challenges for organizations, especially those that operate in multiple states. It is not just about understanding the law; it is also about harmonizing compliance efforts to meet all requirements efficiently.

Part of the complexity stems from the rapid evolution of technology and cyber threats. As digital landscapes change, so does the legal landscape. This necessitates that businesses stay abreast with current state regulations to ensure ongoing Compliance. The dynamism of these laws can be seen as states strive to respond to emerging cyber threats and new data privacy issues.

Given the increasing attention to data privacy and the frequency of cyber-attacks, it is likely that we will see a rise in the number and complexity of state-level regulations in the future. Future developments in this space might be driven by technological advancements, changes in the threat landscape, evolving public sentiment toward privacy, and the response to existing regulations. This creates an additional layer of anticipatory responsibility for businesses, as they must predict and prepare for potential changes in the regulatory landscape.

One noteworthy feature of state-level regulations is their power to influence federal laws and the legal frameworks of other states. They serve as testing grounds for new regulatory ideas and can set precedents that shape broader policy decisions. A single state's approach to a particular issue can create a ripple effect, prompting other states and even the federal government to follow suit.

In this vein, businesses and cybersecurity professionals must not only understand current state-level regulations but also be able to navigate this rapidly evolving landscape. It necessitates an ongoing commitment to learning, adaptation, and a proactive approach to Compliance. Indeed, understanding the current regulations is only half the battle; the other half is being prepared for the future.

Recommendations:

- **Engage in Continuous Learning:** Keep abreast of changes in state-level regulations. This can be done by subscribing to legal and cybersecurity newsletters, attending webinars, and participating in industry forums.
- **Leverage Legal Expertise:** Work with legal professionals experienced in cybersecurity laws across the various states you operate in. This will help ensure you stay in Compliance with all applicable regulations.

- **Implement Robust Compliance Programs:** Build a strong compliance program that addresses current regulations and can adapt to future changes.
- **Advocate for Standardization:** Participate in industry associations and groups that advocate for standardization of cybersecurity laws across states to reduce complexity.
- **Monitor Emerging Trends:** Keep an eye on the emerging trends in data privacy and cybersecurity threats. Understanding these trends will help anticipate potential changes in state-level regulations.

HARMONIZING STATE AND FEDERAL COMPLIANCE

Compliance with cybersecurity regulations is pivotal for businesses, particularly those with multi-jurisdictional operations. Navigating federal and state regulations presents unique challenges due to their intertwined yet distinct requirements. Federal regulations provide a foundational level of protection and general guidelines, while state laws further tailor the criteria based on local needs and perspectives.

A fundamental step toward achieving this harmony is understanding the differences and similarities between state and federal regulations. Some states might only require adherence to federal regulations, while others may impose additional, sometimes stricter, requirements. Therefore, businesses must comprehensively understand both levels of laws to create a harmonized approach to Compliance.

One of the most practical ways to harmonize state and federal compliance is by implementing robust, adaptable, and comprehensive cybersecurity frameworks. These frameworks, such as the National Institute for Science and Technology (NIST) Cybersecurity Framework, offer best practices that align with federal and state regulations. By adhering to these frameworks, organizations can satisfy multiple requirements simultaneously, reducing redundancy in their compliance efforts.

However, not all regulations can be harmonized through these frameworks. Some state regulations may require specific actions not covered by federal laws or general frameworks. Companies should establish distinct processes to ensure they meet these unique requirements in such cases. This approach helps maintain Compliance at both levels and reduces the risk of legal repercussions.

Ensuring ongoing Compliance with state and federal regulations also requires regular reviews and audits. These assessments should verify that the current procedures align with the regulations and identify any changes in the legal landscape that might impact the organization. Regular reviews allow businesses to stay ahead of the regulatory curve and promptly adapt to new requirements.

Creating a culture of Compliance within the organization is also critical to harmonizing state and federal compliance. Everyone, from top-level executives to frontline staff, should understand the importance of Compliance and their roles in maintaining it. This collective responsibility helps ensure Compliance is embedded in the organization's daily operations, reducing the likelihood of breaches and noncompliance.

While harmonizing state and federal compliance can be complex, it is not insurmountable. With careful planning, diligent monitoring, and the right resources, businesses can ensure they meet their regulatory obligations at all levels. As the legal landscape evolves, companies must remain nimble and prepared to adjust their strategies and operations to ensure ongoing Compliance.

Ultimately, harmonizing state and federal compliance should be viewed not as a burden but as an opportunity. It can drive improvements in cybersecurity practices, foster customer trust, and provide a competitive edge for businesses that prioritize and demonstrate their commitment to protecting data.

Recommendations:

- **Grasp the Distinctions:** Make it a priority to understand the differences and similarities between state and federal cybersecurity regulations. A detailed comprehension of both levels of laws will provide a foundation for creating a harmonized approach to compliance.
- **Leverage Cybersecurity Frameworks:** Invest in implementing robust, adaptable, and comprehensive cybersecurity frameworks, like the NIST Cybersecurity Framework. By following such frameworks, your organization can satisfy various regulatory requirements, thus reducing redundancy in compliance efforts.
- **Develop Distinct Processes:** Build separate processes to cater to unique requirements that state regulations might impose, which may not be covered by federal laws or general frameworks. This ensures comprehensive compliance at all levels and mitigates the risk of potential legal repercussions.
- **Implement Regular Reviews:** Conduct regular reviews and audits to ensure your procedures align with existing regulations and to identify any legal changes that might impact your organization. Consistent monitoring will keep your business ahead of the regulatory curve and prepared to adapt to new requirements promptly.
- **Cultivate a Culture of Compliance:** Foster an organizational culture that emphasizes the importance of compliance at all levels, from executives to frontline staff. Encouraging a shared responsibility for compliance can help embed it into daily operations, significantly reducing the likelihood of breaches and noncompliance.

FUTURE DEVELOPMENTS

The future of state-level cybersecurity regulations is a moving target, influenced by various factors, including technological advancements, evolving cyber threats, legislative changes, and shifts in public sentiment about data privacy. Consequently, businesses must adopt a proactive and forward-looking approach to remain compliant.

A significant trend shaping the future of state-level regulations is the ever-increasing interconnectivity driven by the Internet of Things (IoT), cloud computing, and other emerging technologies. These technologies offer numerous benefits, such as improved efficiency and customer service, but they also expand the attack surface for potential cyber threats. As such, we can expect increased regulations focused on securing these new technologies.

Artificial intelligence (AI) and machine learning (ML) are another set of advancements influencing the future of cybersecurity regulations. While these technologies offer potent tools for enhancing cybersecurity, they also raise new privacy and security concerns. Regulatory bodies must grapple with these issues, creating new rules to protect against AI- and ML-based threats and govern these technologies' use in security applications.

The rise in ransomware attacks and other forms of cybercrime will also shape future state-level regulations. States will likely strengthen their laws, imposing harsher penalties for cybercriminals and stricter business security requirements. The increased focus on cybersecurity might also lead to the development of more coordinated efforts at the state level to combat cybercrime.

Additionally, public sentiment toward data privacy and protection is shifting. Consumers are becoming more aware of their digital footprint and are demanding more control over their personal information. This demand will likely spur states to create stricter data collection, storage, and sharing regulations.

Despite the increasing harmonization efforts, the possibility of a federal data privacy law could change the regulatory landscape dramatically. If such a law is enacted, states would need to adjust their regulations to align with federal law, potentially simplifying the compliance process for businesses.

The evolution of cybersecurity threats and the advent of new technologies make it impossible to predict the future of state-level regulations with certainty. However, by staying informed about trends and maintaining a proactive approach, businesses can navigate the changes effectively.

Recommendations:

- **Anticipate Technological Trends:** Stay abreast of technological advancements such as the IoT, cloud computing, and other emerging technologies. Expect increased regulations focused on securing these technologies, and plan to update your cybersecurity strategies accordingly.
- **Understand AI and ML Implications:** Recognize the impact of AI and ML on cybersecurity. Be prepared for new rules addressing AI- and ML-based threats and regulating their use in security applications.
- **Be Vigilant about Cybercrime Trends:** Monitor the rise in ransomware attacks and other forms of cybercrime. Anticipate strengthened laws with harsher penalties for cybercriminals and stricter security requirements for businesses.

- **Acknowledge Shifts in Public Sentiment:** Pay attention to the grow-ing consumer demand for better data privacy and control over personal information. Be prepared for stricter regulations regarding data collec-tion, storage, and sharing.
- **Prepare for Federal Law Changes:** Consider the potential for a federal data privacy law. Such a law could require states to adjust their regula-tions, potentially simplifying the compliance process for businesses. Stay informed and be ready to adapt your compliance strategies.

NOTABLE STATE REGULATIONS

The complexities of state-level cybersecurity regulations cannot be overstated, as they demonstrate a nuanced approach to data protection, reflective of each state's unique challenges and perspectives.

California has been at the forefront of establishing data privacy standards in the United States. The state's introduction of the California Consumer Privacy Act (CCPA) marked a watershed moment in consumer data rights. The CCPA grants consumers a high degree of control over their personal information, fundamentally altering how businesses collect, handle, and share such data. The introduction of the CCPA prompted a ripple effect, pushing other states to establish similar regulations, thereby reshaping the national approach to data privacy.

Following the CCPA, California continued its pioneering efforts by introduc-ing the California Privacy Rights Act (CPRA). This legislation expanded upon the consumer rights outlined in the CCPA and introduced additional obligations for businesses, further strengthening the state's data protection framework. Additionally, California's Data Breach Notification Law (SB-1386) requires businesses to swiftly notify California residents of data breaches, emphasizing the state's commitment to prompt and transparent communication in the wake of security incidents.

In New York, cybersecurity regulations reflect the state's position as a finan-cial hub. The Stop Hacks and Improve Electronic Data Security Act (SHIELD Act) broadens the scope of information covered by breach notification laws and imposes more stringent security requirements on businesses. The SHIELD Act protects consumers from data breaches and encourages businesses to bol-ster their cybersecurity practices.

Further reinforcing New York's commitment to cybersecurity, the Depart-ment of Financial Services Cybersecurity Regulation (23 NYCRR 500) sets stringent cybersecurity requirements for financial services companies. This reg-ulation highlights the importance of industry-specific cybersecurity regulations, requiring financial institutions to establish a robust cybersecurity program, adopt a written cybersecurity policy, and report cybersecurity events promptly.

Massachusetts also prioritizes data security, as evidenced by the Mas-sachusetts Data Breach Notification Law (M.G.L. 93H). This law places strin-gent requirements on businesses to protect personal information and notify residents of data breaches. This proactive legislation represents a significant stride toward enhanced cybersecurity.

Further complementing Massachusetts' approach is the Standards for the Protection of Personal Information (201 CMR 17.00). This regulation mandates businesses to develop, implement, and maintain a comprehensive information security program. The law's comprehensive approach underscores the importance of ongoing, proactive efforts in preserving cybersecurity and protecting sensitive information.

Nevada's unique approach to data protection is embodied in the state's Personal Information Data Privacy Encryption Law (N.R.S. 603A). This legislation mandates businesses to encrypt personal data during electronic transmission, demonstrating a focused and practical approach to mitigating data breaches. Nevada's emphasis on encryption highlights the importance of this fundamental cybersecurity measure in protecting sensitive data during transmission.

In Texas, the comprehensive Identity Theft Enforcement and Protection Act addresses a broad spectrum of identity theft issues, providing important protections for consumer data. This Act emphasizes Texas's commitment to safeguarding consumers from the growing threat of identity theft. Furthermore, the Texas Cybersecurity Act demonstrates a concerted effort to protect consumers and state information resources, showcasing a comprehensive approach to cybersecurity.

The Information Protection Act (FIPA) sets guidelines to protect Floridians' data in Florida. Illinois has enacted the Personal Information Protection Act (PIPA) and the Biometric Information Privacy Act (BIPA), aiming to protect a broad spectrum of personal and biometric data. The Oregon Consumer Identity Theft Protection Act safeguards Oregonians against identity theft, while the Colorado Protections for Consumer Data Privacy Act ensures that Colorado businesses protect consumers' data.

Illinois has made significant strides in personal data protection through the PIPA and the BIPA. PIPA imposes strict obligations on businesses to protect personal information and promptly notify residents in case of a data breach. On the other hand, BIPA is a pioneering law in the United States, requiring consent for collecting and storing biometric data, including fingerprints and facial recognition data, demonstrating Illinois' forward-thinking approach toward emerging technologies.

Oregon's Consumer Identity Theft Protection Act sets forth comprehensive guidelines to protect Oregon residents from identity theft. It mandates businesses to take reasonable measures to protect personal information and promptly notify consumers of a security breach. This proactive law aims to increase transparency and instill confidence in digital interactions, thus promoting a safer cyber environment in Oregon.

In Colorado, the Protections for Consumer Data Privacy Act broadly views personal information and mandates businesses to implement reasonable security procedures to protect this data. It also requires timely notification of data breaches, demonstrating Colorado's commitment to transparency and consumer protection in data security.

Ohio's Data Protection Act is unique as it provides a legal safe harbor to businesses implementing a recognized cybersecurity framework. This approach encourages companies to adopt robust cybersecurity practices, fostering a safer business environment and better protecting Ohio residents from data breaches.

The Maryland PIPA underscores Maryland's commitment to data security. The law mandates businesses to protect personal information through reasonable security procedures and practices. It also requires firms to promptly investigate and notify Maryland residents of any security breach, ensuring transparency in Maryland's digital landscape.

Virginia's Consumer Data Protection Act (CDPA) takes a comprehensive approach to data privacy, providing consumers with substantial control over their data. The CDPA requires businesses to obtain explicit consent before collecting sensitive data and provides consumers with the right to access, correct, delete, and opt out of specific data processing, demonstrating Virginia's commitment to putting data control back into consumers' hands.

Maine's Act to Protect the Privacy of Online Consumer Information is one of the country's strictest internet privacy laws. It prohibits internet service providers from using, disclosing, selling, or permitting access to customers' personal information without express consent, demonstrating Maine's commitment to online privacy and consumer control over personal data.

If enacted, Utah's Consumer Privacy Act will offer comprehensive protections for Utah residents. The proposed Act requires businesses to respect consumers' privacy rights and imposes strict obligations on data collection, usage, and protection, underscoring Utah's commitment to maintaining a safe and trustworthy digital environment.

Recommendations:

- **Comprehensive Understanding:** Make it a priority to understand the cybersecurity regulations in your operating states fully. Familiarize yourself with the specific requirements of each state-level law, such as California's CCPA, Illinois' BIPA, and New York's SHIELD Act. A comprehensive understanding of these regulations will help you develop robust cybersecurity practices that meet and exceed state requirements.
- **Develop State-Specific Compliance Programs:** Create compliance programs tailored to the unique requirements of each state in which your organization operates. For instance, if your organization collects biometric data in Illinois, ensure that your program adheres to BIPA's requirements.
- **Monitor Legislative Changes:** Keep abreast of changes in state-level regulations, such as proposed laws and amendments. Given the rapidly evolving digital landscape, state cybersecurity laws are often updated

to address new threats and technologies. Regularly monitoring these changes will help you maintain compliance and avoid legal issues.

- **Implement Best Practices:** Even without specific state-level laws, adhere to recognized cybersecurity best practices. This may include implementing a recognized cybersecurity framework like the NIST Framework or ISO 27001, regularly auditing your cybersecurity practices, and providing ongoing cybersecurity training for employees.

- **Consult Legal Experts:** Given the complexity of state-level regulations, seeking advice from legal experts specializing in data privacy and cybersecurity can be beneficial. They can provide tailored advice to ensure your compliance efforts align with state requirements and help you navigate potential legal pitfalls.

- **Privacy by Design:** Implement a 'Privacy by Design' approach in your organization's operations. This means integrating data privacy considerations into your operations, from product development to customer service. Adopting such a proactive approach can help your organization stay ahead of regulatory changes and demonstrate a commitment to data privacy, boosting customer trust.

Chapter Conclusion

The challenge for businesses operating across multiple states is to adhere to the varying state laws, which often extend beyond federal requirements. The complex regulatory environment is largely attributed to state-specific needs, the diversity in the business sector, and the fast-paced advancement of technology and cyber threats.

Key state regulations, such as CCPA and the CPRA, ensure consumer data protection and necessitate transparency in data practices. New York's SHIELD Act puts more accountability on businesses to secure private data. In Massachusetts, the Data Breach Notification Law mandates businesses to inform affected individuals and state regulators promptly in case of data breaches. Meanwhile, Nevada's law emphasizes encryption to safeguard consumer data privacy.

Despite these state-specific laws, their collective objective is to enhance consumer data protection, mandating businesses to adopt rigorous protocols for data handling, management, and in cases of security breaches. Achieving harmonious compliance with these various state and federal regulations is indeed a formidable task for businesses. The solution lies in understanding the nuanced differences between state and federal laws, employing sturdy cybersecurity frameworks, conducting frequent audits, and fostering an organizational culture prioritizing compliance.

As for the future of state-level regulations, various factors will be influential. Technological advancements in IoT, AI, and ML, evolving cyber threats, and shifting public sentiments toward data privacy will play significant roles. The constant adaptations in response to the effectiveness of existing regulations will also guide future rules. The rise in cybercrimes will likely lead to more stringent laws, and a potential overarching federal data privacy law could be on the horizon.

Despite the inherent challenges, businesses should approach the task of harmonizing state and federal compliance as a strategic opportunity to enhance their cybersecurity practices and build trust among customers and stakeholders. In the digital age, robust data protection measures can lead to a significant competitive advantage. Therefore, businesses must stay informed, agile, and proactive in navigating this multifaceted and ever-evolving regulatory landscape.

Case Study: Cyberguard's Path to Compliance

CyberGuard Inc., a growing tech startup with a digital footprint across multiple states, realized the importance of complying with the intricate web of state-level cybersecurity regulations. As CyberGuard's Chief Information Security Officer (CISO), Leyla found herself in the throes of this challenge.

The first step in Leyla's path to achieving Compliance involved understanding the cybersecurity laws specific to each state where CyberGuard operated. She dedicated herself to a comprehensive study of notable state regulations, from California's CCPA and New York's SHIELD Act to the unique regulations of states like Massachusetts, Nevada, and Texas. Each law's nuances and implications for CyberGuard's operations were carefully dissected and understood.

Next, Leyla faced the challenge of harmonizing state and federal compliance. She noticed that some regulations overlapped while others were contradictory. The process was complex but necessary to prevent CyberGuard from being exposed to regulatory fines or reputational damage. Leyla collaborated with legal experts to ensure that every facet of CyberGuard's operations adhered to state and federal laws, highlighting the importance of specialist consultation in complex regulatory landscapes.

Aware that the regulatory landscape was ever-evolving, Leyla set up a system to monitor legislative changes continuously. She subscribed to legal bulletins, joined regulatory forums, and liaised with her network of cybersecurity professionals. This proactive approach ensured CyberGuard was always a step ahead and could quickly adapt to new requirements, reflecting the need for ongoing regulatory vigilance.

To ensure that CyberGuard's practices remained robust and in line with industry standards, Leyla integrated a "Privacy by Design" approach.

This approach ensured that privacy measures were embedded in Cyber-Guard's products from the outset, but it also demonstrated a commitment to the security of customer data that strengthened trust with consumers and regulators alike.

Finally, Leyla understood that achieving Compliance was not a one-time task but an ongoing process. She developed state-specific compliance programs that evolved with changing regulations. She regularly conducted audits, addressed gaps, and instilled a culture of cybersecurity awareness within the company.

From this narrative, we learn that comprehending state-specific regulations, harmonizing state and federal laws, monitoring legal changes, implementing best practices, consulting legal experts, and integrating a "Privacy by Design" approach are crucial steps in navigating the complex landscape of state-level cybersecurity regulations. Leyla's proactive and comprehensive approach led CyberGuard Inc. toward a path of robust Compliance.

CHAPTER 17

International Cybersecurity Laws and Regulations

"International cyber laws are like a puzzle that constantly changes its pieces, and as CISOs, we must be the master puzzlers to ensure compliance and protection."

The global cybersecurity landscape is marked by the complexity and constant evolution of international laws and regulations, making it a daunting arena for organizations worldwide. Among these, regulations such as the General Data Protection Regulation (*GDPR*), Personal Information Protection and Electronic Documents Act (*PIPEDA*), the Data Protection Act, China's Cybersecurity Law, and Singapore's Personal Data Protection Act (*PDPA*) stand as prominent pillars. However, there are also several other significant legislations whose business implications warrant careful consideration.

INTERNATIONAL CYBERSECURITY LAWS

In today's interconnected world, international cybersecurity laws have taken center stage and hold unparalleled importance in our increasingly globalized economy. As organizations continue to develop and evolve, they are inherently expanding their digital footprint across national and international borders, operating in multiple jurisdictions simultaneously. This expansion is fueled by numerous advancements in digital technology, which make cross-border operations not just a strategic advantage but a necessity in a world where competition and collaboration are no longer confined to geographical limits. In this context, understanding and complying with a diverse range of regulations becomes pivotal and an operational prerequisite.

Cybersecurity regulations, with their varied implications, span across the globe, each designed in response to their respective countries' unique needs, challenges, and cultural contexts. Various governments worldwide proactively implement laws and regulations to protect citizens' data and secure digital operations within their jurisdiction. These laws may encompass a broad spectrum of elements, such as data privacy, data sovereignty, data breach notification, and requirements for cybersecurity measures, among others. The overarching aim is to establish a safer digital environment where businesses can operate securely, and citizens can trust the digital economy.

The challenge, however, arises when organizations have to navigate this complex regulatory landscape, which is diverse and continually evolving. Adhering to the laws of multiple jurisdictions becomes a tricky task, more so because these laws often have extraterritorial effects. That is, the laws of a country may apply to an organization not physically present within that country, but that deals with the data of its citizens or provides them with goods or services. This means that an organization may need to comply with the cybersecurity laws of the countries where it has physical operations and those of other countries where its digital operations reach.

Therefore, establishing a global cybersecurity compliance program is far from straightforward; it demands a meticulous and complex balance. On the one hand, the organization needs to maintain a uniform cybersecurity stance. This involves establishing a core set of cybersecurity measures, policies, and practices that align with its strategic objectives, risk appetite, and operational context. These might include technical measures such as firewalls and encryption, organizational measures such as access controls and incident response plans, and regulatory measures such as privacy policies and data protection impact assessments.

On the other hand, the organization needs to tweak this uniform stance to comply with regional laws. These tweaks may involve adjusting existing measures, adding new measures, or even removing specific measures, depending on what each jurisdiction's laws require. This often requires extensive knowledge of each jurisdiction's laws, understanding their implications for the organization's operations, and the ability to translate them into actionable measures.

This dual requirement of uniformity and customization can often create tension within the organization's cybersecurity compliance program. The challenge lies in identifying what tweaks are needed for each jurisdiction and ensuring that these tweaks do not compromise the overall effectiveness and consistency of the organization's cybersecurity posture. The solution often lies in a risk-based approach, where the organization identifies its key legal risks in each jurisdiction, prioritizes them based on their potential impact, and addresses them in a way that integrates seamlessly with its overall cybersecurity strategy.

Indeed, establishing a global cybersecurity compliance program is an intricate task requiring a careful balance. It is a task that demands legal expertise and technical knowledge, strategic thinking, project management skills, and a deep understanding of the organization's business model and operations. However, despite the challenges involved, it is a task increasingly becoming a non-negotiable requirement for organizations in today's globalized digital economy.

Recommendations:

- **Embrace the Global Perspective:** Strive to understand the wide array of international cybersecurity laws that span different countries and regions. This comprehensive understanding is fundamental in establishing an effective global cybersecurity compliance program, ensuring your operations abide by varying legal standards.
- **Research and Understand:** Invest time and resources in thoroughly understanding the specific cybersecurity laws applicable to the regions where your organization operates or intends to expand. This deep knowledge helps you navigate the complexities of diverse legal landscapes and align your business operations with local requirements.
- **Seek Expert Help:** Do not hesitate to seek the assistance of legal and cybersecurity experts who specialize in international regulations, especially for regions with complex legal frameworks. Their expertise can guide you in interpreting and implementing these laws effectively, minimizing compliance risks.
- **Establish a Compliance Team:** Assemble a dedicated compliance team whose primary role is to ensure your organization's continuous adherence to relevant international laws. This team can manage the ongoing tasks of monitoring, reporting, and updating your compliance practices as laws evolve and change.
- **Promote Knowledge Sharing:** Foster an environment that encourages regular training and updates on international cybersecurity laws. By informing all employees of these laws and their implications, you can build a corporate culture that values compliance and minimizes the risk of violations.

GENERAL DATA PROTECTION REGULATION (GDPR) – EUROPEAN UNION

The GDPR, introduced by the European Union, represents a transformative shift in data privacy norms within Europe and across the globe. A comprehensive data protection law dramatically alters how businesses, including financial institutions, approach data privacy and protection. This groundbreaking regulation underscored the principle of "privacy by design," a pioneering concept that firmly places privacy at the forefront of business operations rather than as an appended consideration.

The "privacy by design" principle mandates that privacy and data protection are embedded directly into the design specifications of technologies, business practices, and physical infrastructures. This means that from the inception of a new system, service, or process that involves processing personal data, privacy should be one of the core considerations. This principle effectively pushes organizations to take a proactive rather than reactive approach to data privacy, thus leading to higher standards of privacy and better protection for individuals' data.

In addition to emphasizing privacy as a fundamental component of organizational operations, GDPR has also conferred greater control over individuals' data. It offers a series of rights to individuals, including the right to be informed about how their data is being used, the right to access their data, the right to rectify incorrect data, the right to erase data, the right to restrict processing, the right to data portability, the right to object to data processing and rights related to automated decision-making and profiling. These rights place individuals at the center of data processing activities and give them unprecedented control over their data.

While the GDPR was designed and implemented by the European Union, its impact reverberates far beyond the borders of Europe. Its reach extends to all businesses, regardless of location, that process the personal data of individuals located within the EU, thus affecting a broad array of international entities. Consequently, even businesses outside the EU have had to closely examine their data processing activities and ensure they comply with the GDPR requirements if they handle EU citizens' data. This extraterritorial scope has profoundly affected the global business landscape, raising the bar for data protection worldwide.

Financial institutions, in particular, have been significantly affected by the advent of the GDPR. With their vast data repositories, complex data processing activities, and critical economic role, these institutions have had to undertake significant changes to their data handling practices to ensure compliance. Such changes might include revising their data collection and consent procedures, updating their privacy notices, implementing more robust data security measures, establishing processes for reporting data breaches promptly, and creating mechanisms to respond to individuals' requests to exercise their rights under the GDPR.

Given the high stakes involved – with potential fines of up to 4% of global annual turnover or €20 million (whichever is higher) for noncompliance – financial institutions have a considerable interest in developing and implementing robust GDPR compliance strategies. These strategies might involve conducting thorough data audits to understand their data and how it is being used, appointing a data protection officer to oversee compliance activities, implementing privacy impact assessments for high-risk data processing activities, and maintaining comprehensive documentation of their data processing activities.

This section delves deeper into various GDPR compliance strategies, highlighting how these can be applied within the context of financial institutions. It discusses these strategies theoretically and through real-world case studies that illustrate the practical implications of GDPR adherence. These case studies will demonstrate how different institutions have navigated the path to GDPR compliance, their challenges, and the solutions they have implemented, offering valuable insights for other institutions embarking on the same journey.

In essence, the introduction of the GDPR represents a significant milestone in the global data protection landscape, and its implications for financial institutions are vast and complex. As such, these institutions need to understand the regulation, its requirements, and the steps they can take to ensure compliance.

Recommendations:

- **Embrace Privacy by Design:** Prioritize privacy and data protection from the inception of new systems, services, or processes involving personal data. This proactive approach leads to higher privacy standards and better protection for individual data.
- **Understand Individuals' Rights:** Familiarize yourself with the rights conferred by the GDPR, such as the right to be informed, the right to access, and the right to erase data. These rights place individuals at the center of data processing activities, allowing them unprecedented control over their data.
- **Recognize the GDPR's Global Impact:** Regardless of location, any business processing the personal data of individuals located within the EU must comply with GDPR. This extraterritorial reach of the regulation demands compliance from businesses worldwide.
- **Address the Unique Needs of Financial Institutions:** Due to their extensive data repositories and complex data processing activities, financial institutions must make substantial changes to ensure GDPR compliance. These changes could involve revising data collection and consent procedures, enhancing data security measures, and establishing robust processes for reporting data breaches.
- **Develop Robust GDPR Compliance Strategies:** Given the potential high penalties for noncompliance, financial institutions must develop comprehensive compliance strategies. These strategies could involve conducting data audits, appointing a data protection officer, implementing privacy impact assessments, and maintaining detailed documentation of data processing activities.

PIPEDA – CANADA

Canada's stance on data privacy and cybersecurity finds its expression in the Personal Information Protection and Electronic Documents Act (PIPEDA), a legislation that has established the country's approach to data protection. As a federal privacy law for private-sector organizations, PIPEDA lays the groundwork for collecting, using, and disclosing personal information in the context of conducting commercial activities. It sets the standards for how businesses, including financial institutions, should manage and protect personal information, promoting trust and privacy in the digital economy.

PIPEDA was designed to balance individuals' privacy rights and businesses' needs to collect and use personal information for legitimate purposes.

It delineates the principles of fair information practices, which form the basis of how organizations should handle personal information. These principles cover accountability, identifying data collection purposes, obtaining informed consent, limiting collection, ensuring accuracy, implementing adequate security safeguards, being transparent about privacy practices, providing individuals access to their information, and challenging compliance.

A critical feature of PIPEDA is its broad scope, which applies to personal information collected, used, or disclosed during commercial activities across provincial or national borders. This is particularly significant in today's digital age, where data flows freely and quickly across borders, underscoring Canada's commitment to protecting its citizens' personal information regardless of where it is processed. The Act does not just apply to organizations based in Canada and foreign companies with a significant nexus to Canada or process the data of Canadian citizens.

Like any other private-sector businesses, financial institutions operating in Canada are subject to PIPEDA's compliance requirements. Given the nature of their operations, financial institutions often handle large volumes of sensitive personal information. Therefore, they are entrusted with a heightened responsibility to protect this data and ensure their practices comply with PIPEDA. Noncompliance with PIPEDA can have serious consequences, including fines, reputational damage, and loss of customer trust.

Comprehending the implications of these regulations is crucial for financial institutions. For instance, they need to understand what constitutes personal information under PIPEDA, the purposes for which they are permitted to use this information, the extent to which they are required to obtain customer consent, how they should maintain the accuracy of data, what security measures they need to implement, and how they should respond to customers' requests to access or correct their information.

Beyond merely understanding PIPEDA, financial institutions must develop and implement strategies to ensure compliance with the Act. Such strategies might involve conducting privacy impact assessments, implementing robust data security measures, training employees on privacy matters, maintaining transparent privacy practices, and establishing mechanisms to respond promptly to data breaches and customer requests.

Furthermore, we will provide practical strategies to achieve PIPEDA compliance and effectively manage noncompliance risks. These strategies will offer a roadmap to financial institutions, helping them navigate the complexities of PIPEDA compliance and fostering a culture of privacy beyond compliance to build trust and loyalty with their customers.

Recommendations:

- **Balance Privacy Rights and Business Needs:** The PIPEDA balances individuals' privacy rights and the needs of businesses to collect and use personal information. It defines the principles of fair information practices that guide organizations in managing personal information.

- **Understand PIPEDA's Broad Scope:** PIPEDA applies to personal information collected, used, or disclosed during commercial activities across provincial or national borders. It covers both organizations based in Canada and foreign companies that process the data of Canadian citizens.
- **Recognize Financial Institutions' Compliance Requirements:** Financial institutions handling large volumes of sensitive personal information are subject to PIPEDA's compliance requirements. Noncompliance can result in fines, reputational damage, and loss of customer trust.
- **Comprehend the Implications of PIPEDA:** Financial institutions must understand what constitutes personal information under PIPEDA, the permitted uses of this information, customer consent, maintaining data accuracy, necessary security measures, and responding to customers' requests for data access or correction.
- **Develop Compliance Strategies:** Financial institutions must implement strategies to ensure PIPEDA compliance. These may include conducting privacy impact assessments, implementing robust data security measures, employee training, maintaining transparency, and establishing mechanisms for prompt response to data breaches and customer requests.

THE DATA PROTECTION ACT – UNITED KINGDOM

In the United Kingdom, the primary legislation governing the management and protection of personal data is encapsulated in the Data Protection Act. This piece of legislation forms the foundation of the United Kingdom's approach to data privacy and is at the heart of how businesses, including financial institutions, deal with personal data. It sets out the rules for data protection and the rights of individuals, providing a framework for organizations to follow when they process personal data.

However, the United Kingdom's data protection landscape has been substantially affected by the country's departure from the European Union, commonly referred to as Brexit. Post-Brexit, the United Kingdom has endeavored to maintain a data protection framework in line with the GDPR, the EU's comprehensive data protection law. The intention is to ensure data protection continuity and to facilitate the smooth flow of personal data between the United Kingdom and the EU, which is vital for businesses that operate across these jurisdictions.

The GDPR has played a prominent role in global data protection standards, so it has profoundly influenced the United Kingdom's Data Protection Act. The Act embodies many of the principles and provisions of the GDPR, including the concepts of "privacy by design," "data minimization," and "rights of the data subject," among others. Therefore, understanding the relationship between the Data Protection Act and GDPR, particularly in the post-Brexit era, can be complex and requires careful examination.

Financial institutions are among the organizations most significantly impacted by data protection regulations. Given the extensive volumes of personal data they deal with, these institutions must be keenly aware of the requirements of the Data Protection Act and the principles of the GDPR that it upholds. Compliance with these regulations is a legal necessity and a matter of maintaining trust with customers and safeguarding their sensitive information.

This section details the intricacies of the United Kingdom's Data Protection Act. We provide a comprehensive overview of the Act, including its key principles, rights it confers to individuals, and obligations it imposes on organizations. We explore its deep-seated relationship with the GDPR, examining how the two pieces of legislation interact and influence each other, especially in light of the changes brought about by Brexit.

Moreover, we spotlight the specific compliance requirements of the Data Protection Act for financial institutions. From understanding the principles of data processing to knowing the rights of individuals over their data to implementing appropriate security measures, we delve into what it means for financial institutions to comply with the Data Protection Act.

We also highlight the best practices for ensuring data protection compliance within the United Kingdom, providing practical guidance for financial institutions. We explore topics such as implementing privacy by design, managing data breaches, handling subject access requests, and maintaining a robust data protection policy.

This section is designed to equip financial institutions with the knowledge and tools they need to navigate the United Kingdom's data protection landscape effectively, ensuring they comply with the Data Protection Act and continue to foster trust and confidence among their customer base.

Recommendations:

- **Understand the Data Protection Act:** The United Kingdom is the primary legislation governing personal data management and protection. It outlines data protection rules and individuals' rights, providing a framework for organizations processing personal data.

- **Navigate Post-Brexit Changes:** The United Kingdom's departure from the EU has significantly impacted its data protection landscape. To ensure data protection continuity and facilitate personal data flow between the United Kingdom and EU, the United Kingdom aims to maintain a data protection framework in line with the GDPR.

- **Recognize the Influence of GDPR:** The United Kingdom's Data Protection Act embodies many GDPR principles and provisions, including "privacy by design," "data minimization," and "rights of the data subject." Understanding this relationship, especially post-Brexit, is critical.

- **Acknowledge Financial Institutions' Obligations:** Financial institutions handling extensive personal data volumes must comply with the Data Protection Act and uphold the GDPR principles it incorporates. Compliance is both a legal requirement and a trust-building measure with customers.

THE CYBERSECURITY LAW – CHINA

The Cybersecurity Law of the People's Republic of China, enacted in 2017, is a robust and comprehensive piece of legislation that provides a detailed outline of the country's stance on data privacy and cybersecurity. It is not merely a law but a broad legal framework that governs various facets of the digital space, ranging from personal data protection and network security to penal measures for cybercrimes. The law has far-reaching implications, influencing and shaping the actions of domestic and foreign businesses that operate within Chinese cyberspace.

This law has been instrumental in defining China's cybersecurity landscape. It emphasizes the protection of personal data, making it a legal obligation for companies to safeguard this information. Furthermore, the law prioritizes network security, requiring companies to implement measures to protect their network from cyber threats. In addition, it stipulates strict penalties for cybercrimes, thereby enhancing the legal deterrent against cyber misconduct.

Given its broad and all-encompassing nature, the Cybersecurity Law is particularly relevant for foreign financial institutions operating in China. These institutions, which manage vast amounts of personal and financial data, must understand and adhere strictly to the law's provisions to ensure their operations' security and integrity. Understanding the law's nuances and requirements is a regulatory and critical business imperative. Noncompliance not only invites legal penalties but can also erode customer trust, which can have long-term business implications.

In this section, we thoroughly explore the Cybersecurity Law of China. We provide a comprehensive introduction to the law, detailing its history, purpose, and the fundamental principles it upholds. We dissect its main provisions, discussing the various areas of cybersecurity and data privacy it touches upon. We delve into data localization, tiered network protection systems, real-name identification, and more.

We also delve into the law's specific business requirements, focusing on those elements particularly relevant to financial institutions. This includes understanding these institutions' obligations to protect personal information, maintain network security, and respond to cyber threats. We consider how these requirements impact financial institutions collect, store, use, and share data.

The section further explores the impact of the Cybersecurity Law on financial institutions operating in China. We consider how the law influences their data management practices, network security measures, and overall cybersecurity strategy. We also discuss noncompliance penalties, highlighting the potential legal, financial, and reputational risks.

Moreover, we propose practical steps for navigating the stringent landscape of China's cybersecurity regulations. We offer strategies for achieving compliance without compromising operational efficiency or customer service. This includes recommendations on implementing strong data protection measures, maintaining robust network security, managing and responding to cyber threats, and fostering a culture of cybersecurity within the organization.

In sum, this section seeks to provide a detailed examination of China's Cybersecurity Law and its implications for financial institutions. By understanding this law in depth, these institutions can better navigate the Chinese digital landscape, ensure compliance, protect their customers' data, and mitigate cybersecurity risks.

Recommendations:

- **Familiarize Yourself with the Law:** Gain an in-depth understanding of the Cybersecurity Law of China, which provides a broad legal framework governing personal data protection, network security, and penalties for cybercrimes.
- **Prioritize Personal Data Protection:** The law requires companies to protect personal data meticulously. Financial institutions should implement strong policies and controls to handle data securely and responsibly.
- **Enhance Network Security:** The law emphasizes the importance of network security. Institutions should invest in advanced cybersecurity technologies and establish robust protocols to safeguard against potential threats.
- **Stay Abreast of Legal Changes:** Given the evolving nature of cybersecurity, keep up-to-date with the latest amendments and modifications to the law to maintain compliance.
- **Pay Attention to Specific Requirements:** Understand the law's requirements, particularly data localization, tiered network protection system, and real-name identification. Tailor your practices and systems to meet these specific requirements.
- **Prepare for Noncompliance Penalties:** The law stipulates strict penalties for non-compliance. Ensure you understand the potential legal, financial, and reputational implications of failing to comply.
- **Develop a Comprehensive Compliance Strategy:** Create a detailed strategy that covers all aspects of the law. This strategy should include measures to protect personal information, maintain network security, and respond promptly to cyber threats.
- **Foster a Culture of Cybersecurity:** Encourage a culture of cybersecurity within your organization. This culture should emphasize the importance of data privacy and each employee's role in maintaining it.
- **Regularly Review Compliance:** Regularly assess and audit your practices and systems to ensure they remain compliant with the law. Regular reviews will also help you identify and address potential issues promptly.
- **Seek Expert Guidance:** Seek expert legal advice considering the law's complexity. This can help you navigate the law more effectively and ensure your practices meet its requirements.

THE PERSONAL DATA PROTECTION ACT – SINGAPORE

Singapore's PDPA is a comprehensive legislation that governs organizations' collection, usage, and disclosure of personal data. The law, which came into effect in 2012, acts as a vital pillar of Singapore's digital economy, underpinning its efforts to remain competitive and foster a trustworthy business environment in the age of digitalization. The PDPA bolsters Singapore's status as a dependable business hub by setting robust data security and privacy standards. Its implications extend across all sectors of the economy, making it particularly pertinent for financial institutions operating in Singapore to comprehend its intricacies and ensure full compliance.

This section aims to provide a broad and in-depth examination of the PDPA. We begin with a thorough introduction to the Act, including an exploration of its purpose, legislative history, and the fundamental principles it upholds. This includes the Consent Obligation, which demands organizations to seek an individual's permission before collecting, using, or disclosing their data, and the Protection Obligation, which requires organizations to make reasonable security arrangements to protect the personal data they possess or control.

We also dive into the specifics of the PDPA's compliance requirements. This involves an extensive discussion of the various obligations the Act imposes on organizations, such as the need to designate a data protection officer, the rules around data access and correction, and the stipulations for data retention and disposal. We aim to highlight the practical implications of these obligations, particularly for financial institutions that handle sensitive customer data.

Next, we analyze the impact of the PDPA on financial institutions operating in Singapore. We explore how the Act shapes its data management practices and policies, influencing how it collects, stores, uses, and discloses personal and financial data. This includes exploring the potential legal, financial, and reputational risks associated with noncompliance and the need for robust measures to safeguard customer data and trust.

Further, we delve into strategies financial institutions can employ to ensure PDPA compliance. This entails a comprehensive exploration of best practices for data management and protection, plans to embed privacy considerations into organizational processes, and tips for creating a data protection culture within the organization. Additionally, we present case studies and real-world examples to illustrate how these strategies can be applied in practice.

This section aims to equip financial institutions with the knowledge and tools to navigate Singapore's data protection landscape effectively. By understanding the PDPA and its requirements in depth, financial institutions can ensure they comply with the law and promote trust with their customers and stakeholders, enhancing their reputation and competitive advantage in the digital economy.

Recommendations:

- **Comprehend the PDPA:** Understand the PDPA and its requirements to develop effective compliance strategies.

- **Manage Personal Data Responsibly:** Collect, use, and disclose personal data responsibly and in a manner that respects individuals' rights.
- **Establish a Data Protection Policy:** Implement a data protection policy that aligns with PDPA requirements and communicate this policy to stakeholders.
- **Prepare for Breach Notifications:** Develop a robust incident response plan, taking into account the PDPA's breach notification requirements.
- **Maintain Open Channels with the PDPC:** Keep communication lines with Singapore's Personal Data Protection Commission for guidance and compliance help.

OTHER NOTABLE INTERNATIONAL CYBERSECURITY LAWS

In the current worldwide landscape, cybersecurity and data privacy have emerged as cardinal points of concern. Recognizing the urgency and significance of these issues, various countries have introduced many laws and regulations designed to protect personal data, foster digital trust, and enhance cybersecurity. Among these are Australia's Privacy Act, Brazil's General Data Protection Law (*LGPD*), Japan's Act on the Protection of Personal Information (*APPI*), South Korea's Personal Information Protection Act (*PIPA*), and India's Information Technology Act. These legislations testify the collective international response to data privacy and cybersecurity challenges.

This section intends to present a comprehensive yet succinct overview of these laws. It aims to dissect their principal components, shed light on their unique characteristics, and explain their inherent objectives. The purpose is not just to enumerate these laws but to provide a deep understanding of their core tenets and their consequential implications on international organizations' data protection strategies.

First, we delve into Australia's Privacy Act. We explore its 12 Australian Privacy Principles, which set forth a broad framework for appropriately handling personal information by organizations. Furthermore, we discuss the various amendments to the Act over the years and how they reflect Australia's commitment to evolving data protection standards.

Moving on, we explore Brazil's LGPD, which revolutionized the country's data protection regime. We discuss how it mirrors Europe's GDPR in many aspects, signaling Brazil's alignment with international data protection standards. An in-depth examination of the LGPD's principles will be provided, including consent, purpose limitation, and data minimization.

Next, we delve into Japan's APPI Act. This law's purpose and its principle provisions, which balance individual privacy rights with the utilization of personal data for economic and social benefits, will be discussed. The amendments to APPI and their implications for data handling practices will also be highlighted.

Then, we venture into the realm of South Korea's PIPA. We shed light on its rigid principles governing personal data collection, processing, and use and its heavy penalties for violations. The PIPA's impact on South Korea's data protection landscape, including the creating of the Personal Information Protection Commission, will be examined.

Lastly, we dissect India's Information Technology Act. We examine its provisions related to data privacy and the rules for reasonable security practices. Additionally, we look into the Indian government's ongoing efforts to enact a comprehensive data protection law and the potential implications of this development.

By scrutinizing the various nuances of these international laws, we aim to help organizations better understand and navigate the intricate and often overlapping matrix of global cybersecurity compliance. Organizations must have a solid grasp of these laws to ensure smooth cross-border operations, maintain a positive brand reputation, and prevent potential legal repercussions. Furthermore, by adhering to these standards, organizations can reassure their stakeholders of their commitment to data protection and privacy, fostering trust and establishing themselves as leaders in the digital economy.

Recommendations:

- **Understand International Cybersecurity Laws:** Familiarize yourself with the significant cybersecurity laws of the countries in which your organization operates.
- **Implement a Global Compliance Program:** Develop a program considering different laws and regulations across jurisdictions.
- **Align Policies and Practices:** Ensure your cybersecurity policies and practices are aligned with international laws and standards.
- **Continual Monitoring:** Monitor changes in laws and regulations and adjust your compliance program accordingly.
- **Involve Legal Expertise:** Engage legal professionals to ensure comprehensive and accurate understanding and application of international laws.

COORDINATING GLOBAL CYBERSECURITY COMPLIANCE EFFORTS

As the world rapidly shifts toward a globally interconnected economy, businesses face the increasingly intricate challenge of complying with a vast array of cybersecurity laws and regulations spanning numerous jurisdictions worldwide. The need for compliance is not simply about avoiding penalties and reputational damage. It is also about building trust with customers, stakeholders, and partners who are increasingly aware and concerned about the importance of data protection. Thus, addressing this challenge strategically and proactively is crucial to establishing a unified compliance framework, managing international data transfers responsibly, and creating a continuous, organization-wide train-ing and education program. These steps can significantly streamline the efforts needed for global cybersecurity compliance, reducing the risk of breaches and ensuring the ongoing protection of sensitive data.

The following section delves deeper into the strategies to understand and prioritize applicable regulations in this complex global landscape. We explore how to create a unified compliance framework that simplifies the process of adherence to multiple sets of regulations and guidelines. We discuss the necessary measures to manage international data transfers and processing efficiently and securely while ensuring compliance with various national and international laws. Finally, we address the crucial role of continuous education and training for personnel at all organizational levels. These factors are not just about maintaining compliance; they are about instilling a culture of cybersecu-rity awareness that permeates every aspect of the organization.

The ultimate aim is to provide organizations with the knowledge and tools to effectively coordinate their global compliance efforts. In an era where data breaches and cyber threats have the potential to cause substantial damage, both financially and reputationally, a well-coordinated, robust global compli-ance strategy is no longer an option – it is a necessity. By addressing these critical areas, businesses can avoid the costly consequences of noncompliance and establish themselves as trustworthy guardians of their customers' sensi-tive information.

Understanding the regulatory landscape, implementing a compliance frame-work that transcends jurisdictional boundaries, effectively managing interna-tional data transfers, and training staff to maintain and uphold these standards are essential strategies for any organization in today's interconnected digital world. This guide will delve into these elements, providing practical insights and actionable steps to help organizations navigate the complex terrain of global cybersecurity compliance. By doing so, we hope to provide a road map for organizations striving to protect their data, reputation, and future in the face of an ever-evolving cyber threat landscape.

Recommendations:

- **Develop a Unified Compliance Framework:** Establish a framework that aligns with your operating jurisdictions' cybersecurity laws and regulations.
- **Prioritize Regulations:** Understand and prioritize the most impactful reg-ulations for your business.
- **Manage Data Transfers:** Develop a system for managing and monitoring international data transfers and processing.
- **Train Personnel:** Educate and train employees to understand and apply compliance requirements.
- **Stay Updated:** Continually monitor the changing landscape of cyberse-curity regulations and update your policies and practices as needed.

Chapter Conclusion

Different legislative measures have emerged globally, each bearing the unique imprint of their respective cultural, social, and economic backgrounds. Notable examples of these legislative frameworks include the European Union's innovative GDPR, China's comprehensive Cybersecurity Law, Canada's PIPEDA, and Singapore's PDPA. These regulations reflect various interpretations of data protection and cybersecurity in today's digital era, showcasing the diversity of approaches to address the shared challenge of securing information and promoting digital safety.

These distinct legal frameworks pose specific business requirements, covering various obligations. These obligations range from how data is handled to the security measures protecting networks, from the rights of individuals to mandatory reporting mechanisms. These requirements constitute an intricate network of rules that companies must navigate to operate securely and legally. The financial sector, with its heavy reliance on data, provides a clear example of the implications of these laws, demonstrating how critical it is to develop strategies for successful legal compliance.

However, understanding these various regulatory environments extends beyond simply fulfilling legal obligations. It is crucial to recognize the core principle that binds these laws together – protecting personal data. The essence of these laws urges businesses to perceive compliance not merely as a regulatory hurdle but rather as an opportunity.

This perspective allows companies to build trust with their customers, strengthen their brand reputation, and secure operations against a rapidly changing landscape of cybersecurity threats. A deep understanding of the principles of these laws empowers businesses to enhance their cybersecurity, protect their operations, and traverse the digital era with confidence and integrity.

Stay informed about these laws is emphasized as cybersecurity threats evolve, and personal data protection remains a high priority. Recognizing these laws' crucial role in modern business operations is vital for ongoing success. As the digital landscape becomes more complex, the knowledge of these laws will serve as a cornerstone for secure, successful operations in the future.

Case Study: CyberShield Corporation

CyberShield Corporation, a global financial technology company, has recently expanded its operations across the European Union, Canada, the United Kingdom, China, Singapore, and several other countries. With this expansion, they entered a labyrinth of international cybersecurity laws and regulations. They had to manage their data privacy policies effectively to ensure compliance with different jurisdictions. Judy, the newly appointed Chief Information

Security Officer (CISO), guided CyberShield through this complex compliance landscape.

Judy was known for her methodical approach and vast knowledge of cybersecurity and data privacy matters. She understood that noncompliance could result in hefty fines and potentially damage CyberShield's reputation. Judy started by reviewing the key laws applicable to the countries where CyberShield had operations – the GDPR in the EU, the Data Protection Act in the United Kingdom, PIPEDA in Canada, China's Cybersecurity Law, Singapore's PDPA, and various other international laws.

In collaboration with her team, Judy began creating a global cybersecurity compliance program that accounted for the diverse laws. She recognized the need to balance maintaining a uniform cybersecurity stance across the company while accommodating regional regulations. For instance, in handling EU citizens' data, Judy ensured that CyberShield's processes aligned with the GDPR's principle of "privacy by design." She ensured the company comprehended and abided by the robust Chinese Cybersecurity Law for operations in China.

One of Judy's primary goals was to build a culture of data privacy within the organization. She knew this was pivotal to ensuring sustained compliance and establishing a brand trusted by consumers. She confirmed that every level of the organization understood the importance of data protection, the potential threats to data security, and their role in maintaining it.

Judy developed detailed guidelines for each region outlining practical steps for ensuring compliance, including data handling practices, consent mechanisms, data subject rights, and breach reporting protocols. She used case studies to illustrate the practical implications of noncompliance and hosted regular training sessions to ensure that all staff knew their responsibilities in protecting data and maintaining cybersecurity.

Judy's efforts bore fruit when CyberShield faced a potential data breach. Thanks to the comprehensive training, an alert employee could promptly identify and report the issue. With the robust response plan in place, the incident was swiftly contained, and the necessary authorities were informed in line with the relevant jurisdictions' reporting requirements. This incident underscored the importance of Judy's meticulous approach to international cybersecurity compliance and her efforts to imbue a culture of data privacy within CyberShield.

CHAPTER 18

Privacy Laws and Their Intersection with Cybersecurity

"Regulations in cybersecurity are like guardrails on a highway. They're not here to obstruct but to guide us safely as we accelerate into the digital future."

Privacy and cybersecurity are closely entwined in the digital realm, influencing each other significantly. The legal aspects of privacy are a crucial part of this understanding. Privacy laws within the United States and internationally set data protection and personal privacy guidelines. Concepts like "privacy by design" and "privacy by default" also play a vital role. These proactive approaches protect user data from the initial design phase of systems and platforms. Maintaining privacy and ensuring security compliance are challenges faced by businesses and organizations. Applying practical tools and frameworks for privacy management is indispensable to overcoming these hurdles.

THE INTERSECTION OF PRIVACY AND CYBERSECURITY

The connection between privacy and cybersecurity is not merely a casual discussion topic but an issue of expanding interest and critical importance in today's digital world. At the heart of this connection are two elements that have become intertwined due to their shared goal and context. As a concept, privacy involves preserving and protecting personal data and information. This objective of privacy protection forms a core part of cybersecurity's mission, a field primarily focused on safeguarding data, networks, and systems from potential threats and breaches.

The necessity to comprehend the symbiotic relationship between privacy and cybersecurity cannot be overstated. Both domains, in essence, work toward the collective goal of shielding personal data from unauthorized access and breaches. This mutual objective has assumed more significance in an era where the proliferation of digital technology has made protecting personal data a paramount concern.

Organizations today are responsible for implementing cybersecurity measures to fortify personal data protection. This task is of utmost importance in our current environment, where data breaches and cyber threats have become regular occurrences. The urgency of the situation calls for deploying a range of robust measures. These might include implementing advanced encryption technologies, setting up secure access controls, conducting frequent vulnerability assessments, and maintaining constant vigilance through continuous network monitoring. These strategies are indispensable in reducing the potential risks linked with data breaches and cyberattacks.

One must also underline the significance of Privacy Impact Assessments (PIAs). PIAs are proactive measures that organizations can employ to identify potential privacy risks lurking in new projects or upcoming initiatives. This evaluation process enables organizations to spot and tackle these privacy risks before they escalate into detrimental breaches that compromise privacy. Therefore, a PIA's role is cardinal to the intersection of privacy and cybersecurity, forming an essential instrument in the toolkit of organizations committed to safeguarding privacy.

Data breach notification laws represent another significant dimension of the intersection between privacy and cybersecurity. These legal regulations mandate organizations to notify individuals and relevant authorities when a data breach occurs, fostering a culture of transparency and accountability. The stipulations of such laws are ingrained in the broader cybersecurity framework, emphasizing the interdependence between privacy and cybersecurity. Essentially, these laws form a vital bridge linking privacy and cybersecurity, reiterating their commitment to protecting personal data.

Recommendations:

- **Explore the Connection:** Immerse yourself in the intricate network between privacy and cybersecurity. The aim is to comprehend how these two fields intersect, working hand-in-hand to safeguard data and information and how one failure can negatively impact the other.

- **Implement Security Measures:** Executing comprehensive cybersecurity strategies that defend individual data is crucial. These measures should include state-of-the-art encryption techniques to scramble sensitive data, strict access controls to limit who can access the data, and regular network surveillance to ensure that threats are identified and neutralized promptly.

- **Conduct PIAs:** Incorporating PIAs into your organization's everyday operations is a powerful method to discern and alleviate possible privacy risks. PIAs help identify vulnerabilities and devise appropriate mitigation strategies, ensuring that personal data handling meets the highest privacy standards.

- **Understand the Law:** Becoming well-versed with data breach notification laws and their organizational responsibilities is essential. In the event of a breach, organizations must notify affected parties, and understanding these laws helps ensure compliance, protect reputation, and prevent legal ramifications.
- **Ensure Transparency:** An organization should maintain transparency and accountability, which are foundational to strong privacy and cybersecurity protocols. Being transparent about data handling practices and holding oneself accountable for privacy and security mishaps go a long way in building trust and a strong reputation. Explore the Connection: Delve into the interconnected world of privacy and cybersecurity to understand the relationship between these two crucial areas.

PRIVACY AND DATA PROTECTION

A vital initial step in comprehending the broad landscape of cybersecurity involves defining the core concepts of privacy and data protection. The term "privacy" typically denotes an individual's inherent right to exert control over their personal information. This control applies across various dimensions of data handling, encompassing aspects such as the methods employed for data collection, how the data is utilized, and the conditions under which it is shared with third parties. Conversely, data protection represents a proactive practice that guards personal data against potential threats that could lead to its compromise, loss, or misuse.

While privacy and data protection appear as two concepts when initially defined, their spheres of influence overlap significantly in practice. This convergence becomes particularly prominent in the context of digital data. In this digital era, the information individuals generate and exchange often falls under personal data. Due to its nature, such data must be governed by privacy and security principles, underscoring the inseparable connection between these concepts.

The significance of privacy becomes even more pronounced within specific sectors, with the financial industry serving as a prominent example. Given the highly sensitive nature of financial data, measures to protect such data from unauthorized access, misuse, or unwarranted disclosure are critical. The digitization wave that has swept across the financial industry, manifesting in digital banking and financial technologies, has made privacy concerns a paramount issue. As a result, ensuring the confidentiality and security of such data has evolved into a pressing challenge for financial institutions.

The progression of privacy laws and regulations mirrors the dynamic and evolving nature of the digital landscape. As societies have increasingly embraced digital technologies, the demand for robust protections for personal information has grown correspondingly. This transition toward a digital society has generated new challenges, necessitating the development and implementation of more stringent measures to preserve personal data's integrity.

In response to these emerging threats and the associated risks that come with digital data handling, there has been a significant expansion in privacy laws at both national and international levels. These legislative developments seek to combat the security threats due to technological advancements and mitigate the risks associated with personal data management. This continual evolution of privacy laws highlights the importance of keeping abreast of changes and underscores the intricate and evolving relationship between privacy, data protection, and cybersecurity.

Recommendations:

- **Understand the Concepts:** It is crucial to devote time to fully comprehend the principles and subtleties of privacy and data protection. Recognizing how these concepts intertwine within cybersecurity will equip you to build stronger and more comprehensive security strategies.
- **Prioritize Privacy:** Particularly within the finance sector, which deals extensively with sensitive data, prioritizing privacy should be a key aspect of your organization's data handling protocols. Establishing robust privacy controls can help ensure the confidentiality and integrity of your customer's sensitive financial information.
- **Stay Updated:** Regularly monitor the development of privacy laws and regulations. This constant vigilance enables you to stay current with your duties and changes in the legal environment and ensures that your organization can react quickly and appropriately to new regulatory demands.
- **Embrace Compliance:** Compliance with all relevant laws and regulations is nonnegotiable for any organization. This secures your customers' data and helps maintain their trust, fostering long-term relationships and protecting your organization's reputation.
- **Adopt a Forward-thinking Approach:** Adopt a proactive and forward-looking stance toward privacy and data protection challenges. By continually evaluating your existing practices and refining your strategies, you can stay ahead of emerging threats, reduce risk, and ensure your customers' data's ongoing privacy and security.

KEY PRIVACY PRINCIPLES

Consent and data subject rights form the foundational pillars of privacy principles. These principles mandate that individuals maintain autonomous control over their data, encompassing rights such as the right to be duly informed, unrestricted access, and the right to request erasure. These rights lie at the core of privacy laws and regulations, fostering an environment of fairness and transparency in all data processing activities.

Data subject rights are a significant aspect of these principles, highlighting the importance of individual agencies in data management. Individuals should be adequately empowered to control how their data is used, ensuring that personal data handling aligns with their explicit consent, not the whims of the organization holding it. In essence, these rights safeguard against the misuse of personal data, thereby promoting accountability and adherence to ethical standards among data-collecting entities.

Two other cornerstones of privacy principles are data minimization and purpose limitation. Data minimization pertains to collecting only personal data necessary for a specified purpose. This means organizations should restrict themselves to gathering information directly relevant to their operations, avoiding unnecessary or excessive data collection. On the other hand, purpose limitation imposes constraints on how the collected data is utilized, stipulating that the data should be strictly confined to the original purpose for which consent was obtained.

Ensuring the accuracy and integrity of data is another critical aspect of privacy principles that are indispensable for any data processing activity. Organizations are expected to put in place reasonable measures to validate that the personal data they store is accurate, current, and reliable. They are also responsible for safeguarding the data's integrity against unauthorized or unlawful processing. Ensuring accuracy and integrity enhances the data quality and reinforces the trust between the data subjects and the organizations.

Storage limitation and data retention principles come into force to mitigate the risks associated with the indefinite storage of personal data. These principles dictate that personal data should be retained only for the duration necessary for its processing and securely disposed of once it is no longer required. These guidelines are essential to preventing the misuse of outdated or unnecessary data and maintaining the privacy of the data subjects.

Lastly, the principles of confidentiality and security are inherent and indispensable aspects of privacy. They necessitate the protection of personal data from unauthorized access or disclosure, ensuring that sensitive information is kept secure. By employing robust and resilient security measures, organizations can successfully guarantee the confidentiality and security of their data. This safeguards personal data and enhances the organization's reputation as a trusted custodian of sensitive information.

Recommendations:

- **Respect Consent:** Upholding the rights of data subjects begins with respecting their consent. Always obtain clear and explicit consent before gathering and processing their information, ensuring that data subjects are fully aware of how and why their data is being used.

- **Minimize and Limit:** In line with privacy principles, collect only the necessary data required for a given purpose and limit its usage strictly to that purpose. This reduces the amount of data at risk and respects the data subject's privacy by not collecting extraneous information.

- **Maintain Accuracy:** Regular checks and updates of your data are vital to ensure its accuracy and reliability. Accurate data underpins effective decision-making, improves service delivery, and complies with the data quality principles in privacy laws.

- **Define Retention Periods:** Instituting distinct data retention periods in line with legal requirements is an important aspect of data management. Beyond the defined retention period, data should be securely disposed of, preventing unnecessary data buildup and minimizing the risk of breaches.
- **Prioritize Confidentiality:** The confidentiality and security of personal data should be a top priority. Implementing robust security measures such as encryption, access controls, and regular system audits can prevent unauthorized access and maintain the trust of data subjects.

PRIVACY LAWS IN THE UNITED STATES

The terrain of US privacy legislation is broad and multifaceted, making it appear somewhat complex due to its various federal and state laws. When one takes a holistic view of US privacy legislation, a patchwork quilt of sector-specific and overarching privacy laws emerges. Each of these laws has been carefully designed to protect personal data and amplify the rights of individuals, albeit in differing contexts.

The US legislative landscape regarding privacy has seen the creation of several vital laws over the years, addressing the nuanced needs of different industries and sectors. For example, the financial industry is regulated by critical legislation called the Gramm–Leach–Bliley Act (*GLBA*). The GLBA demands that financial institutions provide their customers with clear explanations of their information-sharing practices. Furthermore, this Act mandates these institutions to implement robust safeguards to protect sensitive data.

The healthcare sector, too, has its specific privacy legislation in the form of the Health Insurance Portability and Accountability Act (*HIPAA*). HIPAA is pivotal to protecting personal health information, setting stringent standards for protecting sensitive patient data. It applies to a broad spectrum of entities, including healthcare providers, health insurance companies, and other organizations that deal with patient information. This Act has been instrumental in shaping privacy practices in the healthcare sector, providing a blueprint for maintaining patient data confidentiality and security.

State-level privacy laws complement these federal laws, further fortifying the legal framework protecting personal data. A noteworthy example is the California Consumer Privacy Act (CCPA), which has greatly enhanced California residents' control over their personal information. The CCPA sets a noteworthy precedent, demonstrating how states can strengthen privacy rights, supplementing the protections offered at the federal level.

Different industries often face unique privacy-related challenges due to the specific nature of the data they handle. Therefore, sector-specific privacy regulations have been enacted to address these needs and challenges. These regulations mandate privacy practices tailored to the needs of each industry, ensuring comprehensive data protection across all sectors. Such laws prove that the US privacy legislation landscape is not a monolith but a dynamic and adaptable system that evolves to meet the unique demands of different industries.

In summary, the US privacy legislative landscape is a complex weave of federal and state laws, along with sector-specific regulations, designed to meet the unique needs of different sectors while protecting the privacy of individuals. Although intricate, this web of laws is crucial in today's digital age, offering layered protection to personal data while balancing the operational needs of various sectors. The diversity within the legislative landscape reflects the complexity of modern data privacy challenges, demonstrating the commitment of US lawmakers to ensure comprehensive privacy protection for all.

Recommendations:

- **Navigate Legislation:** It is crucial to comprehensively understand US privacy legislation at both federal and state levels. This knowledge will enable your organization to remain in full compliance, minimizing the risk of penalties and safeguarding your organization's reputation.
- **Familiarize with GLBA:** A thorough understanding of the GLBA and its privacy requirements is essential for organizations operating in the financial sector. The GLBA mandates institutions to protect the confidentiality and integrity of consumer financial information, so a firm grasp of this law will ensure you are adequately safeguarding customer data.
- **Comply with HIPAA:** If your organization deals with health information, it is paramount to fully comprehend the mandates set forth by the HIPAA. HIPAA provides guidelines for protecting and confidential handling of protected health information, and strict compliance is needed to avoid substantial fines and potential legal action.
- **Be Aware of State Laws:** State-level privacy laws such as the CCPA may also apply to your organization. Awareness of these state-specific regulations and ensuring your practices align with them is an important step toward maintaining an overarching compliance strategy.
- **Understand Sector-Specific Regulations:** Sector-specific privacy regulations may apply to your organization depending on your industry. Staying informed about these regulations and strictly adhering to them will help ensure that your data-handling practices remain compliant and that you continue to respect the privacy rights of your clients or customers.

INTERNATIONAL PRIVACY LAWS AND REGULATIONS

While privacy legislation in the United States is decidedly extensive and meticulous, several international privacy laws and regulations also command attention due to their significant impact on the global privacy landscape. Among these, the General Data Protection Regulation (GDPR), implemented by the European Union, holds a prominent position. The GDPR offers an all-encompassing data protection and privacy structure, granting individuals exceptional control over their data. Its far-reaching impact extends to any organization dealing with EU residents' data, whether or not the organization itself is based in the EU.

The GDPR embodies the European viewpoint on privacy rights, considering them fundamental human rights. It encompasses numerous stipulations, including consent requirements, data subject rights, and strict rules for data breach notifications. Additionally, it mandates a "privacy by design and default approach," requiring organizations to incorporate privacy considerations into their products and processes from the onset.

Canada's Personal Information Protection and Electronic Documents Act (*PIPEDA*) is another prominent piece of international privacy legislation. It sets the tone for how organizations should handle personal information, advocating a balance between the right to privacy for individuals and the need for organizations to collect, use, or disclose personal information for legitimate and reasonable purposes. PIPEDA outlines a set of fair information principles that organizations must follow when collecting, using, or disclosing personal information, making it a crucial tool for fostering trust and privacy assurance.

In the United Kingdom, the Data Protection Act (*DPA*) governs the processing of personal data. The DPA is an essential law that offers individuals robust legal rights regarding their personal information. It mandates that organizations process personal data lawfully and transparently, reinforcing the importance of individual autonomy in data processing. Furthermore, it sets specific rules for processing sensitive categories of personal data, including genetic and biometric data, further strengthening individual rights.

In addition, several other key international privacy laws are in various countries and regions. These laws provide different levels of protection and rights concerning personal data and are vital components of the global privacy ecosystem. They range from broad, overarching regulations like GDPR and PIPEDA to more specific laws targeting particular industries or data types.

Awareness and compliance with these international laws are essential for any globally operational organization. These laws protect individual privacy rights and create a level playing field for businesses, providing clear data handling and processing guidelines. The interplay of these international laws and regulations forms a complex yet critical part of the global privacy landscape, shaping organizations' privacy practices and helping to foster trust in an increasingly digital world.

Recommendations:

- **Learn About GDPR:** If your organization has operations within the EU or handles data about EU citizens, it is imperative to understand the GDPR requirements. The GDPR sets stringent data protection and privacy rules, and noncompliance can result in hefty fines and potential reputational damage.
- **Understand PIPEDA:** If your business activities involve handling Canadian personal data, it is crucial to familiarize yourself with the PIPEDA.

This Canadian law governs how private sector organizations collect, use, and disclose personal information during commercial activities.

- **Comply with the DPA:** For organizations operating in the United Kingdom or dealing with UK citizens' data, understanding and complying with the DPA is a must. The DPA provides a framework for the lawful processing of personal data and safeguards individuals' rights concerning their data.
- **Stay Abreast of International Laws:** International privacy laws and regulations continually evolve. Keeping yourself informed about these changes is vital to ensure your organization complies with privacy norms globally and protects your business from penalties and legal repercussions.
- **Cultivate a Culture of Compliance:** Promote a culture of compliance within your organization, underlining the significance of understanding and following privacy laws and regulations worldwide. This culture mitigates legal risks and builds customer trust and confidence in your organization's commitment to privacy.

PRIVACY BY DESIGN AND BY DEFAULT

Privacy by design and default are not merely buzzwords in data privacy and protection; they are crucial principles underpinning robust privacy practices. At its core, privacy by design is a philosophy and approach that insists on embedding privacy considerations into the design and architecture of IT systems, networks, and operational practices right from the beginning. It is a proactive measure, a foresight that anticipates and prevents invasive events before they happen. This fundamental principle of privacy by design encourages the view of privacy as a core functionality rather than a discretionary add-on or an afterthought.

The principle of privacy by design carries even more weight in today's digital age, where technology is deeply woven into everyday life. It suggests that privacy measures should be tacked on to existing systems and integrated into the fabric of technologies and processes. This requires a fundamental shift in the development paradigm – seeing privacy not as a constraint but as a value-adding feature that enhances user trust and business reputation.

Implementing privacy by design in financial institutions, which handle particularly sensitive data, can be pursued through several measures. These include embedding privacy settings into new technologies, ensuring strict access controls, and conducting regular PIAs. Additionally, staff training on data protection practices is crucial to ensure that everyone within the organization understands the importance of privacy and how to protect it. This multifaceted approach is key to building a robust culture of privacy within the institution, fostering trust among customers and compliance with regulatory standards.

On the other hand, privacy by default is the complementary principle to privacy by design. It refers to setting the default settings of products and services to the most privacy-friendly settings. This approach puts the user in control, ensuring that personal data is automatically protected without requiring the user to take additional action.

Beyond theories and principles, real-world examples provide valuable lessons in successfully implementing privacy by design and by default. Best practices and case studies from organizations that have effectively integrated these principles into their operations can guide other businesses looking to bolster their privacy practices.

These tangible examples, drawn from various industries and contexts, illuminate how privacy by design and default can be adapted and applied to different business models and technologies. They demonstrate the feasibility of these principles and highlight the benefits they can bring in terms of enhanced customer trust, reduced risk of data breaches, and improved compliance with privacy laws and regulations. Furthermore, they offer insights into overcoming common challenges and potential pitfalls in implementing these principles, providing a roadmap toward more privacy-centric business practices.

Recommendations:

- **Integrate Privacy by Design:** By incorporating privacy considerations from the onset when designing IT systems, networks, and business practices, you can proactively address potential privacy issues. This approach ensures that privacy is not just an afterthought but an integral part of your system and process design.

- **Apply to Financial Institutions:** Particularly for organizations in the financial sector, it is crucial to weave privacy settings into the fabric of new technologies, conduct regular PIAs, and consistently train staff on data protection. This will help to ensure that privacy protection measures are robust and proactive, safeguarding sensitive financial data.

- **Learn from Others:** Studying best practices and case studies can provide valuable insights into how other organizations have successfully implemented privacy by design and default principles. This knowledge can be a blueprint for shaping your strategies and practices and promoting better privacy outcomes.

- **Train Your Staff:** Regular staff training on the principles of privacy by design helps to cultivate a privacy-conscious culture within your organization. When your team understands and values privacy, they are more likely to apply these principles in their work, further enhancing the effectiveness of your privacy efforts.

- **Continually Evaluate:** Regular reviews and improvements of your privacy practices are key to staying aligned with privacy principles by design and by default. By constantly evaluating and refining your practices, you can ensure that your organization remains up-to-date and responsive to evolving privacy requirements and threats.

CHALLENGES IN MAINTAINING PRIVACY AND SECURITY COMPLIANCE

Keeping up with the rapidly evolving regulatory landscape is undoubtedly one of the most significant challenges in maintaining privacy and security compliance. Laws and regulations governing data privacy and security are not static; they continue to evolve in response to emerging technologies, novel threats, and changing societal expectations. Organizations must be constantly vigilant in this dynamic environment, proactively keeping abreast of the latest changes and updating their compliance programs accordingly. This task is far from easy and requires a dedicated effort, continuous learning, and often the involvement of experts specializing in privacy and security law.

Cross-border data management adds another layer of complexity to privacy and security compliance. With globalization and the proliferation of cloud services, data often flows across national boundaries. Each country has its unique set of privacy laws and regulations, creating a complex web of obligations that organizations must navigate. Understanding these disparate legal landscapes, reconciling their differences, and ensuring compliance in each jurisdiction is a massive challenge that necessitates deep legal expertise and thorough planning.

Organizations face another delicate task to strike the right balance between security and data subject rights. While it is paramount to protect data from security threats, organizations must also respect and uphold the rights of data subjects, such as the right to access, rectify, or delete their data. Striking this balance is not always straightforward and often requires a nuanced understanding of privacy laws and security protocols. Ensuring that stringent security measures do not infringe upon data subject rights requires careful consideration and frequent recalibration.

Responding effectively to data breaches and security incidents is a formidable challenge. When such incidents occur, the response must be swift, comprehensive, and compliant with various legal obligations. These obligations might include notifying affected individuals, reporting the incident to regulatory authorities, and mitigating harm. Furthermore, the response should also include learning from the incident to prevent its recurrence, often necessitating organizational practices or systems changes. This multipronged response requires a robust incident response plan, a well-trained team, and, often, the guidance of legal and technical experts. Preparing for and managing data breaches and security incidents is central to privacy and security compliance and presents unique challenges.

Recommendations:

- **Keep Updated:** It is imperative to stay informed about the latest privacy and security regulations changes to maintain compliance. By keeping abreast of these developments, you can promptly update your organization's policies and procedures, minimizing the risk of noncompliance and associated penalties.

- **Manage International Data:** If your organization operates globally, it is crucial to understand and adhere to the privacy laws in all jurisdictions where you process data. The data privacy landscape varies widely from country to country, and a comprehensive understanding of these diverse regulations will help ensure global compliance.
- **Balance Rights and Security:** It is essential to develop strategies that balance the rights of data subjects with security measures to prevent potential conflicts. Respecting individuals' privacy rights while maintaining strong security protocols is a delicate balancing act but critical to ensure trust and legal compliance.
- **Prepare for Incidents:** Establishing a robust incident response plan is key in dealing effectively and compliantly with data breaches and security incidents. Such a plan should outline roles, responsibilities, and procedures to minimize the impact of a breach and protect your organization's reputation.
- **Foster Compliance Culture:** Cultivating a culture of compliance within your organization can help overcome challenges and ensure strict adherence to privacy and security regulations. This involves continuous training, clear communication, and leadership support to drive home the importance of privacy and security in your organization's operations.

TOOLS AND FRAMEWORKS FOR PRIVACY MANAGEMENT

Managing privacy within an organization is a complex task that demands understanding numerous elements, such as laws, regulations, standards, and best practices. Various tools and frameworks have been developed to aid organizations in meeting their privacy obligations and managing privacy risks. Among these are the National Institute of Standards and Technology (NIST) Privacy Framework and the AICPA Privacy Management Framework, which offer comprehensive and practical guidance.

The NIST Privacy Framework is a voluntary tool aimed at helping organizations identify and manage privacy risks to build innovative products and services while protecting individuals' privacy. This framework offers a flexible, risk-based approach, accommodating different organizational roles, sizes, and sectors.

The NIST Privacy Framework is structured around Core, Profiles, and Implementation Tiers. The Core presents a set of common privacy outcomes and activities across sectors and jurisdictions, helping organizations identify and communicate privacy risks and mitigation strategies. The Profiles help organizations prioritize the outcomes and activities that best meet their privacy values, mission, and risk tolerance. Finally, the Implementation Tiers assist organizations in optimizing resources to manage privacy risks, allowing them to understand and communicate about their current privacy risk management practices.

The ISO/IEC 27701 standard complements the NIST Privacy Framework by providing specific guidance for establishing, implementing, maintaining, and improving a Privacy Information Management System. This international standard is an extension of ISO/IEC 27001 and ISO/IEC 27002 for privacy management within the organization's context. It details a comprehensive set of operational controls that can be mapped against various privacy principles and legal requirements, making it a valuable tool for demonstrating compliance with a wide range of privacy regulations globally.

On the other hand, the American Institute of Certified Public Accountants (*AICPA*) Privacy Management Framework is a helpful tool providing privacy criteria for developing privacy programs. The framework is constructed around nine privacy principles: management, notice, choice and consent, collection, use and retention, access, disclosure to third parties, security for privacy, and quality. Each of these principles encapsulates a different aspect of privacy management, and the framework provides a comprehensive model for managing privacy in an organization.

For instance, the "management" principle deals with the governance of the organization's privacy policies and procedures, requiring that these be defined, documented, communicated, and implemented. "Notice" and "choice and consent" principles deal with informing individuals about the organization's privacy practices and obtaining their consent where necessary. The "security for privacy" principle relates to protecting personal information against unauthorized access, use, or disclosure, requiring the implementation of appropriate technical and organizational measures.

In summary, these tools and frameworks offer a valuable guide to privacy management, and organizations can benefit significantly from their implementation. However, they should not be viewed in isolation but as integral parts of an organization's overall approach to privacy and compliance. Understanding the interconnectedness and complementarity of these frameworks can enable organizations to leverage them effectively in managing privacy risks and meeting compliance obligations. In other words, a comprehensive, integrated approach to privacy management that strategically combines these tools and frameworks is often the most effective strategy for protecting privacy and achieving compliance.

Recommendations:

- **Use the NIST Privacy Framework:** Consider leveraging the NIST Privacy Framework as a strategic tool to manage privacy risks effectively. This framework provides a comprehensive structure for understanding and addressing privacy risks and can assist in aligning your privacy program with your organization's mission and values.

- **Implement ISO/IEC 27701:** To bolster your organization's privacy information management, contemplate implementing the guidelines of ISO/IEC 27701. This international standard provides a framework for establishing,

implementing, maintaining, and continually improving a privacy information management system.

- **Consider the AICPA Framework:** The American Institute of CPAs (AICPA)
Privacy Management Framework can be a valuable resource in constructing a robust privacy program. It provides a comprehensive methodology
that covers privacy governance, risk management, and compliance.

- **Combine Tools:** These tools and frameworks can be used in conjunction for a holistic approach to privacy management. By leveraging the
strengths of each, you can create a robust and comprehensive privacy
management strategy that addresses all aspects of privacy risk.

- **Adapt to Your Needs:** Remember that these tools and frameworks should
be adapted based on your organization's unique needs and risks. Customizing these resources to fit your situation allows for the most effective
and relevant application, ultimately leading to stronger privacy management practices.

Chapter Conclusion

As the digitization of information continues to escalate, so does the focus
on privacy and cybersecurity. They are twin pillars at the intersection of
information technology and personal data protection. At the heart of this
discourse is integrating privacy principles into cybersecurity policies. Given
the rapid evolution of cyber threats and vulnerabilities, organizations need
a well-thought-out strategy that seamlessly fuses cybersecurity measures
with privacy laws. The value of this integrated approach cannot be over-
emphasized. It ensures that organizations not only protect their information
systems and networks from cyber threats but also uphold the rights of individuals to control their personal information.

An essential aspect of implementing this integrated approach involves
continual monitoring and adaptation. The regulatory landscapes that govern
privacy and cybersecurity are far from static, changing in response to technological advancements and evolving societal values. Thus, organizations
must be agile and responsive, always abreast of new laws, standards, and
best practices. Regular audits, risk assessments, and revisions of policies are
instrumental in this regard.

Furthermore, the significance of key privacy principles like data minimization and privacy by design continues to grow. Data minimization, which
involves collecting only the necessary data for specific purposes, reduces the
volume of data that needs to be protected, hence the potential impact of data
breaches. On the other hand, privacy by design ensures that privacy considerations are embedded into the design and operation of IT systems and business practices. These principles are becoming fundamental to privacy and
cybersecurity strategies, underpinning successful data protection initiatives.

Looking to the future, trends in privacy and cybersecurity indicate a growing focus on advanced technologies like Artificial Intelligence (AI) and machine learning. These technologies hold immense potential for enhancing data protection measures. AI can detect unusual activity or anomalies in data patterns that may signify a cyber threat, enabling prompt response. Machine learning can help automate and enhance data privacy controls and processes, improving efficiency and effectiveness.

However, the application of AI and machine learning has challenges. Concerns about data privacy, algorithmic bias, and lack of transparency must be addressed. Therefore, these technologies should be accompanied by robust governance frameworks that align with privacy laws and ethical guidelines.

In conclusion, as organizations continue to navigate the complexities and challenges of digital transformation, the importance of a comprehensive, forward-looking approach to privacy and cybersecurity cannot be overstated. This approach should blend the application of robust cybersecurity measures, adherence to privacy laws and principles, the use of state-of-the-art privacy management tools and frameworks, and the deployment of advanced technologies like AI and machine learning. The goal is to foster a culture of privacy and security that supports the dual objectives of facilitating digital innovation and safeguarding personal data.

Case Study: Privacy and Cybersecurity at DataSage Inc.

DataSage Inc., a rapidly growing technology firm in Silicon Valley's heart, faced a critical challenge. The firm was renowned for its sophisticated data analytics solutions, leveraging machine learning and AI to drive insights for businesses across the globe. However, with the increasing success and scale, a pressing issue surfaced. The company grappled with the complex and vital task of implementing robust privacy and cybersecurity measures. Thus far, DataSage has been fortunate, avoiding any significant data breaches that could have been detrimental. However, the management, headed by Jazlyn, the insightful and proactive Chief Information Officer, realized the significant risks and understood that luck was not a reliable security strategy.

Taking charge of this concern, Jazlyn initiated the process of embedding privacy principles into DataSage's cybersecurity policies as the first order of business. She spearheaded a broad initiative to incorporate foundational privacy principles like data minimization and purpose limitation into all company data-handling procedures and practices. The process was extensive, encompassing every department handling data, from customer relations to the heart of data analytics. To ensure this was not just a temporary focus,

Jazlyn also emphasized adopting a privacy-by-design approach. The goal was to move the organization from treating privacy as an afterthought or add-on to considering it an integral component of any new IT systems development and business practices.

With the changing regulatory landscape posing a significant challenge, Jazlyn adopted a proactive approach to ensure continuous monitoring and adaptation. She meticulously assembled a dedicated team of legal and technical experts to stay abreast of the most recent developments in privacy laws and regulations nationally and internationally. The team's responsibilities went beyond just staying updated. They were tasked with conducting regular audits, vulnerability assessments, and risk assessments to ensure DataSage's practices remained compliant and adapted to these evolving laws and regulatory requirements.

Recognizing the potential of AI and machine learning in data protection, Jazlyn incorporated these technologies into its cybersecurity practices. She championed implementing an AI-driven system to proactively detect anomalous activity and potential cyber threats. Further, machine learning algorithms were employed to automate various data privacy controls. This novel approach significantly improved efficiency, drastically reducing the risk of human error and improving the detection of potential breaches.

Despite the advantages, Jazlyn knew the challenges of implementing these advanced technologies. She developed a comprehensive governance framework to mitigate potential issues concerning data privacy and algorithmic bias. This robust framework provided strict guidelines on ethical AI usage, setting high standards for transparency in machine learning processes and fostering accountability across the board.

EXAMPLE PRIVACY IMPACT ASSESSMENT

This is a simplified example of a Privacy Impact Assessment. An actual PIA may require more detailed and extensive analysis, depending on the nature of the project, the types of data involved, and the applicable legal and regulatory requirements.

Privacy Impact Assessment (PIA) for DataSage Inc.

1. **Overview of the Project:**
   Project Name: Automated Data Analytics System (ADAS)
   Project Description: The project aims to develop an automated data analytics system leveraging artificial intelligence (AI) and machine learning (ML) to provide personalized services to DataSage's clients.
2. **Data Collection:**
   Types of Data Collected: Personal data such as names, addresses, contact details, financial information, as well as sensitive personal data that pertains to the client's business operations.

3. **Data Use and Purpose:**

The collected data will be processed to provide a personalized experience for the clients, deliver more relevant insights, and improve client interaction with DataSage's services.

4. **Data Flow:**

The data will be collected from the clients via a secure web portal and stored in encrypted databases in DataSage's secure cloud environment. The ADAS system will then process the data to generate analytics and insights.

5. **Privacy Risks and Mitigation Measures:**

Risk 1: Unauthorized Access to Personal Data Mitigation: Strict access controls will be implemented, and multifactor authentication will be enforced. Regular security audits will be carried out to ensure the measures remain effective.

Risk 2: Data Breaches Mitigation: Data encryption at rest and in transit, regular vulnerability assessments, and continuous network monitoring will be employed. A response plan for data breaches will be developed and maintained.

Risk 3: Noncompliance with Data Minimization and Purpose Limitation Mitigation: The system will be designed only to collect data necessary for its functioning and strictly for the purpose mentioned. Regular reviews will ensure that these principles are adhered to.

Risk 4: Inaccuracy of Personal Data Mitigation: There will be a system for data subjects to review and correct their data. The data accuracy will be checked regularly using machine learning algorithms.

6. **Legal Compliance:**

The project complies with applicable privacy legislation, including the GDPR, CCPA, HIPAA, and sector-specific regulations.

7. **Engagement with Stakeholders:**

Stakeholder consultation has been conducted with internal and external parties, including the technical team, legal department, clients, and third-party auditors.

8. **Privacy Impact Level:**

The privacy impact level is deemed low after assessing the potential risks and planned mitigation measures.

9. **Sign-off and Approval:**

This Privacy Impact Assessment was conducted by Jazlyn, Chief Information Officer of DataSage Inc., and has been reviewed and approved by DataSage's legal department and the executive board.

Date: July 13, 2023

CHAPTER 19

Auditing Cybersecurity: Guides for Auditors and the Audited

"Auditing is the vigilant sentinel that safeguards the fortress of cyber-security, revealing vulnerabilities, fortifying defenses, and preserving the integrity of digital realms."

Cybersecurity auditing is pivotal for establishing secure information technology practices in the digital age. It encompasses a range of important topics that are critical for both auditors and those being audited. This includes understanding the shifting role of auditors in the contemporary digital environment, grasping essential cybersecurity concepts, and delving into the specifics of audit charters and engagements. In addition, risk-based auditing represents a significant aspect of this landscape, highlighting the need to focus on areas with the highest potential risk in cybersecurity.

THE EVOLVING ROLE OF AUDITORS IN CYBERSECURITY

The modern digital age has brought many changes in how businesses operate. With a vast digital landscape to oversee, the importance of cybersecurity audits and the role of auditors in ensuring cyber resilience have dramatically evolved. The key to understanding the direction of this evolution and how organizations can utilize it for their betterment lies in grasping the scope and objectives of cybersecurity audits in the current era.

Digital transformation has become the norm, with businesses depending heavily on digital infrastructures, regardless of size or sector. As these systems grow in complexity, so does the landscape of cyber threats. Cybersecurity audits have transitioned from a mere regulatory requirement or a reactive measure post-incident to a proactive approach integral to business operations. It is essential for securing digital assets, enhancing stakeholder confidence,

333

upholding brand reputation, and ensuring legal and regulatory compliance. Furthermore, in light of high-profile cyberattacks causing severe financial and reputational damages, the necessity for robust cybersecurity audits has never been more critical.

Auditors now play a pivotal role in the overarching strategy of cyber resilience. They are no longer limited to identifying financial irregularities or compliance with fiscal laws. Today's auditors are expected to traverse the labyrinth of cyber threats, assess the robustness of the controls in place, evaluate the risk management approach, and provide actionable insights for strengthening cybersecurity. They act as frontline warriors in the battle against cyber threats, determining vulnerabilities, identifying loopholes, and suggesting necessary improvements to the existing security protocols.

Understanding the scope and objectives of cybersecurity audits is fundamental for any organization aiming to strengthen its cybersecurity posture. It is not merely about knowing what areas will be under scrutiny but also comprehending what the audit intends to achieve. A clearly defined scope ensures the audit covers all relevant areas of an organization's cybersecurity framework without overlooking potential threat avenues. Articulating the objectives aligns the audit with the organization's strategic goals, ensuring it serves a meaningful purpose beyond compliance. It allows organizations to leverage audits for continual improvement, giving them a roadmap for enhancing their cyber defenses.

Recommendations:

- **Recognize the Importance of Cybersecurity Audits:** Understand the shift in the role of cybersecurity audits, transitioning from a mere regulatory requirement to an integral part of business operations. Acknowledge its significance in securing digital assets, enhancing stakeholder confidence, maintaining brand reputation, and ensuring regulatory compliance.

- **Expand the Role of Auditors:** Recognize the evolving role of auditors, which now goes beyond identifying financial irregularities or fiscal compliance. Expect them to understand the landscape of cyber threats, assess the effectiveness of security controls, evaluate risk management approaches, and provide actionable insights to strengthen cybersecurity measures.

- **Establish the Scope of Cybersecurity Audits:** Define the scope of cybersecurity audits within your organization. Ensure the audit covers all aspects of your cybersecurity framework, considering various elements such as digital infrastructure, data privacy, network security, and cloud security, without overlooking any potential threat avenues.

- **Define the Objectives of Cybersecurity Audits:** Clearly articulate the objectives of cybersecurity audits, aligning them with the organization's strategic goals. The purpose of these audits should go beyond mere compliance; they should also aim at continual improvement, providing a roadmap for enhancing the organization's cyber defenses.

- **Leverage Audits for Cyber Resilience:** Utilize the insights derived from cybersecurity audits to enhance the organization's cyber resilience. Act on the auditor's recommendations for improvements in security protocols and their identification of vulnerabilities and loopholes. This will help the organization mitigate cyber threats and proactively strengthen its cybersecurity posture.

UNDERSTANDING CYBERSECURITY: ESSENTIAL CONCEPTS FOR AUDITORS

The cornerstone for executing an effective cybersecurity audit lies in the auditors' understanding of essential cybersecurity concepts. This understanding is not just a superficial acquaintance with terms but requires a deep and immersive dive into cybersecurity. This expansive journey includes acquiring key terminology, understanding the intricate nuances of cyber threats, vulnerabilities, and risks, and gaining a comprehensive and panoramic view of the cybersecurity control environment. Such comprehensive knowledge empowers auditors with the ability to dissect the organization's cybersecurity fabric and the potential weaknesses therein.

Initiating this journey requires a deep understanding of key cybersecurity terminologies and concepts. These terms and concepts form the backbone and the lexicon of cybersecurity audits. It includes terminologies like threats, vulnerabilities, risks, controls, and many more, which are used extensively and pervasively throughout an audit. However, mere knowledge of these definitions is a starting point, not the end goal. An auditor needs to understand the underlying implications of these terms thoroughly, how they interrelate, and their profound impact on an organization's cybersecurity posture. Moreover, auditors must immerse themselves in cybersecurity standards, frameworks, best practices, and legal requirements pertinent to the organization's industry and geography. This profound knowledge will serve as a benchmark for evaluating the organization's cybersecurity posture, enabling auditors to analyze the organization's cybersecurity framework's robustness critically.

Equally important is understanding cyber threats, vulnerabilities, and risks. Cyber threats represent potential malicious acts that can wreak havoc on an organization's cybersecurity infrastructure. Vulnerabilities are the weaknesses within the system, like hidden chinks in the armor that these threats can exploit, and risks are the potential adverse impacts that can cause significant damage resulting from the successful exploitation of vulnerabilities by threats. Auditors must be able to identify, understand, and assess these elements in the organization's environment. This deep and detailed understanding will empower them to evaluate the organization's exposure to cyber risks and the adequacy of their risk management approach. Thus, this comprehension forms the backbone of an effective cybersecurity audit.

The last piece of the puzzle is understanding the cybersecurity control environment. This environment is a complex ecosystem comprising the various preventive, detective, and corrective measures an organization has to manage its cyber risks. It encompasses many controls, including technical ones like firewalls and encryption, administrative controls such as policies and procedures, and physical controls like secure facilities. An auditor's understanding of how these controls operate, their effectiveness, and their role in mitigating specific threats and vulnerabilities is of paramount importance. Without this knowledge, the auditor's analysis of the organization's cybersecurity posture could be superficial and incomplete.

Recommendations:

- **Review this Book:** Review the Risk Mitigation, Quantum, and AI sections to grasp the technology.
- **Master the Lexicon:** Invest time in understanding key cybersecurity terminologies and concepts. This forms the foundation for understanding and evaluating an organization's cybersecurity posture.
- **Break Down Threats, Vulnerabilities, and Risks:** Develop an intricate understanding of cyber threats, vulnerabilities, and risks. Learn how to identify these and assess their impact on an organization's risk exposure.
- **Stay Current with Standards and Regulations:** Keep yourself updated with the latest cybersecurity standards, frameworks, best practices, and legal requirements relevant to the organization's industry and geography. This will serve as a benchmark for your evaluations.
- **Evaluate the Control Environment:** Learn how to evaluate the adequacy and effectiveness of an organization's cybersecurity control environment. This includes understanding the different types of controls, their functions, and when and how they should be applied.
- **Remain Current:** The world of cybersecurity is rapidly evolving, with new threats and defenses emerging continually. Make it a point to stay abreast of the latest developments, threats, and best practices in the field. This will ensure that your audits remain relevant and effective.

THE AUDIT CHARTER AND AUDIT ENGAGEMENT

The audit charter and audit engagement form the bedrock for a cybersecurity audit. The audit charter is the guiding document that sets the path for the audit. It defines the purpose, scope, and responsibilities of a cybersecurity audit. Simultaneously, the audit engagement outlines the tactical approach and expectations during the audit process. Together, they weave a detailed roadmap for the auditors and the organization being audited, enabling them to tread a clearly defined path leading to a systematic, organized, and comprehensive audit.

The audit charter plays a pivotal role in a cybersecurity audit. It sets the stage for all audit activities, laying the groundwork for what will come. It is a formal document that succinctly articulates the purpose, authority, and responsibility of the audit function within the organization. The charter ensures a mutual understanding of the expectations from the audit and clearly defines the limits and extent of the auditor's duties. By doing so, it brings clarity and focus to the audit process. The charter is an essential tool in preserving the independence and objectivity of the audit function, as it establishes the auditors' reporting lines and defines their access to organizational resources and information.

Determining the scope of the cybersecurity audit engagement is a significant step in the planning phase of the audit. It sets the boundaries for the audit and determines what areas and functions of the organization will be reviewed. It is like a spotlight that illuminates the parts of the organization that will be subjected to the audit process. The scope should be broad enough to cover all the critical aspects of the organization's cybersecurity posture, but it must also be reasonable and attainable. Several factors often influence the scope, including the organization's size, industry, regulations, risk appetite, and past audit findings. Therefore, defining the scope is an intricate balancing act that requires careful consideration.

The engagement objectives and deliverables serve as the roadmap for the audit process. They are like a compass, guiding the auditors in the direction they need to take. The objectives articulate what the audit intends to achieve. It could be confirming compliance with specific regulations, assessing the effectiveness of controls, or identifying vulnerabilities. These objectives should align with the organization's cybersecurity strategy and goals, ensuring the audit is relevant and value-adding.

On the other hand, the deliverables are the tangible outcomes of the audit. They include outputs like the audit report or specific recommendations for improvement. These should provide value to the organization, aiding it in enhancing its cybersecurity posture and meeting its strategic objectives.

Recommendations:

- **Develop a Robust Audit Charter:** Create a comprehensive audit charter defining the function's purpose, authority, and responsibility. Ensure it safeguards the independence and objectivity of the audit.
- **Establish a Clear Scope:** Define the scope of the cybersecurity audit engagement meticulously, ensuring it covers all the critical aspects of the organization's cybersecurity posture.
- **Align Objectives:** Align the engagement objectives with the organization's overall cybersecurity strategy and goals. These objectives should clearly articulate what the audit aims to achieve.
- **Define Valuable Deliverables:** Determine the deliverables to maximize the organization's value. Whether it is the audit report or specific recommendations, these deliverables should assist the organization in enhancing its cybersecurity posture.
- **Review and Update:** Regularly review and update the audit charter, scope, and engagement objectives to reflect changes in the organization's size, industry, regulations, risk appetite, and cybersecurity strategy.

RISK-BASED AUDITING APPROACH IN CYBERSECURITY

Adopting a risk-based auditing approach is a prudent, calculated move in the vast, intricate, and often overwhelming cybersecurity landscape, where potential threats can lurk in any corner. This approach is not a mere procedural step but a comprehensive strategy focusing on the complete understanding, meticulous identification, and thoughtful assessment of cyber risks. Moreover, it ensures that the audit objectives are in harmony with the organization's risk appetite, thus ensuring that its focus aligns with its strategic aims and risk tolerance.

The journey toward a risk-based auditing approach begins with a clear and profound understanding of the method. This type of auditing approach is not a static checklist but rather a dynamic and responsive strategy that evolves in response to the ever-changing risk landscape of the organization. It prioritizes areas with the highest risks during the audit process, ensuring that high-risk areas are adequately addressed. Risk-based auditing, however, is not a simple plug-and-play mechanism. It requires the auditors to have a profound, almost intuitive understanding of the organization's business environment, day-to-day operations, and long-term strategic objectives. Additionally, it requires a comprehensive understanding of the prevailing cybersecurity threats and vulnerabilities relevant to the organization and its sector.

The heart and soul of a risk-based audit lie in identifying and prioritizing cyber risks. This process necessitates auditors to navigate the complex labyrinth of potential threats and vulnerabilities the organization may face. They must understand these risks' potential impact if they materialize and compromise the organization's cybersecurity. The process of risk identification requires more than just surface-level understanding. It calls for a comprehensive understanding of the organization's systems, networks, data, operations, and cyber threat environment. On the other hand, risk prioritization is a strategic process determining which risks pose the most significant potential impact. Therefore, these high-impact risks should be prioritized in the audit process.

Aligning the audit objectives with the organization's risk appetite forms the final part of this risk-based auditing approach. Risk appetite is a measure of the level of risk an organization is willing to accept in the pursuit of its objectives. By understanding the organization's risk appetite, auditors can align the audit objectives accordingly. They can focus the audit efforts on areas where the risk exceeds the defined appetite. Doing this ensures that the audit is not just a procedural activity but provides substantial value to the organization by addressing its most crucial risk areas. The audit thus becomes a strategic tool helping the organization navigate its cyber risk landscape effectively.

Recommendations:

- **Understand Risk-Based Auditing:** Equip yourself with the knowledge and skills needed for risk-based auditing. This will enable you to focus your audit efforts on the areas with the highest cyber risks.

- **Identify and Prioritize Risks:** Make a conscious effort to identify and prioritize the cyber risks the organization faces. Priority should be given to the risks with the most significant potential impact.
- **Align with Risk Appetite:** Understand the organization's risk appetite and align your audit objectives. This ensures your audit addresses the most crucial risk areas for the organization.
- **Stay Updated:** Keep yourself updated with the evolving cyber threat environment. Cyber risks can change rapidly, and staying updated will help ensure your audit remains relevant and effective.
- **Collaborate and Communicate:** Collaborate with the organization's management, IT staff, and risk management team in risk identification and prioritization. Regularly communicate your findings and insights to the relevant stakeholders.

EVALUATING INTERNAL CONTROLS FOR CYBERSECURITY

Internal controls form an organization's cybersecurity landscape's fundamental, almost foundational element. They are crucial safeguards and countermeasures to address, mitigate, and neutralize cyber threats. The evaluation of these controls involves a multifaceted process. It includes assessing their design and implementation, evaluating their effectiveness in mitigating cyber threats, and identifying any deficiencies or gaps that may render them less effective.

The critical initial step in this process involves assessing the design and implementation of these internal controls. Controls should be designed considering the scale, intensity, and potential impacts of the risks they are intended to mitigate. The design should be proportionate to these risks, ensuring adequate defense against potential threats. Moreover, creating these controls should also be in harmony with the organization's strategic objectives, providing a comprehensive and integrated approach to risk management. However, the importance of design is closely followed by its implementation. Auditors must scrutinize how these controls have been implemented across the organization. A brilliant design can be rendered futile if the implementation is flawed, inconsistent, or incomplete. Therefore, design and implementation are vital in establishing effective internal controls.

Following the assessment of design and implementation, the process moves on to evaluate the effectiveness of these controls. Control can only be deemed effective if it adequately mitigates the risk it was designed to address. To ascertain this, auditors must test these controls, observing their functioning and effectiveness first-hand. This testing provides valuable insights into the controls' functionality and helps determine whether they operate as intended. Testing these controls may involve technical tests, such as penetration testing or vulnerability scanning, which directly assess the technical robustness of the controls. It may also involve procedural assessments, like reviewing user access rights or incident response procedures, to ensure that processes associated with the controls function optimally.

Identifying control deficiencies and gaps forms the final stage of this process. This stage is about uncovering instances where the controls are falling short and failing to mitigate the identified risks effectively. Gaps may emerge where necessary controls are missing or have been implemented incorrectly. Identifying these gaps and deficiencies is a critical output of the audit process. This discovery serves as a roadmap guiding the formulation of remedial action plans and recommendations. These plans and recommendations aim to address the identified deficiencies and enhance the organization's overall cybersecurity posture.

Recommendations:

- **Consider Risk During Design:** When assessing the design of controls, ensure that they are proportionate to the potential risks and align with the organization's strategic objectives.
- **Scrutinize Implementation:** Do not just focus on the design of the controls but also scrutinize how they have been implemented across the organization. Check for consistency and completeness of implementation.
- **Evaluate Effectiveness:** Use appropriate tests and procedures to evaluate the effectiveness of the controls. Ensure they are operating as intended and are adequately mitigating the risks.
- **Identify Deficiencies and Gaps:** Vigilantly identify any deficiencies in the controls or gaps in the control environment. Use these findings to formulate remedial action plans and recommendations.
- **Communicate Findings:** Effectively communicate your findings and recommendations to the relevant stakeholders. This will enable timely corrective actions and improvements.

TESTING AND SAMPLING TECHNIQUES IN CYBERSECURITY AUDITING

Testing and sampling techniques are vital, indispensable tools in the arsenal of a cybersecurity audit. These techniques empower auditors to draw insightful, meaningful conclusions about the organization's cybersecurity posture without the impractical need to review every single item or process in depth.

One of the crucial components of this process is the design of audit tests for cybersecurity controls. The tests should not be generic or one-size-fits-all but tailored to the specific controls they assess. The aim is to ascertain the controls' effectiveness in mitigating the targeted cyber risks. These tests can involve various activities, depending on the nature of the control in question. Technical activities, such as penetration testing or firewall configuration reviews, may be necessary for some controls. In contrast, other controls may call for procedural checks, such as reviewing access control processes or incident response procedures. The choice of test should align with the nature and purpose of the control, ensuring a comprehensive evaluation.

Applying suitable sampling techniques is also a crucial factor in the audit process. With the significant volume of data and processes in an organization's cybersecurity environment, reviewing everything thoroughly is often infeasible. This is where the role of sampling techniques becomes evident, as they offer a pragmatic approach to data review. Auditors utilize these techniques to select a representative subset of data or processes for inspection, a sample that should offer an unbiased portrayal of the entire dataset, allowing for drawing meaningful conclusions.

Several sampling techniques can be utilized in practice, including:

1. **Random Sampling:** This technique gives each item in the population an equal chance of being selected. It can help eliminate bias and is especially effective when the population is homogeneous.
2. **Systematic Sampling:** This involves selecting every nth item from the population. It is useful when the population is ordered randomly.
3. **Stratified Sampling:** In this approach, the population is divided into subgroups or 'strata' based on certain characteristics, and samples are taken from each stratum. This can be effective when the population has distinct segments.
4. **Cluster Sampling:** This technique involves dividing the population into clusters and then selecting a few clusters randomly for further sampling. This method can be used when the population is too large or spread out to conduct simple random sampling.
5. **Judgment Sampling:** Also known as purposive sampling, the auditor uses their judgment to select items they believe most represent the overall population.

The final step in this process is the evaluation of test results. Once the tests have been performed and the data has been sampled, auditors have the task of interpreting these results accurately. They must decipher what these results signify in the organization's cyber risk landscape and how they impact its overall cybersecurity posture. The interpretation of these results needs to go beyond mere numbers, diving into their implications for the organization's cyber defense. These results form the basis for the auditors' findings, driving their recommendations. These recommendations enhance the organization's cyber defense, ensuring a robust and resilient cybersecurity posture.

Recommendations:

- **Design Tailored Audit Tests:** Make an effort to design audit tests specific to the cybersecurity controls you are assessing. Rather than using a one-size-fits-all approach, tailor tests to align with the nature and purpose of each control. The goal should be to evaluate the effectiveness of the controls in mitigating targeted cyber risks.
- **Utilize Suitable Sampling Techniques:** Given the large volume of data and processes involved in an organization's cybersecurity environment,

apply appropriate sampling techniques to review data pragmatically. These techniques allow auditors to select a representative subset of data or processes for in-depth inspection.

- **Implement Various Sampling Techniques:** Depending on the characteristics of the data or process, employ different sampling techniques such as random sampling, systematic sampling, stratified sampling, cluster sampling, and judgment sampling. Understand the advantages and applicability of each method and choose accordingly.
- **Interpret Test Results Effectively:** Accurately interpret the results after the tests and the data sampled. Beyond just the numbers, delving into these results' implications for the organization's cyber risk landscape and overall cybersecurity posture.
- **Use Results to Form Recommendations:** Use the findings derived from the test results as a basis for recommendations to enhance the organization's cyber defense. The conclusions drawn should drive actionable recommendations that help ensure a robust and resilient cybersecurity posture within the organization.

COMPLIANCE WITH LEGAL AND REGULATORY REQUIREMENTS

Ensuring compliance with legal and regulatory requirements is a cybersecurity audit's backbone. This task involves more than a mere perfunctory review. Instead, it requires a nuanced and informed understanding of the relevant regulations, a rigorous assessment of the organization's compliance with these norms, and a comprehensive evaluation of potential enforcement actions and penalties.

The auditor's journey begins with a detailed understanding of the laws and regulations that apply to the organization under audit. They must comprehensively understand these regulatory standards, including their intentions, specific provisions, and goals. Such understanding forms the foundation for the auditor's ability to accurately interpret and apply these regulations to the organization's operations and controls.

Interpreting laws and regulations is often challenging due to their complex nature. This complexity is compounded when an organization operates across multiple jurisdictions, each with unique cybersecurity requirements. At this juncture, auditors may need to seek guidance or clarifications. Legal experts, regulatory bodies, and professional organizations such as ISACA and The Institute of Internal Auditors often provide auditors with invaluable insights, guidance, and training materials. These resources play a pivotal role in helping auditors understand the precise application of the laws and regulations.

Following the process of interpretation, the auditor's focus shifts to a detailed examination of the organization's compliance with these norms. This involves an in-depth analysis of various aspects, such as implementing necessary cybersecurity controls, adhering to reporting requirements, and managing incidents in accordance with regulations. This detailed assessment serves a dual purpose. First, it highlights areas of noncompliance, and second, it identifies potential risks associated with such compliance lapses.

The audit process does not end with the identification of noncompliance areas. Understanding the implications of noncompliance, including potential enforcement actions and penalties, is integral to the auditor's role. Regulatory bodies can impose substantial financial penalties for noncompliance. They can even impose restrictions on business operations or cause significant reputational damage. By developing a detailed understanding of these enforcement mechanisms, auditors can effectively assess the severity of the consequences an organization might face in the event of noncompliance.

In summary, the auditor plays a vital role in ensuring regulatory compliance. This responsibility extends from a detailed understanding and interpretation of the laws and regulations to a comprehensive assessment of the organization's compliance and the potential consequences of noncompliance. It is a complex and multifaceted role, but one that is pivotal to the pursuit of a secure and compliant digital landscape.

Recommendations:

- **Understand Relevant Laws and Regulations:** The first step in a cybersecurity audit is to thoroughly understand the laws and regulations applicable to the organization. Gain comprehensive knowledge about these regulatory standards' intent, provisions, and goals, as this will form the foundation for accurate interpretation and application to the organization's operations.

- **Seek Guidance for Interpretation:** Auditors should not hesitate to seek guidance due to the complex nature of laws and regulations, especially when operating in multiple jurisdictions. Legal experts, regulatory bodies, and professional organizations can provide valuable insights, helping auditors understand the precise application of the laws and regulations.

- **Analyze Compliance In Depth:** Auditors should thoroughly examine the organization's compliance once laws and regulations are understood and interpreted. This should include a thorough analysis of the implementation of necessary cybersecurity controls, adherence to reporting requirements, and management of incidents in accordance with regulations.

- **Understand the Implications of Noncompliance:** Auditors must understand the potential enforcement actions and penalties associated with noncompliance as part of the audit process. Regulatory bodies can impose substantial financial penalties and operational restrictions or cause reputational damage. By understanding these enforcement mechanisms, auditors can assess the severity of the potential consequences of noncompliance.

- **Assume a Multifaceted Role:** Realize that the role of an auditor is not limited to merely identifying compliance and noncompliance areas. The role extends to a detailed understanding and interpretation of laws and regulations, a comprehensive assessment of the organization's compliance, and an understanding of the implications of noncompliance. Though complex, this role is vital in maintaining a secure and compliant digital landscape.

REPORTING AND COMMUNICATION OF AUDIT FINDINGS

Compliance with legal and regulatory requirements is fundamental to any cybersecurity audit. Given the complexities of the modern digital world, organizations must adhere to many laws, regulations, and standards. This dynamic regulatory landscape continuously evolves due to technological advancements and emerging threats.

In navigating this intricate landscape, understanding the specifics of the cybersecurity regulatory environment in which an organization operates emerges as the primary task. Every organization exists within a specific legal and regulatory milieu that prescribes the bare minimum standards its cybersecurity practices must meet. This environment could comprise multiple jurisdictions and sectors, each presenting unique cybersecurity requirements. For instance, if an organization operates within the healthcare sector in the United States, it is bound by the Health Insurance Portability and Accountability Act (HIPAA). Meanwhile, if an organization operates within the European region and handles personal data, it must abide by the General Data Protection Regulation (GDPR). Auditors must, therefore, develop a comprehensive understanding of the regulatory environment pertinent to the organization under review to assess its compliance effectively.

The next phase of this regulatory compliance journey involves an exhaustive assessment of the organization's compliance with the applicable laws and regulations. Having understood the specific regulatory requirements, the auditor undertakes a detailed analysis to ascertain whether the organization's cybersecurity practices align with these stipulated norms. This involves thoroughly examining various aspects, such as whether the organization has implemented the necessary cybersecurity controls, meets specific reporting requirements, and manages incidents in alignment with the regulations. This assessment is critical as it helps identify areas of noncompliance and potential risks associated with such lapses.

An integral part of the audit process is the evaluation of enforcement actions and associated penalties. Regulatory bodies can impose stringent penalties for noncompliance, ranging from substantial financial penalties to restrictions on business operations and even causing significant reputational damage. An in-depth understanding of these enforcement mechanisms and the potential implications of noncompliance can aid auditors in assessing the severity of the organization's consequences. This understanding also underscores the importance of robust compliance practices within the organization.

Once the assessment is completed, presenting the findings to the organization forms the next crucial step. Jessica Milliken rightly said, 'Nobody likes it when you call their baby ugly.' Hence, communicating the findings with tact and sensitivity is paramount. However, this does not mean downplaying or obscuring any issues that have been identified. It involves constructively presenting the findings, focusing on the potential improvement areas, and providing actionable insights to rectify the identified lapses.

In some situations, there might be disagreements about the findings. Following a facts-based approach, the auditor must handle these situations professionally and diplomatically. An auditor should be open to discussion, willing to review any additional evidence provided, and be ready to amend findings if new evidence necessitates. The goal is not to enforce an auditor's perspective but to arrive at an accurate representation of the organization's compliance status. While reconciling disagreements, ensuring that the process remains objective, fair, and driven by the pursuit of truth is important. A well-managed audit is about finding noncompliance and fostering a culture of continuous improvement and enhanced cybersecurity posture.

Recommendations:

- **Prepare a Comprehensive Report:** Create a summative report encompassing all audit findings and recommendations. Ensure it is presented professionally and accessible to technical and nontechnical readers. This report will serve as the cornerstone document outlining the audit's outcomes.

- **Present Findings Constructively:** After the assessment, findings should be constructively presented to the organization. This does not involve downplaying or obscuring any identified issues but focuses on potential areas for improvement and providing actionable insights for rectifying the lapses.

- **Handle Disagreements Professionally:** In disagreements regarding findings, auditors must handle these situations professionally and diplomatically. They should be open to discussion, ready to review additional evidence, and willing to amend findings if necessary. The goal is not to enforce an auditor's perspective but to accurately represent the organization's compliance status. The audit process should remain objective, fair, and driven by the pursuit of truth. The ultimate aim is to foster a culture of continuous improvement and enhance the organization's cybersecurity posture.

- **Follow Up:** Do not end the audit process with the report presentation. Follow up with the organization to ensure they are taking appropriate actions based on your findings, facilitating dialogue to address potential challenges.

- **Promote Improvement:** Leverage the audit process to encourage substantial improvements in the organization's cybersecurity posture. Advocate for proactive action and continuous improvement beyond mere compliance.

- **Monitor Progress:** Stay involved with the organization post-audit. Continually assess progress against action plans and be ready to conduct follow-up audits when necessary, ensuring the organization is working toward the recommended improvements.

CONSIDERATION OF THIRD-PARTY RELATIONSHIPS

Third-party relationships can introduce significant cybersecurity risks into an organization's operations. While an organization might have the most robust cybersecurity posture internally, the entire system can become vulnerable if the third-party providers it engages with do not also maintain high cybersecurity standards. This section will delve deeper into evaluating third-party risk management practices, assessing the strength and effectiveness of contracts and service level agreements, and monitoring and oversight mechanisms for third-party providers.

First and foremost is the evaluation of the third-party risk management practices in place within the organization. Most organizations today collaborate with various third-party providers, ranging from suppliers and contractors to partners and affiliates. Each of these relationships, while beneficial, introduces a new set of risks to the organization's cybersecurity posture. Therefore, the organization must implement robust third-party risk management practices to identify and manage the risks associated with each relationship effectively. From an auditor's perspective, assessing these practices is vital to ensure they effectively mitigate the cybersecurity risks emanating from third-party relationships.

Next comes the assessment of the organization's contracts and service level agreements with third-party providers. These contracts and agreements should spell out the cybersecurity obligations of the third-party providers. This could range from requirements related to data protection, incident management, and even compliance with specific regulations or standards. From an auditor's perspective, evaluating these documents is critical to ensure they adequately protect the organization's interests and mitigate potential cybersecurity risks.

Lastly, ongoing monitoring and oversight of third-party providers is of utmost importance. Even with the most robust risk management practices and comprehensive contracts, monitoring third-party providers to ensure they uphold their obligations continually is essential. The auditor must evaluate the organization's monitoring and oversight mechanisms to ensure they effectively maintain the security of the organization's data and systems.

Recommendations:

- **Evaluate Risk Management Practices:** Assess the organization's third-party risk management practices to ensure they effectively identify and manage the risks associated with each relationship.

- **Assess Contracts and SLAs:** Review the organization's contracts and service level agreements with third-party providers to ensure they clearly define the provider's cybersecurity obligations.
- **Monitor and Oversee:** Evaluate the organization's monitoring and oversight practices to ensure they are effective in ensuring that third-party providers are meeting their cybersecurity obligations.
- **Highlight Weaknesses:** Identify and highlight any weaknesses in the organization's third-party risk management practices, contract provisions, or monitoring and oversight practices.
- **Advocate for Robust Practices:** Use the audit process to advocate for robust third-party risk management practices, solid contracts, and effective monitoring and oversight.

QUALITY ASSURANCE AND IMPROVEMENT PROGRAM

A Quality Assurance and Improvement Program (QAIP) is critical for safeguarding and enhancing an organization's cybersecurity posture. The structure and systematic approach of a QAIP involves three primary steps: developing a comprehensive QAIP, conducting detailed internal assessments, and undertaking exhaustive external evaluations and peer reviews.

At the commencement of this process, a QAIP is established, forming the foundation for future cybersecurity activities within the organization. This program, in its essence, is tasked with ensuring the efficacy of an organization's cybersecurity measures while promoting an environment of constant growth and development. A well-implemented QAIP should house mechanisms that allow continuous observation and assessment of the organization's cybersecurity protocols. Such a program must also identify potential areas of concern or avenues for further improvement and implement the necessary changes to enhance the organization's cybersecurity posture.

The second critical aspect of a QAIP is conducting regular internal assessments. These assessments are pivotal to allowing the organization to self-evaluate its cybersecurity practices, comparing them against the established organizational policies and standards. More than just a tool for internal comparison, these assessments should extend to consider relevant external regulations and standards, ensuring the organization remains in compliance with them. This systematic internal review process permits the organization to pinpoint areas of noncompliance or weakness, highlighting the areas requiring immediate attention and remediation.

In pursuing a truly comprehensive QAIP, external evaluations and peer reviews must not be neglected, as they form the final, yet equally crucial, step in this process. External evaluations and peer reviews introduce an unbiased review of the organization's cybersecurity practices. As these are conducted independently, they offer a fresh, objective perspective that internal assessments might fail to provide. Not only do they offer an invaluable third-party perspective, but they also enable the organization to benchmark its cybersecurity practices against industry standards or prevailing best practices. Through this comparison, the organization can discern where it stands relative to its contemporaries and identify further areas for improvement.

In conclusion, a QAIP is a thorough, multifaceted approach that enables an organization to monitor, assess, and improve its cybersecurity practices continually. The three-step approach, involving the establishment of a QAIP, conducting internal assessments, and utilizing external evaluations and peer reviews, offers the organization an opportunity to remain vigilant, compliant, and always improving in an ever-evolving cybersecurity landscape.

Recommendations:

- **Establish a QAIP:** Set up a comprehensive QAIP that oversees the organization's cybersecurity measures. The QAIP should promote constant growth and development, incorporate mechanisms for continuous evaluation, identify potential areas for improvement, and enforce necessary changes to enhance the cybersecurity posture.

- **Conduct Internal Assessments:** Conduct regular internal assessments as a part of the QAIP to self-evaluate the organization's adherence to its policies and standards. Extend these assessments to consider external regulations, identify areas of noncompliance, and spotlight the sections requiring immediate attention and remediation.

- **Undertake External Evaluations and Peer Reviews:** For a well-rounded QAIP, involve external evaluations and peer reviews to provide an unbiased review of cybersecurity practices. Utilize this independent perspective to benchmark against industry standards, understand where the organization stands, and identify potential areas for improvement.

- **Continually Update QAIP:** Ensure the QAIP stays relevant and effective by updating it in response to changes in the organization's cybersecurity landscape. The QAIP should adapt to evolving threats, technology advancements, and changes in regulatory requirements, thus ensuring a dynamic and resilient cybersecurity posture.

- **Promote a Culture of Security:** Use the QAIP to foster a security culture within the organization. The program should not just detect and fix issues but should actively encourage all organization members to prioritize cybersecurity, thus enhancing collective responsibility and awareness.

PROFESSIONAL ETHICS, SKILLS, AND CONTINUING EDUCATION

Professional ethics, competencies, and an ongoing commitment to education are central tenets of an auditor's role in cybersecurity. The intricate intersection of technology, business, and law in this arena makes it a hotbed of ethical concerns – from maintaining sensitive data's privacy to responsibly disclosing discovered vulnerabilities. Consequently, unwavering adherence to high ethical standards is not just expected; it is essential for anyone involved in cybersecurity auditing.

Auditors carry the weight of understanding their impact on the organizations they assess, their stakeholders, and the larger digital ecosystem. Upholding professional ethics can profoundly impact an organization's cybersecurity posture and reputation. Auditors should be deeply familiar with the ethical standards laid out by their professional bodies and display an unwavering commitment to adhere to them. This includes maintaining their independence and objectivity, safeguarding confidential and sensitive information, and clarifying any real or perceived conflicts of interest.

The Enron scandal is a compelling example of the importance of doing what is right. Despite immense pressure and potential personal loss, the auditors at Enron chose to reveal the truth about the company's financial irregularities. This led to the collapse of one of the world's largest corporations, but it also shed light on unethical practices and underscored the importance of ethics in professional practice. This incident is a stark reminder of auditors' role in unmasking unethical behavior, emphasizing the necessity of doing what is right, even when it is difficult.

In addition to a strong ethical foundation, auditors must possess the necessary skills for effective cybersecurity auditing. This includes a comprehensive understanding of IT systems, networks, and cybersecurity principles. Auditors should also be conversant with the specific cybersecurity frameworks, regulations, and standards relevant to the organizations they are assessing. With this technical acumen, they should possess strong analytical and communication skills to evaluate an organization's cybersecurity posture effectively and clearly articulate their findings.

However, given the dynamic nature of cybersecurity, foundational knowledge and skills are not enough. The cyber threat landscape constantly evolves, with new vulnerabilities, threat actors, and attack techniques emerging regularly. At the same time, technological advancements introduce fresh challenges and complexities. To remain effective, auditors must commit to keeping up-to-date with these developments. This commitment to continuing education could include participating in professional training programs, attending industry conferences, or maintaining and updating relevant professional certifications. By continually honing their skills and knowledge, cybersecurity auditors can ensure they are well equipped to navigate the complexities of their profession.

An essential component of a cybersecurity auditor's role is maintaining impartiality and detachment in their assessments. Auditors must avoid allowing personal feelings, preconceived notions, or biases to influence their professional judgment or conclusions.

Auditors should rely heavily on empirical evidence and data in their assessments to accomplish this. Data-driven auditing enables auditors to make objective, accurate, and reliable conclusions about an organization's cybersecurity posture. This method ensures that assessments are based on facts and figures rather than subjective opinions or emotions.

A data-centric approach involves thorough data collection, rigorous analysis, and systematic interpretation. An auditor should identify and evaluate data that accurately represents the organization's cybersecurity practices and controls. This includes but is not limited to reviewing system logs, examining firewall configurations, assessing access control policies, and analyzing incident response procedures. Each piece of data collected should be meticulously analyzed to draw meaningful, objective conclusions about the organization's cybersecurity posture.

Moreover, established audit methodologies and checklists can help auditors maintain objectivity and ensure a systematic, thorough audit process. These standardized approaches provide a roadmap for the audit and ensure that every critical aspect of an organization's cybersecurity is assessed consistently and comprehensively.

However, while relying on data is key, it is also important to interpret this information within its broader context. The auditor must understand the organization's operational environment, business objectives, and risk appetite. This understanding will allow the auditor to provide valuable, relevant recommendations based on the analyzed data.

In conclusion, removing personal feelings and biases from auditing is key to ensuring accurate and fair evaluations. By focusing on data, applying rigorous methodologies, and understanding the broader context, auditors can provide valuable, objective insights into an organization's cybersecurity posture. This approach reinforces trust in the audit process, encouraging organizations to adopt recommended improvements and enhancing overall cybersecurity resilience.

Recommendations:

- **Uphold Ethical Standards:** Auditors should adhere to the ethical standards laid out by their professional bodies. This includes maintaining independence, objectivity, confidentiality, and avoiding conflicts of interest. A commitment to ethics enhances the auditor's credibility and positively influences an organization's cybersecurity posture.

- **Possess Relevant Competencies:** A comprehensive understanding of IT systems, networks, cybersecurity principles, and relevant regulations is essential. Auditors must also demonstrate strong analytical and communication skills. These competencies enable them to effectively evaluate an organization's cybersecurity posture and clearly articulate their findings.

- **Commit to Continuous Education:** With the dynamic nature of cybersecurity, auditors must keep abreast of emerging vulnerabilities, threat actors, and technological advancements. This can be achieved through professional training programs, industry conferences, and maintaining relevant certifications. Continual learning ensures auditors remain effective in their profession.

- **Maintain Impartiality:** Auditors must remain impartial in their assessments, not letting personal feelings or biases influence their judgment. An auditor's assessment should be rooted in empirical evidence and data, promoting accuracy and reliability.
- **Adopt a Data-centric Approach:** Auditors should rely on thorough data collection, rigorous analysis, and systematic interpretation. Data-driven auditing involves evaluating data representing the organization's cybersecurity practices and controls, such as system logs, firewall configurations, access control policies, and incident response procedures.
- **Utilize Established Methodologies:** Standardized audit methodologies and checklists can enhance objectivity and comprehensiveness. These frameworks provide a roadmap for the audit, ensuring that critical aspects of cybersecurity are assessed consistently.
- **Understand Broader Context:** While relying on data is key, auditors should also consider the organization's operational environment, business objectives, and risk appetite. Interpreting data within this broader context allows the auditor to provide relevant and valuable recommendations, enhancing overall cybersecurity resilience.

BEST PRACTICES FOR CYBERSECURITY EXECUTIVES AND TEAMS WHEN INTERFACING WITH AUDITORS

An objective mindset and an openness to criticism underlie an effective interface with auditors. Cybersecurity executives and team members should recognize the value of an audit, understanding that it offers an unbiased, external perspective on existing cybersecurity practices. This insight, viewed from the auditor's perspective, can reinforce defenses if accepted with an open mind. The audit process enhances the organization's cybersecurity; recognizing this is the first step toward effective collaboration.

Preparation is the next critical stage. Proactive preparation for the audit process means assembling necessary documentation and conducting an internal review to identify potential issues. Acknowledging a problem is just the start; delving deeper to comprehend the systemic factors leading to the issue's existence is essential. This not only assists in immediate rectification but also aids in preventing similar issues from arising.

One of the pivotal aspects of this process is how audit findings are handled. It is not a test of an individual or team's professional capabilities, nor should it be taken personally. Instead, findings should be carefully reviewed and seen as opportunities for growth and improvement. Cybersecurity teams should develop and implement an effective remediation plan based on these findings and ensure regular reporting to the auditors, reinforcing a constructive relationship.

Building relationships with auditors is a practice that should not be understated. These relationships cultivate mutual respect and understanding. They foster an environment of ongoing dialogue where information, ideas, and concerns can be exchanged openly and constructively. Effective communication plays a significant role in providing clear, concise, and accurate information to auditors while also asking questions and clarifying any issues as necessary.

A crucial aspect of this dialogue is the capacity to push back on audit findings. This is not a confrontational approach but a healthy discourse and debate on the identified issues. Cybersecurity teams should respond promptly and completely to auditors' requests, providing evidence or context that might have been overlooked, keeping the audit process on track, and ensuring a comprehensive final audit report.

Equally important is not unthinkingly accepting all findings without providing an effective challenge. Audit findings are the starting point of a discussion, not the end. Any challenge should be based on factual evidence and conveyed respectfully, with the mutual goal of improving cybersecurity measures.

An audit aims to enhance a cybersecurity framework's effectiveness, not to find fault. A collaborative and receptive approach to the auditing process can result in a robust, resilient, and secure system. With patience, objectivity, and a willingness to learn and improve, the interface between cybersecurity teams and auditors can become a rewarding experience.

Recommendations:

- **Understand the Auditors' Perspective:** Grasping the auditors' perspective and objectives is crucial for cybersecurity teams. The auditors' external, unbiased viewpoint brings significant value in enhancing the organization's cybersecurity measures. Appreciating this perspective fosters collaboration and mutual understanding during the auditing process.
- **Prepare for the Audit:** Proactive preparation is a fundamental aspect of the process. Cybersecurity teams should assemble all necessary documentation and conduct a thorough internal review to identify potential vulnerabilities and issues. This strategic preparation can streamline the audit process, allowing teams to proactively address any areas of concern.
- **Communicate Effectively:** Communication forms the foundation of a productive interaction with auditors. Cybersecurity teams should aim to provide clear, concise, and accurate information to auditors, fostering an environment of transparency. Simultaneously, they should engage auditors with insightful questions and seek clarification on issues, promoting mutual understanding and reducing ambiguities.
- **Respond Timely:** Responding to auditors' inquiries is crucial to keep the audit process on track. Cybersecurity teams should prioritize prompt and comprehensive responses to auditors' requests, demonstrating their commitment to the auditing process. This approach aids in maintaining the momentum and efficiency of the audit process.
- **Handle Audit Findings Carefully:** Managing audit findings demands careful attention and strategic planning from cybersecurity teams.

They should review audit findings and recommendations meticulously and develop and implement an effective remediation plan. Regular progress reports to the auditors ensure transparency and demonstrate a proactive approach toward enhancing the organization's cybersecurity framework.

Chapter Conclusion

Cybersecurity auditing, a crucial aspect of an organization's overall cybersecurity strategy, is a multifaceted task. It demands a unique blend of key competencies, including deep technical knowledge, analytical prowess, strong adherence to professional ethics, and the capability to collaborate effectively with diverse teams across an organization's structure.

Cybersecurity is marked by its continual evolution in response to a threat landscape that shifts and mutates with relentless frequency. This constant change necessitates that an auditor's role cannot be static. Auditors must persistently stay abreast of these changes, adapting their knowledge and skills to address new challenges and risks as they arise. This adaptive posture underscores the importance of a commitment to continuous learning and professional development, the cornerstone of effective auditing in cybersecurity.

A need for balance further characterizes the auditor's role. On one side of this balance, auditors must provide an independent, objective assessment of an organization's cybersecurity posture, considering the totality of its systems and practices. On the other side, they must also be able to effectively collaborate with the cybersecurity team, sharing insights, making recommendations, and contributing to the improvement process. Striking this balance is not always straightforward, but it is an indispensable aspect of conducting a rigorous and constructive audit.

Building on this notion of balance, the auditing process is symbiotic, benefiting both the auditors and the cybersecurity teams. It allows auditors to shed light on potential vulnerabilities while offering cybersecurity teams a chance to improve their defensive strategies. The goal is not to levy criticism but to foster growth, turning insights and recommendations into actionable steps for bolstering the organization's defenses.

Lastly, perhaps most importantly, auditors must always be guided by their overarching purpose. An audit is not about pinpointing faults for the sake of criticism but about providing observations and recommendations that help organizations strengthen their cybersecurity posture. With a focus on a constructive and supportive approach, auditors should prioritize effective communication, transparency, and collaboration in all their interactions. These practices ensure auditors are integral to the cybersecurity strategy, championing organizational improvement and resilience.

Case Study: Cybersecurity Audit at Techsphere Inc.

TechSphere Inc., a growing tech startup, decided to undertake a comprehensive cybersecurity audit to identify potential vulnerabilities and ensure regulatory compliance. Ayaz, an experienced cybersecurity auditor with a reputation for thoroughness and collaboration, was brought on board to lead the audit.

Ayaz started by conducting a meeting with TechSphere's cybersecurity team. He understood the importance of appreciating their perspective, as highlighted in the guide. He clearly explained his role and objectives – not an adversary but a partner working to enhance the organization's cybersecurity. The team appreciated Ayaz's collaborative approach, and it set a positive tone for the rest of the audit process.

Next, Ayaz guided the team through the preparation phase. As recommended in the guide, he stressed the need for organized documentation and an internal review. Ayaz encouraged the group to proactively identify and address potential issues before the external audit. This proactive approach proved invaluable during the audit, streamlining the procedure and mitigating potential negative findings.

Throughout the audit, Ayaz prioritized effective two-way communication. He ensured that he provided clear and concise information and encouraged the cybersecurity team to do the same. His approach underscored the importance of communication, making the entire process more efficient and fostering a strong sense of collaboration.

When handling the audit findings, Ayaz took a constructive and supportive approach. As the guide recommends, he provided the cybersecurity team with a detailed explanation of identified weaknesses, offering practical recommendations for remediation. His strategy reflected the guide's advice that an auditor's primary goal should be to provide insights that help the organization improve its cybersecurity posture.

Key lessons from this case study echo the guide: the importance of a collaborative approach, effective two-way communication, proactive preparation, and constructive handling of audit findings. Ayaz's successful audit at TechSphere Inc. shows how auditors can apply the recommendations from the guide to real-world situations, delivering tangible benefits to the organizations they work with. Ultimately, his story underscores the potential of cybersecurity auditing, done right, to bolster an organization's defense against digital threats significantly.

CHAPTER 20

The Challenging Role of the Regulator

"Regulators bear the weight of ensuring public safety, scrutinizing every aspect of industries to prevent harm."

Regulators play a pivotal role in cybersecurity, tasked with significant responsibilities while facing diverse opportunities and challenges. They are vital in maintaining industry standards, necessitating continuous learning, adaptation, and fruitful business collaboration. Given the dynamic nature of the field, regulators must be dedicated to constant learning. Numerous resources are available to aid this educational journey, helping them stay updated and effective in their roles. Their responsibilities include guiding businesses, identifying potential obstacles, and finding ways to surmount these challenges. Furthermore, the pursuit of regulatory excellence, an understanding of potential career paths, and achieving a balance between objectivity and advocacy are critical aspects for regulators in cybersecurity. By offering a comprehensive overview of these elements, we can better understand the multifaceted role of regulators in this ever-evolving field.

THE PARAMOUNT ROLE OF THE REGULATOR IN CYBERSECURITY

Regulation occupies an exceptionally critical role within cybersecurity's intricate and multifaceted realm. It establishes the guiding standards and frameworks and enforces a sense of order, thus providing robust protection for all stakeholders involved. It emerges as the first and most vital line of defense in a relentless battle against an increasingly sophisticated and evolving spectrum of cyber threats. This crucial function is aptly fulfilled by the cybersecurity regulators, who undertake a unique, exceedingly challenging, yet immensely rewarding role in achieving and maintaining the delicate balance between technological innovation and comprehensive security.

Regulators in cybersecurity carve out a distinct and profoundly crucial role. They are tasked with ensuring the overall stability and integrity of the enormous, interconnected digital universe we commonly call cyberspace. This responsibility extends to protecting not just individual users but also diverse organizations that form the backbone of today's digital economy. As the vigilant custodians of cybersecurity standards, they navigate the industry's landscape, guiding practices and shaping an environment where cybersecurity can flourish and evolve robustly. These regulators uphold rigorous technical standards while promoting ethical conduct and fostering a culture of appropriate behavior within the cybersecurity industry.

Embarking on a career as a regulator in cybersecurity is both a challenging and rewarding proposition. This role is inherently dynamic, demanding high adaptability, a sharp capacity for critical thinking, and the ability to make informed decisions in complex situations. Given the interdisciplinary nature of cybersecurity, it also requires a comprehensive understanding of technology, legal frameworks, and business principles.

The effectiveness and success of regulators in cybersecurity hinge significantly on their unrelenting commitment to learning and adapting to new circumstances. Cybersecurity as a field is characterized by its volatile nature. The spectrum of threats and the technology used to combat them constantly evolve and mutate. This relentless dynamism necessitates regulators to continuously update their knowledge and skills, ensuring they maintain a robust grasp of this ever-changing landscape and respond to threats appropriately.

Navigating the vast and complex landscape of cybersecurity is an undeniably daunting task. However, armed with the right amalgamation of knowledge, skills, and attitudes, regulators can effectively steer a course through this intricate field. By doing so, they significantly contribute to securing and stabilizing the digital infrastructure that underpins modern society.

Moreover, building and maintaining collaborative relationships with the wider business community is fundamental to a regulator's role. By fostering these relationships, regulators can glean valuable insights into the unique challenges that different businesses face. This understanding enables them to provide relevant, tailored guidance and support, enhancing the overall cybersecurity posture of these organizations.

Recommendations:

- **Pursue Continuous Learning:** Given the dynamic nature of cybersecurity, regulators must commit to continuous learning. Try to stay updated with the latest trends, technologies, threats, and mitigation strategies in the field. Regularly attending webinars, conferences, and training programs can help achieve this.

- **Build Strong Networks:** Regulators should actively seek to build and strengthen relationships within the cybersecurity community. This includes connecting with industry experts, thought leaders, and organizations. These relationships can provide valuable insights and perspectives, improving the regulators' ability to anticipate and respond to emerging threats.
- **Develop Interdisciplinary Knowledge:** Cybersecurity intersects with numerous other disciplines, such as law and business. Regulators should endeavor to broaden their knowledge in these areas to better understand the full implications of their decisions. This can be achieved through additional coursework, self-study, or partnerships with experts in these fields.
- **Encourage Ethical Practices:** Regulators should actively promote and enforce ethical practices within the industry. This includes ensuring companies follow established cybersecurity standards, encouraging transparency, and fostering a culture of accountability. Consider implementing regular audits and feedback mechanisms to monitor compliance.
- **Foster Innovation:** While maintaining security is paramount, regulators should also be advocates for innovation. Strive to create an environment where new ideas and technologies can flourish without compromising security. This might involve working closely with tech startups, supporting academic research, or exploring new ways to integrate emerging technologies into the cybersecurity landscape.

IDENTIFYING KEY FOCUS AREAS IN CYBERSECURITY FOR REGULATORS

As a regulator in the field of cybersecurity, pinpointing key focus areas is not only instrumental for steering practices and sustaining industry standards but also for shaping a robust cybersecurity ecosystem. A deep understanding of the threat landscape is at the heart of these focus areas. As cybersecurity threats morph and mature, regulators must continuously stay informed of the diverse types of attacks, their origins, how they operate, their specific impacts, and their potential future trends. This understanding is pivotal to devising preventative strategies, proactive defense mechanisms, and effective responses to cyber incidents.

A key responsibility of regulators is ensuring compliance and enforcing the established cybersecurity standards. In an era where cyber threats pose substantial risks to businesses and the economy at large, it is incumbent upon regulators to ensure that companies comply with the rules and guidelines devised to maintain cyber hygiene and mitigate risk. This multifaceted role involves drafting and applying regulatory frameworks and their diligent monitoring and enforcing punitive measures when necessary. It involves a continuous, in-depth study of market trends, technological advancements, and shifts in cybercrime techniques, shaping the evolution of these regulations.

Regulators also shoulder the responsibility of promoting best practices in cybersecurity. This role transcends traditional boundaries and delves into education and awareness building. It involves consistently educating the business community about cybersecurity's vital importance, underlining individual actors' roles in the collective cybersecurity effort, sharing insights about potential risks, and offering detailed, accessible, and practical guidance on how organizations can shield themselves effectively against cyber threats.

One of the weapons in the collective fight against cyber threats is the culture of information sharing and incident reporting. Regulators are expected to foster this culture and lead by example. They are tasked with creating an environment of transparency where businesses feel empowered to share their experiences, vulnerabilities, and breaches without the fear of reprisal. This helps in the early detection and mitigation of threats and strengthens the collective cybersecurity framework by encouraging learning from each other's experiences.

Regulators also have a role to play in emerging technologies and associated risks. As technological innovation continues rapidly, it brings many new challenges and threats. Regulators need to stay at the cutting edge of these developments, understand the intricacies of these technologies, assess their potential impacts, and guide businesses on adopting them safely without compromising their cyber defenses.

Recommendations:

- **Understand the Threat Landscape:** Study cyber threats' evolution, diversity, and dynamics. This should involve examining various types of attacks, their origins, modus operandi, specific impacts, and potential future trends. This understanding will form the bedrock of developing preventative strategies, proactive defense mechanisms, and effective responses to cyber incidents.

- **Monitor Compliance and Enforce Standards:** Make it a priority to strictly adhere to established cybersecurity standards and regulations. This encompasses drafting and implementing regulatory frameworks, constantly monitoring their observance, and applying punitive measures where violations occur. Stay abreast of market trends, technological advancements, and shifts in cybercrime techniques to shape the ongoing evolution of these regulations.

- **Promote Best Practices:** Go beyond just setting the rules to actively promoting best practices in cybersecurity. This includes educating the business community about the crucial importance of cybersecurity, highlighting individual roles in the collective cybersecurity effort, and offering detailed and practical guidance on how organizations can effectively shield themselves from cyber threats.

- **Foster a Culture of Information Sharing:** Encourage a transparent environment that promotes sharing experiences, vulnerabilities, and breaches. This involves creating a safe space where businesses can share without fear of reprisal, allowing for early detection and mitigation of threats, and strengthening the collective cybersecurity framework through mutual learning.

- **Stay Ahead with Emerging Technologies:** Remain on the frontline of technological innovation. Understand the intricacies of emerging technologies, assess their potential impacts, and provide guidance on their safe adoption. Keep abreast of the challenges and threats posed by these developments and ensure businesses do not compromise their cyber defenses in the race to adopt new technologies.

UTILIZING FFIEC WORK PAPERS EFFECTIVELY

In the hands of regulators, the Federal Financial Institutions Examination Council (*FFIEC*) work papers are indispensable in ensuring consistent and comprehensive evaluations of cybersecurity practices in businesses. They provide a structured, systematic, uniform approach to assessing an organization's cybersecurity posture. This clarity and uniformity play a crucial role in evaluations, offering an unambiguous lens to observe, analyze, and grade the implementation of cybersecurity practices across businesses.

To effectively align the FFIEC work papers with regulatory objectives, it is crucial to comprehend the overarching goals of cybersecurity regulations. This understanding allows regulators to harness these tools to their fullest potential, directing their attention to areas of most significant risk and concern and consequently driving strategic improvements in cybersecurity. A nuanced understanding of these objectives guides regulators in using the work papers, providing clear pathways to monitor compliance, detect discrepancies, and suggest improvements.

Using FFIEC work papers effectively is not casual but requires careful planning, methodical execution, and thorough analysis. They are not just a series of boxes to be checked off but a tool for gaining a deeper understanding of an organization's cybersecurity practices, strengths and weaknesses, and potential areas for improvement. It involves scrutiny of each aspect of the work papers and correlating it with the actual practices on the ground, identifying gaps, and suggesting improvements.

The role of regulators, however, does not stop at using FFIEC work papers for their evaluations. They also bear the responsibility of encouraging and guiding institutions to use these tools for self-assessment. The work papers can provide businesses with a clear, step-by-step roadmap for maintaining cybersecurity hygiene, identifying potential weaknesses, and fortifying cyber defenses. By promoting these work papers among companies, regulators can empower them to participate proactively in cybersecurity initiatives, transforming them from passive rule-followers to active security proponents.

Recommendations:

- **Understand Regulatory Objectives:** Begin by fully comprehending the overarching goals of cybersecurity regulations. This understanding is instrumental in aligning FFIEC work papers with regulatory objectives, allowing you to harness these tools effectively. With a clear sense of

what the regulations aim to achieve, you can focus on areas of most significant risk, driving strategic improvements in cybersecurity.

- **Use FFIEC Work Papers Strategically:** Rather than treating FFIEC work papers as a checklist, view them as tools for a deeper understanding of an organization's cybersecurity practices. This involves meticulously scrutinizing each aspect of the work papers, correlating it with the actual practices on the ground, identifying gaps, and suggesting improvements.
- **Practice Thorough Analysis:** Dedicate time and resources to analyze the results gathered from the FFIEC work papers thoroughly. Look for patterns, discrepancies, and areas of concern. This level of analysis can help highlight strengths, weaknesses, and potential areas for improvement within an organization's cybersecurity framework.
- **Promote the Use of FFIEC Work Papers:** Encourage and guide institutions to use FFIEC work papers for self-assessment. These tools can provide a clear roadmap for businesses to maintain cybersecurity hygiene, identify potential weaknesses, and fortify cyber defenses. This can transform organizations from passive rule-followers to active security proponents.
- **Foster Proactive Participation:** Use the FFIEC work papers to empower companies to participate in cybersecurity initiatives proactively. By promoting these tools and educating organizations about their use and benefits, you can encourage businesses to maintain their cyber hygiene actively, thus strengthening the overall cybersecurity ecosystem.

DEVELOPING EFFECTIVE COMMUNICATION STRATEGIES

Regulators in the cybersecurity arena are entrusted with developing and maintaining robust communication and interaction strategies with businesses. The trust built through honest, transparent, and frequent communication is the bedrock of such interaction. This trust is vital to cultivating an open environment where businesses feel comfortable sharing sensitive information regarding cybersecurity issues, risks, and incidents without the fear of reprisal. It transforms the regulatory relationship from a unidirectional enforcement mechanism into a collaborative partnership.

A critical part of the trust-building process involves engaging with industry groups and associations. Such engagement allows regulators to understand businesses' challenges in depth and provides opportunities to clarify regulatory expectations. It also helps to dispel misconceptions, promote understanding, and create an atmosphere of shared responsibility. This engagement encourages businesses to willingly adopt cybersecurity best practices and become proactive partners in securing cyberspace rather than just passive recipients of regulation.

Another crucial aspect of effective communication is establishing a common language for cybersecurity. This involves creating and promoting standardized terminologies, frameworks, and procedures that make discussions and instructions clear, unambiguous, and easy to understand. It helps to ensure that all stakeholders are on the same page, thereby minimizing confusion and fostering a more efficient implementation of regulations. Standardization also facilitates consistency in compliance, evaluation, and reporting, creating a cohesive, coherent, and efficient regulatory process that benefits regulators and businesses.

Regulators should also strive to provide constructive feedback and guidance to businesses. This feedback should be timely, clear, relevant, solution-oriented, and framed to facilitate learning and improvement. It should go beyond mere criticism to include recognition of good practices and efforts, as positive reinforcement can be a powerful motivator for businesses to improve their cybersecurity postures continually. This approach transforms the process from a punitive mechanism to continuous learning and improvement.

A fundamental aspect of developing an effective interaction strategy is understanding and considering business constraints and challenges. Regulators should acknowledge that not all businesses have the same resources, capabilities, or risk profiles and adjust their expectations accordingly. This approach requires a delicate balance – it does not mean compromising security but tailoring guidance and support to each business's needs and circumstances. It involves recognizing diversity, understanding unique challenges, and an approach that is as flexible as it is firm.

Recommendations:

- **Build Trust through Communication:** Foster trust with businesses by establishing honest, transparent, and frequent communication channels. Cultivating such trust will create an open environment where businesses feel comfortable sharing sensitive information about cybersecurity risks and incidents. This open communication can transform a regulator's role from a unilateral enforcer into a collaborative partner.

- **Engage with Industry Groups:** Regularly interact with industry groups and associations to understand businesses' challenges better and provide clarity about regulatory expectations. This engagement can dispel misconceptions, foster mutual understanding, and create an atmosphere of shared responsibility. The aim is to encourage businesses to adopt cybersecurity best practices willingly, making them active partners in cybersecurity defense rather than passive recipients of regulation.

- **Establish a Common Language:** Create and promote standardized terminologies, frameworks, and procedures to foster a common language for cybersecurity. This uniform language will make discussions and instructions unambiguous, ensuring all stakeholders are on the same page. This clarity can lead to a more efficient implementation of regulations and consistency in compliance, evaluation, and reporting, benefiting regulators and businesses.

- **Provide Constructive Feedback:** Offer timely, clear, and solution-oriented feedback to businesses. Ensure that this feedback is framed to promote learning and improvement. Going beyond criticism and recognizing good practices and efforts, positive reinforcement can motivate businesses to improve their cybersecurity postures continuously. This approach transforms the regulatory process into one of continuous learning and improvement rather than punishment.
- **Consider Business Constraints:** Understand and consider the constraints and challenges that businesses may face. Recognize that not all businesses have the same resources, capabilities, or risk profiles and adjust regulatory expectations accordingly. This approach does not imply compromising security but tailoring guidance and support to each business's unique needs and circumstances. Strive for an approach as flexible as a firm, recognizing businesses' diversity and unique challenges.

CONTINUOUS IMPROVEMENT AND ADAPTATION FOR REGULATORS

In the rapidly evolving world of cybersecurity, continuous improvement and adaptation are not mere options for regulators – they are vital necessities. Industry trends and developments are in constant flux, and staying in sync with them is crucial for effective regulation. This requires a deep understanding of the sector, which involves tracking the emergence of new technologies, understanding the shifting threat landscape, staying informed about innovations in cybersecurity practices and tools, and maintaining a finger on the pulse of the industry.

A key aspect of continuous improvement and adaptation is the regular revision and updating of regulatory guidelines. As the cybersecurity landscape changes, the regulations that govern it must adapt to reflect these changes. Regular modifications ensure that guidelines remain up-to-date, relevant, and effective in addressing the current risks and challenges. It means the regulatory environment is responsive and resilient, capable of adjusting to changes and addressing new challenges.

Maintaining security is the primary goal of regulators, but they should also encourage innovation within the business community. This delicate balancing act between innovation and security can be achieved by implementing flexible regulatory frameworks that accommodate new technologies and practices without compromising security standards. It involves nurturing an environment that promotes creative problem-solving and encourages the development of novel solutions while still upholding high-security standards.

International collaboration and standards development also offer a strategy for continuous improvement. By working closely with international counterparts, regulators can learn from diverse experiences and perspectives, contribute to developing global standards, and ensure a level playing field in cybersecurity regulations across borders. This collaborative approach brings together the best practices from around the world, contributing to improving cybersecurity regulations.

Providing training and education for regulatory staff is a critical aspect of adaptation. As cybersecurity threats and technologies evolve, so too should the knowledge and skills of the regulatory workforce. Regular training programs, workshops, and seminars can help ensure that regulatory staff are equipped to handle the challenges of the evolving cybersecurity landscape. By focusing on continuous learning, regulators can ensure that their staff remains at the cutting edge of cybersecurity, capable of effectively addressing new threats and leveraging new technologies.

Recommendations:

- **Stay Abreast of Industry Developments:** Maintain a deep understanding of the cybersecurity sector by keeping up with the latest technologies, threat landscapes, and innovations in practices and tools. This means tracking new technology emergence, understanding changes in the threat landscape, staying informed about cybersecurity practices and tool innovations, and keeping a finger on the industry's pulse.
- **Regularly Update Regulatory Guidelines:** Ensure that your regulatory guidelines stay up-to-date, relevant, and effective by revising them regularly. As the cybersecurity landscape changes, the regulations governing it should adapt to reflect these changes. This approach ensures a responsive, resilient regulatory environment that can adjust to changes and tackle new challenges.
- **Balance Innovation and Security:** Foster a delicate balance between encouraging innovation within the business community and maintaining high-security standards. Implement flexible regulatory frameworks that accommodate new technologies and practices without compromising security. This approach nurtures an environment that encourages creative problem-solving and the development of novel solutions while still upholding strict security standards.
- **Collaborate Internationally:** Work closely with international counterparts to learn from diverse experiences, contribute to global standard development, and ensure consistency in cybersecurity regulations across borders. This collaborative approach can lead to an amalgamation of the best practices from around the world, helping to improve cybersecurity regulations overall.
- **Invest in Training and Education:** Regularly train and educate your regulatory staff to ensure they can handle the evolving cybersecurity landscape's challenges. As cybersecurity threats and technologies evolve, so too should the knowledge and skills of your workforce. Continuous learning through regular training programs, workshops, and seminars can help your staff remain at the cutting edge of cybersecurity, ready to address new threats and leverage new technologies effectively.

STAYING INFORMED AND CONTINUOUSLY LEARNING AS REGULATORS

In the ever-evolving cybersecurity landscape, driven by rapid advancements in technology, shifts in threat patterns, and innovations in cybersecurity practices, regulators must remain committed to staying informed and continuously learning. This commitment to continuous learning is not just a necessity but also an acknowledgment of the complexity and multidisciplinary nature of the field. Cybersecurity is intricately intertwined with numerous other disciplines, including information technology, legal aspects, international relations, business practices, and elements of psychology and sociology. A regulator's knowledge base must be broad, up-to-date, and constantly expanding.

A vast array of resources are available for regulators to aid in this continuous learning process. Training programs, for instance, provide a structured, formalized platform to gain new knowledge and skills. Industry conferences and events offer opportunities for learning, networking, and gaining insights into the latest industry trends and developments. Regular newsletters and journals provide a steady stream of up-to-date information on relevant topics, informing regulators about the latest trends, technologies, and threats.

Online courses offer flexibility and the convenience of learning at one's own pace. They are an excellent resource for busy professionals who must balance their learning and work commitments. In addition, membership in professional associations offers several benefits, including access to exclusive resources, opportunities for networking with industry peers, and avenues for contributing to the profession.

Networking and collaborating with peers and industry experts is another essential part of staying informed and continuously learning. These interactions provide opportunities to learn from other's experiences and perspectives, gain insights into best practices, and stay abreast of emerging trends and issues. It opens up opportunities for collaborative problem-solving, knowledge-sharing, and mutual learning.

Finally, regulators can benefit immensely from leveraging research from organizations such as the OCC, FFIEC, Federal Reserve, and FDIC. These institutions conduct extensive research and produce valuable insights that can help regulators understand the changing cybersecurity landscape, anticipate emerging threats, and develop effective regulatory strategies. The rich information contained in these resources can inform and guide regulators in their ongoing efforts to maintain and enhance cyberspace security.

Recommendations:

- **Leverage Training Programs and Industry Events:** Participate in training programs to gain new knowledge and skills in a structured and formalized manner. Industry conferences and events also offer a platform for learning, networking, and gaining insights into industry trends and developments. These opportunities allow for staying informed about the rapid advancements in the cybersecurity field.

- **Regularly Review Newsletters and Journals:** Stay up-to-date with the latest trends, technologies, and threats by regularly reading relevant newsletters and journals. They provide a steady stream of current information on relevant topics in the cybersecurity industry. This continual stream of knowledge will ensure your understanding of the field remains relevant and comprehensive.

- **Use Online Courses and Professional Associations:** Online courses offer flexibility and convenience for busy professionals, allowing you to learn at your own pace. Moreover, becoming a member of professional associations offers access to exclusive resources, networking opportunities with industry peers, and avenues for contributing to the profession. These resources are excellent for balancing work commitments and continuous learning.

- **Network and Collaborate:** Connect with peers and industry experts to stay informed and continuously learn. Interactions with these individuals can provide opportunities to learn from their experiences and perspectives, gain insights into best practices, and stay abreast of emerging trends and issues. This collaborative approach fosters mutual learning and problem-solving and promotes knowledge-sharing.

- **Leverage Research from Reputable Organizations:** Use research findings from organizations like the OCC, FFIEC, Federal Reserve, and FDIC. These institutions conduct extensive research that provides valuable insights into the changing cybersecurity landscape, emerging threats, and effective regulatory strategies. The rich information from these sources can inform and guide regulators in their ongoing efforts to maintain and enhance cyberspace security.

PROVIDING SUPPORT AND GUIDANCE TO THE BUSINESS

Within the multifaceted cybersecurity domain, regulators carry a substantial responsibility, which extends beyond enforcing compliance to support and guide the various businesses within their purview. This support, which is often customized to the particular needs of individual organizations, recognizes the variability between companies in size, available resources, and risk profiles and comprehends that these differences necessitate divergent strategies and solutions to meet their unique requirements.

Regulators lead the charge in encouraging the adoption of cybersecurity best practices, representing one of the principal means through which they offer guidance. By promoting practices that have been tested and found reliable, regulators provide businesses with the tools they need to construct robust and resilient cybersecurity programs. These programs, in turn, safeguard not only the companies' assets but also contribute to the protection of the broader cyberspace, a shared resource upon which all participants in the digital world rely.

A significant segment of regulators' responsibilities is their support to small and medium-sized institutions. Unlike their larger counterparts, these institutions often do not have access to the same depth of resources and might find it a daunting task to satisfy regulatory requirements and effectively manage cybersecurity risks. To help these smaller institutions, regulators can offer guidance tailored to their unique needs, supply them with relevant resources, and offer training that meets their particular circumstances. Additionally, regulators can champion the adoption of cybersecurity solutions that are both accessible and affordable, further aiding these institutions in overcoming the barriers they face.

Another crucial aspect of the support offered by regulators is the monitoring and providing feedback on the cybersecurity programs businesses implement. Regular monitoring conducted by regulators allows for the early identification of potential issues, enabling them to provide timely advice and recommendations. This allows companies to make necessary modifications before problems can escalate. Constructive feedback, on the other hand, assists businesses in comprehending their strengths and weaknesses, paving the way for targeted improvement.

The role of regulators also includes collaborating with institutions to bolster the cybersecurity ecosystem as a whole. Such collaboration can assume various forms, from joint initiatives and information sharing to cooperative research. This engagement contributes to developing a more robust, more resilient cybersecurity ecosystem that benefits all its participants.

Recommendations:

- **Encourage the Adoption of Cybersecurity Best Practices:** As a regulator, your role includes promoting and guiding businesses in adopting cybersecurity best practices. These are practices that have been tested and proven effective. By encouraging these practices, you are providing companies with tools to build robust and resilient cybersecurity programs that protect their assets and contribute to the security of the broader digital ecosystem.

- **Support Small and Medium-Sized Institutions:** Given their limited resources, small and medium-sized businesses often struggle to satisfy regulatory requirements and manage cybersecurity risks effectively. Tailor your guidance to their specific needs and circumstances, provide them with relevant resources, offer targeted training, and promote the adoption of affordable cybersecurity solutions. Your support can help these businesses overcome challenges and enhance their cybersecurity posture.

- **Monitor and Provide Feedback:** Regularly monitor the cybersecurity programs of the businesses under your purview and provide constructive feedback. This approach allows for the early detection of potential issues and enables you to give timely advice and recommendations for improvement. Feedback can also help businesses understand their strengths and weaknesses and chart a path for targeted improvement.

- **Collaborate to Strengthen the Cybersecurity Ecosystem:** Partner with institutions to enhance the resilience of the overall cybersecurity ecosystem. This could involve joint initiatives, information sharing, or cooperative research. Such collaboration fosters shared responsibility for cybersecurity, develops mutual trust, and results in a stronger, more resilient cybersecurity environment that benefits all stakeholders.

- **Champion the Use of Accessible and Affordable Solutions:** The cost of implementing cybersecurity measures can be a major obstacle, especially for smaller institutions. Advocate for adopting accessible and affordable cybersecurity solutions that cater to businesses of all sizes. By making cybersecurity more accessible, you are ensuring that all businesses, regardless of size or resources, can effectively manage their cybersecurity risks and contribute to the overall health of the cyber ecosystem.

CHALLENGES FACED BY REGULATORS AND HOW TO OVERCOME THEM

Regulators frequently confront many challenges when navigating the often complex and rapidly evolving environment of cybersecurity regulation. One such challenge is the delicate balancing act of ensuring security while fostering innovation. Regulators ensure that the businesses they oversee maintain a robust cybersecurity posture. Simultaneously, they must avoid stifling the innovative efforts driving the industry forward. Striking the right balance between encouraging technological advances, which often present new opportunities for growth and competitiveness, and ensuring these advancements do not inadvertently introduce unacceptable levels of risk is no easy task.

Another common challenge faced by regulators is the efficient management of limited resources. Regulators often find their resources stretched thin because of the broad scope of regulatory work, the increasing sophistication of cyber threats, and the constantly evolving cyber landscape. To overcome this challenge, they must focus on efficient resource management, prioritizing critical areas, and leveraging technology to automate processes and increase efficiency wherever possible. This not only helps them manage their resources better but also enables them to respond more swiftly and effectively to emerging threats.

Adapting to the rapid pace of technological changes presents a recurring challenge for regulators. With the exponential rate of technological advancement in the digital era, new vulnerabilities, risks, and threat vectors are constantly emerging. This necessitates regulators to engage in regular training, continuous learning, and staying abreast of industry trends to tackle these challenges effectively. Maintaining a dynamic approach, wherein they constantly learn and adapt to the shifting landscape, becomes a key characteristic of successful regulators.

Conflicting regulatory requirements pose another significant challenge for regulators. Given the presence of various regulators and standards bodies across different countries and regions, businesses often find themselves navigating through a patchwork of regulations. Addressing this challenge, regulators can work toward harmonizing standards and promoting international cooperation. This approach helps minimize conflicts, makes compliance less burdensome for businesses, and ensures a more consistent and effective global response to cybersecurity threats.

Finally, keeping up with the continuously evolving threat landscape remains a constant challenge for regulators. Cyber threats continue to multiply and grow in complexity, sophistication, and potential impact, necessitating regulators to remain vigilant and proactive in managing these threats. Staying one step ahead of the threat landscape requires a deep understanding of the current cyber risks, forecasting future trends, and deploying strategies to mitigate these risks effectively.

Recommendations:

- **Balancing Security and Innovation:** Regulators must skillfully walk a tightrope of fostering innovation while ensuring robust cybersecurity. They must promote technological advancements that bring new growth opportunities and competitive advantages without introducing unacceptable levels of risk. Striking this balance requires thoughtful policymaking, flexibility, and an open dialogue with industry stakeholders.

- **Efficient Resource Management:** With a broad scope of regulatory work, sophisticated cyber threats, and a constantly evolving landscape, regulators often operate with limited resources. Efficient resource management is essential to overcome this challenge. This might involve prioritizing crucial areas, leveraging technology to automate processes, and optimizing workflows to respond swiftly and effectively to emerging threats.

- **Keeping Pace with Rapid Technological Changes:** The exponential rate of technological advancements presents an ongoing challenge for regulators. New vulnerabilities, risks, and threat vectors emerge constantly, necessitating a dynamic approach to regulation. Regulators must invest in regular training, continuous learning, and keeping up-to-date with industry trends to manage these challenges effectively.

- **Harmonizing Conflicting Regulatory Requirements:** Businesses often navigate a patchwork of regulations issued by different regulators and standards bodies across various regions. Regulators can strive to harmonize standards and promote international cooperation to mitigate this challenge. This makes compliance less burdensome for businesses and fosters a consistent global response to cybersecurity threats.

- **Staying Ahead of the Evolving Threat Landscape:** As cyber threats continue to increase in number, complexity, and potential impact, staying ahead of the threat landscape is a constant challenge for regulators. A deep understanding of current cyber risks, the ability to forecast future trends, and the development of effective risk mitigation strategies are all critical to managing these threats effectively.

REGULATORY EXCELLENCE AND FORWARD-LOOKING LEADERSHIP

In an interconnected world that grows more integrated daily, regulators are indispensable in safeguarding our digital landscape's safety and security. Achieving this requires regulatory excellence and forward-thinking leadership. When we speak of regulatory excellence, we refer to the pursuit of best practices, the commitment to maintaining a comprehensive understanding of the cyber landscape, and cultivating a culture centered around continuous improvement and innovation.

Fostering thought leadership within the regulatory community is an integral facet of forward-looking leadership. Thought leadership involves introducing and nurturing new ideas, challenging the status quo, and driving changes that will ultimately shape the future of cybersecurity regulation. It means being bold and creative, willing to think outside the box, and not shying away from challenging existing norms if they no longer serve the best interests of cybersecurity.

Recognizing and nurturing talent is another crucial element in pursuing regulatory excellence. The regulatory field requires individuals with deep knowledge, sharp analytical skills, and the ability to navigate the complex and dynamic field of cybersecurity. Regulators should prioritize talent development by providing continuous learning and professional growth opportunities. They should also strive to create an inclusive and supportive work environment that attracts and retains top talent, thus ensuring that the best minds are working on the most pressing cybersecurity issues.

Integrating technology to enhance regulatory effectiveness is another critical component of regulatory excellence. Advanced analytics, automation, and other innovative tools have the potential to significantly streamline regulatory processes, improve accuracy, and free up valuable human resources for strategic tasks that require human intervention. Embracing these technologies enhances the efficiency and effectiveness of regulatory activities and demonstrates the regulators' commitment to innovation and progress.

Lastly, striving for transparency and accountability in all regulatory activities is crucial. Transparency fosters trust and cooperation from regulated industries, allowing them to understand the regulatory processes and decision-making rationales. Accountability, on the other hand, ensures that regulators are answerable for their actions and decisions. Together, these two elements create a regulatory environment where all stakeholders can work together toward a common goal: enhancing the security of our digital landscape.

Recommendations:

- **Strive for Regulatory Excellence and Champion Thought Leadership:** Regulators are key in ensuring the safety and security of the digital landscape, which requires a commitment to best practices, comprehensive understanding, and a culture of continuous improvement. Thought leadership within the regulatory community is fundamental to this, encouraging the introduction and nurturing of innovative ideas, challenging the status quo, and driving changes that will shape the future of cybersecurity regulation.

- **Recognize and Nurture Talent:** Pursuing regulatory excellence involves identifying and nurturing talent in the field. Regulators should prioritize talent development, providing continuous learning opportunities and fostering professional growth. By creating an inclusive and supportive work environment, regulators can attract and retain top talent, ensuring that the most knowledgeable minds are tackling pressing cybersecurity issues.

- **Integrate Technology:** Integrating technology to enhance regulatory effectiveness is key to achieving regulatory excellence. Advanced analytics, automation, and other innovative tools can streamline regulatory processes, improve accuracy, and allow valuable human resources to focus on strategic tasks. By embracing these technologies, regulators demonstrate their commitment to innovation and progress.

- **Foster Transparency and Ensure Accountability:** Striving for transparency in all regulatory activities fosters trust and cooperation from the regulated industries, allowing them to understand regulatory processes and the rationale behind decisions. Accountability ensures that regulators are answerable for their actions and decisions. Together, these elements foster a collaborative environment where all stakeholders work toward a common goal of enhancing the security of the digital landscape.

BECOMING A REGULATOR: SELECTION, EDUCATION, AND CAREER PATHS

Embarking on a career as a regulator in cybersecurity presents an exciting and challenging opportunity to make a tangible impact on the future of digital security. Understanding the multifaceted role of a regulator is an essential first step on this journey. Regulators play a pivotal role in the financial industry and broader markets. They are responsible for overseeing compliance with rules and standards, maintaining a comprehensive understanding of the industry's inner workings, and identifying and addressing potential risks and vulnerabilities. They also serve as a vital link between the industry and the broader public, ensuring that the industry operates in a manner that is safe, fair, and conducive to overall economic stability.

The educational background and skill sets required for a regulator are specific and varied. The recommended educational backgrounds usually include degrees in Computer Science, Information Systems, Cybersecurity, or related disciplines. These fields provide a strong foundation in the technical aspects of cybersecurity. Essential skill sets for aspiring regulators include strong analytical skills to dissect and understand complex cybersecurity issues, problem-solving abilities to develop and implement effective solutions, excellent communication skills to liaise with different stakeholders effectively, and a deep understanding of cybersecurity principles and practices. Additionally, regulators must be committed to lifelong learning, as ongoing education and professional certifications are key to keeping up with the ever-evolving cybersecurity landscape.

The selection process for regulators can be pretty rigorous, often involving multiple stages and tests. Candidates should be prepared to understand the hiring process, prepare for interviews and assessments, and gain insights into what regulatory bodies look for in potential hires. Many regulatory bodies seek individuals who demonstrate deep knowledge in their chosen field, a strong desire to learn and improve, and the ability to adapt to changing circumstances, all of which are crucial qualities in cybersecurity.

Building a successful career as a regulator typically involves starting with entry-level positions and responsibilities and gradually progressing to roles with greater responsibility and influence. Navigating this career progression can be complex and requires strategic planning, guidance, and mentorship. Networking with professionals in the field, seeking mentorship from experienced regulators, considering long-term career goals, and taking advantage of opportunities for professional growth can all play vital roles in successful career progression. With perseverance and dedication, individuals can rise to influential roles within regulatory bodies, making meaningful contributions to cybersecurity.

Recommendations:

- **Understand the Complex Role of a Regulator:** Starting a career as a regulator in cybersecurity entails understanding the multifaceted role, which involves overseeing compliance with standards, understanding industry workings, and identifying risks and vulnerabilities. Regulators are a vital link between the industry and the public, ensuring that operations are safe, fair, and conducive to economic stability.

- **Acquire the Necessary Educational Background and Skills:** Recommended educational backgrounds for regulators include degrees in Computer Science, Information Systems, Cybersecurity, or related disciplines. Essential skills include strong analytical skills, problem-solving abilities, excellent communication skills, and a deep understanding of cybersecurity principles. Lifelong learning commitment, continued education, and professional certifications are crucial to keep up with the ever-evolving cybersecurity landscape.

- **Navigate the Selection Process Effectively:** The selection process for regulators can be rigorous, involving multiple stages and tests. Candidates need to understand the hiring process, prepare for interviews and assessments, and gain insights into what regulatory bodies look for in potential hires. They seek individuals demonstrating deep knowledge and a strong desire to learn, improve, and adapt to changing circumstances.
- **Strategize for Successful Career Progression:** Building a successful career as a regulator involves starting with entry-level positions and gradually progressing to roles with more responsibility and influence. Navigating this progression requires strategic planning, guidance, mentorship, networking with professionals, seeking mentorship from experienced regulators, considering long-term career goals, and taking advantage of growth opportunities. With perseverance and dedication, individuals can rise to influential roles within regulatory bodies, making meaningful contributions to cybersecurity.

BALANCING OBJECTIVITY AND ADVOCACY

The position of a regulator within the cybersecurity landscape is intricate and multifaceted, necessitating a subtle equilibrium between ensuring impartiality and championing efficacious regulatory strategies. Impartiality, characterized as making judgments and implementing actions that are just, nonpartisan, and grounded in factual data, is vital to the trustworthiness and efficiency of a regulator's function. This impartiality guarantees that every entity engaged in the regulatory process receives fair and equal treatment, fostering trust and integrity in the regulatory framework.

Conversely, advocacy is concerned with advancing efficient regulatory practices and standards. Regulators often advocate for policy changes when current practices no longer adequately address the cybersecurity landscape's evolving needs. This necessitates convincing communication, logical argumentation, and the capacity to use potent arguments favoring the suggested practices or modifications. Advocacy extends beyond merely enhancing the regulatory environment; it also ensures that the regulated sectors comprehend the reasoning and advantages of these practices, thereby nurturing a culture of adherence and collaboration.

Striking a balance between these two elements, impartiality and advocacy, is a critical component of a regulator's responsibilities. Central to maintaining this equilibrium is establishing trust with regulated industries. It is incumbent upon regulators to foster cooperative relationships with these sectors, relationships grounded in reciprocal respect and comprehension. By adhering to principles of impartiality in their decisions and actions while simultaneously championing efficacious practices, regulators can cultivate the industries' trust they supervise. This trust provides the basis for collaborative and constructive interaction, laying the groundwork for a secure and resilient cybersecurity environment that mutually benefits all participants.

The profession of a regulator is a labyrinthine and challenging one, demanding a nuanced interplay between upholding impartiality and promoting effective regulatory methodologies. Impartiality, identified as the process of delivering decisions and executing actions that are equitable, devoid of bias, and reliant on factual substantiation, is integral to the legitimacy and effectiveness of a regulator's role. It ensures that all stakeholders in the regulatory procedure are accorded fair and equal treatment, engendering trust and reliability in the regulatory infrastructure.

In contrast, advocacy refers to promoting robust regulatory practices and tenets. Regulators are often called upon to advocate for alterations when prevailing procedures no longer align with the evolving requirements of cybersecurity. This calls for effective communication, logical deduction, and the capacity to form compelling arguments supporting the proposed practices or alterations. Advocacy does more than refine the regulatory environment; it also guarantees that the regulated industries grasp the reasoning behind and benefits of these practices, thereby fostering a compliance-oriented and collaborative culture.

Maintaining a balance between these principles, impartiality and advocacy, constitutes a crucial aspect of a regulator's function. Building trust with regulated industries is a key part of maintaining this balance. Regulators must develop collaborative ties with these industries, connections based on mutual esteem and comprehension. By keeping the principles of impartiality in their decisions and actions and advocating for robust practices, regulators can secure the trust of the industries they monitor. This trust underpins a cooperative and productive rapport, establishing a secure and resilient cybersecurity environment that benefits all involved parties.

Recommendations:

- **Understand the Complexity of the Regulatory Role:** The role of a regulator in the cybersecurity landscape is intricate, necessitating a careful balance between maintaining impartiality and promoting effective regulatory strategies. Impartiality is vital for ensuring fairness and trust in the regulatory framework, while advocacy is necessary for pushing forward efficient practices that align with evolving cybersecurity needs.

- **Uphold the Principle of Impartiality:** Impartiality is characterized by making judgments and actions that are just, nonpartisan, and based on factual data. It ensures that all entities involved in the regulatory process receive fair and equal treatment, thereby fostering trust and integrity in the regulatory framework.

- **Be an Effective Advocate for Robust Practices:** Advocacy involves promoting robust regulatory practices and standards. Regulators often advocate for policy changes when current practices no longer meet the evolving needs of the cybersecurity landscape. Effective communication, logical argumentation, and strong persuasive skills are necessary for this role. Advocacy ensures that the regulated sectors understand the reasoning and benefits of these practices, fostering a culture of compliance and collaboration.

- **Strike a Balance Between Impartiality and Advocacy:** A balance between impartiality and advocacy is critical to a regulator's responsibilities. Regulators must establish trust with regulated industries by adhering to principles of impartiality in their decisions and actions while championing effective practices.

- **Foster Trust and Collaboration with Industry:** Building trust with regulated industries is central to balancing impartiality and advocacy. Regulators must foster cooperative relationships grounded in mutual respect and understanding. This trust forms the basis for productive interaction, paving the way for a secure and resilient cybersecurity environment that benefits all participants.

- **Adapt and Evolve as a Regulator:** The role of a regulator is complex and demanding, requiring a nuanced interplay between upholding impartiality and promoting effective regulatory methodologies. It is about more than just refining the regulatory environment; it is about ensuring industries understand the rationale behind and benefits of regulatory practices, fostering a compliance-oriented and collaborative culture, and ultimately creating a resilient cybersecurity environment.

Chapter Conclusion

The role of regulators within cybersecurity is progressively adapting to match the evolving landscape of threats and vulnerabilities that continue to test today's industries. The role of a regulator demands an unwavering commitment, robust collaboration, continuous education, and a readiness to adapt. These professionals are responsible for upholding the integrity of digital systems and infrastructure by enforcing stringent standards, guidelines, and best practices.

Nonetheless, the role of a regulator extends far beyond mere enforcement. It also necessitates a deep understanding and empathy to balance the urgent need for high-level security with the real-world business realities confronted by the industries they oversee. It encompasses building trust, encouraging open communication channels, and fostering an environment of mutual respect.

The rapidly changing landscape of cybersecurity dictates that regulators must dedicate themselves to ongoing learning, staying updated with industry trends, and continuously adapting to the advent of new technologies and the emergence of novel risks. They are central in assuring a secure and resilient cyberspace through effective regulation.

In its very essence, a regulator's challenge is fundamentally a leadership challenge. By exemplifying forward-thinking, transparent, and accountable leadership, regulators can ensure that they are not merely enforcing compliance but actively shaping a future where security and technological innovation can coexist seamlessly.

In the same vein, the role of regulators within the cybersecurity landscape is subject to continuous evolution to match the expanding panorama of threats and vulnerabilities that persistently challenge today's industries. This crucial role demands a deep-seated commitment, effective collaboration, lifelong learning, and a capacity to adapt to a dynamic environment. The primary duty of these professionals is to safeguard the integrity of digital ecosystems and infrastructure by enforcing regulatory standards, guidelines, and tried-and-true practices.

However, the function of a regulator transcends the mere act of enforcement. It also necessitates a profound understanding and empathy to balance the pressing demands for comprehensive security and the pragmatic business challenges faced by the industries they regulate. The role involves the cultivation of trust, the facilitation of open dialogue, and the nurturing of mutual respect.

Given the dynamic nature of cybersecurity, regulators must exhibit a steadfast commitment to lifelong learning, keeping abreast of industry trends, and being flexible in adapting to the introduction of new technologies and the rise of novel risks. They are critical to ensure a secure and resilient cyberspace via effective regulation.

In its fundamental core, the regulator's challenge is one of leadership. By embodying progressive, transparent, and accountable leadership styles, regulators can ensure their role is not limited to enforcing compliance but extends to helping shape a future wherein security and innovation can harmoniously coexist.

Case Study: Zephyr Tech

Harold is the Chief Security Officer at Zephyr Tech, a burgeoning tech company, and he has just received a comprehensive review from their industry regulator. With an extensive background in cybersecurity, he understands the critical importance of regulatory compliance and its role in ensuring a secure and resilient digital infrastructure.

However, like many other fast-growing tech companies, Zephyr Tech finds itself balancing driving rapid innovation and ensuring robust cybersecurity. Harold understands that the regulator's role is not just enforcing rules but helping businesses like Zephyr Tech navigate this complex landscape.

Working closely with the regulator, Harold initiates a series of discussions and workshops within Zephyr Tech. The goal is to foster a culture of mutual understanding and respect between the regulator and the company, thus promoting a more cooperative relationship. Open communication channels are established, facilitating more effective feedback and shared learning.

Harold ensures that all the teams within Zephyr Tech are dedicated to continuous learning. He encourages them to stay updated on the latest industry trends and adapt their strategies and technologies in response to emerging risks. They create an efficient, adaptable cybersecurity framework with the regulator's guidance.

Embodying forward-thinking leadership, Harold promotes transparency and accountability within Zephyr Tech. He demonstrates that effective compliance is not just about adhering to rules and shaping a future where innovation and security coexist harmoniously.

This approach culminates in a significant improvement in Zephyr Tech's cybersecurity posture. They drive innovation without compromising security, ensuring their systems remain resilient despite emerging threats. Harold successfully navigates the complex landscape of cybersecurity regulation by embracing the regulator's role as a guide and supporter rather than just an enforcer.

The lessons from this case study are numerous: the importance of understanding and empathy in regulatory relationships, continuous learning and adaptability, and the critical role of forward-thinking leadership in achieving effective compliance. These lessons are invaluable in a world where security and innovation are increasingly intertwined.

CHAPTER 21

Understanding US Regulatory Bodies

"Just as traffic rules maintain order on the roads, cyber regulations establish order in the digital domain, fostering a secure and harmonious digital ecosystem."

It is important to understand the roles and mandates of key US regulatory bodies in the cybersecurity sector. Whether you are a cybersecurity professional, financial institution, or an individual interested in understanding the US regulatory framework for cybersecurity, you will need insights into the Federal Financial Institutions Examination Council (FFIEC), the Office of the Comptroller of the Currency (OCC), the Board of Governors of the Federal Reserve System (Fed), the Federal Deposit Insurance Corporation (FDIC), the Consumer Financial Protection Bureau (CFPB), the Securities and Exchange Commission (SEC), the Financial Industry Regulatory Authority (FINRA), and the National Credit Union Administration (NCUA).

FEDERAL FINANCIAL INSTITUTIONS EXAMINATION COUNCIL (FFIEC)

The FFIEC is a government interagency body that sets the tone for cybersecurity within financial institutions across the United States. The council was created in 1979 to promote uniformity and consistency in the supervision of financial institutions. The FFIEC is pivotal to formulating and establishing principles and standards for examining these institutions. It is crucial for any cybersecurity professional working within a financial institution to have a comprehensive understanding of the FFIEC's function and role.

The FFIEC has a significant role in cybersecurity for financial institutions. Its responsibilities span establishing necessary standards and guidelines for institutions to follow, ensuring the security of customer data, and maintaining the integrity of the information systems of these institutions. The FFIEC aims to protect consumers, maintain confidence in the financial system, and promote stability through its regulatory practices. It has developed a range of tools and resources to aid institutions in identifying their risks and determining their cybersecurity preparedness.

The guidelines and standards issued by the FFIEC play an instrumental role in shaping the cybersecurity landscape within financial institutions. One such critical resource is the FFIEC's Cybersecurity Assessment Tool (CAT), designed to help institutions identify their risk profile and determine the maturity of their cybersecurity practices. The CAT is meant to provide a repeatable and measurable process for financial institutions to measure their cybersecurity preparedness over time.

Another critical resource provided by the FFIEC is the Information Technology Examination Handbook. This handbook comprehensively guides IT-related risks and risk management practices within financial institutions. It covers various topics, including IT governance, information security, operations, and outsourcing. The handbook offers a wealth of information and insight into best practices for managing and mitigating IT-related risks in the financial sector.

As a cybersecurity professional, interaction with the FFIEC can range from ensuring that the institution complies with the FFIEC's guidelines and standards to responding to audits or evaluations conducted by the council. Regular interaction with the FFIEC is necessary to stay abreast of updates to guidelines, standards, or regulations that could impact the institution's cybersecurity policies and practices.

Professionals should also proactively engage with the FFIEC through participation in working groups or committees, attendance at industry events where the FFIEC is present, or direct communication with the FFIEC itself. This proactive engagement can help professionals stay ahead of changes, learn from peers, and ensure their institution is adequately prepared to respond to evolving cybersecurity threats.

Recommendations:

- **Deep Dive into FFIEC's Role:** Invest time in understanding the full spectrum of FFIEC's role in financial institutions' cybersecurity. This includes understanding its mission, responsibilities, and how it impacts your organization's cybersecurity policies and procedures.
- **Utilize the FFIEC's Tools:** Make optimum use of the resources provided by the FFIEC, such as the CAT and the Information Technology Examination Handbook. These resources are designed to help organizations assess and enhance their cybersecurity preparedness.
- **Foster Communication with FFIEC:** Maintain open lines of communication with the FFIEC. Regular interaction is beneficial, whether it is to discuss compliance concerns, seek clarification on guidelines or standards, or prepare for audits.

- **Include FFIEC's Guidelines in Training Programs:** Ensure that all staff within the organization are familiar with the FFIEC's guidelines and standards. Incorporate them into training programs to ensure everyone understands their significance and knows how to apply them in their work.
- **Carry out Regular Audits:** Conduct regular internal audits to ensure FFIEC guidelines and standards compliance. These audits will help identify potential issues or areas of noncompliance, enabling the organization to address them before they escalate or result in penalties.

OFFICE OF THE COMPTROLLER OF THE CURRENCY (OCC)

The OCC, a central entity in the regulatory framework of financial cybersecurity, is an independent bureau within the US Department of the Treasury. With a mandate that covers the chartering, regulation, and supervision of all national banks, federal savings associations, federal branches, and foreign bank agencies, the OCC is a significant pillar of the American financial system's integrity and security.

As part of its mandate, the OCC assumes a powerful role in enforcing compliance with the laws and regulations governing these institutions. This role is essential to the OCC's mission of ensuring these institutions operate safely and soundly. The enforcement powers of the OCC include the ability to examine the banks, issue rules and regulations, take enforcement actions against banks that do not comply with laws or regulations, or refer matters to other law enforcement agencies. An essential aspect of this enforcement power is that the OCC can mandate corrective action if a bank has engaged in unsafe or unsound practices, which could include serious cybersecurity shortcomings.

The OCC's enforcement mandate is focused on maintaining financial stability and soundness but also extends to providing fair access to financial services, fair treatment of customers, and adherence to all relevant laws and regulations. This includes regulations explicitly related to cybersecurity, reflecting the increasing importance of digital security in the contemporary financial landscape.

Considering the highly sensitive nature of the data managed by the institutions it supervises, the OCC places an extraordinary emphasis on cybersecurity. It does so by providing a variety of guidelines, recommendations, and resources designed to assist these institutions in developing and maintaining robust cybersecurity frameworks. Notable among these is the OCC's Bulletin 2013–2029. This Bulletin provides detailed guidance on risk management of third-party relationships, a pivotal aspect of any comprehensive cybersecurity strategy given the interconnected nature of digital business operations and the potential vulnerabilities this can expose.

Furthermore, the OCC also addresses cybersecurity through its Threat and Vulnerability Management program, which assists financial institutions in identifying, assessing, mitigating, and monitoring risks associated with cyber threats. It also offers training resources for financial institutions to understand better evolving cyber threats and how to address them. The OCC's semiannual Risk Perspective report highlights cybersecurity as a significant risk, outlining trends and offering risk-mitigation measures.

Interactions with the OCC necessitate a commitment to regular reporting, open communication, and adherence to the organization's standards and guidelines. The OCC expects the banks to maintain an active cybersecurity risk management framework and promptly disclose any significant cybersecurity incident. They also encourage a risk-based approach, where banks spend more time and resources managing higher-risk areas like cybersecurity.

Moreover, the supervised banks are also subject to regular examinations by the OCC to assess their risk management systems' effectiveness and ensure compliance with these standards. The examination process includes evaluating the quality of the institution's cybersecurity risk governance, risk management processes, network security, and controls over IT systems. Failure to meet these standards can result in enforcement actions, ranging from fines to operational restrictions, underscoring the gravity of OCC's enforcement power in cybersecurity.

In essence, the role of the OCC in governing, regulating, and supervising financial institutions carries significant implications for cybersecurity. It is a testament to the increasingly central role of digital security in the broader regulatory landscape. The organization's guidelines, enforcement powers, and resources collectively strengthen the financial sector's cybersecurity posture and contribute to the overall resilience and integrity of the financial system.

Recommendations:

- **Understand the OCC's Role:** Invest time in comprehending the OCC's function and its impact on your organization's cybersecurity policies and procedures.
- **Familiarize with OCC's Guidelines:** Thoroughly understand the guidelines, bulletins, and advisories issued by the OCC on cybersecurity. Incorporate these guidelines into your organization's cybersecurity policies.
- **Regular Reporting and Communication:** Maintain open lines of communication with the OCC. Regularly report relevant information and developments as required.
- **Prepare for OCC's Examinations:** Develop a solid plan for the OCC's examinations. Regularly review and update your organization's risk management systems to ensure they align with the OCC's expectations.
- **Continuous Learning:** Stay informed about new advisories or bulletins issued by the OCC. Make learning about these updates a part of your continuous professional development.

BOARD OF GOVERNORS OF THE FEDERAL RESERVE SYSTEM

The Board of Governors of the Federal Reserve System, also known as the Federal Reserve Board, plays a significant role in the governance of US financial institutions. As the governing body of the Federal Reserve System, the central banking system of the United States, it guides national monetary policy. It oversees the operation of the Federal Reserve Banks, ensuring stability and integrity in the financial and banking sectors.

In cybersecurity, the Federal Reserve Board's influence is substantial. They enforce laws and regulations related to the security of financial transactions, data protection, and the overall operational resilience of financial institutions. Furthermore, the Federal Reserve Board works closely with other financial regulatory bodies to develop and implement regulatory standards to enhance the cybersecurity posture of the institutions under their supervision.

One such collaborative effort is the development of the FFIEC's CAT, which we discussed earlier. Another example is the participation of the Federal Reserve in the Financial and Banking Information Infrastructure Committee (FBIIC), which coordinates efforts among financial regulators to improve the reliability and security of the financial sector infrastructure. These collaborations underscore the Federal Reserve Board's commitment to improving the financial sector's cybersecurity landscape.

For cybersecurity professionals working in the financial sector, understanding the Federal Reserve Board's role and guidelines can significantly enhance their ability to ensure their organizations' compliance with applicable regulations. This understanding also helps organizations navigate the complexity of the regulatory environment and successfully address the challenges posed by the evolving threat landscape.

Interacting with the Federal Reserve System involves regular communication regarding the organization's compliance with the regulations, guidelines, and standards set by the Federal Reserve Board. This interaction may include participating in audits and inspections conducted by the Federal Reserve, responding to inquiries about the organization's cybersecurity practices, and reporting on its risk management processes and their effectiveness.

Moreover, financial institutions should proactively engage with the Federal Reserve Board through various channels. These could include participation in conferences, workshops, or training programs organized by the Federal Reserve or other regulatory bodies. Such proactive engagement can provide insights into evolving regulatory expectations and emerging cybersecurity trends and strategies, aiding in better preparation and response.

Recommendations:

- **Understand the Regulatory Landscape:** Invest time to comprehend the guidelines, standards, and regulations set by the Federal Reserve Board. Understand how these regulatory requirements impact your organization's cybersecurity policies and procedures.
- **Regular Communication:** Keep a consistent line of communication with the Federal Reserve Board. Regularly update them about your organization's compliance status and any developments that could impact your cybersecurity posture.

- **Be Prepared for Audits:** Conduct internal audits regularly to ensure your organization's cybersecurity practices align with the Federal Reserve Board's expectations. Take corrective measures promptly when discrepancies are identified.
- **Proactive Engagement:** Participate in events organized by the Federal Reserve Board or other regulatory bodies. Such proactive engagement can provide insights into emerging cybersecurity trends and expectations.
- **Foster a Culture of Compliance:** Promote a culture of compliance within your organization. Ensure that everyone understands the importance of adherence to the guidelines and regulations set by the Federal Reserve Board.

FEDERAL DEPOSIT INSURANCE CORPORATION (FDIC)

The FDIC is an independent agency of the US government, created by the Glass–Steagall Act of 1933 in response to bank failures during the Great Depression. The FDIC's primary mission is to maintain stability and public confidence in the nation's financial system. This is accomplished by providing deposit insurance, supervising insured financial institutions for safety and soundness, and resolving failed banks as needed.

An integral part of its supervisory duties, the FDIC diligently monitors the operations of FDIC-insured institutions. The goal is to ensure these financial institutions maintain the safety and soundness necessary to foster trust in the financial system. Over the years, with digital transformation permeating all corners of the banking industry, the FDIC has expanded its role to tackle cybersecurity issues threatening the financial system's stability.

In recent years, the FDIC has played a substantial role in addressing cybersecurity risks by introducing a cybersecurity framework to protect consumers and the integrity of financial systems. Recognizing that cybersecurity issues threaten the financial sector's stability, the FDIC promotes and enforces stringent cybersecurity standards. The agency guides banks in establishing robust cybersecurity frameworks, bolstering the financial sector's resilience against cyber threats.

To ensure that FDIC-insured institutions have the necessary policies and procedures to mitigate cyber threats, the FDIC offers various risk management manuals and guidelines. For example, the FDIC's Risk Management Manual of Examination Policies is a comprehensive document providing banks with exhaustive guidelines. These include cybersecurity risk assessment and management, information security, incident response, vendor management, and more.

Cybersecurity risk management is an overarching theme in the FDIC's supervisory process, as it plays a significant role in ensuring the safety and soundness of financial institutions. One tool at the FDIC's disposal to promote sound cybersecurity practices among banks is the IT Risk Examination (InTREx) Program. FDIC examiners use the InTREx Program as part of their examinations to assess the institution's risk management and the adequacy of its information technology and cybersecurity controls. These examinations are not just cursory checks; they are thorough, probing analyses of the bank's cyber risk management strategies, and any deficiencies identified during the process must be rectified promptly.

The examination process by the FDIC is a critical part of its supervisory role. FDIC examiners conduct routine IT examinations to assess the institution's risk management measures and the adequacy of its IT and cybersecurity controls, but they also work follow-up examinations to ensure that previously identified issues have been adequately addressed. This rigorous and continuous examination process helps maintain the safety and soundness of the financial system and protects it from cybersecurity threats.

Interaction with the FDIC is not a one-way street but a two-way communication channel. On one end, the FDIC communicates expectations, guidelines, directives, and examination results to the banks. These communications offer valuable insights into the regulatory requirements, best practices, and emerging risks that banks must be aware of.

Conversely, banks are expected to communicate their risk management strategies, policies, procedures, and significant incidents to the FDIC. Banks need to provide comprehensive and accurate data to the FDIC, which aids in the risk profiling of each institution. In some instances, the FDIC may issue specific directives to a bank following an examination if they identify deficiencies that need to be addressed.

Noncompliance with FDIC directives can lead to severe consequences. The FDIC can issue various enforcement actions against banks that violate laws or regulations, engage in unsafe or unsound practices, or breach conditions imposed in writing by the agency. These enforcement actions can range from minor penalties, such as fines, to more severe measures, such as removal and prohibition orders.

In sum, the FDIC plays a critical role in the financial sector's cybersecurity, laying down the necessary guidelines, conducting rigorous checks, and enforcing standards. The FDIC's proactive approach to cybersecurity ensures that the financial industry can stay one step ahead of the ever-evolving cyber threats, ensuring that the public can trust a secure and robust financial system.

Recommendations:

- **Familiarize with FDIC's Guidelines:** Develop a deep understanding of the FDIC's guidelines and requirements. Incorporate these into your organization's cybersecurity policies and procedures.
- **Embrace Transparency:** Foster a culture of transparency within your organization. Transparently communicate your risk management strategies, policies, and procedures to the FDIC.
- **Prepare for Examinations:** Develop a robust plan for the FDIC's IT examinations. Please update your risk management systems to align with the FDIC's expectations.

- **Implement Feedback:** After an examination, promptly address any deficiencies or recommendations provided by the FDIC. Implementing their feedback demonstrates your commitment to maintaining a robust cybersecurity posture.
- **Encourage Ongoing Learning:** Stay updated about new directives or bulletins issued by the FDIC. Incorporate learning about these updates into your continuous professional development plan.

CONSUMER FINANCIAL PROTECTION BUREAU (CFPB)

The CFPB is a US government agency created in response to the financial crisis of 2008. It was established under the Dodd–Frank Wall Street Reform and Consumer Protection Act of 2010, marking a significant step in consumer protection in the financial sector. The CFPB's role includes ensuring consumers have clear, accurate information to make sound financial decisions. It also aims to shield consumers from unfair, deceptive, or abusive acts and practices, thereby ensuring the fair operation of markets for consumer financial products and services.

The mandate of the CFPB extends to a broad spectrum of consumer finance markets, including lending, deposit accounts, payment systems, and debt collection, among others. A crucial part of its mission is upholding consumer rights by enforcing federal consumer financial laws and holding financial service providers accountable.

Given the current digital age, the CFPB has had to incorporate a significant focus on cybersecurity, mainly around consumer data protection. As financial services continue to evolve and adapt to digital transformations, the collection and use of consumer data have risen exponentially. Such data can include personal identification information, credit history, transaction history, and more, which, if mishandled or exposed, could lead to severe financial harm or identity theft.

Recognizing the severity of these risks, the CFPB has issued several guidelines regarding collecting, using, and protecting consumer data. These guidelines ensure that financial institutions uphold stringent measures to protect consumers' personal and financial information from cyber threats. For instance, the CFPB's Principles for the Future of Consumer Financial Services, published in 2017, stress the importance of access, control, transparency, and security when handling consumer data.

The interaction with the CFPB goes beyond simple compliance. It involves understanding the agency's relentless focus on consumer protection and incorporating this perspective into an organization's cybersecurity policies and practices. It is also crucial for companies to stay abreast of the CFPB's evolving expectations and regulations. This means that companies should have dedicated teams or individuals responsible for monitoring and implementing changes to their policies and procedures in line with the latest CFPB guidance.

A significant component of engaging with the CFPB involves reporting significant incidents or breaches that may impact consumers' personal or financial information. The CFPB requires companies to promptly report any such incidents and take immediate actions to mitigate the impact. These actions could include notifying affected consumers, offering free credit monitoring services, or making organizational changes to prevent similar incidents.

The CFPB does not just issue guidance and expects compliance. It also has robust enforcement capabilities. Noncompliance with CFPB regulations can lead to investigations and, potentially, severe penalties, including substantial fines. The agency has shown that it is willing to take decisive action against companies that adequately protect their customers' information.

In summary, the CFPB is vital in safeguarding consumers in the financial sector. It establishes the rules of the game, provides guidance on how to comply, and ensures adherence through active monitoring and enforcement. Given the sensitivity of consumer data, particularly in the digital age, the CFPB's role in ensuring cybersecurity in the financial sector is crucial. Understanding and adhering to the CFPB's guidelines and maintaining an open, transparent relationship with the agency will go a long way toward achieving robust consumer data protection.

Recommendations:

- **Understand the CFPB's Focus:** Develop a clear understanding of the CFPB's consumer protection focus and its implications for your organization's cybersecurity practices.
- **Incorporate CFPB Guidelines:** Incorporate the CFPB's data collection, use, and protection guidelines into your organization's cybersecurity policies.
- **Transparent Reporting:** Foster a culture of transparency and promptly report any significant incidents or breaches that may impact consumers' personal or financial information to the CFPB.
- **Emphasize Consumer Protection:** In all your cybersecurity efforts, emphasize the importance of consumer protection. Encourage your team to approach cybersecurity from a consumer protection perspective.
- **Continual Learning:** Stay updated on new directives or guidelines issued by the CFPB and incorporate these updates into your continuous professional development plan.

SECURITIES AND EXCHANGE COMMISSION (SEC)

The SEC is an independent federal government regulatory agency responsible for protecting investors, maintaining fair and orderly functioning of the securities markets, and facilitating capital formation. Given the digitization of securities markets and increasing cyber threats, the SEC has developed a keen focus on cybersecurity, recognizing its significance to the integrity of the needs and investor protection.

In cybersecurity, the SEC's primary role involves formulating and enforcing regulations related to publicly traded companies' disclosure of cybersecurity risks and incidents. They strive to ensure that investors have access to material information about cybersecurity risks and incidents when making investment decisions. The SEC has issued guidelines advising public companies to disclose cybersecurity risks and incidents to investors, even if a cyberattack has not yet targeted them.

The SEC also oversees securities market participants such as broker-dealers, investment advisers, investment companies, self-regulatory organizations (SROs), and alternative trading systems through its Division of Examinations. Cybersecurity forms a significant part of the SEC's examinations, focusing on areas such as governance and risk assessment, access rights and controls, data loss prevention, vendor management, training, and incident response.

Interacting with the SEC involves demonstrating the organization's commitment to cybersecurity, transparency about cybersecurity risks and incidents, and compliance with SEC regulations. Publicly traded companies must include discussions of their cybersecurity risk in their registration and other periodic reports and financial statements. Following a cyber incident, a company should disclose relevant information to help investors understand the incident's impact on the company's financial condition and operations.

Recommendations:

- **Understand the SEC's Focus:** Develop a clear understanding of the SEC's focus on cybersecurity risk disclosure and its implications for your organization's operations. This understanding will guide your cybersecurity policies and practices to align with the SEC's expectations.

- **Incorporate SEC Guidelines:** Incorporate the SEC's guidelines on cybersecurity risk disclosure into your organization's cybersecurity and reporting policies. These guidelines should guide the preparation of your organization's registration statements, financial statements, and other reports.

- **Transparency in Reporting:** Foster a culture of transparency in reporting cybersecurity risks and incidents. Timely and accurately disclosing material cybersecurity risks and incidents can demonstrate your commitment to protecting investors and maintaining market integrity.

- **Prepare for Examinations:** Develop a robust plan for the SEC's cybersecurity examinations. This plan should include regular reviews and updates of your cybersecurity risk management systems to ensure compliance with the SEC's expectations.

- **Foster a Culture of Compliance:** Promote a culture of compliance within your organization. Ensure that everyone understands the importance of adherence to the SEC's guidelines and regulations on cybersecurity risk disclosure.

FINANCIAL INDUSTRY REGULATORY AUTHORITY (FINRA)

The Financial Industry Regulatory Authority, often shortened to FINRA, functions as a nongovernmental organization with the crucial role of overseeing and regulating member brokerage firms and the exchange markets in which they operate. Its primary responsibility lies in safeguarding the interests of investors. It does so by striving to guarantee that the securities industry, a significant sector of the financial landscape, carries out its functions and duties honestly and fairly.

In recent years, the increasing dependency on digital technology in the securities industry has prompted FINRA to underline the significance of robust and reliable cybersecurity practices. With the rise of the digital age, the frequency and intensity of cyber threats have escalated, making it more imperative than ever for companies to have solid protective measures. Recognizing this shift, FINRA has prioritized guiding its member firms in adopting effective cybersecurity measures.

To address the cybersecurity challenge, FINRA creates and propagates rules and guidelines specifically aimed at aiding firms in safeguarding themselves against potential cyber threats. It also conducts regular examinations to test the robustness of firms' cybersecurity strategies and defenses. Additionally, FINRA offers many resources to support and guide firms as they navigate the intricacies of cyber risk management.

One of the most significant contributions from FINRA in this regard is its detailed Cybersecurity Checklist. This checklist is designed to serve as a comprehensive guide for firms as they develop and implement their cybersecurity programs. As laid out in this checklist, the organization's guidelines stress several key aspects. These include identifying and assessing cybersecurity threats, establishing a governance framework to manage these threats, developing effective incident response plans, and carefully managing relationships with vendors, all of which have significant implications for a firm's cybersecurity stance.

Interactions with FINRA are multifaceted and can involve various steps. An organization must comply with the cybersecurity guidelines laid down by FINRA. This is not only about adhering to the rules but also involves demonstrating readiness and preparation to protect against cyber threats. In doing so, the organization underlines its commitment to maintaining the integrity of the financial system and the trust of its clients.

Another key aspect of interaction with FINRA is the requirement for timely reporting of cyber incidents. This allows FINRA and the organization to promptly address any breaches and ensure minimal impact on the business operations and clients. Cooperation during FINRA's cybersecurity examinations is also expected, ensuring a comprehensive assessment of the organization's cybersecurity measures.

Such a comprehensive interaction process helps ensure alignment with the industry standards set by FINRA. Additionally, it aids in the quick detection and resolution of any identified deficiencies in the organization's cybersecurity measures. This process, thus, helps maintain investors' confidence in the industry and ensures a secure and robust financial system.

Recommendations:

- **Familiarize Yourself with FINRA's Guidelines:** Take time to understand FINRA's guidelines on cybersecurity. Incorporate these guidelines into your organization's cybersecurity policies and procedures.
- **Embrace Transparency:** Develop a culture of transparency within your organization. Openly communicate your cybersecurity practices and any significant incidents to FINRA.
- **Prepare for Examinations:** Prepare for FINRA's cybersecurity examinations by regularly reviewing and updating your cybersecurity practices. This preparation can ensure a smooth examination process and help identify areas for improvement.
- **Implement Feedback:** Act promptly to implement any recommendations or directives issued by FINRA following an examination. This responsiveness demonstrates your commitment to maintaining a robust cybersecurity posture.
- **Encourage Ongoing Learning:** Stay updated on any new guidelines or resources FINRA provides. Use these updates as learning opportunities to enhance your organization's cybersecurity measures.

NATIONAL CREDIT UNION ADMINISTRATION (NCUA)

The National Credit Union Administration, or the NCUA, operates as an independent federal agency. Its principal responsibilities are to regulate, charter, and provide supervision for federal credit unions across the United States. The NCUA's mission revolves around ensuring the safety and soundness of the credit union system, a task that involves overseeing the financial health of credit unions, protecting member rights, and promoting credit union growth. Given the significant role of digital technology in the credit union system, the NCUA has a vital interest in the cybersecurity posture of credit unions.

The NCUA is not a passive observer but takes an active and engaged role in helping credit unions understand, manage, and mitigate the various cybersecurity risks they may face. In today's digital age, cybersecurity has become a cornerstone of operational safety for financial institutions, and credit unions are no exception. Recognizing this, the NCUA has prioritized formulating guidelines and regulations to ensure credit unions implement and maintain robust cybersecurity measures.

One of the key resources that the NCUA provides to assist credit unions in bolstering their cybersecurity readiness is the Automated Cybersecurity Examination Tool (ACET). This tool is built upon the foundation of the CAT developed by the FFIEC. The ACET demonstrates the NCUA's commitment to providing credit unions with concrete resources to assess and enhance their cybersecurity readiness.

The ACET presents a repeatable and measurable process that allows credit unions to gauge their cybersecurity preparedness continually. This iterative approach enables credit unions to monitor their progress, ensuring they can adapt and update their cybersecurity practices to meet evolving threats. The tool's key focus is to provide credit unions with a reliable method to track their cybersecurity strategies and actions, thereby fortifying their ability to protect their operations and members from cyber threats.

Interacting with the NCUA involves several crucial steps that credit unions must understand and follow. These include a thorough understanding of the agency's regulations and guidelines, especially cybersecurity-related ones, and a commitment to adhere to them. Adherence means implementing security measures and maintaining an ongoing review and improvement process.

Another significant aspect of the interaction with the NCUA is the requirement for timely reporting of substantial cybersecurity incidents. Prompt and accurate reporting enables the NCUA to help the credit union respond effectively, minimize damage to the institution and its members, and also help inform the wider credit union community about potential threats.

The credit unions are also expected to collaborate during NCUA cybersecurity examinations. These examinations, which may utilize tools such as the ACET, help the NCUA evaluate a credit union's cybersecurity readiness and offer improvement guidance. Understanding and familiarity with the NCUA's examination processes, including the ACET, prove highly beneficial for credit unions. This knowledge can help credit unions prepare for these examinations and ensure that their cybersecurity practices meet the standards set forth by the NCUA.

Recommendations:

- **Understand NCUA's Focus:** Invest time in understanding NCUA's focus on cybersecurity and how it applies to your organization. This understanding can help shape your cybersecurity policies and practices to align with the NCUA's expectations.
- **Incorporate NCUA Guidelines:** Incorporate the NCUA's guidelines and tools, such as the ACET, into your organization's cybersecurity program. These tools can provide valuable insights to enhance your organization's cybersecurity readiness.
- **Foster a Culture of Transparency:** Foster a culture of transparency within your organization. Communicate your cybersecurity strategies, procedures, and any significant incidents to the NCUA promptly.
- **Prepare for Examinations:** Develop a comprehensive plan for the NCUA's cybersecurity examinations. Regularly review and update your cybersecurity risk management systems to ensure they align with the NCUA's expectations.

- **Encourage Continuous Learning:** Stay updated on new directives, guidelines, or tools the NCUA provides. Incorporate learning about these updates into your professional development plan to continuously enhance your organization's cybersecurity readiness.

THE FEDERAL TRADE COMMISSION

The Federal Trade Commission, often called the FTC, is an independent agency of the US government. Its principal mandate is to enforce antitrust laws and promote consumer protection. With the significant role that digital technology plays in businesses and the lives of consumers, the FTC has a crucial interest in cybersecurity, particularly with its relevance to consumer protection.

Unlike agencies with a narrower focus, the FTC does not merely observe the market but actively helps businesses understand, manage, and mitigate the various cybersecurity risks they may face. In an era where cybersecurity is increasingly important for the operational safety of all enterprises, the FTC recognizes the significance of developing guidelines and regulations to ensure businesses, particularly those handling sensitive consumer data, implement and maintain robust cybersecurity measures.

One of the most critical resources the FTC provides to assist businesses in strengthening their cybersecurity readiness is the Start with Security guide. Based on lessons from the FTC's 50+ data security cases, this guide is a foundation for businesses to create a sound and reliable data security plan. It exemplifies the FTC's commitment to ensuring businesses have tangible resources to assess and improve cybersecurity readiness.

The Start with Security guide provides businesses with a clear and actionable process to continually gauge their cybersecurity preparedness. This process allows businesses to monitor their progress over time, ensuring they can adapt their cybersecurity practices to address evolving threats. The guide's main focus is to provide businesses with a roadmap to formulate and implement their cybersecurity strategies and actions, strengthening their capacity to protect their operations and consumer data from cyber threats.

Interactions with the FTC involve several crucial steps that businesses must understand and adhere to. These include understanding the agency's regulations and guidelines, especially cybersecurity-related ones, and committing to follow them. Compliance entails implementing necessary security measures and necessitates maintaining a regular review and improvement process.

Another significant aspect of interaction with the FTC is the requirement for timely reporting of substantial cybersecurity incidents. Swift and accurate reporting allows the FTC to assist businesses in responding effectively to breaches, minimizing damage to the institution and its customers, and informing the broader business community about emerging threats.

Businesses are also expected to cooperate during FTC cybersecurity investigations. These investigations help the FTC evaluate a business's cybersecurity readiness and offer improvement guidance. Familiarity with the FTC's investigation processes, including understanding the lessons from the Start with Security guide, proves invaluable for businesses. This understanding can help businesses prepare for these investigations and ensure their cybersecurity practices meet the standards set forth by the FTC.

Recommendations:

- **Understand the Role of FTC:** Familiarize yourself with the FTC's mission and its relation to cybersecurity. Understand that the FTC enforces antitrust law and promotes consumer protection, and acknowledge the agency's active role in helping businesses manage cybersecurity risks.
- **Utilize FTC Resources:** Make good use of the resources provided by the FTC, such as the Start with Security guide. This guide, informed by over 50 data security cases, will help your business create a comprehensive data security plan, thus improving your cybersecurity readiness.
- **Regularly Review FTC Guidelines:** Develop a regular habit of reviewing the FTC's guidelines and regulations, particularly cybersecurity-related ones. Commit to these guidelines and maintain a regular review and improvement process to ensure ongoing compliance.
- **Cooperate with FTC Examinations:** Be prepared for possible FTC investigations into your cybersecurity practices. Understand the FTC's investigation processes and cooperate fully. Use insights from the Start with Security guide to help your business prepare for these investigations.
- **Timely Incident Reporting:** Establish a protocol for swiftly and accurately reporting significant cybersecurity incidents to the FTC. This allows the FTC to assist in responding to breaches and keeps the broader business community informed about emerging threats. Timely reporting minimizes damage to your institution and its customers.

Chapter Conclusion

In the constantly evolving world of financial cybersecurity, various regulatory bodies operate with distinct mandates, guidelines, and focus areas. Entities ranging from the FFIEC to the NCUA play significant roles in shaping the cybersecurity landscape of the financial sector.

The FFIEC, a critical interagency body, formulates and promotes uniform principles and standards for examining financial institutions. The FFIEC's CAT is noteworthy, offering a systematic approach for organizations to evaluate and enhance their cybersecurity readiness.

Meanwhile, the OCC is tasked with ensuring the safety and stability of the national banking system. Its proactive stance is demonstrated by issuing timely alerts and bulletins about emerging cyber threats and shaping cybersecurity frameworks in banking institutions.

The CFPB focuses on consumer protection within the financial sector. It emphasizes collecting, utilizing, and protecting consumer data, reinforcing the importance of prioritizing consumer data protection in cybersecurity endeavors.

The Federal Reserve's responsibility involves supervising and regulating financial institutions and promoting stability, integrity, and efficiency within the nation's monetary, financial, and payment systems. Its cybersecurity guidelines assist financial institutions in managing and mitigating cyber risks effectively.

The role of the FDIC in maintaining public confidence and stability in the nation's financial system is essential. The FDIC's guidelines on establishing a solid cybersecurity framework reflect its commitment to enabling institutions to respond to cyber threats effectively.

The SEC focuses on protecting investors by disclosing cybersecurity risks. The SEC highlights the intersection of cybersecurity and investor protection by emphasizing the transparency of cybersecurity risks and incidents in corporate disclosures.

The FINRA, a nongovernmental body, underscores the need for industry self-regulation, regulating member brokerage firms and exchange markets. Its detailed Cybersecurity Checklist is valuable for firms developing and implementing effective cybersecurity programs.

Lastly, the NCUA works to ensure the safety and soundness of the credit union system. The NCUA's ACET showcases the agency's proactive approach to providing resources for credit unions to evaluate their cybersecurity readiness.

In summary, understanding these regulatory bodies' roles, guidelines, and expectations is crucial for cybersecurity professionals in the financial sector. Active engagement with these agencies, policy adherence, and transparent communication help build strong cybersecurity frameworks and demonstrate a firm commitment to cybersecurity. This proactive approach promotes trust among consumers, investors, and regulators, which is key to the financial sector's integrity, resilience, and success.

ONLINE REGULATORY RESOURCES

Remember, while these resources provide valuable information, they should be used with professional advice when making business decisions. The financial industry's regulatory landscape is complex and subject to change, making continuous learning and professional consultation essential to staying compliant.

Office of the Comptroller of the Currency (OCC)

1. **OCC's Official Website:** The site provides a comprehensive understanding of the OCC's mission, regulations, guidelines, and latest updates.

2. **OCC's Handbook:** Provides guidance and procedures for bank examiners and supervised institutions.

3. **OCC Bulletin:** Contains all the bulletins issued by OCC for the national banks and federal savings associations.

4. **Annual Report:** The OCC's Annual Report discusses the condition of the federal banking system, its regulatory activities, and policy initiatives.

Federal Deposit Insurance Corporation (FDIC)

1. **FDIC's Official Website:** This website is an invaluable resource for learning about the FDIC's regulations, guidelines, and the latest updates.

2. **FDIC's Risk Management Manual of Examination Policies:** Provides the FDIC's comprehensive guidelines, including cybersecurity risk assessment and management.

3. **FDIC Consumer News:** Contains articles and resources aimed at helping consumers make informed decisions about their money.

4. **FDIC's Bank Data and Statistics:** Provides data and analytical tools related to banking statistics.

Consumer Financial Protection Bureau (CFPB)

1. **CFPB's Official Website:** Provides insights into the CFPB's mission, regulations, guidelines, and the latest updates.

2. **CFPB's Regulations:** Contains final rules issued by the CFPB.

3. **CFPB's Consumer Tools:** Offers a variety of resources to help consumers make informed financial decisions.

4. **CFPB Blog:** Contains news and updates about the agency's latest initiatives and resources.

5. **CFPB Reports:** Contains the agency's research on consumer behavior, financial products, and policy implications.

Financial Industry Regulatory Authority (FINRA)

1. **FINRA's Official Website:** This website is the best place to learn about FINRA's work, rules, and regulations.

2. **FINRA Rulebook:** Contains all FINRA's regulatory notices, rules, and guidelines.

3. **FINRA Compliance Tools:** Offers tools to help firms understand and comply with FINRA rules.

4. **FINRA Newsroom:** Features the latest news, speeches, testimonies, and videos of FINRA's operations.

Federal Reserve System (Fed)

1. **Federal Reserve's Official Website:** Provides comprehensive information on the Fed's functions, regulations, and latest updates.
2. **Federal Reserve's Supervision and Regulation Report:** Provides insights into the Fed's supervisory and regulatory activities.
3. **Federal Reserve Education:** Provides resources to understand the role of the Federal Reserve in the US economy.
4. **Fed's Monetary Policy Report:** Explores the conduct of monetary policy and economic developments and prospects for the future.

Federal Financial Institutions Examination Council (FFIEC)

1. **FFIEC's Official Website:** Features FFIEC's guidelines, regulations, and latest updates.
2. **FFIEC IT Examination Handbook:** Provides a comprehensive guide for IT examination, including cybersecurity.
3. **FFIEC Press Releases:** Offers the latest news and announcements about the council's work.
4. **FFIEC Reports:** Features reports on various aspects of the financial industry.

National Credit Union Administration (NCUA)

1. **NCUA's Official Website:** Provides a wealth of information about the NCUA's rules, regulations, and latest updates.
2. **NCUA Regulations:** Features all regulations and guidance applicable to credit unions.
3. **NCUA Examiner's Guide:** Offers a detailed NCUA examination process guide.
4. **NCUA News:** Contains the latest news and updates from the NCUA.

Securities and Exchange Commission (SEC)

1. **SEC's Official Website:** Provides comprehensive information about the SEC's functions, rules, and regulations.
2. **SEC EDGAR Database:** Contains filings from companies regulated by the SEC.
3. **SEC** http://Investor.gov: Provides resources for individual investors to understand the securities market.
4. **SEC Newsroom:** Features the latest news, statements, and announcements from the SEC.

CHAPTER 22

Managing Regulatory Visits and Requests for Information

"Do not underestimate the power of effective response. By crafting well-thought-out and timely responses to regulatory visits and requests, you can demonstrate your organization's commitment to compliance and protecting sensitive data."

Managing regulatory visits and information requests is crucial to cybersecurity governance, risk management, and compliance procedures. These activities encompass a broad spectrum of topics – understanding what these visits and requests entail, preparing for them appropriately, responding to them effectively, and fostering a cooperative and constructive relationship with regulators. Practical strategies and actionable recommendations are needed to ensure organizations of all sizes and types can effectively navigate these activities. These not only aid in understanding the complexities of regulatory visits and information requests but also equip organizations with the knowledge to handle them proficiently. The ultimate goal is to ensure compliance with regulations and secure sensitive data, key components in maintaining a robust cybersecurity posture.

REGULATORY VISITS AND REQUESTS FOR INFORMATION

Regulatory visits and requests for information are crucial parts of cybersecurity governance, significantly impacting an organization's compliance status and relationship with regulatory bodies. In understanding the nuances of regulatory visits, organizations must acknowledge their primary goal, which predominantly involves affirming the organization's adherence to set cybersecurity standards and regulations. The spectrum of these visits varies, from conventional audits to in-depth investigations propelled by specific incidents or identified risks.

The nature of typical requests for information usually encompasses aspects like policies, protocols, and security measures adopted by the organization. These could comprise requests for substantiation of data protection practices, incident reports detailing breaches, or protocols surrounding user access control. Addressing these requests meticulously helps organizations present a robust image of their cybersecurity framework to regulators.

Undoubtedly, the cornerstone of a beneficial relationship between an organization and its regulators lies in cooperation and adherence to compliance. Promoting an open line of communication, responding promptly to information requests, and cooperating fully during regulatory visits contribute to building a positive rapport with regulatory bodies. These practices not only enhance the regulators' perception of the organization's compliance but also create a foundation for constructive dialogue in the future.

At the same time, an important aspect that organizations must navigate is the dichotomy between maintaining transparency with regulators and safeguarding sensitive information. An optimal balance must be struck, where the company must be transparent and cooperative with regulators while protecting sensitive data. Achieving this balance necessitates a strategy finely aligned with cybersecurity best practices on the one hand and the organization's overarching business objectives on the other. Such a strategy requires thoughtful planning and regular reassessment, ensuring that these critical aspects of the organization's operations are given equal weight.

Recommendations:

- **Develop a Clear Understanding:** Make efforts to understand the objectives, types, and importance of regulatory visits and requests for information. This knowledge will inform the development of effective strategies for managing them.
- **Embrace Transparency:** Upholding a high degree of transparency in your communication with regulatory authorities strengthens their trust in your organization and unequivocally signals your dedication to adhering to compliance requirements. Regular, open disclosure of information, including any challenges or issues, can foster better relationships with regulators and assist in collaborative problem-solving.
- **Safeguard Sensitive Information:** Establish protocols for handling sensitive data during regulatory visits or information requests. This measure ensures that only necessary information is disclosed, protecting your organization's proprietary and sensitive information.
- **Foster Cooperation:** Encourage an organizational culture that values cooperation and compliance. This attitude will contribute to smoother regulatory visits and more effective management of requests for information.
- **Be Proactive:** Do not wait for a regulatory visit or an information request to prepare. Be proactive in reviewing and updating your policies, ensuring they align with current regulations.

PREPARING FOR REGULATORY VISITS

Preparing for regulatory visits is vital to cybersecurity governance, a multifaceted task requiring in-depth planning and rigorous execution. The preparation commences with a thorough understanding of the visit's purpose and scope. This could range from a routine check to ensure an organization's compliance with cybersecurity standards and regulations to an in-depth investigation triggered by a specific incident or suspected vulnerability. The nature and extent of the visit profoundly influence the degree of preparation required. For a routine audit, the preparation might focus more on ensuring that regular processes are up-to-date and adequately documented. However, the preparation might need to delve deeper into specific incidents or practices for a more targeted investigation.

Following this initial assessment, identifying the relevant personnel and their responsibilities forms a significant part of the preparatory process. This step ensures that the right individuals are on hand to answer questions, provide necessary documents, and engage in meaningful discussions during the regulatory visit, but it also helps the organization present a united and organized front. It can be helpful to develop a clear roster of responsibilities ahead of time, detailing who will be responsible for which aspects of the visit. This might include a specific person for providing physical or virtual access to facilities or systems, another person explaining certain practices or procedures, and perhaps a spokesperson to provide official responses on behalf of the organization.

Keeping the organization's policies and procedures up-to-date forms another essential pillar in this preparation process. This task extends beyond merely updating the procedures related to cybersecurity. It also encompasses data protection, privacy, incident response policies, and other areas that might come under the regulatory microscope. This could involve reviewing each policy and procedure to ensure it is current, ensuring that changes in the regulatory environment have been appropriately reflected, and confirming that policies are being followed in practice.

Internal assessments and mock audits often prove invaluable in readying an organization for regulatory visits. Such self-inspections serve as an effective tool to unearth gaps in policies, procedures, or implementations that may have escaped routine checks. They provide an opportunity to rectify these issues well before the regulator's visit. Beyond merely identifying gaps, these internal audits can also help test the organization's response mechanisms, offering valuable insights that could be instrumental during the actual regulatory visit.

In parallel with the above tasks, compiling and organizing the requested documentation in a timely manner is integral to successful communication with regulators. This action demonstrates the organization's readiness and commitment to compliance and helps ensure a smooth and efficient visit. Compiling and organizing documents also provides an opportunity to review the content of the documents, ensuring that they are accurate, up-to-date, and complete.

Lastly, but not least importantly, staff communication and training significantly contribute to the overall preparation. Employees must understand their roles during the visit, the importance of the visit, and the potential impact on the organization. This goes beyond merely instructing them on what to do during the visit – it also involves explaining why their cooperation and professionalism are essential and how their actions can contribute to the organization's overall compliance and relationship with regulators. The training should also instill confidence in the employees, ensuring they understand that the visit is a normal part of business operations and not something to fear. These combined efforts will help ensure the organization is fully prepared and ready to handle regulatory visits effectively and efficiently.

Recommendations:

- **Understand the Purpose:** Strive to understand the purpose and scope of a regulatory visit. This knowledge will aid in shaping your organization's preparation strategy and ensure the appropriate focus areas are addressed.
- **Identify Relevant Personnel:** Identify and brief the personnel directly involved in the visit. This ensures that the right individuals are available and prepared to assist during the regulatory visit.
- **Review Policies and Procedures:** Regularly update your organization's policies and procedures. This practice ensures that your organization complies with current regulations and is ready to demonstrate this compliance during a visit.
- **Conduct Internal Assessments:** Make a habit of conducting internal assessments and mock audits. These exercises identify potential compliance gaps and provide an opportunity for proactive mitigation.
- **Organize Documentation:** Prioritize the timely compilation and organization of all requested documentation. This aids in effective communication with the regulators and exhibits your organization's preparedness and commitment to compliance.
- **Communicate and Train Staff:** Ensure open communication and comprehensive training for your staff regarding the regulatory visit. This preparation helps employees understand their roles and the potential impact of the visit on the organization.

RESPONDING TO REQUESTS FOR INFORMATION

Receiving and processing requests for information is a nuanced task that necessitates great care and accuracy. Understanding the essence of the request, its relevance, and the legal implications are fundamental to crafting an appropriate response. This process calls for a holistic approach that includes analyzing the nature of the information requested, considering the potential outcomes of various responses, and foreseeing the legal and practical consequences of sharing particular information.

Timeliness is another vital aspect when responding to information requests. Respecting the designated timeframes and deadlines is crucial to demonstrate the organization's efficiency and commitment. Adhering to these timelines can foster stronger relationships with regulators and other parties. Conversely, delayed responses can have adverse effects, implying noncompliance or lack of preparedness, negatively impacting the organization's reputation.

A critical measure in processing information requests is the verification of their legitimacy. An organization needs to understand the request's source and confirm its authenticity. This step protects the organization from inadvertently disclosing sensitive information to unauthorized entities. Moreover, it helps the organization control its intellectual property and other proprietary data.

The stage of gathering and evaluating the requested information is intricate and demanding. The approach should be exhaustive, precise, and focused to ensure that the collected information is comprehensive and accurate. The ultimate aim is to provide information responsive to the request and detailed and enlightening to the requesting party.

When responding to requests, it is paramount that the response strictly aligns with the scope of the request. The response should not be overly broad or exceed the specifics of the request, as this could unintentionally subject other areas of the business to scrutiny. Thus, it is important to thoroughly understand the request, maintain precision in the information gathered, and provide clear and concise responses that satisfy the query without diverging into potentially sensitive territories.

Balancing transparency with protecting sensitive information and intellectual property is complex yet essential. Organizations must strike a balance between maintaining transparency and protecting sensitive information. This entails discerning which information should be disclosed and withheld to avoid potential legal disputes or loss of competitive advantage.

Documenting and tracking responses to information requests is an essential last step. This practice ensures consistency in dealing with such requests and allows for easy reference in the future. It serves as a rich knowledge base for similar future requests and contributes to informed decision-making, setting a precedent for future actions. The documentation process strengthens not only the organization's informational structure but also its regulatory compliance.

Recommendations:

- **Prioritize Understanding:** Commit to thoroughly understanding the essence, relevance, and legal implications of every information request received. Incorporate a systematic analysis of the information requested, potential responses, and the foreseeable consequences of sharing specific information. This deep understanding will enable crafting appropriate and legally sound responses.

- **Uphold Timeliness:** Respect all designated timeframes and deadlines when responding to information requests. Ensure systems and processes are efficient enough to meet these deadlines, fostering stronger relationships with regulators and other parties. Remember that timely responses demonstrate commitment and preparedness, enhancing the organization's reputation.

- **Verify Request Legitimacy:** Make it a standard procedure to verify the authenticity of every information request received. By understanding the source of each request and confirming its legitimacy, you can protect your organization from inadvertently disclosing sensitive information to unauthorized entities and maintain control over your intellectual property.

- **Maintain Response Precision:** Adopt a rigorous, precise, and focused approach while gathering and evaluating the requested information. Ensure the data collected is comprehensive and accurate. Aim to provide responses that are not just in line with the request but also detailed and enlightening to the requester.

- **Document and Track:** Implement a robust system for documenting and tracking responses to information requests. This practice ensures consistency, provides an easy reference for future similar requests, and contributes to informed decision-making. Not only does this fortify your organization's informational structure, but it also reinforces regulatory compliance.

BEST PRACTICES DURING REGULATORY VISITS

Regulatory visits play a critical role in an organization's cybersecurity compliance journey, and the roles and responsibilities of key personnel, including compliance officers and legal counsel, become even more pronounced during these events. Compliance officers act as the primary liaison between the organization and the regulators, guiding the process, managing communications, and coordinating the fulfillment of requests. They need to be well-versed in the regulatory landscape, fully aware of the organization's policies and procedures, and able to manage potential challenges effectively.

Legal counsel, on the other hand, provides legal oversight of the entire process. They work closely with the compliance officers, contributing to legal interpretations of regulations and ensuring the organization's legal obligations are met. They also play a critical role in managing any sensitive situations that may arise during the visit. The synergy between the compliance officers and legal counsel forms the backbone of a successful regulatory visit, laying the groundwork for a positive and cooperative interaction with regulators.

Communication is a vital component during regulatory visits. The exchange of information between the organization and regulators should be clear, concise, and open. Transparent communication fosters understanding and builds a strong foundation for a positive relationship with regulators. It helps prevent misunderstandings, resolves issues promptly, and promotes mutual respect and cooperation. Organizations should strive for clarity in communication, avoiding jargon or overly technical language and ensuring that the regulators' queries and concerns are fully addressed.

Effective management can significantly enhance the experience for both parties when it comes to on-site interviews and inspections. The goal should be to minimize disruptions to daily operations while ensuring that the objectives of the visit are met. This involves coordination and planning, such as scheduling interviews at convenient times, preparing relevant staff for their roles in the inspection, and setting up conducive environments for the regulators to conduct their work. By effectively managing these on-site activities, organizations can balance their operational needs with the requirements of the regulatory visit.

Encountering unexpected or ambiguous requests during a regulatory visit is not uncommon. However, it is vital to handle these situations with grace and professionalism. Instead of responding defensively or evasively, seeking clarity and confirming the regulators' needs is better. This may involve asking follow-up questions or requesting additional time to gather the necessary information. The aim is to provide satisfactory responses while maintaining a cooperative and respectful attitude.

Finally, documenting the visit for internal records is more than just a good practice – it is a vital tool for continuous improvement. Detailed documentation of the regulatory visit can be invaluable, including the discussions, information shared, issues raised, and actions agreed upon. This documentation aids in post-visit reviews and can inform preparations for future visits. It also provides a historical record that can be referred to when needed, enhancing the organization's ability to respond effectively to regulatory concerns and strengthen its compliance practices over time.

Recommendations:

- **Understand and Communicate Roles:** Make an effort to understand and clearly define the roles and responsibilities of compliance officers and legal counsel during regulatory visits. This clarity is paramount for efficient and streamlined communication and operations. Knowing who is responsible for what allows for a well-structured response to regulators' queries and ensures that your organization's stance is correctly represented during discussions.

- **Encourage Transparency and Candor:** Encourage a culture of openness and respect in communications with regulators. Open communication includes a willingness to share information, ask questions, and accept feedback. This approach fosters a cooperative relationship with the regulators and builds a foundation of trust, which can significantly ease the process of regulatory visits.

- **Formulate a Strategy for Interviews:** Establish a well-thought-out and structured process for managing on-site interviews and inspections. This strategy should include logistics, allocation of resources, and timelines. A well-structured process can help reduce stress, prevent misunderstandings, and ensure that all pertinent areas are covered during the visit.

- **Prepare for the Unexpected:** Regulatory visits often include unforeseen questions or requests. Having a strategy in place is crucial to handle unexpected or ambiguous requests. This strategy may involve taking time to understand the question, consulting with internal experts, and then crafting a comprehensive and compliant response.

- **Make Documentation a Priority:** Accurate documentation of each regulatory visit is essential for internal records. The documentation should include the purpose of the visit, individuals involved, areas inspected, questions asked, and responses given. This practice allows for thorough post-visit reviews, identifying areas for improvement, and preparing more effectively for future visits.

DEVELOPING INTERNAL PROCESSES FOR MANAGING REGULATORY REQUESTS

Managing regulatory requests efficiently is critical to maintaining a robust cybersecurity posture. A key component of this management is establishing a request management team. This team should ideally be composed of members drawn from various departments within the organization, such as IT, legal, compliance, and business units. The team's diversity helps ensure a comprehensive understanding of the implications of the request, given the various aspects of the business it may impact. Additionally, the individuals selected should possess the necessary skills and knowledge to handle regulatory requests effectively. Their roles would include understanding the nature of the request, gathering the required data or information, validating the data for accuracy and completeness, and facilitating the response to the regulator.

Developing standard operating procedures (SOPs) for handling regulatory requests ensures consistency, efficiency, and compliance across the organization. These SOPs should provide a clear blueprint for handling all aspects of a regulatory request. They should define the initial process for receiving and acknowledging the request, set out the responsibilities of the various individuals and teams involved, establish timelines for the various stages of response, and set out the final process for delivering the response to the regulator. The SOPs should also stipulate quality checks and review processes to ensure the integrity and accuracy of the information provided to the regulators.

Implementing a robust tracking system is beneficial to aid in managing current and future reference regulatory requests. This system could be a part of the broader cybersecurity management framework or a stand-alone solution tailored to the unique needs of regulatory request handling. The system should track all incoming requests, the stages of the response process, the individuals or teams involved, the timelines, and the final responses. This tracking system should be easily accessible to all relevant personnel and provide real-time updates on the status of various requests.

Staff training and education on regulatory interactions are integral to enhancing their understanding and improving the speed and accuracy of responses. This training should cover the fundamentals of regulatory requests, the significance of these requests, the organization's process for handling them, and the staff's specific roles and responsibilities. Additionally, real-life examples and case studies can highlight potential challenges and the best practices for addressing them.

Lastly, managing regulatory requests should be seen as an evolving process incorporating a continuous improvement and feedback loop for optimization. Regular reviews and updates based on internal feedback, regulatory changes, and industry best practices ensure the process remains effective and compliant. These reviews might identify areas where the process can be streamlined for efficiency, gaps where additional controls are needed, or opportunities for leveraging technology to improve the speed and accuracy of responses. By embedding a culture of continuous improvement, organizations can ensure that their regulatory request management process remains robust and resilient in the face of an ever-changing regulatory landscape.

Recommendations:

- **Form a Dedicated Team:** Form a dedicated request management team composed of individuals with the proper knowledge and skills. This centralization not only aids in quick and efficient responses but also ensures consistency in interpreting regulatory requests and formulating responses.
- **Create Comprehensive SOPs:** Take the time to develop detailed SOPs for handling regulatory requests. These procedures should define the process flow, designate responsibilities, and stipulate timelines. Detailed SOPs ensure consistency and efficiency in responses and provide a reference for staff during training.
- **Use Technology for Tracking:** Implement a robust tracking system for managing requests and responses, possibly leveraging technology. This system should be capable of logging requests, tracking progress, and archiving responses. It enables better organization, helps avoid missed deadlines, and provides valuable data for future reference.
- **Invest in Staff Training:** Regular training and education for staff on regulatory interactions should be a priority. Training programs should cover understanding regulatory requests, the organization's response process, and individual responsibilities. Well-trained employees are better equipped to handle regulatory visits or requests for information, reducing the risk of miscommunication or noncompliance.
- **Encourage a Learning Culture:** Promote continuous learning, improvement, and feedback. This culture encourages staff to learn from past experiences, share knowledge, and suggest edits. Regular reviews of the response process and updates based on feedback ensure the process remains effective and aligned with regulatory changes.

BUILDING AND MAINTAINING RELATIONSHIPS WITH REGULATORS

Building and maintaining a healthy relationship with regulators is essential for an organization's cybersecurity governance strategy. A critical component of this relationship is fostering a spirit of cooperation. This is accomplished through regular, transparent, and constructive communication with regulatory bodies. Regular updates on the organization's cybersecurity measures, implementing new policies, and resolving potential issues demonstrate compliance and a willingness to engage proactively. This transparency fosters trust and can contribute to more constructive interactions during regulatory visits and audits.

Regular participation in industry groups and regulatory forums can significantly enhance the organization's understanding of the regulatory landscape. These platforms provide insights into upcoming regulatory changes, industry trends, and best practices adopted by peers. Active involvement also offers networking opportunities with industry leaders and regulators, opening up avenues for sharing and learning. Furthermore, participation can also provide a chance for the organization to influence industry standards or regulations by offering insights from their practical experiences and challenges.

Proactively seeking clarification and guidance from regulators on compliance and regulatory obligations shows initiative and responsibility. This action may involve reaching out to regulatory bodies for explanations of new regulations, interpretations of existing guidelines, or how a specific regulation applies to a particular business scenario. This proactive approach helps prevent misunderstandings that may lead to noncompliance and underscores the organization's commitment to regulatory requirements.

An organization's demonstrated commitment to compliance and security significantly impacts the regulator's perception. This commitment can manifest in various ways – from implementing robust cybersecurity measures, promptly addressing identified issues, and continuously educating and training staff to transparent reporting and proactive communication with regulators. Such commitment builds trust with regulators and enhances the organization's image and reputation. It signals to all stakeholders, including customers, partners, and investors, about the organization's seriousness in ensuring data protection and cybersecurity, strengthening their confidence in its operations.

In all these activities, it is essential to remember that building and maintaining relationships with regulators is an ongoing, long-term process. It requires consistent efforts, open communication, and a genuine commitment to uphold the highest compliance and cybersecurity standards. This relationship forms a crucial part of an organization's overall cybersecurity strategy, impacting its ability to effectively manage cybersecurity risks and demonstrate its commitment to maintaining a secure and compliant environment.

Recommendations:

- **Encourage Cooperation:** Through regular, transparent, and constructive communication, foster cooperation with regulators. Keep regulatory bodies updated about your cybersecurity measures, new policies, and potential issue resolutions. This openness promotes trust and aids in more productive regulatory visits and audits.

- **Actively Participate:** Engage actively in industry groups and regulatory forums to enhance understanding of the regulatory landscape. Leverage these platforms for insights into regulatory changes, industry trends, and peer best practices. Such participation also provides networking opportunities and a chance to influence industry standards or regulations with your unique insights.

- **Seek Regulatory Guidance:** Proactively contact regulators to clarify compliance and regulatory obligations. This could involve understanding new regulations, interpreting existing guidelines, or seeking advice on specific regulations in particular business scenarios. This proactive behavior helps prevent noncompliance and shows your commitment to meeting regulatory requirements.

- **Demonstrate Commitment:** Show your dedication to compliance and security in tangible ways, such as implementing robust cybersecurity measures, addressing issues promptly, training staff consistently, and transparently reporting to regulators. This commitment enhances your image and reputation, strengthening stakeholder confidence in your organization's cybersecurity efforts.

- **Invest Long-term:** Recognize that building and maintaining relationships with regulators is a continual, long-term endeavor requiring consistent efforts, open communication, and commitment to upholding compliance and cybersecurity standards. These relationships are crucial to your cybersecurity strategy, influencing your ability to manage risks and maintain a secure, compliant environment.

Chapter Conclusion

Regulatory interactions can significantly enhance an organization's relationship with the regulatory bodies when managed effectively. This constructive rapport can boost its overall stance on compliance and align it more effectively with regulatory requirements.

Regulatory visits verify an organization's compliance with established cybersecurity standards. The nature of these visits can vary substantially – they could be part of routine audits adhering to a regular regulatory schedule or detailed investigations initiated by specific incidents or concerns. During these visits, regulators often seek comprehensive information about the organization's cybersecurity policies, operating procedures, and security measures.

To build a successful relationship with regulators, an organization must communicate promptly and transparently and provide timely, accurate responses to inquiries. However, this openness should not compromise safeguarding sensitive, proprietary information. Thus, a delicate balance between transparency and protecting sensitive data must be maintained.

Effective preparation for these regulatory visits is a complex and multistep process. It starts with comprehending the specific objectives the regulatory visit aims to achieve. The organization needs to assign appropriate personnel-specific responsibilities to handle every aspect of the visit. Ensuring that the organization's policies and procedures are up-to-date and that internal audits are routinely carried out to identify and rectify compliance gaps is crucial.

During regulatory visits, the roles of compliance officers and legal counsel are of utmost importance as they guide the process and interactions with regulators. They must ensure clear and concise communication with regulators, efficiently manage on-site interviews, and ensure smooth inspection oversight. It is critical to seek clarity for any unexpected requests without attempting to evade or ignore them. After each visit, documenting the proceedings and any observations made for future reference and review is important in maintaining compliance.

Organizations should establish a dedicated request management team to handle regulatory requests efficiently. This team should develop SOPs, implement a tracking system for managing requests and responses, and provide staff with the necessary training to handle regulatory inquiries. The approach should not be static but encourage continuous improvement, incorporating regular process updates based on feedback and any changes in regulatory rules.

Building a positive, cooperative relationship with regulators is fundamental to regulatory compliance. Regular communication and updates, active participation in industry groups and regulatory forums, proactively seeking clarification and guidance, and demonstrating a tangible commitment to compliance and security are all key strategies to foster this relationship. By adopting these strategies, an organization can establish a positive relationship with regulators, underlining its commitment to upholding cybersecurity standards.

Case Study: Orchid Technologies

Orchid Technologies, a promising startup in the Artificial Intelligence sector, was preparing for its first regulatory visit. Gideon, the newly appointed Chief Information Security Officer (CISO), was tasked with ensuring that Orchid Technologies was ready for this crucial event.

Gideon began by clearly understanding the visit's purpose and scope across the team. He knew the visit was routine, designed to ensure the startup followed industry-standard cybersecurity practices and complied with data protection regulations. He communicated the importance and objectives of the visit to his team and the wider organization, setting the stage for a coordinated approach.

Drawing on the best practices from "The Ultimate Cybersecurity Guide to Governance, Risk, and Compliance," Gideon established a dedicated team comprising individuals skilled in the company's cybersecurity governance. This included network engineers, data privacy experts, compliance officers, and legal counsel. Each person was assigned specific roles and responsibilities for the visit, ensuring that every query or requirement from the regulators could be promptly and accurately addressed.

Gideon also spearheaded a comprehensive review of Orchid's policies and procedures, updating them to match the current cybersecurity landscape and regulatory requirements. He arranged for internal assessments and mock audits to test their robustness, helping the company identify and fix gaps before the regulators' visit.

One of the critical insights Gideon employed from the guide was implementing a robust tracking system for managing requests and responses. This system helped Orchid keep track of all interactions with regulators, from receiving the initial notice of the visit to submitting required documentation.

As the regulatory visit approached, Gideon took the initiative to maintain regular communication with the regulators, updating them on the company's preparations. This proactive communication strategy fostered a positive relationship, demonstrating Orchid's commitment to compliance and cooperation. During the visit, Gideon ensured that all interactions with the regulators were guided by openness, clarity, and respect, creating a positive impression.

The regulatory visit concluded successfully, with Orchid Technologies receiving commendation for its preparedness, transparency, and effective process handling. The experience strengthened Orchid's relationship with the regulators and reinforced its reputation as a company committed to stringent cybersecurity governance.

CHAPTER 23

Understanding Regulatory Penalties

"Addressing regulatory penalties is a chance to learn, improve, and strengthen your organization's cybersecurity posture. Use these experiences to identify vulnerabilities, enhance your security infrastructure, and demonstrate your commitment to compliance."

Exploring the consequences of noncompliance with cybersecurity regulations, specifically regulatory penalties, is crucial. These penalties are significant deterrents against inadequate security practices and mirror the regulatory landscape's fluidity. This is an array of regulatory penalties, including Matters Requiring Attention (MRAs), Consent Orders, Civil Money Penalties (CMPs), Cease and Desist Orders, and other potential enforcement actions. It is imperative to develop a comprehensive understanding of the purpose and procedure associated with each penalty and strategize on how to address them to ensure continued compliance.

OVERVIEW OF REGULATORY PENALTIES

Regulatory penalties are the tool for enforcing cybersecurity standards and regulations across industries. These penalties are levied by various governing bodies and regulatory agencies to ensure that entities comply with established cybersecurity norms and rules. In this context, compliance is nonnegotiable and is the basis for achieving an optimal state of cybersecurity.

The types and severity of penalties vary, often depending on the nature of the infraction, the organization's size, and its compliance history. These penalties can range from fines to orders mandating corrective actions or even suspension of business operations in severe cases. Understanding the breadth and depth of these penalties is crucial to the overall cybersecurity governance, risk, and compliance (GRC) strategy.

Furthermore, the purpose of these penalties extends beyond punishment. They act as effective deterrents, ensuring organizations invest in robust security measures and frameworks. They also play a crucial role in setting industrywide expectations and holding corporations accountable for their actions or lack thereof.

However, penalties are not arbitrarily imposed. Regulators usually adopt a systematic approach when determining the nature and extent of the penalty. They consider factors such as the severity of the violation, the duration, whether the breach was intentional or resulted from negligence, and the organization's response.

Notably, some penalties may be preventable or negotiable. In the face of impending regulatory action, proactive engagement with the regulators can often lead to less severe outcomes. This involves understanding the regulatory landscape, early and ongoing compliance efforts, effective communication, and demonstration of due diligence.

While the idea of penalties is daunting, understanding their context can illuminate how businesses can avoid or mitigate them. Organizations can transform these challenges into opportunities for improving their security posture by aligning governance, risk management, and compliance strategies.

Recommendations:

- **Understand the Regulatory Scope:** Develop a comprehensive understanding of the regulatory landscape pertinent to your organization. This includes knowing the various penalties and the circumstances under which they may be imposed.
- **Engage with Regulators:** Instead of adopting a reactive approach, maintain open lines of communication with regulators. This not only aids in understanding their expectations but also fosters trust.
- **Invest in Regulatory Compliance:** A robust cybersecurity program is not just about risk mitigation and compliance. Invest in systems, processes, and training that help you comply with industry norms and regulations.
- **Mitigate Compliance Risks Proactively:** Risk management should be a continuous process, not a one-time activity. By identifying and addressing vulnerabilities promptly, you can reduce the likelihood of regulatory penalties.
- **Plan for Regulatory Penalties:** Despite your best efforts, penalties may be inevitable. Have a plan to respond to regulatory actions effectively, including the financial implications, operational impact, and public relations strategy.

REGULATORY PENALTIES AND ENFORCEMENT ACTIONS

Regulatory authorities can impose various penalties and enforcement actions to uphold the integrity of cybersecurity standards and ensure compliance.

These punitive actions can take many forms, ranging from financial penalties to orders requiring remedial actions or changes to business practices. However, not all penalties are monetary. Some enforcement actions are corrective, compelling organizations to address shortcomings in their cybersecurity practices.

Financial penalties or fines are among the most common forms of regulatory sanctions. These can be either predetermined, based on the type and severity of the violation, or discretionary, allowing the regulator to determine the amount based on individual circumstances. Fines can be substantial, often reaching millions of dollars, particularly for severe or repeated violations.

Another type of enforcement action is the requirement for remedial action. In these cases, the regulator identifies areas where the organization falls short of compliance and orders necessary corrective measures. These could range from revising cybersecurity policies and procedures, investing in new technologies or security measures, to providing additional staff training.

In extreme cases, regulators can impose operational penalties, including revoking licenses, ordering a halt to specific business activities, or initiating legal proceedings. While these are less common, their potential impact makes understanding and avoiding them vital.

Lastly, it is important to note that regulatory penalties are not just about financial loss or operational disruption. They also have a significant impact on an organization's reputation. The public announcement of regulatory sanctions can lead to a loss of customer trust, shareholder value, and potential business opportunities.

These diverse penalties underline the imperative for a robust, proactive approach to cybersecurity GRC. Understanding them can help organizations implement effective strategies to prevent, respond to, and recover from potential enforcement actions.

Recommendations:

- **Understand Penalties:** Acquaint yourself with the varying penalties and enforcement actions that regulatory authorities can impose. These punitive measures can range from financial penalties to orders requiring remedial actions or changes to business practices. Recognizing the diverse types of penalties helps anticipate the potential consequences of noncompliance.

- **Consider Financial Impacts:** Financial penalties or fines are among the most common regulatory sanctions. Understand that these can either be predetermined based on the severity of the violation or discretionary based on individual circumstances, often reaching substantial amounts for severe or repeated violations.

- **Prepare for Remedial Actions:** Be ready to be ordered to take remedial action. Regulatory authorities may identify areas of noncompliance and demand corrective measures such as revising cybersecurity policies, investing in new security technologies, or providing additional staff training.

- **Mitigate Operational Risks:** Familiarize yourself with extreme enforcement actions such as revoking licenses, halting specific business activities, or initiating legal proceedings. Although less common, their potential impact makes understanding and mitigating these risks crucial.
- **Safeguard Reputation:** Regulatory penalties can significantly impact an organization's reputation. Public announcements of sanctions can lead to a loss of customer trust, shareholder value, and potential business opportunities. Therefore, proactively managing compliance and demonstrating a commitment to cybersecurity is crucial.

UNDERSTANDING THE AUTHORITY BEHIND ENFORCEMENT ACTIONS

When discussing regulatory penalties, it is essential to understand who holds the authority to enforce these penalties. The power to implement cybersecurity regulations and impose penalties resides with various regulatory bodies, depending on the sector, jurisdiction, and specific rules. In the United States, for example, numerous federal and state agencies have authority over different aspects of cybersecurity.

In the broader regulatory landscape, authorities such as the Office of the Comptroller of the Currency (OCC), the Federal Deposit Insurance Corporation (FDIC), and the Consumer Financial Protection Bureau (CFPB) in the United States, among others, have significant roles in imposing cybersecurity regulations and their corresponding penalties.

The OCC, an independent bureau within the US Department of the Treasury, regulates all national banks and federal savings associations. The OCC has taken stringent action against financial institutions that violate cybersecurity norms, often in conjunction with other regulators like the FDIC. For instance, in 2016, the OCC, the FDIC, and the Federal Reserve fined a large global bank $185 million following a fraudulent sales practice scandal involving significant customer data breaches.

Meanwhile, the FDIC is an independent agency of the US federal government that preserves and promotes public confidence in the US financial system. The FDIC has enforcement authority over FDIC-insured banks and has exercised this authority to penalize noncompliant behaviors. This can be seen in the $600 million penalty levied on a leading bank in 2019, alongside other regulators, for failing to implement an effective compliance program, leading to a significant breach of customer information.

On the other hand, the CFPB, another US government agency, is responsible for consumer protection in the financial sector. The CFPB has been known to issue fines and Consent Orders against noncompliant financial institutions. An example of this was in 2017 when the CFPB fined a prominent credit reporting agency $100 million following a massive data breach, highlighting the hefty penalties that can result from noncompliance.

Additionally, the European Union's General Data Protection Regulation (GDPR) has had a substantial global impact, with heavy penalties for noncompliance, affecting any company that deals with E.U. citizens' data. One high-profile example occurred in 2019 when the UK's Information Commissioner's Office (ICO), which enforces the GDPR in the United Kingdom, proposed a fine of £183 million against a major airline for a significant data breach involving customer data.

As you can see, the landscape of regulatory authority is not just broad but also remarkably complex, covering multiple sectors and jurisdictions. Each regulatory body has its unique focus, regulations, and enforcement mechanisms, making it crucial for organizations to understand the specific obligations applicable to their operations.

At the banking level, regulators like the OCC and FDIC, alongside the Federal Reserve, are renowned for their stringent oversight and the enforcement of regulations to maintain the banking system's safety and soundness. Noncompliance can lead to Consent Orders, CMPs, and other serious repercussions, as demonstrated in numerous instances.

In contrast, agencies like the FTC, SEC, and CFPB focus on consumer protection, enforcing regulations designed to safeguard consumers' privacy and financial interests. Noncompliance penalties can also be severe, often involving substantial fines and potentially damaging Consent Orders.

On the state level, authorities in states like California and New York have made a significant impact with rigorous privacy laws, such as the California Consumer Privacy Act (CCPA) and the New York Department of Financial Services (NYDFS) cybersecurity regulations. These regulations are some of the most stringent in the nation, underscoring the trend toward a greater regulatory focus on data privacy and security at the state level.

Further, the influence of self-regulatory organizations (SROs), like the Financial Industry Regulatory Authority (FINRA) and the Payment Card Industry Security Standards Council (PCI SSC), cannot be ignored. These SROs often have substantial enforcement authority within their respective sectors and have been known to levy severe penalties for noncompliance.

Given this complex and multifaceted landscape, it becomes increasingly evident that understanding the regulatory authority is an essential part of an organization's cybersecurity strategy. This understanding should go beyond knowing the potential penalties for noncompliance to include comprehension of the jurisdiction, specific requirements, and expectations of each regulatory body. With a comprehensive and proactive approach, organizations can navigate this complex regulatory landscape, mitigate risks, and ensure ongoing compliance with cybersecurity regulations.

Regulatory enforcement authority is constantly evolving, and the landscape is becoming increasingly complex. New regulations are continually being introduced, and existing ones are regularly updated to reflect technological changes and threat landscapes. Therefore, staying abreast of the latest developments, maintaining open communication with regulatory bodies, and seeking expert legal and compliance advice are essential in navigating this complex landscape.

Recommendations:

- **Maintain Awareness:** Keep up-to-date with the latest regulatory developments and the enforcement authorities in your industry. Regular reviews and updates of your compliance program to align with the changing landscape will ensure you stay ahead of potential regulatory actions. Be proactive and treat compliance as a continuous journey rather than a destination.

- **Establish Communication Channels:** Actively maintain open lines of communication with relevant regulatory bodies. This helps understand their expectations and signals your commitment to cybersecurity and compliance. Regular interaction can also provide early warning signs of potential issues and allow for proactive resolution before penalties are enforced.

- **Seek Expert Guidance:** Regulatory compliance can be complex, particularly when multiple authorities are involved. Seek advice from legal and compliance experts who can guide you through the intricacies of the regulations that apply to your business. This includes understanding the nuances of each regulatory body's enforcement authority, interpreting complex regulatory language, and ensuring your cybersecurity practices meet the standards required.

THE IMPORTANCE OF UNDERSTANDING PENALTIES AS PART OF COMPLIANCE EFFORTS

A comprehensive understanding of regulatory penalties is a linchpin in managing compliance efforts, forming a cornerstone of effective GRC strategies. As we delve deeper into the implications of these penalties, we find that they serve dual roles: they are not only punitive mechanisms for noncompliance but also powerful deterrents to discourage organizations from adopting a lackadaisical approach toward their cybersecurity responsibilities.

The penalties associated with regulatory noncompliance underline the weight and seriousness of the regulatory landscape. They embody the potential repercussions of noncompliance, operating as potent reminders for businesses of the dire need to adhere to their cybersecurity obligations. Indeed, facing hefty fines, sanctions, or reputational damage can spur companies into action, prompting the establishment and maintenance of comprehensive cybersecurity strategies.

Simultaneously, these penalties are intended to deter laxity in cybersecurity practices. The threat of substantial financial and reputational costs often drives organizations to enforce stringent security measures proactively. Such actions can play a decisive role in curbing the risk of data breaches and other security incidents that could otherwise lead to regulatory penalties.

Deepening our understanding of the wide range and depth of potential penalties aids organizations in making informed decisions about their cybersecurity strategies. It highlights the potential ramifications of various choices or lack of action, enabling a comprehensive risk–benefit analysis - a process at the heart of effective GRC. Businesses can better understand the potential fallout from inadequate or ineffective cybersecurity measures by quantifying noncompliance risk. Such awareness allows for a more strategic allocation of resources toward bolstering cybersecurity defenses, which can significantly mitigate the risk of penalties.

But this understanding of penalties transcends mere avoidance of punitive actions. It fosters a broader perspective of the regulatory environment and how it influences business operations. With this insight, strategic decision-making can be more informed, guiding considerations such as budget allocations for cybersecurity initiatives or creating robust incident response plans incorporating potential regulatory implications.

Furthermore, it is not just about internalizing the fear of punishment or the drive to evade penalties. An in-depth understanding of the regulatory penalties fosters an organization's compliance culture. It creates an environment where regulations are respected and followed not solely due to fear of sanctions but because of an ingrained recognition of the inherent value of robust cybersecurity practices.

Understanding penalties helps shape an organization's compliance narrative in the broader picture of the organizational scheme. It promotes a proactive culture of risk management, where potential risks are identified, evaluated, and mitigated before they can culminate in breaches or violations. This proactive approach to risk management and a deep understanding of the implications of noncompliance can strengthen the organization's overall cybersecurity posture.

Ultimately, knowing regulatory penalties helps establish a holistic approach to cybersecurity beyond simply avoiding noncompliance. It fosters a deeper understanding of the regulatory landscape and the corresponding risks, guiding strategic decision-making, risk management, and resource allocation. It enhances the broader cybersecurity ecosystem within an organization, promoting an ingrained culture of compliance and proactive risk management. Doing so significantly reinforces the organization's cybersecurity defenses, paving the way for a more secure and compliant operational environment.

Recommendations:

- **Prioritize Understanding:** Make understanding penalties a priority within your compliance efforts. This understanding will provide a more holistic view of the regulatory environment, which can inform strategic decisions and foster a culture of compliance. Knowing the potential repercussions of noncompliance is essential in emphasizing the importance of cybersecurity within the organization.
- **Foster a Compliance Culture:** Use the potential penalties as a tool to foster a culture of compliance within your organization. When employees understand the possible consequences of noncompliance, they are more likely to adhere to cybersecurity policies and procedures. This increased

awareness can significantly reduce the risk of breaches and other incidents that could lead to regulatory penalties.

- **Leverage Penalties in Risk Management:** Include potential penalties in your risk management assessments. Understanding the potential costs of noncompliance can inform your decisions about where to allocate resources and how to prioritize various cybersecurity initiatives. By factoring in these potential costs, you can make more informed, strategic decisions about your cybersecurity posture.

MATTERS REQUIRING ATTENTION (MRAS)

MRAs form a critical component of the regulatory landscape, often surfacing during regulatory examinations as issues that require immediate remediation. They serve as a primary tool for regulators to point out weaknesses and areas of noncompliance within an organization, thus requiring immediate action.

MRAs are typically issued when a regulator identifies a practice, condition, or deficiency that could potentially risk a bank's safety, soundness, or compliance with laws and regulations. They serve as the initial warning from the regulator, prompting the entity to correct its course. Responding to and addressing MRAs effectively is crucial to maintaining regulatory compliance and avoiding further enforcement actions.

Addressing MRAs is not a simple task of ticking boxes; it requires an in-depth understanding of the regulator's expectations and a comprehensive plan to remediate identified deficiencies. Institutions are expected to address the root cause of the issues identified in the MRA rather than merely addressing the symptoms. This could entail changes to policies, procedures, systems, or even organizational structures and often requires the commitment of significant resources.

Moreover, responding to MRAs can be complex, with multiple stages and involving various stakeholders. The process may include creating a detailed action plan, regularly reporting progress to regulators, and demonstrating the effectiveness of remediation actions. Additionally, it is crucial to remember that failure to address an MRA adequately could result in more severe enforcement actions, including consent orders or CMPs.

MRAs indicate regulatory expectations and allow organizations to correct their course before more stringent enforcement actions are taken. Understanding the significance of MRAs, the process for addressing them, and the potential implications of not addressing them effectively can help organizations navigate regulatory examinations and maintain a strong compliance posture.

In conclusion, MRAs are a key component of the regulatory environment and carry significant implications for institutions under regulatory scrutiny. They demand immediate action and necessitate a proactive and comprehensive response. A clear understanding of MRAs, the expectations they set, and the processes to address them effectively is essential for maintaining compliance and avoiding more severe enforcement actions. The real-world examples of Citigroup, Wells Fargo, and JPMorgan Chase underline the urgency and importance of addressing MRAs adequately and swiftly.

Recommendations:

- **Treat MRAs Seriously:** Treat MRAs as high-priority items that demand immediate attention. Their significance in the regulatory process must not be taken lightly. Failure to address MRAs promptly and effectively can lead to more severe enforcement actions.
- **Engage with Regulators:** If your organization receives an MRA, engage with the regulatory agency to understand their concerns and expectations thoroughly. Open and proactive communication can aid in effectively addressing the issues raised and demonstrate your commitment to compliance.
- **Implement Remedial Actions:** Develop and implement a plan of action to address the issues identified in the MRA. This may involve revising your cybersecurity policies, enhancing security controls, or providing additional employee training. The action plan should be comprehensive, addressing the root cause of the issues, not just the symptoms.

CONSENT ORDERS

Consent Orders are a regulatory tool frequently utilized by authorities like the OCC and the FDIC to enforce compliance. These are formal, legally binding agreements voluntarily agreed upon by the regulator and the regulated entity to resolve alleged violations of regulations. Typically, these violations could range from noncompliance with data protection standards to lapses in privacy regulations, and the party under scrutiny neither admits nor denies the accusations. Understanding Consent Orders is paramount as their far-reaching implications affect the organization's operations, reputation, and financial stability.

In a cybersecurity context, Consent Orders carry significant weight. They often mandate specific remedial actions to correct the identified deficiencies. These corrective measures could be substantial and multifaceted, from altering data protection measures to restructuring business operations and investing heavily in cybersecurity infrastructure. Additionally, these orders often involve ongoing compliance monitoring, leading to increased regulatory scrutiny. This continuous supervision necessitates maintaining an up-to-date and robust cybersecurity infrastructure to meet heightened regulatory expectations.

A notable real-world example occurred in 2020 when the OCC issued a Consent Order against Capital One in response to a high-profile data breach that exposed the data of over 100 million customers. Besides paying a hefty penalty, the bank was ordered to enhance its risk management program, internal governance, and controls. This Consent Order underscored the significant ramifications for businesses and the critical need to comply with all the stipulated terms and conditions.

Another instance of a Consent Order is the case involving Wells Fargo in 2016. The FDIC and OCC jointly issued a Consent Order in response to the unauthorized account scandal, which involved employees opening millions of fraudulent savings and checking accounts without customers' consent. The Order required Wells Fargo to pay restitution to all victims and implement an enterprise-wide compliance risk management program, highlighting the broad and impactful changes that can come from such regulatory actions.

Implementing a Consent Order signifies the beginning of a highly regulated period for an organization. The terms and expectations embedded within the Consent Order require a comprehensive understanding to ensure strict adherence. Any misinterpretation or noncompliance could lead to severe consequences, such as increased penalties or the onset of additional enforcement actions. Therefore, it is crucial for organizations to collaborate closely with their legal and compliance departments and often seek advice from external consultants or legal experts to ensure a complete understanding and compliance.

An important aspect to remember is that a Consent Order, while resolving a specific regulatory issue, does not serve as a blanket absolution from future regulatory scrutiny or enforcement actions. Even after issuing a Consent Order, ongoing and heightened compliance efforts are necessary. Organizations must continually demonstrate their commitment to fulfilling regulatory obligations and their ability to promptly identify and address potential compliance issues.

Finally, the termination of a Consent Order is a process that is typically prolonged and stringent. Regulators generally demand proof of substantial progress and a consistent track record of compliance over an extended period before they consider terminating a Consent Order. The journey to removing a Consent Order necessitates a long-term commitment to investing resources, time, and effort.

For example, in 2018, after seven years, the OCC lifted a Consent Order it had imposed on U.S. Bank following a money laundering scandal. The termination followed after years of demonstrating substantial improvements in its anti-money laundering controls and commitment to establishing a robust compliance culture.

In summary, Consent Orders play a significant role in the regulatory enforcement landscape. The ramifications of receiving a Consent Order are substantial and lasting, requiring organizations to demonstrate their ability to remediate past mistakes and their commitment to maintaining a robust and proactive compliance posture in the future. This underlines the importance of understanding Consent Orders fully and comprehensively, equipping businesses to handle these regulatory tools effectively. Real-world examples, such as Capital One, Wells Fargo, and U.S. Bank, illustrate the grave implications of Consent Orders and the intense commitment required to navigate their terms successfully.

Recommendations:

- **Understand Consent Orders:** If your organization is issued with a Consent Order, it is vital to understand its terms fully and the implications for your business. Engage legal and compliance professionals who can guide your response and ensure that all relevant personnel understand the Order and their responsibilities under it.

- **Implement Remedial Measures:** Take swift action to address the issues identified in the Consent Order. This could involve many measures, from overhauling your cybersecurity framework to providing additional employee training. Be thorough in your response, and aim to address the root causes of the issues rather than merely treating the symptoms.
- **Engage with Regulators:** Maintain open lines of communication with the regulatory authorities throughout the Consent Order. Show that you are proactive in addressing the issues, and be transparent about your progress. This can help to build trust with the regulators and could potentially influence their decision when it comes to lifting the Order.

CIVIL MONEY PENALTIES (CMPS)

CMPs are an essential enforcement mechanism employed by regulatory authorities to enforce compliance with cybersecurity and other regulations. These financial penalties are levied against organizations that are noncompliant with specific regulatory standards, serving as punitive measures to drive compliance and deter future noncompliance. Often, CMPs are not standalone enforcement actions but are used with other regulatory tools, such as Consent Orders or cease and desist orders, to create a comprehensive compliance enforcement strategy.

CMPs, depending on the severity of the noncompliance, the potential harm caused, and several other factors, can vary significantly in their monetary value. Some CMPs may be relatively small, acting as a slap on the wrist for minor infractions, while others can be substantial, reaching into the millions or even billions of dollars for egregious or persistent violations. The significant variability in CMPs is one reason why understanding them is crucial for organizations.

There are several factors that regulatory authorities take into account when deciding to issue a CMP and in determining the amount. These include the severity of the noncompliance, the duration for which the noncompliance persisted, the harm caused to consumers or the public, and the organization's prior history of compliance or noncompliance. An organization's actions after discovering noncompliance, including the speed and effectiveness of its response, can also influence the regulators' decisions.

In the case of major financial institutions, regulatory bodies such as the OCC and the FDIC have imposed substantial CMPs. For instance, in 2019, the OCC levied a $400 million civil money penalty against Citibank for its risk management, internal controls, and audit program deficiencies. In the same year, the FDIC imposed a CMP of $614 million on USAA Federal Savings Bank for noncompliance with the Bank Secrecy Act and anti-money laundering laws. These examples illustrate the potentially enormous financial implications of CMPs and the need for organizations to fully understand and comply with all relevant regulations.

When an organization is faced with a CMP, it is imperative to respond proactively and professionally. This response includes immediate engagement with the regulatory authorities, a thorough understanding of the reasons behind the issuance of the CMP, and swift and effective action to address and rectify the identified issues. A well-handled response to a CMP can not only mitigate the immediate impact of the penalty but can also demonstrate the organization's commitment to compliance, thereby reducing the risk of future penalties.

Moreover, organizations should not view CMPs purely as punitive measures but as invaluable opportunities to learn and improve. CMPs highlight specific areas where an organization's compliance efforts may have fallen short, providing clear, tangible guidance on where improvements are needed. By taking lessons from these experiences, organizations can strengthen their compliance programs, adjust their cybersecurity strategies, and reduce the risk of future penalties.

In summary, CMPs are a potent tool used by regulators to enforce compliance and penalize noncompliance. Their potential financial impact can be substantial, making it crucial for organizations to understand the circumstances under which they might be issued and how to respond if they are effective. Ultimately, by viewing CMPs not just as punitive measures but also as opportunities for improvement, organizations can leverage them to strengthen their overall compliance programs and cybersecurity posture.

Recommendations:

- **Learn from CMPs:** If your organization faces a Civil Money Penalty, view it as a learning opportunity. Use it to identify and address gaps in your compliance program and strengthen defenses against future enforcement actions. Remember, the goal is not just to resolve the current issue but to prevent similar problems in the future.
- **Respond Proactively:** Do not ignore a CMP or delay your response. Engage with the regulators, understand the reasons behind the penalty, and develop a plan to address the issues identified. A proactive response can help mitigate the penalty's impact and reduce the risk of future penalties.
- **Review Compliance History:** Regularly review your organization's compliance history, including past CMPs. Understanding your compliance track record can help you to anticipate potential issues, avoid repeat mistakes, and demonstrate your commitment to continuous improvement in your compliance efforts.

CEASE AND DESIST ORDERS

Cease and Desist Orders, often issued by regulatory bodies, are powerful tools designed to protect consumers and maintain the integrity and fairness of the market. These orders typically require an organization to halt practices that violate regulations, including cybersecurity-related ones. Such orders can mandate a halt to practices posing a risk to data security, consumer privacy, or those that otherwise infringe upon established cybersecurity standards.

Understanding the nature, application, and potential implications of Cease and Desist Orders is paramount for organizations. Noncompliance with these orders can lead to severe penalties, often encompassing substantial fines and business restrictions. Further, Cease and Desist Orders can significantly blow an organization's reputation. A tarnished reputation can lead to a loss of consumer trust and potential market share erosion, affecting the organization's bottom line.

When a Cease and Desist Order is issued, the organization should seek to fully comprehend the reasons behind the issuance of the Order and the specific actions or practices required to cease. Cease and Desist Orders are not recommendations; they are directives that must be taken seriously. Immediate action should be taken to comply with the terms of the Order to prevent exacerbation of the situation.

An excellent example of a Cease and Desist Order is the one issued by the NYDFS against the digital currency company Bittrex in 2019. NYDFS issued the Order due to deficiencies in the company's compliance program related to anti-money laundering standards, causing the firm to cease its operations in New York State. Another example is when the Federal Trade Commission (FTC) issued a Cease and Desist Order against Facebook in 2011. The Order required Facebook to stop misrepresenting the privacy and security of users' personal information.

In the wake of a Cease and Desist Order, it is prudent for the organization to undertake a comprehensive review of all its practices. This exercise can help ensure that all other operations comply with the pertinent regulations. Such proactive steps not only help to ward off further regulatory problems but can also demonstrate the organization's commitment to regulatory compliance. It communicates that the organization is serious about meeting its regulatory obligations, potentially leading to a more favorable view from regulatory bodies and the public.

However, the journey does not end with compliance with the Cease and Desist Order. Lifting such an order can often be a complex and protracted process. It typically requires the organization to exhibit sustained compliance with regulations over a significant period and may involve continuous monitoring by regulatory authorities. This commitment to long-term compliance further emphasizes the need for organizations to allocate sufficient resources to managing and navigating the compliance landscape effectively.

Lastly, organizations should note that while Cease and Desist Orders are impactful and carry significant implications, they can also serve as opportunities for learning and improvement. By carefully analyzing the circumstances leading to an order and proactively taking steps to address these issues, an organization can emerge with more robust cybersecurity practices, a more profound commitment to regulatory compliance, and a more substantial reputation in the long term.

Recommendations:

- **Respond Swiftly:** Respond quickly and decisively if your organization is issued a Cease and Desist Order. Understand the reasons behind the Order, cease the identified practices, and take steps to ensure that all other practices comply with regulations.
- **Review Practices:** Conduct a thorough review of your organization's practices in response to a Cease and Desist Order. This can help to identify and address other potential issues before they attract regulatory attention. Remember, the goal is to prevent further regulatory matters, not just to resolve the current ones.
- **Prepare for the Long Term:** Be prepared for the fact that lifting a Cease and Desist Order can be a long-term process. Plan for ongoing compliance efforts and monitoring, and allocate sufficient resources to manage this process effectively. A proactive and committed approach can help expedite the Order's lifting and reduce the risk of future regulatory issues.

OTHER ENFORCEMENT ACTIONS

As we delve deeper into the spectrum of regulatory enforcement measures, it becomes evident that regulatory bodies possess many tools to ensure adherence to the rules they set forth. These enforcement mechanisms can vary depending on many factors, including jurisdiction, sector, and the specifics of the regulations in question. While we have already discussed standard methods such as Consent Orders, CMPs, and Cease and Desist Orders, enforcement actions can also encompass a range of other measures. These may include the revocation of licenses, imposition of business restrictions, requirement for mandatory audits, or other intervention methods.

For instance, license revocations can be particularly impactful, preventing businesses from legally operating in their field until they meet regulatory compliance standards. On the other hand, business restrictions can limit the scope of an organization's operations, often enforcing changes to business models or practices. Mandatory audits can require companies to undergo rigorous and comprehensive examinations of their operations and compliance practices, usually carried out by independent auditors, and these audits can unearth further areas for regulatory scrutiny.

Further to this, it is worth noting that regulators are increasingly favoring a 'carrot and stick' approach when enforcing compliance. This strategy involves pairing punitive measures, such as previously mentioned, with incentives to encourage better compliance behavior. For example, some regulators may offer reduced penalties or other benefits to organizations that self-report violations or that can demonstrate a reasonable faith effort to improve their compliance. This approach penalizes noncompliant behavior, rewards proactive compliance efforts, and promotes a culture of regulatory adherence.

An instance of this approach is the "Amnesty Program" run by the Securities and Exchange Commission (SEC), which offers protections to whistleblowers who voluntarily provide the SEC with unique and useful information that leads to a successful enforcement action. This incentivizes employees to report any regulatory breaches they uncover, promoting a culture of transparency and compliance within organizations.

Despite the wide range of potential enforcement actions and the variability in their application, the central message remains the same: regulators wield significant powers to enforce compliance, and noncompliance can lead to severe and potentially business-altering consequences. Given the gravity of potential repercussions, it becomes abundantly clear that adopting a proactive, diligent, and comprehensive approach to regulatory compliance is essential for any organization.

In the end, navigating the labyrinth of regulatory enforcement requires understanding the law's letter and the ethos behind it. It necessitates not only the knowledge of potential penalties but also an appreciation for regulators' incentives. Ultimately, it calls for a commitment to creating and nurturing a culture of compliance throughout the organization, reinforcing the notion that regulatory compliance is not just a requirement but a cornerstone of ethical and responsible business practices.

Recommendations:

- **Stay Informed:** Keep abreast of the regulatory landscape in your sector and jurisdiction. Understand the potential enforcement actions that regulators can take and their implications. This knowledge can help you to anticipate potential issues and take proactive steps to avoid them.
- **Be Proactive:** Do not wait for a regulatory enforcement action to motivate your compliance efforts. Be proactive in your approach, continually evaluating and improving your compliance program. This can help to prevent regulatory issues and demonstrate your commitment to compliance.
- **Please seek Expert Advice:** Regulatory compliance can be complex, and it is often helpful to seek expert advice. Whether it is legal counsel, a compliance consultant, or a cybersecurity specialist, these professionals can provide valuable insights and guidance to help you navigate the regulatory landscape effectively.

OTHER ENFORCEMENT ACTIONS

The complexity of regulatory actions in cybersecurity often calls for specialized knowledge and experience. This is where consultants and experts come into play. Their expertise can prove instrumental in navigating the intricacies of regulatory actions, helping organizations understand their obligations, anticipate potential issues, and craft effective responses.

Engaging consultants provides several advantages. First, they bring a wealth of knowledge and expertise, often derived from years of experience in the field. This specialized understanding can illuminate regulations' nuances and enforcement, offering clarity amid complexity. Experts are familiar with the regulatory landscape and are often adept at interpreting and applying laws and regulations in practical, operational terms.

Second, consultants offer an external perspective that can help identify areas of risk that may be overlooked internally. They can provide a fresh set of eyes to evaluate an organization's cybersecurity posture and compliance efforts, enabling a more thorough assessment.

Thirdly, consultants can aid in the crafting of robust and effective compliance strategies. They can guide organizations through developing policies and procedures that meet regulatory requirements and align with the organization's unique goals and operational context.

Moreover, consultants can provide invaluable assistance when facing enforcement actions such as Consent Orders or Cease and Desist Orders. They can help interpret the terms of the Order, develop a plan of action, and liaise with regulators, helping to ensure a professional and proactive response.

However, the use of consultants is not without potential pitfalls. One of these is the risk of over-reliance. While consultants can provide valuable guidance, organizations must maintain ownership of their compliance efforts. Outsourcing should not mean abdicating responsibility.

In addition, consultants may not always be fully aware of the organization's specific operational context or culture. This can lead to advice that is theoretically sound but challenging to implement in practice. Therefore, organizations must ensure that consultants understand their specific operational environment, business objectives, and risk appetite.

Moreover, considering the critical role they play, the selection of consultants should be done with care. Not all consultants are created equal. The competency and integrity of these consultants are paramount, as their advice can significantly impact the organization's compliance status and overall cybersecurity posture.

Lastly, it is important to note that while consultants can provide expert advice and guidance, the ultimate decision-making power lies with the organization. Consultants can offer recommendations, but it is up to the organization to evaluate these recommendations and decide on the best course of action.

Recommendations:

- **Harness Expertise:** Leverage the specialized knowledge of consultants to gain a nuanced understanding of the regulatory landscape and its implications. This will aid you in deciphering complex regulatory issues, enabling you to navigate the multifaceted world of cybersecurity regulations and compliance more confidently.
- **Maintain Ownership:** Even as you benefit from external expertise, control your compliance efforts. It is crucial to remember that while consultants can provide valuable guidance, the ultimate responsibility for compliance

resides within your organization. Do not abdicate this responsibility; use consultants as advisors and facilitators in your compliance journey.

- **Select with Care:** Exercise prudence when choosing consultants. The quality of their advice can significantly influence your organization's compliance status and overall cybersecurity health. Ensure that they have a proven track record, demonstrate a high level of competence, and uphold the highest standards of professional integrity.

- **Contextual Understanding:** Make sure consultants know your organization's unique operational context, business objectives, and risk appetite. This understanding can ensure that their advice is theoretically sound, practically implementable, and aligned with your specific needs.

- **Decision-Making Power:** Recognize that consultants are advisors, not decision-makers. They can offer recommendations, but your final decision should always remain. Evaluate their advice critically and make informed decisions that align with your organization's goals and compliance obligations.

Chapter Conclusion

The role of regulatory compliance in the sphere of cybersecurity management cannot be overstated. It forms a critical element of an organization's overarching strategy as a keystone in establishing and maintaining secure systems and processes. An in-depth comprehension of the regulatory environment, including the prospective enforcement measures and penalties for noncompliance, empowers organizations to architect more effective, proactive, and robust compliance strategies.

Beyond merely sidestepping regulatory penalties, these strategies can contribute to the fortification of cybersecurity defenses, safeguarding an organization's data, reputation, and bottom line from potential breaches. In the intricate web of today's digital world, a single security breach can lead to catastrophic outcomes, damaging not just the finances but also the credibility of an organization in the public eye. Hence, a proactive approach toward compliance is a potent shield, insulating the organization from potential vulnerabilities and risks.

However, it is crucial to remember that the journey toward compliance is not a sprint but a marathon. It is not a single task to be checked off a list but rather a continual commitment that must be integrated into an organization's operations. Compliance is an ongoing evaluation, adaptation, and improvement process, a never-ending cycle of learning and evolving that mirrors the dynamic nature of the cybersecurity landscape.

Cybersecurity is characterized by its rapid and relentless evolution, with new threats emerging and old ones morphing into more potent versions. As such, staying compliant necessitates staying vigilant, adaptable, and proactive. It requires organizations to stay ahead of the curve, anticipating potential threats and updating their defenses accordingly. It also demands flexibility, as organizations must adapt their strategies to changing regulations and evolving threat landscapes.

Additionally, the path toward compliance is not an isolated journey. It involves open lines of communication with regulatory bodies and an understanding of their expectations and requirements. It requires collaboration and coordination across different departments within the organization, ensuring a collective, unified effort toward a common goal.

Sometimes, it may also involve collaboration with other organizations, industry bodies, and government agencies to share knowledge, best practices, and insights. These collaborative efforts can help to raise the bar for cybersecurity compliance across entire industries, creating a safer and more secure digital environment for all.

Moreover, practical compliance efforts can also yield business benefits. Besides avoiding penalties, a robust compliance program can build trust with customers, partners, and stakeholders, showing them that the organization is committed to protecting their data. It can also offer a competitive advantage, particularly in sectors where consumer data security is a crucial concern.

Regulatory compliance in cybersecurity is much more than a necessary obligation. It is an opportunity to strengthen defenses, build trust, and create a culture of excellence and responsibility. When embarked upon with diligence and commitment, it is a journey that can lead to a more robust, safer, and more successful organization. Therefore, as we continue to navigate the complex and ever-changing landscape of cybersecurity, let us remember that compliance is not just about following rules – it is about leading the way toward a more secure and resilient digital future.

Case Study: Phoenix Corporation and Robust Compliance

Phoenix Corporation, a multinational firm in the technology sector, faced an intricate web of cybersecurity regulations spanning multiple jurisdictions. Flynn, the company's newly appointed Chief Information Security Officer (CISO), found himself at the helm of a complex task: ensuring that Phoenix Corporation fully complies with all applicable regulations while safeguarding the company's cybersecurity posture.

Flynn's first step was to stay informed about the evolving regulatory landscape. He made it a point to regularly update himself on the existing and emerging cybersecurity regulations pertinent to Phoenix's operations. He became adept at understanding the potential enforcement actions regulators could take and their implications, which allowed him to anticipate potential issues and develop proactive strategies. However, he recognized that the complexity of the task demanded specialized expertise.

To this end, Flynn brought in a team of regulatory consultants. They had the requisite knowledge of the regulatory landscape and its implications, helping Phoenix decipher complex issues and navigate compliance requirements confidently. However, Flynn ensured that the company maintained ownership of its compliance efforts. He worked with the consultants as advisors, using their guidance to aid the company's decisions, but always ensured that the ultimate responsibility remained within the organization.

With the consultants' assistance, Phoenix could understand and respond to various regulatory actions, such as Consent Orders, CMPs, and Cease and Desist Orders. They also helped understand the broad array of enforcement tools regulators could use, including license revocations, business restrictions, and mandatory audits. By treating regulatory penalties as learning opportunities, Phoenix was able to identify the gaps in its compliance program and bolster its defenses.

In conclusion, Flynn's journey underscored the importance of regulatory compliance as an integral aspect of Phoenix's cybersecurity management. By understanding the regulatory landscape, including potential enforcement actions and penalties for noncompliance, Phoenix was able to develop effective and proactive compliance strategies. Flynn's story highlighted that staying compliant means staying vigilant, adaptable, and proactive in an ever-evolving world of cybersecurity.

CHAPTER 24

Addressing and Remediating Regulatory Findings

"When faced with regulatory feedback and findings, approach them as valuable insights rather than obstacles. Embrace the opportunity to learn, adapt, and continuously improve your cybersecurity measures."

Addressing and rectifying regulatory findings involves several critical steps. The first stage is understanding regulatory penalties and the best practices to avoid them. This is followed by managing regulatory feedback and results and formulating a remediation plan. Allocating resources and responsibilities for remediation is another key step in this process. The path then leads to monitoring progress and compliance and reporting to the regulator. Individuals can learn how to constructively respond to regulatory findings by covering these areas. Furthermore, they can allocate resources appropriately and manage the remediation process effectively. The goal is to provide a clear path toward managing regulatory issues and completing remediation and compliance tasks.

RECEIVING AND REVIEWING REGULATORY FEEDBACK AND FINDINGS

Managing regulatory findings is a comprehensive process that necessitates a deep understanding of the feedback and findings provided by the regulatory bodies. This journey of experience commences with identifying the types of regulatory findings. These findings vary widely in nature and severity, from minor observations requiring minimal corrective action to serious noncompliance issues threatening the organization's operations and reputation.

This initial recognition is far from a cursory glance at the issues raised. It involves detailed analysis and comprehension of the findings, their basis, and their implications. In this context, communication plays a pivotal role. Understanding these findings and ensuring that all relevant organizational stakeholders clearly understand the issues is important. This involves educating them on the problems identified, their potential impact, the potential consequences of inaction, and the remediation plan.

Analyzing the implications of findings is a multilayered process that demands a comprehensive perspective. It involves an examination of the extent of the problem, determining which areas of the organization it impacts, and anticipating the potential repercussions if the issues remain unaddressed. This complex task calls for a multidisciplinary approach, drawing on the expertise and insights of your cybersecurity team and the legal, operations, and management teams. This collective approach ensures that all potential implications are considered, and no stone is left unturned.

In responding to regulatory bodies, promptness and respect are key. Your organization should acknowledge the findings and convey your commitment to rectifying the identified issues as soon as they are received and understood. This acknowledgment should be communicated in a manner that displays professionalism and dedication to compliance. It goes a long way in demonstrating your organization's seriousness about maintaining high cybersecurity standards and adherence to regulations.

Once the findings are thoroughly understood and communicated, the next phase involves gathering additional information and data relevant to the results. This task is expansive and can encompass a range of data sources, including past audit reports, specific system logs, incident reports, employee feedback, and more. The aim is to collect data and comprehensively understand the problems identified. This holistic view enables your organization to formulate an informed, effective remediation plan. It ensures that the remedial actions you take are not just reactive but targeted, strategic measures that address the root causes of the issues, thereby preventing their recurrence.

Recommendations:

- **Identify Regulatory Findings:** Begin by recognizing and understanding the types of regulatory findings your organization receives. These can range from minor observations to severe noncompliance issues. A comprehensive understanding of the findings, their basis, and implications is the first step in effectively managing them.
- **Communicate Findings Internally:** Ensure all relevant organizational stakeholders are educated about the identified regulatory findings. They must understand the issues, their potential impact, the consequences of inaction, and the remediation plan. Clear internal communication facilitates a coordinated response and a swift resolution.
- **Analyze Implications:** Conduct a detailed examination of the extent of the regulatory findings and the areas they impact within the organization. Utilize a multidisciplinary approach involving your cybersecurity,

legal, operations, and management teams to understand potential repercussions and ensure no aspect is overlooked.

- **Acknowledge Findings:** Display promptness and respect in responding to the regulatory bodies. Acknowledge the findings and commit to rectifying the identified issues as soon as possible. This approach demonstrates your organization's commitment to maintaining high cybersecurity standards and adherence to regulations.

- **Gather Relevant Data:** After understanding the regulatory findings, gather additional information from past audit reports, system logs, incident reports, and employee feedback. This comprehensive data collection helps you understand the problems deeper, enabling your organization to devise an effective, targeted remediation plan that addresses the root causes and prevents recurrence.

CREATING A REMEDIATION PLAN

Devising a strategic remediation plan following a comprehensive understanding of regulatory findings is an intricate and crucial task. It signifies not just a reaction to problems that have been identified but the inception of a well-structured plan designed to address root causes and prevent future instances of noncompliance. This beginning phase, which resembles the initiation stage in project management, includes identifying the problem, recognizing its dimensions, establishing clear objectives, and understanding the stakeholders involved.

In project management, this initiation phase also includes the creation of a project charter, a formal document that outlines the purpose, objectives, stakeholders, and planned approach of the project. This would involve detailing the regulatory findings and creating a document that sets the groundwork for the remediation efforts. It is a roadmap that offers a clear overview of what will be achieved and how the organization plans to get there. This charter serves as a reference point throughout the remediation process.

The next step in this complex process is the identification of the root causes of the identified compliance issues. The intention is to delve deeper than the superficial symptoms and understand why these problems have arisen. This crucial stage requires a detailed, methodical examination of all the systems, processes, and human factors that may have contributed to these issues, much like the planning stage in project management. This planning also entails conducting a thorough risk assessment, defining roles and responsibilities, and determining a suitable remediation budget.

After identifying the root causes, the remediation process defines the objectives. This process is a mirror image of the goal-setting step in project planning. The remediation objectives could span from enhancing a weak process, mitigating an overlooked risk, or improving the organization's overall compliance posture. It is paramount that these objectives are articulated, pertinent to the identified issues, and in alignment with the organization's broader strategic goals.

With the clear articulation of objectives, the focus then shifts to the prioritization of actions, similar to project management tasks that involve organizing based on importance and impact. A systematic, risk-based analysis and ranking of the issues based on their level of risk and severity is essential. The evaluation ensures that the most critical issues are addressed first, and that resources are effectively allocated. A prioritized list of actions helps ensure that resources and efforts are directed toward the highest risk and biggest impact areas.

As the planning process continues, the next phase is the development of remediation strategies and tactics. In project management, the project plan includes details about how the project will be executed, monitored, and controlled. Similarly, in the remediation plan, it is crucial to ensure that the strategies and tactics for each action item are specific, measurable, achievable, relevant, and time-bound (SMART). Setting SMART objectives makes the plans practical, trackable, and aligned with the previously defined objectives.

Continuing with the project plan, it is also important to establish clear timelines and milestones for the remediation activities. These benchmarks act as a guide for tracking progress and maintaining momentum throughout the remediation process. They provide the team with a clear path forward, including key dates and targets. Consider regulatory deadlines, ensuring the timelines align with these external parameters.

Finally, each task in the remediation plan should have a designated owner, an approach that mirrors the assignment of tasks in project management. Assigning ownership and accountability for each action item promotes efficiency in task management and instills a sense of responsibility among team members. It creates a framework where everyone involved knows their role, their part in achieving compliance, and their contribution to the broader objectives of the remediation plan. This fosters a commitment to the process and a dedication to successfully implementing the remediation plan.

Organizations can apply structured, effective, and efficient methodologies proven in other contexts by adopting a project management approach to designing a remediation plan. This process facilitates communication, streamlines decision-making, and bolsters the overall management of the remediation process. Ultimately, it ensures the success of the remediation plan, leading to improved compliance and reduced risk for the organization.

Recommendations:

- **Initiate the Remediation Plan:** Begin by identifying the problem, recognizing its dimensions, establishing clear objectives, and understanding the stakeholders involved. Create a project charter outlining the remediation plan's purpose, objectives, and planned approach, similar to the initiation phase in project management.
- **Identify Root Causes:** Go beyond the superficial symptoms and delve into the fundamental reasons causing the compliance issues. Conduct a detailed examination of systems, processes, and human factors, and

perform a thorough risk assessment. This stage mirrors the planning phase in project management.

- **Define Objectives:** Articulate clear remediation objectives relevant to the identified issues and aligned with the organization's strategic goals. This mirrors the goal-setting step in project planning.
- **Prioritize Actions:** Conduct a systematic, risk-based analysis and rank the issues based on their level of risk and severity. This helps ensure resources and efforts are directed toward areas of highest risk and biggest impact, similar to how tasks are prioritized in project management.
- **Develop SMART Remediation Strategies:** Create SMART strategies and tactics for each action item. This makes the plans practical and trackable and aligns them with the defined objectives, similar to how a project plan is developed.
- **Establish Clear Timelines and Milestones:** Create benchmarks for tracking progress and maintaining momentum throughout the remediation process. These should consider regulatory deadlines, ensuring timelines align with these external parameters.
- **Assign Task Owners:** Designate an owner for each task in the remediation plan. This promotes efficiency and instills a sense of responsibility among team members, mirroring the assignment of tasks in project management.
- **Apply Project Management Methodologies:** Incorporate structured, effective, and efficient methodologies from project management to facilitate communication, streamline decision-making, and improve the overall management of the remediation process. This approach leads to the success of the remediation plan, improved compliance, and reduced risk.

ALLOCATING RESOURCES AND RESPONSIBILITIES FOR REMEDIATION

Upon developing and approving a robust remediation plan, the following stage involves the meticulous identification of the necessary resources for remediation, coupled with strategic allocation. These resources, key components in the successful execution of your remediation plan, span a broad spectrum. They might encompass tangible assets like advanced hardware or software solutions critical to addressing technological shortcomings. On the other hand, human assets, which refer to the personnel intricately executing various aspects of the remediation process, are also paramount. Remember that your identified resources should be sufficient to cater to the demands of the remediation tasks and readily available when needed. This ensures that the remediation process does not hit roadblocks due to resource limitations, facilitating a smooth, efficient operation.

Moving to a more fiscal perspective, budget allocation and strategic financial planning play a pivotal role in resource allocation. This involves looking at the cost implications of the remediation plan, including the price tags attached to new hardware or software, the cost of training programs, external consultant fees, or even overtime compensation for your team. Every potential cost associated with the remediation process should be estimated and included in a comprehensive budget. In addition, it is judicious to establish a contingency fund designed to cater to any unexpected costs that may arise during the execution of the plan. This ensures financial resilience and readiness to tackle unforeseen events without destabilizing your organization's finances.

Following the identification and allocation of resources, there is the task of assigning roles and responsibilities to the personnel involved in the remediation process. This step should be conducted precisely and echo the ownership and accountability defined in the remediation plan. Everyone involved must know their role, expectations, and how their performance will be measured. This fosters a sense of personal investment and accountability, ultimately driving the efficient execution of tasks.

Moreover, training and skill development for personnel should not be overlooked. It is crucial to ensure they are adequately equipped to execute their roles effectively, both in knowledge and skills. This may necessitate organizing tailored training sessions workshops or even bringing in external consultants. These efforts enhance the team's competence and boost their confidence in handling their assigned tasks, leading to better performance and outcomes.

Lastly, establishing effective communication channels and reporting structures is vital in steering the remediation process toward success. Effective communication fosters transparency, enhances coordination, and ensures that all stakeholders stay informed about the progress of the remediation process. Regular updates, meetings, and progress reports help keep everyone on the same page, promoting mutual understanding and collaboration. Furthermore, a well-defined reporting structure ensures that information flows smoothly from one level to another, facilitating quick decision-making and problem-solving.

Recommendations:

- **Identify and Allocate Resources:** Determine the necessary resources for executing your remediation plan, including tangible assets like hardware or software solutions and human assets like personnel. Ensure these resources are sufficient and readily available to prevent roadblocks during remediation.

- **Plan Budget and Financial Resources:** Analyze the cost implications of the remediation plan, including new hardware or software, training programs, consultant fees, or overtime compensation. Develop a comprehensive budget and establish a contingency fund to cater to unexpected costs, ensuring financial resilience.

- **Assign Roles and Responsibilities:** Precisely assign roles and responsibilities to personnel involved in the remediation process. Each individual should know their role, expectations, and how their performance will be measured to foster a sense of personal investment and accountability.

- **Train and Develop Skills:** Equip personnel with the necessary knowledge and skills for their roles. This might involve organizing training sessions, workshops, or bringing in external consultants. These efforts enhance team competence and confidence, leading to better performance and outcomes.

- **Establish Communication and Reporting Structures:** Develop effective communication channels and reporting structures to foster transparency, enhance coordination, and keep all stakeholders informed about the progress of the remediation process. Regular updates, meetings, and progress reports ensure everyone stays on the same page. A well-defined reporting structure facilitates quick decision-making and problem-solving.

MONITORING PROGRESS AND COMPLIANCE

Once crafting a comprehensive remediation plan has been completed and the necessary resources have been judiciously allocated, attention must be shifted to establishing robust mechanisms to monitor progress and ensure compliance diligently. Setting up sophisticated monitoring and tracking tools or systems, which are designed to provide real-time visibility into the execution of the remediation plan, is a key element in this process. Such tools can assist in closely observing the implementation of various actions, identifying deviations from the set path, or promptly spotting any potential roadblocks. This level of close supervision facilitates early detection of issues, enabling swift action and ensuring the process stays on track.

In addition to having the right tools for tracking progress, it is equally vital to have a mechanism for regular status updates and progress reporting. Such a practice fosters transparency and keeps all stakeholders, from the board members to the employees involved in the remediation process, in the loop about the progress. This way, everyone remains on the same page, reducing the chances of confusion and misinformation. Furthermore, as you monitor the progress, a vigilant approach toward identifying and addressing roadblocks and challenges should be maintained. Swift resolution of these issues aids in keeping the remediation process on schedule and prevents minor problems from escalating into major setbacks.

As the remediation plan rolls out, it is important to remember that the risk landscape is not static but dynamically changing. Hence, ongoing risk assessments during the remediation process become critical. These assessments are meant to identify any emerging risks that could potentially impact the success of the remediation process. Early identification allows for timely mitigation, ensuring these new risks do not derail the process or escalate existing problems.

In parallel with all these activities, it is essential to continually gather evidence of compliance and remediation efforts. This evidence, such as audit reports, system logs, meeting minutes, or even email correspondences, will prove the actions taken to remediate compliance issues. This documentation will be vital when reporting back to the regulator, and it provides validation for the actions taken, building credibility in your organization's commitment to regulatory compliance.

Finally, change management is crucial to consider during the remediation process. Remediation efforts often involve significant changes in processes, systems, or personnel roles. These changes must be managed effectively to ensure smooth implementation and acceptance by all stakeholders. Well--planned change management strategies can help minimize resistance, increase buy-in, and foster a smoother transition, ultimately contributing to the successful implementation of the remediation plan.

Recommendations:

- **Establish Monitoring Tools:** Implement sophisticated monitoring and tracking tools to provide real-time visibility into the remediation process. These tools assist in closely observing action implementation, identifying deviations, and promptly spotting potential roadblocks, facilitating swift action and keeping the process on track.

- **Regular Updates and Reporting:** Create a mechanism for regular status updates and progress reports. This practice fosters transparency and keeps all stakeholders informed about the progress, reducing the chances of confusion and misinformation. Vigilantly identify and address roadblocks and challenges for timely resolution and keeping the process on schedule.

- **Ongoing Risk Assessments:** As the risk landscape is dynamically changing, conduct ongoing risk assessments during the remediation process. Identify any emerging risks that could potentially impact the success of the remediation process for timely mitigation.

- **Document Compliance Evidence:** Continually gather evidence of compliance and remediation efforts. This documentation, such as audit reports or meeting minutes, validates the actions taken and will be vital when reporting back to the regulator, enhancing your organization's credibility in regulatory compliance.

- **Manage Change:** Remediation efforts often involve significant changes in processes, systems, or personnel roles. Manage these changes effectively to ensure smooth implementation and acceptance by all stakeholders. Well-planned change management strategies can minimize resistance, increase buy-in, and foster a smoother transition.

REPORTING BACK TO THE REGULATOR

An essential part of the remediation process is reporting back to the regulator providing them with detailed information about the actions taken to address the compliance issues they identified. This involves preparing a comprehensive remediation report that outlines all the steps taken, the resources allocated, and the outcomes achieved.

The remediation report should be carefully crafted. It must clearly articulate how your organization identified the root causes, developed and implemented the remediation plan, allocated resources, and tracked progress. Also, it should include evidence of the remediation efforts and the results achieved. Remember that this document is evidence of your organization's commitment to compliance and could significantly influence the regulator's perception of your compliance culture.

Data included in the remediation report should be validated and verified. This means cross-checking data for accuracy and completeness and ensuring that it aligns with the evidence gathered during the remediation process. It is essential to maintain integrity and honesty throughout this process. Any discrepancies found later could harm your organization's credibility with the regulator, potentially leading to additional compliance issues.

When communicating with regulators, certain best practices should be followed. First, communication should be respectful and professional. Also, ensure that all communications are accurate, timely, and clear. Miscommunications can lead to misunderstandings, potentially complicating the compliance situation.

Once your remediation report has been submitted, you may need to negotiate or discuss your remediation efforts with the regulator. This is an opportunity for dialogue and clarification, and it can help build a more constructive relationship with the regulator. Your organization should be prepared to respond to feedback on the remediation provided by the regulator.

Finally, it is essential to understand the possible outcomes and responses from the regulator after submitting your remediation report. The regulator might accept the report, close the issue, request more information or clarification, or indicate that further remediation is needed. Your organization should be prepared for any of these scenarios and have plans in place to respond appropriately.

Recommendations:

- **Prepare Detailed Remediation Report:** Create a comprehensive report outlining the steps taken, allocated resources, and achieved outcomes. The report should articulate how your organization identified root causes, developed and implemented the remediation plan, allocated resources, and tracked progress. Include evidence of the remediation efforts and results.

- **Validate and Verify Report Data:** Cross-check the data in the remediation report for accuracy and completeness. Ensure it aligns with the evidence gathered during the remediation process. Maintain integrity and honesty throughout this process to uphold your organization's credibility with the regulator.

- **Communicate Professionally with Regulators:** All communication with regulators should be respectful, professional, accurate, timely, and clear. Avoid miscommunications that can lead to misunderstandings and potentially complicate the compliance situation.

- **Engage in Discussion with the Regulator:** Be prepared to negotiate or discuss your remediation efforts with the regulator. This opportunity for dialogue and clarification can help build a constructive relationship with the regulator. Be ready to respond to feedback provided by the regulator.
- **Understand Possible Outcomes:** The regulator might accept the report, close the issue, request more information or clarification, or indicate that further remediation is needed. Be prepared for any of these scenarios and plan to respond appropriately.

Chapter Conclusion

Understanding and responding adequately to regulatory findings is critical to ensuring robust cybersecurity governance, risk management, and compliance. It is a process that necessitates meticulous attention to detail, comprehension, and actionable steps. This involves beginning with a thorough understanding of feedback and findings, intending to grasp the implications of the identified regulatory issues completely.

Subsequently, the development of an effective remediation strategy is necessary. This strategy should be grounded in the insights from the received feedback and findings. It should address all areas of concern, consider all regulatory stipulations, and plot a clear roadmap to rectify the identified issues.

After developing the remediation plan, resources and responsibilities must be allocated. This step requires judicious thought and planning to ensure appropriate resources are deployed and individuals with the right skills are given the correct tasks. This division of responsibilities should aim to optimize the efficiency and effectiveness of the remediation process.

Once resources and responsibilities are designated, it becomes vital to monitor progress consistently. This stage involves regular reviews of the remediation process, adjusting as necessary. The aim is to confirm that all tasks are being executed on schedule and that the process is advancing as intended.

Finally, the process necessitates a detailed report to the respective regulatory bodies. This comprehensive report should outline the remedial measures taken, the progress achieved, and how the identified issues have been resolved. It serves as an opportunity to showcase the organization's dedication to rectifying the findings and upholding compliance with regulatory standards.

Remember that this process is not singular but iterative, necessitating continuous learning and enhancement. While the suggestions provided are a general guide to streamline the process and bolster effectiveness, your organization's specific circumstances and unique regulatory environment will significantly shape your approach.

Responding to and rectifying regulatory findings is a task that demands a meticulously structured plan, clear and consistent communication, efficient resource allocation, diligent monitoring of progress, and comprehensive reporting. Understanding and applying best practices and recommendations can significantly enhance your organization's compliance posture. It can help mitigate regulatory risks and foster a more robust relationship with the regulatory bodies.

Adherence to these guidelines and principles will not only serve to address current regulatory findings but also act as a strong foundation for future interactions with regulatory bodies. This process, while demanding, is ultimately rewarding as it ensures that your organization operates within the required regulatory framework, thereby reducing potential risks and reinforcing its standing in the eyes of regulatory bodies.

Case Study: XYZ Corporation's Remediation Plan

A mid-sized fintech company, XYZ Corporation, faced a significant regulatory hurdle after a routine compliance audit identified several cybersecurity gaps. Vernon, the Chief Information Security Officer (CISO), was tasked with addressing these regulatory findings and implementing remedial measures.

Vernon recognized the urgency and sensitivity of the situation and approached it methodically, adhering to the best practices and recommendations provided in this chapter. His first step was to understand the regulatory findings and their implications thoroughly. He communicated these findings to all relevant stakeholders in the organization, including the board of directors, to ensure everyone understood the gravity of the situation.

Next, Vernon focused on creating a remediation plan. He led a team to identify the regulatory findings' root causes, define the remediation plan's objectives, and prioritize actions based on risk and severity. After formulating the strategies and tactics for remediation, he established clear timelines and milestones and assigned ownership and accountability for each action.

As CISO, Vernon understood that having the right resources and a well-prepared team was crucial for the successful execution of the remediation plan. He worked with the finance department to allocate the budget required for remediation. He ensured all personnel were well equipped through relevant training and skill development programs. Clear communication channels were established, and a robust reporting structure was implemented to keep everyone informed about the progress.

Throughout the remediation process, Vernon continuously monitored the progress and compliance. He used state-of-the-art monitoring and tracking tools to identify any roadblocks or challenges early, enabling the team to resolve them promptly and stay on track. He emphasized the importance of ongoing risk assessments and ensured sufficient evidence of compliance and remediation efforts were gathered.

Finally, it was time to report back to the regulator. Vernon worked meticulously preparing a comprehensive remediation report detailing all the actions taken, resources used, and the outcomes achieved. All the data included in the report was validated and verified for accuracy. Vernon communicated with the regulators professionally, keeping all discussions respectful, accurate, and timely.

Through Vernon's dedicated efforts, XYZ Corporation was able to address and remediate all regulatory findings successfully. They received positive feedback from the regulators, which boosted their credibility and compliance culture.

EXAMPLE REGULATORY FINDING REMEDIATION PLAN

Regulatory Finding: Inadequate Cybersecurity Governance and Risk Management.

Root Cause Analysis: Intensive analysis has determined that the root cause of this regulatory finding lies in the lack of a robust governance structure and a poorly defined risk management strategy. This has led to gaps in cybersecurity policies and procedures, ineffective communication and coordination, and insufficient risk identification and mitigation efforts.

Objectives of the Remediation Plan:

1. Strengthen Cybersecurity Governance: Establish a robust governance structure to streamline cybersecurity processes and enhance overall security posture.
2. Improve Risk Management: Develop a comprehensive risk management strategy to identify, assess, mitigate, and monitor cybersecurity risks effectively.

Priority Actions Based on Risk and Severity:

1. Review and update cybersecurity policies and procedures.
2. Establish a dedicated cybersecurity governance committee.
3. Develop a risk management framework aligned with industry best practices.
4. Implement regular cybersecurity training and awareness programs.

Remediation Strategies and Tactics:

1. Review and Update Cybersecurity Policies and Procedures

Our current policies and procedures have been identified as being inadequate. The remediation action will thoroughly review and update these policies to ensure they are comprehensive, clear, and aligned with current cybersecurity standards. This process will include input from various stakeholders, including IT, legal, operations, and management teams.

2. Establish a Dedicated Cybersecurity Governance Committee

A strong governance structure is key to addressing the regulatory finding. A dedicated cybersecurity governance committee with representatives from different business units will be established. This committee will oversee all cybersecurity initiatives, ensure alignment with business goals, and promote effective communication and coordination.

3. Develop a Risk Management Framework

A key aspect of the remediation plan is developing a risk management framework. This framework will align with industry best practices, such as NIST's Risk Management Framework, and provide guidelines for consistently identifying, assessing, mitigating, and monitoring risks.

4. Implement Regular Cybersecurity Training and Awareness Programs

The final remediation action will involve implementing regular cybersecurity training and awareness programs. These programs will ensure that all employees have the necessary knowledge and skills to adhere to our cybersecurity policies and contribute to risk management.

Timelines and Milestones:

1. Review and Update Cybersecurity Policies and Procedures

This remediation action is set to commence immediately after the approval of the remediation plan and will span two months.

- Week 1–2: Initial meetings with stakeholders to understand the specific areas that require revision. This period will also include collecting all existing policy and procedure documents for review.
- Week 3–4: Detailed review and identification of gaps in current policies and procedures. This will involve meetings and discussions with the IT team and key stakeholders.
- Week 5–6: Development of updated policies and procedures. Drafts will be prepared for each policy and procedure identified in the previous stage.
- Week 7: Review drafts by the cybersecurity governance committee, legal team, and other relevant stakeholders.
- Week 8: Incorporation of feedback, finalization, and approval of updated policies and procedures.

2. Establish a Dedicated Cybersecurity Governance Committee

This action will take one month and commence concurrently with reviewing and updating cybersecurity policies and procedures.

- Week 1: Identification and nomination of committee members. This will involve discussions with department heads and other leaders in the organization.

- Week 2: Initial committee meeting to discuss roles, responsibilities, and operational guidelines.
- Week 3–4: Establishment of meeting schedules, development of committee charter, and finalizing the committee structure.

3. Develop a Risk Management Framework

The development of a risk management framework will be initiated after establishing the cybersecurity governance committee and will take three months.

- Month 1: Research and benchmarking. This will involve studying industry best practices and risk management frameworks like the NIST Risk Management Framework.
- Month 2: Development of the initial draft of the risk management framework. This will include identifying risk categories, risk assessment methods, risk response strategies, and monitoring procedures.
- Month 3: Review the draft by the cybersecurity governance committee and other relevant stakeholders. Incorporating feedback, finalizing, and approving the risk management framework will follow this.

4. Implement Regular Cybersecurity Training and Awareness Programs

This is an ongoing action that will commence after the approval of the risk management framework.

- Month 1–2: Identifying training needs and developing a training calendar. This will involve discussions with various departments to understand their specific training requirements.
- Month 3 onwards: Commencement of the training programs. The programs will be conducted regularly, and their effectiveness will be evaluated periodically to ensure they meet the intended objectives.

The above timelines and milestones provide a detailed roadmap for the execution of our remediation plan. By adhering to this timeline, we aim to fully address the regulatory finding within six months. During this period, we will ensure regular communication with all stakeholders about the progress of the remediation actions. This will not only keep everyone informed but will also help in promptly identifying and addressing any issues or challenges that may arise.

Ownership and Accountability:

1. CISO will oversee the overall remediation process and will be responsible for establishing the cybersecurity governance committee.
2. Under the IT Director's leadership, the IT team will be accountable for reviewing and updating the cybersecurity policies and procedures and developing the risk management framework.
3. In coordination with the IT team, HR will be responsible for implementing cybersecurity training and awareness programs.

Resource Allocation:

A budget for the remediation process will be allocated, covering resources like workforce, technology, and training materials. The CISO will be responsible for financial planning and resource allocation, ensuring adequate resources are available for each remediation action.

Monitoring Progress and Compliance:

The CISO, with the cybersecurity governance committee, will monitor the progress of the remediation actions. Regular updates will be provided to all stakeholders. Any roadblocks or challenges encountered will be promptly addressed to keep the remediation process on track.

CHAPTER 25

Cybersecurity Architecture

"Strong cybersecurity architecture is the bedrock upon which secure systems are built, protecting digital landscapes from the storm of cyber threats. Let us construct a foundation that fortifies our networks, defends our data, and shields our future."

Cybersecurity architecture is a complex field that forms the foundation for creating secure systems. Understanding the concept and importance of cybersecurity architecture is vital, as it plays a significant role in corporate security and intersects with business and security objectives. Exploration of this topic involves diving into basic concepts, architectural components, and layers – ranging from network to application architecture. However, the study does not confine itself to traditional realms of cybersecurity architecture but also expands into the evolving areas of cloud, mobile, and IoT security. Threat modeling and risk management are also indispensable in designing architecture and modifications to tackle emerging threats. Furthermore, discussing future trends and innovations in the sector provides a comprehensive perspective on cybersecurity architecture, offering readers a holistic view of the subject.

CYBERSECURITY ARCHITECTURE

Cybersecurity architecture represents a broad and strategic approach toward the comprehensive protection of an organization's digital assets, aiming to shield these precious resources against growing cyber threats. This involves the thoughtful and deliberate arrangement of security principles across numerous layers of an information system, from the network periphery to the user interface and every touchpoint in between. The effectiveness of an organization's cybersecurity measures and initiatives can often be traced back to the soundness of its cybersecurity architecture – it is, in essence, the backbone that provides structure and resilience to a secure system.

In the context of enterprise security, the role of cybersecurity architecture becomes even more pronounced. The architecture maps out a coherent and systematic approach to designing, implementing, and managing the organization's vast security processes, technologies, and strategies. It ensures that every element, whether hardware, software, policies, or user behavior, is tuned toward the common data protection objective. By synchronizing and aligning these often disparate elements, the architecture enables a holistic, 360-degree defense mechanism, encapsulating the organization's entire information systems and networks.

The necessity for a cybersecurity architecture to align with business objectives is paramount. Every organization is unique, with its strategic goals, operational processes, and risk factors. The cybersecurity architecture should reflect this individuality by addressing the organization's security needs and risk profile. Whether protecting intellectual property, ensuring customer data privacy, or safeguarding operational continuity, the architecture encapsulates the organization's security priorities and supports its business goals.

Despite its vital importance, implementing cybersecurity architecture can face several challenges. The landscape of cyber threats is fast-paced, dynamic, and continually evolving. New vulnerabilities and attack vectors emerge as new technologies and practices emerge. The complexity of modern IT environments, with their myriad interconnected devices, systems, and platforms, further compounds these challenges. These multifaceted, high-stakes complexities necessitate a sophisticated and adaptable cybersecurity architecture.

Furthermore, budget constraints and the well-documented shortage of skilled cybersecurity professionals add a practical layer to these challenges. There is often a significant gap between what is needed and what resources are available. Bridging this gap requires strategic planning, prioritization, and the efficient allocation of resources, all of which are guided by the cybersecurity architecture.

Perhaps the most nuanced challenge in developing a secure architecture is striking the right balance between security and operational efficiency. The purpose of cybersecurity is to enable the business to operate securely, not to hinder its operations. An overly restrictive security posture can impede productivity, stifle innovation, and create user frustration. On the other hand, a lax approach to security can leave the organization open to cyber threats with potentially devastating consequences. Hence, the cybersecurity architecture plays a crucial role in modulating the security controls in line with the organization's risk tolerance and strategic objectives. It is about creating a secure environment that enables, rather than inhibits, the business.

Cybersecurity architecture is the lynchpin that holds an organization's cyber defenses together. It is an evolving discipline that seeks to counteract increasingly sophisticated threats while facilitating the organization's operational and strategic objectives. Despite the challenges, developing a robust cybersecurity architecture is necessary and integral to any modern enterprise's successful and secure functioning.

Recommendations:

- **Understand the Basics:** Familiarize yourself with the principles of cybersecurity architecture and how it operates on different layers of an information system. Recognize its significance in strengthening an organization's cybersecurity measures.
- **Align Security with Business Goals:** Ensure your cybersecurity architecture supports the organization's strategic goals and operational processes. Identify the organization's security needs and risk profile, and let these guide your strategies.
- **Stay Informed and Adaptable:** Be mindful of the ever-evolving landscape of cyber threats. Keep abreast of new technologies and practices and anticipate potential vulnerabilities. Make sure your cybersecurity architecture is adaptable to these changes.
- **Efficient Resource Allocation:** Address the challenges of budget constraints and the shortage of skilled cybersecurity professionals. Implement strategic planning and efficient allocation of resources to bridge the gap between what is needed and what resources are available.
- **Balance Security and Efficiency:** Strive to strike a delicate balance between maintaining security and facilitating operational efficiency. While ensuring robust security controls, also prioritize operational continuity and innovation.
- **Build a Dynamic Security Environment:** Emphasize creating a cybersecurity architecture that enables rather than hinders the business. The architecture should foster a secure environment that aligns with the organization's risk tolerance and strategic objectives.
- **Embrace the Evolution:** Accept that cybersecurity architecture is an evolving discipline. Stay committed to refining and developing your architecture to counteract sophisticated threats while facilitating the organization's operational and strategic objectives.

FUNDAMENTAL CONCEPTS

The concept of "Defense in Depth," sometimes called the castle approach, takes inspiration from a time-honored military strategy that banks on layering defenses to fortify security. In a digital context, this strategy calls for applying multiple security measures across every facet of the system – akin to a castle's high walls, moat, and guard towers working in unison to keep intruders at bay. By embedding defensive mechanisms at different layers, the security structure can deter, detect, delay, and react effectively to cyberattacks. Even if one layer gets breached, the remaining layers provide protection, buying valuable time to respond to and mitigate the threat.

The "Least Privilege" principle is another cornerstone of cybersecurity architecture. It advocates for limiting the access rights for users, applications, or processes to the bare minimum necessary for performing their functions. In other words, every component should have just enough privileges to perform its duties, but no more. This principle limits the potential avenues malicious actors can exploit by strictly controlling access. Furthermore, if an account or process is compromised, the damage is confined, as the perpetrator's reach is restricted to the minimum privileges assigned to that particular account or process.

Security zones and segmentation are fundamental components of robust network architecture. They help organize networks and resources, establishing clear boundaries that segregate sensitive information from the rest. Segmentation works by partitioning the network into smaller subnetworks or segments. If a system within a segment is compromised, the threat is contained within that segment, reducing the possibility of lateral movement across the network. This arrangement creates smaller, more manageable blocks of systems that can be individually fortified and monitored.

Network Access Control (NAC) supplements the security zones and segmentation strategy by enforcing policy-based access controls. In essence, NAC serves as a gatekeeper, scrutinizing every device trying to connect to the network. Based on predefined policies, it validates the device's compliance status and user credentials before granting access. By doing so, NAC helps safeguard the network from potentially vulnerable, compromised, or unauthorized devices that could threaten the system.

Data Flow Analysis is a crucial analytical tool used to visualize and understand the movements and interactions of data within a system. Organizations can better understand their systems' functioning by tracing the data flow from origin to destination. This enables them to detect any potential vulnerabilities, misconfigurations, or anomalies that might present exploitable opportunities for cyber threats. Moreover, data flow analysis ensures that data handling processes adhere to the organization's security and compliance policies.

These principles and methodologies contribute to a multilayered and adaptable cybersecurity architecture. Organizations can build a resilient, comprehensive defense system capable of countering a broad spectrum of cyber threats through the combined application of Defense in Depth, Least Privilege, security zones and segmentation, NAC, and Data Flow Analysis. This holistic approach boosts the organization's security profile and empowers it to respond effectively to security incidents.

Recommendations:

- **Implement Defense in Depth:** Consider a multilayered defensive strategy in your cybersecurity architecture. By embedding defensive mechanisms at different system layers, you can enhance your ability to deter, detect, delay, and respond effectively to cyberattacks.
- **Please adhere to the Principle of Least Privilege:** Limit the access rights of users, applications, and processes to only what is necessary for them

to perform their functions. By controlling access strictly, you can minimize the potential avenues exploitable by cyber threats.

- **Utilize Security Zones and Segmentation:** Organize your network and resources by establishing clear boundaries and segregating sensitive information from the rest. Network segmentation helps in containing threats and managing blocks of systems more effectively.

- **Apply Network Access Control:** Implement policy-based access controls to scrutinize every device connecting to your network. By validating device compliance status and user credentials, NAC can help safeguard your system from potentially vulnerable or unauthorized devices.

- **Conduct Data Flow Analysis:** Use this analytical tool to understand the movements and interactions of data within your system. Through this analysis, you can detect potential vulnerabilities or anomalies and ensure that your data handling processes comply with your organization's security policies.

- **Integrate Strategies for a Comprehensive Defense:** Build a resilient cybersecurity architecture by combining the principles of Defense in Depth, Least Privilege, security zones and segmentation, NAC, and Data Flow Analysis. A holistic approach fortifies your organization's security profile and enhances your ability to respond effectively to security incidents.

ARCHITECTURAL COMPONENTS AND LAYERS

This section explores various facets of security architecture, including network, system, application, and mobile/IoT security architectures, Identity and Access Management (IAM), cloud security, and threat modeling. Network architecture involves the design of a computer network and includes elements like network topologies, firewalls, Intrusion Detection and Prevention Systems (IDPS), and Virtual Private Networks (VPNs) that enhance network security. System architecture involves designing and functioning a computer system, and it considers key components such as operating systems, hardware security modules (HSMs), and modern techniques like virtualization and containerization for optimal security. Application architecture focuses on the design and implementation of software applications, with security considerations playing a crucial role, involving secure software development practices, application layer security, and modern architectural models such as microservices. IAM ensures authorized individuals have appropriate organizational access. Cloud security emphasizes securing cloud computing environments against various threats, understanding different cloud deployment models, and incorporating the shared responsibility model. Mobile and IoT security architectures focus on protecting portable and internet-connected devices, with the former involving Mobile Device Management (MDM) and the latter addressing the security of diverse, connected devices. The text also highlights threat modeling and risk management as proactive processes to systematically identify, understand, and address potential threats, promoting a more robust security posture.

Network Architecture

The term "Network Architecture" encapsulates the layout and composition of a computer network, both in terms of its physical and logical constructs. It involves various elements, such as network topologies, firewalls, IDPS, and VPNs, each contributing to the overall resilience and effectiveness of the network.

Network topologies represent the architectural design of a network. The structure can follow different formats, including star, ring, and bus. Each topology presents unique advantages, and their strategic implementation can lead to increased operational efficiency. However, potential vulnerabilities also exist, requiring a deep understanding of these topologies and their intricacies to mitigate associated risks.

Firewalls act as the initial line of defense against cyber threats, scrutinizing network traffic based on predetermined security rules. These vital devices control incoming and outgoing network traffic, protecting unauthorized access. Moreover, they can be strategically configured to achieve maximum efficiency without significantly impacting the network's performance.

IDPS extend the security capabilities of a network. These sophisticated systems constantly monitor network activities, detecting and mitigating potential threats and policy violations. Sometimes, they can even prevent or report these actions in real time, enabling quick responses to security incidents.

VPNs are crucial tools in today's interconnected world, especially given the increased remote work and internet dependency. VPNs establish secure, encrypted connections across public networks, ensuring data confidentiality and integrity during transit. They play an integral role in safeguarding digital communications from eavesdropping and other forms of cyberattacks.

System Architecture

System architecture encompasses both the design and functioning of a computer system. Key components such as the operating system, HSMs, and modern techniques like virtualization and containerization collectively determine a system's security posture.

Operating systems are at the heart of any computing device, providing the necessary platform for running applications. They come equipped with multiple security features like user authentication, access controls, and system integrity checks that can be leveraged to enhance the system's overall security. Implementing and managing these features directly influences the system's vulnerability to cyber threats.

HSMs add an extra layer of security to systems. These physical devices manage, process, and store cryptographic keys securely. By securing these keys, HSMs safeguard against the loss, corruption, or unauthorized access of sensitive data, adding a sturdy layer of protection.

Virtualization and containerization are groundbreaking technologies that revolutionize applications' deployment and management. By abstracting the hardware, these techniques enable multiple operating systems or applications to coexist independently on a single physical host. The resultant benefits – including isolation and segmentation, quick application deployment, and streamlined disaster recovery – significantly bolster system security.

Application Architecture

Application architecture involves the design and implementation of software applications, with security considerations playing a vital role. It encompasses secure software development practices, application layer security, and modern architectural models such as microservices and API security.

Secure software development practices are foundational to creating robust, specific applications. This includes secure coding practices that eliminate common coding vulnerabilities, code reviews that catch security issues early, and thorough testing strategies that scrutinize the application for potential security flaws.

Even with the most secure development practices, applications require security mechanisms at the operational level. Application layer security entails several techniques, including input validation, output encoding, and session management. These practices provide a vital security layer to prevent common web-based attacks like SQL injection, Cross-Site Scripting (XSS), and session hijacking.

As software architecture evolves toward microservices, new security challenges emerge. Microservices architecture breaks an application into more minor, independently running services, each communicating via lightweight mechanisms, typically HTTP APIs. With this architectural shift, securing individual services and their APIs becomes critical to overall application security.

Identity and Access Management

IAM is a comprehensive framework that manages digital identities and their organizational access. It ensures authorized individuals access the right resources at the right times and for valid reasons. This involves implementing robust processes for authentication (identity verification), authorization (access granting based on identity), and accounting (tracking and logging user activities).

IAM also introduces mechanisms such as single sign-on (SSO) and federated identity. SSO simplifies user authentication by allowing users to authenticate once and gain access to multiple applications, thereby improving user experience while maintaining security. Federated identity extends SSO capabilities across organizational boundaries, enabling seamless business collaboration.

Privileged access management is another integral part of IAM that manages and monitors access rights for privileged users. These users, such as system administrators, have broad access to systems, making them prime targets for cyber threats. Thus, controlling and auditing their access is critical to mitigating potential security risks.

Cloud Security Architecture

Cloud security focuses on securing cloud computing environments against a variety of threats. It encompasses understanding different cloud deployment models, such as public, private, and hybrid clouds, and their respective security considerations. Knowledge of these models and their associated vulnerabilities is paramount to formulating a secure cloud strategy.

The shared responsibility model is a cornerstone of cloud security. This model specifies that while the cloud provider ensures the security of the cloud infrastructure, the user is responsible for security within the cloud – this includes securing data and applications hosted in the cloud. Thus, understanding the shared responsibility model is crucial to avoid security gaps in cloud deployments.

Several best practices and tools can enhance cloud security. For instance, secure access controls ensure only authorized individuals can access cloud resources. Encryption protects data at rest and in transit, reducing the risk of data breaches. Security analytics tools provide insights into the cloud environment, enabling the early detection and mitigation of security threats.

Mobile and IoT Security Architecture

Mobile and IoT Security architecture focuses on securing portable and internet--connected devices. Implementing robust security measures for these devices becomes critical as we rely heavily on mobile and IoT devices.

Mobile security protects personal and business information stored on and transmitted from mobile devices such as smartphones, tablets, and laptops. MDM is vital, enabling organizations to manage and secure mobile devices remotely. This includes enforcing security policies, managing app usage, and controlling data access on these devices.

IoT security, conversely, involves securing a vast array of internet-connected devices and networks. Given the diversity of IoT devices and their widespread use, securing them presents significant challenges. These challenges range from the lack of standard security protocols and the scale of deployment to issues around data privacy and the inherent vulnerabilities of some devices.

Threat Modeling and Risk Management in Architecture

Threat modeling and risk management are proactive processes to systematically identify, understand, and address potential threats. Incorporating these into security architecture ensures that security measures align with potential threats, promoting a more robust defensive posture.

Threat modeling methodologies, such as STRIDE (Spoofing, Tampering, Repudiation, Information Disclosure, Denial of Service, and Elevation of Privilege) and DREAD (Damage, Reproducibility, Exploitability, Affected Users, and Discoverability), help identify and prioritize potential vulnerabilities. They allow organizations to take a more strategic, risk-based approach to cybersecurity.

Attack tree analysis visually represents potential threats and their execution paths. Security professionals can devise more robust defenses and response strategies by understanding a threat actor's possible routes to exploit a system. This method also helps perform cost–benefit analyses of different defense measures, enabling organizations to allocate resources more effectively.

Integrating threat modeling into security architecture ensures that the defensive measures are in sync with the threat landscape. It allows security professionals to anticipate and address threats proactively rather than reacting to incidents after they occur. By continually identifying and assessing hazards, organizations can stay ahead of attackers, reducing the likelihood of successful attacks.

Recommendations:

- **Explore Different Security Architectures:** Deep dive into various aspects of security architecture such as network, system, application, mobile/IoT security architectures, IAM, and cloud security. Also, familiarize yourself with threat modeling and risk management to proactively identify and mitigate potential threats, reinforcing your security posture.

- **Master the Network Architecture:** Develop a comprehensive understanding of the structure and composition of a computer network, including elements like network topologies, firewalls, IDPS, and VPNs. Appreciate how these elements contribute to the resilience and effectiveness of the network.

- **Enhance Your System Architecture:** Broaden your understanding of a computer system's design and functioning. Acquaint yourself with key components such as operating systems, HSMs, and modern techniques like virtualization and containerization. These elements collectively determine a system's security posture.

- **Optimize Application Architecture:** Design and implement software applications with security considerations at the forefront. This includes secure software development practices, application layer security, and modern architectural models such as microservices and API security. Ensure secure coding practices, perform thorough testing strategies, and validate application layer security.

- **Focus on Identity and Access Management:** Implement a comprehensive IAM framework that ensures authorized individuals have appropriate access to resources within the organization. Incorporate robust processes for authentication, authorization, and accounting. Also, introduce mechanisms such as SSO, federated identity, and privileged access management to improve security and user experience.

SECURITY REFERENCE MODELS AND FRAMEWORKS

Security reference models and frameworks play an instrumental role in the strategic planning and execution of an organization's security measures. They delineate key principles and methodologies and offer an overarching guideline to sustain secure systems in an ever-evolving cyber landscape.

One such extensive model is the SABSA (Sherwood Applied Business Security Architecture). This is a highly versatile and adaptable framework for designing risk-driven enterprise information security and assurance architectures. SABSA employs a top-down approach, defining business needs before diving into risk and security requirements. Its architectural layers address different aspects of the organization, from business strategy to operational considerations, ensuring that security initiatives align with business objectives. Additionally, it encapsulates the entire security journey – from conceptualization and design to implementation, management, and continuous assessment. By offering such a holistic approach, SABSA enables organizations to effectively structure their cybersecurity measures, integrate them with business strategies, and adapt to changing security landscapes.

TOGAF, which stands for The Open Group Architecture Framework, is a highly recognized enterprise architecture framework that provides a comprehensive approach to the design, planning, implementation, and governance of an enterprise's IT architecture. Developed by The Open Group, an independent IT industry consortium, TOGAF has emerged as a critical tool for helping organizations create a structure that aligns IT with business goals.

The foundation of TOGAF is its Architecture Development Method (ADM), a proven, step-by-step approach to developing enterprise architecture. The ADM includes several phases, starting with the architecture vision and ending with architecture change management. Each phase has specific objectives and outcomes, and they all collectively aim to ensure the successful creation and implementation of a robust, future-proof enterprise architecture. The ADM's iterative nature allows for continuous monitoring and improvement, making it adaptable to changing business needs and technology trends.

TOGAF also emphasizes the importance of establishing a comprehensive architecture repository. This repository is a single source of truth for architectural artifacts, including principles, vision, and standards. By maintaining all architecture-related documentation in a centralized location, organizations can ensure consistency and continuity in their IT architecture strategies, leading to improved decision-making and efficiency. It further facilitates communication across business units, creating a shared understanding of the organization's architectural landscape.

Moreover, TOGAF encourages a holistic view of enterprise architecture, considering business, data, application, and technology domains. This comprehensive approach ensures that all aspects of an organization's IT are aligned with its overall business objectives. By providing a high-level, strategic context for the evolution of the IT system in response to the ever-changing needs of the business environment, TOGAF helps organizations achieve strategic goals and deliver value through effective IT architecture management. Ultimately, implementing TOGAF can lead to cost-effective IT operations, better returns on IT investments, and a more efficient and effective IT infrastructure that supports the organization's business objectives.

The NIST (National Institute of Standards and Technology) Cybersecurity Framework offers a risk-based approach to managing cybersecurity risk. It integrates industry standards and best practices to aid organizations in managing their cybersecurity risks. Complementing existing business and cybersecurity operations, the NIST Framework provides clear guidelines for identifying, protecting, detecting, responding to, and recovering from cybersecurity incidents. While a brief overview is provided here, reviewing the entire chapter is recommended to fully grasp the potential and application of the NIST CSF.

Understanding and implementing these models can significantly enhance an organization's cybersecurity posture. They present structured guidance and a strategic roadmap that help to improve security operations, fortify defenses, and elevate the organization's response to cybersecurity threats. When employed correctly, these frameworks can provide a resilient shield against potential cyber threats, ensuring business continuity and building stakeholder trust.

Recommendations:

- **Embrace Holistic Security Models:** Organizations should consider adopting comprehensive security models like SABSA that offer a top-down approach, beginning with defining business needs before detailing risk and security requirements. These models ensure that security initiatives align with business objectives and adapt to evolving security landscapes, providing a complete view of security from conceptualization and design to implementation and ongoing assessment.

- **Utilize the TOGAF Framework:** Aiming for a well-structured IT architecture that aligns with business goals is essential. TOGAF, with its ADM, allows for a step-by-step approach to developing a robust, future-proof enterprise architecture. Its iterative nature provides continuous monitoring and improvement, making it adaptable to changing business needs and technology trends.

- **Develop an Architecture Repository:** In line with TOGAF's guidelines, organizations should establish a comprehensive architecture repository as a single source of truth for architectural artifacts. This repository will enhance decision-making efficiency and consistency in IT strategies. Furthermore, it can facilitate communication across different business units, fostering a shared understanding of the organization's architectural landscape.

- **Implement a Comprehensive View of Enterprise Architecture:** To align all aspects of an organization's IT with its overall business objectives, it is crucial to consider all architectural domains, as TOGAF advises. This holistic view provides a strategic context for the evolution of the IT system, helping organizations achieve strategic goals and deliver value through effective IT architecture management.

- **Explore the NIST Cybersecurity Framework:** Organizations should delve into the NIST Cybersecurity Framework to effectively manage cybersecurity risks. This framework offers a risk-based approach integrating industry standards and best practices. It complements existing operations, providing guidelines for identifying, protecting, detecting, responding to, and recovering from cybersecurity incidents. It is recommended to thoroughly review the entire chapter on the NIST CSF for a deep understanding of its potential and applications.

BUILDING AND EVOLVING CYBERSECURITY ARCHITECTURE

The in-depth evaluation of the current cybersecurity architecture is the first step in comprehending an organization's security posture. This evaluation is a multifaceted process that involves a meticulous examination of the existing policies, security controls, and operational technologies that the organization uses. It is a crucial part of an organization's cybersecurity strategy as the starting point from which other actions are formulated. The objective of this step is not merely to observe but to discern and pinpoint vulnerabilities that may exist within the organization's digital landscape. Each vulnerability can expose the organization to cyber threats and compromises, making this process a significant determinant in the subsequent steps to fortify cybersecurity.

After thoroughly auditing the organization's current cybersecurity setup, determining the specific security requirements becomes the next important stage. These requirements must be carefully defined, considering they should align with the organization's business objectives and applicable regulatory obligations. This determination process involves an astute understanding of the business's goals and objectives and a keen awareness of the relevant local, national, and international regulatory standards. The chosen requirements thus form a balanced, comprehensive perspective that fortifies the organization's cybersecurity stance while maintaining compliance with regulatory bodies.

Once the security requirements have been established, these form the basis for selecting and applying suitable controls. The controls that are selected can span a wide spectrum, from the implementation of sophisticated technological solutions to the introduction of policy-driven approaches. Technological controls might include cutting-edge solutions such as advanced intrusion detection systems, strengthened firewall capabilities, or state-of-the-art encryption mechanisms. On the other hand, policy-based controls could include initiatives such as comprehensive employee training programs, stringent access control policies, or robust data handling and storage procedures. The key is to ensure that each selected control serves the dual purpose of mitigating identified risks and vulnerabilities and bolstering the overall security architecture.

However, ensuring the long-term robustness and effectiveness of the cybersecurity architecture is not a task that ends with implementing controls. It demands a process of continual monitoring and enhancement. Maintaining the cybersecurity architecture is a perpetual activity, not a singular event. Regular revision, reassessment, and modification of the architecture are critical to keeping up with the rapidly changing cyber landscape. Emerging threats, technological changes, and evolving business requirements are all factors that necessitate this ongoing improvement cycle. By staying vigilant and adaptable, an organization can maintain a fortified cybersecurity architecture resilient against the myriad cyber threats in the digital age.

Recommendations:

- **Perform an Exhaustive Evaluation of Current Architecture:** Start your journey toward a robust cybersecurity posture by thoroughly evaluating the existing architecture. This would involve a detailed investigation of currently implemented policies, controls, and technologies. Identifying potential weak points will enable you to formulate effective counter-measures and reinforce your security stance.
- **Define Clear Security Requirements:** The next step is establishing clear and actionable security requirements after identifying potential vulnerabilities. These should align with your business objectives and comply with any regulatory obligations. Doing this ensures that your security measures are effective and customized to your organization's needs and goals.
- **Implement Appropriate Controls:** Select and implement appropriate controls based on the established security requirements. These could range from technological solutions to policy-driven approaches. These controls must be theoretically effective, feasible, and sustainable in your business operations.
- **Establish a Routine for Continuous Monitoring:** To maintain the effectiveness of your cybersecurity architecture, establish a routine for consistent monitoring. This will ensure that any emerging threats, technological changes, and evolving business needs are accounted for. Keeping a proactive stance will help you stay ahead of potential cybersecurity issues.
- **Emphasize Continuous Improvement:** Alongside monitoring, stress the importance of continuous improvement. The cybersecurity landscape is ever-changing, and so should your approach to maintaining security. Regularly review and update the architecture based on the insights gained from your monitoring efforts, thereby ensuring that your cybersecurity measures are always up-to-date.

ADAPTING ARCHITECTURE TO EMERGING THREATS

Adapting to the ever-changing cybersecurity landscape requires a multi-pronged approach incorporating technological solutions, policy structures, and human factors. This entails persistently staying updated with the latest developments in cybersecurity, understanding risk intelligence, and being aware of emerging and evolving threats, as well as the inventive defensive mechanisms utilized across different sectors. A vigilant approach to promptly updating and patching all systems is part of this strategy. This is critical because software that is not kept current creates opportunities for cyberattackers to exploit. A well-structured incident response strategy that detects, isolates, eliminates, and recovers from a cyber incident is also paramount. In addition, secure and effective communication channels must be ensured to facilitate swift incident response. Furthermore, cultivating a security-oriented culture within the organization is critical. This encourages every member to develop secure behaviors and actively participate in maintaining the organization's cyber hygiene.

This comprehensive approach to cybersecurity management is essential to establishing a secure, robust, and trustworthy cyber environment within any organization. Each component augments the others, forming a solid defense against cyber threats. Keeping abreast of the latest trends and threat intelligence in cybersecurity enables an organization to be prepared for and combat emerging threats. Regular system updates and patch management remove potential vulnerabilities that cyberattackers could exploit. Effective incident response strategies ensure the organization can quickly bounce back from incidents with minimal impact. Finally, fostering a security-conscious culture ensures that every individual contributes to maintaining cybersecurity, resulting in an enhanced security stance.

Navigating the complex and evolving world of cybersecurity necessitates a flexible strategy that weaves together technological tools, policy initiatives, and the human element. This means maintaining a pulse on the latest advancements in cybersecurity, risk intelligence, emergent and changing threats, and cutting-edge defensive strategies used throughout various industries. It necessitates a diligent and prompt system of updates and patches, given that outdated software becomes an attractive target for cyberattackers. The development and implementation of rigorous incident response protocols, capable of identifying, quarantining, eliminating, and bouncing back from a cyber incident, are indispensable. Additionally, secure and effective communication channels must be maintained for rapid incident response. A significant aspect is creating a culture within the organization that prioritizes security, motivating every team member to embrace secure practices and contribute to the organization's cyber hygiene.

Such a holistic view of cybersecurity management is critical to fostering an organization's secure, resilient, and reliable cyber ecosystem. These elements supplement each other and, when combined, create a formidable barrier against a wide range of cyber threats. The most current knowledge about cybersecurity trends and threat intelligence enables organizations to anticipate and counter emerging threats. Regularly updating and patching systems eliminates exploitable vulnerabilities that cyberattackers might target.

Robust incident response strategies ensure the organization can quickly recover from incidents with minimal disruption. Lastly, promoting a culture of security consciousness ensures that every person within the organization plays their part in upholding cybersecurity, thereby leading to a more robust security posture.

Recommendations:

- **Stay Current with Cybersecurity Trends:** It is essential to keep yourself updated with the latest trends and developments in cybersecurity. Subscribe to reputable cybersecurity news outlets, blogs, reports, and newsletters. Participate in cybersecurity forums, webinars, and conferences to learn about the latest threats and how other organizations tackle them.
- **Develop a Robust Patch Management Process:** Patching is not just about applying updates; it is a process that requires careful planning and execution. Develop a robust patch management process that includes regular scanning for vulnerabilities, prioritizing patches based on risk, testing patches before deployment, and auditing and reporting on patch compliance.
- **Implement Incident Response Strategies:** Be prepared for a cyber incident with a well-planned and tested incident response strategy. This should include procedures for detecting, reporting, containing, and recovering from an incident and a communication plan for informing stakeholders and authorities.
- **Invest in Cyber Threat Intelligence:** Cyber threat intelligence can provide valuable information about the types of threats your organization faces, who is likely to attack, and how they might do it. Investing in threat intelligence services can help you stay one step ahead of cybercriminals and take proactive steps to protect your organization.
- **Promote a Security-Conscious Culture:** Fostering a security culture within your organization is essential. This can be achieved through regular training and awareness programs, promoting good security habits, and rewarding employees for adhering to security policies and practices.

Chapter Conclusion

The architecture of cybersecurity is a complex and perpetually evolving domain. It is an intricate weave of principles, strategies, and technologies, all interplaying to create a defensive bulwark against an ever-growing landscape of cyber threats. From understanding the nature of network and system structures and the nuances of threat modeling to the pivotal role of Artificial Intelligence (AI) and emerging technologies, each facet contributes to the overarching goal of securing an organization's cyber domain.

One of the foundational elements in creating a secure cyber architecture is a profound comprehension of network and system structures. A grasp of the intricacies of network typologies, firewalls, IDPS, and various other protective measures is instrumental in building a formidable defense. The network and system structures are the backbone of an organization's cybersecurity architecture. Any lapse in their security can lead to a potential breach, causing extensive damage.

In parallel, threat modeling is a crucial aspect of cybersecurity. It involves identifying potential threats, assessing the vulnerabilities that might be exploited, and developing strategies to mitigate them. A well-constructed threat model provides a realistic view of the possible attack vectors an adversary could use, enabling organizations to devise defensive plans proactively. In essence, it transforms the reactive approach of cybersecurity to a proactive one, empowering organizations to stay one step ahead of the attackers.

AI and emerging technologies' role in cybersecurity architecture cannot be overstated. AI, machine learning, and other advanced technologies can provide significant advantages in identifying, predicting, and mitigating cyber threats. They automate threat detection, streamline incident response, and reduce human error. Additionally, they continuously learn from each interaction, which enables them to adapt and evolve in the face of new and sophisticated threats.

It is equally important to emphasize the dynamic nature of cybersecurity. Maintaining a static cybersecurity architecture is insufficient, with threats continuously evolving and new vulnerabilities emerging. Organizations must ensure they are consistently updated on the latest developments in the field. This involves regular training for staff, updating policies, and continuously reassessing and upgrading security controls.

Adopting robust models and frameworks forms another crucial pillar of a strong cybersecurity architecture. Standards such as ISO 27001, the NIST cybersecurity framework, and others provide a structured approach to managing cybersecurity risks. They offer a set of best practices that help organizations establish, implement, monitor, and continually improve their Information Security Management Systems (ISMS).

Lastly, fostering an ethos of continuous learning and improvement is vital. Cybersecurity is a marathon, not a sprint. Organizations need to learn from each incident, each near-miss, and even from the successes. This continuous learning feeds into the system, strengthening the security posture over time.

In summary, navigating the labyrinth of the cybersecurity landscape can be challenging. However, by keeping up-to-date, adopting robust models and frameworks, and fostering a culture of continuous learning and improvement, organizations can remain a step ahead of potential threats, securing their digital frontier in the face of an uncertain and volatile cyber world.

Case Study: Orchid Enterprises and Robust Cybersecurity

Orchid Enterprises, a prominent player in the e-commerce industry, realized the significance of cybersecurity when a minor breach exposed the vulnerabilities in their existing system. As the newly appointed Chief Information Security Officer (CISO), Ken had been entrusted with the formidable task of bolstering the company's cybersecurity infrastructure. He knew that his job involved far more than merely plugging a few security gaps. Ken needed a comprehensive plan that would align with Orchid Enterprises' business objectives and cover all aspects discussed in the chapter.

Ken's first task was to carry out a thorough assessment of the current architecture. With a focus on understanding the current security posture, he led a team that conducted an in-depth review of all implemented policies, controls, and technologies. They meticulously scrutinized the existing network and system structures, identifying potential vulnerabilities and assessing the effectiveness of the deployed security measures. This painstaking process led to a better understanding of the organization's security posture and identifying areas of vulnerability, reinforcing the chapter's emphasis on the need for a comprehensive assessment.

Next, Ken moved toward establishing security requirements aligned with Orchid Enterprises' business and regulatory objectives. He collaborated closely with various stakeholders, including business heads, regulatory compliance teams, and IT teams, to create a list of requirements. These requirements guided the selection and implementation of appropriate controls, including technological measures and policy-based approaches. The efficacy of this approach underscored the chapter's emphasis on aligning security measures with business objectives and regulations.

Understanding the evolving cybersecurity landscape, Ken realized that continuous monitoring and improvement were crucial to maintaining a robust cybersecurity architecture. He implemented a system that regularly reviews and updates the architecture based on emerging threats, technological changes, and business needs. He also established a robust incident response team and used AI and other advanced technologies to automate threat detection and incident response. Furthermore, he ensured the company was consistently updated on the latest cybersecurity trends and threat intelligence, and systems were regularly patched. This multipronged approach echoed the chapter's assertion of the need for continuous learning and adaptation in the face of changing threats.

Ken also put significant emphasis on fostering a security-conscious culture within Orchid Enterprises. He initiated regular training sessions, updated policies, and encouraged employees to adopt secure habits. He realized that cybersecurity was not the sole responsibility of the IT department; instead, it was an organization-wide responsibility. This focus on the human element of cybersecurity tied in with the chapter's emphasis on the importance of a security-aware culture.

Finally, Ken used robust models and frameworks like the NIST cybersecurity framework. He believed in the power of these frameworks to provide a structured approach to managing cybersecurity risks. By adopting these best practices, Orchid Enterprises established, implemented, monitored, and continually improved its ISMS, reflecting the chapter's emphasis on using structured frameworks.

Ken's journey at Orchid Enterprises practically demonstrated the principles discussed in the chapter. His approach reinforced the importance of comprehensive assessment, alignment with business objectives, continuous adaptation, the significance of a security-conscious culture, and the use of robust frameworks. By successfully navigating the complex cybersecurity landscape, Ken fortified Orchid Enterprises' cybersecurity infrastructure and stayed one step ahead of potential threats. His actions underline the importance of a versatile, forward-thinking approach to cybersecurity, bringing to life the key lessons of the chapter.

CHAPTER 26

Risk Mitigation

"The cost of a security incident far outweighs the investment in risk mitigation. Leaders must convey this message to stakeholders, emphasizing the importance of allocating resources to protect the organization's reputation, customer trust, and bottom line."

Risk mitigation forms a critical part of any organization's cybersecurity strategy. This study delves into the fundamentals of understanding and developing effective risk mitigation strategies, from choosing the right controls to implementing them effectively. Key areas covered include the role of policies, standards, and procedures in risk mitigation and the importance of inventory and classification of assets. The study also explores methods to mitigate interconnectivity risks and the application of user security controls. Emphasizing the role of physical security, network controls, change management within the IT environment, and end-of-life management, the study offers actionable recommendations for each section. This in-depth exploration aims to furnish a thorough understanding of risk mitigation in cybersecurity.

RISK MITIGATION BASICS

Risk mitigation is the bedrock upon which the edifice of cybersecurity stands. As cyber threats continue to evolve and become increasingly complex, there is a growing need to understand the nuances of risk mitigation, develop comprehensive strategies, and implement these effectively to safeguard an organization's assets.

Understanding risk mitigation begins with recognizing it as a systematic process of identifying, assessing, and prioritizing risks, followed by the concerted application of resources to curtail, observe, and manage the probabilities or consequences of unforeseen events. It is a crucial element of risk management, from merely recognizing potential risks to actively decreasing their potential for damage. This involves looking at the organization's operations holistically, understanding the interplay between various elements, and the vulnerabilities each element may expose.

Risk mitigation strategies are the next pillar in this foundational cybersecurity subject. Developing a strategy requires diligent effort, a profound understanding of the organization's workings, and a deep awareness of the potential threats in the cyber landscape. Developing a risk mitigation strategy is not a 'one-size-fits-all' solution but a bespoke plan tailored to an organization's needs and vulnerabilities. It involves detailed risk analysis, which includes identifying potential risks, assessing the likelihood of these risks manifesting, and understanding the potential impact should they do so. Once this groundwork is laid, measures can be determined and implemented to prevent or reduce the risk.

This leads us to the critical aspect of selecting appropriate controls. In a risk mitigation context, controls refer to the measures and procedures to manage identified risks. The selection of these controls should be rooted in a keen understanding of the specific risks faced by the organization and the potential impact of these risks. Choosing the right controls requires careful analysis, often involving input from multiple organizational stakeholders. A selected control's effectiveness, cost, and feasibility are all important factors.

Implementing the selected risk mitigation measures is not a process to be taken lightly. This stage demands a concerted effort, clear communication, and meticulous planning. The chosen controls must be integrated effectively into the organization's operational fabric, with all stakeholders fully aware of their roles and responsibilities. These measures must be implemented not to disrupt the organization's normal functioning but to augment and strengthen it.

Evaluating the effectiveness of implemented measures is the final step in the risk mitigation process but is not the least important. Regular monitoring and evaluation provide insights into the efficacy of the measures and the need for any adjustments. This step is not a static, one-time process but a dynamic, ongoing activity that evolves with organizational changes and the risk landscape.

Recommendations:

- **Enhance Understanding:** Actively encourage an organizational culture that values understanding risk mitigation. Conduct educational seminars, workshops, or training sessions that underscore its importance in cybersecurity governance.

- **Craft a Risk Mitigation Strategy:** Create a comprehensive risk mitigation strategy tailored to your organization's risk profile. Regularly reassess and update this strategy to remain abreast of evolving threats.

- **Prioritize Appropriate Control Selection:** Do not underestimate the importance of selecting the proper controls for identified risks. This process might require external expertise, but it is essential for managing risks effectively.

- **Implement Measures Methodically:** When implementing your control, be systematic and deliberate. Your plan should enable effective integration into the organization's existing processes without causing undue disruption.
- **Regularly Evaluate and Adapt:** Keep a constant check on the effectiveness of your risk mitigation measures. Use these insights to fuel ongoing improvements to your risk mitigation strategy, adapting to changes in the risk environment and the organization.

POLICIES, STANDARDS, AND PROCEDURES

The next integral part of risk mitigation revolves around establishing and managing policies, standards, and procedures. These components are the linchpin of any organization's risk management endeavors, underpinning the entire security infrastructure.

The role of these elements in risk management cannot be overstated. Policies, standards, and procedures articulate an organization's expectations concerning its security posture. They outline how risks should be identified, assessed, and managed, ensuring that all organization members work from the same blueprint. Furthermore, they establish a common language and understanding of risk management practices, which can be crucial for maintaining a consistent approach across various departments and teams.

The process of developing and approving these documents is a critical step. It requires a deep understanding of the organization's risk landscape, operational parameters, and overall strategic objectives. Involvement from various stakeholders, from executives to operational staff, is crucial to ensure these documents are comprehensive and practical. Developing policies, standards, and procedures is not a one-off task; these documents should be reviewed and updated regularly to ensure they remain relevant and effective in the face of evolving threats.

Communication and training form a crucial part of this process. All staff members, regardless of their roles, need to understand these documents and the expectations they set out. This understanding can only be achieved through effective communication and ongoing training programs. Without adequate knowledge and experience, even the most well-conceived policies and procedures will fail to deliver the desired risk mitigation outcomes.

Compliance with these policies, standards, and procedures is essential for effective risk mitigation. Mechanisms must be in place to ensure that all organization members adhere to these documents. Regular audits, checks, and balances are essential for maintaining compliance and identifying and addressing gaps or shortcomings.

Finally, these policies, standards, and procedures must be reviewed and updated periodically. The cyber risk landscape is not static; new threats emerge, and old threats evolve. The organization's risk management documents must reflect these changes to remain effective. A procedure for regular review and updates should be in place, and this process should involve input from various stakeholders across the organization.

Recommendations:

- **Stakeholder Engagement:** Involve stakeholders at all levels in developing and approving policies, standards, and procedures. Their insights can help ensure that these documents are both comprehensive and practical.
- **Effective Communication:** Communicate your organization's policies, standards, and procedures clearly and effectively. Ensure all organization members understand these documents and their role in implementing them.
- **Ongoing Training:** Establish ongoing training programs to ensure all staff members understand the risk management policies and procedures and their role in implementing them.
- **Compliance Mechanisms:** Implement mechanisms to ensure compliance with your organization's policies, standards, and procedures. Regular audits can help identify and address any gaps or shortcomings.
- **Regular Reviews:** Review and update your policies, standards, and procedures regularly to ensure they remain effective in the face of evolving threats. Involve various stakeholders in this process to ensure a comprehensive approach.

INVENTORY AND CLASSIFICATION OF ASSETS

The third critical aspect of risk mitigation is the inventory and classification of assets. This process is a cornerstone in establishing a robust risk mitigation strategy as it helps an organization understand what needs to be protected and prioritizes risk mitigation resources effectively.

The importance of an asset inventory cannot be overstated. Each piece of hardware, software, data, or other organizational resource could be vulnerable. Thus, keeping a comprehensive and updated inventory of these assets is the first step in assessing and managing the associated risks. The asset inventory must include details such as the asset's location, users, criticality, and potential vulnerabilities. Regular updates to this inventory are crucial as assets are added, modified, or retired.

Once an asset inventory has been established, asset classification can begin. This involves categorizing assets based on various criteria, such as their importance to the organization, sensitivity, or potential risk. This process helps prioritize risk mitigation efforts and resources. For example, an asset that holds sensitive data or is critical to the organization's operations would typically be given a higher priority than an asset that holds nonsensitive data or is not critical to operations.

Asset management processes are crucial in maintaining the asset inventory and classification. These processes include procedures for adding new assets to the inventory, updating the details of existing assets, and retiring assets that are no longer in use. Proper asset management also involves regular asset inventory audits to ensure accuracy and completeness.

Asset risk assessment is a vital part of the asset management process. Once an asset has been added to the inventory and classified, the risks associated with the asset need to be assessed. This involves identifying potential threats to the asset, evaluating the likelihood of them materializing, and the potential impact if they do. The results of the asset risk assessment should guide the selection of controls and other risk mitigation measures.

Finally, monitoring and reporting are crucial for effective asset management. Regular monitoring helps identify any changes to assets or new threats that may emerge. Reporting ensures that stakeholders know the assets' status and associated risks.

Recommendations:

- **Maintain Asset Inventory:** Keep a comprehensive and regularly updated inventory of all organizational assets, such as hardware, software, and data. The inventory should include asset location, users, criticality, and potential vulnerabilities.

- **Classify Assets:** Once an asset inventory is established, begin the process of asset classification. Categorize assets based on their importance to the organization, sensitivity, or potential risk. This classification helps prioritize risk mitigation resources and efforts.

- **Implement Asset Management Processes:** Procedures for adding new assets to the inventory, updating existing assets' details, and retiring unused assets are vital. Regular asset inventory audits to ensure accuracy and completeness are also key to asset management.

- **Perform Asset Risk Assessment:** Once an asset has been inventoried and classified, conduct an assessment of the risks associated with it. Identify potential threats, evaluate their likelihood, and understand the possible impact if they materialize. Use the results to guide the selection of controls and risk mitigation measures.

- **Monitor and Report:** Regular monitoring of assets helps identify changes or new threats. Reporting ensures that stakeholders are informed about the status of assets and associated risks.

MITIGATING INTERCONNECTIVITY RISK

The fourth aspect of risk mitigation, particularly pertinent in our interconnected digital world, involves mitigating the risk arising from interconnectivity. This includes managing risks from internal connections between different systems within an organization and external connections with third parties such as vendors, suppliers, or customers. Interconnectivity risks extend to using APIs (Application Programming Interfaces), as they form the bridges connecting disparate systems and services.

Understanding interconnectivity risks is the foundation for managing them effectively. In cybersecurity, one must remember that a network is only as secure as its most vulnerable connection point. Risks can arise from various sources, including unsecured APIs, connections to untrusted networks, and third-party vendors with poor security practices. Recognizing these potential pitfalls forms the groundwork for developing and implementing an effective risk mitigation strategy.

Identifying dependencies comes next in this process. Every connection or API an organization employs, whether internally or externally, establishes a dependency. These dependencies can lead to potential risks if not managed correctly. An important part of the risk mitigation strategy is identifying and mapping these dependencies, which includes a deep understanding of API usage and dependencies.

Third-party risk management is a crucial element in mitigating interconnectivity risks. With many organizations relying heavily on third-party providers for various services, including APIs, these third parties can potentially expose the organization to many risks. Having robust processes for third-party risk management becomes critical. This process includes thorough due diligence before onboarding a third-party API, regular audits and security assessments of third-party services, and comprehensive contractual agreements that cover data security and risk management.

The implementation of controls to manage interconnectivity risks is equally important. These controls could range from technical measures such as firewalls, encryption, secure API, and network configurations to organizational measures, including developing strong policies and procedures, comprehensive staff training on secure API usage, and robust governance structures.

Lastly, monitoring and response mechanisms need to be established. Given the dynamic nature of interconnectivity risks, it is crucial to regularly monitor the security status of all connections, including APIs. This can be facilitated by utilizing API monitoring tools, which provide real-time visibility into API security. Equally important is establishing an effective response mechanism to quickly address identified risks, which can involve automated security incident responses and well-defined procedures for managing identified vulnerabilities in APIs.

Recommendations:

- **Understand Interconnectivity Risks:** Recognize that a network's security hinges on its most vulnerable connection point. Identify potential sources of risk, including unsecured APIs, connections to untrusted networks, and third-party vendors with inadequate security practices.
- **Identify Dependencies:** Ascertain and map out all internal and external connections or APIs your organization relies upon. Understanding these dependencies, especially API usage and dependencies, is a significant part of risk mitigation.

- **Manage Third-party Risks:** Establish robust processes to manage risks associated with third-party providers. This includes conducting due diligence before integrating a third-party API, performing regular audits and security assessments, and establishing detailed contractual agreements that address data security and risk management.
- **Implement Controls:** Develop and deploy controls ranging from technical measures like firewalls, encryption, and secure API/network configurations to organizational measures such as strong policies and procedures, comprehensive staff training on secure API usage, and robust governance structures.
- **Establish Monitoring and Response Mechanisms:** Regularly monitor the security status of all connections, including APIs, utilizing API monitoring tools for real-time visibility. Set up an effective response mechanism to address identified risks promptly, incorporating automated security incident responses and clear-cut procedures for managing identified vulnerabilities in APIs.

USER SECURITY CONTROLS

Risk mitigation in any organization is a complex task, and the fifth stage is devoted to establishing and maintaining comprehensive user security controls. These controls are vital to an organization's overall security framework as they manage the potential risks arising from users of its systems and data. Such users may span various categories, including employees, contractors, vendors, and occasionally customers.

Identity and Access Management (IAM) is a critical component of user security controls. IAM focuses on ensuring that only approved individuals gain access to the organization's systems and data, with the granted access being strictly limited to the necessities of their role. This crucial security measure incorporates various methods for creating, managing, and deactivating user accounts and assigning and managing user privileges. IAM technology, such as Microsoft Azure Active Directory or Okta, facilitates the effective implementation of these processes, providing automated workflows, role-based access control, and granular permissions.

Another pivotal aspect of user security controls is user authentication. This practice involves validating the identity of users before they are granted access to systems or data. Techniques utilized for authentication range from simple password-based authentication to more sophisticated multi-factor authentication (MFA) mechanisms. MFA technologies, such as Google Authenticator or Duo Security, incorporate a combination of multiple verification methods, including something the user knows (like a password), something the user has (like a physical token or a mobile device), or something the user is (like a fingerprint or facial recognition).

Privileged Account Management (PAM) is fundamental in managing user security risks. Privileged accounts, often belonging to administrators, possess high-level access rights and, if mishandled, can pose a significant risk to an organization's security. Special controls must be in place to manage these accounts, such as robust authentication measures, usage monitoring, and regular audits. PAM technologies, such as CyberArk or Thycotic, offer effective solutions to manage, control, and monitor privileged accounts.

User training and awareness are essential parts of user security controls, with technologies such as learning management systems (LMS) playing a role in their implementation. Users, often the most vulnerable link in the organization's security chain, can unintentionally engage in risky behaviors due to a lack of awareness. Implementing regular training programs, made possible by platforms like Moodle or SAP Litmos, can ensure users are fully informed about the organization's security policies and procedures, the potential risks they may encounter, and methods to circumvent them.

Finally, it is necessary to monitor and regularly review user activities. This can help detect unusual or risky behaviors and initiate corrective measures before significant damage occurs. User and Entity Behavior Analytics (UEBA) tools use machine learning and advanced analytics to detect deviations from normal behavior, helping security teams spot potential threats early on.

In conclusion, every aspect of user security controls – from IAM to user awareness training – is crucial for effective risk mitigation. The use of technologies associated with these controls, including IAM systems, MFA tools, PAM solutions, LMS platforms, and UEBA tools, can greatly enhance the effectiveness of an organization's security framework.

Recommendations:

- **Implement Identity and Access Management (IAM):** Ensuring only approved individuals can access an organization's systems and data. This involves creating, managing, and deactivating user accounts and assigning and managing user privileges. IAM technology facilitates the effective implementation of these processes.

- **Establish User Authentication:** Validating the identity of users before granting access to systems or data. Authentication techniques range from simple password-based authentication to MFA mechanisms, which involve multiple verification methods.

- **Manage Privileged Accounts:** High-level access accounts, if mishandled, pose a significant security risk. It is important to have controls for these privileged accounts, including robust authentication measures, usage monitoring, and regular audits. PAM technologies provide solutions for this purpose.

- **Train Users and Raise Awareness:** Users can unintentionally engage in risky behaviors due to a lack of awareness. Implement regular training programs to ensure users understand the organization's security policies, potential risks, and how to avoid them. LMS can assist in implementing these programs.

- **Monitor and Review User Activities:** Regularly observe user activities to detect unusual or risky behaviors, allowing for early detection and prevention of potential threats. UEBA tools use machine learning and advanced analytics to spot deviations from normal behavior.

PHYSICAL SECURITY

The sixth component of the broader concept of risk mitigation is physical security. This aspect, though frequently given less attention in debates revolving around cybersecurity, plays an integral role in formulating any well-rounded risk mitigation strategy. It is vital to recognize the importance of physical security in protecting an organization's assets and resources from internal and external threats.

Physical security is multifaceted, involving various components. A pivotal component of this is facility access control. It refers to the process of managing and regulating who can access the physical premises of an organization. These premises might include offices, data centers, or any other physical facilities that belong to the organization. Access control can be implemented in numerous ways. The simplest way is perhaps using traditional lock and key mechanisms, but organizations might resort to advanced biometric access controls in more sophisticated settings. These biometric systems add an extra layer of security, making unauthorized access incredibly difficult.

Maintaining physical security is another important aspect of constant monitoring and vigilant surveillance. Using security apparatus like security cameras forms the backbone of this process. Furthermore, Intrusion Detection Systems (IDS) that alert for any unauthorized entries or activities, frequent security patrols to manually check for discrepancies, and various other measures work in unison to detect and deter unauthorized access. These mechanisms also serve as a psychological deterrent to potential intruders, adding further protection.

Moreover, environmental controls constitute another significant aspect of physical security. These systems protect the organization's premises and valuable assets from environmental hazards. Such hazards might include fire, flood, power failures, or natural disasters. Fire suppression systems, flood defenses, and backup power systems are typical examples of such measures. These controls prevent damage and minimize the interruption to operations during an environmental incident.

Emergency response planning is another critical facet of physical security. A robust emergency response plan is essential during a physical security breach or an environmental hazard. A plan ensures that the organization can respond quickly and effectively to emergencies. This could significantly minimize the impact of such events, allowing for a swift return to regular operations, thus limiting any potential loss.

Lastly, routine audits of physical security measures are integral to a comprehensive security strategy. These audits test the effectiveness of the existing measures and can help identify any potential weaknesses, gaps, or vulnerabilities. Regular audits also encourage the continual improvement and updating of physical security measures, ensuring they remain up-to-date with evolving threats.

Recommendations:

- **Implement Facility Access Control:** Managing and regulating who can access an organization's physical premises, such as offices or data centers, is crucial. While traditional lock and key mechanisms can be used, more advanced settings might require biometric access controls for an extra layer of security.

- **Establish Continuous Monitoring and Surveillance:** This involves using security apparatus like cameras, IDS, and frequent security patrols to detect and deter unauthorized access. These measures can also serve as a psychological deterrent to potential intruders.

- **Install Environmental Controls:** Systems that protect an organization's premises and assets from environmental hazards like fire, flood, power failures, or natural disasters are vital. Implementing fire suppression systems, flood defenses, and backup power systems can prevent damage and minimize operational interruption during an environmental incident.

- **Develop Emergency Response Plans:** A robust plan for responding to physical security breaches or environmental hazards can minimize their impact, enabling a swift return to regular operations. This could substantially limit any potential loss.

- **Conduct Routine Physical Security Audits:** Regular audits test the effectiveness of the existing measures and can help identify any potential weaknesses, gaps, or vulnerabilities. They encourage continual improvement and updating of physical security measures, ensuring they remain current with evolving threats.

NETWORK CONTROLS

The seventh facet of risk mitigation zeroes in on the crucial responsibility of installing and maintaining robust network controls. In a world where our reliance on digital networks is ever-increasing, these networks play a critical role in enabling an organization's functions and services. Given this, network-related risks must be effectively managed. This requires various measures and procedures to mitigate potential risks while ensuring the network remains high-performing.

The front line of defense in any network begins with the strategic deployment of firewalls and the division of the network through segmentation. Firewalls essentially function as barricades between trusted internal and external networks that could be untrusted. They examine and regulate the data packets that come in and out of the network based on predefined rules, thus shielding the network from malicious activity. Network segmentation, conversely, involves breaking up a network into numerous smaller parts or segments. The objective of this division is to limit the fallout of a potential breach, ensuring that an attack on one segment does not necessarily jeopardize the entire network. This strategy of firewall implementation and network segmentation requires careful planning, management, and regular audits to ensure they effectively mitigate potential network risks without hindering the performance and functionality of the network.

Further bolstering network security are tools such as IDS and Intrusion Prevention Systems (IPS), essential components of a strong network control setup. IDS tools function as a network's watchtowers; they monitor network traffic and scan for patterns indicating a network or system attack from an individual or a program attempting to breach or compromise the system. IPS tools, however, are more proactive. They step in to deflect these potential threats, nipping them in the bud before they can infiltrate the network and cause damage.

Another key factor in fortifying network security is the implementation of secure network configurations. This involves ensuring all network devices – routers, switches, firewalls, and servers – are correctly configured to minimize potential vulnerabilities. These configurations should be based on industry-recognized best practices and guidelines and subjected to regular reviews to ensure they continually provide the highest level of security.

Virtual Private Networks (VPNs) and remote access protocols are becoming increasingly common, allowing employees to securely connect to the business network from various global locations. While this facilitates flexible working arrangements, it also introduces additional security considerations that must be managed. This necessitates the implementation of robust policies and technical controls to ensure that remote connections are secure and that access to the network is granted strictly to authorized individuals.

Lastly, actively monitoring and analyzing network traffic is indispensable for detecting and responding to security threats. Consistent observation of the network helps identify unusual traffic patterns or behavior that could indicate a security incident. Anomalies or deviations from the norm can thus be rapidly detected, and appropriate remedial measures can be initiated promptly to mitigate the risk and impact of any potential security breach.

In conclusion, the seventh facet of risk mitigation, implementing robust network controls, is a multipronged process involving various tools, strategies, and proactive measures to ensure network integrity and security. This is not a static, one-time effort but a continuous, dynamic process of adaptation and evolution to stay ahead of potential threats and vulnerabilities.

Recommendations:

- **Deploy Firewalls and Segment the Network:** Firewalls are barriers between trusted internal networks and potential untrusted external networks. They monitor and regulate data traffic based on predefined rules, thus protecting the network from harmful activities. Network segmentation divides a network into smaller segments to limit the impact of a potential breach.

- **Implement Intrusion Detection and Prevention Systems (IDS/IPS):** IDS and IPS are crucial to network security. IDS monitors network traffic for suspicious activity, and IPS actively blocks these threats before they can infiltrate the network and cause harm.

- **Secure Network Configurations:** Ensuring all network devices – such as routers, switches, firewalls, and servers – are correctly configured minimizes potential vulnerabilities. Regular reviews of these configurations are necessary to maintain a high level of security.

- **Establish Secure Remote Access Protocols:** As VPNs and other remote access protocols become common, they bring additional security considerations. Implementing robust policies and technical controls is necessary to ensure secure remote connections and restrict network access to authorized individuals.

- **Monitor and Analyze Network Traffic:** Continuously observing the network helps identify unusual traffic patterns or behaviors that may signal a security incident. Rapid detection of anomalies allows for quick responses and mitigates the impact of potential security breaches.

CHANGE MANAGEMENT WITHIN THE IT ENVIRONMENT

The eighth facet of risk mitigation pivots around the complex task of managing change within the IT environment. Change is given in a technological landscape where advancements are made at breakneck speeds. However, if these changes are not expertly managed, they can introduce new risks to the environment or aggravate existing ones, undermining the very purpose of the change. Therefore, a robust change management process is a critical risk mitigation strategy that can have profound implications for the organization's resilience and long-term success.

Change management starts with the careful identification and comprehensive documentation of proposed changes. These changes can exist on a wide spectrum, ranging from minor tweaks, such as updates to software or patches to systems, to more significant transformations, like implementing entirely new technologies or systems or even decommissioning and replacing outdated systems. Regardless of the scale, each change needs to be clearly defined, its purpose and expected impact carefully articulated, and its implementation steps meticulously planned.

Once proposed changes are identified, risk assessment becomes a cornerstone of the change management process. The proposed change must be scrutinized to understand the potential risks it could introduce to the IT environment. This assessment includes a comprehensive analysis of how the change might interact with the existing systems, any potential for conflicts, disruptions, or security vulnerabilities it might introduce, and the readiness of the organization to accommodate the change. The assessment should also estimate the cost, time, and resources required to implement the change. The ultimate decision to approve the change hinges on thoroughly evaluating these factors. In other words, the change should only get the green light if the benefits it brings to the table significantly outweigh the potential risks or if the risks, once identified, can be adequately managed and mitigated.

The Change Advisory Board (CAB) is crucial in this phase. Comprising key stakeholders from various departments, including IT, business operations, and risk management, the CAB is responsible for reviewing the proposed change, considering the risk assessment, and giving the final approval. They can offer diverse perspectives and insights, ensuring a well-rounded and balanced decision.

Before the approved changes are implemented, it is of paramount importance to conduct thorough testing and validation. Testing should occur in a controlled, simulated environment that mimics the real-world scenario as closely as possible. This testing phase allows for the early identification of issues or bottlenecks that might impact system performance or security, and these can be addressed before the change is rolled out on a larger scale. Conversely, validation ensures that the change achieves its intended outcome without causing any adverse effects on the IT environment. It verifies that the change works as planned and does not disrupt other systems or processes.

The change can be implemented once testing and validation have been satisfactorily completed. This step should be executed per the planned schedule and process, with every step carefully logged and documented for future reference. However, implementation is not solitary but closely tied to clear and timely communication. It is essential to inform all relevant stakeholders – from the project team to the end users – about the change. This communication includes information about why the change is happening, when and how it will occur, its expected impact, and who to contact for any issues or queries. This can help to manage expectations, facilitate smooth transitions, and minimize resistance or pushback.

Post-implementation, the work is far from over. Monitoring and review are critical activities that must be carried out once the change has been implemented. This involves continuously tracking the effects of the change on the IT environment, watching for any unexpected consequences or issues that may crop up, and evaluating how the change has impacted risk mitigation. It is important to remember that the IT environment is a dynamic and interdependent ecosystem; changes can have ripple effects that may not be immediately apparent. Therefore, this monitoring and review should be continuous, not a one-off task.

Moreover, the change management process is incomplete without a post-implementation review, sometimes called a "post-mortem." This is a structured review to analyze the change management process – what went well, what did not, and what lessons can be learned for future changes. These insights feed back into the overall risk mitigation strategy, enabling it to evolve and improve with each change.

In conclusion, the eighth facet of risk mitigation, managing change within the IT environment, is a comprehensive and methodical process. It involves several phases – from identification and risk assessment to implementation and review – each as crucial as the next. Each step must be meticulously planned, executed, and reviewed, ensuring the change enhances the IT environment and strengthens the organization's overall risk mitigation approach.

Recommendations:

- **Identification and Documentation of Changes:** Changes in the IT environment, from minor updates to significant system transformations, must be clearly defined, documented, and planned meticulously. The purpose, expected impact, and implementation steps for each change should be carefully articulated.

- **Risk Assessment:** A comprehensive risk analysis of the proposed changes is a cornerstone of the change management process. This includes understanding how the change interacts with existing systems, potential conflicts or disruptions it may cause, and whether the organization is ready to accommodate it. The decision to approve a change hinges on these factors.

- **Change Advisory Board (CAB) Review:** The CAB, comprising key stakeholders, is responsible for reviewing the proposed change and risk assessment before giving final approval. They ensure a well-rounded decision, considering diverse perspectives and insights.

- **Testing and Validation:** Thorough testing and validation in a controlled environment should occur before any approved change is implemented. This allows for early identification of potential issues and ensures the change achieves its intended outcome without adverse effects.

- **Implementation and Communication:** The approved change is implemented per the planned schedule and process, and all steps are carefully logged and documented. Clear and timely communication with all stakeholders about the change is essential for smooth transitions and managing expectations.

- **Monitoring and Review:** Post-implementation, continuous tracking of the change's effects on the IT environment and its impact on risk mitigation is crucial. Unexpected consequences or issues should be monitored; this monitoring and review should be continuous.

- **Post-Implementation Review:** Also known as a "post-mortem," this structured review analyzes what went well and what did not during the change management process, providing valuable lessons for future changes.

END-OF-LIFE MANAGEMENT

The final component of risk mitigation is managing the end of life (EOL) for systems and technologies. Not correctly managing EOL can expose the organization to various risks, including unsupported systems, potential data loss, and regulatory noncompliance.

Planning for EOL is the first step in the process. This involves identifying systems nearing their EOL, understanding the potential risks, and developing a plan to transition away from these systems.

Data migration and archival are a critical part of EOL management. Before a system is decommissioned, it is essential to ensure that any data it holds is either migrated to a new system or securely archived. This prevents data loss and provides continued access to data for business or regulatory purposes.

Decommissioning and disposal involve taking the system out of service and disposing of it in a secure and environmentally friendly manner. This requires careful planning and execution to ensure data is not inadvertently exposed and disposal complies with environmental regulations.

Consideration of compliance issues is an integral part of EOL management. Many regulations require businesses to retain certain types of data for specified periods. Understanding these requirements can ensure that data is properly managed and compliance is maintained throughout the EOL process.

Lastly, lessons learned from managing EOL can provide valuable insights for future planning. This can involve identifying what went well, what could have been done better, and how the process can be improved for future EOL transitions.

Recommendations:

- **Planning for End of Life (EOL):** The first step in EOL management is to identify systems nearing their EOL, understand potential risks associated with these systems, and create a plan for transitioning away from them. This is a proactive approach, allowing for smoother transitions and minimizing potential disruptions.

- **Data Migration and Archival:** Before decommissioning a system, it is crucial to ensure that any stored data is either migrated to a new system or securely archived. This action is important to prevent data loss and provide ongoing data access for operational and regulatory reasons.

- **Decommissioning and Disposal:** This involves taking the system out of operation and disposing of it securely and environmentally responsibly. Proper planning and execution are essential to ensure that data is not accidentally exposed during this process and that all disposal activities comply with environmental regulations.

- **Compliance Considerations:** Complying with regulations is an integral part of managing EOL. Many regulations necessitate the retention of

specific types of data for certain periods. Awareness of these requirements and incorporating them into the EOL plan can help ensure that
data management adheres to all relevant regulations during and after
the EOL process.

- **Lessons Learned:** After the EOL process has been completed, it is beneficial to review and identify what went well, what could have been
improved, and how the process can be further enhanced for future EOL
transitions. These insights are valuable for continuous improvement and
more efficient EOL management.

Chapter Conclusion

In today's digitally interconnected era, the protection of valuable assets and
the sustainability of business operations have grown to depend heavily on
robust risk mitigation strategies. An understanding of the threats we face,
alongside the selection and implementation of appropriate controls, underpin an effective, comprehensive risk mitigation approach. Adopting a proactive stance is not merely optional but crucial to remain a step ahead of
potential cyber threats.

Understanding the role of policies, standards, and procedures in risk management offers a holistic perspective on cybersecurity. Developing, approving,
communicating, training, compliance enforcement, reviewing, and updating
these elements are the backbone of the integrity of an organization's cybersecurity environment. They are indispensable to any risk management program, ensuring its fluidity and effectiveness.

Asset management takes a central stage in risk mitigation. It involves
knowing the whereabouts and value of the assets, thus forming the first
line of defense. Asset inventory, classification, management processes, risk
assessment, monitoring, and reporting are key components in establishing a
solid defensive line against potential breaches.

The interconnected nature of the modern world significantly broadens
an organization's attack surface. It is paramount to understand these risks
and implement measures to mitigate them. Key strategies include identifying dependencies, managing third-party risks, implementing controls, and
adopting active monitoring and responsive measures.

User security controls play a critical role, particularly when the human
factor emerges as a significant vulnerability. Highlighted areas include
identity and access management, user authentication, PAM, user training, awareness, and constant monitoring and review. Similarly, physical
security controls are often overlooked yet vital to risk mitigation. Facility
access control, monitoring and surveillance, environmental controls, emergency response planning, and physical security audits play key roles in
this respect.

Network controls stand at the forefront of the digital battleground, requiring constant vigilance. The crucial role of firewalls and network segmentation, intrusion detection and prevention systems, secure network configuration, VPNs, remote access, and traffic monitoring and analysis cannot be overstated.

Managing changes within the IT environment requires understanding the potential risks associated with these changes. It is a multifaceted process encompassing risk assessment and approval, testing and validation, implementation, communication, and a keen eye for monitoring and review. Lastly, end-of-life management, a topic often forgotten, is as crucial as the inception of systems and technologies. Planning for end-of-life, data migration, archival, decommissioning and disposal, compliance considerations, and lessons learned are all pivotal.

In essence, risk mitigation is a multidimensional, complex task that calls for a comprehensive and pragmatic approach that is adaptive, responsive, and proactive. With ever-evolving cybersecurity challenges, ensuring that our strategies evolve in sync is crucial, keeping us ahead of the curve and, most importantly, the threats.

Case Study: Risk Mitigation at SkyTech Solutions

Rose worked as a cybersecurity officer at SkyTech Solutions, a rapidly growing technology company with a diverse portfolio. Despite the company's phenomenal success in the tech world, Rose recognized a glaring concern – SkyTech's approach toward risk mitigation lacked depth and comprehensiveness. Understanding that this could significantly expose the company to cyber threats, she spearheaded a company-wide cybersecurity overhaul to elevate SkyTech's risk mitigation strategies to meet the industry's best standards.

She began by revisiting SkyTech's risk mitigation basics, emphasizing the importance of understanding risk mitigation, developing a risk mitigation strategy, selecting appropriate controls, implementing mitigation measures, and evaluating their effectiveness. She strived to embed these principles into the very DNA of SkyTech's risk mitigation approach. To ensure this, she planned a series of workshops and training sessions, disseminating the cruciality and methods of proactive risk mitigation among employees at all levels.

One of the critical steps Rose took was in the realm of policies, standards, and procedures. She knew that these guidelines formed the backbone of the risk management strategy. Working with her team and involving every department head, she initiated a thorough review and revision of existing protocols. This move ensured that all policies were up-to-date, effective, and enforceable, fortifying SkyTech's risk posture.

However, Rose knew implementing controls and standards was only part of the battle. She recognized the human factor as a substantial vulnerability and initiated comprehensive training and awareness programs. These programs were tailored to include various aspects like identity and access management, PAM, and user security controls, enhancing the overall user-based security.

Rose also took steps to revamp the physical security protocols of Sky-Tech, realizing the potential threats material breaches could pose to the company. She engaged a security consultancy to audit the current measures and recommend improvements. Following the audit, SkyTech saw a systematic upgrade of its physical security controls, including better facility access control, efficient monitoring and surveillance, implementation of environmental management, and robust emergency response planning.

Lastly, Rose was keen to manage the risk associated with technological transitions. She put a particular emphasis on EOL management. She championed practices like thorough planning for EOL, secure data migration and archival, compliant decommissioning and disposal, and systematic analysis of lessons learned. This ensured a seamless transition during EOL and reduced potential vulnerabilities that could have been exploited.

The transformation at SkyTech was significant and noticeable. Under Rose's guidance, the company adopted a more robust, comprehensive risk mitigation strategy, becoming an industry benchmark. This case underscores the value of a well-rounded, proactive approach to risk mitigation, proving that understanding, managing, and mitigating risk is not a one-time event but an ongoing, evolving process. From policies and procedures to end-of-life management, every aspect of risk mitigation holds its unique importance, contributing to the resilient fabric of cybersecurity in the organization.

CHAPTER 27

Cloud Security

"Cloud computing, the alchemist of our era, transmutes raw data into golden insights, empowering organizations to make informed decisions, turning bits and bytes into the currency of progress."

Cloud security represents a vast field, covering everything from the fundamentals of cloud computing and its benefits and challenges to a thorough analysis of top cloud service providers and their security protocols. Key cloud security challenges are explored to familiarize nontechnical executives with various cloud services and related security considerations, and an array of tools and techniques are introduced to tackle them. The study concludes with a review of cloud security standards and best practices and an outlook on future trends. Essential takeaways and informative case studies are presented to ensure a well-rounded understanding. Overall, the aim is to offer a comprehensive understanding of the complex landscape of cloud security.

CLOUD COMPUTING

In the digitized world we live in today, cloud computing has positioned itself as the fulcrum of modern businesses. By providing efficient management of IT resources, such as storage, databases, applications, and networking, cloud computing has become an indispensable part of the operational strategy for many organizations. Over time, cloud computing has moved beyond its initial function as a mere data storage solution to become a complex and comprehensive platform that underpins many services. This dynamic technology offers several key advantages, including cost-effectiveness, scalability, and direct access to the latest technological advancements. However, the convenience and power of the cloud come with their challenges, encompassing concerns around data privacy, a lack of comprehensive visibility, and complexities of ineffective management and governance.

One of the primary challenges is the cloud's impact on governance, risk, and compliance (GRC) – key pillars that ensure the overall health of an organization. As the cloud becomes deeply entrenched in organizational processes, it inevitably has profound implications on these critical areas. Governance, which guides the usage and management of IT resources, becomes more complex due to the virtual nature of the cloud and the need to integrate with pre-existing IT policies and procedures. Risk management must evolve to address the unique threats inherent in cloud environments, including data security, privacy, and compliance issues. Compliance, too, becomes a more complicated issue with the cloud due to the diverse jurisdictions and laws applicable to cloud data storage and transmission.

Understanding and adhering to the Shared Responsibility Model is crucial to cloud security. This model delineates the security tasks within the cloud service provider's domain and those the customer needs to handle. In its simplest form, while the provider is generally responsible for the security "of" the cloud, customers are responsible for ensuring security "in" the cloud. This refers to the security of their data, applications, and other digital assets hosted on the cloud platform.

Recognizing the nuances between cloud deployment models – including public, private, hybrid, and community clouds – is vital in making well-informed decisions. This knowledge can dictate which type of cloud is best suited to meet a specific business requirement and how to secure it optimally. Each model has its strengths and weaknesses, and understanding these can enable a more tailored, risk-aware approach to cloud usage and governance.

Recommendations:

- **Invest in Knowledge:** Make a deliberate effort to familiarize yourself with the Shared Responsibility Model. Explore its principles, its applications, and its relevance in the context of cloud security. Understanding this model will lay the groundwork for effective cloud governance and risk management.

- **Embrace Holistic Governance:** Develop a comprehensive governance framework that incorporates cloud computing. This framework should align with existing IT governance while addressing the unique needs of the cloud environment. A solid governance framework will streamline management and ensure cloud usage aligns with strategic goals.

- **Continually Assess Risk:** Implement a robust risk management process to identify, assess, and mitigate cloud-specific risks. Regularly review and update this process to reflect evolving threats and vulnerabilities. By doing so, you will maintain a secure and resilient cloud environment.

- **Prioritize Compliance:** With data in the cloud potentially crossing multiple jurisdictions, prioritize compliance with relevant laws and regulations.

Understand the compliance requirements of each jurisdiction in which you operate. An informed compliance strategy will minimize legal and operational risks.

- **Optimize Your Cloud Model:** Understand the strengths and weaknesses of the different cloud deployment models to determine which best suits your business needs. Regularly reassess this choice as your needs evolve. Choosing the suitable cloud model will maximize the benefits of cloud computing while minimizing its challenges.

MAJOR CLOUD SERVICE PROVIDERS

Several major service providers in cloud computing have established themselves as industry leaders. Each provider brings unique offerings, driving innovation in cloud services and playing significant roles in defining and shaping security standards and best practices. Let us delve a bit deeper into the history, services, and security features of each one.

Amazon Web Services (AWS) is a pioneer in the cloud computing industry. Launched in 2006, it has continuously evolved to offer a mix of Infrastructure as a service (IaaS), Platform as a service (PaaS), and packaged Software as a service (SaaS) solutions. AWS has played a significant role in popularizing the cloud model among businesses worldwide. It offers extensive security features like Identity and Access Management (IAM), Virtual Private Cloud (VPC), AWS Key Management Service, AWS Shield, AWS WAF, AWS CloudTrail, and Amazon CloudWatch. Users should follow best practices for AWS security, which include data encryption, managing IAM policies, regular rotation of security credentials, implementing security groups and network ACLs, and maintaining compliance within the AWS environment.

Next in line is Microsoft Azure, another dominant player in the cloud service provider market. Azure was launched in 2010, four years after AWS, but quickly gained traction thanks to Microsoft's extensive enterprise customer base and deep software stack. Like AWS, Azure offers a wide range of cloud services, including IaaS, PaaS, and SaaS. It provides robust security measures such as Azure Active Directory, Azure Key Vault, Network Security Groups, Azure Application Gateway, Azure Firewall, and Azure Security Center. Adopting best practices for Azure security is essential, and these include utilizing Role-Based Access Control (RBAC), securing data with Azure Storage Service Encryption, implementing Multi-Factor Authentication (MFA), continuously monitoring with Azure Monitor, and maintaining compliance with industry standards.

The Google Cloud Platform (GCP) emerged in 2011 as a strong competitor in the cloud computing arena. Leveraging Google's advanced data centers and global network, GCP offers an impressive array of services, including computing, storage, data analytics, machine learning, and networking. Key security features of GCP include Cloud IAM, Google Cloud's operations suite for logging and monitoring, Google Cloud's security command center, and VPC Service Controls. GCP users must understand and follow the best practices around these features, like least privilege access principles, encryption at rest and in transit, secure interservice communication, and compliance monitoring.

The IBM Cloud, another significant contributor to cloud computing, emerged in 2011. It combines Infrastructure from SoftLayer (acquired by IBM in 2013) with the platform services from IBM Bluemix. IBM Cloud's security offerings include IBM Key Protect, IBM Cloud Activity Tracker, and IBM Cloud Security Advisor. Users of IBM Cloud should follow the recommended best practices like securing the cloud infrastructure, using activity tracking for cloud resources, and managing security advisories.

Oracle Cloud, launched in 2012, provides a comprehensive suite of integrated applications for Sales, Service, Marketing, Human Resources, Finance, Supply Chain, Manufacturing, and Highly Automated and Secure Oracle Cloud Infrastructure featuring the Oracle Autonomous Database. Oracle Cloud's security features include Oracle Identity Cloud Service, Oracle Cloud Infrastructure Key Management, Oracle Cloud Guard, and Oracle Cloud Infrastructure Web Application Firewall. Best practices include IAM principles, using key management for encryption, maintaining a security posture with Oracle Cloud Guard, and protecting web applications with the web application firewall.

In conclusion, whether you are using AWS, Azure, GCP, IBM Cloud, or Oracle Cloud, understanding the history, services, and security features each provider offers is key. Regardless of your chosen provider, adherence to their respective best practices and compliance measures is crucial for maintaining a secure cloud environment.

Recommendations:

- **Conduct Research:** Familiarize yourself with each significant cloud service provider, including AWS, Azure, GCP, IBM Cloud, and Oracle Cloud. Dive into their histories, the services they offer, and their respective security features. This groundwork will allow you to make a more informed decision about which cloud service provider aligns best with your specific needs.

- **Explore Security Measures:** Understand the unique security measures that each cloud service provider offers. These can range from IAM, key management services, network ACLs, and firewalls to web application firewalls. Learning about these measures and how to implement them correctly can significantly enhance the security of your cloud environment.

- **Embrace Best Practices:** Make it a point to adhere to the best practices recommended by each cloud service provider. This can include implementing RBAC, data encryption, regular rotation of security credentials, interservice communication security, and compliance with industry standards. Incorporating these practices can significantly contribute to the safety and efficiency of your cloud-based operations.

- **Leverage Unique Offerings:** Each cloud provider offers unique services like specific applications, machine learning capabilities, or advanced data centers. Consider your business's requirements and choose a provider that best suits your needs. Leveraging these unique offerings can allow you to drive innovation and performance in your industry.

- **Continual Monitoring and Compliance:** Ensure continuous monitoring of your cloud environment and maintain compliance with the standards set by your chosen cloud service provider. This can involve monitoring tools like AWS CloudTrail, Azure Monitor, Google Cloud's operations suite, IBM Cloud Activity Tracker, or Oracle Cloud Guard. This vigilance is critical to identifying potential security threats and maintaining a robust cloud environment.

TYPES OF CLOUD SERVICES

The world of cloud computing encompasses several types of services, each designed with specific benefits, potential use cases, and inherent security implications. Understanding these different service types is essential when choosing the right service to meet your organization's unique needs and formulating the appropriate security strategies for protecting your cloud assets.

IaaS provides the basic building blocks for cloud IT, supplying businesses with networks, storage, servers, and services like virtualization and data center management. IaaS providers include AWS, Microsoft Azure, and GCP. It gives organizations complete control over their Infrastructure, which makes it highly flexible and scalable. However, with this freedom comes increased responsibility for security. In the IaaS model, while the service provider manages the underlying physical Infrastructure, the user is responsible for securing the operating systems, data, and applications that run on the Platform. This includes system patching, network and firewall configurations, IAM, and intrusion detection.

PaaS delivers a framework developers can leverage to create, test, and deploy applications. Examples of PaaS include AWS Elastic Beanstalk, Microsoft Azure App Services, and Google App Engine. PaaS abstracts much of the underlying infrastructure management, freeing developers to focus on writing and managing applications. However, even though the service provider handles security at the infrastructure layer, the customer still needs to secure the applications they run and manage, the runtime environment, and the data they handle on the Platform. Therefore, considerations for PaaS extend to areas such as application security, data protection, encryption, and managing user access controls.

SaaS is a delivery model in which applications are hosted and managed in a service provider's data center, paid for on a subscription basis, and accessed via a browser over the internet. Examples of SaaS include Salesforce, Microsoft Office 365, and Google Workspace. In this model, the application's security is primarily managed by the service provider, but users must still be mindful of areas under control. These include managing the security settings of the SaaS application, ensuring secure user access, monitoring user activities, protecting the data they generate and store in the application, and maintaining compliance with applicable regulations.

Function as a Service (FaaS), or serverless computing, provides a platform to execute pieces of function (code) in response to specific events, scaling as needed. Examples of FaaS include AWS Lambda, Google Cloud Functions, and Azure Functions. FaaS abstracts almost all the infrastructure management tasks, leaving developers free to focus on individual functions in their application code. However, users should consider security aspects such as securing the application code, protecting data in transit and at rest, managing third-party dependencies, and ensuring the triggering events are secure and authorized.

Each cloud service model – IaaS, PaaS, SaaS, and FaaS – brings unique advantages and challenges, including the extent of control users have over the services and the corresponding responsibilities for security. Choosing the suitable service model depends on an organization's specific needs regarding control, flexibility, scalability, and the resources they can dedicate to manage and secure the service. As cloud computing evolves and becomes more sophisticated, staying informed and updated about these services and their security implications is crucial.

Recommendations:

- **Determine Service Needs:** Consider your organization's requirements and resources before selecting a type of cloud service. Understand the unique advantages and challenges of IaaS, PaaS, SaaS, and FaaS. Ensure your choice aligns with your control, flexibility, scalability, and security needs.

- **Understand Security Responsibilities:** Recognize that each cloud service type has different security implications. With IaaS, the user is responsible for securing operating systems, data, and applications, while PaaS users need to secure the applications and data they handle on the Platform. In the SaaS model, the user should manage secure access and protect data, and FaaS users should secure the application code and safeguard data in transit and at rest.

- **Regularly Update and Patch Systems:** In models like IaaS and PaaS, where users have significant control over their applications and runtime environments, apply system patches regularly. This includes network and firewall configurations, IAM, and intrusion detection systems. Regular patching can help prevent security vulnerabilities.

- **Prioritize Application Security:** Especially in PaaS and FaaS models, focus on application-level security. Implement robust access controls, protect data at rest and in transit, manage third-party dependencies securely, and ensure that triggering events for functions are secure and authorized.

- **Continuous Learning:** As cloud computing evolves and becomes more sophisticated, stay informed and updated about these services and their security implications. Regularly revise your security strategies to meet each type of service's unique needs and challenges. Continuous learning will help you maintain a secure cloud environment.

CLOUD SECURITY CHALLENGES

While cloud services offer considerable benefits in terms of cost efficiency, scalability, and accessibility, they also bring to the fore a distinct set of security challenges that organizations must tackle to safeguard their digital assets. These challenges, ranging from data privacy to vulnerability management, can significantly impact an organization's ability to utilize the cloud's power securely.

One of the major concerns in cloud computing is data privacy and compliance. In a cloud environment, data is stored and processed in remote servers, spanning multiple geographical regions. As a result, maintaining privacy becomes a significant challenge. For instance, consider a company operating in the healthcare sector. The remote storage and processing of sensitive patient data bring about privacy concerns that may not have been present in a traditional on-site data center. Furthermore, compliance with regulations like the General Data Protection Regulation (GDPR) in Europe and the Health Insurance Portability and Accountability Act (HIPAA) in the United States necessitates a clear understanding of where data resides, who can access it, and how it is protected. For instance, under GDPR, companies must obtain explicit consent from users before processing their data, and under HIPAA, healthcare providers must implement strict safeguards to protect patient information.

Another key challenge lies in IAM. Ensuring the right individuals have access to appropriate resources and preventing unauthorized access is crucial in the cloud environment. For instance, consider a large enterprise using a SaaS solution like Salesforce. Managing access for hundreds or thousands of users with distinct roles and permissions can be intricate. Moreover, there is the risk of "permission creep," where users accumulate more access rights over time, potentially leading to situations where they have more access than necessary, thereby increasing the potential damage in case of a breach.

Cloud environments are also at risk of data breaches and data loss. Cyberattackers might exploit vulnerabilities to gain unauthorized access to sensitive data. For example, a recent breach at a major company occurred when attackers gained access through a misconfigured web application firewall, exposing sensitive user data. Meanwhile, technical issues, such as server failures or data corruption, could lead to data loss. This situation was exemplified when a cloud service provider suffered a significant outage, causing permanent data loss for some customers.

The issue of insider threats, whether intentional or accidental, poses a significant challenge in cloud environments. Employees with access to sensitive resources can misuse them, leading to a potential breach. For example, a disgruntled employee might intentionally leak confidential company data, or an employee could accidentally make sensitive data publicly accessible due to a misunderstanding of cloud storage settings.

Vulnerability management is another crucial challenge in the cloud. Keeping track of all cloud assets and their security vulnerabilities becomes daunting, considering cloud environments' dynamic and scalable nature. For instance, in a large organization using multiple cloud services, tracking and patching vulnerabilities across numerous servers, containers, databases, and applications can be herculean.

Network security in cloud environments often involves complex configurations and can be challenging to manage effectively. Insecure configurations can expose the network to attacks. For example, an improperly configured cloud-based database could inadvertently be left accessible from the internet, making it an easy target for cybercriminals.

Related to network security, cloud misconfigurations are a common problem leading to security incidents. Due to human error, these misconfigurations can expose sensitive data. A notable instance of this was when a major corporation had a significant amount of confidential data leaked because a database on a cloud server was incorrectly configured to be publicly accessible.

Finally, navigating cloud security's legal and regulatory landscape can be challenging. Different countries and regions have other laws and regulations around data privacy, and complying with them can be complex. For example, a company operating in multiple countries will need to navigate the data privacy regulations of each of these countries, including the GDPR in the European Union, the Personal Data Protection Act in Singapore, and the California Consumer Privacy Act in the United States. Understanding and complying with these disparate regulations require considerable effort and expertise, further amplifying cloud security challenges.

Recommendations:

- **Enhance Data Privacy and Compliance:** Take steps to understand where your data resides, who can access it, and how it is protected in your cloud environment. For industries with sensitive data, like healthcare, focus on meeting specific regulations like GDPR and HIPAA. Implement strict safeguards like data encryption and seek explicit user consent for data processing.

- **Improve Identity and Access Management:** Utilize IAM tools to control who has access to what resources in your cloud environment. Regularly review user access rights to prevent 'permission creep' and establish a principle of least privilege. Using MFA can also bolster security and prevent unauthorized access.

- **Prioritize Data Protection Measures:** Mitigate data breaches and loss risks by regularly monitoring and updating security measures. Implement robust firewalls, run routine vulnerability scans, and backup data regularly. Ensure data recovery procedures are in place during an unexpected outage or data corruption.

- **Address Insider Threats:** Create a security-aware culture within your organization to minimize the risk of accidental breaches. Implement strict controls and monitoring systems for high-privilege users and provide regular training for employees about the secure usage of cloud resources.

- **Focus on Vulnerability Management:** Develop a robust vulnerability management strategy to stay on top of all security vulnerabilities in your cloud environment. Use automated tools to track and patch vulnerabilities across various cloud services, servers, containers, databases, and applications.

- **Strengthen Network Security:** Ensure network configurations in the cloud environment are secure. Regular audits can help identify and rectify insecure configurations before they are exploited.

- **Prevent Cloud Misconfigurations:** Establish procedures and controls to prevent misconfigurations in your cloud environment. Regular audits and automated tools can help detect and correct misconfigurations and thus prevent unintended data exposure.

- **Understand Legal and Regulatory Landscape:** If operating internationally, familiarize yourself with the data privacy regulations of all relevant countries. Consult with legal and data privacy experts to ensure compliance with complex laws like GDPR, PDPA, and CCPA. Staying updated with these regulations is crucial to avoid legal complications and penalties.

SECURITY TOOLS AND TECHNIQUES FOR CLOUD ENVIRONMENTS

Many sophisticated tools and techniques can be employed to alleviate the security challenges inherent in cloud environments. From encryption and key management to cloud-native security services, these mechanisms provide robust protective layers and visibility into potential vulnerabilities and threats, ensuring the safe usage of cloud resources.

First and foremost, encryption and key management are foundational to data protection within the cloud. This strategy involves encrypting data at rest and in transit, ensuring that even if data is accessed illicitly, it cannot be read or exploited without the associated decryption keys. For instance, a company might use Advanced Encryption Standard (AES) encryption to protect sensitive data. In this system, the data is scrambled using a secret key, which can only be unscrambled – or decrypted – by someone who possesses that key. Implementing a robust key management strategy is equally important. For example, Hardware Security Modules (HSMs) can protect encryption keys by storing them in a highly secure physical device, thus preventing unauthorized access.

Security monitoring and logging tools are crucial in maintaining visibility into cloud activities and ensuring a robust security posture. These solutions allow organizations to detect anomalous activities that might indicate a security incident. For example, if a user who typically logs in during work hours suddenly logs in late at night, this could be a sign of a compromised account. Similarly, a large data transfer from a company's cloud storage might indicate a potential data breach. A specific example of such a tool would be a Security Information and Event Management (SIEM) solution, which aggregates and analyzes log data from various sources, helping security teams identify and respond to threats.

Cloud Access Security Brokers (CASBs) provide visibility into your cloud applications and services, helping enforce security policies and detect and respond to threats. Consider an organization that uses multiple SaaS solutions, such as Office 365, Salesforce, and Slack. A CASB solution, like those offered by companies like McAfee or Netskope, can provide a single pane of glass through which the organization can view and control how these services are used, ensuring that security policies are consistently applied across all services.

Cloud Security Posture Management (CSPM) tools are specialized solutions designed to identify and remediate risks arising from cloud misconfigurations. For instance, a CSPM tool might automatically detect if a cloud storage bucket is inadvertently made publicly accessible or if security group rules in a cloud environment are overly permissive, thereby exposing the system to potential attacks. Remediation could involve automatically modifying the configuration or alerting the responsible team to make the necessary changes. Companies such as Check Point and Palo Alto Networks offer such solutions.

IAM tools are critical for managing user identities and controlling access to resources within the cloud environment. These tools enable organizations to ensure that only authorized individuals have access to specific cloud resources, and they can manage this access at a granular level. For instance, Google's Cloud Identity or AWS's IAM enables organizations to assign specific permissions to each user, controlling which actions they can perform on which resources. This can range from read-only access to a storage bucket to full administrative privileges for a virtual machine.

Cloud-native security service providers can offer seamless integration and efficient security management. These services are designed to work optimally within the provider's cloud environment, reducing the complexities often associated with third-party tools. For example, Amazon's AWS Shield is a managed Distributed Denial of Service (DDoS) protection service that safeguards applications running on AWS. Google Cloud Armor is another such service, defending against DDoS and web attacks for Google Cloud applications.

In summary, while cloud environments pose a unique set of security challenges, a comprehensive suite of tools and techniques is explicitly designed to address these issues. Through the strategic implementation and management of these resources, organizations can fortify their cloud environments against potential threats, thereby harnessing the power of the cloud with increased confidence and security.

Recommendations:

- **Implement Encryption and Key Management:** Use encryption for data at rest and in transit using techniques like AES encryption. For example, ensure robust key management to prevent unauthorized decryption through HSMs.

- **Utilize Security Monitoring and Logging Tools:** Deploy solutions that detect anomalous activities, indicating potential security incidents. SIEM tools can help promptly identify and respond to threats.
- **Deploy Cloud Access Security Brokers (CASBs):** Use CASB solutions to gain visibility into cloud applications and services, enforce security policies consistently, and respond to threats. These solutions ensure that all cloud services adhere to the organization's security standards.
- **Leverage Cloud Security Posture Management (CSPM) Tools:** These specialized solutions identify and remediate risks from cloud misconfigurations, such as publicly accessible storage buckets or overly permissive security group rules.
- **Use Identity and Access Management (IAM) Tools:** Manage user identities and control access to cloud resources. Tools like Google's Cloud Identity or AWS's IAM can assign specific permissions to each user, ensuring only authorized access.
- **Integrate Cloud-Native Security Services:** Cloud-native services like AWS Shield or Google Cloud Armor can offer optimal security management within the provider's environment. They simplify the complexities associated with third-party tools and efficiently protect against DDoS attacks.

CLOUD SECURITY STANDARDS AND BEST PRACTICES

Compliance with established cloud security standards and best practices is integral to maintaining a resilient security posture. These standards, developed by globally recognized organizations, provide thorough guidance for organizations to understand better, manage, and mitigate the risks associated with cloud computing. By adhering to these standards, organizations can ensure high security while proving their commitment to protecting their stakeholders' sensitive data.

The Cloud Security Alliance (CSA) is a leading organization offering exhaustive guidance for cloud security. The CSA's recommendations span multiple domains, including information governance, operations management, and threat and vulnerability management. For instance, in information governance, the CSA recommends a comprehensive data classification scheme where data is tagged based on sensitivity and business impact, guiding appropriate security controls. In operations management, CSA encourages the adoption of methodologies like DevSecOps, where security is integrated into the entire software development life cycle. Regarding threat and vulnerability management, the CSA promotes continuous monitoring and threat intelligence to stay ahead of emerging risks. The CSA's Security Guidance and Cloud Controls Matrix are two essential resources that provide a structured approach to cloud security.

The National Institute of Standards and Technology (NIST) offers the Cloud Computing Security Reference Architecture, a detailed framework designed to assist organizations in understanding, managing, and mitigating risks in their cloud environments. This framework presents a systematic approach to security, underscoring the criticality of risk assessment and management. For instance, it emphasizes the importance of regular risk assessments, incorporating measures to mitigate identified risks, and an ongoing review and update process to account for changes in the threat landscape or business requirements. NIST's framework also advocates for the principle of "least privilege," where users are given the minimum levels of access necessary to perform their tasks, thereby reducing the risk of unauthorized data access.

ISO/IEC 27017 is a cloud-specific standard that delineates guidelines on the information security facets of cloud computing. It offers controls and implementation guidance for cloud service providers and users of cloud services, promoting a shared responsibility model. For example, it prescribes security controls around network security, asset management, access control, and incident response for cloud service providers. It also guides cloud customers on securely using cloud services, such as managing their data, handling user credentials, and monitoring the service provider's security performance.

Lastly, maintaining compliance in the cloud environment is a vital requirement. Compliance with regulations such as the GDPR and the HIPAA is pivotal to protecting sensitive data and circumventing hefty fines. Under GDPR, for example, organizations must ensure the privacy and protection of EU citizens' data. This may involve implementing stringent data security controls, reporting breaches within 72 hours, and providing data portability. HIPAA, on the other hand, focuses on protecting health information. Entities dealing with such data must ensure proper encryption, establish access controls and audit trails, and have Business Associate Agreements (BAAs) in place with third parties handling the data.

These guidelines, standards, and compliance measures form a comprehensive and rigorous framework organizations can adhere to establish and maintain a robust cloud security posture. Not only do they provide a pathway to secure cloud operations, but they also help foster Trust among stakeholders, including customers, partners, and regulators.

Recommendations:

- **Adhere to Cloud Security Alliance (CSA) Recommendations:** CSA provides detailed guidance for cloud security, spanning multiple domains like information governance, operations management, and threat/vulnerability management. Essential resources include the CSA's Security Guidance and Cloud Controls Matrix.

- **Follow the NIST Cloud Computing Security Reference Architecture:** This framework helps understand, manage, and mitigate risks in cloud environments. It emphasizes regular risk assessments, the principle of "least privilege," and updating processes to account for changes in the threat landscape.

- **Comply with ISO/IEC 27017 Standard:** This standard outlines guidelines on cloud computing's information security aspects. It provides controls and implementation guidance for cloud service providers and users, advocating a shared responsibility model.

- **Ensure Regulatory Compliance:** Compliance with regulations such as GDPR and HIPAA is crucial for protecting sensitive data and avoiding potential fines. Key actions may involve implementing stringent data security controls, reporting breaches promptly, ensuring data portability, and having proper agreements with third parties handling sensitive data.

FUTURE TRENDS IN CLOUD SECURITY

The field of cloud security is in constant flux, driven by technological innovation, evolving threat landscapes, and changing regulatory environments. Recognizing future trends and their implications is crucial for organizations to prepare effectively for impending challenges and leverage opportunities for improved security postures.

One major trend is the rise of cloud-native security solutions. As organizations progressively embrace cloud services, security solutions purpose-built for the cloud environment are gaining prominence. Traditional security tools, often designed for on-premises infrastructure, sometimes struggle to adapt to cloud services' scalability, dynamism, and diversity. In contrast, cloud-native security solutions are inherently designed to integrate seamlessly with the cloud ecosystem, enhancing security while promoting efficiency. They leverage cloud service providers' APIs to gain visibility into cloud environments and enforce security controls. For instance, solutions like Prisma Cloud by Palo Alto Networks or Security Hub by AWS are cloud-native tools that offer a broad array of capabilities, including threat detection, vulnerability management, and compliance assessment.

Integrating artificial intelligence (AI) in cloud security marks another significant trend. AI can enhance the automation of detecting and responding to security threats, making security operations more efficient and reducing response times. Machine learning, a subset of AI, is instrumental in identifying patterns and anomalies that might indicate a security incident. For example, an AI-powered security tool could learn normal user behavior patterns and flag any deviations as potential security threats. AI can also speed up incident response by automating routine tasks such as patch applications or isolating affected systems. Companies like Darktrace and Cylance are pioneering the use of AI in security, providing advanced threat detection and response capabilities.

The concept of Zero Trust is another trend experiencing significant evolution in the context of cloud security. Zero Trust, founded on the principle of "never trust, always verify," is being more widely adopted in cloud environments to bolster security. Rather than granting access based on network location, as traditional models do, Zero Trust verifies the identity and context of each request, regardless of its origin. This approach significantly reduces the risk of unauthorized access, even if a threat actor has infiltrated the network. Zero Trust architecture involves MFA, IAM, and micro-segmentation. Okta and Duo Security offer Zero Trust solutions that provide robust user authentication and secure access control.

These trends are reshaping the cloud security landscape, presenting challenges and opportunities. As organizations become more reliant on cloud services, the importance of understanding and embracing these trends grows. By integrating cloud-native solutions, harnessing the power of AI, and implementing Zero Trust principles, businesses can navigate the evolving landscape, ensuring their cloud environments are secure, compliant, and resilient against future threats.

Recommendations:

- **Embrace Cloud-Native Security Solutions:** As you further integrate cloud services into your organization, consider adopting cloud-native security solutions. These tools are designed specifically for the cloud environment, offering enhanced visibility, scalability, and effectiveness compared to traditional security tools.
- **Invest in AI-Enhanced Security Tools:** AI can significantly improve your organization's ability to detect and respond to threats quickly. Look for security tools that leverage machine learning to identify patterns and anomalies indicative of security incidents.
- **Adopt a Zero Trust Security Model:** A Zero Trust approach – "never trust, always verify" – can significantly enhance cloud security. This method requires verification for every user and device, regardless of network location. Invest in solutions that provide robust MFA, identity, and access management, and consider implementing network microsegmentation.
- **Regularly Update and Train Your Team:** Given the fast-paced nature of technological developments and evolving threat landscapes, ensure your team is up-to-date with the latest cloud security trends and practices. Regular training sessions can help ensure they are well equipped to manage and respond to potential security incidents.
- **Comply with Security Standards and Regulations:** Make sure your organization complies with internationally recognized cloud security standards, such as those outlined by the CSA, the NIST, and ISO/IEC 27017. Regular compliance audits can help ensure that your security controls are up to standard and that sensitive data is well protected.

Chapter Conclusion

Delving into the intricacies of cloud security, one must start from the rudiments of cloud computing. An evaluation of its journey from conception to widespread adoption across various industry sectors provides a fascinating view. The compelling virtues of cloud computing, including its cost efficiency, scalability, and nimbleness, are recognized. However, it is also crucial to be aware of the challenges it presents, such as the technological barriers and cultural shifts necessary for its adoption. The shared responsibility model, a cornerstone of cloud security, distinguishes how security tasks are distributed between cloud service providers and customers, outlining various aspects of cloud security allocation.

Next, an in-depth exploration of different cloud service models – IaaS, PaaS, SaaS, and FaaS – is conducted. Each model's unique characteristics and the security implications they pose are examined. For instance, the IaaS model requires customers to manage security from the operating system layer upward, whereas the SaaS model leaves a larger portion of security management to the provider, with users mainly responsible for data and access protection.

The assessment compares prominent cloud service providers like AWS, Microsoft Azure, GCP, IBM Cloud, Oracle Cloud, Alibaba Cloud, and Salesforce. The distinct security features, services, and proposed best practices for secure cloud usage of each provider are analyzed. For example, the breadth of security services and tools AWS provides, such as AWS Shield for DDoS protection and AWS IAM for access control, is highlighted.

The journey then shifts toward cloud security's challenges, from data privacy and compliance issues to IAM, data breaches and loss, insider threats, vulnerability management, network security, cloud misconfigurations, and complex legal and regulatory challenges. Detailed discussions backed with real-world examples highlight the ramifications of these issues. The exploration then segues into potential remedies, from encryption and key management to CASBs and CSPM tools.

Toward the end, the spotlight shines on emerging trends in cloud security. This involves evaluating the growing importance of cloud-native security solutions designed for seamless integration with cloud environments, the rising utilization of AI to automate and enhance security operations, and the expanding role of the Zero Trust model in strengthening cloud security. These trends are scrutinized in depth, supported with specific instances and potential impacts. Such a comprehensive walk-through ensures a robust understanding of cloud security, ranging from foundational principles, key hurdles, and viable solutions to the future course of this ever-evolving domain.

Case Study: Moving to the Cloud with Aurora Innovations
Derek was in the hot seat as the CISO of Aurora Innovations, a rapidly growing Internet of Things (IoT) industry start-up. Aurora Innovations decided to adopt cloud computing to handle the massive data their IoT devices were generating, a choice that would scale their business while improving the

efficiency of their operations. However, this transition also brought various security challenges that Derek was tasked to overcome.

The first challenge he faced was selecting suitable cloud service models from IaaS, PaaS, SaaS, and FaaS, each with distinct characteristics and security implications. After analyzing the requirements of different departments within Aurora, Derek proposed combining IaaS for hosting the company's data-intensive servers, PaaS for the development and deployment environment, and SaaS for standard business processes such as email and CRM.

After defining the service model mix, Derek set about finding a suitable cloud service provider. He compared AWS, Azure, GCP, IBM Cloud, Oracle Cloud, Alibaba Cloud, and Salesforce based on their security features, range of services, scalability, and best practices. After a thorough evaluation, Derek partnered with AWS due to its robust security measures, comprehensive services, and ability to grow with Aurora's expanding needs.

With the provider selected, Derek faced the daunting challenge of securing the data in the cloud. She understood that data privacy, compliance, IAM, and data loss prevention were pivotal issues in cloud security. He implemented robust encryption protocols and key management practices to ensure data privacy. He introduced logging and CSPM tools to monitor suspicious activities. He also implemented IAM systems to control resource access effectively.

The security challenges did not end there. Derek had to grapple with the issue of cloud misconfigurations and vulnerability management, two common pitfalls that could expose Aurora's sensitive data to threats. To address these issues, he utilized CASBs to gain visibility into cloud applications and services, enforce security policies, and use CSPM tools to identify and remediate risks arising from misconfigurations.

Even as he dealt with these challenges, Derek understood the importance of keeping up with future trends in cloud security. Derek saw the rise of cloud-native security solutions and the integration of AI in cloud security. Recognizing the potential of these developments, he pushed for adopting AI-powered security solutions to automate threat detection and response. Also, he initiated the transition toward a Zero Trust model, which follows the principle of "never trust, always verify."

In conclusion, Derek's story is a case study for managing cloud security challenges. His approach, from selecting the right service models and providers addressing various security concerns to staying abreast with future trends in cloud security, serves as a comprehensive roadmap for organizations planning their cloud journey.

CHAPTER 28

Artificial Intelligence in Cybersecurity

"In AI, limitations are merely stepping stones towards limitless possibilities. Embrace the challenges, unlock your curiosity, and let your innovation shape a future where the extraordinary becomes the norm."

Artificial Intelligence (AI) and cybersecurity interact in complex ways, with AI potentially significantly enhancing cybersecurity protocols. It can shape the cyber threat landscape and is often surrounded by misconceptions regarding its role in cybersecurity. A thorough analysis of AI's transformative impact on cyber defense strategies offers insights into how it could redefine the cybersecurity product landscape. Moreover, the practical applications of AI have distinguished it from science fiction portrayals, with several real-world AI systems currently making significant contributions. With a balanced understanding of AI's role in cybersecurity, its historical development, and practical manifestations, actionable recommendations can be formulated to effectively harness AI in a business environment.

UNRAVELING THE AI-CYBERSECURITY CONUNDRUM

Since its inception, AI has been a force to reckon with in numerous fields, and cybersecurity is no exception. The capabilities introduced by AI in the realm of cybersecurity are unprecedented. They have not only transformed the methods of threat detection and response but have also allowed us to conceive the future of cybersecurity in ways never imagined.

Nevertheless, AI in cybersecurity, often regarded as a panacea for all cyber threats, has its own set of limitations and misconceptions. These misconceptions may lead to unrealistic expectations and unsatisfactory outcomes if not addressed. Simply put, AI is not the magic wand it is often perceived as. For instance, while AI is extraordinarily adept at detecting patterns and anomalies in large datasets, it still requires human input and judgment to distinguish between an actual threat and a false positive. It is also crucial to remember that AI algorithms, like any other software, can contain bugs that might lead to unintentional consequences.

The advent of AI has dramatically reshaped the cyber threat landscape. When used judiciously, it is a potent tool that can drastically enhance threat detection and response capabilities. Traditional cybersecurity measures often struggle with the sheer volume and complexity of data they need to process. With its superior processing power and machine learning algorithms, AI can sift through this data much more efficiently, helping identify potential threats that might have otherwise gone unnoticed. A noteworthy example of AI's potential is its use by the cybersecurity firm Darktrace. By employing AI-powered threat detection, Darktrace has identified and thwarted potential threats in real time, well before they could inflict substantial damage.

However, the transformative power of AI is a double-edged sword. While it offers immense benefits in threat detection and mitigation, it can also be exploited by malicious actors to execute highly sophisticated cyberattacks. The same algorithms that detect cyber threats can also learn to create them. We have already seen glimpses of this darker side of AI with the emergence of AI-powered phishing attacks that are far more convincing and harder to detect than their human-crafted counterparts.

The potential of AI in cybersecurity extends beyond just automated threat detection. AI's predictive capabilities, harnessed through machine learning algorithms, are poised to redefine cybersecurity. Rather than simply reacting to threats as they occur, AI can learn from past incidents to predict and prevent future attacks. This shift from reactive to proactive cybersecurity holds enormous promise for the future.

Despite its significant potential, integrating AI into cybersecurity is not without challenges. The inherent complexity of AI systems and a widespread shortage of AI expertise can make implementation daunting. In addition, ethical and legal considerations must be addressed to ensure the responsible use of AI. Privacy, consent, and accountability issues can become potential stumbling blocks in AI integration.

Furthermore, AI systems, while powerful, are not infallible. They are as good as the data they are trained on, and biased or erroneous data can lead to flawed predictions and analyses. This challenge was starkly demonstrated in the 2016 case of Tay, Microsoft's AI chatbot, which started spewing offensive tweets after being manipulated by users. This incident underscores the importance of rigorous testing and constant monitoring of AI systems.

The road to AI integration in cybersecurity is a complex journey, fraught with unprecedented opportunities and considerable challenges. It is a delicate balance that calls for a well-considered approach, with a clear understanding of what AI can and cannot bring. In the following sections, we will delve deeper into these aspects, aiming to provide a comprehensive perspective on the role of AI in cybersecurity.

Recommendations:

- **Augment AI with Human Insight:** While AI can process vast amounts of data and detect patterns effectively, human judgment remains critical. For example, distinguishing between false positives and actual threats often requires human insight. Viewing AI as a tool that complements human effort rather than a replacement is essential.
- **Be Prepared for AI-Driven Threats:** The power of AI can be exploited by malicious actors to launch sophisticated cyberattacks. For example, AI-driven phishing attacks can be more convincing than traditional ones. Organizations should be prepared for such advanced threats and implement countermeasures like AI-driven threat detection and response systems.
- **Leverage Predictive Capabilities:** AI's ability to learn from past incidents and predict future threats can revolutionize cybersecurity, moving it from a reactive to a proactive stance. Organizations should invest in AI technologies that can predict and prevent potential cyberattacks.
- **Address Ethical and Legal Issues:** Integrating AI in cybersecurity also brings ethical and legal considerations such as privacy, consent, and accountability. Organizations must address these issues in their AI implementation strategies to ensure the responsible use of AI technologies.
- **Ensure Rigorous Testing and Monitoring:** AI systems, while robust, are prone to errors if trained on biased or incorrect data. Regular testing and monitoring of AI systems are essential to identify and correct potential flaws. The incident of Microsoft's AI chatbot, Tay, which started generating offensive content, is a stark reminder of this need.

A HISTORICAL TAPESTRY: TRACING THE ORIGINS AND EVOLUTION OF AI

The history of AI dates back to the mid-twentieth century, with its roots planted firmly in the fertile cross-section of diverse fields such as computer science, mathematics, psychology, and even philosophy. In 1956, the term "Artificial Intelligence" was first coined by John McCarthy during the Dartmouth Conference, a seminal event that many consider the birth of AI as an independent field.

However, the seeds of AI were sown even before that. As early as the 1940s, pioneers such as Alan Turing contemplated machines that could mimic human intelligence. Turing's eponymous test, conceived in 1950, set a benchmark for a machine's ability to exhibit intelligent behavior equivalent to or indistinguishable from a human's.

AI's journey since its inception has been a roller coaster ride characterized by ebbs and flows of optimism, progress, disillusionment, and subsequent resurgence. The early years, often called the "golden age" of AI, were marked by significant optimism. Projects like the Logic Theorist and the General Problem Solver, aimed at simulating human problem-solving techniques, laid the groundwork for AI research.

The 1960s and 1970s saw a branching out of AI into various sub-disciplines and applications. Expert systems, AI programs that answer questions and solve problems in a specific domain, began flourishing. Prominent among these were DENDRAL, designed to deduce the molecular structure of organic compounds, and MYCIN, which aided doctors in identifying bacteria causing severe infections and suggesting treatments.

Despite these successes, AI's progress did not go uninterrupted. Periods known as "AI winters" saw reduced interest and funding due to disillusionment with unfulfilled promises and technical challenges. The first occurred in the mid-1970s, triggered by the limitations of expert systems and a critique by Marvin Minsky and Seymour Papert of the then-popular perceptron model for neural networks.

The 1980s saw a resurgence of interest in AI with the advent of machine learning. The concept shifted from creating machines that mimic human intelligence to developing systems that can learn from and improve their interactions with data over time. The Japanese Fifth Generation Computer project, ambitious in its goal to create intelligent machines using logic programming, typified this era's optimism.

However, the excitement was short-lived. The end of the 1980s brought about another AI winter, characterized by the time's limitations of machine learning techniques and the conclusion of expensive projects like the Fifth Generation Computer project.

The dawn of the twenty-first century brought another resurgence, often termed the "AI Spring." This resurgence was fueled by several factors – a massive increase in computational power, availability of large volumes of data, and significant algorithmic advancements, especially in neural networks.

Deep learning, a subset of machine learning that mimics the human brain's neural networks, has been at the forefront of this AI Spring. It has powered many of the AI applications we see today, from virtual assistants like Amazon's Alexa to autonomous vehicles like Waymo.

Throughout history, AI has often been conflated with science fiction, fostering misconceptions of sentient robots and superintelligent systems that could potentially outsmart or threaten humanity. While such notions make for captivating cinema and literature, real-world AI is far from achieving such capabilities.

Today's AI systems are tools designed to perform specific tasks. They lack consciousness or the ability to understand or experience the world as humans do. This is often referred to as Narrow AI. For instance, IBM's Watson, a highly sophisticated AI system, excels at tasks such as parsing and interpreting vast amounts of data in fields as diverse as healthcare, finance, and weather forecasting.

Another powerful AI system is Google's AlphaGo, which made headlines by defeating the world champion Go player in 2016. This was a landmark event in AI's history as Go, with its complexity and enormous possibility space, was considered a formidable challenge for AI.

Then there is OpenAI's GPT, a cutting-edge language model that uses machine learning to generate human-like text. This AI has wide-ranging applications, from drafting emails to creating written content, and is a testament to how far AI has come in understanding and generating language.

In computer vision, AI algorithms power facial recognition systems like those used by Facebook for photo tagging and security agencies for identification and tracking. These algorithms can process and analyze vast amounts of visual data, performing tasks that would be impossible for humans to accomplish in a reasonable timeframe.

Tesla's Autopilot system is a prime example of AI in the autonomous vehicles domain. This advanced driver-assistance system leverages AI to analyze real-time sensor data, make decisions, and control the vehicle, bringing us closer to a future where self-driving cars are commonplace.

In conclusion, while AI has often been conflated with the fantastical realm of science fiction, its actual trajectory and capabilities are rooted in rigorous research, progressive innovation, and tangible real-world applications. From its early beginnings and through periods of hype and disillusionment, AI has evolved into an integral part of our technological landscape, profoundly transforming various industries and shaping our everyday lives. As we stand on the threshold of AI's future, it is crucial to separate myth from reality and harness the power of AI responsibly and ethically.

Recommendations:

- **Learning from the Past:** Understanding the history of AI, including its cycles of enthusiasm and disillusionment, can provide valuable insights for future research and development. From the "AI winters" to the "AI Spring," each phase offers lessons on managing expectations, the importance of persistent innovation, and the role of societal and technological factors in AI's development.

- **Maintaining Realistic Expectations:** While AI has brought unprecedented advancements, separating science fiction from reality is critical. Today's AI systems, even the most advanced ones, operate within the realm of Narrow AI, performing specific tasks without possessing consciousness or a human-like understanding of the world.

- **Diversified Applications:** AI has demonstrated its potential across various domains, from language processing to autonomous vehicles and healthcare. The successful deployment of AI in these areas serves as a blueprint for identifying and harnessing AI's potential in other sectors.

- **Responsible and Ethical Use:** AI's power also brings ethical challenges, such as privacy in facial recognition systems. Navigating these issues responsibly is crucial, balancing technological advancement and ethical considerations.

- **Fostering AI Literacy:** Given AI's profound impact on society, promoting a broader understanding of its capabilities, limitations, and implications among the general public and decision-makers is essential. This understanding will allow informed decision-making and foster responsible AI integration into various aspects of our lives.

THE AI REVOLUTION: TRANSFORMING CYBER DEFENSE

AI is leading an extraordinary revolution within the domain of cyber defense. Traditionally, cybersecurity efforts have focused on identifying and countering attacks, often in a reactive manner. With AI, this approach is undergoing a fundamental shift. AI-driven cyber defense systems move beyond just reacting to breaches and threats. Instead, they are designed to predict and pre-empt potential attacks, allowing businesses to adopt a more proactive stance against cyber threats.

This transformation is not simply about integrating another tool into the cybersecurity armamentarium. It represents a sea change in our perception and handling of cybersecurity threats. This shift is akin to moving from a manual, labor-intensive process to an automated, intelligent system that learns from its environment and enhances its capabilities over time.

For instance, consider the case of an AI-driven intrusion detection system (IDS). Traditional IDS solutions depend on rule-based methods and signature detection, often failing to detect zero-day exploits and sophisticated threats. On the other hand, AI-driven IDS solutions leverage machine learning algorithms to learn from past incidents and adapt to new threat patterns, enabling the early detection of novel and evolving threats.

Defense-in-depth is a tried and tested strategy that aims to create multiple layers of defense to counter varying degrees of cyber threats. The integration of AI into these frameworks has the potential to enhance their robustness significantly. However, such integration requires careful planning and execution.

AI's proactive capabilities can fortify defense-in-depth strategies, turning them from passive shields into active, intelligent systems that adapt and evolve in response to the threat landscape. For example, AI can enhance network security, one of the layers in a defense-in-depth framework, by predicting potential attack paths, identifying anomalies in network traffic, and automating responses to detected threats.

However, AI's rapid evolution in cybersecurity raises an important question: What happens to current cybersecurity products as AI becomes more entrenched in cybersecurity strategies? AI's advancement threatens to make some traditional security tools and methods obsolete, necessitating an adaptation of existing products or the development of new ones that can effectively harness the power of AI.

Integrating AI into cybersecurity solutions is already disrupting the cybersecurity product landscape. For instance, the proliferation of AI-enabled security analytics tools challenges the relevance of traditional security information and event management (SIEM) solutions. While SIEM tools help gather and analyze security data, their reliance on rule-based systems and manual input makes them less efficient than AI-enabled tools, which can learn and adapt over time to identify and respond to threats more effectively.

In essence, as we move further into the era of AI-powered cybersecurity, the roles and relevance of traditional cybersecurity products will likely be reassessed. Some may need to evolve to stay relevant, while others may give way to more sophisticated, AI-driven solutions. As we tread this path, it becomes vital for organizations and cybersecurity professionals to stay abreast of these developments, embracing change while critically assessing AI's promises and potential pitfalls in cybersecurity.

Recommendations:

- **Adopting a Proactive Stance:** AI's predictive capabilities allow for a shift from reactive to proactive cybersecurity measures. Businesses should embrace this potential, adapting their strategies to anticipate and prevent attacks rather than simply responding.

- **Planning and Execution:** Integrating AI into cybersecurity is not a mere addition of another tool; it represents a significant shift in threat perception and handling. As such, careful planning and execution are required to integrate AI effectively into existing cybersecurity frameworks.

- **Evolution of Existing Tools:** As AI becomes more entrenched in cybersecurity, existing products must adapt or evolve to remain relevant. Businesses should proactively update their tools and methods, replacing obsolete technologies with more advanced, AI-driven solutions where necessary.

- **Continuous Learning:** AI's rapid advancement necessitates constant learning and adaptation for cybersecurity professionals. Keeping abreast of new developments in AI-enabled cybersecurity can ensure they are well-prepared to handle evolving threats.

- **Critical Assessment of AI:** While AI holds great promise in cybersecurity, it is crucial to assess its potential pitfalls critically. A balanced understanding of AI's capabilities, limitations, and implications can help make informed decisions and ensure AI's responsible and effective use in cybersecurity.

AI-POWERED CYBERSECURITY SOLUTIONS

Intrusion Detection Systems (IDS): AI has significantly transformed intrusion detection systems (IDS), making them more effective at identifying unusual or suspicious network traffic that might indicate a cyber threat. These AI-powered

systems leverage machine learning algorithms, learning from historical network traffic data, which helps establish a baseline of normal behavior. Any
deviations from this baseline can then be flagged as potential anomalies. This
ability to recognize irregularities enables AI-powered IDS to alert cybersecurity teams about likely intrusion attempts in real time, thereby enhancing an
organization's defense mechanisms.

Antivirus Software: Modern antivirus software is a notable example of
how AI is used in cybersecurity. Traditional antivirus software used signatures to identify malware but struggled against new or modified variants. AI
comes into play by analyzing patterns in the behavior and code of applications, enabling it to identify and isolate malicious software even if it has not
been previously cataloged. This approach provides robust protection against
previously unseen or zero-day threats, further bolstering the organization's
security posture.

Security Information and Event Management (SIEM): AI has revolutionized Security Information and Event Management (SIEM) platforms by enabling
the real-time analysis of security alerts generated by network hardware and
applications. With many signals generated every minute, identifying threats
can be like finding a needle in a haystack. AI's pattern recognition capabilities assist in reducing false positives, aggregating related alerts, and detecting threats that might otherwise go unnoticed. This significantly improves the
speed and accuracy of threat detection and response.

Phishing Detection: Phishing attempts have grown more sophisticated and
harder to detect, but AI technologies have risen to the challenge. By analyzing
elements such as email text, sender details, and embedded links, AI-powered
phishing detection tools can identify subtle indicators of phishing attempts that
traditional spam filters may overlook. This capability drastically reduces the
likelihood of successful phishing attacks and enhances email security.

User and Entity Behavior Analytics (UEBA): In internal security, AI-powered
User and Entity Behavior Analytics (UEBA) solutions offer an advanced level
of protection. These tools monitor and learn from the behavior of users and
other entities, such as devices and applications, within a network. The AI algorithms establish a baseline of regular activity, making it easier to detect unusual
behaviors or patterns that might indicate a compromised user account or an
internal threat.

AI in Digital Forensics: AI has profoundly impacted the field of digital forensics. Forensic investigators often have to analyze vast volumes of data, which
can be significantly expedited with the help of AI. By identifying patterns, correlations, and anomalies in the data, AI can provide insights into malicious activities, thus speeding up investigations and helping organizations respond more
effectively to security incidents.

Automated Threat Hunting: AI-powered automated threat-hunting tools
have substantially boosted Proactive cybersecurity efforts. These tools can
comb through massive amounts of data to identify potential threats, a task
that would be overwhelming for human analysts. AI-driven threat hunting can

significantly enhance an organization's proactive defense capabilities by identifying subtle patterns and correlations that may indicate a hidden threat.

Secure User Authentication: AI brings a new layer of security to user authentication by facilitating biometric verification methods such as facial recognition, voice recognition, and fingerprint scanning. These AI-powered systems can analyze intricate details that would be nearly impossible for a human to review, making them far more reliable and harder for attackers to bypass.

Advanced Persistent Threat (APT) Detection: Advanced Persistent Threats, or APTs, are sophisticated, long-term attacks on specific targets. AI-powered tools are increasingly being used to detect these stealthy threats. By continuously learning and adapting to new information, AI can identify unusual patterns of behavior that might signal the presence of an APT, even if the attack was designed to evade traditional detection methods.

Data Loss Prevention (DLP): AI has also been applied to Data Loss Prevention (DLP) solutions, helping to prevent the unauthorized exfiltration of sensitive information. By learning what normal data transfer activities look like within an organization, an AI-powered DLP tool can detect and alert about any unusual activity, potentially preventing a data breach before it occurs.

Real-Time Risk Assessment: AI algorithms can conduct real-time risk assessments, identifying potential vulnerabilities and threats as they emerge. By analyzing patterns and anomalies in vast amounts of data, AI can provide insights into the current security status of an organization, allowing for immediate action to be taken against identified risks.

Deepfake Detection: Deepfakes are synthetic media where a person in a video or image is replaced by someone else's likeness using AI algorithms. As deepfakes become more sophisticated, AI-based tools are being developed to detect them, analyzing inconsistencies in appearance or behavior that might reveal the media as falsified.

Automated Security Policy Generation: The increasing complexity of cybersecurity environments has increased the need for automated security policy generation tools. These AI-powered systems can analyze the organization's infrastructure, understand the interrelationships between different components, and suggest optimal security policies. This simplifies the security management process and helps ensure that no critical security policy is overlooked.

Secure Software Development: AI has also made its way into secure software development with tools that can automatically identify potential security flaws in code. Using machine learning algorithms to understand what secure code should look like, these tools can flag areas of the code that deviate from these standards, thereby assisting in the early detection and remediation of potential vulnerabilities.

Insider Threat Detection: AI is being used to address one of the most challenging aspects of cybersecurity: insider threats. These tools monitor user behavior within the organization, identifying anomalies that could indicate malicious activities. AI can more accurately remember suspicious actions that could lead to a security incident by learning what constitutes normal behavior for each user.

Cyber Threat Intelligence: AI significantly enhances cyber threat intelligence efforts by automating the collection and analysis of threat data from various sources. By identifying patterns and trends in this data, AI can provide actionable insights into potential threats, helping organizations stay one step ahead of cybercriminals.

Predictive Analytics: Predictive analytics tools powered by AI can analyze historical cyberattack data and identify patterns that can help predict future attacks. These tools provide organizations with a proactive defense approach, enabling them to take preventive measures before an attack occurs.

Security Orchestration, Automation, and Response (SOAR): Security Orchestration, Automation, and Response (SOAR) platforms leverage AI to streamline the incident response process. By automating routine tasks and providing decision support for complex tasks, AI can help cybersecurity teams respond to incidents more effectively and efficiently, reducing the time from detection to remediation.

Privacy Enhancing Technologies (PETs): AI-powered Privacy Enhancing Technologies (PETs) are designed to protect user data while maintaining utility. These tools can automate the process of de-identifying data, stripping it of personally identifiable information to ensure privacy and compliance with data protection regulations.

Quantum Computing for Cybersecurity: While not a typical AI technology, quantum computing's potential implications for cybersecurity cannot be ignored. Quantum computers could potentially break many current encryption algorithms, necessitating the development of quantum-resistant encryption. On the flip side, quantum computing could also provide new, advanced methods for secure communication. The intersection of AI, quantum computing, and cybersecurity is an emerging field that is expected to have significant implications in the future.

Recommendations:

- **Evaluate your cybersecurity needs:** Different AI technologies serve different purposes. Before selecting a technology, clearly define your cybersecurity needs and understand how other technologies can meet these needs.

- **Invest in training:** AI cybersecurity technologies can only be effective if your team knows how to use them. Invest in training to ensure your cybersecurity personnel can leverage these technologies to their fullest potential.

- **Please do not rely solely on AI:** While AI can significantly enhance your cybersecurity capabilities, it should not be the only line of defense. Continue to invest in other cybersecurity measures and ensure that AI is integrated into a multi-layered defense strategy.

- **Stay updated on technological advancements:** AI in cybersecurity is evolving rapidly. Stay updated on the latest improvements to ensure you leverage the most effective and up-to-date technologies.
- **Involve all stakeholders:** When integrating AI into your cybersecurity strategy, involve all relevant stakeholders, including IT personnel, executives, and end users. This will ensure that the technology is effectively implemented and everyone understands their role in maintaining cybersecurity.

Chapter Conclusion

Integrating AI into cybersecurity is a double-edged sword, presenting many advantages and challenges. The most notable advantage is AI's remarkable transformation to cybersecurity strategies, elevating their effectiveness through improved threat detection and accelerated response times. It has also initiated a crucial transition from reactive to proactive defense mechanisms. Nevertheless, AI is not a universal solution to all cybersecurity concerns. Inherent complications come with AI adoption, such as the possibility of AI being manipulated for more potent and complex cyberattacks.

Understanding AI, its capabilities, and its limitations is not complete without debunking numerous prevalent myths. AI is often misconstrued as a practical tool due to its exaggerated portrayals in science fiction. To fully comprehend its scope and potential, it is essential to study the evolutionary trajectory of AI, which provides a historical lens into the development of this influential technology. Numerous applications of AI are now embedded in our everyday lives, from virtual assistants like Alexa to autonomous vehicles like Waymo and data analysis systems like IBM's Watson to language models such as GPT developed by OpenAI.

As AI technology progresses rapidly, it inevitably forces us to rethink the future of existing cybersecurity products. Some traditional cybersecurity solutions may become obsolete in the face of advanced AI technologies, urging organizations to embrace adaptability and foster a culture of continuous learning to thrive in this fluctuating landscape.

It is crucial to heed recommendations to successfully navigate this radical shift driven by AI in cybersecurity. These include developing an understanding of AI's history and projected trajectory, dispelling misconceptions perpetuated by science fiction, and learning from the functioning of existing AI systems to glean valuable insights. Additionally, considering the field's rapid evolution, it is vital to consider the ethical implications of AI usage and remain committed to learning.

In summary, capitalizing on the rising wave of AI in cybersecurity goes beyond simply adopting a trending technology. It necessitates a balanced understanding of AI's potential, pitfalls, and practical applications. With a nuanced comprehension of AI, businesses are better equipped to chart their course, enabling them to effectively and responsibly harness AI's power in shaping their cybersecurity strategies. This amplifies their defensive capacities and empowers them to navigate the intricacies of this revolutionary technology.

Case Study: Embracing AI in Cybersecurity at FuturaTech

As the Chief Information Officer (CIO) of FuturaTech, a leading software firm expanding rapidly, Lynn had always been acutely aware of the changing dynamics in cybersecurity, and her years of experience had taught her the importance of staying ahead of the curve in a world where the nature of cyber threats was constantly evolving. When she noticed the increasing limitations of their traditional security methods in the face of growing digital assets and novel cyber threats, Lynn realized it was time for a change. She had often heard about the transformative impact of AI on cybersecurity and wondered if this was the key to strengthening her organization's defense capabilities.

Deciding to explore AI was the first step. But before diving headfirst into implementing it, Lynn knew she had to understand the technology at a deeper level. She decided to delve into the history of AI, tracing its roots from the Dartmouth Conference in the 1950s to its evolution over the decades. Through this study, Lynn uncovered a pattern of hype and disillusionment but also of undeniable progress. She learned how AI had transformed from a concept in theoretical research to practical applications across various industries, including cybersecurity. This historical perspective gave her a more grounded understanding of AI, dispelling the misconceptions generated by its portrayal in science fiction and allowing her to form realistic expectations about its potential in cybersecurity.

Once Lynn better understood AI and its capabilities, she studied real-world AI systems. She explored IBM's Watson, known for its advanced data analysis capabilities, and OpenAI's GPT-3, famed for its groundbreaking natural language processing prowess. Lynn also looked into more niche applications, like Darktrace's enterprise immune system that leverages AI for cyber defense. By studying these systems, Lynn could see first-hand what AI could achieve within a cybersecurity context. She began understanding how AI could enhance threat detection and response and predict and prevent attacks, a game-changer for FuturaTech's cyber defense strategies.

However, Lynn was also conscious of the ethical implications of using AI. She recognized that AI, if misused, could pose significant privacy risks and, in the hands of the wrong people, could even become a tool for launching more sophisticated cyberattacks. To mitigate these risks, Lynn emphasized the importance of ethical AI usage at FuturaTech. She worked closely with the legal and compliance teams to establish ethical AI usage guidelines and integrated them into their corporate policies. These guidelines ensured transparency, accountability, and fairness in all their AI operations.

Recognizing the rapid advancement in AI technology, Lynn knew her journey with AI would be continuous learning and adaptation. She committed to staying up-to-date with the latest developments in AI and its applications in cybersecurity, realizing that a tool or strategy that was effective today might become obsolete tomorrow. To facilitate this, Lynn initiated regular training sessions and workshops for her team and subscribed to leading AI and cybersecurity journals and reports for the latest research and trends.

THE CISO'S AI PREPARATION CHECKLIST

1. **AI Strategy and Planning**
   - Define the organization's AI vision and align it with overall business objectives.
   - Develop a roadmap for AI implementation, considering budget, timeline, resources, and potential risks.
   - Establish a cross-functional AI team, including data scientists, data engineers, IT professionals, security experts, and business stakeholders.

2. **AI Risk Assessment**
   - Identify potential cybersecurity risks associated with AI technologies and assess their potential impact.
   - Review whether the AI system can be weaponized to carry out malicious activities or whether it might introduce new vulnerabilities into your system.
   - Consider the implications of data privacy and compliance regulations on AI system deployment.

3. **AI Data Management**
   - Define data collection, storage, and processing policies in line with data privacy regulations.
   - Ensure AI systems use high-quality, unbiased data to avoid skewed decision-making.
   - Check data encryption policies and practices to safeguard sensitive data.

4. **AI Algorithm and Model Validation**
   - Assess the transparency, interpretability, and accountability of AI algorithms.
   - Validate and test AI models before deployment to ensure they work as expected.

- Regularly monitor AI performance post-deployment to identify any issues early on.

5. **AI Ethical and Legal Considerations**
    - Understand the ethical implications of AI decision-making and ensure the technology is not used discriminatively.
    - Review relevant AI legislation and ensure compliance with all applicable laws and regulations.
    - Ensure clear lines of AI accountability and responsibility within the organization.

6. **AI Vendor Evaluation**
    - If using third-party AI solutions, evaluate the vendor's security protocols, data privacy policies, and their alignment with your company's standards.
    - Review the vendor's track record, financial stability, and the robustness of their solution.
    - Define responsibilities and liabilities concerning data breaches and cyberattacks in the vendor contract.

7. **AI Incident Response Plan**
    - Develop an incident response plan that includes AI-specific scenarios.
    - Regularly test and update the incident response plan.
    - Train your team on how to respond effectively to an AI-related incident.

8. **AI Employee Training**
    - Provide regular training for employees about AI and its potential security risks.
    - Develop a culture of security and data privacy across the organization.
    - Encourage open communication about potential AI risks and vulnerabilities.

9. **AI System Life Cycle Management**
    - Regularly audit and update AI systems to keep them secure and effective.
    - Ensure appropriate decommissioning procedures for outdated AI technologies, including secure data deletion.

10. **AI Governance Framework**
    - Establish a clear governance framework to manage AI deployment and use.
    - This should cover decision-making processes, roles, responsibilities, and guidelines for AI's ethical and transparent use.

CHAPTER 29

Quantum Computing: A New Frontier

"Quantum computing has the potential to disrupt the field of cyberse-curity, rendering encryption obsolete. The intricate interplay of qubits exposes weaknesses, leaving digital defenses powerless against this quantum onslaught."

Quantum computing represents an emerging paradigm in cybersecurity with potentially transformative impacts on businesses and governments. An initial understanding of quantum computing and a comparison to classical com-puting sets the foundation for further exploration. The connection between quantum computing and cryptography is another area of focus, outlining how quantum technologies could influence current cryptographic methods and lead to the development of quantum-resistant cryptography. The study also delves into the geopolitical and strategic aspects of the global "quantum race" and emphasizes the need for a quantum-ready cybersecurity framework.

QUANTUM COMPUTING – AN EMERGING PARADIGM IN CYBERSECURITY

Quantum computing, an emerging field with the potential to cause a seismic shift in information technology, operates on principles that deviate significantly from those of classical computing. This deviation begins with the unit of data. While classical computing relies on bits, each holding a value of 0 or 1, quantum computing introduces quantum bits or qubits. The revolutionary characteristic of qubits is their ability to exist in multiple states at once, a phenomenon known as superposition. Through superposition, a qubit can be in a state representing 0, a state representing 1, or any superposition of these states. This enables the representation and manipulation of a vast array of data far beyond the binary constraints of classical bits.

Further separating quantum computing from classical computing is the concept of entanglement, another fundamental quantum principle. Entanglement creates a unique bond between qubits, such that the state of one qubit can instantaneously affect another, no matter the physical distance separating them. This quantum correlation results in a highly interconnected system, where the state of the whole cannot be described independently of its components. This interconnectedness dramatically amplifies the processing capacity of quantum computers, allowing for computations that would be prohibitively complex or time-consuming for classical machines.

The differential processing power and speed between quantum and classical computing open the door to a transformative era in information processing. Quantum computers, leveraging their unique properties of superposition and entanglement, are poised to tackle problems currently insoluble by classical computers. Whether factorizing large numbers, simulating complex quantum systems, or optimizing large-scale logistical problems, quantum computers are predicted to outperform classical ones. This transformative potential extends to a myriad of fields, including cryptography, artificial intelligence, and pharmaceuticals, to name a few.

Recognizing the potential of quantum computing, especially in cryptography, is strategically vital to nations and organizations globally. Quantum computing carries the promise of radically transforming cryptographic techniques. Current cryptographic systems rely heavily on the hardness of mathematical issues like the factorization of large primes or the logarithm problem in finite fields. Quantum computers, however, can solve these problems much more efficiently than classical computers, threatening to break the existing cryptographic schemes.

As a result, any significant advance in practical quantum computing could render current cryptographic defenses vulnerable, thus compromising the security of all digital communications. Awareness of this potential upheaval underscores why quantum computing has been earmarked as a critical national security and strategic competition area. Countries worldwide are investing heavily in quantum research to protect their digital infrastructure and gain the upper hand in what is fast becoming a quantum supremacy race.

Recommendations:

- **Grasp Quantum Basics:** Initiate your journey into quantum computing by understanding the basics, especially the concepts of qubits, superposition, and entanglement. These principles underpin the transformative power and potential of quantum computing. Such foundational knowledge will prepare you to delve deeper into the field and its applications.

- **Study Quantum Algorithms:** After familiarizing yourself with the basic principles of quantum computing, shift your focus to quantum algorithms, particularly those that can factorize large numbers or simulate complex quantum systems. Understanding these algorithms will allow you to appreciate better why quantum computers can outperform classical ones in specific tasks.

- **Understand Quantum Computing's Impact on Cryptography:** Considering quantum computing's potential to revolutionize cryptography, endeavor to learn how it could break existing cryptographic schemes. A comprehensive understanding of this relationship can help foresee the impact of quantum advances on global digital security, positioning you to develop or advocate for quantum-resistant cryptographic strategies.

- **Monitor Developments in Quantum Research:** Stay abreast of global developments in quantum research, as this is a rapidly evolving field with significant implications for national security and strategic competition. Monitoring research progress will help you keep pace with advances, potential breakthroughs, and their likely consequences for different sectors.

- **Advocate for Quantum Preparedness:** Given the transformative potential of quantum computing, encourage your organization or nation to invest in quantum research, education, and infrastructure. This could help secure a competitive edge in the quantum era, prepare for the potential upheaval in cryptography, and capitalize on quantum computing's potential benefits in fields like AI and pharmaceuticals.

THE QUANTUM-CRYPTOGRAPHY NEXUS: A SHIFT IN THE CYBERSECURITY PARADIGM

Quantum computing's potential impact on existing cryptographic methods is profound. Many current encryption protocols are founded on computational problems that challenge even the most influential classical computers. One of these problems is the difficulty of factorizing large composite numbers into their prime factors. Classical computers, limited by their linear processing capabilities, take exponentially increasing time to factorize as the number increases. This mathematical challenge is the cornerstone of many encryption schemes, including widely used public-key cryptosystems such as RSA and elliptic-curve cryptography.

However, quantum computing, utilizing quantum algorithms like Shor's algorithm, can factorize large numbers significantly faster than classical computers. By outperforming classical machines in these computationally heavy tasks, quantum computers directly threaten our current encryption standards. This means that once sufficiently powerful and stable, quantum computers could decrypt messages encrypted with today's cryptographic systems, rendering them obsolete.

Consequently, quantum-resistant or post-quantum cryptography has emerged as a necessary field of study, intending to develop cryptographic systems resilient to quantum attacks. This field aims to construct encryption algorithms based on mathematical problems that even quantum computers find hard to solve. Lattice-based cryptography, for instance, rests on the complexity of specific problems in lattice theory, while code-based cryptography is built upon the hardness of decoding randomly generated linear codes. Multivariate polynomial cryptography, on the other hand, leverages the difficulty of solving systems of multivariate polynomials over finite fields.

Despite the potential these techniques show, they remain in the developmental stages. Standardization is an ongoing process, with the National Institute of Standards and Technology (NIST) currently conducting an evaluation to identify secure and efficient quantum-resistant algorithms. Furthermore, the real-world implementation of these algorithms remains challenging due to the processing power, bandwidth, and memory requirements, which can be significantly higher than existing methods.

Therefore, strategic preparedness for the arrival of the quantum era is a priority that should command the attention of businesses and governments alike. This preparedness is not limited to understanding the potential threats quantum computing could pose to current encryption methods. It also involves proactive steps such as investing in quantum-resistant technologies, encouraging research into quantum-safe cryptographic techniques, and developing quantum strategies that address the potential disruption. Ensuring data security in the quantum era will require a comprehensive approach that includes keeping abreast of emerging cryptographic standards, planning for their integration, and understanding their impact on various facets of operations, from data storage to digital communication.

Recommendations:

- **Understand Quantum Threats:** Familiarize yourself with quantum computing's potential to disrupt existing cryptographic methods, especially public-key cryptosystems such as RSA and elliptic-curve cryptography. Recognizing how quantum computers, aided by algorithms like Shor's, can factorize large numbers much faster than classical computers will help you comprehend the looming threat to current encryption standards.

- **Learn about Post-Quantum Cryptography:** Study emerging fields like post-quantum or quantum-resistant cryptography. These fields are devising new encryption algorithms based on mathematical problems that remain hard for quantum computers, such as lattice-based, code-based, and multivariate polynomial cryptography. Understanding these methods will enhance your knowledge of potential quantum-resistant solutions.

- **Follow Standardization Efforts:** Keep track of the ongoing efforts by organizations like the NIST to standardize secure and efficient quantum-resistant algorithms. Staying informed about these developments will aid you in preparing for the transition to new cryptographic standards when they emerge.

- **Anticipate Implementation Challenges:** Acknowledge that the practical implementation of quantum-resistant algorithms may pose challenges due to higher processing power, bandwidth, and memory requirements. By being aware of these potential hurdles, you can more effectively strategize on overcoming them when planning to integrate new cryptographic methods into your operational systems.
- **Advocate for Quantum Readiness:** Encourage your organization or government to invest in quantum-resistant technologies, promote research into quantum-safe cryptographic methods, and develop quantum strategies to mitigate potential disruptions. A comprehensive approach to data security in the quantum era will involve integrating emerging cryptographic standards, understanding their operational impacts, and keeping pace with advances in the field.

THE QUANTUM RACE: STRATEGIC AND SECURITY IMPLICATIONS

The global landscape of quantum computing showcases intense competition, with stakes high for technological supremacy and national security. Nations, including the United States, China, and members of the European Union, are engaged in an unprecedented push to advance quantum research. Similarly, private-sector tech behemoths such as Google and IBM are investing heavily in quantum computing capabilities. The objective of this race is not merely scientific discovery or commercial advantage; it is the potential to redefine global cybersecurity.

The winner of this quantum race could possess the ability to decrypt all current secure communication, considering the vulnerability of current cryptographic systems to the computational power of quantum computers. This immense potential to unravel encrypted data has national security implications, creating a power dynamic where the leader in quantum computing could have a significant strategic advantage. This reality makes the quantum computing race not just a technological challenge but a geopolitical one.

Creating a quantum-ready cybersecurity framework is an indispensable step toward preparing for a future where quantum computers are shared. The foundation of such a framework rests on several pillars. One is the development and implementation of quantum-resistant algorithms, cryptographic systems capable of withstanding the computational abilities of quantum computers. The second pillar involves securing quantum communication, a field where principles of quantum mechanics are utilized to enable secure communication channels, with Quantum Key Distribution (QKD) being a prime example.

Furthermore, a quantum-ready cybersecurity framework requires a workforce skilled in quantum mechanics and quantum computing. Quantum literacy among cybersecurity professionals will be essential to understanding, developing, and implementing quantum-resistant measures and securing quantum communication systems.

Transitioning to this new framework, however, is fraught with challenges. Standardizing new cryptographic systems across different industries and sectors is a complex task. These systems must also ensure backward compatibility with existing technology and communication infrastructure. Alongside these technical hurdles, economic considerations should be made regarding the cost of implementing new technologies. Policymakers must also navigate the implications of quantum advancements, creating regulations that protect security and privacy without stifling innovation.

Preparing for the quantum era is not just about surviving the quantum computing race. Still, it also involves building a resilient cybersecurity infrastructure that can adapt to the revolutionary changes quantum computing will bring. As the quantum era approaches, nations, businesses, and individuals must prepare for a shift in the cybersecurity paradigm.

Recommendations:

- **Track Global Quantum Efforts:** Stay informed about the international quantum computing race, with nations and major tech companies like Google and IBM investing heavily in research and development. By tracking these developments, you can better understand the global landscape of quantum computing and its implications for technological supremacy and national security.

- **Develop Quantum-Resistant Infrastructure:** Prioritize developing and implementing quantum-resistant algorithms as part of your cybersecurity framework. These cryptographic systems, designed to withstand quantum computing's computational power, will be crucial in securing data in the quantum era.

- **Foster Quantum Literacy:** Promote the education and training of a workforce skilled in quantum mechanics and quantum computing. Quantum literacy among cybersecurity professionals will be crucial to understanding, developing, and implementing quantum-resistant measures and securing quantum communication systems.

- **Consider Implementation Challenges:** Be aware of the challenges transitioning to a quantum-ready framework will entail, such as standardizing new cryptographic systems, ensuring backward compatibility with existing infrastructure, and addressing economic considerations related to new technology implementation. Preparing for these hurdles can facilitate a smoother transition when the time comes.

- **Advocate for Balanced Policy:** Encourage policymakers to navigate the implications of quantum advancements carefully. The creation of regulations should aim to protect security and privacy without stifling innovation, helping to create a resilient cybersecurity infrastructure that can adapt to the revolutionary changes that quantum computing will bring.

Chapter Conclusion

Quantum computing is an emerging technology with the transformative potential to redefine the rules of computation and data security. This game-changing potential is marked by its profound influence on current cryptographic systems, which are under threat due to the computational capabilities of quantum computers. Quantum computers, operating on principles of superposition and entanglement, could solve mathematical problems that underpin modern cryptography much faster than traditional machines, rendering our current security systems vulnerable.

The transition to a quantum world does not only involve technical innovation; it also presents a dynamic geopolitical theater with the ongoing global race for quantum supremacy. We have looked into this contest, a struggle for power and influence among nations and large tech companies, each seeking the enormous advantage of mastering quantum technologies. This race is not just about economic or technological dominance; it is also about control over information in the future, as the winner could potentially decipher all existing secure communications.

Quantum computing introduces a new frontier in cybersecurity, pushing the boundaries of what is possible and redefining our approach to secure communication. This transformation necessitates strategic foresight from both government and industry leaders. As the quantum era draws closer, it is imperative to commit substantial investments in quantum research and development to keep pace with rapid advancements and contribute actively to shaping the quantum future.

This strategic preparation involves developing and implementing quantum-resistant cryptographic systems, the new guardrails for data security in a quantum age. Quantum-resistant or post-quantum cryptography strives to create encryption algorithms that even quantum computers cannot break. This field is crucial in proactively preparing for the inevitable quantum disruption, ensuring our security systems can withstand the quantum threat.

As quantum technology continues to evolve at a staggering pace, its transformative influence on the cybersecurity landscape cannot be overstated. Quantum computing is not a distant, abstract concept; it is a rapidly approaching reality. The developments in quantum computing are set to change how we think about data security, encryption, and information privacy. This technological revolution demands our attention, readiness, and active participation to navigate and shape the impending quantum future. As we stand at the precipice of this quantum era, it is clear that the game's rules are changing, and so must we.

Case Study: Preparing for Quantum

Kelly was recently appointed Chief Information Security Officer (CISO) at CyberNova Industries, a rising tech start-up known for innovative digital solutions. Armed with a profound understanding of the cybersecurity landscape and a vision for the future, Kelly was acutely aware of the potential upheaval that quantum computing could bring to the world of cybersecurity. She recognized the double-edged nature of this emerging technology. While it promised unparalleled computational speed and the potential for groundbreaking innovation, it also threatened to dismantle the very foundations of current cryptographic systems. The quantum era, she knew, was as much a security challenge as it was a technological breakthrough.

In her first board meeting in the new role, Kelly used the platform to educate the directors about the seismic shift approaching in the form of quantum computing. She meticulously detailed the computational prowess of quantum machines, illustrating how their ability to process and factor large numbers with relative ease could potentially break the company's RSA and elliptic-curve cryptography. She didn't stop there – she went on to paint a broader picture of the global quantum race, explaining how nations and large corporations were in a fierce competition to achieve quantum supremacy. This was a timely wake-up call about the imminent quantum revolution for the board members, who were primarily engrossed in immediate operational and security concerns.

To prepare CyberNova Industries for the forthcoming quantum era, Kelly proposed a strategic roadmap for the company's transition to quantum-ready cybersecurity. Central to her strategy was the development and implementation of quantum-resistant cryptographic systems. These systems, she argued, would be an essential line of defense against potential quantum attacks. Kelly also underscored the need for quantum-secured communication channels, emphasizing the importance of QKD in ensuring the privacy and integrity of the company's digital communication.

Additionally, Kelly recommended substantial investment in quantum-related research and development, citing the need for the company to keep pace with and contribute to the evolving quantum technology landscape. She advocated for partnerships with academic institutions and research organizations, envisioning a talent pipeline to equip CyberNova with professionals well-versed in quantum mechanics and quantum computing – an essential ingredient for a quantum-ready future.

Embracing Kelly's visionary approach, CyberNova Industries embarked on an ambitious strategic transformation journey. The company launched dedicated projects to explore and implement post-quantum cryptographic solutions, ensuring their systems would resist quantum computational threats. They formed alliances with local universities, fostering a culture of continuous learning and research within the company and setting up internship programs to nurture a new generation of cybersecurity professionals. These initiatives represented a paradigm shift in the company's approach to cybersecurity, grounded in the reality of the impending quantum era.

The Kelly and CyberNova Industries case study is a practical application of the lessons explored in this chapter. It emphasizes the importance of recognizing the transformative potential of quantum computing and its impact on current cryptographic systems. It underscores the geopolitical and strategic implications of the global race to quantum supremacy and highlights the urgent need to establish a robust, quantum-ready cybersecurity framework. Through Kelly's strategic foresight and CyberNova's proactive approach, this case study illustrates the necessity of preparing for the quantum era – not as a distant possibility but as an imminent reality that requires immediate action and long-term planning. In the rapidly evolving world of cybersecurity, embracing the quantum shift is not just an option; it is an imperative for survival and growth.

THE CISO'S QUANTUM PREPARATION CHECKLIST

1. 1.**Quantum Computing Strategy and Planning**
   - Understand and define how quantum computing fits the organization's overall IT strategy.
   - Develop a roadmap for QC implementation that includes budget, timeline, resources, and potential risks.
   - Establish a team of quantum computing experts, data scientists, IT professionals, and security experts.
2. **Quantum Risk Assessment**
   - Identify the potential security risks associated with quantum technologies and assess their potential impact.
   - Understand the implications of quantum computers on traditional encryption methods and potential vulnerabilities.
   - Conduct regular risk assessments to keep up with the rapidly evolving quantum landscape.
3. **Quantum Data Management**
   - Implement robust data management strategies to ensure quantum--processed data is kept secure.
   - Consider encryption techniques that are quantum-resistant for data storage and transmission.
   - Establish policies for the secure collection, storage, and processing of quantum data.
4. **Quantum System Validation**
   - Test quantum systems for accuracy and validity before deployment.
   - Monitor quantum systems regularly post-deployment for any changes in performance or potential security issues.

5. **Quantum Ethical and Legal Considerations**
   - Understand the ethical implications of quantum computing and ensure its use does not violate any laws or regulations.
   - Ensure clear lines of accountability for quantum-related decisions and actions within your organization.

6. **Quantum Vendor Evaluation**
   - When using third-party quantum solutions, evaluate the vendor's security protocols and data privacy policies.
   - Review the vendor's track record, their solutions' stability, and their quantum offering's robustness.
   - Clearly define responsibilities and liabilities in the vendor contract concerning quantum-related incidents.

7. **Quantum Incident Response Plan**
   - Develop an incident response plan tailored for quantum computing scenarios.
   - Regularly test and update the incident response plan, considering the unique aspects of quantum computing.
   - Train your team on how to respond effectively to quantum-related incidents.

8. **Quantum Computing Training**
   - Provide regular training for employees about quantum computing and its potential security risks.
   - Foster a culture of security awareness concerning quantum technologies.
   - Encourage open communication about potential quantum risks and vulnerabilities.

9. **Quantum System Life Cycle Management**
   - Regularly audit and update quantum systems to keep them secure and effective.
   - Have a secure decommissioning process in place for outdated quantum technologies.

10. **Quantum Governance Framework**
    - Establish a clear governance framework for managing quantum computing within your organization.
    - This framework should cover decision-making processes, roles, responsibilities, and guidelines for the ethical and transparent use of quantum computing.

CHAPTER 30

Incident Response and Recovery

"Cybersecurity is not just about preventing incidents; it's about how swiftly and effectively we respond when they occur. Like a well-rehearsed symphony, incident response harmonizes expertise, coordination, and resilience to turn chaos into an opportunity for growth."

Incident response and recovery are fundamental aspects of cybersecurity, involving meticulous planning, preparation, detection, analysis, containment, eradication, and recovery. The process begins with creating an incident response plan (IRP) and training personnel, then identifying and analyzing potential security incidents. The active response phase involves limiting the impact and eliminating the threat, leading to the recovery stage, which focuses on system restoration and preventive measure implementation. Effective communication throughout the stages is critical, ensuring informed actions from all parties involved.

PLANNING AND PREPAREDNESS

Incident response planning is the bedrock upon which effective cybersecurity management programs are built. The starting point for any effective response to a cybersecurity incident is a well-articulated incident response policy. This policy is the guiding doctrine, setting the ground rules for how an organization responds to cyber threats. It forms the cornerstone of the company's stance on cybersecurity, clearly outlining its commitment to safeguarding its digital assets. It acts as the reference guide during an incident, providing a clear roadmap for employees at all levels of the organization.

A comprehensive incident response policy includes defining what constitutes an incident in the organization's specific context, delineating the severity levels of incidents, and establishing protocols for escalated response actions. It also encompasses the responsibilities of individuals and teams during an incident and the decision-making authority for actions during various stages of incident response. The policy should highlight the importance of communication during a crisis and provide protocols for internal and external communication. This ensures that all stakeholders are kept informed and the organization speaks with a unified voice, reducing the chances of confusion and misinformation.

Forming an incident response team is vital to the policy creation process. This team serves as the primary action group during a cybersecurity incident. The incident response team should comprise representatives from various departments – IT, legal, HR, and public relations (PR) – each contributing their unique skills and perspectives to tackle potential cyber threats effectively. For instance, while IT personnel would address the technical aspects of an incident, legal experts would guide the organization on any legal implications and compliance requirements. At the same time, PR representatives would manage communications with external stakeholders, including the media, to protect the organization's reputation.

The IRP is a detailed, step-by-step action plan that provides explicit directions for handling cybersecurity incidents. It goes beyond the policy to offer an operationally focused, tactical approach to managing an incident. The plan's Scope is determined by the organization's risk profile, the nature of its digital assets, and the potential impact of an incident on its operations and reputation. The IRP also identifies potential risks and vulnerabilities the organization may face, outlining specific procedures for addressing each type of threat. This includes everything from the initial detection of an incident to its Containment, eradication, recovery, and subsequent review.

The IRP should also provide clear guidelines for reporting and communication during an incident. This includes reporting to management, other internal stakeholders, and external entities such as regulators, customers, or the general public, as required. The plan should be tailored to the organization's unique context, considering its size, industry, regulatory environment, and specific threat landscape. Notably, the IRP should be a living document that is continually updated based on evolving threats, lessons learned from previous incidents, and changes in the organization's environment or operations.

Training and exercises form the lifeblood of the incident response framework. Continuous learning and practice are vital to ensure that the incident response team and other key personnel are fully prepared to deal with an incident when it occurs. Regular training sessions covering various topics, such as the latest threat intelligence, technological advancements, and legal and regulatory updates, ensure the team is equipped with the most recent skills and knowledge to combat emerging threats.

Practical exercises are equally important as they help bridge the gap between theoretical knowledge and real-world application. These could include tabletop activities, discussion-based sessions where team members brainstorm responses to a hypothetical incident, simulations, which are real time, scenario-based exercises, and drills, where the team goes through the motions of an actual incident response. These exercises allow the team to understand how to apply their training practices, identify gaps in their skills or the organization's procedures, and continuously improve their preparedness.

Coordination with third-party entities forms the outer circle of the incident response ecosystem. An organization does not exist in a vacuum; its incident response efforts can benefit the community. This may include law enforcement agencies, which can support in cases where a cyber incident has legal implications or requires criminal investigation; regulators, who need to be informed about incidents impacting customer data or critical infrastructure; cybersecurity experts, who can provide specialist knowledge or skills; and other relevant stakeholders such as industry bodies, peers, or partners. Collaborating with these entities allows the organization to take a holistic view of the threat landscape, benefit from shared intelligence or expertise, and ensure a well-rounded, comprehensive response to cyber incidents.

Recommendations:

- **Prioritize Incident Response Policy:** Develop a comprehensive incident response policy that outlines the organization's commitment to cybersecurity and serves as the primary guide during cyber incidents. This policy should define what constitutes an incident, establish protocols for different severity levels, and clarify roles, responsibilities, and decision-making authority.

- **Assemble a Diverse Response Team:** Form an incident response team with representatives from various departments such as IT, legal, HR, and PR. Each team member contributes unique skills and perspectives, tackling potential cyber threats from multiple angles, including technical, legal, and communication.

- **Implement an Incident Response Plan (IRP):** Create a detailed IRP that provides a tactical, step-by-step approach to managing incidents. The IRP should identify potential risks and vulnerabilities, outline specific procedures for each type of threat, and include clear internal and external communication guidelines. Regularly update the IRP to reflect evolving threats and organizational operations changes.

- **Emphasize Continuous Learning:** Ensure regular training sessions and practical exercises for the incident response team and key personnel. Covering the latest threat intelligence, technological advancements, and legal updates can enhance the team's readiness. Tabletop exercises, simulations, and drills bridge the gap between theoretical knowledge and real-world application.

- **Collaborate with External Entities:** Coordinate incident response efforts with third-party entities like law enforcement agencies, regulators, cybersecurity experts, and industry bodies. Such collaboration allows the organization to take a holistic view of the threat landscape, benefit from shared intelligence or expertise, and ensure a comprehensive response to cyber incidents.

DETECTING AND ANALYZING INCIDENTS

In cybersecurity, effective incident detection is not a single action but a series of strategically orchestrated efforts. It necessitates a blend of the right tools, techniques, and people to identify potential threats accurately and in real time. Vital to this process are state-of-the-art tools such as intrusion detection systems (IDS), which monitor network traffic for suspicious activities, and Security Information and Event Management (SIEM) solutions, which aggregate and analyze data from multiple sources to identify unusual behavior or events. Other tools include advanced behavioral analytics that can track and analyze user behavior to identify anomalies that deviate from established norms. A robust detection framework does not rely on a single tool or technique but takes a layered approach. This approach combines various detection mechanisms to form a protective shield, making it difficult for any potential security incident to go unnoticed.

Upon detecting an incident, immediate categorization based on its severity, potential impact, and the type of threat involved becomes the next step. This process aids in creating a clear roadmap for dealing with the incident at hand and forms the backbone of the response strategy. A well-defined categorization and prioritization process provides a rational basis for response actions, first focusing on the most significant risks. This prioritization system is guided by several factors, like the criticality of the affected systems, the sensitivity of the data involved, the potential impact on the organization's operations, the threat's potential propagation, and the broader risk landscape. By considering these factors, an organization ensures that resources are deployed where they are needed most, enhancing the efficiency and effectiveness of the response process.

Digging deeper, incident analysis and investigation involve understanding the incident's nature, origins, and potential impact. This process uses digital forensic tools and techniques to gather, preserve, and analyze evidence. The purpose is to identify the incident's root cause, determine the extent of the incident, understand how it occurred, and assess its potential damage. The findings from this investigation are invaluable for managing the current incident and bolstering the organization's resilience against future ones.

Moreover, it offers insights into the strategies and tactics of adversaries, equipping the organization with the knowledge to preempt similar threats. Analyzing incidents can also reveal systemic weaknesses, allowing the organization to fortify its defenses and make it more resilient to future threats.

The role of documentation and communication during the incident response phase is as significant as any technical aspect. Proper documentation involves meticulously capturing all actions, findings, decisions, and timelines to ensure accountability and traceability. This provides a written record for internal reference and is necessary for legal and regulatory Compliance, facilitating communication with all stakeholders.

Detecting and Analyzing Incidents 525

Communication must be clear, timely, factual, and consistent during an incident. Internal communication helps keep all relevant parties within the organization informed and coordinated. At the same time, external communication, whether with customers, partners, regulators, or the general public, should be managed carefully to protect the organization's reputation and maintain trust. Miscommunication or lack of communication can exacerbate the situation, leading to confusion, unnecessary panic, and further damage.

Lastly, integrating threat intelligence into the incident detection and analysis process can significantly amplify the organization's ability to anticipate, detect, and respond to incidents. Threat intelligence is more than just information; it is processed data that provides insights about emerging threats, tactics, techniques, and procedures (TTPs) used by cybercriminals, indicators of compromise (IOCs), and vulnerabilities that need attention.

When fed into the organization's security systems, these insights can help identify known threats, detect new variants of malware, or identify patterns that could indicate a cyberattack. Furthermore, threat intelligence can also aid in post-incident review, helping the organization learn from each incident, improve its defenses, and reduce its future risk.

Recommendations:

- **Embrace Layered Detection:** Utilize various tools such as IDS, SIEM solutions, and advanced behavioral analytics for real-time threat identification. A robust detection framework employs a layered approach, combining different detection mechanisms for a comprehensive protective shield.

- **Categorize and Prioritize Incidents:** Upon detecting a security incident, immediately categorize and prioritize it based on its severity, potential impact, and threat type. This process enables an efficient response strategy and ensures that resources are deployed where needed most.

- **Conduct Thorough Incident Analysis:** Use digital forensic tools and techniques to deeply understand an incident's nature, origins, and potential impact. The insights from this analysis are crucial for managing the current incident, bolstering future resilience, understanding adversary tactics, and revealing systemic weaknesses.

- **Prioritize Documentation and Communication:** Meticulously document all actions, findings, decisions, and timelines during an incident response for accountability, traceability, and regulatory Compliance. Maintain clear, timely, factual, and consistent internal and external communication to ensure effective coordination and trust.

- **Integrate Threat Intelligence:** Incorporate processed data about emerging threats, cybercriminal tactics, IOCs, and vulnerabilities into your incident detection and analysis process. Threat intelligence can enhance the ability to anticipate, detect, and respond to incidents and improve defenses for future risk reduction.

CONTAINMENT, ERADICATION, AND RECOVERY

Once a cybersecurity incident strikes, effective management of the situation calls for a swift and robust containment plan. Containment strategies play a crucial role in mitigating the impact of an incident and protecting unaffected systems. A primary step in this process is to isolate the affected systems promptly, which helps to prevent the spread of the threat to other areas of the network. It is akin to putting up a virtual quarantine around the compromised systems, preventing the intrusion from proliferating.

Implementing temporary countermeasures is another critical containment strategy, including blocking specific IP addresses, turning off certain services, or changing access credentials. While these actions might disrupt normal operations, they are often necessary to prevent further harm. Furthermore, Containment is not just about stopping the threat but also about preserving the crime scene. By carefully collecting and preserving digital evidence, organizations can help law enforcement and cyber forensic experts trace the attackers and learn from the incident. Depending on the severity and nature of the incident, Containment can be a short-term measure aimed at reducing the immediate risk or a long-term solution requiring more resources and time for a more comprehensive fix.

Following Containment, the eradication process commences. Eradication involves purging the threat from the system entirely, a digital cleansing that ensures no remnants of the malicious entity remain. This could affect the removal of malware, closure of exploited access points, or patching of vulnerabilities that have been exploited. Depending on the incident's extent, this may require simple actions such as deleting infected files or more drastic measures like reformatting hard drives or replacing hardware components. Given the tenacity of modern cyber threats, it is vital to ensure that the threat has been entirely eradicated before transitioning to the recovery phase. This is to avoid a relapse, where the threat reemerges and causes a secondary breach.

The recovery phase signifies restoring systems and operations to their pre-incident states. This could involve restoring systems from clean backups, replacing compromised files, or, in severe cases, rebuilding entire systems. The recovery process should be conducted with a focus not just on returning to normalcy but also on fortifying systems against future threats. This involves ensuring that all systems, software, and applications are patched and updated to the latest versions to prevent a similar threat from exploiting the same vulnerabilities.

Data restoration is an indispensable component of the recovery phase. This process involves retrieving and implementing data from backups, and the integrity and confidentiality of this data should be maintained during restoration. The incident underscores the importance of a solid backup strategy, with regular, encrypted, and off-site backups considered best practices. Backups serve as a lifeline in the aftermath of an incident, enabling organizations to bounce back with minimal data loss.

Once the dust has settled and normal operations have been restored, a post-incident review is conducted. This retrospective analysis is akin to an autopsy of the incident, dissecting the event, the response, and the recovery process to identify strengths, weaknesses, and areas for improvement. The post-incident review aims to turn the incident into a learning opportunity, creating actionable recommendations for bolstering the organization's incident response capabilities.

The lessons learned from this review should prompt updates to incident response policies, plans, procedures, and even training programs. This reflective phase allows organizations to learn from their experiences and improve their cybersecurity posture. It embodies the spirit of continual improvement, which lies at the heart of effective cybersecurity governance. By learning from each incident, organizations can evolve their defenses, becoming more resilient and prepared for future threats.

Recommendations:

- **Swift Containment:** The first step following a cybersecurity incident is to isolate affected systems to prevent the threat from spreading. Containment strategies might include implementing temporary countermeasures such as blocking specific IPs, turning off certain services, or changing access credentials. During this stage, preserving digital evidence for future investigation is also crucial.

- **Thorough Eradication:** This involves completely purging the threat from the system. It can range from removing malware and closing exploited access points to drastic measures like reformatting hard drives or replacing hardware components. The goal is to ensure that no remnants of the threat remain, preventing a potential relapse.

- **System Recovery:** Restoring systems and operations to pre-incident states is critical. Recovery could involve restoring systems from clean backups, replacing compromised files, or rebuilding entire systems. The focus should be returning to normal operations and fortifying systems against future threats.

- **Data Restoration:** Retrieve and implement data from backups while maintaining data integrity and confidentiality. The importance of a robust backup strategy becomes evident in this phase, with regular, encrypted, and off-site backups considered as best practices.

- **Post-Incident Review:** Conduct a retrospective analysis of the event, response, and recovery process to identify strengths, weaknesses, and areas for improvement. This review turns the incident into a learning opportunity and should promptly update incident response policies, plans, procedures, and training programs.

- **Continual Improvement:** Learn from each incident to evolve defenses and become more resilient against future threats. This continuous learning and improvement process is central to effective cybersecurity governance.

COMMUNICATION AND REPORTING REQUIREMENTS

At the helm of a cybersecurity incident, managing communication effectively can be as important as resolving the technical aspects of the breach. An internal communication strategy should act as a beacon, guiding the organization through the storm. This strategy should outline the process of disseminating crucial information across the organization, defining who needs to be informed, what they need to know, the timing of the information dissemination, and the means of communication. This can range from formal reporting to management and the board to updates to teams and individual contributors. The key is to provide timely, accurate, and clear information that helps maintain order, manage expectations, and minimize disruptions within the organization.

While internal communication focuses on controlling the narrative within the organization, external communication and notifications target entities outside the organization and need a different level of sensitivity; this includes communication with customers, partners, regulators, law enforcement, cybersecurity experts, and the media. The nature of the incident often dictates the Scope and the scale of the external communication. These notifications should embody a balance of transparency and discretion, providing factual information about the incident and the steps being taken for resolution without revealing sensitive operational details. They should also emphasize the organization's commitment to resolving and protecting stakeholders' interests.

Compliance with legal and regulatory reporting requirements is another crucial aspect of managing cybersecurity incidents. With varying legal frameworks across different regions and industries, organizations must be well-versed in their specific obligations to report incidents to regulatory bodies or government authorities. Factors such as the type and severity of the incident, the nature of data involved, the potential impact on stakeholders, and the organization's industry and location all influence these reporting obligations. Non-compliance with these requirements can result in significant penalties and damage the organization's reputation.

Simultaneously, PR management aims to shield the organization's reputation during the incident and its aftermath. The PR strategy involves steering the narrative around the incident, portraying the organization's proactive steps toward resolution, and demonstrating resilience. Transparency is key, but it should be balanced with not disclosing sensitive details that might unnecessarily aid other threat actors or alarm stakeholders. A well-executed PR strategy can even turn a crisis into an opportunity, showcasing the organization's robust incident response capabilities and stakeholder commitment.

Lastly, capturing and reporting on lessons learned post-incident is a cornerstone of continual improvement in the cybersecurity framework. This involves meticulous analysis of the incident, the response measures employed, their effectiveness, and the steps taken to recover and prevent a recurrence. By doing so, the organization not only enhances its IRP but also contributes to the broader learning of the community, providing valuable insights to other organizations and helping strengthen collective defenses against cyber threats. A well-documented lessons-learned report serves as a treasure trove of wisdom, assisting organizations to evolve and bolster their cyber resilience.

Recommendations:

- **Internal Communication:** Craft a strategy that outlines the process of sharing crucial information across the organization, defining who needs to know what and when. The focus should be on providing timely, accurate, and clear information to maintain order and manage expectations.
- **External Communication:** Manage communications with external entities such as customers, partners, regulators, law enforcement, cybersecurity experts, and the media. This communication should balance transparency and discretion, providing factual details without revealing sensitive operational information.
- **Compliance Reporting:** Fulfill legal and regulatory reporting requirements for your organization's region and industry. Factors like the incident's type, severity, data involved, potential impact on stakeholders, and the organization's industry and location influence these reporting obligations.
- **Public Relations Management:** Steer the narrative around the incident to protect the organization's reputation. Emphasize the proactive steps taken, demonstrate resilience, and balance transparency with discretion to prevent aiding other threat actors or causing unnecessary alarm.
- **Lessons Learned Reporting:** Document a detailed analysis of the incident, response measures, their effectiveness, and the steps taken for recovery and prevention. This report enhances the organization's IRP and contributes to collective learning in the community, strengthening overall cyber defenses.

WORKING WITH LEGAL FIRMS

Bringing a legal firm into the picture during a cybersecurity incident might initially seem like an additional layer of complexity in an already tumultuous situation. However, involving legal expertise can provide invaluable benefits, facilitating the navigation of the intricate maze of legal obligations and strategic decision-making.

One of the key benefits of a legal consultation is safeguarding sensitive discussions under the shield of Attorney–Client Privilege. This legal principle provides a sanctuary for communications between an attorney and their client, allowing for candid discussion and strategy development. In the context of a cybersecurity incident, such privilege can protect sensitive conversations about the incident from public disclosure. This confidentiality is vital, especially during the initial stages of incident response when the organization is still trying to grasp the extent of the intrusion and its potential repercussions.

Furthermore, legal firms can bring much-needed discretion and strategic direction to the incident response process. When faced with a security incident, the organization is thrust onto a tightrope, walking the thin line between transparency and preserving business integrity. Legal firms can guide navigating this precarious path, advising on what information should be publicly disclosed, how to effectively communicate with affected parties and the optimal timing for such communications. Doing so ensures legal obligations are met without compromising the organization's reputation or giving away information that might aid adversaries.

Legal firms also offer external validation to strengthen the organization's credibility during a cybersecurity incident. It signals to stakeholders – customers, partners, regulators, or potential adversaries – that the organization is tackling the incident with the gravity it deserves. It shows a commitment to resolving the issue and an openness to seek external expertise to do so effectively. This can reassure stakeholders that the organization is equipped to manage the incident and is transparent and accountable.

Moreover, legal firms specializing in cybersecurity incidents can bring knowledge from previous experiences. They can provide insights into best practices, common pitfalls, and practical strategies for incident response, contributing to a more comprehensive and practical approach. Their expertise also aids in understanding and complying with the myriad of legal obligations, which can vary widely depending on the nature of the incident, the type of data involved, and the geographic and industry context of the organization.

In summary, involving a legal firm during a cybersecurity incident can be a strong support pillar. They offer a trifecta of benefits: protecting sensitive discussions under Attorney-Client Privilege, guiding strategic decision-making and communication, and providing an external validation that can enhance credibility. Thus, they help the organization navigate the difficult path of incident response with confidence and effectiveness.

Recommendations:

- **Attorney–Client Privilege:** One key benefit of involving a legal firm during a cybersecurity incident is safeguarding sensitive discussions under this legal principle, allowing for candid strategy development without fear of public disclosure.
- **Strategic Guidance:** Legal firms offer essential discretion and direction in balancing transparency and preserving business integrity. They advise on what information to disclose, how to communicate effectively with affected parties, and when to release these communications to meet legal obligations without compromising the organization's reputation.
- **External Validation:** A legal firm's involvement signals stakeholders that the organization is addressing the incident seriously, showcasing a commitment to resolution and a willingness to seek external expertise.

This boosts the organization's credibility and assures stakeholders of its capability to manage the incident transparently and responsibly.

- **Experienced Insights:** Legal firms specializing in cybersecurity incidents bring valuable knowledge from past experiences. They can advise on best practices, potential pitfalls, and effective strategies for incident response. Their expertise also aids in understanding and adhering to various legal obligations, which may depend on the nature of the incident, the data involved, and the organization's geographic and industry context.

Chapter Conclusion

Incident Response and Recovery in cybersecurity is a comprehensive sequence of stages that begins with the initial detection of an incident and continues until the situation is fully resolved. In this process, great emphasis is placed on having a meticulously documented Incident Response Policy. A dedicated team of experts, trained and prepared to handle cybersecurity incidents, is integral to this process. The emphasis on being proactive rather than reactive underscores the importance of readiness and preparedness in the face of potential cybersecurity threats.

Creating an effective IRP is a pivotal part of the process, serving as a vital blueprint for addressing cybersecurity threats. This plan, detailed and specific to an organization's unique needs, lays out the step-by-step procedures to be followed when a cybersecurity incident occurs. In addition, training drills designed to test and enhance the organization's response capabilities play a key role. Third-party coordination and collaboration further enhance the robustness of the incident response framework, forming a broader and more holistic defense mechanism against potential cyberattacks.

The detection and subsequent analysis of cybersecurity incidents involve amalgamating various tools and techniques for effective incident identification. This multilayered detection mechanism allows organizations to rapidly identify potential security threats and incidents. Once identified, the incidents are categorized and prioritized systematically, ensuring an efficient allocation of resources. This systematic approach to resource management allows organizations to focus their efforts where they are most needed. Understanding an incident's nature, origins, and potential impact is a critical part of the process. Such understanding provides a foundation for immediate incident mitigation and formulating strategies to prevent future occurrences.

The strategies employed for incident response and recovery extend well beyond the technical aspects of containment and eradication. Effective communication management is a fundamental part of the response strategy. A well-planned and executed internal communication strategy ensures that everyone is well informed and aligned. External communication and notification systems must be managed tactfully to maintain public trust and regulatory compliance. Legal and regulatory reporting requirements are underscored, highlighting the importance of complying with relevant laws and regulations.

A thorough post-incident review is an important part of the process. This review allows organizations to learn from their experiences and adapt their response policies and procedures accordingly. By examining the strengths and weaknesses of the incident response process, organizations can make necessary improvements to their incident response strategies. Legal consultation during this process is also recommended. The benefits of such consultation range from privileged attorney–client communication and strategic guidance on communication and disclosure to an external validation from a respected legal entity. This adds a layer of protection and strategic direction, proving invaluable in handling cybersecurity incidents effectively.

Case Study: NexTech Corporation's Journey

NexTech Corporation, a growing fintech company, recently experienced a potentially devastating cyberattack. Thankfully, their Incident Response Manager, Ceylin, was well prepared and ready to face the challenge. The following case study examines how she applied the recommendations detailed throughout the Incident Response and Recovery chapter to mitigate the incident and improve NexTech's overall cybersecurity posture.

At the onset of her tenure, Ceylin recognized the importance of preparedness in cybersecurity management. She crafted a robust IRP, laying out clear roles and responsibilities for the company's incident response team, which included representatives from different departments, bringing unique skills and perspectives. They trained together, engaging in simulations and tabletop exercises, building a cohesive team ready to tackle potential cyber threats.

When the cyberattack hit NexTech, the company's advanced IDS and SIEM solutions and behavioral analytics detected the anomaly swiftly. Thanks to the IRP, the team quickly categorized the incident based on its potential impact and severity, ensuring the right resources were allocated to address the threat. Ceylin oversaw the incident analysis, using forensic tools and techniques to understand the threat's nature, origins, and potential damage. She ensured all actions, findings, and decisions were meticulously documented, facilitating clear, factual, and timely communication with internal and external stakeholders.

Containment was Ceylin's first line of defense. She promptly isolated the affected systems to prevent the threat from spreading further, implementing temporary countermeasures and collecting evidence for further analysis. After confirming that the threat was contained, she moved on to eradication. With her team, they removed the malware, closed exploited access points, and patched vulnerabilities. Throughout the process, Ceylin emphasized maintaining thorough documentation and clear communication.

Once the threat was eradicated, Ceylin focused on recovery. She implemented clean backups, replaced compromised files, and ensured all systems were updated to prevent the same threat from reoccurring. To manage external communications during the incident, Ceylin coordinated with the company's legal and PR teams, who guided her on what to disclose publicly and when. They effectively communicated NexTech's commitment to resolving the issue while maintaining the company's reputation.

After the incident was fully resolved, Ceylin initiated a comprehensive post-incident review. The team studied their response's effectiveness, identified areas of strength and weakness, and documented lessons learned. This review led to several improvements in their incident response procedures, refining their IRP and enhancing their training exercises.

Ceylin's story highlights several key lessons from the chapter: the importance of a well-structured IRP, the need for a trained and diverse incident response team, the effectiveness of advanced detection mechanisms and thorough incident analysis, the crucial roles of Containment, eradication, and recovery in incident management, and the value of a comprehensive post-incident review. By applying these principles, NexTech was able to turn a potential catastrophe into an opportunity for growth and improvement in its cybersecurity posture.

EXAMPLE CYBERSECURITY INCIDENT RESPONSE PLAN – FOR NexTech CORPORATION

I. Introduction
   A. Purpose of the plan: This plan aims to provide a structured framework for NexTech Corporation to respond to cyber incidents effectively, minimize their impact, and maintain business continuity.
   B. Scope and applicability: This plan applies to all employees, systems, and networks within NexTech Corporation, including remote employees and third-party contractors.
   C. Definitions and terminology: A comprehensive glossary of incident response-related terms and definitions will be included in the plan to ensure clarity and consistency.

II. Incident Response Team
   A. Composition and roles: The incident response team consists of the following members:

1. Ceylin – Incident Response Manager: Responsible for overseeing the incident response process, coordinating team activities, and ensuring timely resolution of incidents.
2. Brennan – IT Administrator: Managed and secured the company's IT infrastructure, assisting in incident containment and system restoration.
3. Merle – Network Security Specialist: Responsible for monitoring network activity, identifying potential threats, and assisting in incident analysis and network forensics.
4. David – Legal Counsel: Provides legal guidance during incident response, ensuring Compliance with applicable laws and regulations and managing any legal implications arising from incidents.

B. Contact information: The contact details for each incident response team member, including alternate contact information, will be documented and maintained in a central repository accessible to all team members.

III. Preparatory Measures
A. Risk assessment and threat intelligence: NexTech Corporation conducts regular risk assessments, leveraging threat intelligence sources and industry best practices to identify potential vulnerabilities and emerging threats.
B. Incident response policies and procedures: NexTech Corporation has documented incident response policies and procedures that outline the steps to be taken during incident detection, response, and recovery. These policies are regularly reviewed and updated to align with evolving threat landscapes.
C. Incident response tools and technologies: NexTech Corporation maintains a comprehensive suite of incident response tools and technologies, including intrusion detection systems, SIEM solutions, and malware analysis platforms, to facilitate efficient incident response and investigation.
D. Training and awareness programs: NexTech Corporation conducts regular training sessions and awareness programs for employees, focusing on incident reporting, phishing awareness, and best practices for incident response. These programs aim to ensure that all employees are knowledgeable and equipped to respond appropriately in the event of an incident.
E. Communication protocols and channels: NexTech Corporation has established clear communication protocols and designated channels for incident reporting and escalation. Employees are educated on these protocols for efficient and effective communication during incidents.

IV. Incident Identification and Reporting
A. Indicators of compromise (IOCs): NexTech Corporation maintains a constantly updated repository of IOCs obtained from threat

intelligence feeds, internal incident investigations, and security vendors. These IOCs detect and identify potential incidents across the organization's networks and systems.

B. Reporting channels and escalation procedures: NexTech Corporation employees are educated on the designated incident reporting channels, including a dedicated incident response hotline and an incident reporting email address. Clear escalation procedures are established, ensuring incidents are promptly escalated to the incident response team for immediate action.

C. Incident categorization and prioritization: NexTech Corporation employs a robust incident categorization and prioritization framework to assess the severity and impact of incidents. This framework considers potential data loss, service disruption, financial impact, and regulatory compliance implications, enabling the incident response team to allocate appropriate resources and prioritize incident response efforts effectively.

V. Incident Assessment and Initial Response

A. Incident triage and assessment: Upon receipt of an incident report, the incident response team, led by Ceylin, promptly initiates the incident triage process. This involves assessing the nature and Scope of the incident, identifying affected systems, and determining the potential impact on business operations.

B. Containment and isolation of affected systems: The incident response team takes immediate steps to contain and isolate affected systems to prevent further spread of the incident and mitigate additional damage. This may involve network segmentation, deactivating compromised accounts, or isolating infected hosts from the network.

C. Preservation of evidence: To support incident investigation and potential legal proceedings, the incident response team ensures the preservation of relevant evidence. This includes logging system and network activity, taking snapshots of affected systems, and securing any physical or digital evidence associated with the incident.

D. Notification of relevant stakeholders: The incident response team, in collaboration with the communications team, promptly notifies relevant stakeholders, including senior management, legal counsel, affected departments, and external parties, as necessary. Clear communication channels and templates are established to ensure consistent and timely notifications.

E. Activation of the incident response team: Once an incident is confirmed, the incident response team is activated according to predefined procedures. This involves convening a virtual or physical war room, where the team coordinates and executes incident response activities, including communication, analysis, Containment, and recovery efforts.

F. Documentation of initial actions: The incident response team diligently documents all initial actions taken during the incident
response process. Detailed logs, incident timelines, and task assign-
ments are maintained to provide a comprehensive record for future
analysis, reporting, and potential legal requirements.

VI. Incident Investigation and Analysis

A. Forensic analysis and evidence collection: The incident response
team conducts thorough forensic research to understand the root
cause of the incident, the extent of the compromise, and the TTPs
employed by the attacker. This may involve examining system logs,
analyzing network traffic, and utilizing digital forensics tools.

B. Malware analysis and reverse engineering: In cases involving malicious software, the incident response team performs malware
analysis and reverse engineering to identify the functionality and
behavior of the malware. This analysis helps understand the impact,
persistence mechanisms, and potential mitigation strategies.

C. System and network log analysis: The incident response team
reviews system and network logs to identify anomalous activities,
unauthorized access attempts, or other IOCs. Log correlation and
analysis tools identify patterns and potential attack vectors.

D. Vulnerability assessment and penetration testing: As part of the
incident investigation, the incident response team performs vulnerability assessments and penetration testing to identify any underlying vulnerabilities or weaknesses the attacker may have exploited.
This helps address the root causes and implement appropriate
security measures to prevent future incidents.

E. Threat intelligence analysis: The incident response team leverages
internal and external sources of threat intelligence to gain insights
into the threat actor's tactics, tools, and motivations. This analysis
aids in enhancing incident response capabilities and proactively
defending against future attacks.

F. Attribution and identification of the attacker: While challenging, the
incident response team collaborates with external cybersecurity
organizations and law enforcement agencies to attribute the attack
to a specific threat actor or group. This information assists in potential legal actions and strengthens defenses against future attacks.

VII. Incident Mitigation and Recovery

A. Remediation of affected systems: The incident response team works
closely with the IT department to implement necessary remediation
measures, such as patching systems, updating security configurations, and removing or neutralizing malicious artifacts.

B. Patch management and vulnerability remediation: NexTech Corporation establishes robust patch management procedures to ensure
the timely application of security patches and updates. Vulnerability scanning and remediation processes address identified weaknesses and reduce the attack surface.

C. System restoration and data recovery: NexTech Corporation maintains comprehensive backups of critical systems and data. The incident response team orchestrates the restoration and recovery process, verifying the integrity of backups and ensuring that affected systems are returned online securely.

D. Configuration management: To strengthen the security posture, NexTech Corporation emphasizes robust configuration management practices. The incident response team reviews and enhances security configurations, hardening systems, networks, and applications to minimize future vulnerabilities.

E. Post-incident system hardening: After incident resolution, the incident response team implements additional security measures, such as deploying advanced monitoring and IDS, conducting security awareness training, and implementing stricter access controls.

F. Lessons learned and process improvement: A post-incident review led by the incident response team identifies lessons learned, areas for improvement, and recommended changes to incident response procedures, policies, and technologies. These findings are documented, and appropriate actions are taken to enhance future incident response capabilities.

VIII. Communication and Stakeholder Management

A. Internal communication protocols: NexTech Corporation maintains clear internal communication protocols to ensure effective collaboration and information sharing among relevant stakeholders during incident response. Regular updates, incident briefings, and post-incident reports are disseminated to keep all employees informed.

B. External communication with customers, partners, and regulatory bodies: In collaboration with the communications and legal teams, the incident response team manages external communications during incidents. As applicable laws and regulations require, timely and accurate notifications are provided to customers, partners, regulatory bodies, and other relevant parties.

C. Public relations and media management: NexTech Corporation engages in PR public relations and media management to maintain trust and transparency. The incident response team works closely with the PR team to ensure consistent messaging and coordinated responses to media inquiries.

D. Notification and coordination with the cyber insurance company: In the event of a cyber incident, NexTech Corporation promptly notifies their cyber insurance company as part of the external communication process. The incident response team collaborates with the legal team to ensure the insurance company receives the necessary information and documentation related to the incident. This includes incident details, impact assessment, forensic findings, and other relevant information required for insurance claims and coverage.

E. Cyber insurance coordination: The incident response team works closely with the cyber insurance company throughout the incident response process. This may involve coordinating with insurance company representatives, providing necessary evidence and documentation for claim assessment, and following any specific requirements or procedures outlined by the insurance policy. The incident response team ensures effective communication and collaboration with the insurance company to facilitate a smooth claims process and maximize the benefits of cyber insurance coverage.

IX. Legal and Regulatory Considerations
A. Compliance with applicable laws and regulations: NexTech Corporation ensures Compliance with relevant laws, regulations, and industry standards about incident response, data protection, and privacy. The incident response team collaborates with legal counsel to navigate legal and regulatory requirements during incidents.
B. Data breach notification requirements: In a data breach involving personal information, NexTech Corporation adheres to applicable data breach notification requirements, promptly notifying affected individuals, regulators, and other relevant parties as required by law.
C. Coordination with legal counsel: The incident response team maintains close coordination throughout the incident response process. Legal counsel guides legal implications, evidence preservation, regulatory obligations, and potential legal actions.

X. Training, Testing, and Exercises
A. Regular training and awareness programs: NexTech Corporation conducts regular incident response training and awareness programs for all employees, including tabletop exercises and simulated incident scenarios. These activities enhance preparedness and ensure a well-informed workforce.
B. Tabletop exercises and simulations: The incident response team organizes tabletop exercises and simulations periodically to test the effectiveness of the IRP, validate response procedures, and identify areas for improvement. These exercises involve realistic incident scenarios and encourage cross-functional collaboration.
C. IRP review and update: The IRP is reviewed and updated regularly to incorporate lessons learned from incidents, changes in the threat landscape, emerging technologies, and organizational changes. The incident response team is responsible for maintaining an up-to-date and accurate plan.

XI. Plan Maintenance and Review
A. Plan review frequency: The IRP is reviewed annually or whenever significant changes occur in the organizational environment, such as changes in technology, regulatory requirements, or organizational structure.

    B.   Plan update procedures: The incident response team is responsible for initiating plan updates and ensuring the timely incorporation of changes. Updated plan versions are disseminated to all stakeholders, and obsolete copies are securely archived.

    C.   Documentation management: NexTech Corporation maintains a centralized repository for all incident response documentation, including incident reports, logs, communications, and post-incident review findings. Document versioning, access controls, and retention policies are implemented to ensure document integrity and confidentiality.

XII. Appendices

    A.   Contact lists: The plan includes comprehensive contact lists of incident response team members, key stakeholders, external partners, and relevant authorities.

    B.   Incident response tool documentation: Detailed documentation of incident response tools and technologies, including installation guides, configuration instructions, and troubleshooting procedures, is provided as a reference for incident responders.

    C.   Incident response templates and forms: Standardized templates and forms, such as incident reporting templates, evidence preservation forms, and post-incident review templates, are included to streamline incident response activities and ensure consistency.

    D.   Reference materials and resources: A list of relevant references, industry best practices, guidelines, and external resources is provided for further reading and research.

CHAPTER 31

Navigating the Cyber Insurance Maze

"In a world of complex digital ecosystems, cybersecurity insurance isn't an option. It's a necessity."

Cyber insurance is a complex domain increasingly relevant in today's digital landscape. It begins with differentiating it from traditional business insurance and recognizing its critical role in contemporary business operations. Delving into the uses and misuses of cyber insurance unveils beneficial use cases, potential pitfalls, misunderstandings, and common missteps in the application and claim process. Navigating claim settlement involves dissecting why insurance companies may resist paying, comprehending the intricate details of policies and clauses, and developing effective strategies for claim management.

CYBER INSURANCE: A PRIMER FOR BUSINESSES

The advent of the digital age has ushered in a new era of risks and challenges for businesses across the globe. The proliferation of digital technologies and the internet has transformed how companies operate, opening up many opportunities. However, this digital transformation has also exposed businesses to various cyber threats. Cyber threats, data breaches, online fraud, and various forms of cyberattacks are now an unfortunate part of digital reality, making cyber insurance an indispensable part of modern risk management strategies.

Cyber insurance is a specialized form of insurance designed to protect businesses from internet-based risks and, more broadly, risks relating to information technology infrastructure and activities. This form of insurance is a relatively new addition to the insurance landscape, emerging in response to the unique challenges posed by the digital age. It is tailored to address businesses' cyber risks, providing coverage not typically included in traditional insurance policies.

In contrast to traditional business insurance, which primarily covers physical assets such as buildings, machinery, and inventory, cyber insurance is designed to protect digital assets. This is a crucial distinction as the value of digital assets, such as customer data, proprietary software, and online platforms, can often exceed the value of a company's physical assets. Cyber insurance covers a wide range of cyber incidents, including data breaches, business interruption due to a network outage, cyber extortion, and even reputational damage resulting from a cyber incident. It can cover the costs of investigating a cyber incident, legal fees, notification costs, credit monitoring services for affected customers, and public relations efforts to manage reputational damage.

In today's interconnected world, the importance of cyber insurance cannot be overstated. Businesses increasingly rely on digital platforms and technologies to operate and compete effectively, regardless of size or industry. This increased reliance on digital technologies has, in turn, increased the potential for cyber threats. Cyberattacks are not only becoming more frequent but also more sophisticated, posing a significant threat to businesses. Cyber insurance serves as a safety net in this risky digital environment, providing financial support and expert resources in the event of a cyber incident. It can help businesses recover from a cyber incident more quickly and efficiently, minimizing disruption and financial loss.

However, it is important to note that while cyber insurance provides valuable protection, it is not a substitute for implementing robust cybersecurity measures. Businesses must continue to invest in cybersecurity technologies, policies, and training to prevent cyber incidents and mitigate their impact. Cyber insurance should be viewed as a component of a comprehensive cybersecurity strategy, providing a final layer of protection in case all other defenses fail.

Recommendations:

- **Understand Cyber Insurance:** Develop a clear understanding of what cyber insurance is, how it differs from traditional business insurance, and what it covers. It is important to know that cyber insurance is tailored to protect digital assets like customer data, proprietary software, and online platforms against cyber threats. It can cover investigation, legal fees, notification costs, credit monitoring services, and public relations efforts after a cyber incident.

- **Assess Your Business Risks:** Evaluate your business for potential cyber risks and threats. Look into areas of vulnerability, such as network security, data protection, and the security practices of any third-party service providers. This assessment will help you understand the level and type of cyber insurance coverage your business might require.

- **Implement Cybersecurity Measures:** Do not rely solely on cyber insurance for protection. Invest in effective cybersecurity measures like firewalls, antivirus software, secure networks, and encryption. Regularly updating your security protocols and training your staff on cybersecurity best practices is also crucial.

- **Incorporate Cyber Insurance into Your Strategy:** Cyber insurance should be a part of your overall cybersecurity strategy, not a stand-alone solution. It should serve as the last line of defense, complementing other cybersecurity measures and mitigating financial loss in case of a cyber-attack. Your strategy should be comprehensive, involving prevention, detection, response, and recovery.

- **Consult an Insurance Professional:** To ensure your business gets the best cyber insurance policy, consult an insurance professional. These professionals understand the cyber risk landscape and can guide you in selecting a policy that best fits your business needs and mitigates your unique cyber risks.

EXPLORING THE USES AND MISUSES OF CYBER INSURANCE

Cyber insurance can be a powerful tool in a company's risk management arsenal when used correctly. It can cover a wide range of expenses associated with a cyber incident. This includes the costs of investigating a cyber incident, which can involve hiring external experts to identify the source and extent of a breach. It can also cover business interruption losses, which can occur if a cyber incident results in downtime for a company's network or systems. Cyber insurance can also cover the costs of notifying customers affected by a data breach, a requirement under many data protection laws, and providing credit monitoring services to these customers. In the case of a ransomware attack, some cyber insurance policies may even cover the ransom payment. However, this is a controversial coverage area due to concerns that it may encourage more ransomware attacks.

However, it is crucial to understand that cyber insurance is not a panacea for all cyber threats. It is not a substitute for implementing robust cybersecurity measures. Cyber insurance should be seen as a comprehensive risk management strategy component, complementing but not replacing cybersecurity best practices such as regular system updates, employee training, and strong access controls. Relying solely on cyber insurance to protect against cyber threats can lead to a false sense of security and potentially costly mistakes.

Misunderstandings about what cyber insurance covers can lead to costly mistakes. For instance, not all policies cover all types of cyber incidents. Some policies may exclude coverage for incidents resulting from unpatched software, arguing that the company failed to take reasonable steps to prevent the breach. Similarly, some policies may not cover breaches involving non-encrypted data because the company did not adequately protect sensitive data. It is crucial to thoroughly understand the terms and conditions of your policy, including any exclusions or conditions of coverage, to ensure that your company has the protection it needs.

The application and claim process for cyber insurance can be complex and requires careful attention. Companies must provide detailed information about cybersecurity practices when applying for cyber insurance. Common missteps in this process include not fully disclosing the company's cybersecurity practices or not accurately representing the company's risk level. This can lead to a denial of coverage if a claim is made. Similarly, it is essential to notify the insurer promptly if a cyber incident occurs. Failure to do so could result in a denial of the claim.

In conclusion, while cyber insurance can provide valuable protection against the financial impact of cyber incidents, it is essential to understand its limitations and use it as part of a broader risk management strategy. By understanding the terms and conditions of their policies, companies can avoid costly misunderstandings and ensure they have the coverage they need.

Recommendations:

- **Understand the Scope of Cyber Insurance:** Familiarize yourself with the wide range of expenses a cyber insurance policy can cover, including investigation costs, business interruption losses, customer notification and credit monitoring services, and even potential ransom payments. However, not all cyber insurance policies are the same, and not all cyber incidents may be covered.

- **Implement Robust Cybersecurity Measures:** Treat cyber insurance as a supplement to, not a replacement for, comprehensive cybersecurity measures. Regularly update your systems, provide cybersecurity training for your employees, and establish strong access controls. Relying on cyber insurance alone can lead to a false sense of security and put your company at risk.

- **Understand Your Policy:** Review your cyber insurance policy thoroughly to understand what is covered and what is not. Note any exclusions or conditions, as some policies may not cover incidents resulting from unpatched software or involving non-encrypted data. It is important to understand your coverage to avoid unexpected costs.

- **Be Transparent During Application and Claims Processes:** When applying for cyber insurance, provide accurate and detailed information about your company's cybersecurity practices. Avoid misrepresenting your company's risk level, as it could lead to denial of coverage. Similarly, notify your insurer promptly if a cyber incident occurs to prevent claim denial.

- **Integrate Cyber Insurance into Broader Risk Management Strategy:** Use cyber insurance as a comprehensive risk management strategy. By thoroughly understanding your policy's terms and conditions, you can ensure your company is adequately protected and avoid costly misunderstandings. Continually improve your cybersecurity measures and maintain a robust cyber insurance policy.

THE COMPLEX DANCE OF CLAIM SETTLEMENT: UNRAVELING THE TRUTH

Claim settlement in cyber insurance can be a complex and often daunting process. The path from filing a claim to receiving a payout is rarely straightforward and is often fraught with challenges. Insurers may resist paying claims for a variety of reasons. One such reason could be policy exclusions. These are specific situations or circumstances that are not covered by the policy. For example, a policy may exclude coverage for incidents resulting from unpatched software or breaches involving non-encrypted data. The insurer may resist paying the claim if a claim is filed for a cyber incident that falls under these exclusions.

Another reason insurers may resist paying is due to inadequate documentation of the incident. Cyber insurance claims often require extensive documentation to prove the claim's validity. This can include evidence of the breach, records of the response to the incident, and documentation of the costs incurred due to the incident. The insurer may resist paying the claim if this documentation is not thorough or provided promptly.

Noncompliance with policy conditions can also lead to resistance from insurers. Cyber insurance policies often include requirements the policyholder must meet, such as maintaining specific cybersecurity measures or promptly reporting incidents. The insurer may resist paying the claim if the policyholder does not comply with these conditions.

Understanding the fine print of your policy is crucial to avoid disputes during the claim process. Policies and clauses in cyber insurance can be intricate and filled with industry jargon. It is essential to understand what is covered, what is excluded, and under what conditions a claim will be paid. This understanding can help businesses prepare for a cyber incident, respond effectively when one occurs, and manage the claim process more effectively.

Formulating strategies for effective claim management is vital to a smooth claim process. This includes maintaining comprehensive records of cybersecurity measures. These records can provide evidence of compliance with policy conditions and support a claim's validity. Promptly reporting incidents is also crucial. Many policies require that incidents be reported within a specific timeframe, and failure to do so can result in a denial of the claim. Providing complete and accurate information during the claim process can also facilitate a smooth claim process and increase the likelihood of a favorable outcome.

Recommendations:

- **Be Aware of Policy Exclusions:** Understand the specifics of your cyber insurance policy, including any exclusions. These are conditions under which the policy will not provide coverage. For example, unpatched software or breaches involving non-encrypted data might not be covered. Knowing these exclusions can help prevent disputes when filing a claim.

- **Document Every Incident Thoroughly:** When a cyber incident occurs, ensure comprehensive documentation of the breach, response, and costs incurred. Cyber insurance claims often require extensive documentation to substantiate their validity. Providing thorough, timely documentation can reduce resistance from insurers and increase the likelihood of successful claim settlement.
- **Comply with Policy Conditions:** Adhere strictly to the conditions of your cyber insurance policy. This might include maintaining specific cybersecurity measures or promptly reporting incidents. Insurers may deny claims if these conditions are not met, so understanding and complying with them is crucial for a successful claim process.
- **Understand Your Policy:** Review the fine print of your policy carefully to fully understand what is covered, what is excluded, and under what conditions a claim will be paid. Familiarity with your policy's terms and conditions can better equip you to manage a cyber incident and effectively navigate the claim process.
- **Strategize for Effective Claim Management:** Develop a proactive approach toward claim management. This includes maintaining records of your cybersecurity measures, which can prove compliance with policy conditions. Promptly report any incidents, as policies often require reporting within a specific timeframe. Also, provide complete and accurate information during the claim process to facilitate a smoother process and increase the chances of a favorable outcome.

Chapter Conclusion

Navigating cyber insurance's intricate labyrinth can be complex but not insurmountable. With a clear and comprehensive understanding of its fundamental principles, potential uses and misuses, and the often intricate process of claim settlement, businesses can effectively harness the power of cyber insurance to bolster their organizational safety and resilience.

Cyber insurance has emerged as a critical tool in the modern business landscape. In an era where digital threats are increasingly prevalent and sophisticated, cyber insurance provides a much-needed safety net. It offers financial support after a cyber incident, helping businesses manage the often substantial costs of responding to and recovering from a cyberattack. Additionally, many cyber insurance policies provide access to expert resources, such as forensic investigators, legal counsel, and public relations professionals, further aiding businesses in their recovery efforts.

However, it's crucial to understand that cyber insurance is not a magic bullet that can solve all cyber threats. It should not be viewed as a standalone solution but as a comprehensive risk management strategy component. This strategy should also include robust cybersecurity measures, such as regular system updates, employee training, and strong access controls, to prevent cyber incidents and mitigate their impact. Cyber insurance should be seen as a final layer of protection, providing support when all other defenses have failed.

Understanding the terms and conditions of cyber insurance policies is crucial in avoiding costly misunderstandings and managing claims effectively. Procedures can often be complex and filled with industry jargon, making it easy to overlook important details. Businesses must take the time to thoroughly review their policies, ask questions, and seek clarification on any points of confusion. This understanding can help companies to ensure they have the coverage they need and can help facilitate a smoother claim process.

As the digital landscape continues to evolve, so will the cyber insurance field. New cyber threats will emerge, existing threats will evolve, and the regulatory environment will change. Businesses must stay informed about these changes and adapt their cyber insurance strategies accordingly. Regularly reviewing and updating cyber insurance policies can ensure they remain relevant and effective in this constant change.

In the end, while the world of cyber insurance can be complex, it is also a world of opportunity. By understanding its intricacies and leveraging its benefits, businesses can navigate the cyber insurance maze and harness its power for organizational safety.

Case Study: Navigating the Cyber Insurance Maze with TechGuard Inc.

Whitney, the Chief Information Officer (CIO) of TechGuard Inc., a mid-sized tech company specializing in cloud-based solutions, had always been proactive about cybersecurity. She had spearheaded numerous initiatives to strengthen the company's digital defenses, including regular system updates, employee training programs, and the implementation of strong access controls. However, the increasing frequency and sophistication of cyber threats in the digital landscape and the high-profile breaches in the news made her realize that the risk of a cyber incident could never be eliminated despite the best preventive measures. This sobering realization made her consider cyber insurance a critical part of TechGuard's comprehensive risk management strategy.

Whitney began her journey into cyber insurance by thoroughly educating herself on its fundamentals. She spent countless hours researching and consulting with experts to understand the nuances of this specialized form of insurance. She understood that unlike traditional business insurance, which covered physical assets such as buildings and equipment, cyber insurance was designed to protect digital assets. This included coverage for a wide range of cyber incidents, including data breaches, business interruption due to a network outage, cyber extortion, and even reputational damage resulting from a cyber incident. She also realized the critical importance of cyber insurance in today's interconnected world, where businesses increasingly rely on digital platforms and technologies.

However, Whitney was also acutely aware of the potential misuse of cyber insurance. She knew it was not a magic bullet to solve all cyber threats. It was not a substitute for implementing robust cybersecurity measures but rather a safety net that provided financial support and expert resources during a cyber incident. It should be seen as a comprehensive risk management strategy component, not a solution to all cyber threats. She also understood that misunderstandings about what cyber insurance covers could lead to costly mistakes. Therefore, she thoroughly understood the terms and conditions of TechGuard's Policy, even consulting with a legal expert to ensure she fully understood the policy's fine print.

When it came to the application and claim process for cyber insurance, Whitney was meticulous. She knew that the process could be complex and required careful attention. She ensured full disclosure of TechGuard's cybersecurity practices during the application process, providing detailed information about their cybersecurity measures, incident response plans, and employee training programs. She also understood the importance of promptly notifying the insurer when a cyber incident occurred. She established a protocol to ensure that any potential cyber incidents would be reported to the insurer as soon as possible.

When TechGuard experienced a minor data breach, Whitney was prepared. She promptly reported the incident to their cyber insurance provider and provided comprehensive documentation and their response. This included evidence of the breach, records of their response to the incident, and documentation of the costs incurred due to the incident. As a result, the claim process was smooth, and TechGuard could recover from the incident quickly and efficiently, with minimal disruption to its operations.

Glossary

This section furnishes definitions for numerous key terms and concepts, establishing a robust foundation for readers. Nonetheless, it is pivotal to remember that these definitions are a compass, and interpretations can fluctuate based on context. For unequivocal interpretations, always refer back to your organization's specific glossary or authoritative industry glossaries, such as those supplied by the National Institute of Standards and Technology (NIST), the Control Objectives for Information and Related Technologies (COBIT), the International Organization for Standardization (ISO), and other acknowledged bodies in the cybersecurity domain. We aspire to cultivate a comprehensive and flexible comprehension of this intricate field by recognizing various sources and interpretations.

Agile Project Management   is a project management approach that leverages Agile methodologies, typically used in software development, to handle and manage change efficiently. Agile project management emphasizes flexibility, collaboration, customer satisfaction, and high-quality delivery of projects.

AI-Powered Cybersecurity Solutions: These solutions leverage Artificial Intelligence (AI) to detect, analyze, and mitigate potential security threats. AI can assist in automating threat detection, analyzing large volumes of data for patterns, and making predictive analyses to anticipate future threats.

Asset Inventory and Classification: Asset inventory involves identifying and categorizing an organization's assets, including hardware, software, data, and other resources. Asset classification assigns value and sensitivity levels to these assets, which helps determine appropriate security controls.

Audit Charter: This formal document defines the internal audit activity's purpose, authority, and responsibility within an organization. It establishes the internal audit's position within the organization and the nature of the chief audit executive's functional reporting relationship with the board.

Audit Engagement: Refers to a specific audit assignment, task, or review activity, such as an internal audit, control self-assessment review, fraud examination, or consultancy. An audit engagement typically includes a defined scope, objective, and duration.

Board of Directors: The board of directors is a group of individuals elected by shareholders to oversee the management of a corporation and make significant decisions. They play a critical role in setting the organization's cybersecurity strategy and ensuring its effective implementation.

Business Continuity: Refers to ensuring the continuous operation of a business before, during, and after a disruption or disaster. This may involve business continuity planning (BCP), disaster recovery (DR), and incident response plans.

Business Objectives: These are the specific, measurable goals a company aims to achieve over a specified period. In cybersecurity, business objectives might include ensuring the integrity and availability of data, complying with regulations, and protecting the organization's reputation.

Cloud Computing: Cloud computing is a model for enabling on-demand access to a shared pool of computing resources. These resources can be rapidly provisioned and released with minimal management effort or service-provider interaction.

Cloud Security: Refers to the set of policies, controls, procedures, and technologies designed to protect data, applications, and infrastructure associated with cloud computing. It addresses physical and virtual security across the software, platform, and infrastructure service models.

Compliance: In cybersecurity, compliance refers to the adherence to laws, regulations, and standards designed to protect information and data. Compliance efforts may involve implementing specific controls, maintaining certain policies, and conducting periodic audits.

Control Families (in the context of NIST SP 800-53):   These are groups of related security controls defined in NIST Special Publication 800-53. Each family addresses a different security aspect, such as access control, incident response, or system and information integrity.

Core Functions and Categories (in the context of NIST CSF):   In the context of the NIST Cybersecurity Framework (CSF), core functions refer to the five main activities: Identity, Protect, Detect, Respond, and Recover. Each function is further divided into categories: groups of cybersecurity outcomes closely tied to programmatic needs and particular activities.

Cyber Insurance: This type of insurance is designed to help businesses mitigate risk exposure by offsetting costs involved with recovery after a cyber-related security breach or similar event. It may cover financial losses, the cost of incident response, legal fees, and more.

Cybersecurity: Cybersecurity refers to the practice of protecting systems, networks, and programs from digital attacks. These attacks often aim to access, change, or destroy sensitive information, interrupt normal business processes, or enable illicit transactions.

Cybersecurity Architecture: This involves the design of IT systems and processes for managing and improving network and data security. It includes the system's structure, processes, security measures and protocols implemented, and logical software layout of technologies and data.

Cybersecurity Certifications: These qualifications demonstrate a professional's or an organization's adherence to specific cybersecurity standards and best practices. Certifications can help validate knowledge, skills, and abilities in various cybersecurity domains, such as CompTIA Security+, Certified Information

Systems Security Professional (CISSP), or Certified Information Security Manager (CISM).

Cybersecurity Culture and Awareness: This term refers to an organizational mindset or attitude toward cybersecurity. An effective cybersecurity culture promotes employee awareness about cyber threats and emphasizes individual responsibility for maintaining the organization's cybersecurity.

Cybersecurity Governance: This is how an organization's cybersecurity policies are directed and controlled. It includes the distribution of rights and responsibilities among different roles in the organization, such as the board, executives, and managers, and the rules and procedures for making decisions about cybersecurity.

Cybersecurity Leadership refers to guiding and directing an organization's cybersecurity strategy, policy, and practices. Leaders are typically responsible for fostering a security culture, making key risk and resource allocation decisions, and ensuring compliance with laws and regulations.

Cybersecurity Maturity refers to an organization's development and readiness to deal with cybersecurity threats. Maturity can be assessed based on various factors, such as the comprehensiveness of the cybersecurity program, the level of integration into business processes, and the organization's ability to adapt to changing threats.

Cybersecurity Metrics: These are measurements used to quantify the effectiveness and efficiency of an organization's cybersecurity controls and processes. They might include metrics related to incident response time, the number of detected threats, or the percentage of employees trained in cybersecurity awareness.

Cybersecurity Program and Project Management: This involves planning, executing, and overseeing projects to improve an organization's cybersecurity posture. These projects can range from implementing a new security technology to conducting a cybersecurity risk assessment or training program.

Cybersecurity Reference Models: These are frameworks or blueprints to guide development and implementation of cybersecurity strategies, policies, and controls. Examples include the NIST Cybersecurity Framework and the ISO/IEC 27000 standards.

Cybersecurity Risk Appetite: This is the level of cyber risk that an organization is willing to accept in pursuit of its business objectives. Risk appetite is typically defined by senior management and informs the organization's approach to risk management, including the level of investment in cybersecurity measures.

Cybersecurity Risk Assessment: Identifying, analyzing, and evaluating cybersecurity risks. It involves understanding potential threats to the organization, assessing the vulnerabilities that these threats could exploit, and evaluating the impact a breach or incident could have on the organization.

End-of-Life Management: This refers to managing the final stages of a product or service life cycle. Cybersecurity often involves ensuring that obsolete, unsupported, or unpatched software and hardware are phased out and replaced to minimize the risk of security vulnerabilities.

FFIEC: The Federal Financial Institutions Examination Council (FFIEC) is a U.S. government interagency body that sets standards for examining financial institutions. FFIEC guides managing cybersecurity risks, and compliance with its recommendations is often mandatory for financial institutions.

GRC Culture   refers to an organizational culture supporting governance, risk, and compliance (GRC) objectives. A healthy GRC culture emphasizes transparency, integrity, and accountability and encourages employees to manage risks and comply with applicable laws and regulations proactively.

GRC Frameworks and Standards: These structured guidelines detail the processes, policies, and controls needed for effective governance, risk management, and compliance. Examples include the COSO Framework, ISO 31000 for risk management, and ISO/IEC 27001 for information security management.

GRC Implementation: This involves applying GRC principles in a practical setting within an organization. It includes establishing relevant policies and procedures, setting up risk assessment and compliance monitoring systems, and integrating GRC processes into the organization's daily operations.

GRC Tools and Technologies: These software applications and technological solutions support governance, risk management, and compliance processes. They might assist with policy management, risk assessment, compliance reporting, incident management, and auditing.

Governance and Risk Management Framework: This is a structured set of guidelines for establishing an organization's governance and risk management system. It provides a roadmap for defining roles and responsibilities, setting strategic objectives, identifying and managing risks, and ensuring compliance with laws and regulations.

Governance, Risk Management, and Compliance (GRC):   GRC is a strategic approach for aligning IT with business objectives, effectively managing risk, and meeting compliance requirements. A robust GRC program helps organizations achieve their goals, prevent data breaches, and maintain stakeholder trust.

Incident Containment, Eradication, and Recovery: These are phases in the incident response process. Containment involves limiting the scope and impact of the incident; eradication consists in removing the threat from the environment; and recovery involves restoring systems to regular operation and implementing measures to prevent future incidents.

Incident Detection and Analysis: This is the process of identifying potential security incidents, confirming they are actual incidents, and understanding their nature and potential impact. It involves using various detection methods, such as intrusion detection systems and log analysis, and may also include root cause analysis to determine how the incident occurred.

Incident Management: This is a systematic process for responding to and managing the life cycle of an incident. It includes all activities from initial detection to resolution and post-incident analysis, aiming to limit damage and reduce recovery time and costs.

Incident Reporting refers to documenting and communicating information about a security incident. Reporting may be internal within the organization or involve external parties such as law enforcement, regulators, or affected customers.

Interconnectivity Risk: This is associated with the interconnectedness of IT systems and networks within and outside the organization. Increased inter-connectivity can bring business benefits, but it also creates potential points of vulnerability and increases the potential impact of cybersecurity incidents.

IT Change Management: This refers to a structured approach to managing changes in an IT environment. It seeks to minimize the impact of disruptions and prevent errors that could lead to security vulnerabilities. Change manage-ment includes assessing and approving proposed changes, testing changes before implementation, and reviewing the success after implementation.

Key Performance Indicators (KPIs): Measurable values demonstrate how effectively a company achieves key business objectives. In cybersecurity, KPIs might measure the effectiveness of security controls, the speed of incident response, or the level of employee compliance with security policies.

Key Risk Indicators (KRIs): KRIs are measures organizations use to provide an early signal of increasing risk exposure in various areas of the enterprise. In cybersecurity, KRIs might include the number of unpatched systems, the num-ber of failed logins, or the number of detected malware incidents.

Network Controls: These are safeguards or countermeasures to protect a network's integrity, confidentiality, availability, and data. Network controls can include physical measures (e.g., secure cabling), technical measures (e.g., fire-walls, encryption), and administrative measures (e.g., user access controls and security policies).

Physical Security: This involves the measures taken to protect personnel, hardware, software, networks, and data from physical actions and events that could cause severe damage or loss to an enterprise. These measures include access control, surveillance, and testing.

Policies, Standards, and Procedures: In cybersecurity, policies are high-level statements of what an organization wants to achieve with its cybersecurity program; standards are specific, mandatory requirements for meeting the pol-icy goals; and procedures are detailed instructions for performing tasks that comply with the standards.

Privacy by Design and Default: This principle requires that privacy and data protection measures are embedded into products and services from the earliest stages of development. The strictest privacy settings automatically apply once a customer acquires a new product or service (i.e., "by default").

Privacy Laws and Data Protection: Privacy laws are regulations designed to protect personal data from unauthorized access, use, or disclosure. Data protection involves implementing controls to ensure compliance with these laws and protecting data from threats like loss, corruption, or breach.

Regulatory Expectations: These are the requirements and standards that regulatory bodies expect organizations to meet. In cybersecurity, regulatory expectations might include maintaining specific security controls, reporting security incidents, or demonstrating compliance with specific cybersecurity frameworks or standards.

Regulatory Penalties: These are sanctions imposed by regulatory bodies for noncompliance with legal or regulatory requirements. Penalties can include fines, imprisonment, or other sanctions and can be applied to organizations and individuals.

Risk Approvals: This involves obtaining a formal agreement to proceed with an activity or decision that carries an identified risk. In a cybersecurity context, risk approval is typically given by a senior executive or a risk committee based on an understanding of the potential impact and likelihood of the risk, as well as the cost and benefit of mitigation options.

Risk Assessment and Analysis: Risk assessment involves identifying and evaluating risks, while risk analysis involves understanding the nature of identified risks, their potential impact, and the likelihood of their occurrence. Together, these processes inform decision-making about risk responses and controls.

Risk Management: Identifying, assessing, and controlling threats to an organization's capital and earnings. In a cybersecurity context, risk management includes implementing measures to detect, prevent, and mitigate the impact of cybersecurity threats.

Risk Management Life Cycle: This refers to the ongoing process of identifying, assessing, responding to, and monitoring risk. The risk management life cycle is typically repeated periodically to ensure that risks are continually identified and managed as an organization's risk environment changes.

Security Reference Models   are blueprints or frameworks that detail an organization's security architecture. They provide an overview of the organization's security controls and how they interact to protect it from threats.

Strategic Planning   involves setting strategic goals and determining a plan to achieve them. Strategic planning might involve defining cybersecurity objectives, assessing current capabilities, and planning initiatives to close gaps in cybersecurity.

Third-Party Risk Management: This involves identifying and managing the risks associated with third parties, such as suppliers, service providers, or business partners. In a cybersecurity context, third-party risks can include data breaches at a vendor, software vulnerabilities in third-party applications, or inadequate security practices at a service provider.

User Security Controls: These are measures taken to ensure that users within an organization can only access and modify the data and systems they are authorized to. Controls may include user authentication measures, access controls, user training, and user activity monitoring.

Cybersecurity Resources

The complexities of today's cybersecurity landscape can daunt businesses of all sizes and sectors. Recognizing this reality, this appendix has been dedicated to exploring a range of significant cybersecurity resources readily available to organizations. It thoroughly dissects resources such as the U.S. Cybersecurity & Infrastructure Security Agency (CISA), the National Institute of Standards and Technology (NIST), and the National Vulnerability Database (NVD), among others. By clarifying their functions, services, and the most effective methods for their utilization, it serves as a guiding light, assisting in navigating the intricate maze of cybersecurity resources.

U.S. Cybersecurity and Infrastructure Security Agency (CISA) – [https://www.cisa.gov]

The U.S. Cybersecurity & Infrastructure Security Agency, commonly known as CISA, is pivotal to our nation's cybersecurity defense mechanism. Founded to protect the nation's critical infrastructure from physical and cyber threats, CISA is integral in securing government networks and enhancing the resilience of the broader cybersecurity ecosystem. By understanding its mission and structure, we can gain valuable insights into the policies, practices, and approaches that shape the US cybersecurity landscape.

CISA's resources span a vast spectrum, providing private and public entities with a robust arsenal of tools, guidelines, and services to counteract cyber threats. This includes comprehensive risk management services, cybersecurity training, incident response support, and other resources. These services are calibrated to offer proactive defense mechanisms against many cyber threats, enabling organizations to fortify their cybersecurity stance and improve their overall risk management.

Using CISA's resources is a strategic move that promises significant benefits. Organizations can substantially enhance their threat detection and mitigation capabilities with access to in-depth, actionable threat intelligence. This access is facilitated by an extensive suite of cyber tools and information provided by CISA, designed to amplify cybersecurity awareness and foster an environment of proactive defense.

However, reaping the benefits of these resources requires a clear understanding of how to incorporate them into existing security practices. Tailoring these resources to an organization's specific needs and integrating them into its risk management framework can substantially boost the efficacy of its cybersecurity strategies. This involves understanding each tool's purpose, function, and optimal use case and aligning it with the organization's unique security requirements.

Given the rapidly evolving threat landscape, keeping abreast of the latest developments and trends in cybersecurity is paramount. In this regard, CISA's role extends beyond merely providing resources. It also operates as a primary source of information and updates regarding emerging threats, incident reports, vulnerability advisories, and more. Staying informed about these updates can help organizations stay one step ahead of potential threats.

In conclusion, CISA is a vital ally in the fight against cyber threats. Its extensive resources and comprehensive approach toward threat intelligence and risk management make it an indispensable component of an effective cybersecurity strategy. Organizations leveraging these resources can strengthen their defenses, mitigate risks, and better prepare for the Future.

National Institute Of Standards and Technology (NIST) – [https://www.nist.gov]

The NIST is a critical resource in the cybersecurity space, renowned for its comprehensive guidelines and standards. Established as a nonregulatory agency within the U.S. Department of Commerce, NIST aims to promote innovation and competitiveness by advancing measurement science, standards, and technology. Its work in cybersecurity has profoundly influenced security policies and practices across industries.

One of NIST's most notable contributions is the NIST Cybersecurity Framework, a guide designed to assist organizations in managing and reducing cybersecurity risk. The Framework hailed for its practicality and versatility, can be tailored to suit organizations of various sizes and sectors. In addition to the Framework, NIST also publishes many standards, guidelines, and special publications that delve into specific aspects of information security and risk management.

The advantages of leveraging NIST resources are multifold. Organizations can gain a structured and strategic approach to managing cyber risks by adopting the NIST Cybersecurity Framework. The Framework's core functions – Identify, Protect, Detect, Respond, and Recover – provide a roadmap for organizations to build their cybersecurity programs and ensure continuous improvement. Moreover, the other publications offer in-depth insights on various cybersecurity topics, allowing for targeted improvements in specific areas.

Yet, while NIST provides an extensive suite of resources, understanding how to integrate them into an organization's cybersecurity program effectively is complex. Each organization's security needs are unique, requiring the Framework and other resources to be tailored and implemented strategically. Achieving this requires a deep understanding of the organization's risk profile, business objectives, and security posture.

Furthermore, the applicability of NIST resources extends beyond US borders. Organizations worldwide use their guidelines and standards to enhance their security practices. This global acceptance speaks volumes about the quality and effectiveness of NIST's work. Organizations can align security practices with internationally recognized best practices by adopting these standards.

In essence, NIST is a goldmine of cybersecurity wisdom organizations can use to strengthen their defenses. Its meticulously crafted guidelines and standards and dedication to promoting innovative security solutions make it a cornerstone of the global cybersecurity community. Utilizing NIST resources effectively can significantly enhance an organization's resilience against cyber threats, paving the way for a secure and prosperous future.

National Vulnerability Database (NVD) – [https://nvd.nist.gov]

The NVD, operated by NIST, is a critical cybersecurity resource, offering a comprehensive collection of vulnerabilities and corresponding metadata. As an extension of the Common Vulnerabilities and Exposures (CVE) dictionary, NVD provides additional analysis, such as severity scores, impact metrics, and remediation guidance, making it an essential tool in the cybersecurity landscape.

By providing a comprehensive overview of known vulnerabilities, NVD allows organizations to approach their cybersecurity efforts proactively. By integrating NVD data into their security operations, organizations can actively monitor their systems for these known vulnerabilities, swiftly implementing patches or workarounds as they become available. This can significantly reduce the window of opportunity for attackers, thereby enhancing the organization's overall security posture.

Effective vulnerability management using NVD entails a cyclical process of identifying, classifying, prioritizing, and remediating vulnerabilities. To support this, NVD provides various tools and feeds that can be integrated into vulnerability management and threat intelligence platforms. These enable automated scanning, identification, and prioritization of vulnerabilities based on severity scores, helping organizations focus their remediation efforts where they matter most.

Integrating NVD data into an organization's security practices involves a strategic blend of people, processes, and technology. On the one hand, it requires a commitment from the organization to prioritize vulnerability management and foster a culture of security. On the other hand, it involves setting up processes for regular vulnerability scanning and remediation, bolstered by the right technological tools.

The NVD also plays a crucial role in the broader cybersecurity community, contributing to collective defense efforts by fostering transparency and information sharing. By making vulnerability data publicly accessible, NVD empowers organizations across industries to enhance their defenses and join in the collective fight against cyber threats. This collaborative approach to security significantly raises the bar for potential attackers, making cyber intrusions increasingly challenging to achieve.

In essence, NVD serves as an indispensable tool for organizations seeking to enhance their cybersecurity defenses. Its rich repository of vulnerability data, coupled with its suite of analysis tools and feeds, allows organizations to level up their vulnerability management practices. By effectively integrating NVD data into their security practices, organizations can significantly reduce their exposure to cyber risks and enhance their resilience against potential attacks.

National Cybersecurity and Communications Integration Center (NCCIC) – [https://us-cert.cisa.gov]

The National Cybersecurity and Communications Integration Center (NCCIC) is crucial to the U.S. Department of Homeland Security. The NCCIC serves as a centralized source for cybersecurity coordination, information sharing, and incident response within the federal government. The center aims to empower private and public sector partners by providing timely information about security issues, vulnerabilities, and exploits.

One critical service the NCCIC provides is its comprehensive incident reporting and response mechanism. Organizations can report cyber incidents to the NCCIC, which coordinates the federal response and offers technical assistance where necessary. By doing so, the NCCIC enhances the national response to cyber incidents and helps limit the impact of potential cyberattacks.

The NCCIC also offers various services and support options to strengthen the nation's cybersecurity infrastructure. This includes vulnerability coordination, incident response assistance, technical reports, and cybersecurity evaluations. By availing these services, organizations can bolster their cybersecurity defenses and stay abreast of the latest cyber threats and vulnerabilities.

However, the efficacy of these resources largely depends on how effectively they are integrated into an organization's cybersecurity strategy. Properly using these resources can result in better threat detection capabilities, enhanced incident response, and improved security posture. This requires an understanding of the resources offered by the NCCIC and a strategic approach toward their implementation.

Given the evolving nature of the cyber threat landscape, having up-to-date information on potential threats and vulnerabilities is crucial. The NCCIC provides real-time threat and vulnerability information, cybersecurity tips, and alerts. By staying updated with these resources, organizations can ensure they are well prepared to tackle the latest threats.

In conclusion, the NCCIC is a critical player in the national cybersecurity ecosystem, providing resources and services that enhance the nation's ability to respond to and mitigate cyber threats. By leveraging these resources, organizations can improve their cybersecurity posture and contribute to the nation's collective cyber resilience.

Federal Bureau Of Investigation (FBI) – Internet Crime Complaint Center (IC3) – [https://www.ic3.gov]

The Internet Crime Complaint Center (IC3), under the jurisdiction of the Federal Bureau of Investigation (FBI), is a resource designed to provide the public with a reliable and convenient reporting mechanism for suspected cybercrime. The IC3 serves as a centralized hub for receiving, developing, and referring complaints regarding internet-based crime, playing a significant role in the broader mission of the FBI to protect the United States against cyber threats.

An introduction to the IC3 reveals a range of resources and services aimed at public awareness, education, and protection against cybercrime. The IC3's key offerings include reporting mechanisms for internet crime, public service announcements, and annual reports outlining the prevalent trends in cyber-crime. These resources are valuable tools for organizations and individuals looking to understand and mitigate cyber risks.

The IC3's robust internet crime reporting system allows victims of cyber-crime to submit complaints online, providing a streamlined mechanism for the public to report internet-related crimes. The information gathered from these reports assists the FBI and law enforcement agencies in investigating and combating cybercrime. Victims must report cybercrime incidents promptly, pro-viding detailed information, enhancing the chances of apprehending the cul-prits, and recovering lost funds or data.

However, simply reporting internet crimes is not enough. Understanding how to utilize IC3 resources effectively for awareness and protection against cyber threats is essential. This entails regularly visiting the IC3's website, stay-ing abreast of public service announcements, and perusing the annual reports to understand the evolving cyber threat landscape. These practices can help individuals and organizations identify prevalent cyber threats and take appro-priate precautionary measures.

The IC3 also emphasizes the importance of cyber hygiene and security edu-cation, underscoring that awareness is the first defense against cyber threats. By offering tips and guidelines on various topics, such as online scams, ran-somware, and social engineering tactics, the IC3 helps the public understand the nature of these threats and how to avoid falling victim to them.

In summary, the FBI's IC3 serves as a critical resource in the fight against cybercrime, offering various tools and services for public protection and edu-cation. By understanding and leveraging these resources, individuals and organizations can significantly enhance their cybersecurity posture and resil-ience against cyber threats, contributing to a safer and more secure digital environment.

The Sans Institute – [https://www.sans.org]

The SANS Institute is a trusted and significant player in cybersecurity. Established in 1989, the institute offers a wide range of resources related to information security, including training, education programs, certification courses, and a wealth of free resources available through its Reading Room and webcasts. The SANS Institute has made invaluable contributions to the cybersecurity community, empowering professionals with knowledge and skills to tackle evolving cyber threats.

The SANS Institute offers a myriad of training and education programs in various fields of cybersecurity. Its courses are designed for multiple exper-tise levels, from beginners to seasoned professionals. The instructors at SANS are practicing professionals in the area, offering practical insights, real-world examples, and hands-on training. This high-quality training can significantly enhance an individual's cybersecurity skills and knowledge, enabling them to respond to cyber threats more effectively.

The SANS Reading Room and webcasts are additional resources that offer free, in-depth, and insightful content on a range of cybersecurity topics.

The Reading Room features over 3000 articles written by the SANS faculty, while the webcasts provide the opportunity to learn from industry experts on various cybersecurity issues. By regularly accessing these resources, cybersecurity professionals can keep themselves updated on the latest trends, techniques, and best practices in the field.

However, merely accessing these resources is not enough. They must be incorporated into an ongoing learning process to extract maximum value. Cybersecurity professionals must integrate this knowledge into their daily practices and strategies, applying learned concepts to real-world scenarios. This can improve their skill set continuously and enhance their organization's overall cybersecurity posture.

Moreover, the SANS Institute fosters a robust community for cybersecurity professionals. Networking opportunities arise from various events, forums, and online platforms managed by SANS, allowing professionals to connect, share experiences, and learn from each other. This sense of community strengthens cybersecurity, promoting collective learning and growth.

The SANS Institute is invaluable for deepening their cybersecurity knowledge and skills. By fully engaging with the SANS resources and community, professionals can stay at the forefront of the field, armed with the latest knowledge and best practices to counter the ever-evolving world of cyber threats.

Center for Internet Security (CIS) – [https://www.cisecurity.org]

The Center for Internet Security (CIS) is a nonprofit organization that plays a pivotal role in enhancing the cybersecurity posture of individuals and organizations globally. Its mission is to identify, develop, validate, promote, and sustain best practices in cybersecurity. CIS achieves this through various offerings, including the CIS Controls, CIS Benchmarks, and membership and community involvement opportunities.

CIS Controls and Benchmarks provide prioritized and industry-accepted security measures that organizations of all sizes can adopt to improve their cybersecurity defenses. CIS Controls outline a set of 20 actionable controls that are universally applicable and can significantly reduce an organization's risk profile. The CIS Benchmarks are consensus-based, best-practice security configuration guidelines spanning numerous technologies.

Membership in CIS provides a range of benefits that enhance cybersecurity awareness and capabilities. Members gain access to additional resources and insights, can influence the development of CIS Controls and Benchmarks, and can network with cybersecurity experts worldwide. Such participation can significantly enhance an organization's cybersecurity posture by leveraging shared knowledge and expertise.

CIS's contribution extends beyond the resources it offers. The organization's commitment to promoting a culture of cybersecurity in communities through awareness campaigns, workshops, and training programs plays a vital role in enhancing collective cybersecurity resilience. Engagement with the CIS community can provide organizations with insights into the cybersecurity landscape, helping them adapt to evolving threats and trends.

The proactive application of CIS Controls and Benchmarks can substantially reduce an organization's cyber risk profile. These resources provide a roadmap for organizations to prioritize their cybersecurity efforts. They offer a practical approach applicable across various industry sectors, regardless of an organization's size or the complexity of its systems.

In conclusion, the CIS is a cornerstone in the cybersecurity community, providing invaluable resources and creating platforms for collaboration. Organizations can bolster their cybersecurity defenses and contribute to a broader cybersecurity awareness and resilience culture by utilizing CIS's resources and becoming involved in its community.

Electronic Frontier Foundation (EFF) – [Https://Www.eff.org]

The Electronic Frontier Foundation (EFF) is a leading nonprofit organization dedicated to defending civil liberties in the digital world. Since its inception in 1990, the EFF has been at the forefront of primary policy debates, court challenges, and advocacy efforts concerning online privacy, free speech, and other critical digital rights issues.

Much of the EFF's work involves providing legal support for individuals and organizations facing legal challenges related to online activities. This includes cases involving censorship, surveillance, and intellectual property. EFF's legal team uses these cases to set precedents that protect and expand digital rights, contributing to a free and open internet.

The EFF offers numerous resources aimed at preserving privacy and freedom online. These include practical tools, guides, and information on various topics, including secure communication, data protection, and online tracking. By utilizing these resources, individuals and organizations can better understand their digital rights and learn how to safeguard their online privacy and freedom.

Understanding and leveraging the EFF's resources and services requires a proactive approach to digital rights and online privacy. This involves regularly checking the EFF's website for updates, utilizing its tools and guides, and staying informed about relevant legal and policy developments. This knowledge can empower individuals and organizations to exercise their digital rights confidently and responsibly.

The EFF also advocates to influence policies and legislation that impact digital rights. This includes campaigning against laws and practices that infringe upon online freedoms and promoting policies that enhance digital rights and internet freedom. Participation in these advocacy efforts can enable individuals and organizations to contribute to shaping the Future of the digital world.

The EFF is a vital resource for anyone looking to understand and exercise their digital rights. The EFF plays a pivotal role in defending and promoting digital rights and freedoms through its legal support, educational resources, and advocacy efforts. Engaging with the EFF can equip individuals and organizations with the knowledge and tools to navigate the digital world safely and responsibly.

Mitre Corporation – [https://www.mitre.org]

The MITRE Corporation is a not-for-profit organization that operates federally funded research and development centers (FFRDCs) in the United States.

MITRE's work includes contributing significantly to the cybersecurity landscape with two of its most notable offerings: the CVE program and the Adversarial Tactics, Techniques, and Common Knowledge (ATT&CK) framework.

The CVE program, managed by MITRE, provides a dictionary of publicly known cybersecurity vulnerabilities. This standardizes how vulnerabilities are identified, allowing security professionals worldwide to speak a common language when discussing and managing vulnerabilities. The CVE program is integral to the cybersecurity community and forms the backbone of many vulnerability management systems.

MITRE's ATT&CK framework is a curated knowledge base and model for cyber adversary behavior. Security teams widely use it to develop threat models and methodologies in their networks, driving a wide range of security improvements. The ATT&CK framework's practicality and effectiveness have made it a go-to resource for organizations seeking to bolster their defense strategies.

Engaging with MITRE's resources involves more than just utilizing the CVE and ATT&CK databases. It requires understanding the principles underlying these resources, implementing them into the organization's security strategies, and staying updated with their regular updates. This can significantly enhance an organization's ability to effectively identify, prevent, and respond to cyber threats.

MITRE also encourages community involvement, providing opportunities for cybersecurity professionals to contribute to its resources. This collaborative approach ensures that its resources are kept up-to-date and relevant, reflecting the collective knowledge and expertise of the cybersecurity community. Professionals can contribute to the broader cybersecurity landscape by participating in this community while learning from their peers.

The MITRE Corporation is a critical contributor to the cybersecurity ecosystem, providing key resources that inform and shape security practices globally. Organizations can significantly improve their cybersecurity defenses and contribute to the broader cybersecurity community's collective knowledge and resilience by leveraging and contributing to MITER's resources.

The Open Web Application Security Project (OWASP) – [https://owasp.org]
The Open Web Application Security Project (OWASP) is a nonprofit organization dedicated to improving software security. It is best known for its "OWASP Top Ten," a list of the most critical security risks to web applications, which has become a vital resource for developers and security professionals around the globe.

The OWASP Top Ten is regularly updated to reflect the evolving web application security landscape. By understanding and addressing the vulnerabilities listed in the Top Ten, developers can significantly enhance the security of their web applications. The Top Ten is just one of many OWASP projects aimed at improving software security, with other resources including the OWASP Testing Guide, the OWASP Code Review Guide, and the OWASP Cheat Sheet Series.

Beyond offering these resources, OWASP operates local chapters worldwide and organizes conferences that provide opportunities for networking, learning, and sharing best practices among security professionals. Involvement in these activities can significantly expand a professional's knowledge base and keep them up-to-date on the latest threats and mitigation techniques.

Utilizing OWASP resources effectively requires a commitment to continuous learning and adaptation. Web application security is a dynamic field that constantly changes as new threats emerge and old ones evolve. By staying abreast of OWASP updates and actively participating in its community, developers can stay ahead of these changes and continually enhance their applications' security.

In addition, OWASP offers a range of resources that help organizations build security into the software development life cycle. These include guides on threat modeling, security testing, secure coding practices, and more. By integrating these resources into their processes, organizations can significantly reduce their risk of a security breach.

In conclusion, OWASP is critical to web application security, providing numerous resources and community platforms that help developers create secure software. By actively engaging with OWASP, developers and organizations can stay ahead of the rapidly changing threat landscape and improve their ability to build secure applications.

Other Resources

For-profit cybersecurity resources also play a significant role in enhancing cybersecurity defenses. These resources often come from cybersecurity companies and include blogs, threat intelligence reports, and a range of other resources that offer insights into the latest cybersecurity threats and trends. For example, FireEye's Threat Research Blog, Symantec's Official Blog, and McAfee's Blog Central are some of the popular for-profit resources available.

FireEye's Threat Research Blog is a prime example of how cybersecurity companies disseminate knowledge. The blog regularly features analysis of the latest threats and security incidents, often providing in-depth technical breakdowns. This information is helpful for security professionals looking to understand the threat landscape and learn about advanced threat detection and response techniques.

Symantec's Official Blog is another example. It contains a wealth of information on various cybersecurity topics, including threat intelligence, cybersecurity best practices, and security awareness. Symantec's blog can be a valuable resource for technical and nontechnical audiences seeking to broaden their cybersecurity knowledge.

McAfee's Blog Central is a comprehensive resource covering various cybersecurity topics. From advanced threat research to practical tips for securing personal devices, the blog provides information valuable to enterprises and individuals. This mix of content makes it a versatile resource for anyone interested in improving their cybersecurity posture.

Utilizing these resources effectively involves more than just casual reading. It requires active engagement, including following these blogs, reading them regularly, understanding the information they provide, and applying that knowledge to improve cybersecurity practices. It may also involve participating in the comment sections of these blogs to ask questions, share insights, and learn from other readers' perspectives.

Threat intelligence platforms are essential tools in the modern cybersecurity landscape. They provide actionable insights about the latest threats and help organizations understand, prevent, and respond to security incidents. Examples of these platforms include Recorded Future, ThreatConnect, and CrowdStrike Falcon X.

Recorded Future is a threat intelligence platform that offers real-time threat intelligence. It uses machine learning and natural language processing to collect and analyze data from various sources, providing insights to help organizations anticipate and mitigate cyber threats. Recorded Future can provide contextual intelligence on threats, making it a vital tool for cybersecurity professionals.

ThreatConnect is another platform that provides comprehensive threat intelligence services. Its platform allows for aggregating and correlating data from various sources, enabling organizations to view their threat landscape comprehensively. ThreatConnect also provides tools for incident response, making it a versatile platform for cybersecurity operations.

CrowdStrike Falcon X is a cybersecurity platform that combines threat intelligence, automation, and endpoint protection. It provides threat intelligence reports, malware search capabilities, and incident response tools, all within a single interface. CrowdStrike Falcon X can help organizations streamline their cybersecurity operations and respond more quickly to threats.

Leveraging these platforms requires integrating them into an organization's security practices. This means understanding how they work, configuring them appropriately, and training relevant personnel to use them effectively. When utilized properly, threat intelligence platforms can significantly enhance an organization's ability to anticipate and respond to cyber threats.

In conclusion, threat intelligence platforms are powerful tools that provide organizations with actionable insights about the latest cyber threats. Organizations can use these platforms to enhance their cybersecurity defenses and respond more effectively to security incidents.

Community-driven cybersecurity resources are a vital part of the cybersecurity ecosystem. These resources include security forums and communities, social media, meetups, and conferences, all providing platforms for cybersecurity professionals to share knowledge, learn from each other, and collaborate on solving cybersecurity challenges.

Security forums and communities are excellent resources for novice and seasoned cybersecurity professionals. They offer a platform to ask questions, share experiences, and learn from others in the field. Examples include the Reddit r/netsec community, the Stack Exchange Information Security forum, and the SecLists.Org security mailing list.

Social media can also be valuable for staying updated on cybersecurity news and trends. Many cybersecurity professionals and organizations maintain active social media profiles where they share updates, insights, and discussions about cybersecurity. Following these profiles can help individuals and organizations stay informed and engaged with the cybersecurity community.

Meetups and conferences provide opportunities for in-person networking and learning. The Black Hat, DEF CON, and RSA conferences feature presentations by leading cybersecurity experts, hands-on workshops, and networking events. Participation in these events can significantly enhance a professional's knowledge and skills and expand their professional network.

Ready-to-Use KPI Examples

This appendix is your comprehensive toolkit to an array of ready-to-use Key Performance Indicator (KPI) examples that can be directly implemented into your performance tracking strategy. Each KPI is divided into 10 sections, detailing everything from the KPI title, objective, and metric summary to the measurement formula, quantifiable measure, and benchmark or target measure. We also delve into the necessary timeframe, data source, and recommended visual representation to aid analysis. Lastly, the insights and actions segment guides translating the collected data into actionable steps. This systematic approach ensures a complete understanding and effective use of each KPI in real-world scenarios.

1. **KPI Title:** The title of each KPI acts as the first point of entry in understanding its essence. The KPI Title is carefully chosen to be succinct yet descriptive, outlining the specific aspect of cybersecurity it addresses. The title must be clear, setting the tone for the following details. The title should intuitively resonate with the security goal it is aligned with and must enable the reader to gauge the underlying theme of the KPI without ambiguity quickly.

2. **KPI Objective:** Under this section, the prime objective or goal that the KPI aims to accomplish is thoroughly elucidated. It explains why this particular indicator is significant in the broader context of cybersecurity. The objectives usually align with the overarching cybersecurity goals of an organization. Understanding the objective is foundational, explaining why this metric is being measured. This section will lay the groundwork by correlating the KPI with real-world security concerns and how tracking this KPI can provide valuable insights.

3. **Metric Summary:** The Metric Summary provides an in-depth exploration of the KPI. It outlines what the KPI measures and explains how this measurement is significant in achieving security objectives. The summary considers how the KPI is intertwined with different aspects of cybersecurity and provides a rationale for its selection. It serves as a narrative that bridges the gap between the theoretical aspects of the KPI and its practical application in a real-world scenario.

4. **Possible Measurement Formula:** A mathematical formula or method for calculating the KPI is presented here. The section breaks down the formula's components and explains each variable. It also guides how

to compute the KPI using the data collected accurately and might offer formula variations for different contexts or scenarios.

5. **Quantifiable Measure:** The discussion focuses on ensuring that the KPI can be measured quantitatively. It explains how a quantifiable measure, whether in numbers, percentages, or other units, is crucial for objective assessment and analysis. This allows for a clear understanding of the organization's goals.

6. **Benchmark or Target Measure:** This part details the performance thresholds or benchmarks the organization aims to achieve for the KPI. It elaborates on what would be considered a "good" or "bad" value for the KPI and how these values are derived. This section is integral in setting realistic and achievable targets and facilitates the organization in measuring how far or close they are to attaining their cybersecurity goals.

7. **Timeframe:** This section discusses the importance of defining a specific timeframe for measuring and analyzing the KPI. It explains how selecting an appropriate timeframe is essential to ensure the data is relevant and reflects the current state of security affairs. The section elaborates on how different timeframes suit daily, weekly, or monthly KPIs.

8. **Data Source:** This segment highlights the importance of identifying and validating the data sources that will be used to measure the KPI. It discusses the various possible data sources, such as logs, reports, and audits, and how to ensure their reliability and accuracy. The significance of data integrity in making informed decisions is emphasized.

9. **Visualization Recommendation:** This section explores the importance of visually representing KPIs. It explains how visual aids like charts, graphs, and dashboards can effectively describe the data. This not only aids in quickly assimilating information but also helps identify trends and patterns that might not be evident in tabular data.

   (a) **Type of Graph/Chart:** Explain which type of visualization, such as line graph, bar chart, heatmap, etc., is most appropriate for the KRI. Different types of KRIs might be best represented in different ways. For instance, trends over time might be best visualized with line graphs, while distributions might be more effectively represented with histograms.

   (b) **Axes Representation:** Guides what should be represented on the x-axis and y-axis. Typically, time is on the x-axis, but there could be cases where a different representation is more insightful. The y-axis typically represents the measurement of the KRI, but sometimes it could also be helpful to represent relative change, percentages, etc.

   (c) **Scale and Limits:** Discuss the appropriate scale for the y-axis. This can sometimes make a big difference in how the data is perceived. Also, provide recommendations if there should be any limits on the graph. For instance, having a maximum limit on the y-axis might be helpful to make specific patterns more apparent.

(d) **Threshold Lines or Markers:** Explain if horizontal or vertical lines should represent triggers or breaches in the KRI. This can help in immediately identifying points of concern on the graph.

(e) **Color and Highlighting:** Recommend using color or other highlighting techniques to make certain aspects of the data stand out, such as using a different color for data points above a certain threshold.

10. **Insights and Actions:** This section deals with interpreting the data and converting the analysis into actionable insights. It discusses how KPI data should be the driving force behind decisions and strategies. This section bridges the gap between measurement and action, providing a clear path for utilizing KPI data effectively.

KPI Title: Mean Time to Respond (MTTR)

KPI Objective: Mean Time to Respond (*MTTR*) aims to gauge the efficiency and effectiveness of an organization's response to security incidents. The organization can evaluate its preparedness and agility in dealing with threats by assessing the average time to respond to and mitigate a security incident. This is critical in minimizing potential damage, maintaining customer trust, and ensuring business continuity. A well-defined MTTR ensures that the organization is committed to a timely incident resolution and can adapt and streamline its response procedures.

Metric Summary: MTTR is an essential KPI for assessing the organization's incident response capabilities. In cybersecurity, the speed at which an organization can respond to a security incident is often as critical as the ability to detect it in the first place. Security incidents can substantially impact an organization's reputation, customer data, and operational integrity, and the MTTR serves as a key indicator of how effectively the organization can minimize these impacts. Reducing the MTTR should be a continuous effort, as it directly reduces the risk and consequences of security incidents. This KPI is crucial for incident response planning, resource allocation, and improving communication and coordination during incident handling.

Possible Measurement Formula: MTTR = sum of all response times for incidents/total number of incidents.

Suggested Frequency: Monthly.

Quantifiable Measure: The MTTR is measured in time, commonly hours or minutes.

Benchmark or Target Measure: This depends on the nature of incidents and the organization's capabilities, but continuous reduction should be the goal.

Timeframe: This KPI is usually measured monthly to assess trends and make timely adjustments.

Data Source: Incident response logs, ticketing systems.

Visualization Recommendation: For MTTR, a line graph is most effective, with the x-axis depicting time and the y-axis showing the average time taken to respond to security incidents. Use a uniform scale for the y-axis, with either hours or days as units. Introduce a horizontal threshold line to indicate target response times and utilize color to highlight instances when the MTTR exceeds this threshold, alerting to areas needing expedited response mechanisms.

Insights and Actions: An increasing MTTR trend or a consistently high MTTR indicates potential bottlenecks or inefficiencies in the incident response process. This requires in-depth analysis to identify the underlying issues – such as lack of resources, ineffective communication, or inadequate tools – and develop strategies for improvement. Conversely, a decreasing trend in MTTR reflects positive improvements but should not lead to complacency. Continuous review and practice, leveraging automation where possible, and ensuring updated training and documentation are essential in maintaining an effective incident response capability. Additionally, it is important not solely to focus on speed but also on the quality and thoroughness of the response, ensuring that incidents are fully resolved and that lessons are learned for future prevention and response.

Next KPI Title: Number of Security Incidents

KPI Objective: The objective of the Number of Security Incidents KPI is to monitor and record the total number of security incidents reported within a given period. This KPI is crucial in evaluating the security landscape faced by the organization and the effectiveness of preventive measures. By tracking the frequency and types of incidents, the organization can allocate resources more effectively, identify trends, and implement targeted security improvements. A consistent reduction or a low number of security incidents indicates a robust security posture.

Metric Summary: Monitoring the Number of Security Incidents is essential for any organization to understand its risk landscape. It reflects the challenges faced in maintaining security and indicates the effectiveness of security controls and preventive measures. Not only is it essential to track the sheer number, but categorizing incidents by type and severity provides a more granular understanding, enabling more targeted response and prevention strategies. Organizations can prioritize their security investments and focus on the most significant risks by understanding the most common types of incidents. Furthermore, understanding the source of incidents, external attacks, or insider threats can provide invaluable context.

Possible Measurement Formula: Number of Security Incidents = sum of all security incidents reported within a specific time frame.

Suggested Frequency: Monthly.

Quantifiable Measure: The Number of Security Incidents is a numerical value representing the count of incidents.

Benchmark or Target Measure: Targets should be set based on historical data, industry standards, and the organization's risk appetite. The goal is generally to minimize the number of incidents.

Timeframe: Monthly tracking is common, though more frequent monitoring may be necessary in high-risk environments.

Data Source: Security incident reports, incident management systems, logs.

Visualization Recommendation: A bar graph is ideal for visualizing the Number of Security Incidents, with the x-axis showing time and the y-axis representing the count of security incidents. The graph should have a consistent scale and no predefined limits to allow for natural fluctuations. Incorporate a horizontal threshold line and utilize color coding, such as red, for critical incidents to differentiate the severity of incidents over time.

Insights and Actions: Increasing security incidents demand immediate attention and analysis. Are the incidents of a particular type? Are they targeting a specific system or data? Understanding the specifics can guide the response. Perhaps new security controls are required, or existing controls must be adjusted. It might also indicate the need for additional employee training. A decreasing trend in security incidents might suggest that current security measures are effective, but it is essential not to become complacent. Continuous evaluation of the threat landscape is crucial as new threats and vulnerabilities emerge. It is also beneficial to benchmark against industry peers and adopt best practices. Engaging in threat intelligence sharing and keeping abreast of new security technologies can further enhance the organization's security posture.

KPI Title: Security Incident Resolution Rate

KPI Objective: The Security Incident Resolution Rate KPI aims to quantify the organization's efficiency and effectiveness in successfully resolving security incidents within a specific timeframe. This is essential in assessing the organization's incident response capabilities and ensuring that security incidents do not remain unresolved, posing ongoing risks. An efficient incident resolution process protects organizational assets, minimizes downtime, and maintains customer trust.

Metric Summary: The Security Incident Resolution Rate measures how effectively an organization can resolve identified security incidents. When a security incident occurs, timely and effective resolution is critical to minimize impact. This KPI helps understand whether the incident response team is sufficiently equipped and skilled and if the processes are streamlined for effective resolution. Analyzing trends in the resolution rate over time can indicate if improvements or changes in strategies are needed. This KPI also necessitates a focus on the resolution quality – ensuring incidents are closed quickly and thoroughly investigated and resolved, mitigating any risks they pose.

Possible Measurement Formula: Security Incident Resolution Rate (%) = (number of security incidents successfully resolved within a specific timeframe/total number of security incidents) × 100.

Suggested Frequency: Monthly.

Quantifiable Measure: Expressed as a percentage reflecting the proportion of successfully resolved security incidents.

Benchmark or Target Measure: Target of maintaining a close to 100% resolution rate.

Timeframe: This KPI is generally measured monthly.

Data Source: Incident response logs, ticketing systems, and security incident reports.

Visualization Recommendation: To visualize the Security Incident Resolution Rate, a line graph is fitting, where the x-axis represents time, and the y-axis shows the percentage of incidents resolved within a given timeframe. Employ a scale from 0% to 100% on the y-axis and a consistent time unit on the x-axis. Implement a threshold line indicating the desired resolution rate and use color coding to distinguish between above and below-threshold performance.

Insights and Actions: A low-Security Incident Resolution Rate signals that incident resolution processes may need enhancement. It is essential to delve into the underlying reasons – is it due to insufficient resources, skills, or inefficient processes? A high-resolution rate indicates effective incident handling, but ensuring that resolution quality is not sacrificed for speed is essential. Constant training, comprehensive documentation, and regular drills can enhance incident resolution capabilities. Additionally, post-incident reviews should be conducted to gather lessons and continuously improve the incident resolution process. Monitoring this KPI alongside the MTTR can provide a comprehensive view of incident response capabilities.

KPI Title: Patch Compliance

KPI Objective: Patch Compliance is pivotal in maintaining the security of systems and applications. This KPI measures the percentage of systems and software applications installed with the latest security patches. Ensuring high patch compliance rates is essential for safeguarding against known vulnerabilities and threats, thereby protecting organizational assets and information.

Metric Summary: Patch Compliance plays a significant role in an organization's vulnerability management program. As vulnerabilities are discovered, vendors release patches to address these security gaps. However, merely releasing a patch does not secure an environment; the patch must be applied. This KPI measures how effectively an organization keeps its systems and software applications updated with the latest security patches. By maintaining high patch compliance, an organization reduces the attack surface available to malicious actors. Moreover, patch compliance is often a requirement in regulatory compliance frameworks and is a hallmark of a mature cybersecurity program. Keeping track of patch compliance across different systems and software can help prioritize patching efforts and allocate resources efficiently.

Possible Measurement Formula: Patch Compliance (%) = (number of systems with the latest security patches installed/total number of systems) × 100.

Suggested Frequency: Monthly.

Quantifiable Measure: Expressed as a percentage representing the proportion of systems patched.

Benchmark or Target Measure: Close to 100%, though this might vary based on the criticality of systems and organizational risk tolerance.

Timeframe: Typically measured monthly.

Data Source: Patch management systems, vulnerability scanning tools, inventory management systems.

Visualization Recommendation: For Patch Compliance, a line graph is recommended. The x-axis should represent time, and the y-axis should display the patched percentage of systems and applications. A 0%–100% scale on the y-axis is ideal. Utilize a horizontal line to mark the desired compliance rate and color-code data points below this threshold to emphasize areas requiring attention.

Insights and Actions: High patch compliance indicates that the organization is vigilant in protecting against known vulnerabilities. However, it is important to recognize that 100% compliance at all times may not be realistic due to various factors such as compatibility issues or patch stability. Low patch compliance necessitates immediate attention. Are there bottlenecks in the patch management process? Are certain systems consistently noncompliant? Addressing these issues can help improve compliance. Automating patch management, where feasible, can also increase compliance rates. Focusing on quantity and quality is important – ensuring that the most critical patches are applied first. Regular communication between the security team and other IT and business units is crucial to understand dependencies and ensure that patching does not disrupt business processes.

KPI Title: Phishing Click Rate

KPI Objective: The Phishing Click Rate KPI measures the percentage of employees who fall for phishing attempts, typically through email links. This KPI is crucial for assessing the effectiveness of cybersecurity awareness training and understanding the organization's susceptibility to social engineering attacks. A lower Phishing Click Rate indicates a more cyber-aware workforce that is vigilant in recognizing and avoiding phishing scams.

Metric Summary: Phishing attacks are among the most prevalent cybersecurity threats, often as the initial entry point for more extensive security incidents. The Phishing Click Rate KPI helps organizations understand the extent to which their employees can recognize and avoid these scams. This KPI is not just a measure of employee behavior; it reflects training effectiveness and the organization's security culture. Monitoring this KPI can help identify departments or groups that might be more susceptible and need targeted training. It also provides insights into the types of phishing attacks that are more likely to succeed, which can guide training content and technical controls. Organizations must create an environment where employees feel comfortable reporting potential phishing attempts, contributing to more accurate data for this KPI.

Possible Measurement Formula: Phishing Click Rate (%) = (number of phishing emails clicked/total number of phishing emails sent) × 100.

Suggested Frequency: Quarterly.

Quantifiable Measure: Expressed as a percentage representing the proportion of phishing emails clicked.

Benchmark or Target Measure: The target should be as low as possible, indicating high employee awareness.

Timeframe: This KPI is generally measured quarterly, following phishing simulation exercises.

Data Source: Phishing simulation tools, security awareness training platforms, incident reports.

Visualization Recommendation: A line graph effectively visualizes the Phishing Click Rate, with time on the x-axis and the percentage of phishing clicks on the y-axis. Set the y-axis scale between 0% and an upper limit representing the worst-case scenario, and add a horizontal threshold line to signify the acceptable click rate. Employ color coding for points above the threshold as a warning for periods requiring additional training or measures.

Insights and Actions: A decreasing Phishing Click Rate over time can indicate that security awareness training is effective and that employees are more adept at recognizing phishing attempts. Conversely, an increasing or high click rate indicates a need for action. In such cases, analyzing which types of phishing emails are being clicked on is essential as tailoring the training content accordingly. Engaging, regular, and diverse training content can be more effective. Encouraging and incentivizing reporting of phishing attempts can also be beneficial. From a technical perspective, ensuring that email security controls are configured to minimize the number of phishing emails that reach the users in the first place is crucial.

KPI Title: User Awareness Training Completion Rate

KPI Objective: The User Awareness Training Completion Rate KPI measures the percentage of employees who complete cybersecurity awareness training within a given period. This KPI is essential for ensuring the workforce is educated and aware of cybersecurity best practices, threats, and the importance of adhering to the organization's security policies. A well-informed workforce acts as a strong line of defense against cyber threats.

Metric Summary: Human error is often considered the weakest link in cybersecurity. User Awareness Training is a fundamental element in mitigating this risk. The User Awareness Training Completion Rate KPI measures how effectively an organization educates its workforce. It is not just a measure of compliance with training requirements; it is an indicator of the organization's commitment to cybersecurity culture. An assessment of the quality and effectiveness of the training should accompany high completion rates. Different roles may require different types of training, and ensuring that the training is relevant and engaging is crucial. Moreover, regular training that keeps pace with the evolving threat landscape is important. This KPI can also be broken down by department or role to identify areas needing additional focus.

Possible Measurement Formula: User Awareness Training Completion Rate (%) = (number of employees who completed the training/total number of employees required to take the training) × 100.

Suggested Frequency: Annually or after each training cycle.

Quantifiable Measure: Expressed as a percentage representing the proportion of employees completing the cybersecurity awareness training.

Benchmark or Target Measure: The target should be close to 100% completion.

Timeframe: Typically measured annually or after each training cycle.

Data Source: Learning management systems, HR records, training completion records.

Visualization Recommendation: Utilize a line graph to represent the User Awareness Training Completion Rate, with time on the x-axis and completion rate percentage on the y-axis. The y-axis should have a 0%–100% scale. Implement a horizontal threshold line that represents the desired completion rate, and use colors to differentiate between periods when the rate is above or below this threshold.

Insights and Actions: High completion rates are desirable, but it is equally important to evaluate the effectiveness of the training. Are employees retaining and applying the knowledge? Are there particular groups with lower completion rates that need targeted interventions? Feedback from employees on the training content and delivery can be invaluable in enhancing effectiveness. If completion rates are low, exploring different training formats or creating incentives for completion might be worthwhile. Additionally, integrating cybersecurity awareness into the broader organizational culture, beyond formal training, can help ingrain good cybersecurity habits in daily workflows.

KPI Title: Firewall Rule Compliance

KPI Objective: Firewall Rule Compliance assesses the percentage of firewall rules that comply with defined security policies. A robust firewall configuration is critical for protecting networks from unauthorized access and potential threats. This KPI ensures that firewalls are effectively configured according to organizational security standards, reducing the risk of breaches and unauthorized data transmission.

Metric Summary: Firewalls act as critical security controls, preventing unauthorized access to and from a network. The Firewall Rule Compliance KPI evaluates whether an organization's firewall rules adhere to the established security policies. Properly configured firewalls are crucial for safeguarding sensitive data and services. Over time, as the network evolves, firewall rules can become outdated or conflicting, potentially leading to security risks. Regularly assessing and updating firewall rules to ensure they align with the current network structure and security policies is essential. This KPI helps identify areas where firewall rules may need adjustment or optimization and ensures firewalls effectively fulfill their role in the security posture.

Possible Measurement Formula: Firewall Rule Compliance (%) = (number of firewall rules compliant with security policies/total number of firewall rules) × 100.

Suggested Frequency: Quarterly.

Quantifiable Measure: Expressed as a percentage representing the proportion of firewall rules in compliance with security policies.

Benchmark or Target Measure: The target should be close to 100% compliance.

Timeframe: Typically measured quarterly.

Data Source: Firewall management systems, security policy documentation, configuration audits.

Visualization Recommendation: A line graph is suitable for visualizing Firewall Rule Compliance. Have time on the x-axis and compliance percentage on the y-axis, which should be scaled from 0 to 100%. Add a horizontal threshold line representing the target compliance rate, and use color coding to indicate when compliance falls below this desired level.

Insights and Actions: Achieving high Firewall Rule Compliance is indicative of a well-maintained and secured network perimeter. However, it is important to continuously monitor this KPI as network changes and evolving threats can necessitate rule updates. A lower compliance percentage requires immediate attention to identify and rectify noncompliant rules. Regular firewall rule reviews, preferably automated, can help maintain high compliance. It is also important to document the purpose and necessity of each rule and remove or update any obsolete or overly permissive rules. Collaboration between network and security teams is critical to ensure firewall configurations support business needs and security requirements.

KPI Title: Intrusion Detection System (IDS) Alerts

KPI Objective: The Intrusion Detection System (IDS) Alerts KPI measures the number of alerts generated by the IDS within a specified period. This KPI is crucial for monitoring potential security incidents and gauging the effectiveness of IDS configurations. Timely response to legitimate IDS alerts can prevent breaches and mitigate damage.

Metric Summary: An IDS monitors network traffic for suspicious activity or policy violations and generates alerts. The IDS Alerts KPI is an indicator of the quantity of these alerts. A sudden alert increase could indicate an ongoing attack, while consistently high numbers might suggest configuration issues or an overly permissive network. It is important to focus not only on the number of alerts but also on their quality and relevance. Frequent false positives can lead to alert fatigue and the risk of overlooking critical alerts. Regularly tuning IDS configurations to reduce false positives and ensure that the system effectively identifies genuine threats is essential. This KPI should be analyzed with other data sources for effective incident response.

Possible Measurement Formula: Number of IDS Alerts = total number of alerts generated by the IDS in a specified period.

Suggested Frequency: Weekly or Daily.

Quantifiable Measure: Expressed as a raw number representing the total alerts generated.

Benchmark or Target Measure: There is no fixed benchmark, as this can vary based on network size, traffic, and threat landscape.

Timeframe: Typically measured weekly or daily.

Data Source: IDS logs.

Visualization Recommendation: Use a bar graph for IDS Alerts, with the x-axis indicating time and the y-axis showing the number of alerts. There should be no predefined limits to allow natural fluctuations. Use color coding to represent different types of alerts, and add a horizontal threshold line to indicate when the number of alerts exceeds a level that requires attention.

Insights and Actions: The number of IDS alerts should be monitored continuously, and any sudden spikes or unusual patterns should be investigated. It is equally important to gauge the quality of alerts; frequent false positives can cause desensitization to alerts and potentially lead to overlooking genuine threats. Regularly tuning IDS configurations to align with the evolving threat landscape and reduce false positives is critical. Additionally, integrating IDS data with other security tools and conducting periodic threat-hunting exercises can help proactively identify and mitigate threats.

KPI Title: Malware Detection Rate

KPI Objective: The Malware Detection Rate KPI measures the rate at which malware is detected and mitigated within an organization's network. Malware poses significant risks, including data breaches, system damage, and ransom demands. This KPI is vital in evaluating the effectiveness of anti-malware solutions and ensuring timely detection and response to malware infections.

Metric Summary: Malware, which encompasses viruses, worms, ransomware, and other malicious software, continues to be a prevalent cyber threat. The Malware Detection Rate KPI helps organizations understand how effectively they identify and deal with malware. Not only is the speed of detection critical, but the rate at which detected malware is subsequently mitigated or removed is equally important. By monitoring the Malware Detection Rate, an organization can assess the effectiveness of its security controls and be agile in addressing any malware that manages to penetrate its defenses. Regularly updating anti-malware solutions, employing multilayered security controls, and promptly patching systems are important components of an effective malware defense strategy.

Possible Measurement Formula: Malware Detection Rate = number of malware instances detected and mitigated/time period.

Suggested Frequency: Weekly.

Quantifiable Measure: Expressed as a rate showing the number of malware instances detected and mitigated over a specified time period.

Benchmark or Target Measure: Specific benchmarks may vary, but an increasing detection rate over time may indicate improving security controls or a rising threat level.

Timeframe: Typically measured weekly.

Data Source: Anti-malware solutions, security incident and event management (*SIEM*) systems, and incident response records.

Visualization Recommendation: For Malware Detection Rate, use a line graph where the x-axis represents time and the y-axis shows the Malware Detection Rate. Utilize a linear scale and no preset limits on the y-axis. Implement a horizontal threshold line to represent the acceptable rate and employ colors to signify periods when the rate exceeds this threshold, requiring further investigation.

Insights and Actions: An increasing Malware Detection Rate could indicate increased attacks or improved detection capabilities. Conversely, a decreasing rate might suggest that preventative measures are successful or that detection capabilities are waning. Understanding the context is crucial. Organizations should consistently review and update their anti-malware solutions and configurations. Employing a multilayered defense, user education, and network segmentation can further bolster defenses. Additionally, integrating threat intelligence and ensuring efficient incident response processes can enhance an organization's ability to react rapidly to evolving malware threats.

KPI Title: Data Loss Prevention (DLP) Policy Violations

KPI Objective: The Data Loss Prevention (*DLP*) Policy Violations KPI quantifies the number of incidents where sensitive data is mishandled or leaked, violating established DLP policies. Ensuring the confidentiality and integrity of sensitive data is crucial for any organization. This KPI is essential in monitoring and mitigating data loss or leakage risks.

Metric Summary: DLP policies are essential for safeguarding sensitive information such as personally identifiable information (*PII*), intellectual property, or financial data. The DLP Policy Violations KPI tracks the effectiveness of these policies by monitoring instances where sensitive data is improperly handled, whether through inadvertent mistakes or malicious intent. It helps organizations identify potential vulnerabilities and take corrective actions to prevent data exfiltration. Analyzing trends and patterns in DLP policy violations can also help refine policies and controls. Training and awareness among employees, especially regarding handling sensitive data, are critical in reducing DLP policy violations.

Possible Measurement Formula: DLP Policy Violations = number of incidents violating DLP policies within a specified period.

Suggested Frequency: Monthly.

Quantifiable Measure: The raw number represents the total incidents violating DLP policies.

Benchmark or Target Measure: Aim for a downward violation trend over time.

Timeframe: Typically measured monthly.

Data Source: DLP solutions, incident records, and network monitoring tools.

Visualization Recommendation: Visualize DLP Policy Violations using a bar graph, with time on the x-axis and the number of violations on the y-axis. Employ a consistent scale on the y-axis and incorporate a horizontal threshold line. Utilize color coding for different types of violations or when violations exceed a certain number, aiding in quickly identifying areas of concern.

Insights and Actions: DLP policy violations can indicate process weaknesses, insufficient training, or malicious actions. Analyzing the nature and source of violations is essential for determining corrective measures. Regular employee training, especially for those handling sensitive data, is crucial. Additionally, DLP policies and tools should be regularly reviewed and adjusted to align with changes in the data environment and threat landscape. In cases where violations are due to malicious actions, appropriate disciplinary measures and potentially legal action may be required. Integrating DLP tools with other security systems for a comprehensive security posture is also beneficial.

KPI Title: Security Audit Findings

KPI Objective: The Security Audit Findings KPI measures the number of findings or noncompliance issues identified during security audits. Regular security audits are crucial for evaluating an organization's security posture and ensuring compliance with internal policies and external regulations. This KPI helps organizations identify vulnerabilities and areas for improvement in their security controls.

Metric Summary: Security audits systematically evaluate an organization's security policies, procedures, and controls. They are vital in identifying vulnerabilities, noncompliance, and potential security risks. The Security Audit Findings KPI aggregates the issues identified during these audits. These findings can range from minor policy violations to critical vulnerabilities. Analyzing and addressing audit findings is essential for maintaining a strong security posture and ensuring compliance with regulatory requirements. Beyond merely tracking the number of findings, categorizing them by severity and area of impact can provide better insights into the organization's security state.

Possible Measurement Formula: Security Audit Findings = total number of findings identified in security audits within a specified period.

Suggested Frequency: Annually or after each audit cycle.

Quantifiable Measure: Expressed as a raw number representing the total findings identified.

Benchmark or Target Measure: Aim for a downward trend in critical findings.

Timeframe: Typically measured annually or after each audit cycle.

Data Source: Security audit reports, compliance management systems.

Visualization Recommendation: For Security Audit Findings, use a stacked bar graph with time on the x-axis and the number of findings on the y-axis. This depicts the total number of findings and their breakdown by categories such as severity or type. Employ a consistent scale on the y-axis, and use colors to differentiate between various categories of audit findings.

Insights and Actions: Regularly conducting security audits and diligently addressing the findings are crucial for an organization's cybersecurity health. Pay special attention to critical findings that pose immediate risks. Create an action plan for resolving findings and assign responsibilities and timelines. Collaboration between different departments is often necessary to address audit findings. Monitor the progress and ensure that improvements are made. Additionally, use the findings as a learning opportunity to improve future security policies and practices and consider engaging external experts for an unbiased perspective.

KPI Title: Compliance with Regulatory Requirements

KPI Objective: The Compliance with Regulatory Requirements KPI measures the extent to which the organization complies with relevant cybersecurity regulations. Noncompliance can result in legal penalties, loss of customer trust, and reputational damage. This KPI is vital for avoiding these consequences and ensuring the organization fulfills its legal and ethical obligations regarding cybersecurity.

Metric Summary: Regulatory compliance is an important aspect of cybersecurity, particularly for organizations that handle sensitive financial or personal data. Numerous cybersecurity regulations, such as GDPR, HIPAA, or PCI-DSS, and noncompliance can have severe consequences. This KPI tracks the organization's adherence to these regulations. Regularly assessing compliance and addressing any gaps is critical. This KPI should consider not only compliance status but also the severity and potential impact of any noncompliance.

Possible Measurement Formula: Compliance Level (%) = (number of ful-filled regulatory requirements/total number of applicable regulatory requirements) × 100.

Suggested Frequency: Annually or as required by specific regulations.

Quantifiable Measure: Expressed as a percentage representing the proportion of regulatory requirements met.

Benchmark or Target Measure: Aim for 100% compliance.

Timeframe: Typically measured annually or as required by specific regulations.

Data Source: Compliance assessment reports, regulatory bodies' feedback, and legal department records.

Visualization Recommendation: A gauge chart is ideal for visualizing Compliance with Regulatory Requirements. This chart type provides an at-a-glance view of the organization's proximity to full compliance. Divide the gauge into segments representing ranges of compliance levels, such as red for low, yellow for medium, and green for high. Add markers to indicate specific regulatory thresholds.

Insights and Actions: Achieving and maintaining regulatory compliance should be a priority. Regularly review the regulations applicable to your industry and jurisdiction, and ensure that your policies, processes, and controls align with these requirements. Address any compliance gaps as soon as they are identified. Consider engaging legal counsel or compliance experts for advice on complex regulatory matters. Employee training and awareness programs related to compliance obligations are also important. Keep documentation of your compliance efforts as evidence in case of audits or investigations by regulatory bodies.

KPI Title: Mean Time to Patch (MTTP)

KPI Objective: The Mean Time to Patch ($MTTP$) KPI measures the average time taken to apply security patches after their release. Timely patching is essential for protecting systems against known vulnerabilities. This KPI helps in evaluating the organization's Patch Management Efficiency and effectiveness.

Metric Summary: Patching is one of the most effective ways to secure systems against known vulnerabilities. The MTTP KPI tracks how quickly an organization can apply security patches once available. A shorter MTTP reduces the window of opportunity for attackers to exploit known vulnerabilities, whereas a longer MTTP indicates a higher risk. Effective patch management requires a balance between speed and caution, as hastily applied patches can sometimes cause system issues.

Possible Measurement Formula: MTTP = sum of (patch application date − patch release date) for all patches/total number of patches applied.

Suggested Frequency: Monthly.

Quantifiable Measure: Expressed in days or hours represents the average time to apply patches.

Benchmark or Target Measure: Industry benchmarks can vary; aim for a downward trend in MTTP.

Timeframe: Typically measured monthly.

Data Source: Patch management systems, vulnerability management systems, vendor patch release notes.

Visualization Recommendation: Use a line graph to visualize MTTP, with time on the x-axis and the average time to patch on the y-axis. Employ a consistent scale for the y-axis in hours or days. Introduce a horizontal threshold line to indicate desired patching times and use colors to highlight instances when MTTP exceeds this threshold, signaling the need for more efficient patch management.

Insights and Actions: A shorter MTTP is generally better, but it is important to ensure that patches are tested for compatibility issues before being widely deployed. Develop a systematic patch management process, including rapidly assessing patches' criticality. For critical patches, consider implementing an expedited process. Regularly review and improve your patch management procedures, and ensure that you have a rollback plan in case a patch causes issues. Additionally, maintaining an up-to-date inventory of systems and software can make the patch management process more efficient.

KPI Title: Percentage of Systems with Updated Antivirus Software

KPI Objective: This KPI measures the percentage of systems with up-to-date antivirus software. Antivirus software is a fundamental security control for defending against malware. Keeping antivirus software updated is crucial for ensuring its effectiveness.

Metric Summary: Antivirus software protects systems from malware by using signatures and heuristics. However, its effectiveness depends on having the latest signatures to detect new threats. This KPI tracks the percentage of systems with up-to-date antivirus software, providing insight into the organization's basic security hygiene. A high percentage indicates that the organization maintains fundamental security controls, whereas a low percentage suggests a heightened risk from malware and other threats.

Possible Measurement Formula: Percentage of Systems with Updated Antivirus Software (%) = (number of systems with updated antivirus software/ total number of systems) × 100.

Suggested Frequency: Monthly.

Quantifiable Measure: Expressed as a percentage representing the proportion of systems with updated antivirus software.

Benchmark or Target Measure: Aim for close to 100%.

Timeframe: Typically measured monthly.

Data Source: Antivirus management systems, system inventory records.

Visualization Recommendation: For this KPI, a line graph is appropriate, with the x-axis depicting time and the y-axis showing the percentage of systems with updated antivirus software. The y-axis should be scaled from 0% to 100%. A threshold line can represent the target percentage, and color coding can highlight periods when the percentage falls below the threshold.

Insights and Actions: Maintaining updated antivirus software is a fundamental security practice. If this KPI is below target, investigate the reasons and take corrective action. This may include automating antivirus updates, implementing policies for regular updates, and educating users on the importance of updates. Monitor the status of antivirus software across the organization, especially on critical systems, and establish alerts for systems that are not up-to-date. Also, review and ensure that the antivirus software configurations are optimized for maximum effectiveness without causing operational disruptions.

KPI Title: Ransomware Attacks

KPI Objective: The Ransomware Attacks KPI measures the number of ransomware attacks detected and prevented by the organization. Ransomware attacks, where malicious software encrypts an organization's data and demands payment for its release, threaten business continuity and data integrity. Actively monitoring and defending against ransomware attacks is crucial.

Metric Summary: Ransomware attacks are increasingly prevalent and can devastate organizations, including financial loss, reputational damage, and operational disruption. This KPI measures the number of ransomware attacks that have been detected, whether successful or thwarted. By tracking this KPI, organizations can gauge the frequency and severity of ransomware threats and assess the effectiveness of preventive measures. Counting attacks and analyzing the attack vectors, payloads, and targeted assets are essential to develop better defenses.

Possible Measurement Formula: Ransomware Attacks = total ransomware attacks detected within a specified period.

Suggested Frequency: Monthly.

Quantifiable Measure: The raw number represents the total ransomware attacks detected.

Benchmark or Target Measure: Aim for a downward trend or maintenance of low numbers.

Timeframe: Typically measured monthly.

Data Source: Incident response records, SIEM systems.

Visualization Recommendation: Visualize Ransomware Attacks using a bar graph, where the x-axis represents time and the y-axis displays the number of attacks. No predefined limits should be set, allowing natural fluctuations to be visible. Differentiate the types of ransomware attacks using color coding and add a threshold line to indicate the level at which an in-depth review is required.

Insights and Actions: Monitoring the number of ransomware attacks is essential, but taking proactive measures to prevent them is equally important. Regularly back up critical data, educate users on the dangers of phishing emails and keep systems and antivirus software updated. When an attack is detected, analyze how it occurred and use this information to improve defenses. Engage with cybersecurity communities and threat intelligence sources to stay informed on the latest ransomware threats and best practices for defense.

KPI Title: Third-Party Vendor Security Assessments

KPI Objective: The Third-Party Vendor Security Assessments KPI measures the number of security assessments conducted on third-party vendors.

Organizations often rely on third-party vendors, which can introduce security risks if these vendors do not have adequate security measures. Regular assessments are necessary for managing this risk.

Metric Summary: Third-party vendors can be a weak link in an organization's security posture. The Third-Party Vendor Security Assessments KPI tracks the number of security assessments conducted on these vendors. Regular assessments ensure vendors adhere to the organization's security standards and take appropriate measures to protect any data they handle. These assessments can be in the form of questionnaires, interviews, documentation reviews, or onsite audits.

Possible Measurement Formula: Third-Party Vendor Security Assessments = total number of security assessments conducted on third-party vendors within a specified period.

Suggested Frequency: Annually.

Quantifiable Measure: The raw number represents the total number of third-party vendor security assessments conducted.

Benchmark or Target Measure: This varies depending on the number of vendors and the criticality of their services.

Timeframe: Typically measured annually.

Data Source: Vendor management systems, security assessment records.

Visualization Recommendation: A bar graph is recommended for Third-Party Vendor Security Assessments. The x-axis should represent time, and the y-axis should represent the number of assessments conducted. Use color coding to differentiate between types of assessments or vendors and implement a threshold line if there is a target number of assessments to be conducted within a certain period.

Insights and Actions: Conducting third-party vendor security assessments is essential for managing the risks associated with outsourcing and partnerships. Develop a structured process for these assessments, including criteria for evaluating vendor security practices. Prioritize assessments based on the criticality of the vendor's services and the sensitivity of the data they handle. If a vendor does not meet the organization's security standards, work with them to address the gaps or consider finding an alternative vendor. Engage legal counsel to ensure that security requirements are stipulated in vendor contracts.

KPI Title: Security Incident Response Plan (IRP) Testing

KPI Objective: The Security Incident Response Plan (*IRP*) Testing KPI measures the frequency of testing the effectiveness of the IRP through simulations and drills. A well-prepared IRP is essential for an organization's ability to respond effectively to security incidents. Regular testing and refinement of this plan are crucial.

Metric Summary: An IRP is a structured approach for handling and managing the aftermath of a security breach or cyberattack. The Security IRP Testing KPI monitors how often the organization tests its IRP. Regular testing through simulations and drills is critical for evaluating and improving the IRP's effectiveness, ensuring that personnel are familiar with their roles during an incident, and identifying areas for improvement.

Possible Measurement Formula: Security IRP Testing = number of IRP tests conducted within a specified period.

Suggested Frequency: Semiannually or annually.

Quantifiable Measure: Expressed as a raw number representing the total number of IRP tests conducted.

Benchmark or Target Measure: At least semiannually, but may vary based on organizational risk profile.

Timeframe: Typically measured semiannually or annually.

Data Source: Incident response records, training, and exercise logs.

Visualization Recommendation: A bar graph is suitable for this KPI, with the x-axis representing time and the y-axis depicting the number of IRP tests performed. Color coding can indicate the success or failure of these tests, while a horizontal threshold line can represent the minimum number of tests that should be performed within a specific timeframe.

Insights and Actions: Testing the IRP is critical for ensuring that it is effective and that the organization is prepared for security incidents. Schedule regular tests, such as tabletop exercises or full simulations, and ensure they are realistic and challenging. After each test, conduct a thorough debrief to identify what went well and what did not. Use this feedback to refine the IRP and address any identified gaps. Training and awareness for staff involved in incident response are also crucial, as is ensuring that the IRP is aligned with industry best practices and regulatory requirements.

KPI Title: Employee Security Training Effectiveness

KPI Objective: The Employee Security Training Effectiveness KPI gauges the improvement in employees' knowledge and understanding of cybersecurity best practices after completing security training. It is crucial to ensure the completion and efficacy of the security training programs, as employees often act as the first line of defense against cyber threats.

Metric Summary: Employee Security Training Effectiveness goes beyond merely checking if employees have completed training. It assesses whether the training has improved employees' knowledge and understanding of cybersecurity. Pre- and post-training assessments, feedback surveys, and practical exercises can measure this. Evaluating the quality and effectiveness of training content and delivery methods is important. An effective training program should be engaging and relevant and empower employees to recognize and respond to security threats.

Possible Measurement Formula: Employee Security Training Effectiveness (%) = ((average post-training assessment score − average pre-training assessment score)/average pre-training assessment score) × 100.

Suggested Frequency: Annually or after each training cycle.

Quantifiable Measure: Expressed as a percentage representing employee knowledge improvement after the training.

Benchmark or Target Measure: Positive percentage indicating improvement; specific targets may vary.

Timeframe: Typically measured annually or after each training cycle.

Data Source: Training assessments and employee feedback surveys.

Visualization Recommendation: For Employee Security Training Effectiveness, a radar chart is recommended, as it can simultaneously display multiple metrics that contribute to effectiveness, such as knowledge retention, practical skills, and attitude changes. Use axes to represent these categories and plot values for different training sessions, using color to distinguish between different periods or groups.

Insights and Actions: Measuring Employee Security Training Effectiveness helps ensure that training investments deliver value. If the effectiveness is lower than desired, consider revamping the training content, employing more engaging delivery methods, or targeting training more specifically to roles and responsibilities. Employee feedback is invaluable for understanding which aspects of the training work and which are not. Additionally, staying abreast of evolving threats and updating training material is crucial to ensure relevance. The ultimate goal is to foster a culture of security where employees are vigilant and proactive in protecting organizational assets and data.

KPI Title: Critical Asset Identification

KPI Objective: The Critical Asset Identification KPI measures the percentage of critical assets identified and prioritized for protection within an organization. Identifying and prioritizing critical assets is fundamental to effective cybersecurity, enabling organizations to focus their security resources where they are needed most.

Metric Summary: Critical Asset Identification is a cornerstone of risk management and involves identifying and categorizing assets based on their importance to the organization's mission and operations. This KPI measures how effectively an organization has identified and cataloged critical assets, such as sensitive data, key systems, and vital infrastructure. This process should be thorough and systematic, forming the foundation for subsequent risk assessments, protective measures, and incident response planning. Understanding what is critical helps make informed decisions about allocating security resources and efforts.

Possible Measurement Formula: Critical Asset Identification (%) = (number of critical assets identified/total number of assets) × 100.

Suggested Frequency: Annually.

Quantifiable Measure: Expressed as a percentage representing the proportion of critical assets identified.

Benchmark or Target Measure: Aim for 100% identification of critical assets.

Timeframe: Typically measured annually.

Data Source: Asset inventories, risk assessments.

Visualization Recommendation: Use a line graph for Critical Asset Identification, with time on the x-axis and the percentage of critical assets identified on the y-axis. Scale the y-axis from 0% to 100% and implement a threshold line representing the desired identification rate. Utilize color coding to distinguish between periods when identification is above or below the desired level.

Insights and Actions: Identifying critical assets is an essential first step but must be coupled with ongoing management and protection efforts. Regularly review and update the inventory of critical assets, especially during changes in the organizational environment or technology stack. Engage different departments to ensure that all perspectives are considered in determining the criticality of assets. After identification, conduct risk assessments for these critical assets and implement appropriate security controls. Align critical asset protection with business objectives to ensure security efforts contribute positively to the organization's mission and goals.

KPI Title: Incident Containment Time

KPI Objective: The Incident Containment Time KPI measures the average time to contain a security incident after it has been detected. Rapid containment is essential to minimize the impact of security incidents on the organization.

Metric Summary: Incident Containment Time is a critical metric for evaluating the responsiveness and effectiveness of an organization's incident response capability. Once a security incident is detected, it is imperative to contain it quickly to prevent further damage or data loss. This KPI tracks the average time taken to achieve containment after detection. Organizations must have clear procedures and skilled personnel in place for this phase of incident response, as rapid containment can significantly mitigate the consequences of security incidents.

Possible Measurement Formula: Incident Containment Time (average in hours) = total hours taken to contain incidents/number of incidents contained.

Suggested Frequency: Monthly.

Quantifiable Measure: Expressed in hours representing the average time taken to contain security incidents.

Benchmark or Target Measure: Aim for the shortest time possible; industry benchmarks can provide context.

Timeframe: Typically measured monthly.

Data Source: Incident response records, SIEM systems.

Visualization Recommendation: A line graph effectively visualizes Incident Containment Time, with time on the x-axis and average containment time on the y-axis. Use a consistent scale, such as hours or days, and implement a threshold line for target containment times. Utilize color to highlight periods when containment times exceed this threshold.

Insights and Actions: Shortening Incident Containment Time is vital for minimizing the impact of security incidents. Develop, practice, and refine incident response procedures to ensure the organization can act swiftly and decisively when an incident occurs. Regular training and tabletop exercises can help prepare staff for real-world incidents. Automate containment procedures where possible and ensure clear communication channels during incidents. Analyze past incidents to identify any bottlenecks or delays in containment and address these issues proactively. It is also valuable to benchmark your organization's containment times against industry standards to understand if you are performing at an acceptable level. Collaboration with external partners, such as cybersecurity firms and law enforcement, can also enhance containment capabilities.

KPI Title: Encryption Adoption Rate

KPI Objective: The Encryption Adoption Rate KPI tracks the percentage of encrypted sensitive data in storage and during transmission. Encryption is a fundamental security control that protects the confidentiality and integrity of data, reducing the risk of unauthorized disclosure or alteration.

Metric Summary: Encryption is essential in safeguarding sensitive information from unauthorized access and protecting it during network transmission. The Encryption Adoption Rate measures how much of the organization's sensitive data is encrypted. For robust security, it is crucial that encryption is applied both to data at rest (e.g., stored on hard drives) and data in transit (e.g., being transferred over the internet). The goal is to ensure that even if data is accessed unauthorizedly, it cannot be easily read or altered without the encryption keys.

Possible Measurement Formula: Encryption Adoption Rate (%) = (amount of sensitive data encrypted/total amount of sensitive data) × 100.

Suggested Frequency: Quarterly.

Quantifiable Measure: Expressed as a percentage representing the proportion of encrypted sensitive data.

Benchmark or Target Measure: Aim for 100%, meaning all sensitive data is encrypted.

Timeframe: Typically measured quarterly.

Data Source: Data management systems, encryption solutions, IT asset inventories.

Visualization Recommendation: For Encryption Adoption Rate, use a line graph, with time on the x-axis and adoption rate percentage on the y-axis, scaled from 0% to 100%. Include a threshold line to represent the target adoption rate and use color coding to indicate when the adoption rate falls below this threshold.

Insights and Actions: An Encryption Adoption Rate close to 100% is ideal, as encryption is a fundamental layer of protection for sensitive data. Ensure encryption standards and solutions are current and widely recognized for their strength. It is also important to securely manage encryption keys and regularly review who has access to them. Engage IT and business units to understand the data types that should be classified as sensitive. Educate employees on the importance of encryption and provide them with tools and guidance on encrypting data. When lower-than-expected Encryption Adoption Rates are observed, investigate and address any technical or organizational barriers to encryption adoption.

KPI Title: Security Control Effectiveness

KPI Objective: Security Control Effectiveness measures the performance of security controls in preventing, detecting, and responding to security incidents. It aims to evaluate whether the deployed security measures effectively mitigate risks and protect organizational assets.

Metric Summary: Security controls are the mechanisms and processes to protect data and systems' confidentiality, integrity, and availability. These controls may include firewalls, antivirus software, IDSs, etc. The Security Control Effectiveness KPI is essential in understanding how well these controls perform in real-world scenarios. By evaluating control effectiveness, organizations can ensure they get the desired security outcomes from their investments and make data-driven decisions on where improvements or changes are needed.

Possible Measurement Formula: Security Control Effectiveness can be measured using various methods such as incident reduction rate, fewer false positives/negatives, red teaming, and security testing.

Suggested Frequency: Quarterly.

Quantifiable Measure: This can be expressed in various formats, such as percentage reduction in incidents, depending on the chosen measurement method.

Benchmark or Target Measure: A higher effectiveness percentage or reduced incidents indicate better performance.

Timeframe: Typically measured quarterly.

Data Source: Security incident reports, control logs, and testing results.

Visualization Recommendation: Use a radar chart to visualize Security Control Effectiveness, where each axis represents a different security control, and the values depict their effectiveness levels. Use color coding for different periods or benchmark comparisons. This provides an overview of how effective various security controls are relative to each other.

Insights and Actions: Regularly assess security controls through testing, audits, and real-world performance data. Where controls are underperforming, investigate the causes – it may be due to misconfiguration, lack of staff training, or the control being unsuited to the current threat environment. Ensure the security team is informed and trained on the latest security control technologies and practices. Continually evolve and adapt controls in response to new threats and business requirements. Collaboration between cybersecurity, IT, and business teams is essential for ensuring that controls are aligned with organizational objectives and risk tolerance.

KPI Title: Security Assessment Coverage

KPI Objective: The Security Assessment Coverage KPI measures the percentage of systems, applications, and networks assessed for security vulnerabilities. Regular security assessments are crucial for identifying and remediating vulnerabilities before they can be exploited.

Metric Summary: Security assessments are critical in identifying system, application, and network vulnerabilities. These assessments can include automated vulnerability scanning, penetration testing, and security audits. The Security Assessment Coverage KPI tracks how much of the organization's technology environment is being assessed. Security assessments must be comprehensive and cover the full breadth of the organization's technology stack, as vulnerabilities in any component can potentially be exploited to compromise systems and data.

Possible Measurement Formula: Security Assessment Coverage (%) = (number of systems/applications/networks assessed/total number of systems/applications/networks) × 100.

Suggested Frequency: Quarterly.

Quantifiable Measure: Expressed as a percentage representing the proportion of the environment assessed.

Benchmark or Target Measure: Aim for 100% coverage.

Timeframe: Typically measured quarterly.

Data Source: Security assessment reports, IT asset inventories.

Visualization Recommendation: Use a line graph for Security Assessment Coverage, where the x-axis represents time and the y-axis displays the percentage of systems assessed. The y-axis should have a 0%–100% scale. Include a horizontal threshold line to signify the desired coverage level, and employ color coding for values that are below this threshold.

Insights and Actions: A high-Security Assessment Coverage rate is essential for ensuring that the organization has visibility into the security posture of its technology environment. Regularly update and review the systems, applications, and networks inventory to ensure that new assets are included in security assessments. Create a schedule for security assessments that balances comprehensiveness with operational impact. When gaps in coverage are identified, work to understand why these areas have not been assessed and take steps to include them in future assessments. Ensure that results from security assessments are acted upon, and vulnerabilities are mitigated promptly. Establishing a collaborative environment among security, IT, and business teams is also important, ensuring that everyone understands the importance of security assessments and contributes to the process.

KPI Title: Mean Time Between Failures (MTBF)

KPI Objective: The Mean Time Between Failures (*MTBF*) KPI measures the average time between cybersecurity-related failures. This KPI is essential for understanding the reliability and resilience of the organization's cybersecurity infrastructure and helps predict and prevent future security incidents.

Metric Summary: MTBF is a critical KPI for analyzing the stability and reliability of cybersecurity systems. A failure is considered any event that causes a disruption or breach of security. By calculating the average time between these failures, organizations can better understand the resilience of their cybersecurity infrastructure. A longer MTBF indicates a more stable and reliable environment. This KPI is vital for understanding the current state and predicting when future failures might occur, allowing for preventative actions to be taken before a security incident occurs. It also aids resource allocation, ensuring proper investments are made in areas where frequent failures occur.

Possible Measurement Formula: MTBF (in hours) = (total operational time in hours – total downtime in hours)/number of failures.

Suggested Frequency: Monthly or Quarterly.

Quantifiable Measure: Typically measured in hours.

Benchmark or Target Measure: Higher is generally better, but the target can vary based on the nature of the systems and industry benchmarks.

Timeframe: Typically measured monthly or quarterly.

Data Source: Incident management systems, system logs, maintenance records.

Visualization Recommendation: Visualize MTBF with a line graph, where the x-axis shows time and the y-axis depicts the average time between failures. Employ a consistent scale on the y-axis in hours or days. A horizontal threshold line can represent the desired MTBF, with color coding used to signify periods below this threshold.

Insights and Actions: A longer MTBF indicates a more stable and reliable cybersecurity environment. Regularly analyze MTBF data to identify trends or patterns indicating underlying issues. Conduct root cause analyses for failures to understand their causes and implement corrective actions to prevent recurrence. Use MTBF data to make informed decisions about resource allocation, ensuring investments are targeted at areas that maximize reliability and security. Engage in proactive maintenance and continuous monitoring to further extend the MTBF and enhance the resilience of your cybersecurity infrastructure.

KPI Title: Security Incident Recovery Time

KPI Objective: The Security Incident Recovery Time KPI measures the average time to recover systems and operations after a security incident. This metric is vital for understanding the organization's ability to restore normalcy after a breach or attack.

Metric Summary: Security Incident Recovery Time is crucial in understanding the effectiveness of the organization's IRP and the ability to minimize the impact of security incidents. This KPI reflects the time required to rectify the immediate technical issues and ensure that operations can resume at full capacity. A lower Security Incident Recovery Time indicates a more effective and efficient incident response capability. By keeping this metric low, organizations can reduce the impact of security incidents on operations, reputation, and revenue. Understanding this KPI is essential for the continuous improvement of incident response strategies.

Possible Measurement Formula: Security Incident Recovery Time (in hours) = sum of (recovery completion time – incident detection time) for each incident/total number of incidents.

Suggested Frequency: Monthly or Quarterly.

Quantifiable Measure: Typically measured in hours.

Benchmark or Target Measure: Lower is better, but targets should be based on industry benchmarks and the systems' criticality.

Timeframe: Typically measured monthly or quarterly.

Data Source: Incident management systems, recovery logs, operational records.

Visualization Recommendation: Use a line graph to visualize Security Incident Recovery Time. The x-axis should represent time, and the y-axis should represent the average recovery time in hours or days. Implement a horizontal threshold line to indicate the target recovery time and use color coding to high-light instances exceeding this threshold.

Insights and Actions: A lower Security Incident Recovery Time indicates a strong incident response capability. Regularly review and test IRPs to ensure they are effective and up-to-date. Conduct post-incident reviews to identify areas for improvement in the incident response process. Ensure that communication lines are established for efficient coordination during recovery efforts. Develop relationships with third-party vendors, law enforcement, and other stakeholders that may be involved in the recovery process. Investing in automation and employee training can also significantly reduce Security Incident Recovery Time. This KPI should be a focal point in incident response exercises and simulations, with efforts to reduce recovery times through practice and optimization.

KPI Title: Password Strength and Complexity

KPI Objective: The Password Strength and Complexity KPI tracks the percentage of user accounts secured with strong and complex passwords. This is critical as passwords are often the first defense in protecting sensitive data and systems.

Metric Summary: Passwords are often the most direct form of security for user accounts and system access. The strength and complexity of these passwords are vital in protecting against unauthorized access. This KPI monitors the proportion of passwords within the organization that meet predefined criteria for strength and complexity (such as length, mix of characters, and avoidance of common words). A higher percentage indicates a more secure environment, but it is also important to ensure that policies regarding password complexity are balanced with usability.

Possible Measurement Formula: Password Strength and Complexity (%) = (number of user accounts with strong and complex passwords/total number of user accounts) × 100.

Suggested Frequency: Quarterly.

Quantifiable Measure: Expressed as a percentage.

Benchmark or Target Measure: Aim for a high percentage, close to 100%.

Timeframe: Typically measured quarterly.

Data Source: User account management systems, active directory.

Visualization Recommendation: For Password Strength and Complexity, use a bar graph with the x-axis representing different categories of password strength and the y-axis showing the percentage of user accounts. Scale the y-axis from 0% to 100%. Use color coding to differentiate between different password strength categories, such as weak, moderate, and strong.

Insights and Actions: A high percentage of strong and complex passwords indicates a robust frontline defense against unauthorized access. Regularly educate employees on the importance of strong passwords and guide them on creating them. Employ tools such as password managers to aid in creating and storing complex passwords. Consider implementing multifactor authentication to add a layer of security. Regularly audit user accounts for password compliance and require periodic password changes. Balance security and usability – overcomplicated requirements may lead to user frustration and circumvention of policies.

KPI Title: Security Incident Response Team (SIRT) Performance

KPI Objective: The Security Incident Response Team (SIRT) Performance KPI evaluates the effectiveness and efficiency of the SIRT in handling and mitigating security incidents. This KPI is crucial for ensuring rapid and effective responses to security threats.

Metric Summary: The SIRT is critical to an organization's defense against cybersecurity threats. Their performance directly affects the organization's ability to quickly contain and remediate security incidents. This KPI evaluates the team based on response time, containment success, and post-incident analysis quality. It is essential that the SIRT is well-trained, adequately resourced, and operates based on well-defined procedures.

Possible Measurement Formula: SIRT Performance can be measured using a combination of metrics such as MTTR, the success rate in containing incidents, and stakeholder feedback.

Suggested Frequency: Quarterly.

Quantifiable Measure: This can be expressed as a score or rating.

Benchmark or Target Measure: Higher scores or ratings indicate better performance.

Timeframe: Typically measured quarterly.

Data Source: Incident reports, response time logs, stakeholder feedback.

Visualization Recommendation: Use a radar chart for SIRT Performance, with axes representing performance metrics such as response time, resolution rate, and communication effectiveness. Use color coding to represent different periods or benchmarks. This gives a comprehensive overview of the team's performance across various aspects.

Insights and Actions: High performance by the SIRT is essential for minimizing the impact of security incidents. Regular training and exercises are crucial in keeping the team sharp. Equip the team with the tools and resources needed for rapid response. Maintain clear and well-practiced procedures for incident response. Post-incident analysis and lessons learned should be incorporated back into training and procedures. Foster a collaborative environment with other stakeholders to ensure coordinated responses to incidents.

KPI Title: Security Investment Return on Investment (ROI)

KPI Objective: The Security Investment Return on Investment (ROI) KPI quantifies the return on investment for cybersecurity initiatives, helping to justify the financial investments made in cybersecurity efforts.

Metric Summary: Understanding the financial return on security investments is key for justifying and optimizing security spending. This KPI helps demonstrate the value of security investments by comparing the costs of security initiatives with the monetary benefits obtained, such as reduced incidents, less downtime, and avoidance of regulatory fines. A positive ROI indicates that the security investments generate value for the organization.

Possible Measurement Formula: Security Investment ROI (%) = [(monetary benefits − cost of security investment)/cost of security investment] × 100.

Suggested Frequency: Annually.

Quantifiable Measure: Expressed as a percentage.

Benchmark or Target Measure: A positive ROI is desirable, but targets vary based on industry and organization size.

Timeframe: Typically measured annually.

Data Source: Financial records, incident reports, regulatory fines avoided.

Visualization Recommendation: A bar graph is suitable for visualizing Security Investment ROI, with the x-axis representing different security investments and the y-axis showing the ROI percentage. Use color coding to differentiate between investments with positive ROI and those without, helping identify the most beneficial investments.

Insights and Actions: A positive Security Investment ROI indicates that security spending generates value. Regularly review security spending to ensure it is aligned with risk and business objectives. Review the cost-effectiveness of security tools and practices when ROI is lower than expected. Engage with business units to understand the impact of security initiatives on business operations and value. Continually optimize security investments by focusing on initiatives that yield the highest ROI. Security ROI should be seen in direct financial returns, reputational protection, and regulatory compliance.

KPI Title: Third-Party Vendor Security Assessments

KPI Objective: The Third-Party Vendor Security Assessments KPI tracks the number of security assessments conducted on third-party vendors to ensure they meet the organization's security standards. This is essential as vendors can often be a weak link in security.

Metric Summary: Third-party vendors often have access to an organization's sensitive data and systems. Ensuring the security of these vendors is vital in protecting against data breaches and other security incidents. This KPI tracks the number of security assessments conducted on vendors. Regular assessments are important to ensure that vendors comply with the organization's security requirements and identify areas where security needs strengthening.

Possible Measurement Formula: Third-Party Vendor Security Assessments = number of security assessments conducted on third-party vendors.

Suggested Frequency: Quarterly.

Quantifiable Measure: Expressed as a number of assessments conducted.

Benchmark or Target Measure: This should be based on the number of vendors and the criticality of the data and systems they have access to. Regular assessments are desirable.

Timeframe: Typically measured quarterly.

Data Source: Vendor management systems, security assessment reports.

Visualization Recommendation: A bar graph is recommended for Third-Party Vendor Security Assessments. The x-axis should represent time, and the y-axis should represent the number of assessments conducted. Use color coding to differentiate between types of assessments or vendors and implement a threshold line if there is a target number of assessments to be conducted within a certain period.

Insights and Actions: Regular assessments of third-party vendor security are essential to mitigate the risk they pose to your organization. Establish a vendor management program that includes criteria for security assessments. Prioritize assessments based on the criticality and sensitivity of the data and systems the vendors have access to. When gaps or issues are identified in vendor security, work with the vendor to address these issues promptly. Regularly review the criteria for security assessments to ensure they reflect current threats and best practices. Vendor security assessments should be integrated into the overall security management process, and findings should be communicated to relevant stakeholders.

KPI Title: Security IRP Testing

KPI Objective: This KPI measures the frequency of testing the effectiveness of the Security IRP through simulations and drills. Regular testing is essential to ensure that the IRP is effective and that the organization is prepared for security incidents.

Metric Summary: The Security IRP is critical in guiding the organization's response to security incidents. Regular testing through simulations and drills is essential to ensure that the plan is effective, that roles and responsibilities are clear, and that the organization is prepared for security incidents. This KPI tracks the frequency of these tests. Regular testing is essential for identifying and addressing gaps in the IRP before a real incident occurs.

Possible Measurement Formula: Security IRP Testing = number of IRP tests conducted.

Suggested Frequency: Quarterly or Semiannually.

Quantifiable Measure: Expressed as a number of tests conducted.

Benchmark or Target Measure: This should be based on the organization's risk profile and industry best practices, but regular testing is recommended.

Timeframe: Typically measured quarterly or semiannually.

Data Source: IRPs, testing records, simulation results.

Visualization Recommendation: A bar graph is suitable for this KPI, with the x-axis representing time and the y-axis depicting the number of IRP tests performed. Color coding can indicate the success or failure of these tests, while a horizontal threshold line can represent the minimum number of tests that should be performed within a specific timeframe.

Insights and Actions: Regular Security IRP testing is critical for preparedness. Ensure that tests are comprehensive and realistic. Conduct post-test reviews to identify gaps and areas for improvement in the IRP. Update the IRP based on the findings from tests and simulations. Ensure that all relevant staff are trained on the IRP and that roles and responsibilities are clear. Establish metrics for evaluating the success of IRP tests and use these metrics to drive continuous improvement. Engage with external stakeholders such as law enforcement and vendors as part of the testing process.

KPI Title: Employee Security Training Effectiveness

KPI Objective: The Employee Security Training Effectiveness KPI measures the improvement in employees' knowledge and understanding of cybersecurity best practices. This is crucial for ensuring that the human element of cybersecurity is strong.

Metric Summary: Employees are often considered the weakest link in cybersecurity. Effective security training is essential for ensuring employees understand cybersecurity best practices and their role in protecting the organization. This KPI measures employee knowledge and understanding improvement due to security training. This can be measured through pre- and post-training tests, surveys, and monitoring security incidents involving human error.

Possible Measurement Formula: Employee Security Training Effectiveness (%) = [(post-training score – pre-training score)/pre-training score] × 100.

Suggested Frequency: Annually or after each training session.

Quantifiable Measure: Expressed as a percentage improvement in knowledge.

Benchmark or Target Measure: Improvements are desirable, with targets based on industry benchmarks and the organization's security objectives.

Timeframe: Typically measured annually or after each training session.

Data Source: Training records, test scores, surveys.

Visualization Recommendation: For Employee Security Training Effectiveness, a radar chart is recommended, as it can simultaneously display multiple metrics that contribute to effectiveness, such as knowledge retention, practical skills, and attitude changes. Use axes to represent these categories and plot values for different training sessions, using color to distinguish between different periods or groups.

Insights and Actions: Improving Employee Security Training Effectiveness indicates a more security-aware workforce. Regularly review and update training content to reflect current threats and best practices. Use various training methods to engage employees and cater to different learning styles. Conduct regular assessments to evaluate employees' knowledge and understanding of cybersecurity. Provide feedback and additional training where necessary. Create a security-aware culture within the organization where cybersecurity is everyone's responsibility. Recognize and reward employees who demonstrate strong cybersecurity practices.

KPI Title: Vulnerability Discovery Rate

KPI Objective: The Vulnerability Discovery Rate KPI measures the rate at which vulnerabilities are discovered and assessed within an organization's systems and applications. An organization must identify and manage vulnerabilities proactively to mitigate potential exploitation by malicious entities. Organizations can allocate appropriate resources, prioritize remediation efforts, and improve security by monitoring and assessing the Vulnerability Discovery Rate.

Metric Summary: The Vulnerability Discovery Rate reflects the efficiency and effectiveness of the organization's vulnerability management process. In the constantly evolving threat landscape, new vulnerabilities emerge frequently. Being vigilant and proactive in discovering these vulnerabilities is a cornerstone of cybersecurity. This KPI indicates the thoroughness of the vulnerability scanning and assessment processes. It helps organizations understand if they are discovering vulnerabilities at a pace consistent with or better than the emergence of new threats. The granularity is essential: understanding which vulnerabilities are being discovered and which systems can guide targeted improvement efforts. Analyzing trends in this KPI over time can indicate the effectiveness of improvements or the need for new strategies.

Possible Measurement Formula: Vulnerability Discovery Rate = total number of new vulnerabilities discovered in a specific period.

Suggested Frequency: Monthly.

Quantifiable Measure: Expressed as a numerical value representing the count of discovered vulnerabilities.

Benchmark or Target Measure: There is no specific target as it depends on the threat landscape, but consistency and upward trends in discovery are positive.

Timeframe: Typically measured monthly.

Data Source: Vulnerability scanning tools and vulnerability assessment reports.

Visualization Recommendation: A line graph is recommended for the Vulnerability Discovery Rate. The x-axis should represent time, typically in weeks or months, and the y-axis should represent the number of vulnerabilities discovered. This graph should have a linear scale and no preset limits to depict fluctuations accurately. Using a color-coded approach with a red line as a threshold can help identify periods with unusually high vulnerabilities. Highlight points of interest, such as when a new system was introduced, to help analyze factors that might have contributed to the trend.

Insights and Actions: A high Vulnerability Discovery Rate might initially seem concerning, but it can also indicate an effective discovery process. The critical aspect is how the organization responds to these discoveries. Organizations should ensure an efficient process for risk-ranking the vulnerabilities and patching the most critical ones first. A low discovery rate might mean the vulnerability scanning process is not comprehensive enough. It is essential to keep scanning tools up-to-date and ensure that they cover the entire environment. Understanding the root causes of vulnerabilities can help in designing more secure systems. Benchmarking against industry data can also provide insights into how well the organization is discovering vulnerabilities compared to peers.

KPI Title: User Security Training Completion Rate

KPI Objective: The User Security Training Completion Rate KPI measures the percentage of employees who have completed mandatory cybersecurity training. As human error is often a significant factor in security incidents, educating employees on security and best practices is critical for reducing risk.

Metric Summary: Cybersecurity is not just about technology; it is also about people. Employees are often the first defense against cyber threats, and their actions can mitigate or exacerbate security risks. The User Security Training Completion Rate KPI tracks the extent to which the workforce is being educated about security best practices. This includes training on phishing, password poli-cies, data protection, and more. Regular security awareness training is essential for ensuring employees know they must act as effective guardians of organiza-tional data and systems.

Possible Measurement Formula: User Security Training Completion Rate (%) = (number of employees who have completed security training/total num-ber of employees required to complete the training) × 100.

Suggested Frequency: Annually or after each training cycle.

Quantifiable Measure: Expressed as a percentage representing the pro-portion of employees who have completed mandatory cybersecurity training.

Benchmark or Target Measure: Aim for close to 100%.

Timeframe: Typically measured annually or after each training cycle.

Data Source: Learning management systems, HR records.

Visualization Recommendation: Visualize Ransomware Attacks using a bar graph, where the x-axis represents time and the y-axis displays the num-ber of attacks. No predefined limits should be set, allowing natural fluctuations to be visible. Differentiate the types of ransomware attacks using color cod-ing and add a threshold line to indicate the level at which an in-depth review is required.

Insights and Actions: A high User Security Training Completion Rate indi-cates a security-conscious workforce, an invaluable asset in defending against cyber threats. If the completion rate is low, it may be necessary to reevaluate the training program to make it more engaging or to accommodate employees' schedules better. Leadership support is also critical in emphasizing the impor-tance of security training. Additionally, consider incorporating practical exer-cises such as simulated phishing attacks to assess employees' ability to apply what they have learned. Regularly update training content to address evolving threats and to keep the material fresh and engaging for repeat participants.

KPI Title: Patch Management Efficiency

KPI Objective: The Patch Management Efficiency KPI measures the per-centage of critical systems that have been patched or updated within a spec-ified timeframe after the release of a patch. Keeping systems and software patched is essential for protecting against known vulnerabilities.

Metric Summary: Patch Management Efficiency is a critical aspect of cybersecurity hygiene. As vulnerabilities are discovered in systems and soft-ware, vendors release patches to address these vulnerabilities. This KPI tracks the organization's efficiency in applying these patches to critical systems. Delays in patching can expose the organization to known vulnerabilities, which adversaries can exploit. Organizations must have a systematic approach to patch management, prioritizing critical assets and ensuring patches are deployed promptly.

Possible Measurement Formula: Patch Management Efficiency (%) = (num-ber of critical systems patched within specified timeframe/total number of critical systems requiring patches) × 100.

Suggested Frequency: Monthly.

Quantifiable Measure: Expressed as a percentage representing the efficiency of patching critical systems.

Benchmark or Target Measure: Aim for near 100%, recognizing that some delays may be inevitable due to testing and deployment logistics.

Timeframe: Typically measured monthly.

Data Source: Patch management systems, IT asset inventories.

Visualization Recommendation: For the Patch Management Efficiency KPI, it is recommended to use a combination chart with time on the x-axis. The y-axis on the left should represent the percentage of systems patched (0%–100%), which can be visualized using a line graph. The y-axis on the right should indicate the number of patches applied, which can be represented by bars. Incorporate a horizontal threshold line to mark the target efficiency level. Differentiate between timely and delayed patches using color coding; this will help in recognizing the efficiency and timeliness of the patch management process. This combo chart approach helps analyze the coverage and volume aspects of patch management over time.

Insights and Actions: Efficient patch management is essential for minimizing exposure to known vulnerabilities. Develop a structured patch management process that includes monitoring patch releases, prioritizing patches for critical systems, testing patches in a controlled environment, and then deploying them broadly. Communicate and coordinate with relevant stakeholders to minimize operational disruptions during patch deployment. Automation can also significantly improve Patch Management Efficiency, especially in large environments. Finally, it is important to monitor for any issues or conflicts caused by patches and have rollback procedures in place if needed.

Ready-to-Use KRI Examples

This appendix is your comprehensive toolkit for an array of ready-to-use Key Risk Indicator (KRI) examples that can be directly implemented into your risk monitoring strategy. Each KRI is divided into 11 sections, detailing everything from the KRI title, objective, and metric summary to the measurement formula and trigger or breach measure. We also delve into the necessary timeframe, data source, and recommended visual representation to aid analysis. Lastly, the insights and actions segment guides translating the collected data into actionable steps. This systematic approach ensures a complete understanding and effective use of each KRI in real-world scenarios.

STRUCTURE OF KRIS

Each KRI typically includes several components:

1. **KRI/KPI Title:** This is a succinct label for the metric.
2. **Specific Risk:** This outlines the particular cybersecurity risk that the KRI monitors. This section should provide a precise and concise statement of the specific risk that the KRI is designed to track. Understanding the specific risk is critical as it establishes the purpose and context of the KRI. This must be clearly articulated so that all stakeholders understand what is being measured and why.
3. **Metric Summary:** A brief description of why the KRI is valuable. This should include an overview of why this particular KRI is a good measure of the specific risk it is associated with. It should highlight the importance of tracking this metric over time and how it can provide insights into the organization's security posture. This section should articulate how the KRI fits into the broader risk management strategy and how it can support decision-making.
4. **Understanding the Risk:** This section provides background on why the specific risk is important and the potential consequences of the risk materializing. It is crucial to delve into the nature of the risk, historical instances where it has been realized in real-world scenarios, and the potential impact it can have on the organization. The objective is to give stakeholders a solid grasp of why this risk warrants attention and the negative outcomes that could arise if it is not adequately managed.
5. **Mitigating the Risk:** Here, guidance is given on what actions organizations should take to prevent the risk from materializing. This part should

599

outline best practices, controls, and countermeasures that can be used to reduce the likelihood or impact of the risk. It should also touch on how the KRI can be used to assess the effectiveness of these mitigations over time.

6. **Possible Measurement Formula:** This formula can be used to calculate the KRI. This section should provide a clear and easy-to-follow mathematical formula or method for calculating the KRI. It should also guide the data sources required, any assumptions or estimations included in the formula, and any normalization or weighting that might be applied to the raw data.

7. **Suggested Frequency:** This indicates how often the KRI should be measured. It is important to strike a balance between obtaining timely data and over-monitoring. The frequency should reflect the risk volatility and the measurement cost. For instance, KRIs for rapidly evolving risks might need to be measured more frequently than those that change slowly.

8. **Trigger/Breach Information:** This section contains two subsections:

   (a) **Trigger:** The point at which you might want to investigate the metric for potential issues. This is a threshold that, if reached, signals the need for closer examination or preliminary action.

   (b) **Breach:** The point at which the risk materializes and immediate action is needed. This should be a clearly defined point for initiating a formalized incident response process.

9. **Visualization Recommendation:** This section guides effectively visualizing the KRI data to convey the most meaningful insights to stakeholders. Visualization is an important aspect of KRI reporting as it can often make trends and patterns more apparent than raw data alone. In this section, it is important to describe the type of graph or chart most appropriate for the data and what the axes should represent. It is crucial to consider the time frame for which the data is represented and how it can be most understandable to the intended audience. Here are the aspects to focus on in this section:

   (a) **Type of Graph/Chart:** Explain which type of visualization, such as line graph, bar chart, heatmap, etc., is most appropriate for the KRI. Different types of KRIs might be best represented in different ways. For instance, trends over time might be best visualized with line graphs, while distributions might be more effectively represented with histograms.

   (b) **Axes Representation:** Typically, time is on the x-axis, but there could be cases where a different representation is more insightful. The y-axis typically represents the measurement of the KRI, but sometimes it could also be helpful to represent relative change, percentages, etc.

   (c) **Scale and Limits:** Discuss the appropriate scale for the y-axis. This can sometimes make a big difference in how the data is perceived. Also, provide recommendations if there should be any limits on the graph. For instance, having a maximum limit on the y-axis might be helpful to make certain patterns more apparent.

(d) **Threshold Lines or Markers:** Explain if horizontal or vertical lines should represent triggers or breaches in the KRI. This can help in immediately identifying points of concern on the graph.

(e) **Color and Highlighting:** Recommend using color or other highlighting techniques to make certain aspects of the data stand out. For instance, using a different color for data points above a certain threshold.

10. **Quantifiable, Measurable, and Accurate:** Describes how to ensure the metric is quantifiable, measurable, and accurate. This section should delve into the data quality aspects of the KRI. The data used in KRI calculations must be of high quality and reliability. This section should discuss how to ensure that the data is consistently measured and recorded, what kinds of data validation should be in place, and how to deal with any data anomalies or missing data.

11. **Insights and Actions:** Provides information on how the KRI can be interpreted and what actions could be taken based on its value. This final section explores the practical application of the KRI in depth. It should discuss how to interpret changes in the KRI, what they might indicate regarding the underlying risk, and what actions should be taken in response. It is important to consider short-term and long-term trends and how the KRI interacts with other KRIs and risk indicators. This section should also discuss how to incorporate the insights from the KRI into broader risk management and decision-making processes.

KRI Title: Number of Data Breaches

Specific Risk: Unauthorized access and potential exfiltration of sensitive data.

Metric Summary: The number of data breaches is a critical metric that helps organizations understand how often their sensitive data is exposed to unauthorized parties. Monitoring this metric closely is important because it reflects the effectiveness of an organization's cybersecurity posture. A decrease in the number of data breaches over time suggests the success of security measures, while an increase could indicate vulnerabilities or gaps in the security infrastructure.

Understanding the Risk: Data breaches can have devastating consequences for organizations. They involve unauthorized access to sensitive data such as customer information, trade secrets, and other valuable assets. The repercussions can range from financial losses due to fines and customer compensations to reputational damage, which might lead to a loss of customer trust and competitiveness.

Mitigating the Risk: Organizations should continuously monitor their network for signs of intrusion and employ multilayered security measures such as firewalls, intrusion detection systems, and encryption. Regular security audits and penetration testing should also be conducted to identify and fix vulnerabilities. In addition, it is vital to educate employees on the importance of cybersecurity and how to recognize and report potential security threats.

Possible Measurement Formula: Number of Data Breaches = total number of confirmed incidents with unauthorized access to sensitive data.

Suggested Frequency: Monthly.

Trigger: One data breach.

Breach: Any number greater than one.

Visualization Recommendation: For visualizing the Number of Data Breaches, a line graph can be used where the x-axis represents time (monthly or quarterly) and the y-axis represents the number of breaches. It is recommended that the y-axis starts at 0 to depict any changes accurately. An additional horizontal line can be included to indicate an acceptable threshold; any data points above this line should be cause for concern.

Quantifiable, Measurable, and Accurate: The metric can be quantified by counting the number of confirmed data breaches. It is measurable, providing a concrete number that can be tracked over time. To ensure accuracy, organizations must have clear criteria for what constitutes a data breach and employ rigorous verification processes before classifying an incident as a data breach.

Insights and Actions: Monitoring the number of data breaches provides insights into the organization's security posture. An increase in data breaches could indicate the need for an immediate review and strengthening of security protocols. Organizations should have a well-established incident response plan to address data breaches and minimize their impact promptly. Furthermore, the insights gained from analyzing the data breaches can guide necessary modifications to security policies and procedures.

KRI Title: Number of Unpatched Vulnerabilities

Specific Risk: Exploitation of known security vulnerabilities.

Metric Summary: Tracking the number of unpatched vulnerabilities is essential for understanding the exposure of an organization's systems and applications to known security risks. This metric is valuable because it directly influences the organization's cyberattack susceptibility. Many unpatched vulnerabilities indicate a greater attack surface for malicious actors.

Understanding the Risk: Unpatched vulnerabilities are known weaknesses in systems and applications that have not been addressed or patched. They present an open invitation to attackers, who can exploit these vulnerabilities to gain unauthorized access, disrupt services, or exfiltrate sensitive data. These attacks can cause severe financial loss, data breaches, and reputational harm.

Mitigating the Risk: Organizations should implement a systematic vulnerability management program, which includes regular scanning for vulnerabilities and timely application of patches. It is essential to prioritize patching based on the severity of vulnerabilities and the criticality of the affected systems to the business. In some cases, additional layers of security controls may be required to mitigate the risk associated with unpatched vulnerabilities.

Possible Measurement Formula: Number of Unpatched Vulnerabilities = total number of known vulnerabilities that have not been patched.

Suggested Frequency: Monthly.

Trigger: More than five unpatched high-severity vulnerabilities.

Breach: Any critical unpatched vulnerability present for more than 30 days.

Visualization Recommendation: For the Number of Unpatched Vulnerabilities, the x-axis can represent time (e.g., in weeks or months), and the y-axis can represent the number of unpatched vulnerabilities. Set the y-axis to 0, and include a horizontal threshold line representing the maximum acceptable number of unpatched vulnerabilities.

Quantifiable, Measurable, and Accurate: This metric is quantifiable as it involves counting the known vulnerabilities that have not been patched. It is measurable, and trends can be analyzed over time. For accuracy, a clear definition of what constitutes an unpatched vulnerability and the use of reliable scanning tools is essential.

Insights and Actions: This metric provides insight into the organization's vulnerability management effectiveness. A consistently high number of unpatched vulnerabilities might indicate a need for process improvement or resource allocation for timely patching. Organizations should apply patches, implement compensating controls, or isolate vulnerable systems to reduce the risk.

KRI Title: Cost of Cyber Incidents

Specific Risk: Financial loss due to cyberattacks and security incidents.

Metric Summary: The cost of cyber incidents encompasses the financial losses incurred due to cybersecurity incidents. This metric is valuable as it directly indicates the monetary impact of cyber incidents on the organization. Analyzing this cost helps in decision-making regarding investment in cybersecurity and understanding the ROI of security measures.

Understanding the Risk: Cyber incidents such as data breaches, malware infections, or denial of service attacks can impose various costs on an organization. These costs include incident response, legal fees, regulatory fines, customer compensation, and loss of business due to reputational damage. The cumulative financial loss can be substantial and, in extreme cases, threaten the organization's solvency.

Mitigating the Risk: Organizations should invest in robust cybersecurity programs encompassing preventive measures, detection capabilities, and incident response plans. Regular security training for employees and advanced security solutions can reduce the likelihood and impact of cyber incidents. It is also advisable to have cyber insurance to mitigate the financial impact of incidents.

Possible Measurement Formula: Cost of Cyber Incidents = sum of (incident response costs + legal fees + regulatory fines + customer compensation + business loss) for all cyber incidents in a given period.

Suggested Frequency: Quarterly.

Trigger: Costs reaching 75% of the predefined budget.

Breach: Costs exceeding the predefined budget.

Visualization Recommendation: On the line graph, the x-axis should represent time, typically in months or quarters, while the y-axis should represent the cost of cyber incidents in dollars. A horizontal line indicating the budget allocated for cyber incidents can be added, and points above this line indicate exceeding the budget.

Quantifiable, Measurable, and Accurate: The cost of cyber incidents is quantifiable by summing the expenses associated with various aspects of the incidents. It is measurable over time and can be benchmarked against industry averages. Accuracy depends on meticulous record-keeping and including all relevant costs, both direct and indirect.

Insights and Actions: Tracking the cost of cyber incidents provides insights into the financial effectiveness of an organization's cybersecurity program. Organizations should use this data to optimize spending on cybersecurity, ensuring that investments are aligned with risk. The insights can also inform decisions on cyber insurance and prompt actions to strengthen security measures if costs are escalating.

KRI Title: Number of Failed Logins

Specific Risk: Unauthorized attempts to gain access to systems or data.

Metric Summary: Monitoring the number of failed login attempts is crucial for detecting potential unauthorized system access. A sudden spike or a consistently high number of failed logins might indicate a brute force attack or attempts by unauthorized individuals to guess passwords to gain access to sensitive systems or data.

Understanding the Risk: Failed logins, especially large volumes, may signify an attacker trying to gain unauthorized access by guessing credentials. If successful, this unauthorized access can lead to data breaches, information theft, or malicious activities within the network, such as installing malware or ransomware.

Mitigating the Risk: Organizations should have strict account lockout policies in place, where after a certain number of failed attempts, the account gets locked for a specific duration. Implementing multifactor authentication adds an extra layer of security. Monitoring and alerting systems should be used to detect and notify of any unusual failed login patterns.

Possible Measurement Formula: Number of Failed Logins = total unsuccessful login attempts within a given period.

Suggested Frequency: Daily.

Trigger: 5% of total login attempts are failed logins.

Breach: 10% of total login attempts are failed logins.

Visualization Recommendation: Visualize the Number of Failed Logins with time (days, weeks, or months) on the x-axis and the number of failed logins on the y-axis. Starting the y-axis at 0 is recommended. A horizontal threshold line can be set at a level where an investigation should be launched if it is exceeded.

Insights and Actions: Many failed logins should trigger an investigation to determine if it is an attack or a configuration issue. If an attack is underway, the organization should take immediate steps to block the source of the attack and assess if any accounts were compromised.

KRI Title: Number of Compromised Credentials

Specific Risk: Unauthorized access to systems or data using stolen credentials.

Metric Summary: The number of compromised credentials represents how many user account credentials have been exposed or stolen. This is a valuable metric because compromised credentials are a common attack vector. Attackers can use these credentials to impersonate legitimate users, bypassing security controls, and gaining unauthorized access to systems and data.

They understand the Risk: When attackers obtain legitimate user credentials, they can access systems without raising alarms. This can lead to data breaches, theft, and further attack propagation within the organization. Compromised credentials can be used for malicious activities such as stealing intellectual property, committing fraud, or installing malware.

Mitigating the Risk: Organizations should implement multifactor authentication to reduce the risk of compromised credentials. Monitoring and auditing login activities to detect unusual access patterns is essential. Employees should be trained to recognize phishing attempts and encouraged to use strong, unique passwords. Additionally, periodic password changes and using password managers can be beneficial.

Possible Measurement Formula: Number of Compromised Credentials = total number of user account credentials confirmed to be exposed or stolen.

Suggested Frequency: Monthly.

Trigger: One compromised credential.

Breach: More than one compromised credential.

Visualization Recommendation: Use time on the x-axis and the number of compromised credentials on the y-axis. You should include a horizontal line indicating the threshold beyond which a breach investigation is warranted.

Quantifiable, Measurable, and Accurate: The number of compromised credentials is quantifiable and can be counted based on confirmed incidents. It is measurable over time to assess trends. Accuracy in this metric is reliant on effective detection mechanisms and verifiable reports of compromised credentials.

Insights and Actions: Monitoring compromised credentials provides insight into an organization's exposure to account-based attacks. When compromised credentials are detected, the organization should immediately reset passwords, investigate the scope of the compromise, and implement additional security measures as needed.

KRI Title: Percentage of Systems Not Compliant with Security Policies

Specific Risk: Increased vulnerability due to systems not adhering to established security policies.

Metric Summary: The percentage of systems not compliant with security policies indicates how well an organization's systems adhere to established security standards and policies. A high percentage suggests that the organization's systems are more vulnerable to security risks, as they may not be configured or protected according to best practices.

Understanding the Risk: When systems are not configured or maintained according to security policies, they can become vulnerable to attacks. Noncompliant systems might lack necessary security controls, patches, or configurations, leading to unauthorized access, data breaches, and other security incidents.

Mitigating the Risk: Organizations should regularly audit and monitor systems for compliance with security policies. Automated compliance checks and reporting tools can facilitate this process. When noncompliance is detected, remediation processes should be initiated to bring the systems into compliance. Ensuring security policies are current and aligned with industry best practices is vital.

Possible Measurement Formula: Percentage of Systems Not Compliant with Security Policies = (number of noncompliant systems/total number of systems) × 100.

Suggested Frequency: Monthly.

Trigger: 5% of systems are not compliant.

Breach: More than 10% of systems are not compliant.

Visualization Recommendation: For this KRI, the x-axis should represent time (monthly or quarterly), and the y-axis should depict the percentage of noncompliant systems. A threshold percentage line should be included; readings above this line should trigger compliance reviews.

Quantifiable, Measurable, and Accurate: This metric is quantifiable as it involves calculating the ratio of noncompliant systems to total systems. It is measurable, and trends can be analyzed over time. Accuracy depends on comprehensive and regular audits of systems against the established security policies.

Insights and Actions: This metric provides insight into the organization's adherence to its security policies. A high percentage of noncompliance might indicate a need for process improvement, training, or resource allocation for remediation efforts. Actions should be taken to bring noncompliant systems into compliance and to review and update security policies as needed regularly.

KRI Title: Time to Detect Security Incidents

Specific Risk: Delays in detecting security incidents increase the potential impact of the incident.

Metric Summary: Time to Detect Security Incidents measures the average time it takes for an organization to discover a security incident from the time it occurred. Rapid detection is crucial to minimizing the damage caused by security incidents. A longer detection time may allow an attacker to exfiltrate data, move laterally through the network, or cause more damage.

Understanding the Risk: The longer it takes to detect a security incident, the more time an attacker has to achieve their objectives. This can lead to more extensive data breaches, financial losses, and significant reputational damage.

Mitigating the Risk: Implementing effective monitoring and alerting systems is key to reducing the time to detect security incidents. Conducting regular security assessments and training staff to recognize signs of a security incident can also help in early detection. Organizations should also participate in threat intelligence sharing to be aware of new threats and vulnerabilities.

Possible Measurement Formula: Time to Detect Security Incidents = sum of (detection times for each incident)/total number of incidents.

Suggested Frequency: Monthly.

Trigger: Detection time exceeds 4 hours.

Breach: Detection time exceeds 24 hours.

Visualization Recommendation: For the Average Time to Detect, the x-axis should represent time, and the y-axis should represent the average time (in hours or days) taken to detect a security incident. A horizontal threshold line should indicate the maximum acceptable average time.

Quantifiable, Measurable, and Accurate: This metric is quantifiable, measuring the time in hours or days, and can be tracked over time. Accuracy depends on effective incident logging and reporting processes.

Insights and Actions: Monitoring the Time to Detect Security Incidents helps an organization understand its capability to detect incidents promptly. If this metric shows a trend of increasing detection time, the organization should evaluate and possibly upgrade its monitoring and alerting systems and conduct additional staff training.

KRI Title: Employee Security Training Participation Rate

Specific Risk: Lack of employee awareness and training leading to security incidents.

Metric Summary: The Employee Security Training Participation Rate indicates the percentage of employees participating in security training programs. Employee awareness and training are essential components of a security program, as attackers can often exploit human error or lack of knowledge.

Understanding the Risk: Employees not well-informed about security risks and best practices may inadvertently expose the organization to threats by clicking on phishing links, using weak passwords, or mishandling sensitive data.

Mitigating the Risk: Organizations should implement regular security awareness and training programs for all employees. These programs should be engaging and relevant and provide practical knowledge that employees can apply daily. Tracking participation rates and ensuring high engagement levels is critical for these programs' effectiveness.

Possible Measurement Formula: Employee Security Training Participation Rate = (number of employees who participated in security training/total number of employees) × 100.

Suggested Frequency: Annually.

Trigger: Less than 90% participation rate.

Breach: Less than 85% participation rate.

Visualization Recommendation: For visualizing the Employee Security Training Participation Rate, the x-axis should represent time (monthly or quarterly), and the y-axis should represent the participation rate in percentage. Include a horizontal threshold line to indicate the minimum acceptable participation rate, ensuring that most employees are engaged in security training.

Quantifiable, Measurable, and Accurate: This metric is quantifiable and can be calculated as a percentage. It can be tracked over time to assess trends in employee engagement with security training. Accuracy depends on having a reliable method for tracking participation.

Insights and Actions: If the Employee Security Training Participation Rate is low, the organization should investigate the reasons for low engagement and make necessary adjustments to the training program. This could include changing the format, content, or training schedule to make it more appealing and accessible to employees.

KRI Title: Third-Party Vendor Security Incidents

Specific Risk: Security incidents involving third-party vendors accessing an organization's systems or data.

Metric Summary: The Third-Party Vendor Security Incidents metric tracks the number of security incidents that involve or originate from third-party vendors. Many organizations rely on vendors for various services, and these vendors often have access to sensitive data or systems. A security incident involving a vendor can potentially affect the organization.

Understanding the Risk: Third-party vendors may not always have the same level of security controls as the organization, and their access to the organization's systems and data makes them a potential weak link in the security chain. An incident with a third-party vendor can lead to data breaches or other security incidents affecting the organization.

Mitigating the Risk: Organizations should thoroughly vet the security practices of third-party vendors before granting them access to systems or data. Regular security audits of vendors, establishing clear security requirements in contracts, and monitoring vendor activities are important for mitigating this risk.

Possible Measurement Formula: Third-Party Vendor Security Incidents = total number of security incidents involving third-party vendors within a given period.

Suggested Frequency: Quarterly.

Trigger: One incident involving a third-party vendor.

Breach: More than one incident involving a third-party vendor.

Visualization Recommendation: On the line graph for Third-Party Vendor Security Incidents, the x-axis should represent time, and the y-axis should represent the number of security incidents associated with third-party vendors. A horizontal threshold line representing the maximum acceptable number of incidents is recommended to monitor vendor-related risks.

Quantifiable, Measurable, and Accurate: This metric is quantifiable by counting the incidents involving third-party vendors. It is measurable over time and can provide insights into trends and patterns. Accuracy depends on effective incident tracking and communication with vendors.

Insights and Actions: A trend of increasing security incidents involving third-party vendors may indicate a need to reevaluate vendor relationships and security requirements. The organization should work closely with vendors to address security issues and may need to consider changing vendors if security incidents persist.

KRI Title: Number of Legal and Regulatory Compliance Violations

Specific Risk: Legal repercussions and penalties due to noncompliance with cybersecurity regulations.

Metric Summary: The Number of Legal and Regulatory Compliance Violations metric tracks the total number of instances where the organization fails to comply with legal or regulatory requirements related to cybersecurity. This metric is crucial for gauging an organization's adherence to standards and understanding potential legal liabilities.

Understanding the Risk: Noncompliance with legal and regulatory requirements can result in penalties, loss of customer trust, and reputational damage. Additionally, it may indicate weaknesses in the organization's cybersecurity posture, leading to a higher risk of data breaches or other security incidents.

Mitigating the Risk: Regular audits and reviews should be conducted to ensure compliance with relevant legal and regulatory requirements. Establishing a compliance management program and training employees on compliance requirements is essential.

Possible Measurement Formula: Number of Legal and Regulatory Compliance Violations = total number of compliance violations within a period.

Suggested Frequency: Quarterly.

Trigger: One compliance violation.

Breach: More than one compliance violation.

Visualization Recommendation: The x-axis should represent time, and the y-axis should represent the count of legal and regulatory compliance violations. A threshold line can be set to the maximum acceptable violations within the period.

Quantifiable, Measurable, and Accurate: This metric is quantifiable and can be tracked over time to observe trends. Accuracy depends on thorough documentation and understanding of compliance requirements.

Insights and Actions: If this metric shows a trend of increasing compliance violations, it may indicate a need to strengthen the compliance management program. Actions should include reviewing and updating policies, enhancing training, and ensuring compliance is a priority at all levels of the organization.

KRI Title: Data Exposure Events

Specific Risk: Unauthorized disclosure of sensitive data.

Metric Summary: Data Exposure Events measure the number of incidents in which sensitive data is exposed to unauthorized parties. This metric is important for understanding the organization's risk of data breaches and unauthorized data disclosure.

It understands the Risk: Data exposure can lead to the loss of sensitive information, which may result in financial losses, damage to reputation, legal penalties, and loss of customer trust. Various factors, including misconfigurations, software vulnerabilities, or human error, can cause it.

Mitigating the Risk: Regular audits should correctly implement access controls and security configurations. Organizations should also employ data encryption, educate employees on security practices, and establish incident response plans.

Possible Measurement Formula: Data Exposure Events = total number of data exposure incidents within a given period.

Suggested Frequency: Monthly.

Trigger: One data exposure event.

Breach: More than one data exposure event.

Visualization Recommendation: Visualize Data Exposure Events with time on the x-axis and the number of data exposure events on the y-axis. A horizontal threshold line should indicate the acceptable limit for such events.

Quantifiable, Measurable, and Accurate: This metric is quantifiable and should be tracked over time to identify trends. Accuracy depends on vigilant monitoring and thorough documentation of incidents.

Insights and Actions: An increasing trend in data exposure events may indicate underlying security weaknesses. Actions should include an assessment of security controls, staff training, and possibly the introduction of additional security solutions like Data Loss Prevention (DLP) tools.

KRI Title: Number of Systems Running Outdated Software

Specific Risk: Increased cyberattack vulnerability due to systems running outdated or unsupported software.

Metric Summary: The Number of Systems Running Outdated Software metric tracks the number of systems within an organization running software versions that are no longer supported or have not been updated with the latest security patches. This metric is important for gauging the organization's exposure to vulnerabilities associated with outdated software.

Understanding the Risk: Running outdated software can leave systems vulnerable to exploits and attacks. Outdated software may have known vulnerabilities patched in later versions, and attackers can exploit these vulnerabilities to gain unauthorized access or disrupt services.

Mitigating the Risk: Organizations should have a patch management program to ensure that software is regularly updated. Additionally, inventory and monitoring of software versions should be conducted to identify and update systems running outdated software.

Possible Measurement Formula: Number of Systems Running Outdated Software = total number of systems running outdated or unsupported software versions within a given period.

Suggested Frequency: Monthly.

Trigger: One system was identified as running outdated software.

Breach: More than five systems running outdated software.

Visualization Recommendation: On a line graph, the x-axis should depict time, and the y-axis should represent the number of systems running outdated software. A threshold line should be present, and points above this line indicate a critical number of systems needing updates.

Quantifiable, Measurable, and Accurate: This metric is quantifiable and can be accurately measured through asset inventories and automated scanning tools. Tracking the metric over time can reveal trends and help assess the effectiveness of patch management efforts.

Insights and Actions: If the metric reveals an increasing number of systems running outdated software, it indicates a failure in the patch management process. The organization should reassess and improve its patch management strategy, ensure compliance with internal policies, and consider automation to keep software updated.

KRI Title: Increase in Attack Surface

Specific Risk: Increased exposure to cyber threats due to expanding the organization's attack surface.

Metric Summary: The Increase in Attack Surface metric tracks changes in the size of an organization's attack surface over time. The attack surface includes all the points where an unauthorized user can attempt to enter or extract data from the environment.

Understanding the Risk: An increase in attack surface may result from adding new devices and applications or opening network ports, among others. The larger the attack surface, the more opportunities for attackers to exploit vulnerabilities or infiltrate the network.

Mitigating the Risk: Organizations should employ network segmentation, limit unnecessary functionalities, conduct regular audits of network assets, and apply the principle of least privilege to minimize the attack surface.

Possible Measurement Formula: Increase in Attack Surface = (attack surface at the end of the period − attack surface at the start of the period)/attack surface at the start of the period.

Suggested Frequency: Quarterly.

Trigger: More than a 10% increase in attack surface.

Breach: More than a 25% increase in attack surface.

Visualization Recommendation: For an Increase in Attack Surface, use time on the x-axis and a relevant measure (such as the number of exposed endpoints or open ports) on the y-axis. Set a threshold line to indicate when the attack surface becomes too large and warrants action.

Quantifiable, Measurable, and Accurate: This metric can be quantified by comparing snapshots of the attack surface over time. Automation tools and network scanning can assist in the measurement.

Insights and Actions: A significant increase in attack surface should prompt a security review to determine the causes and assess the risks. Actions may include decommissioning unnecessary systems, closing ports, or implementing additional security controls.

KRI Title: Number of Lost or Stolen Devices

Specific Risk: Unauthorized access to sensitive data due to the loss or theft of organizational devices.

Metric Summary: The Number of Lost or Stolen Devices metric counts how many organization-owned devices (such as laptops, smartphones, and tablets) are lost or stolen within a specific period. Tracking this metric is crucial for understanding the risks associated with the physical security of devices that may contain sensitive data.

Understanding the Risk: If improperly secured, lost or stolen devices can lead to unauthorized access to sensitive information. This may result in data breaches, intellectual property theft, and loss of customer trust.

Mitigating the Risk: Organizations should implement security measures such as encryption, remote wiping capabilities, and ensuring that devices require strong authentication. Additionally, employees should be trained on the importance of physical security and promptly reporting lost or stolen devices.

Possible Measurement Formula: Number of Lost or Stolen Devices = total number of organization-owned devices reported lost or stolen within a given period.

Suggested Frequency: Monthly.

Trigger: One device was reported lost or stolen.

Breach: More than two devices were reported lost or stolen.

Visualization Recommendation: With time on the x-axis and the number of lost or stolen devices on the y-axis, include a horizontal line representing the maximum acceptable number of lost or stolen devices within a specific period.

Quantifiable, Measurable, and Accurate: This metric is quantifiable and should be accurately documented through incident reports. Tracking over time is important to identify trends or areas where physical security may need improvement.

Insights and Actions: If lost or stolen devices increase is observed, organizations should review and possibly strengthen their physical security policies and controls. Additional training for staff on the importance of device security and the procedures for reporting lost or stolen equipment should be considered.

KRI Title: Percentage of High-Risk Third Parties/Vendors

Specific Risk: Data breaches or security incidents due to vulnerabilities in third-party vendors.

Metric Summary: The Percentage of High-Risk Third Parties/Vendors metric calculates the proportion of third-party vendors that pose a high risk to the organization's cybersecurity. Understanding and monitoring this metric is essential to managing the cybersecurity risks associated with outsourcing or partnering with external entities.

Understanding the Risk: Third-party vendors with access to an organization's network or data can introduce vulnerabilities if they do not have adequate security controls. A breach by a third-party vendor can lead to a data breach within the organization.

Mitigating the Risk: Perform regular risk assessments of third-party vendors. Establish criteria for categorizing risk levels and ensure contracts with third parties include clauses about cybersecurity requirements. Monitor the security practices of high-risk vendors closely.

Possible Measurement Formula: Percentage of High-Risk Third Parties/ Vendors = (number of high-risk third-party vendors/total number of third-party vendors) × 100.

Suggested Frequency: Quarterly.

Trigger: 10% of third-party vendors are categorized as high risk.

Breach: More than 20% of third-party vendors are categorized as high risk.

Visualization Recommendation: Visualize this KRI with time on the x-axis and the percentage of high-risk third parties/vendors on the y-axis. Add a horizontal threshold line to indicate the maximum acceptable percentage.

Quantifiable, Measurable, and Accurate: The metric is quantifiable through vendor risk assessments. Keeping accurate records of assessments and categorization is essential.

Insights and Actions: Increased high-risk third-party vendors may indicate a need to reassess vendor selection criteria and security requirements. Actions could include strengthening contractual security obligations, conducting frequent risk assessments, or seeking alternative vendors with stronger security controls.

KRI Title: Number of Insider Threat Incidents

Specific Risk: Unauthorized access, data leakage, or other security incidents due to actions or negligence by employees, contractors, or other individuals within the organization.

Metric Summary: The Number of Insider Threat Incidents metric quantifies how many security incidents have been caused by individuals within the organization. This helps assess the risks related to insider threats, known for their potential to cause significant damage.

Understanding the Risk: Insider threats can be malicious or unintentional. Malicious insiders have the potential to steal data or sabotage systems, while unintentional insider threats include individuals who inadvertently cause security incidents due to negligence or lack of awareness.

Mitigating the Risk: Organizations should conduct regular security awareness training, enforce the principle of least privilege, monitor user behavior, and implement stringent access controls. A reporting mechanism for suspicious behavior should also be in place.

Possible Measurement Formula: Number of Insider Threat Incidents = total number of security incidents caused by insiders within a given period.

Suggested Frequency: Monthly.

Trigger: One insider threat incident.

Breach: More than three insider threat incidents in a given period.

Visualization Recommendation: For visualizing the Number of Insider Threat Incidents, the x-axis should represent time, and the y-axis should represent the number of incidents. Include a horizontal threshold line representing the maximum acceptable number of incidents.

Quantifiable, Measurable, and Accurate: This metric can be quantified by collecting incident reports and logs. Accurate categorization of incidents as insider-related is essential for measurement.

Insights and Actions: An increase in insider threat incidents may indicate a need for enhanced security training, better access controls, or more rigorous background checks for employees with access to sensitive data.

KRI Title: Customer Data Requests and Complaints

Specific Risk: Reputation damage, loss of customer trust, and potential regulatory action due to inadequate handling of customer data or privacy concerns.

Metric Summary: The Customer Data Requests and Complaints metric tracks the number of customer inquiries and complaints regarding their data. It can indicate customer concerns about how their data is being handled, and a high number could suggest a lack of confidence in the organization's data handling practices.

Understanding the Risk: Customers are increasingly aware of the importance of data privacy. An increase in customer data requests or complaints may indicate that customers are concerned about how their data is used or protected. This can lead to reputation damage and potential regulatory scrutiny.

Mitigating the Risk: Organizations should have transparent policies regarding data handling and comply with data protection laws. They should also have efficient processes to respond promptly to customer data requests and complaints.

Possible Measurement Formula: Customer Data Requests and Complaints = total number of customer data requests and complaints received within a given period.

Suggested Frequency: Monthly.

Trigger: A noticeable increase in customer data requests and complaints.

Breach: More than double the average number of customer data requests and complaints received in previous periods.

Visualization Recommendation: On the line graph, the x-axis should represent time, and the y-axis should represent the number of customer data requests and complaints. A horizontal line indicating the maximum acceptable number within a specific period can be added.

Quantifiable, Measurable, and Accurate: This metric is quantifiable through customer support logs and communications. Tracking trends and analyzing the data for insights into customer concerns is vital.

Insights and Actions: An increasing trend in customer data requests and complaints should prompt a review of data handling practices and customer communication strategies. Improving transparency and data protection may help alleviate customer concerns and rebuild trust.

KRI Title: Number of Unresolved Security Vulnerabilities

Specific Risk: Increased likelihood of a security breach due to unpatched vulnerabilities in systems and applications.

Metric Summary: The Number of Unresolved Security Vulnerabilities metric quantifies the number of known security vulnerabilities within an organization's network, systems, or applications that have not yet been resolved or mitigated. Monitoring this metric is critical for understanding and managing an organization's exposure to potential cyberattacks.

Understanding the Risk: Unresolved security vulnerabilities can be exploited by attackers to gain unauthorized access, steal data, or disrupt services. The longer vulnerabilities remain unresolved, the higher the risk of exploitation.

Mitigating the Risk: Organizations should employ a vulnerability management program that includes regular scanning for vulnerabilities, risk assessment, and timely patching or mitigation of identified vulnerabilities.

Possible Measurement Formula: Number of Unresolved Security Vulnerabilities = total number of known vulnerabilities that have not been resolved or mitigated within a given period.

Suggested Frequency: Monthly.

Trigger: Any high or critical severity vulnerability remaining unresolved for over 30 days.

Breach: More than five high or critical severity vulnerabilities unresolved for over 60 days.

Visualization Recommendation: The x-axis should depict time, while the y-axis represents the number of unresolved security vulnerabilities. Add a horizontal line to represent the maximum acceptable number of unresolved vulnerabilities.

Quantifiable, Measurable, and Accurate: This metric is quantifiable through vulnerability scanning tools and patch management systems. It is important to categorize vulnerabilities by severity and focus on resolving the most critical ones first.

Insights and Actions: If the number of unresolved security vulnerabilities increases, this may indicate a failure in the vulnerability management process. Actions should include prioritizing and accelerating the patching process and possibly reassessing the resources allocated to vulnerability management.

KRI Title: Percentage of Systems Patched Against Known Vulnerabilities

Specific Risk: Exposure to security breaches due to failure to apply patches to known system vulnerabilities.

Metric Summary: The Percentage of Systems Patched Against Known Vulnerabilities metric measures the proportion of systems in an organization that has been updated or patched to address known security vulnerabilities. A high percentage indicates a proactive approach to vulnerability management, while a low percentage suggests potential security risks.

Understanding the Risk: Failure to patch known vulnerabilities increases the risk of exploitation by attackers, potentially leading to data breaches, service interruptions, or other malicious activities. Timely patching is critical for maintaining a strong security posture.

Mitigating the Risk: Organizations should implement a patch management process that includes regular vulnerability assessments, patch testing, and timely deployment of patches to production systems.

Possible Measurement Formula: Percentage of Systems Patched Against Known Vulnerabilities = (number of patched systems/total number of systems) × 100.

Suggested Frequency: Monthly.

Trigger: Below 90% of systems patched against known vulnerabilities.

Breach: Below 80% of systems are patched against known vulnerabilities.

Visualization Recommendation: Visualize this KRI with time on the x-axis and the percentage of systems patched on the y-axis. A threshold line should indicate the minimum acceptable percentage for patched systems.

Quantifiable, Measurable, and Accurate: Utilize vulnerability scanning tools and patch management systems to ensure accurate data collection and reporting. It is essential to focus on patching high-severity vulnerabilities as a priority.

Insights and Actions: Low percentages indicate a need for improvement in the patch management process. Consider allocating additional resources, improving patch testing procedures, and setting more aggressive patch deployment schedules.

KRI Title: Average Time to Detect (TTD) a Security Incident

Specific Risk: Increased impact of a security incident due to delays in detection.

Metric Summary: Average Time to Detect (TTD) measures the average time to detect a security incident. Shorter detection times indicate a more effective security monitoring and incident response program, whereas longer times may signify potential weaknesses in detection capabilities.

Understanding the Risk: Delays in detecting security incidents allow attackers more time to move through the network, exfiltrate data, or perform other malicious activities, potentially resulting in greater damage.

Mitigating the Risk: Organizations should have robust monitoring and alerting mechanisms and regularly review and adjust detection capabilities to keep pace with evolving threat landscapes.

Possible Measurement Formula: Average TTD = sum of (detection time for each incident)/total number of incidents.

Suggested Frequency: Monthly.

Trigger: TTD exceeding 4 hours.

Breach: TTD exceeding 24 hours.

Visualization Recommendation: For the Average TTD, the x-axis should represent time, and the y-axis should represent the average time (in hours or days) taken to detect a security incident. A horizontal threshold line should indicate the maximum acceptable average time.

Quantifiable, Measurable, and Accurate: Maintaining accurate logs and using security information and event management (SIEM) tools can help quantify this metric.

Insights and Actions: If TTD is increasing or exceeding acceptable thresholds, consider revising monitoring strategies, enhancing alerting mechanisms, and conducting additional training for security operations center (SOC) staff.

KRI Title: Average Time to Respond (TTR) to a Security Incident

Specific Risk: Escalation of the impact and scope of security incidents due to delays in response.

Metric Summary: Average TTR measures the average time taken to respond to a security incident after it has been detected. A shorter TTR implies an effective incident response capability, while a longer TTR suggests inefficiencies in incident management processes.

Understanding the Risk: Delays in response times can allow security incidents to escalate, potentially leading to more extensive damage, data loss, and reputational harm. Quick response is crucial to mitigate the impact of security incidents.

Mitigating the Risk: Organizations should establish an incident response plan, conduct regular drills, and ensure that the incident response team is adequately trained and equipped to deal with various security incidents.

Possible Measurement Formula: Average TTR = sum of (response time for each incident)/total number of incidents.

Suggested Frequency: Monthly.

Trigger: TTR exceeding 8 hours.

Breach: TTR exceeding 24 hours.

Visualization Recommendation: Visualize this KRI with time on the x-axis and the average time to respond to an incident on the y-axis (in hours or days). A threshold line should indicate the maximum acceptable average time.

Quantifiable, Measurable, and Accurate: This metric can be quantified by tracking incident timestamps from detection to resolution. Ensuring that all timestamps are accurately recorded for all incidents is crucial.

Insights and Actions: If TTR is too high, organizations should review and improve their incident response plans, conduct training and simulations, and consider automated response solutions to reduce the time to respond to incidents.

KRI Title: Phishing Click-through Rate

Specific Risk: Compromise of user accounts and potentially wider network breaches due to users interacting with phishing emails.

Metric Summary: Phishing Click-through Rate represents the percentage of users clicking links within phishing emails. This metric is important for assessing the effectiveness of security awareness training and understanding the susceptibility of an organization's workforce to phishing attacks.

Understanding the Risk: Phishing attacks are a common vector used to steal credentials and gain unauthorized network access. High click-through rates indicate a significant risk of successful phishing attacks.

Mitigating the Risk: Regular security awareness training should be provided, particularly on recognizing and reporting phishing attempts. Additionally, implementing email security controls can help to minimize the volume of phishing emails that reach users.

Possible Measurement Formula: Phishing Click-through Rate = (number of clicks on phishing email links/total number of phishing emails sent) × 100.

Suggested Frequency: Quarterly.

Trigger: Above 10%.

Breach: Above 20%.

Visualization Recommendation: On the line graph, the x-axis should represent time, and the y-axis should represent the click-through rate in percentage. A threshold line should be set to indicate the maximum acceptable rate.

618 Ready-to-Use KRI Examples

Quantifiable, Measurable, and Accurate: Conduct simulated phishing campaigns to measure how many users are clicking on phishing emails. Analyze the data to ascertain the effectiveness of awareness programs.

Insights and Actions: If the phishing click-through rate is high, it suggests that security awareness training may not be effective, and a review and improvement of training content and delivery methods should be considered.

KRI Title: Patch Management Compliance Rate

Specific Risk: Security breaches due to ineffective patch management.

Metric Summary: Patch Management Compliance Rate is the percentage of systems compliant with the organization's patch management policy. This metric is essential for evaluating the effectiveness of the organization's patch management process and identifying areas that may require attention or improvement.

Understanding the Risk: Ineffective patch management can leave systems vulnerable to known security issues that vendors have patched. This can result in security breaches, data loss, and compliance issues.

Mitigating the Risk: Organizations should have a comprehensive patch management policy and process. This includes regular patching cycles, timely application of critical security patches, and regular compliance checks.

Possible Measurement Formula: Patch Management Compliance Rate = (number of systems compliant with patch policy/total number of systems) × 100.

Suggested Frequency: Monthly.

Trigger: Below 90% compliance.

Breach: Below 80% compliance.

Visualization Recommendation: For visualizing the Patch Management Compliance Rate, use time on the x-axis and compliance rate in percentage on the y-axis. Include a horizontal threshold line to indicate the minimum acceptable compliance rate.

Quantifiable, Measurable, and Accurate: Use automated tools for patch management and compliance checks to ensure accurate and up-to-date information. Monitor and report on compliance across all systems.

Insights and Actions: If the Patch Management Compliance Rate is low, consider reviewing and updating the patch management policy and ensuring adequate resources are allocated to patch management activities.

KRI Title: Password Policy Compliance Rate

Specific Risk: Unauthorized access due to weak or compromised passwords.

Metric Summary: Password Policy Compliance Rate measures the percentage of user accounts that comply with the organization's password policy. This metric is important to ensure that users are adhering to best practices for password complexity and change frequency.

Understanding the Risk: Noncompliance with password policies can result in weak passwords that are easy for attackers to guess or crack, leading to unauthorized access and potential data breaches.

Mitigating the Risk: Enforce a strong password policy with complexity requirements and regular password changes. Provide user education on the importance of strong passwords.

Possible Measurement Formula: Password Policy Compliance Rate = (number of user accounts compliant with password policy/total number of user accounts) × 100.

Suggested Frequency: Monthly.

Trigger: Below 90% compliance.

Breach: Below 80% compliance.

Visualization Recommendation: With time on the x-axis and the compliance rate in percentage on the y-axis, a horizontal threshold line should be added to indicate the minimum acceptable compliance rate.

Quantifiable, Measurable, and Accurate: Use tools to monitor and enforce password policies. Regular audits should be conducted to ensure compliance.

Insights and Actions: If the Password Policy Compliance Rate is low, consider revising the password policy, implementing technical controls, and conducting training and awareness programs.

KRI Title: Unauthorized Access Attempts

Specific Risk: Potential security breaches due to unauthorized attempts to access systems or data.

Metric Summary: Unauthorized Access Attempts metric counts the number of attempts to access systems or data that were not authorized. This metric is critical for detecting potential attacks and assessing the effectiveness of access controls.

Understanding the Risk: Many unauthorized access attempts may indicate that the organization is under attack. It can also indicate that internal users are attempting to access resources they should not.

Mitigating the Risk: Implement strong access controls, monitor for unauthorized access attempts, and have an incident response plan to address any successful breaches.

Possible Measurement Formula: Unauthorized Access Attempts = sum of all unauthorized access attempts over a period of time.

Suggested Frequency: Weekly.

Trigger: More than 10 unauthorized attempts in a week.

Breach: More than 20 unauthorized attempts in a week.

Visualization Recommendation: Visualize Unauthorized Access Attempts with time on the x-axis and the number of unauthorized access attempts on the y-axis. Include a horizontal line representing the threshold for maximum acceptable attempts.

Quantifiable, Measurable, and Accurate: Use SIEM systems or other monitoring tools to track and report unauthorized access attempts. Ensure logging is enabled and retained for sufficient time.

Insights and Actions: A high number of unauthorized access attempts could indicate a targeted attack or insufficient access controls. Organizations should investigate the source of these attempts and may need to implement additional security measures or conduct internal awareness training.

KRI Title: Data Leakage Incidents

Specific Risk: Unauthorized disclosure of sensitive data.

Metric Summary: Data Leakage Incidents are the count of instances where sensitive data is disclosed to unauthorized parties, either intentionally or unintentionally. This metric is crucial for understanding the organization's data protection and confidentiality risk exposure.

Understanding the Risk: Data leakage can result in reputational damage, loss of customer trust, and legal consequences. It can occur through various means, such as email, cloud storage, external devices, etc.

Mitigating the Risk: Implement DLP tools, train employees on data handling practices, and enforce access controls and encryption for sensitive data.

Possible Measurement Formula: Data Leakage Incidents = sum of all recorded data leakage incidents over a period of time.

Suggested Frequency: Monthly.

Trigger: 1 incident in a month.

Breach: More than 2 incidents in a month.

Visualization Recommendation: For Data Leakage Incidents, the x-axis should represent time, and the y-axis should represent the number of data leakage incidents. Include a horizontal line indicating the acceptable threshold.

Quantifiable, Measurable, and Accurate: Use DLP tools and incident tracking systems to accurately record and analyze data leakage incidents. Regular audits can help validate the accuracy of this metric.

Insights and Actions: Increased data leakage incidents might indicate the need for improved data handling policies, employee training, and technological safeguards such as encryption and access controls.

KRI Title: Encryption Usage Rate

Specific Risk: Data breaches and unauthorized access to sensitive information due to lack of encryption.

Metric Summary: Encryption Usage Rate is the percentage of encrypted systems and data, according to the organization's encryption standards. This metric is essential for understanding the extent to which sensitive data is secured against unauthorized access.

Understanding the Risk: Lack of encryption can lead to sensitive data being accessed, stolen, or altered by unauthorized parties, resulting in data breaches, compliance issues, and reputational damage.

Mitigating the Risk: Deploy encryption across all systems and data, particularly where sensitive information is stored or transmitted. Regularly review and update encryption algorithms and keys.

Possible Measurement Formula: Encryption Usage Rate = (number of systems and data encrypted/total number of systems and data that should be encrypted) × 100.

Suggested Frequency: Monthly.

Trigger: Below 90% encryption rate.

Breach: Below 80% encryption rate.

Visualization Recommendation: Visualize the Encryption Usage Rate with time on the x-axis and usage rate with percentage on the y-axis. Include a horizontal line to indicate the minimum acceptable encryption usage rate.

Quantifiable, Measurable, and Accurate: Automated tools can be used to track encryption implementation across systems and data. Regular audits should be conducted to ensure that encryption is implemented correctly and according to the organization's standards.

Insights and Actions: A low Encryption Usage Rate could indicate that sensitive data is at risk of unauthorized access. Actions to take include reviewing encryption policies, implementing encryption where it is lacking, and ensuring that employees know encryption protocols and their importance in data protection.

KRI Title: Time to Contain Security Incidents

Specific Risk: Extended exposure to security threats due to delays in containing security incidents.

Metric Summary: Time to Contain Security Incidents measures the average time to contain a security incident after it has been detected. A shorter containment time limits the potential damage caused by security incidents and indicates an effective incident response process.

Understanding the Risk: Delayed containment of security incidents can result in prolonged unauthorized access to systems and data, increasing the severity of data breaches and escalating recovery costs and reputational damage.

Mitigating the Risk: Develop and maintain a well-documented incident response plan, conduct regular incident response drills, and ensure clear communication channels during incidents.

Possible Measurement Formula: Time to Contain Security Incidents = sum of (time to contain each incident)/number of incidents.

Suggested Frequency: Monthly.

Trigger: More than 4 hours.

Breach: More than 12 hours.

Visualization Recommendation: For Time to Contain Security Incidents, use time on the x-axis and the average time to contain incidents on the y-axis (in hours or days). Include a threshold line indicating the maximum acceptable average time.

Quantifiable, Measurable, and Accurate: Use incident management tools to accurately record the time of detection and containment for security incidents. Regularly review and analyze this data for process improvement.

Insights and Actions: An increase in Time to Contain Security Incidents might indicate inefficiencies in the incident response process. Organizations should review their incident response plans, conduct training, and consider deploying automated tools to aid in rapid containment.

KRI Title: Data Backups Success Rate

Specific Risk: Data loss and service disruption due to unsuccessful data backups.

Metric Summary: Data Backups Success Rate measures the percentage of successful data backups compared to the total number of planned data backups. This metric ensures the organization can recover data during hardware failure, corruption, or other incidents.

Understanding the Risk: Failure to successfully backup data can result in permanent data loss, service disruptions, and an inability to recover from incidents promptly, which can have severe business consequences.

Mitigating the Risk: Regularly test backup procedures, monitor the success rates of backups, and have redundancy in place for critical data. Ensure that backups are stored in secure and geographically diverse locations.

Possible Measurement Formula: Data Backups Success Rate = (number of successful backups/total number of planned backups) × 100.

Suggested Frequency: Weekly.

Trigger: Below 90% success rate.

Breach: Below 80% success rate.

Visualization Recommendation: On the line graph, the x-axis should represent time, and the y-axis should represent the success rate in percentage. Add a horizontal threshold line indicating the minimum acceptable success rate for data backups.

Quantifiable, Measurable, and Accurate: Use backup management software to track backups' success and failure rates. Regularly review backup logs for anomalies and errors.

Insights and Actions: If the Data Backups Success Rate is low, investigate the causes of backup failures, such as hardware issues or configuration errors, and take corrective action. It is also important to regularly test data restoration procedures to ensure they are effective.

KRI Title: Number of Security Policy Exceptions

Specific Risk: Increased vulnerability and noncompliance due to deviations from security policies.

Metric Summary: The number of Security Policy Exceptions measures the count of instances where exceptions to the organization's security policies have been made. This is critical for managing and understanding deviations that could impact the security posture. The number of exceptions below will depend on the size of the enterprise and may need to be increased accordingly.

Understanding the Risk: Allowing exceptions to security policies can create vulnerabilities and increase risk exposure. This may also result in noncompliance with regulatory requirements and frameworks.

Mitigating the Risk: Exceptions to security policies should be documented, justified, and regularly reviewed to assess their impact. Implement compensating controls where necessary.

Possible Measurement Formula: Number of Security Policy Exceptions = count of documented exceptions to security policies.

Suggested Frequency: Monthly.

Trigger: 3–5 exceptions.

Breach: More than 5 exceptions.

Visualization Recommendation: For the Number of Security Policy Exceptions, the x-axis should represent time, and the y-axis should represent the number of exceptions. A horizontal line indicating the maximum acceptable number of exceptions should be included.

Quantifiable, Measurable, and Accurate: Maintain a centralized record of security policy exceptions and regularly review them to ensure they are still relevant and justified.

Insights and Actions: An increase in the Number of Security Policy Exceptions could indicate a need to review and possibly update security policies. Exceptions should be assessed for risk, and compensating controls should be implemented where necessary.

KRI Title: Percentage of Users With Multi-Factor Authentication Enabled

Specific Risk: Unauthorized access due to compromised credentials.

Metric Summary: The percentage of Users With Multi-Factor Authentication Enabled measures the proportion of user accounts with MFA (Multi-Factor Authentication) enabled. This is important for reducing the risk of unauthorized access due to compromised credentials.

Understanding the Risk: Without MFA, accounts are vulnerable to access by unauthorized users if credentials are compromised. MFA adds a layer of security by requiring additional verification.

Mitigating the Risk: Enforce MFA for all user accounts, especially for privileged accounts and accounts with access to sensitive data.

Possible Measurement Formula: Percentage of Users With Multi-Factor Authentication Enabled = (number of users with MFA enabled/total number of user accounts) × 100.

Suggested Frequency: Monthly.

Trigger: Below 90% of users with MFA enabled.

Breach: Below 80% of users with MFA enabled.

Visualization Recommendation: Visualize this KRI with time on the x-axis and the percentage of users with multifactor authentication enabled on the y-axis. A horizontal threshold line should indicate the minimum acceptable percentage.

Quantifiable, Measurable, and Accurate: Use identity and access management (IAM) tools to monitor the use of MFA across user accounts. Ensure that reports are accurate and reflect the current state of MFA deployment.

Insights and Actions: A low percentage of users with MFA enabled indicates a higher risk of unauthorized access due to compromised credentials. The organization should enforce MFA across all user accounts, train users on the importance of MFA, and monitor compliance.

KRI Title: Time to Patch Critical Vulnerabilities

Specific Risk: Exploitation of known vulnerabilities in systems and applications.

Metric Summary: Time to Patch Critical Vulnerabilities measures the average time to apply patches to known critical vulnerabilities from when they are identified. Minimizing this time is crucial for reducing the window of opportunity for attackers to exploit vulnerabilities.

Understanding the Risk: A delay in patching known vulnerabilities provides attackers with the opportunity to exploit these vulnerabilities, potentially leading to data breaches, unauthorized access, or disruption of services.

Mitigating the Risk: Implement a vulnerability management process, prioritize patching based on risk, and use automated patch management tools.

Possible Measurement Formula: Time to Patch Critical Vulnerabilities = sum of (time to patch each critical vulnerability)/number of critical vulnerabilities patched.

Suggested Frequency: Monthly.

Trigger: Between 7 and 14 days.

Breach: More than 14 days.

Visualization Recommendation: For the Time to Patch Critical Vulnerabilities KRI, the x-axis should represent time, while the y-axis should represent the average time to patch critical vulnerabilities, typically measured in days. Include a horizontal threshold line to indicate the maximum acceptable average time for patching, as taking too long to patch critical vulnerabilities can expose the organization to risks.

Quantifiable, Measurable, and Accurate: Use vulnerability scanning and patch management tools to monitor the time to patch vulnerabilities. Ensure that logs and records are accurate and up-to-date.

Insights and Actions: An increased time to patch critical vulnerabilities could indicate inefficiencies in the vulnerability management process. Actions include reviewing the patch management process, allocating more resources to patching, and using automated tools to streamline patch deployment.

KRI Title: Network Traffic Anomalies Detected

Specific Risk: Undetected network intrusions and malicious activity.

Metric Summary: The Network Traffic Anomalies Detected metric monitors unusual patterns or spikes in network traffic, which may indicate malicious activity such as data exfiltration, DDoS attacks, or unauthorized access.

Understanding the Risk: Anomalies in network traffic can be indicative of cyberattacks. These attacks can go unnoticed without adequate monitoring, leading to data breaches, system outages, or the compromise of sensitive information.

Mitigating the Risk: Use network monitoring tools, establish a baseline for normal network traffic patterns, and configure alerts for unusual activity. Regularly review network logs and conduct traffic analysis.

Possible Measurement Formula: Network Traffic Anomalies Detected = Count of detected network traffic anomalies.

Suggested Frequency: Daily.

Trigger: 4–6 anomalies detected daily.

Breach: More than 6 anomalies are detected daily.

Visualization Recommendation: On the line graph, the x-axis should represent time, and the y-axis should represent the number of network traffic anomalies detected. Add a horizontal threshold line to indicate the maximum number of anomalies that are considered acceptable before action is necessary.

Quantifiable, Measurable, and Accurate: Use network security monitoring tools that automatically detect anomalies based on predefined thresholds and heuristics. Ensure that the tools are properly calibrated to reduce false positives.

Insights and Actions: An increased detected network traffic anomalies may indicate an ongoing attack. Investigate each anomaly and assess whether it is malicious or benign. Take corrective actions such as blocking malicious IPs or tightening security controls.

KRI Title: Phishing Detection Rate

Specific Risk: Successful phishing attacks leading to data breaches or fraud.

Metric Summary: The Phishing Detection Rate measures the ability of an organization's security systems to identify and block phishing emails. High detection rates help in preventing phishing attacks.

Understanding the Risk: Phishing attacks are common methods attackers use to gain unauthorized access or steal sensitive data. Failure to detect these attacks may lead to data breaches, financial fraud, or malware infections.

Mitigating the Risk: Implement email security solutions to detect and block phishing emails. Conduct regular security awareness training for employees to recognize phishing attempts.

Possible Measurement Formula: Phishing Detection Rate = (number of phishing emails detected/total number of emails received) × 100.

Suggested Frequency: Weekly.

Trigger: Below 98% detection rate.

Breach: Below 95% detection rate.

Visualization Recommendation: For visualizing the Phishing Detection Rate, the x-axis should represent time, and the y-axis should represent the detection rate in percentage. Include a horizontal line to indicate the minimum acceptable detection rate.

Quantifiable, Measurable, and Accurate: Use email security solutions with reporting capabilities to measure the detection rate of phishing emails. Regularly update and calibrate the solutions to adapt to evolving phishing tactics.

Insights and Actions: A decrease in the phishing detection rate might indicate that the email security solution is not effectively identifying phishing emails. Review the solution's configuration and consider additional employee training on recognizing phishing attempts.

KRI Title: Number of Privileged Access Violations

Specific Risk: Unauthorized access and actions within systems, potentially leading to data breaches or system damage.

Metric Summary: The Number of Privileged Access Violations metric tracks instances where privileged accounts violate established policies, indicating potential insider threats or compromised accounts.

Understanding the Risk: Privileged accounts have elevated permissions and can significantly change systems. Misuse of these accounts can lead to data breaches, system outages, or compliance violations.

Mitigating the Risk: Implement strict controls over privileged accounts, including multifactor authentication, regular audits, and least privilege principles.

Possible Measurement Formula: Number of Privileged Access Violations = count of instances where privileged accounts were used in violation of policies.

Suggested Frequency: Weekly.

Trigger: 2–3 violations weekly.

Breach: More than 3 violations weekly.

Visualization Recommendation: In this visualization, the x-axis should represent time, and the y-axis should represent the number of privileged access violations. Include a horizontal line indicating the maximum acceptable number of violations.

Quantifiable, Measurable, and Accurate: Use IAM tools along with SIEM systems to track and report on privileged access violations. Ensure logs are accurate and regularly reviewed.

Insights and Actions: Increased privileged access violations may indicate insider threats or compromised accounts. Investigating each violation, revoking inappropriate privileges, and implementing stricter controls are critical.

KRI Title: Data Classification Errors

Specific Risk: Inappropriate handling or exposure of sensitive data due to misclassification.

Metric Summary: Data Classification Errors measure the instances where data is incorrectly classified, which could lead to inadequate security controls for sensitive data.

Understanding the Risk: Incorrect data classification can lead to inadequate protection of sensitive information. This could result in unauthorized access, data breaches, and noncompliance with data protection regulations.

Mitigating the Risk: Implement and enforce a data classification policy. Use data classification tools and regularly review the classification labels on data to ensure accuracy.

Possible Measurement Formula: Data Classification Errors = count of data instances being incorrectly classified.

Suggested Frequency: Monthly.

Trigger: 3–5 classification errors monthly.

Breach: More than 5 classification errors monthly.

Visualization Recommendation: For Data Classification Errors, the x-axis should represent time, and the y-axis should represent the number of data classification errors. Include a horizontal threshold line to indicate the maximum acceptable number of errors.

Quantifiable, Measurable, and Accurate: Use data classification tools to automate the classification process and reduce human error. Regularly review data classifications and correct any errors.

Insights and Actions: An increase in data classification errors could indicate a lack of understanding or adherence to the data classification policy. Consider additional training for staff and review the data classification tools and policies.

KRI Title: Number of Unprotected Endpoints

Specific Risk: Compromise of network endpoints leading to data breaches or malware infections.

Metric Summary: The Number of Unprotected Endpoints metric tracks the count of devices that do not have adequate security controls, such as antivirus software or firewalls, making them vulnerable to cyberattacks.

Understanding the Risk: Unprotected endpoints can easily be exploited by attackers, leading to data breaches, malware infections, or further penetration into the network.

Mitigating the Risk: Ensure all endpoints have essential security controls, including antivirus, firewalls, and regular patching. Use endpoint detection and response (EDR) solutions.

Possible Measurement Formula: Number of Unprotected Endpoints = count of endpoints without adequate security controls.

Suggested Frequency: Weekly.

Trigger: 6–10 unprotected endpoints weekly.

Breach: More than 10 unprotected endpoints weekly.

Visualization Recommendation: For visualizing the Number of Unprotected Endpoints, the x-axis should represent time, and the y-axis should represent the number of unprotected endpoints. Include a horizontal line to indicate the maximum number of unprotected endpoints considered acceptable.

Quantifiable, Measurable, and Accurate: Use EDR solutions and network scanning tools to identify unprotected endpoints. Ensure that the tools are properly configured and that the data is accurate.

Insights and Actions: Many unprotected endpoints indicate a significant risk to the network. It is critical to implement security controls on these endpoints and investigate the reasons for the lack of protection. Regularly assess and enforce endpoint security policies and controls.

KRI Title: Percentage of Security Incidents Detected by Internal Controls

Specific Risk: Failure of internal controls to detect and prevent security incidents, leading to data breaches or system compromises.

Metric Summary: The Percentage of Security Incidents Detected by Internal Controls metric gauges the effectiveness of an organization's internal security controls in identifying and mitigating security incidents.

Understanding the Risk: Internal controls' failure to detect security incidents increases the risk of undetected breaches or compromises. This can result in data losses, financial penalties, and reputational damage.

Mitigating the Risk: Regularly review and update internal controls. Conduct internal security assessments and use security monitoring tools to enhance the detection capabilities of internal controls.

Possible Measurement Formula: Percentage of Security Incidents Detected by Internal Controls = (number of security incidents detected by internal controls/ total number of security incidents) × 100.

Suggested Frequency: Monthly.

Trigger: Between 80% and 90% of security incidents are detected by internal controls.

Breach: Below 80% of security incidents are detected by internal controls.

Visualization Recommendation: For this KRI, the x-axis should represent time, and the y-axis should represent the percentage of security incidents detected by internal controls. A horizontal threshold line should indicate the minimum acceptable percentage.

Quantifiable, Measurable, and Accurate: Use security incident management tools and conduct regular audits of security controls to ensure that the data is accurate and that the internal controls are effective.

Insights and Actions: If the percentage of security incidents detected by internal controls is low, this indicates a need for immediate review and enhancement of the internal controls. Undertake a thorough review of the controls and security monitoring tools and make necessary adjustments to improve detection capabilities. Conduct regular security awareness training for employees.

KRI Title: Frequency of Cybersecurity Risk Assessments

Specific Risk: Failure to identify and mitigate evolving cybersecurity threats and vulnerabilities due to infrequent risk assessments.

Metric Summary: The Frequency of Cybersecurity Risk Assessments metric measures how often an organization conducts formal cybersecurity risk assessments. Regular risk assessments are vital for identifying and mitigating potential cybersecurity risks.

Understanding the Risk: Cybersecurity threats and vulnerabilities are constantly evolving. Failure to conduct regular risk assessments can result in an organization not being aware of new risks and not taking appropriate measures to mitigate them.

Mitigating the Risk: Organizations should schedule regular cybersecurity risk assessments and ensure they are conducted thoroughly. They should also consider conducting ad-hoc assessments in response to significant changes in the threat landscape.

Possible Measurement Formula: Frequency of Cybersecurity Risk Assessments = count of cybersecurity risk assessments conducted within a specific period (e.g., quarterly).

Suggested Frequency: Quarterly.

Trigger: Less than one cybersecurity risk assessment in six months.

Breach: No cybersecurity risk assessment was conducted within a year.

Visualization Recommendation: On the line graph, the x-axis should represent time, while the y-axis should represent the number of cybersecurity risk assessments conducted within a given time frame. While this may not require a horizontal threshold, ensuring that the frequency aligns with the organization's policy and the dynamic nature of cybersecurity risks is important.

Quantifiable, Measurable, and Accurate: Use calendars, reminders, and project management tools to schedule and track the conduct of cybersecurity risk assessments. Ensure the assessments are thorough and properly documented.

Insights and Actions: If risk assessments are not being conducted regularly, this indicates a potential lack of understanding of the evolving threat landscape. Organizations should prioritize these assessments and take action based on the findings to mitigate risks.

KRI Title: IoT Device Security Compliance Rate

Specific Risk: IoT device compromise leads to data breaches or network intrusions.

Metric Summary: The IoT Device Security Compliance Rate measures the percentage of IoT devices within an organization that comply with security policies and standards. Ensuring that IoT devices are not the weakest link in an organization's security is crucial.

Understanding the Risk: IoT devices often have limited security capabilities and can be an entry point for cyberattacks. A compromised IoT device can be used to gain unauthorized access to the network and sensitive data.

Mitigating the Risk: Ensure all IoT devices are configured according to security policies, regularly updated, and monitored for signs of compromise. Employ network segmentation to isolate IoT devices from critical systems.

Possible Measurement Formula: IoT Device Security Compliance Rate = (number of IoT devices compliant with security policies/total number of IoT devices) × 100.

Suggested Frequency: Monthly.

Trigger: Between 90% and 95% compliance.

Breach: Below 90% compliance.

Visualization Recommendation: For the IoT Device Security Compliance Rate, the x-axis should represent time, and the y-axis should represent the compliance rate in percentage. Add a horizontal threshold line that represents the minimum acceptable compliance rate. This is crucial as IoT devices often present additional security challenges, and ensuring a high compliance rate is essential for mitigating associated risks.

Quantifiable, Measurable, and Accurate: Utilize automated device management and security monitoring tools to evaluate the security posture of IoT devices. Regularly audit and assess IoT devices to ensure compliance with security policies.

Insights and Actions: A low IoT Device Security Compliance Rate indicates that IoT devices may be vulnerable to attacks. Organizations should review and enforce security policies for IoT devices, conduct regular assessments, and isolate them from critical systems.

KRI Title: User Accounts with Excessive Permissions

Specific Risk: Unauthorized access and actions due to overly permissive user accounts.

Metric Summary: User Accounts with Excessive Permissions count the number of user accounts with more permissions than required. This metric is crucial for managing the risk of unauthorized actions or access to sensitive data.

Understanding the Risk: User accounts with excessive permissions can lead to unauthorized actions, including data alteration, theft, and even the escalation of privileges. This poses both internal and external security threats.

Mitigating the Risk: Implement the principle of least privilege, conduct regular permissions audits, and promptly revoke unnecessary permissions.

Possible Measurement Formula: User Accounts with Excessive Permissions = count of user accounts with permissions exceeding the required level for their role.

Suggested Frequency: Monthly.

Trigger: More than 5 user accounts with excessive permissions.

Breach: More than 10 user accounts with excessive permissions.

Visualization Recommendation: Visualize User Accounts with Excessive Permissions with time on the x-axis and the number of user accounts on the y-axis. Add a horizontal threshold line indicating the maximum acceptable number of such accounts.

Quantifiable, Measurable, and Accurate: Use IAM tools to monitor and report on permissions. Regular audits should be conducted to verify permissions.

Insights and Actions: If the number of User Accounts with Excessive Permissions is high, organizations should audit user permissions and implement stricter access controls.

The End

```
01010100 01101000 01100001 01101110 01101011 00100000 01111001
01101111 01110101 00100000 01100110 01101111 01110010 00100000
01110010 01100101 01100001 01100100 01101001 01101110 01100111
00100000 01101111 01110101 01110010 00100000 01100110 01101001
01110010 01110011 01110100 00100000 01100010 01101111 01101111
01101011 00101110 00100000 01001000 01100101 01110010 01100101
00100000 01100001 01110010 01100101 00100000 01110011 01101111
01101101 01100101 00100000 01110011 01110000 01101111 01101001
01101100 01100101 01110010 01110011 00100000 01100001 01101110
01100100 00100000 01100001 00100000 01100111 01101001 01100110
01110100 00101110 00100000 01000100 01100001 01110010 01110100
01101000 00100000 01010110 01100001 01100100 01100101 01110010
00100000 01101001 01110011 00100000 01001100 01110101 01101011
01100101 00100111 01110011 00100000 01000110 01100001 01110100
01101000 01100101 01110010 00101100 00100000 01010100 01101000
01100101 00100000 01010111 01101001 01111010 01100001 01110010
01100100 00100000 01101111 01100110 00100000 01001111 01111010
00100000 01101001 01110011 00100000 01001010 01110101 01110011
01110100 00100000 01100001 00100000 01001101 01100001 01101110
00101100 00100000 01001001 01110100 00100000 01110111 01100001
01110011 00100000 01000101 01100001 01110010 01110100 01101000
00100000 01000001 01101100 01101100 00100000 01000001 01101100
01101111 01101110 01100111 00100000 01100001 01101110 01100100
00100000 01101110 01101111 01110100 00100000 01110100 01101000
01100101 00100000 01010000 01101100 01100001 01101110 01100101
01110100 00100000 01101111 01100110 00100000 01110100 01101000
01100101 00100000 01000001 01110000 01100101 01110011 00101100
00100000 01010011 01101111 01111001 01101100 01100101 01101110
01110100 00100000 01000111 01110010 01100101 01100101 01101110
00100000 01101001 01110011 00100000 01010000 01100101 01101111
01110000 01101100 01100101 00101100 00100000 01001110 01101111
01110010 01101101 01100001 01101110 00100000 01000010 01100001
01110100 01100101 01110011 00100000 01101001 01110011 00100000
01001000 01101001 01110011 00100000 01001101 01101111 01110100
01101000 01100101 01110010 00101100 00100000 01010011 01101110
01100001 01110000 01100101 00100000 01001011 01101001 01101100
01101100 01110011 00100000 01000100 01110101 01101101 01100010
```

ledore, Bruce Willis is a Ghost in 6th Sense, Tyler Durden Isn't Real, Tony Stark Dies a Hero. Your gift: https://jason-edwards.me/gift

Index